Children's 10 Rights to Excellent Reading Instruction

Children have a right to appropriate early reading instruction based on their individual needs. Children have a right to reading instruction that builds both the skill and the desire to read increasingly complex materials. Children have a right to well-prepared teachers who keep their skills up to date through effective professional development. Children have a right to access a wide variety of books and other reading material in classroom, school, and community libraries. Children have a right to reading assessment that identifies their strengths as well as their needs and involves them in making decisions about their own learning. Children who are struggling with reading have a right to receive intensive instruction from professionals specifically trained to teach reading. Children have a right to reading instruction that involves parents and communities in their academic lives. Children have a right to reading instruction that makes meaningful use of their first language skills. Children have the right to equal access to the technology used for the improvement of reading instruction. Children have a right to classrooms that optimize learning opportunities.

Improving Reading

Interventions, Strategies, and Resources

Fifth Edition

CD Enclosed

Contains Activities, Reproducibles, and Resources

Jerry L. Johns
Northern Illinois University, *Emeritus*

Susan Davis Lenski
Portland State University

Kendall Hunt
publishing company

Book Team

Chairman and Chief Executive Officer   Mark C. Falb
President and Chief Operating Officer
Chad M. Chandlee
Vice President, Higher Education   David L. Tart
Director of National Book Program   Paul B. Carty
Editorial Manager   Georgia Botsford
Vice President, Operations   Timothy J. Beitzel
Assistant Vice President, Production Services
Christine E. O'Brien
Senior Production Editor   Carrie Maro
Permissions Editor   Colleen Zelinsky
Cover Designer   Marilyn Kupferschmidt

Books by Jerry L. Johns and Susan Davis Lenski

Teaching Reading Pre K–Grade 3 (three editions with Laurie Elish-Piper)
Comprehension and Vocabulary Strategies for the Elementary Grades (two editions with Roberta L. Berglund)
Reading and Learning Strategies: Middle Grades through High School (three editions with Mary Ann Wham and Micki M. Caskey)
Improving Writing: Resources, Strategies, and Assessments (two editions)
Celebrating Literacy: The Joy of Reading and Writing (with June E. Barnhart, James H. Moss, and Thomas E. Wheat)
Language Arts for Gifted Middle School Students

Ordering Information

Address: Kendall Hunt Publishing Company
4050 Westmark Drive
Dubuque, IA 52002
Telephone: 800-247-3458, ext. 4
Website: www.kendallhunt.com
Fax: 800-772-9165

Books by Jerry L. Johns

Basic Reading Inventory (ten editions)
Fluency: Strategies & Assessments (three editions with Roberta L. Berglund)
Visualization: Using Mental Images to Strengthen Comprehension (with Linda L. Zeigler)
Strategies for Content Area Learning (two editions with Roberta L. Berglund)
Enhancing Writing through Visualization (with Linda L. Zeigler and Virginia R. Beesley)
Spanish Reading Inventory
Balanced Reading Instruction: Teachers' Visions and Voices (edited with Laurie Elish-Piper)
Secondary & College Reading Inventory (two editions)
Literacy for Diverse Learners (edited)
Handbook for Remediation of Reading Difficulties
Informal Reading Inventories: An Annotated Reference Guide (compiled)
Literacy: Celebration and Challenge (edited)

Author Information for Professional Development and Workshops

Jerry L. Johns
Reading Consultant
2105 Eastgate Drive
Sycamore, IL 60178
E-mail: *jjohns@niu.edu*

Susan Davis Lenski
Professor
Portland State University
Graduate School of Education
P.O. Box 751
615 SW Harrison
Portland, OR 97207-0751
E-mail: *sjlenski@pdx.edu*
503-725-5403

ISBN 978-0-7575-6833-6

Printed in the United States of America
10 9 8 7 6 5 4 3 2

Brief Contents

Contents

CD Contents

Additional Books and Book Listings

Preface

Improving Reading: Interventions, Strategies, and Resources has been a useful tool for teachers, reading teachers, reading coaches, interventionists, tutors, and teacher candidates for many years. When we conceptualized the first edition, we decided to organize the teaching strategies around typical behaviors that teachers see every day with readers who struggle. We list these behaviors inside the front cover of the book so teachers can use them for a quick and easy reference. As teachers observe the listed behaviors of their students, they can turn to that section in the book and find strategies, ideas, games, and resources to help solve the student's reading problems. Teachers have been using *Improving Reading* for whole group and small group instruction for years. Now, they can also use *Improving Reading* as they plan interventions for struggling readers using the Response to Intervention (RTI) model.

What Is Response to Intervention (RTI)?

Response to Intervention (RTI) is a federal initiative that is part of the 2004 reauthorization of the Individuals with Disabilities Education Act (IDEA). According to Allington and Walmsley (2007), RTI is an attempt by the federal government to decrease the number of students identified with disabilities. Previously, students with learning disabilities were identified using a discrepancy model. That means that students who had a measurable difference between their intelligence quotient (IQ) and their reading achievement were considered learning disabled. The RTI model changes the method of identification. The RTI model is based on the idea that some students who struggle with reading do not really have a learning disability but rather have not had sufficient opportunities for learning (Vellutino & Fletcher, 2005). The legislation is designed to give students multiple opportunities to learn before referring them for special education testing.

What Does RTI Look Like?

At the time of this writing, there were no federal legal requirements about the implementation of RTI. Many states, however, have designed frameworks for reading that encourage teachers to use a certain model. The three-tier model is presently the most popular way to determine which students have trouble learning and should be considered for special education.

In the three-tier RTI model, Tier 1 focuses on providing effective classroom reading instruction for all students. This instruction could come from a core reading program, literature, or a combination of the two. Tier 2 is when teachers identify students who are not responding to instruction. Teachers provide these struggling readers with intensive, small-group instruction. If students still do not respond to instruction, they are given individualized instruction in Tier 3. If teachers can document that students have not responded to the interventions at Tier 3, they will most likely be considered to have a learning disability and may be referred for additional testing (Fuchs, Fuchs, & Vaughn, 2008).

Many states and districts have adopted the three-tier system of assessment and intervention. This multitiered system provides students with ample opportunities to learn. If students have difficulty with the targeted interventions, they might have a disability that is preventing them from responding. The number of tiers that teachers use, however, is not important, nor is it federally mandated. Allington and Walmsley (2007) remind us that RTI was designed so that struggling readers have the opportunity for targeted, expert instruction before they are labeled as students with disabilities regardless of the framework that teachers are using to document the instruction.

Improving Reading as a Resource for Interventions

Response to Intervention (RTI) has changed the way teachers think about struggling readers. Instead of teaching a program, teachers are adopting a problem-solving approach. The teacher identifies the student's problem behaviorally, formulates an academic goal, and then implements an intervention (Vaughn & Denton, 2008). Some teachers prefer to place students in a purchased program, but Allington (2009) believes that teachers would do better to use a more adaptable approach, such as the kind of teaching called a responsive intervention or problem-solving design. In this type of teaching, the teacher selects instructional materials and decides which interventions and strategies to use based on the needs of the reader (Bender & Shores, 2007). This is where *Improving Reading* can help.

The interventions that are required for RTI must be scientifically valid. According to Mesmer and Mesmer (2008/2009), "RTI requires that instructional interventions be scientifically valid, public, implemented with integrity and systematically evaluated. The content of the intervention should be designated, the teacher responsible for implementing it identified, and the assessments determined" (p. 284). Many teachers need ideas as they develop these interventions; very few teachers can design all of their lessons for struggling readers without a good resource book.

A Personal Invitation from the Authors . . . MAKE IT YOUR BOOK!

Improving Reading will support teachers who are looking for ideas for interventions as well as for general classroom instruction. After you have determined the kinds of behaviors to teach, you can turn to the section on those behaviors for a variety of strategies, ideas, and resources that can be used for interventions.

The format allows you to quickly find teaching interventions, strategies, ideas, and resources to help students strategize their reading. Teachers attending our presentations and workshops thank us for the friendly and useful organizational scheme as well as the hundreds of evidenced-based strategies.

Many teachers have told us, "I use this book all the time, but I've never read the entire book." Those teachers were using *Improving Reading* as a practical tool to strengthen their teaching, and we applaud that approach—quickly finding what was needed and using it. Many teachers tell us they tag often-used pages for easy references. **MAKE IT YOUR BOOK!**

Who Will Use This Book?

- Preservice teachers, practicing teachers, and professionals who fulfill special resource roles appreciate the user-friendly approach we have taken in *Improving Reading: Interventions, Strategies, and Resources*. This book is grounded on sound reading theory and contains the five core areas identified in the report of the National Reading Panel:

  - ☐ phonemic awareness
  - ☐ phonics
  - ☐ fluency
  - ☐ vocabulary
  - ☐ comprehension

  From our experiences, we have identified other areas important in reading instruction and included strategies to address concerns in these areas:

  - ☐ motivating and engaging students in reading
  - ☐ mastering a variety of word-identification strategies
  - ☐ strengthening oral reading
  - ☐ expanding comprehension

- College and university students use this book in their classes and in the classroom. *Improving Reading* provides practical ideas in courses for preservice and practicing teachers to use in their quest to help students improve their reading abilities.
- Educators in school and district professional development programs have given *Improving Reading* high marks for enabling them to give classroom teachers the assistance they need to help their students improve their reading scores.

What Are Some of the Unique Characteristics of This Book?

Improving Reading: Interventions, Strategies, and Resources is the most comprehensive, useful reading resource available, chock full of ideas for teachers who work with entire classes, individual students, or groups of students in reading. This book is divided into seven chapters that correlate with the main components of a comprehensive reading curriculum. Within each chapter are 5 to 14 sections that provide teaching interventions, strategies, activities, and resources to help students overcome a specific reading problem.

CD

This edition has a dual platform CD. The reproducible student pages and teacher resources provided in this book can be printed directly from the CD. In response to comments from teachers that the book is beginning to be a bit overwhelming in size, we have provided additional resources and book listings on the CD as well.

What Grade Levels Do the Strategies Address?

Improving Reading does not focus on distinct grade levels. This comprehensive strategy book provides suggestions for use from Pre-K through high school. Use the **Quick Reference Guide** to identify the problem and then use the recommended strategy to address the problem.

Again, we invite you to . . . MAKE IT YOUR BOOK!

Sample of Contents

You also can use *Improving Reading* to help one or more students with a specific reading problem. For example, say a student has difficulty in reading fluently. Check the **Quick Reference Guide** (see the sample below) and look at the chapter on fluency (see sample at the bottom of page xvii). Under the chapter heading are several behaviors that a student could be exhibiting. Scan the list of behaviors on the **Quick Reference Guide** (inside front cover and page i) to determine which one best describes the student's reading problem. Then turn to that section to find interventions and strategies to use with the student.

Sample of Quick Reference Guide

Chapter 1 Motivation, Engagement, Interests, and Attitudes 1

1.1 The student can read but chooses not to read. 3

1.2 The student does not like to read or exhibits a negative attitude toward reading. 20

1.3 The student does not find much of interest to read. 38

1.4 The student has a low level of confidence in his or her reading ability. 51

1.5 The student does not set reading goals. 62

You will see that most chapters are arranged in the same format:

- Overview
- Numbered section heading (see bottom right page)
- Student learning goal (behavior observed and anticipated outcome)
- Background or Perspectives and Strategies information
- Numbered teaching strategies

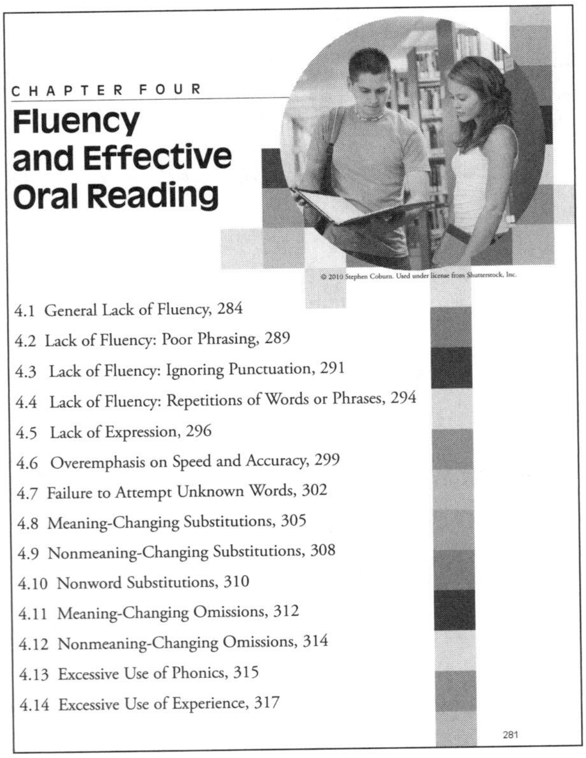
CHAPTER FOUR

Fluency and Effective Oral Reading

© 2010 Stephen Coburn. Used under license from Shutterstock, Inc.

4.1 General Lack of Fluency, 284
4.2 Lack of Fluency: Poor Phrasing, 289
4.3 Lack of Fluency: Ignoring Punctuation, 291
4.4 Lack of Fluency: Repetitions of Words or Phrases, 294
4.5 Lack of Expression, 296
4.6 Overemphasis on Speed and Accuracy, 299
4.7 Failure to Attempt Unknown Words, 302
4.8 Meaning-Changing Substitutions, 305
4.9 Nonmeaning-Changing Substitutions, 308
4.10 Nonword Substitutions, 310
4.11 Meaning-Changing Omissions, 312
4.12 Nonmeaning-Changing Omissions, 314
4.13 Excessive Use of Phonics, 315
4.14 Excessive Use of Experience, 317

281

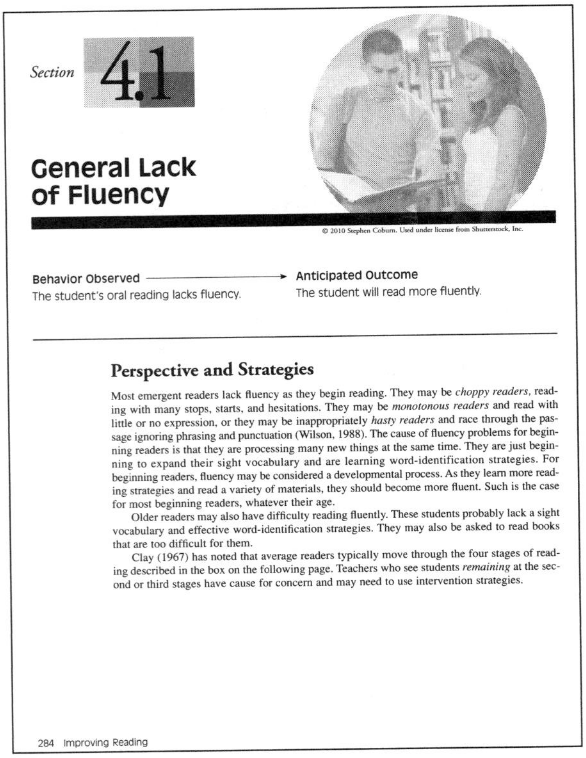
Section 4.1

General Lack of Fluency

© 2010 Stephen Coburn. Used under license from Shutterstock, Inc.

Behavior Observed → Anticipated Outcome
The student's oral reading lacks fluency. The student will read more fluently.

Perspective and Strategies

Most emergent readers lack fluency as they begin reading. They may be *choppy readers*, reading with many stops, starts, and hesitations. They may be *monotonous readers* and read with little or no expression, or they may be inappropriately *hasty readers* and race through the passage ignoring phrasing and punctuation (Wilson, 1988). The cause of fluency problems for beginning readers is that they are processing many new things at the same time. They are just beginning to expand their sight vocabulary and are learning word-identification strategies. For beginning readers, fluency may be considered a developmental process. As they learn more reading strategies and read a variety of materials, they should become more fluent. Such is the case for most beginning readers, whatever their age.

Older readers may also have difficulty reading fluently. These students probably lack a sight vocabulary and effective word-identification strategies. They may also be asked to read books that are too difficult for them.

Clay (1967) has noted that average readers typically move through the four stages of reading described in the box on the following page. Teachers who see students *remaining* at the second or third stages have cause for concern and may need to use intervention strategies.

284 Improving Reading

There is a **numbered section** heading (e.g., 4.1 General Lack of Fluency).

The **behavior observed** and **anticipated outcome** for the section are identified below the heavy black line.

Background or **Perspective and Strategies** information is given to aid in reaching the goal.

Teaching strategies form the heart of this book. These strategies are carefully described and often use examples. For each goal, you will find one or more strategies. Practice and reinforcement activities are also included.

denotes group activities.

identifies materials in chapter resources.

highlights book lists on the CD.

CD Contents

Chapter-by-Chapter Reproducibles

Includes reproducible sheets to use with students (denoted by a student reading icon), and teacher resources (denoted by an apple icon). These pages can also be found within chapters.

Additional Books and Book Listings

Part A: Books without Words
Part B: Alphabet Books
Part C: Pattern Books
Part D: Recent Picture Books

What You Will Find in *Improving Reading*

An easy-to-use **Quick Reference Guide** inside the front cover that lists 69 student behaviors in reading.

Over 200 **strategies and interventions,** linked to the 69 student behaviors that you can use to help students become better readers.

More than 425 **practice and reinforcement activities** that expand the strategies and interventions to help you enhance student learning.

About the Authors

Jerry L. Johns has been recognized as a distinguished teacher, writer, outstanding teacher educator, and popular professional development speaker for schools, school districts, and conferences. His more than 700 presentations have involved travel throughout the United States and 12 countries. He has taught students from kindergarten through graduate school and also served as a reading teacher. Professor Johns spent his distinguished career at Northern Illinois University. He was also a Visiting Professor at Western Washington University and the University of Victoria in British Columbia.

Professor Johns served in leadership positions at the local, state, national, and international levels. He has been president of the International Reading Association, the Illinois Reading Council, the College Reading Association, and the Northern Illinois Reading Council. He also served on the Board of Directors for each of these organizations as well as the American Reading Forum. In addition, Dr. Johns has served on numerous committees of the International Reading Association and other professional organizations.

Dr. Johns has authored or coauthored nearly 300 articles, monographs, and research studies as well as numerous professional books. His *Basic Reading Inventory*, now in the tenth edition, is widely used in undergraduate and graduate classes as well as by practicing teachers. Among his more than 15 coauthored books to help teachers strengthen their reading instruction are *Teaching Reading Pre-K–Grade 3, Fluency: Strategies & Assessments, Comprehension and Vocabulary Strategies for the Elementary Grades,* and *Reading and Learning Strategies: Middle Grades through High School.* Professor Johns currently serves on the editorial advisory boards for *Reading Psychology* and the *Illinois Reading Council Journal.*

Dr. Johns has been the recipient of numerous awards for his contributions to the profession. The Illinois Reading Council honored him with the induction into the Reading Hall of Fame. Other recognitions include the Alpha Delta Literacy Award for Scholarship, Leadership, and Service to Adult Learners and the A.B. Herr Award for outstanding contributions to the field of reading. He also received the Outstanding Teacher Educator in Reading Award presented by the International Reading Association, the Champion for Children Award presented by the HOSTS Corporation, and the Laureate Award from the College Reading Association for life-long contributors to the field of reading. In 2007, the International Reading Association renamed the Outstanding Teacher Educator in Reading Award in his honor.

Susan Davis Lenski is a Professor at Portland State University. Dr. Lenski has taught in public schools for 20 years. Her teaching experiences include working with children from kindergarten through high school. Dr. Lenski currently teaches graduate reading and language arts courses.

Professor Lenski has been recognized by several organizations for her commitment to education. Among her numerous awards, Dr. Lenski was presented with the Nila Banton Smith Award from the International Reading Association (IRA) for her work in integrating content area subjects with reading instruction in secondary school. As an elementary school reading specialist, Dr. Lenski was instrumental in her school receiving an Exemplary Reading Program Award from the International Reading Association. She served on the Board of Directors of the IRA from 2004–2007.

Professor Lenski's research interests are in improving reading and writing instruction in elementary and secondary schools. She has conducted numerous inservice presentations and has presented at many state and national conferences. Dr. Lenski has written more than 60 articles for professional journals and 15 books.

Acknowledgments

We would like to thank all the teachers, professors, reading teachers, consultants, and curriculum coordinators who have used our work to help make reading instruction more responsive to students. We value your partnership, support, and encouragement. Thanks!

Jerry & Sue

CHAPTER ONE

Motivation, Engagement, Interests, and Attitudes

Overview

Reading for pleasure correlates strongly with academic achievement. Students who engage in pleasure reading are better readers than nonreaders. And those students who read for pleasure on a daily or weekly basis score better on reading tests than infrequent readers. These findings, based on a report by the National Endowment for the Arts, were highlighted by Gambrell (2008). Clearly, it is not enough that students read with fluency and comprehension. They must also find pleasure in reading. Good teachers "know about the role of motivation and interest in their students' success" (Snow, 2008, p. xiii).

> Motivated readers are better readers.

"If only my students were more motivated to read." Teachers of young children through young adults have the same goal: they desire their students to *want* to read. Teachers intuitively know what research bears out—that motivated readers are better readers (Guthrie et al., 1999). And because teachers want their students to be good readers, they also want their students to be motivated to read. The question for most teachers, however, is *how* to motivate and engage students in reading.

Reading motivation is a multifaceted combination of a student's personal goals, values, and beliefs interacting with topics, processes, and outcomes of reading (Guthrie & Wigfield, 2000). Motivated and engaged readers want to read. They find reading enjoyable and choose to read during some of their free time. Motivated and engaged readers recognize that they learn through reading. Reading is attractive to them because they find topics of interest in books and other types of printed material. Motivated and engaged readers set learning goals. They find ways to challenge themselves through reading. Motivated and engaged readers also read outside of the school setting. They not only choose to read in school, but they also read at home, in the library, and wherever they can take a book. Such readers have a combination of personal qualities that make them motivated (Miller & Faircloth, 2009).

> One way to value reading is to become a reading role model.

Because reading motivation and engagement is so complex, it is situational and often fragile. Cole (2000) has used the term "literacy personalities" to highlight the unique variety of motivators for students. Teachers find that activities that are motivational and engaging at the beginning of the school year sometimes lose their appeal by December. Furthermore, motivation and engagement can change in individual students. First-grade teachers frequently find almost all of their students highly motivated to read. However, reading motivation and engagement tends to decline in many students as they progress through school (Wigfield et al., 1997). Therefore, it's important that teachers recognize how motivation changes and flexibly apply a variety of strategies that will motivate their students to read. It is also important that teachers themselves cultivate the reading habit. Applegate and Applegate (2004), in a study of 195 preservice teachers, found that many of them were not avid readers. This lack of engagement may be passed on to their students.

Not every student will become an avid reader, but we believe that teachers can make a profound difference in the motivational dispositions of their students. There are many ways that teachers can create an interest in reading among their students (Gambrell, 1996). One of the most effective ways to motivate and engage students is to value reading in the classroom (Rasinski & Padak, 2000). One way to value reading is to become a reading role model. Teachers need to model for their students a genuine love of reading and a desire to read. They can model their love of reading in many ways. Teachers can discuss books and other printed materials they have read for personal enjoyment; they can discuss their reading habits (e.g., reading before going to bed); and they can tell their students about authors they particularly enjoy. Teachers who exhibit a passion for reading are taking the first step in motivating their students to read.

For students to become effective, lifelong readers, they must have both the skill and the will to read. Therefore, an important role of the teacher is to provide activities and strategies that encourage students to read. This chapter focuses on ways teachers can help motivate their students to read and engage them in reading so that it becomes personally satisfying.

Section 1.1

Lack of Motivation and Engagement

Behavior Observed →
The student can read but chooses not to read.

Anticipated Outcome
The student will become more motivated to read and will begin to choose reading as an activity.

Background

In recent years, there has been increased attention to the important role that motivation plays in students' learning (Bempechat, 2008). Cunningham and Cunningham (2002) note that engagement is "probably the most common term used to talk about the relationship between motivation and learning" (p. 89). Some students can read, but they do so infrequently. They may be called *reluctant* or *aliterate* readers. Such readers generally comprise two groups. One group is composed of students who are not particularly good readers. They can read but they are reading below grade level; moreover, they do not appear interested in improving their reading. Instead, they prefer to watch television, play video games, and participate in activities that do not involve reading.

The second group of reluctant readers is comprised of students who can read quite well but who choose not to read. These students are reading at or above grade level; however, they are not apt to read in their leisure time. Reading does not provide the same satisfaction as nonreading activities. Such students frequently appear to their teachers as bored or apathetic.

Reluctant Readers

- Students who are not good readers
- Students who read well but choose not to read

To encourage reluctant readers, it may be helpful to consider two types of motivation: internal (intrinsic) and external (extrinsic). Reluctant readers, by definition, possess little intrinsic motivation to become engaged with books and other reading materials. Whatever the causes, these students have become indifferent or antagonistic toward reading. Because many reluctant readers possess little or no intrinsic motivation for reading, one of the central tasks of teachers is to use techniques to bring students and books together.

Extrinsic motivation may be needed because reluctant readers, on their own, have not found much satisfaction in reading. Teachers, therefore, must develop strategies that move these students toward books and other types of printed materials in order for students to gain a tangible reward. As reading becomes a more pleasant and satisfying experience, it is hoped that extrinsic motivation will be replaced with intrinsic motivation to read. Teachers who seek to motivate and engage the reluctant reader is consciously trying to change the student's behavior and attitude toward reading from one of apathy to one of self-satisfaction and involvement. Teachers should also use techniques that will encourage the student to view reading as an activity that merits his or her time and energy. The following strategies and activities should be useful.

These students are motivated and engaged readers.

© 2010 Monkey Business Images. Under license from Shutterstock, Inc.

READING ROLE MODELS

1. Tell students that many people love to read and that you will be bringing in special speakers who will tell them about the kinds of books they read. Explain to students that you will be bringing in two Reading Role Models a month. Ask students to help make scheduling decisions about when the Reading Role Models will speak to the class.
2. Prepare a speakers' schedule and begin asking people if they would be interested in telling your class about their reading habits. To find special speakers, contact local police officers or fire fighters, city council members, newspaper writers, radio or TV personalities, sports stars, and even your local football team (Cunningham & Allington, 1999). As you contact potential speakers, tell them something like what follows.

   > *I'm making a concerted effort this year to motivate my students to read. I know that my students look up to you, and they would be mightily impressed if you could come to school and tell them about the reading you do in your life.*

   You will find so many individuals interested in helping you motivate your students that you will probably have a waiting list.
3. Tell your speakers that you want them to talk about all of the different types of reading that they do. Stress the variety of reading people do throughout the day, not just book reading. You might tell your speakers about your reading preferences and habits as an example of the kind of thing you want them to tell your students. For example, you might say what follows.

   > *I read every chance I get. I read the newspaper during breakfast in the morning. When I get to school, I get a cup of coffee and spend some time reviewing my teaching lessons. If I have time, I then reread the literature selection of the day. When the students come into the classroom, I read the notes they bring me, the announcements, and the lunch menu. Throughout the day I read students' papers. After school, I read professional journals and news magazines. I might also read a cookbook if I'm making something new for dinner. In the evening I grade my students' papers for an hour or so; then I read to my children. After the children are in bed, I snuggle up with the latest* New York Times *best seller until I go to bed.*

4. After you have scheduled your speakers, print T-shirts with a catchy slogan such as "Real Men Read Books" or "Real Women Love to Read." Give the special speakers a T-shirt to wear as they tell your class about their reading habits.

MOTIVATION TO READ PROFILE: READING SURVEY

1. Tell students you are interested in their views about reading. Explain to students that you will be giving them a survey to take that will help you understand how they feel.
2. Reproduce and distribute copies of the Motivation to Read Profile (MRP) beginning on the next page (Gambrell, Palmer, Codling, & Mazzoni, 1996).
3. Ask students to write their names in the space provided and tell them something like what follows.

    I am going to read some sentences to you. I want to know how you feel about your reading. There are no right or wrong answers, so tell me honestly what you think. I will read each sentence twice. Do not mark your answer until I tell you to. After I read the sentence the first time, I want you to think about the best answer for you. Then after I read the sentence the second time, I want you to fill in the space beside your best answer. Mark only one answer.

4. Have students complete the survey and collect them. Score them by assigning a numerical value for each item: 1 point for the first answer, 2 points for the second answer, 3 points for the third answer, and 4 points for the fourth answer. For some of the questions the scoring is reversed. Recode the answers that have an asterisk next to them on the MRP Reading Survey Scoring Sheet found on page 10.
5. Interpret your students' scores on the Motivation to Read Profile by calculating the students' scores about their self-concept as a reader and the value they place on reading. Use the results of the surveys to tailor your motivational interventions for individual students as well as for your class.

Students are happy to share their reading interests.
Photo by S. Johns.

MOTIVATION TO READ PROFILE: READING SURVEY

Name ____ Date ____________________

Sample 1: I am in ____________.

- ☐ Second grade
- ☐ Third grade
- ☐ Fourth grade
- ☐ Fifth grade
- ☐ Sixth grade

Sample 2: I am a ____________.

- ☐ boy
- ☐ girl

1. My friends think I am ____________.
   - ☐ a very good reader
   - ☐ a good reader
   - ☐ an OK reader
   - ☐ a poor reader
2. Reading a book is something I like to do.
   - ☐ Never
   - ☐ Not very often
   - ☐ Sometimes
   - ☐ Often
3. I read ____________.
   - ☐ not as well as my friends
   - ☐ about the same as my friends
   - ☐ a little better than my friends
   - ☐ a lot better than my friends
4. My best friends think reading is ____________.
   - ☐ really fun
   - ☐ fun
   - ☐ OK to do
   - ☐ no fun at all
5. When I come to a word I don't know, I can ____________.
   - ☐ almost always figure it out
   - ☐ sometimes figure it out
   - ☐ almost never figure it out
   - ☐ never figure it out
6. I tell my friends about good books I read.
   - ☐ I never do this.
   - ☐ I almost never do this.
   - ☐ I do this some of the time.
   - ☐ I do this a lot.

(continued)

Gambrell, L.B., Palmer, B.M., Codling, R.M., & Mazzoni, S.A. (1996). Assessing reading motivation. *The Reading Teacher*, *49*, 518–533.

MOTIVATION TO READ PROFILE: READING SURVEY *(continued)*

7. When I am reading by myself, I understand ___________.
   - ☐ almost everything I read
   - ☐ some of what I read
   - ☐ almost none of what I read
   - ☐ none of what I read
8. People who read a lot are ___________.
   - ☐ very interesting
   - ☐ interesting
   - ☐ not very interesting
   - ☐ boring
9. I am ___________.
   - ☐ a poor reader
   - ☐ an OK reader
   - ☐ a good reader
   - ☐ a very good reader
10. I think libraries are ___________.
    - ☐ a great place to spend time
    - ☐ an interesting place to spend time
    - ☐ an OK place to spend time
    - ☐ a boring place to spend time
11. I worry about what other kids think about my reading ___________.
    - ☐ every day
    - ☐ almost every day
    - ☐ once in a while
    - ☐ never
12. Knowing how to read well is ___________.
    - ☐ not very important
    - ☐ sort of important
    - ☐ important
    - ☐ very important
13. When my teacher asks me a question about what I have read, I ___________.
    - ☐ can never think of an answer
    - ☐ have trouble thinking of an answer
    - ☐ sometimes think of an answer
    - ☐ always think of an answer

(continued)

Gambrell, L.B., Palmer, B.M., Codling, R.M., & Mazzoni, S.A. (1996). Assessing reading motivation. *The Reading Teacher*, *49*, 518–533.

Motivation to Read Profile: Reading Survey *(continued)*

14. I think reading is ________.
    - ☐ a boring way to spend time
    - ☐ an OK way to spend time
    - ☐ an interesting way to spend time
    - ☐ a great way to spend time
15. Reading is ________.
    - ☐ very easy for me
    - ☐ kind of easy for me
    - ☐ kind of hard for me
    - ☐ very hard for me
16. When I grow up I will spend ________.
    - ☐ none of my time reading
    - ☐ very little of my time reading
    - ☐ some of my time reading
    - ☐ a lot of my time reading
17. When I am in a group talking about stories, I ________.
    - ☐ almost never talk about my ideas
    - ☐ sometimes talk about my ideas
    - ☐ almost always talk about my ideas
    - ☐ always talk about my ideas
18. I would like for my teacher to read books out loud to the class ________.
    - ☐ every day
    - ☐ almost every day
    - ☐ once in a while
    - ☐ never
19. When I read out loud I am a ________.
    - ☐ poor reader
    - ☐ fair reader
    - ☐ good reader
    - ☐ very good reader
20. When someone gives me a book for a present, I feel ________.
    - ☐ very happy
    - ☐ sort of happy
    - ☐ sort of unhappy
    - ☐ unhappy

Gambrell, L.B., Palmer, B.M., Codling, R.M., & Mazzoni, S.A. (1996). Assessing reading motivation. *The Reading Teacher*, *49*, 518–533.

MRP READING SURVEY SCORING SHEET

Student's Name ______________________________

Grade ____________ Teacher ______________________________

Administration Date ______________________________

Recoding Scale

1 = 4
2 = 3
3 = 2
4 = 1

Self-Concept as a Reader		**Value of Reading**	
*recode	1. _____		2. _____
	3. _____	*recode	4. _____
*recode	5. _____		6. _____
*recode	7. _____	*recode	8. _____
	9. _____	*recode	10. _____
*recode	11. _____		12. _____
	13. _____		14. _____
*recode	15. _____		16. _____
	17. _____	*recode	18. _____
	19. _____	*recode	20. _____

SC raw score: _____ /40 **V raw score:** _____ /40

Full survey raw score (Self-Concept & Value): _____ /80

Percentage scores

Percentage scores	Self-Concept	[ ]
	Value	[ ]
	Full Survey	[ ]

Comments: ______________________________

____

____

Gambrell, L.B., Palmer, B.M., Codling, R.M., & Mazzoni, S.A. (1996). Assessing reading motivation. *The Reading Teacher*, *49*, 518–533.

THUMBS-UP OR THUMBS-DOWN

1. Tell students that their opinions about the books they read are important and that you will be providing them with an opportunity to share their views with others in the class.
2. Duplicate and distribute the Thumbs-Up (Good) and Thumbs-Down (Not So Good) reproducibles that follow this strategy. Have students cut out the picture of the hand that best represents their view of a book they have recently read.
3. Ask students to write the title of the book, the name of the author, a one-sentence plot summary, and the reason for their rating on the hand picture. Tell students that all of their reasons will be considered valid as long as they can justify their opinions.
4. Display the Thumbs-Up and Thumbs-Down pictures in your room at the students' eye level. Encourage students frequently to read their class members' opinions about books. From time to time, highlight a particularly good book that students have enjoyed.
5. Provide additional copies of the Thumbs-Up and Thumbs-Down pictures for students to use on an ongoing basis.

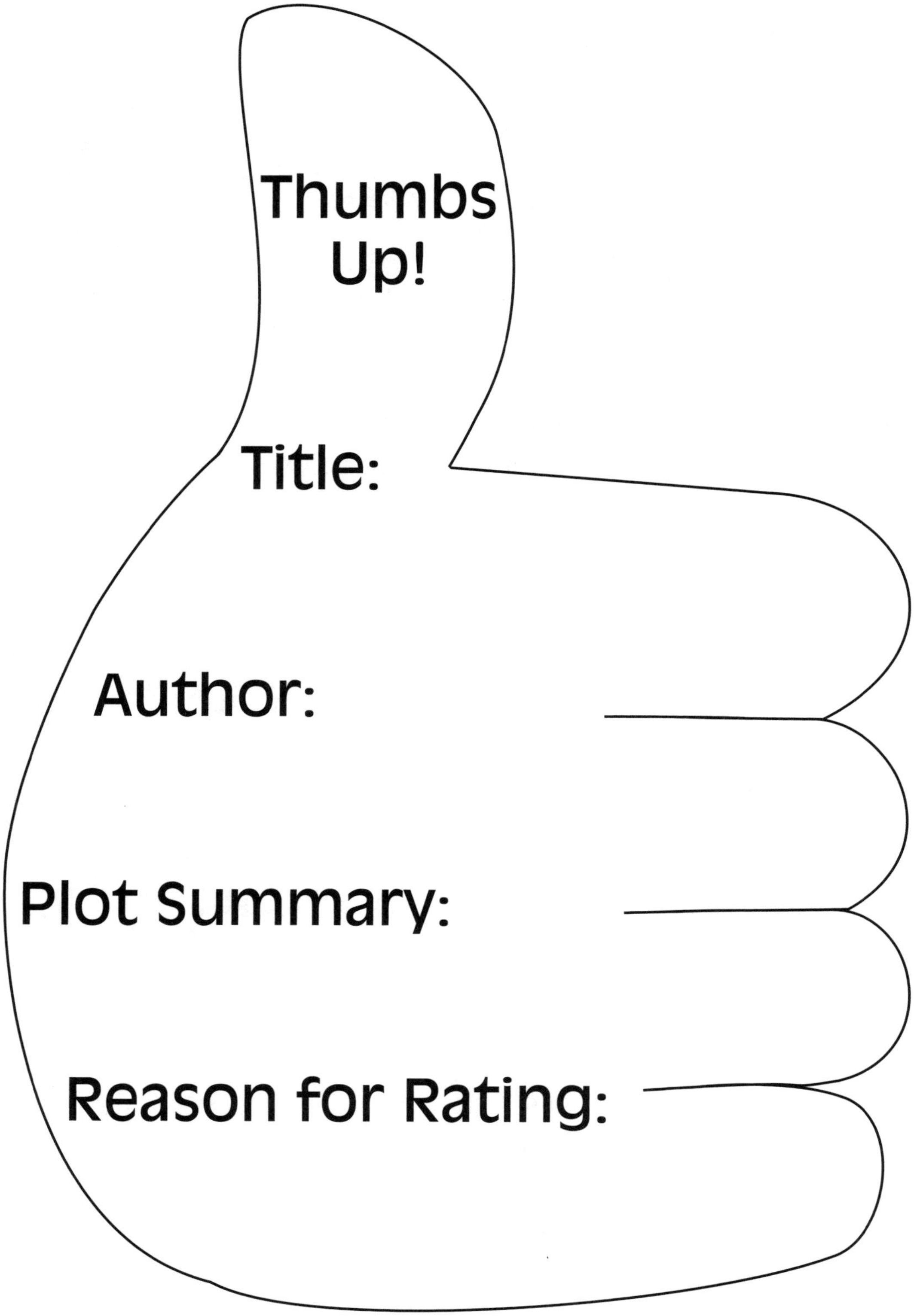
Thumbs
Up!
Title:
Author:
Plot Summary:
Reason for Rating:

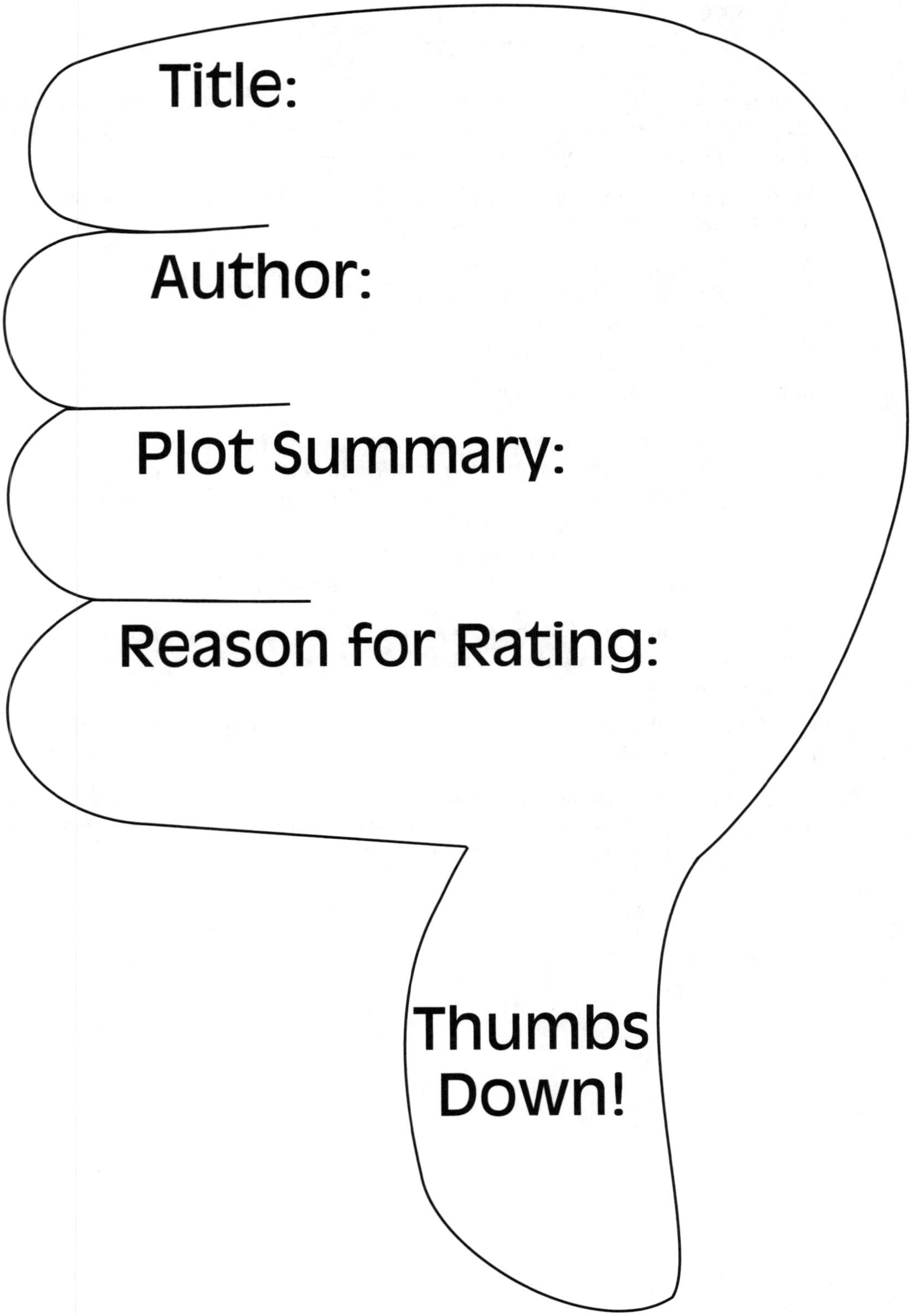
Title:
Author:
Plot Summary:
Reason for Rating:
Thumbs
Down!

YOU'LL LIKE THIS BOOK

1. Your recommendations can motivate students to read a book or story. Set aside a few minutes each week to introduce and share several books or other reading materials. The goal should be to create an interest in the materials and to promote reading.
2. Select a variety of reading materials (e.g., fiction, nonfiction, magazine articles, newspaper items). Use something like the following to create interest.
   - an object that relates to the material
   - an interesting part from the material
   - something about the topic, event, or main character
   - an engaging or interesting question
3. Introduce your first item. Below is an example.

   > *Look at what I'm holding. Who knows what it is? You're right, it's a Lego brick. You can read this brief article* [show article] *that's about the lost city of Atlantis and learn about some of the things built with Lego bricks. You might be interested in seeing what was made with more than 77,000 Lego bricks. After reading the article, you can use the computer to log on to* www.LEGOLAND.com *to learn more about this theme park.*

4. Continue sharing other books and materials. After you have finished, invite student volunteers to request the materials to read. You could also place them in a prominent place in the classroom library.
5. Check back with students who have selected the materials and invite them to share their reactions with you.
6. As the school year progresses, students can be invited to promote their favorite reading materials. Be sure that students are well prepared before they share. Often a time limit of 60 to 90 seconds is helpful to keep students engaged.

JUST ASK!

1. Gather a wide variety of poetry books and anthologies. Select and introduce a few poems to students from the various sources. Initially, choose short poems that are likely to appeal to students who are reluctant readers.
2. Repeat the above process over several days, tagging the pages and encouraging students to read poems you have shared and to select additional poems that are of interest. Read some of the student-selected poems to the class.
3. After a variety of poems and/or books have been shared, invite students to find a poem that they really enjoy. Be ready for selections of humorous verse, slap-stick humor, or simple verses. Students can then be invited to copy the poem on a sheet of paper, or you can use the reproducible on the following page.
4. Once the poems are written on a sheet of paper, have students carry their paper with them throughout the day. You should also select a poem and write it on paper.
5. At appropriate times (e.g., getting in line, just before dismissal), invite students to share their poems with each other. Some ideas for asking and sharing are listed below.
   - Would you like to hear my poem?
   - Just ask if you'd like me to share my poem.
   - Would you please share your poem with me?
   - Let's read each other our poems. You go first.
   - I have a poem about ______________________ that I'd like to share with you.
6. Encourage students to select new poems to share from time to time. Poems can be selected that relate to other topics being studied (e.g., the weather, holidays, wishes/dreams). Poems shared previously can be placed on a bulletin board titled *Poems We Have Shared.*

JUST ASK! (POETRY SHEET)

Name ____ Date ______________

Poet ______________________________

Poem Title ____

Practice and Reinforcement Activities

1. Have students bring in a photograph of themselves, family members, or pets. Tell students that they will be using the photograph and that it will not be returned. Give students copies of precut bookmarks made out of plain construction paper. Have students cut a picture from the photograph that will fit on the bookmark and glue the picture in place. Then have students decorate their bookmarks.
2. Provide a wide variety of reading materials. Paperback books, magazines, newspapers, and high-interest, low-vocabulary materials often help motivate students to read.
3. Design attractive book displays and bulletin boards with information about books and authors. Students may find something of interest on them.
4. Read orally to students. Such reading may pique students' interests and encourage them to read independently. Introduce a new book periodically and read only the beginning to students or highlight interesting chapters. This procedure may entice a reluctant reader to borrow the featured book.
5. Provide reading corners with comfortable cushions, a rug, bean-bag chairs, or a couch. Students can plan and decorate the area. Use cardboard boxes of various sizes or boards and bricks as bookshelves.
6. Bring in thought-provoking objects that will stimulate questions and prompt students' desire to read books about specific topics. Many such objects can be found in closets, other storage areas, and at garage sales.
7. Use appropriate popular music to inspire interest in reading by having students write down and examine the lyrics. Use the lyrics for discussions and lessons.
8. Provide periods of time for independent silent reading so students can interact directly with printed materials of their own choice. Gambrell (2007) highlights innovative adaptations of traditional sustained silent reading (SSR) programs: conferring with students, providing individual guidance, and allowing time at the end of the SSR period for students to share their reading with a partner. Silent reading has been introduced to students using acronyms. Numerous examples follow.

SSR	Sustained Silent Reading
RIP	Read in Peace
DEAR	Drop Everything and Read
SQUIRT	Sustained Quiet Uninterrupted Independent Reading Time
RABBIT	Read a Book Because It's There
WALTER	We All Like the Extra Reading
SURE	Sustained Uninterrupted Reading Enjoyment
GRAB	Go Read a Book
FRED	Free Reading Every Day
WAR	We All Read
RINGO	Reading Is Now Going On
RIOT	Reading Is Our Thing
OSCAR	Our School Cares About Reading
GRINCH	Good Reading Is Now Coming Here
RIBET	Reading Is Bringing Everyone Together
SUPER	Silent Undisturbed Private Entertainment Reading
FRISBEE	Free Reading in School by Everyone Everywhere
SAFARI	Students and Faculty All Read Independently
ZYLAR	Zip Your Lips and Read

9. Encourage adult family members to set aside a few minutes each day when everyone in the family reads self-selected materials. The program could be called FRED: Family Reading Every Day.
10. A student may be motivated to read materials designed to help him or her accomplish a task of interest (for instance, model building or cooking).

11. Emphasize the practical nature of reading. For example, an older student may be motivated to read a driver's manual if he or she hopes to obtain a driver's license. Younger students can be encouraged to read environmental print.
12. Show enthusiasm for reading. Perhaps the most important ingredient in motivating the reluctant reader is your own attitude toward books and reading. Your enthusiasm for reading may naturally be passed on to your students.
13. For a set period of time (six to eight weeks), hold a weekly reading challenge. Brainstorm with your students about ideas for topics of reading that are interesting to the students. Topics that work well are sports, animals, fantasy stories, and so on. Have students read books about the class topics. On a bulletin board, keep track of the books the students have read for each topic.
14. Have a reading riot. In the center of the room, place many books that are easy to read. Have two or three students come to the pile of books and, in 30 seconds, choose one book to read. After each student has a book, give them time to read.
15. Stress the idea that reading can be a fun and rewarding activity.
16. Develop classroom libraries with a wide range of reading levels in various genres. Be sure to include magazines, brochures, newspapers, and other forms of print.
17. Sprinkle your teaching with comments that are intrinsically motivating by including comments of anticipation, novelty, security, completion, identification, and feedback (Rinne, 1998). For example, a comment that includes the idea of novelty, or something out of the ordinary, would be "I've never read *Holes* to a fifth-grade class before, but I think you will really enjoy it." The resource chart on the following page has additional suggestions of motivational comments.
18. Encourage students to visit websites of their favorite authors. Students can find out more about authors and their latest books.
19. Alert students to popular authors of series books. Such books generally feature a repeating cast of characters.

Suggested Motivational Comments

Possible Intrinsic Appeals in Subject Matter	Description	Examples of Cue Words
Novelty	The opposite of routine	■ Here's something different . . . ■ For the very first time this year, we are going to . . . ■ I'll bet you have never met anybody like the characters you'll meet in this book . . .
Surprise	An unexpected turn of events	■ You will not believe your eyes . . . ■ You will be delighted . . . ■ Just wait until you see this . . .
Anticipation	Prompts curiosity and suspense	■ Today we are going to . . . ■ See if . . . ■ Can you figure out how to . . . ■ Be sure to watch for . . . ■ I can't wait to share . . .
Security	The reassurance of familiarity, safety, and efficacy	■ You already know . . . ■ If you have difficulty, I will be here to help you . . . ■ This is just like we did . . . ■ You have the skills to . . .
Challenge	A problem that begs to be solved, a question that resists an answer, an obstacle that needs to be overcome, a goal that might be reached	■ Can you do it like the experts? ■ I wonder how that could be done. ■ Can you . . . ■ You can only use . . . ■ What makes it behave that way? ■ What do you think?
Completion	One part of the lesson is used in another part of the same lesson	■ You're wondering why we are doing this now? Because later . . . ■ After you finish this task, use it as you . . . ■ Complete this job so you will be ready to . . . ■ I am teaching you . . . so . . .
Application	Using the skills somewhere outside the lesson	■ You can use this someday when . . . ■ People often find this useful when . . . ■ As you do this, you are doing what (engineers, scientists, librarians, authors) do . . .
Feedback	Sees the immediate results of engagement with the content	■ You will know immediately whether you were correct . . . ■ If everything goes as planned, you should be able to see/hear . . . ■ Yes, that is exactly what we are looking for . . .
Identification a. Possession b. Belonging c. Achievement d. Projection	The personal tie between content and the self-image of the student a. Ownership b. A place, status, sense of self c. Mega-cognition of achieving mastery d. Identification with a role model, a hero/heroine, an adventure	■ Show/demonstrate your (possession) to the class . . . ■ Your team . . . ■ You will be a member of . . . ■ You are all in this together . . . ■ See if you can beat your own record . . . ■ When you have finished, you will find you can . . . ■ Teach someone else . . . ■ Pretend you are . . . ■ If you were ____________, what would you do?
Competition	"Winning"	■ The way to win is . . . ■ Whoever comes in first . . . ■ Whoever does the best . . .

Adapted from Rinne, C. (1998). Motivating students is a percentage game. *Phi Delta Kappan, 79*, 620–627.

Section 1.2

Negative Attitude Toward Reading

Behavior Observed → **Anticipated Outcome**

Behavior Observed	Anticipated Outcome
The student does not like to read or exhibits a negative attitude toward reading.	The student will gain a more positive attitude toward reading.

Background

A student who does not like to read or who exhibits a negative attitude toward reading is not necessarily unmotivated to read. Motivation is different from attitude toward reading (McKenna, Kear, & Ellsworth, 1995). Think about students who are motivated to do well in school. They keep trying even though they may not like what they are doing. Those students are motivated but have a negative attitude. On the other hand, there are students who may not be motivated but who have a positive attitude. It might be useful to think about yourself for this example. Perhaps you like to exercise and you know you should exercise, but you just don't. You probably aren't very motivated even though you have a positive attitude. This example illustrates the distinction between motivation and attitude.

> Motivation is different from attitude.

A student who has a negative attitude toward reading is often—but not always—having difficulty with reading. Some students have a positive attitude toward reading regardless of their reading ability. However, many students may have a negative attitude toward reading because reading is difficult for them. When something is difficult, there seems to be a natural tendency to avoid or shy away from it. Other students may not have had enough positive experiences with reading to know what a wonderful activity reading is. These students may have a negative attitude simply because they were not introduced to the joys of reading in their early years.

Whatever the reasons why students have negative attitudes toward reading, you can listen actively and observe to find out why they don't like to read. These clues may provide a means of working with students to explore ways of helping them. Most teachers can tell when a student has a negative attitude toward reading, and there are surveys to help teachers assess students' attitudes toward reading. Teachers can use the results of surveys as a basis for experiences or materials to help their students develop more positive attitudes toward reading.

ATTITUDE SURVEYS

1. Look at the two surveys that follow and determine which one is more appropriate for your students. The Elementary Reading Attitude Survey is typically popular with young students, and the Rhody Secondary Reading Attitude Assessment is more appropriate for students in middle school and high school. Duplicate the survey that you have chosen. Additional surveys and a conversational interview can be found in Chapter 1 Resources (pages 78–92).
2. Tell students that you would like to find out how they feel about reading. Emphasize that this survey is not a test and that there are no "right" or "wrong" answers. Encourage honesty.
3. If you have chosen the Elementary Reading Attitude Survey, distribute the survey forms and, if you wish to monitor the attitudes of specific students, ask them to write their names in the space at the top. Hold up a copy of the survey so that students can see the first page. Point to the picture of Garfield at the far left of the first item. Ask students to look at this same picture on their own survey. Discuss with them the mood Garfield seems to be in (very happy). Then move to the next picture and again discuss Garfield's mood (this time, a little happy). In the same way, move to the third and fourth pictures and talk about Garfield's moods—a little upset and very upset. It is helpful to point out the position of Garfield's mouth, especially in the middle two figures.
4. Have students complete the survey independently as you read the statements to them. Ask students to respond with the answer that best describes how they feel.
5. If you have chosen the Rhody Secondary Reading Attitude Assessment, have students follow the directions on the survey.
6. Score the surveys using the scoring instructions that follow each of the surveys.
7. Use the information from the surveys to determine students' attitudes toward reading. Then take steps to help students build more positive attitudes toward reading using the ideas and strategies in this section.

ELEMENTARY READING ATTITUDE SURVEY

Name ______________________________ Date ______________

1. How do you feel when you read a book on a rainy Saturday?

2. How do you feel when you read a book in a school during free time?

3. How do you feel about reading for fun at home?

4. How do you feel about getting a book for a present?

2

5. How do you feel about spending free time reading?

6. How do you feel about starting a new book?

7. How do you feel about reading during summer?

8. How do you feel about reading instead of playing?

3

9. How do you feel about going to a bookstore?

10. How do you feel about reading different kinds of books?

11. How do you feel when the teacher asks you questions about what you read?

12. How do you feel about doing reading workbook pages and worksheets?

4

13. How do you feel about reading in school?

14. How do you feel about reading your school books?

15. How do you feel about learning from a book?

16. How do you feel when it's time for reading in class?

5

17. How do you feel about the stories you read in reading class?

18. How do you feel when you read out loud in class?

19. How do you feel about using a dictionary?

20. How do you feel about taking a reading test?

Elementary Reading Attitude Survey

Michael C. McKenna and Dennis J. Kear

Scoring and Interpretation

1. To score the survey, count four points for each leftmost (happiest) Garfield circled, three for each slightly smiling Garfield, two for each mildly upset Garfield, and one point for each very upset (rightmost) Garfield. Three scores for each student can be obtained: the total for the first 10 items, the total for the second 10, and a composite total. The first half of the survey relates to attitude toward recreational reading; the second half relates to attitude toward academic aspects of reading.
2. You can interpret scores in two ways. One is to note informally where the score falls in regard to the four points on the scale. A total score of 50, for example, would fall about midway on the scale, between the slightly happy and slightly upset figures, indicating a relatively indifferent overall attitude toward reading. The other approach is more formal. It involves converting the raw scores into percentile ranks by means of Table 1.1 on page 29. Be sure to use the norms for the right grade level and to note the column headings (Rec = recreational reading, Aca = academic reading, Tot = total score). If you wish to determine the average percentile rank for your class, average the raw scores first; then use the table to locate the percentile rank corresponding to the raw score mean. Percentile ranks cannot be averaged directly.

Norms for the Elementary Reading Attitude Survey

To create norms for the interpretation of the Elementary Reading Attitude Survey scores, a large-scale study was conducted late in January 1989, at which time the survey was administered to 18,138 students in Grades 1–6. Several steps were taken to achieve a sample that was sufficiently stratified (that is, reflective of the American population) to allow confident generalizations. Children were drawn from 95 school districts in 38 states. The number of girls exceeded by only 5 the number of boys. Ethnic distribution of the sample was also close to that of the U.S. population in 1989. The proportion of Blacks (9.5%) was within 3% of the national proportion, whereas the proportion of Hispanics (6.2%) was within 2%.

Percentile ranks at each grade for both subscales and the full scale are presented in Table 1.1 on page 29. These data can be used to compare individual students' scores with the national sample, and they can be interpreted like achievement-test percentile ranks.

McKenna, M.C., & Kear, D.J. (1990). Measuring attitude toward reading: A new tool for teachers. *The Reading Teacher, 43,* 626–639. Reprinted with permission of Michael C. McKenna and the International Reading Association.

ELEMENTARY READING ATTITUDE SURVEY SCORING SHEET

Student's Name ____

Teacher ____

Grade ______________ Administration Date ______________________________

Scoring Guide

4 points	Happiest Garfield
3 points	Slightly smiling Garfield
2 points	Mildly upset Garfield
1 point	Very upset Garfield

Recreational reading	Academic reading
1. _____	11. _____
2. _____	12. _____
3. _____	13. _____
4. _____	14. _____
5. _____	15. _____
6. _____	16. _____
7. _____	17. _____
8. _____	18. _____
9. _____	19. _____
10. _____	20. _____
Raw score: _____	Raw score: _____

Total raw score (Recreational + Academic): _____

	Percentile Ranks
Recreational	
Academic	
Full scale	

TABLE 1.1

Mid-Year Percentile Ranks by Grade and Scale

Raw Score	Grade 1			Grade 2			Grade 3			Grade 4			Grade 5			Grade 6		
	Rec.	Aca.	Tot.	Rec.	Aca.	Tot.	Rec.	Aca.	Tot.	Rec.	Aca.	Tot.	Rec.	Aca.	Tot.	Rec.	Aca.	Tot.
80			99			99			99			99			99			99
79			95			96			98			99			99			99
78			93			95			97			98			99			99
77			92			94			97			98			99			99
76			90			93			96			97			98			99
75			88			92			95			96			98			99
74			86			90			94			95			97			99
73			84			88			92			94			97			98
72			82			86			91			93			96			98
71			80			84			89			91			95			97
70			78			82			86			89			94			96
69			75			79			84			88			92			95
68			72			77			81			86			91			93
67			69			74			79			83			89			92
66			66			71			76			80			87			90
65			62			69			73			78			84			88
64			59			66			70			75			82			86
63			55			63			67			72			79			84
62			52			60			64			69			76			82
61			49			57			61			66			73			79
60			46			54			58			62			70			76
59			43			51			55			59			67			73
58			40			47			51			56			64			69
57			37			45			48			53			61			68
56			34			41			44			48			57			62
55			31			38			41			45			53			58
54			28			35			38			41			50			55
53			25			32			34			38			46			52
52			22			29			31			35			42			48
51			20			26			28			32			39			44
50			18			23			25			28			36			40
49			15			20			23			26			33			37
48			13			18			20			23			29			33
47			12			15			17			20			26			30
46			10			13			15			18			23			27
45			8			11			13			16			20			25
44			7			9			11			13			17			22
43			6			8			9			12			15			20
42			5			7			9			10			13			17
41			5			6			7			9			12			15
40	99	99	4	99	99	5	99	99	6	99	99	7	99	99	10	99	99	13
39	92	91	3	94	94	4	96	97	5	97	98	6	98	99	9	99	99	12
38	89	88	3	92	92	2	94	95	4	95	97	5	96	98	8	97	99	10
37	86	85	2	88	89	2	90	93	3	92	95	4	94	98	7	95	99	8
36	81	79	2	84	85	2	87	91	2	88	93	3	91	96	6	92	98	7
35	77	75	1	79	81	1	81	88	2	84	90	3	87	95	4	88	97	6
34	72	69	1	74	78	1	75	83	2	78	87	2	82	93	4	83	95	5
33	65	63	1	68	73	1	69	79	1	72	83	2	77	90	3	79	93	4
32	58	58	1	62	67	1	63	74	1	66	79	1	71	86	3	74	91	3
31	52	53	1	56	62	1	57	69	0	60	75	1	65	82	2	69	87	2
30	44	49	1	50	57	0	51	63	0	54	70	1	59	77	1	63	82	2
29	38	44	0	44	51	0	45	58	0	47	64	1	53	71	1	58	78	1
28	32	39	0	37	46	0	38	52	0	41	58	1	48	66	1	51	73	1
27	26	34	0	31	41	0	33	47	0	35	52	1	42	60	1	46	67	1
26	21	30	0	25	37	0	26	41	0	29	46	0	36	54	0	39	60	1
25	17	25	0	20	32	0	21	36	0	23	40	0	30	49	0	34	54	0
24	12	21	0	15	27	0	17	31	0	19	35	0	25	42	0	29	49	0
23	9	18	0	11	23	0	13	26	0	14	29	0	20	37	0	24	42	0
22	7	14	0	8	18	0	9	22	0	11	25	0	16	31	0	19	36	0
21	5	11	0	6	15	0	6	18	0	9	20	0	13	26	0	15	30	0
20	4	9	0	4	11	0	5	14	0	6	16	0	10	21	0	12	24	0
19	2	7		2	8		3	11		5	13		7	17		10	20	
18	2	5		2	6		2	8		3	9		6	13		8	15	
17	1	4		1	5		1	5		2	7		4	9		6	11	
16	1	3		1	3		1	4		2	5		3	6		4	8	
15	0	2		0	2		0	3		1	3		2	4		3	6	
14	0	2		0	1		0	1		1	2		1	2		1	3	
13	0	1		0	1		0	1		0	1		1	2		1	2	
12	0	1		0	0		0	0		0	1		0	1		0	1	
11	0	0		0	0		0	0		0	0		0	0		0	0	
10	0	0		0	0		0	0		0	0		0	0		0	0	

Rhody Secondary Reading Attitude Assessment

Regina Tullock-Rhody and J. Estill Alexander

Purpose

To acquire a quantitative idea of students' attitudes toward reading. The assessment can be used with students in grades 7 through 12.

Administration

1. Reproduce the sheet titled "Rhody Secondary Reading Attitude Assessment" on the following page.
2. Assure students that the score will not affect their grades in any way.
3. Tell students how they should mark their answers. Use the directions on the students' copy.
4. Read each of the statements aloud as students read them silently and give students ample time to mark their responses.

Scoring and Interpretation

1. Assign numerical values to each of the 25 items as follows:

	Type and Number of Item	*Numerical Values*				
		SD	D	U	A	SA
Positive:	4, 5, 6, 7, 8, 10, 15, 17, 20, 22, 23, 24, 25	1	2	3	4	5
Negative:	1, 2, 3, 9, 11, 12, 13, 14, 16, 18, 19, 21	5	4	3	2	1

2. Add the numerical scores for all the statements. The student's score is a quantitative reflection of his or her attitude toward reading. The possible range of scores is 25 to 125. Interpret the score informally.
3. Items on the scale have been grouped into clusters to help teachers understand students' feelings toward areas of the reading environment. Use the cluster data informally.

Cluster	*Item Number*
School related reading	11, 18
Reading in the library	9, 20
Reading in the home	4, 10
Other recreational reading items	5, 17, 22, 24, 25
General reading	1, 2, 3, 6, 7, 8, 12, 13, 14, 15, 16, 19, 21, 23

4. Consult the original article for further information on the development of the attitude assessment.

Tullock-Rhody, R., & Alexander, J.E. (1980). A scale for assessing attitudes toward reading in secondary schools. *Journal of Reading, 23,* 609–614. Reprinted with permission of Regina Tullock-Rhody and the International Reading Association.

RHODY SECONDARY READING ATTITUDE ASSESSMENT

Name ______________________________ Date ______________

Directions: This is a survey to tell how you feel about reading. The score will not affect your grade in any way. You read the statements silently as I read them aloud. Then put an ☒ in the box under the letter or letters that represent how you feel about the statement.

SD = Strongly Disagree
D = Disagree
U = Undecided
A = Agree
SA = Strongly Agree

	SD	D	U	A	SA
1. You feel you have better things to do than read.	☐	☐	☐	☐	☐
2. You seldom buy a book.	☐	☐	☐	☐	☐
3. You are willing to tell people that you do not like to read.	☐	☐	☐	☐	☐
4. You have a lot of books in your room at home.	☐	☐	☐	☐	☐
5. You like to read a book whenever you have free time.	☐	☐	☐	☐	☐
6. You get really excited about books you have read.	☐	☐	☐	☐	☐
7. You love to read.	☐	☐	☐	☐	☐
8. You like to read books by well-known authors.	☐	☐	☐	☐	☐
9. You never check out a book from the library.	☐	☐	☐	☐	☐
10. You like to stay at home and read.	☐	☐	☐	☐	☐
11. You seldom read except when you have to do a book report.	☐	☐	☐	☐	☐
12. You think reading is a waste of time.	☐	☐	☐	☐	☐
13. You think reading is boring.	☐	☐	☐	☐	☐
14. You think people are strange when they read a lot.	☐	☐	☐	☐	☐
15. You like to read to escape from problems.	☐	☐	☐	☐	☐
16. You make fun of people who read a lot.	☐	☐	☐	☐	☐
17. You like to share books with your friends.	☐	☐	☐	☐	☐
18. You would rather someone just tell you information so that you won't have to read to get it.	☐	☐	☐	☐	☐
19. You hate reading.	☐	☐	☐	☐	☐
20. You generally check out a book when you go to the library.	☐	☐	☐	☐	☐
21. It takes you a long time to read a book.	☐	☐	☐	☐	☐
22. You like to broaden your interests through reading.	☐	☐	☐	☐	☐
23. You read a lot.	☐	☐	☐	☐	☐
24. You like to improve your vocabulary so you can use more words.	☐	☐	☐	☐	☐
25. You like to get books for gifts.	☐	☐	☐	☐	☐

Tullock-Rhody, R., & Alexander, J.E. (1980). A scale for assessing attitudes toward reading in secondary schools. *Journal of Reading, 23,* 609–614. Reprinted with permission of Regina Tullock-Rhody and the International Reading Association.

Strategy 2 SECTION 1.2

PICTURE BOOK SONGS

1. Explain to students that many popular songs have been made into picture books (Towell, 1999, 2000). Show students examples of songs made into picture books such as *The Ants Go Marching* or *This Old Man*. (A list of additional picture books made from songs follows on page 33.) Play or sing the songs for the students.
2. Identify a picture book song that students would enjoy singing. Write the words of the song on a chart, an overhead transparency, or sentence strips.
3. Teach students the words of the song by reading the written words.
4. Teach the tune of the song using a tape, CD, or a keyboard.
5. Listen to the music as you show the illustrations of the book. Track each line of the song as the students look at the words and listen to the music.
6. Ask students to sing along with the music. Practice a few lines at a time; then sing the entire song.
7. Make the book and tape available at the classroom listening center for students to use independently.

Strategy 3 SECTION 1.2

USING HUMOR

1. Set up a humorous literature center in your classroom (Klesius, Laframboise, & Gaier, 1998). You might use a countertop, a desk, or even the chalkboard ledge. Tell students that this area will be devoted to fun reading.
2. Stock the humorous literature center with joke books, riddles, humorous poetry, and books of word play. Include books with a variety of reading levels. (Examples of humorous literature follow on page 34.)
3. Introduce students to the types of books in the humorous literature center. For example, read a riddle from one of the riddle books.
4. Invite students to read books from the humorous literature center during independent reading time. Tell students that they don't have to read any of the books from the first page to the last page but that they can read selectively in these types of books.
5. Provide students with the opportunity to share some of the fun from these books with other class members. You might give students five minutes at the end of independent reading time to share a joke, riddle, or poem.
6. Change the selection of books in the humorous literature center every few weeks. Invite students to submit books to the center as well.

Picture Books Made from Songs

B-52s. *Wig!* New York: Hyperion, 1995. (available on tape)

Bates, Katharine Lee. *O Beautiful for Spacious Skies.* San Francisco: Chronicle, 1994.

Carpenter, Mary Chapin. *Halley Came to Jackson.* New York: HarperCollins, 1998. (with tape)

Collins, Judy. *My Father.* Boston: Little, Brown, 1968. (available on CD)

Garcia, Jerry, & Grisman, David. *The Teddy Bears' Picnic.* New York: HarperCollins, 1996. (with tape)

Judd, Naomi. *Love Can Build a Bridge.* New York: HarperCollins, 1999. (with tape)

Messenger, Jannat (illustrator). *Twinkle, Twinkle, Little Star.* New York: Piggy Toes, 1997. (with music)

Parton, Dolly. *A Coat of Many Colors.* New York: HarperCollins, 1994. (music available on CD)

Raffi. *Down by the Bay.* New York: Crown, 1990. (tape is available)

Rounds, Glen (illustrator). *Old MacDonald Had a Farm.* New York: Holiday House, 1989.

Trapani, Iza. *The Itsy Bitsy Spider.* Dallas: Whispering Coyote, 1993.

Weeks, Sarah. *Follow the Moon.* New York: Laura Geringer, 1995. (with tape)

Weiss, George David, & Thick, Bob. *What a Wonderful World.* New York: Atheneum, 1996.

Westcott, Nadine. *The Lady With the Alligator Purse.* Boston: Little, Brown, 1998.

Wood, Don and Audrey. *Piggies.* San Diego: Voyager, 1991. (with tape)

Books for Mood Music

de Paola, Tomie. *Fin M'Coul—the Giant of Knockmany Hill.* New York: Holiday House, 1982. (Irish music)

Downing, Julie. *Mozart Tonight.* New York: Bradbury, 1991. (classical music)

Gatti, Anne. *The Magic Flute.* San Francisco: Chronicle, 1997. (music by Mozart, comes with CD)

London, Jonathan. *Hip Cat.* San Francisco: Chronicle, 1993. (jazz)

Nichol, Barbara. *Beethoven Lives Upstairs.* New York: Orchard Books, 1993. (classical music)

Pinkney, Andrea Davis. *Duke Ellington.* New York: Hyperion, 1998. (swing, ragtime music)

Pratt, Kristin Joy. *A Walk in the Rainforest.* Nevada City: Dawn, 1992. (rainforest music)

Sheldon, Dyan. *The Whale's Song.* New York: Dial, 1990. (ocean music)

Yolen, Jane. *Owl Moon.* New York: Philomel, 1987. (classical music)

From Towell, J.H. (1999, 2000). Motivating students through music and literature. *The Reading Teacher, 53,* 284–287.

Recommended Humorous Literature

Barrett, Judi. *Animals Should Definitely Not Wear Clothes.* New York: Macmillan, 1970.

Bathroom Readers' Institute. *Uncle John's Bathroom Reader for Kids Only.* Ashland, OR: Bathroom Readers' Press, 2002.

Berenstein, Stan & Jan. *The Bike Lesson.* New York: Random House, 1964.

Berger, Melvin. *101 Wacky State Jokes.* New York: Scholastic, 1991.

Birdseye, Tom. *A Regular Flood of Mishaps.* New York: Holiday House, 1994.

Bridwell, Norman. *Clifford, the Big Red Dog.* New York: Scholastic, 1963.

Day, Alexandra. *Carl Goes to Daycare.* New York: Farrar, Straus & Giroux, 1993.

Gelman, Rita. *More Spaghetti, I Say.* New York: Scholastic, 1987.

Gwynne, Fred. *A Chocolate Moose for Dinner.* New York: Prentice-Hall, 1976.

Hepworth, Cathi. *Antics: An Alphabetical Anthology.* New York: G. P. Putnam's Sons, 1991.

Kowitt, Holly. *Fairly Odd Jokes.* New York: Simon Spotlight, 2004.

Lyon, George. *The Outside Inn.* New York: Orchard, 1991.

Macauley, David. *Why the Chicken Crossed the Road.* Boston: Houghton Mifflin, 1987.

Mayer, Mercer. *Little Critter's Joke Book.* New York: Golden Book, 1993.

Meddaugh, Susan. *Martha Speaks.* Boston: Houghton Mifflin, 1992.

Monsell, Mary. *Underwear.* Morton Grove, IL: Albert Whitman, 1988.

Most, Bernard. *The Cow That Went Oink.* New York: Harcourt Brace Jovanovich, 1990.

Noble, Trinka Hakes. *Jimmy's Boa and the Big Splash Birthday Bath.* New York: Trumpet, 1989.

Phillips, Bob. *Slam Dunk Jokes for Kids.* Eugene, OR: Harvest House, 2004.

Phillips, Bob, & Russo, Steve. *Jammin' Jokes for Kids.* Eugene, OR: Harvest House, 2004.

Pinkwater, Daniel. *The Wugglie Norple Story.* New York: Trumpet, 1980.

Sachaar, Louis. *Sideways Stories from Wayside School.* New York: Avon, 1978.

Schwartz, Amy. *Bea and Mr. Jones.* Scarsdale, NY: Bradbury, 1982.

Shaw, Nancy. *Sheep in a Jeep.* Boston: Houghton Mifflin, 1986.

Terban, Marvin. *Hey, Hay! A Wagonload of Funny Homonym Riddles.* New York: Clarion, 1991.

Thaler, Mike. *The Teacher from the Black Lagoon.* New York: Scholastic, 1989.

The Usborne Book of Animal Jokes. Saffron Hill, London: Usborne Publishing, 2003.

Van Laan, Nancy. *Possum Come A-knockin'.* New York: Trumpet, 1990.

Willis, Jeanne. *Earth Weather as Explained by Professor Xargle.* New York: Dutton, 1991.

Yoe, Craig. *Mighty Big Book of Knock Knock Jokes.* New York: Price Stern Sloan, 2002.

Klesius, J., Laframboise, K.L., & Gaier, M. (1998). Humorous literature: Motivation for reluctant readers. *Reading Research and Instruction, 37,* 253–261. Books published after 2002 were not in the original article.

Strategy 4
I HAVE THE KEY!

1. Use a locked cabinet, chest, or closet that can hold a variety of specially selected books and other reading materials. These materials should have the potential to appeal to all students, especially reluctant readers. Begin with a small number of items and add more as the school year progresses. Rearrange materials and provide some new items each week. You may also want to include objects related to selected books.
2. Create student interest by posting a sign on the cabinet that reads, "Locked Reading Materials." Use your key to open the door a bit and put in some covered reading materials so students are unable to read or see the selected titles. Repeat this process over several days to create greater interest. Add and arrange additional materials when students are not in the classroom.
3. As students express interest in the contents of the cabinet, you might say something like the following.

   I know many of you want to be able to read the books and other materials that are in the locked cabinet, but they aren't quite ready. In a few days, you'll see a sign-up sheet on the cabinet. Please be patient.

4. Continue to build interest in the locked cabinet. You might want to invite some reluctant readers to be among the first to sign up to select and check out materials.
5. As students begin selecting and reading the materials, keep interest high by adding more reading materials, including two or three copies of some titles. When there are multiple copies of the same title, and at least one of your students who is a reluctant reader selects that title, offer the books with the same title to the entire class. Select the reluctant reader and two other students to have the books first. Say something like what follows.

   I have two books with the same title as the one Cody selected. Who else might like to read this book?

   Encourage the students to read and discuss the books together. They could also discuss the books after all students have finished.
6. Adapt the locked cabinet idea in ways to interest and engage students in reading.

Strategy 5 PERSONAL INVITATION

1. Identify a particular student's interests and select an appropriate book or other reading material with that student in mind. To determine your students' interests, use observation, informal conversations, and/or selected items from the Resources for Chapter 1.
2. Meet with the student one-on-one and present the material you have selected. You might say something like the following.

   I've noticed that you seem to have an interest in art and drawing. I was thinking about you when I saw this book in the school library and thought you might like it. There are some tips on how to draw different types of animals along with step-by-step illustrations. I'd be happy to loan you the book if you'd like.

3. If the student declines your invitation, do not try to force the book.

   That's okay. I'll keep my eyes open for something else you might like. Is there anything in particular you would like me to look for?

   Return at a later time with a different book and another personal invitation.
4. If the student accepts your invitation, invite the student to share with you when he or she is finished with the book.

   I'd be interested in seeing one or more of your drawings and learning more about the book. You can just let me know when you would like to meet and share for a minute or two.

5. Continue to share Personal Invitations to help create a more favorable attitude toward reading. Be patient and do not force materials on the student. As the student shares, you will have an excellent opportunity to build positive rapport.

Practice and Reinforcement Activities

1. Have students write, illustrate, and bind their own books. Good titles for books might be *All About Me* or *An Experience I Had*. Write the stories on paper or use a computer. Let students illustrate their stories and share them with one another. Some students may prefer to illustrate their stories before they write or dictate them to help maintain the story line. Also, remember that some students may write more easily when topics are general and abstract. Provide this option.
2. Have a book scavenger hunt. Divide the class into teams and give each team a copy of the same book. Give students 15 minutes to find the page numbers of particular objects, events, or people in the book. After the time is over, have students share their results.
3. Give positive reinforcement when students read. Encourage students to share what was read.
4. Create a book nook where students can display their favorite books. Encourage students to make murals, pictures, or original book jackets to promote their books. Big pillows and bean-bag chairs can help make the book nook inviting. These displays may help reluctant readers realize that many of their peers enjoy reading.
5. Choose a picture book with a small amount of text to read to your students. Read the picture book to your students without telling them the title or showing them the cover. After reading the book, divide the class into groups of three or four students and have students brainstorm a title for the book. Share the titles that the students created and then show students the title and cover of the book.
6. Invite guest speakers to tell students how they use reading in jobs or everyday situations. (See page 5 in this chapter.)
7. Model your love of reading to your students. Bring copies of books you read for pleasure and read aloud appropriate short passages from the books. Share other types of printed materials that you read.
8. Invite a storyteller to your classroom. Explain to students that before books were available people shared stories by telling them to others. Discuss ways books have made stories accessible to more people.
9. Arrange students' chairs back to back in a semicircle. Place a book under each chair. Have students sit on the chairs without looking at the books. Play some music that students like. Tell students to walk around the chairs while the music is playing and to stop and sit in the nearest chair when the music stops. Have students preview the book that is under the chair by reading the title and the first page and paging through the rest of the book. Repeat this procedure more than once. Place the books on the chalkboard ledge or at another accessible place for students to read during independent reading time.
10. Provide informal opportunities for students to share their reading in literature circles or discussions.

Section 1.3

Limited Reading Interests

Behavior Observed → **Anticipated Outcome**

Behavior Observed	Anticipated Outcome
The student does not find much of interest to read.	The student will expand his or her interests in reading.

Background

"Most students develop strong interests in topics that they really want to learn about—not only lawn mowers or the body, but bugs, earthworms, airplanes, dolls, soccer, the U.S. Civil War, video games, music, and many other things" (Fischer & Fusaro, 2008, p. 64).

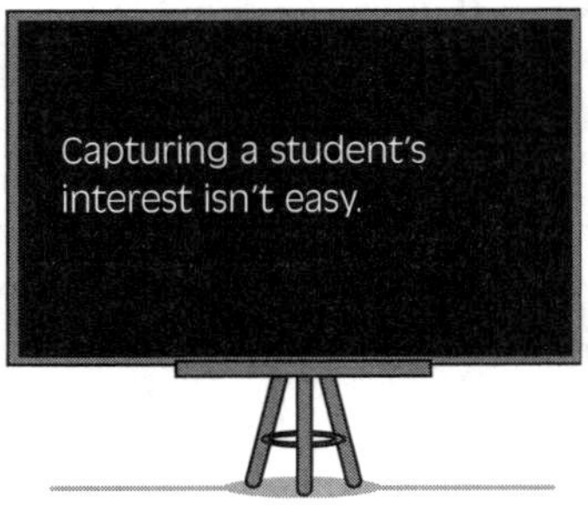
Capturing a student's interest isn't easy.

What contributes to a student's interests? It's hard to say why one student might be fascinated with rocks while another can't stand the topic. Certainly, familiarity may be a contributing factor to the formation of interests. Students who have spent hours with an adult collecting different kinds of rocks may have a natural interest in them. However, that doesn't always work. Sometimes spending time experiencing or learning about a topic doesn't increase one's interest.

Interest is not only hard to define; it's also changeable. What interests a student in fourth grade may not be interesting in fifth grade. Indeed, many students go through phases in reading and learning. There are trends and fads in literature just as there are in other social events. Capturing a student's interest isn't easy.

Although it may be difficult to identify students' interests, learning about what interests them is important. Students who read texts that are interesting to them tend to spend more time reading (McLoyd, 1979). Furthermore, students tend to have higher achievement in a topic that interests them (McPhail et al., 2000). Therefore, teachers should take the time to tailor students' reading to their interests. This section provides teaching strategies and activities to help in this undertaking.

INTEREST INVENTORY

1. Choose an Interest Inventory to administer to your students. News About Me (pages 40–41) is typically popular with elementary students and the Inventory of Experiences (pages 42–43) is more appropriate for upper elementary and middle school students.
2. Duplicate and distribute the appropriate Interest Inventory.
3. Explain to students that you would like them to complete either the News About Me or the Inventory of Experiences. Say something like the following.

   I would like to know more about you and what interests you. I want to know so I can find books that fit your interests and study the topics you want to learn. Please complete the inventories and include as many details as possible.

4. Allow adequate time for students to complete the Interest Inventory. (You may need to read it to some students.)
5. After the students have completed the inventory, have them discuss their interests with class members. Divide the class into groups of three or four students. Tell students to share their responses with their group members. Ask one of the group members to list the interests shared in discussion.

6. Have students share their interest lists with the entire class. After each entry, ask the class if others are interested in the topic. For example, if one student states that ice hockey is interesting, ask how many other students are interested in ice hockey. Encourage students with similar interests to share their knowledge about the topic. Jot down the names of students who share interests so you can use this knowledge to expand your classroom library and use the information when teaching.
7. Find books and other printed materials about many of the topics of interest. A librarian may help you. Place the books and materials in a visible place in the classroom and allow students time to read about topics that interest them.
8. Administer the interest inventories every few months. Interests change and you will find it useful to assess your students' current interests throughout the year. You may also want to carefully observe students to learn their new and emerging interests.

NEWS ABOUT ME

A News Story About ____

(write your name here)

News About My Family

I have ________ brothers and sisters.

They are ________________ years old.

I like to play with ______________________.

My family and I like to __________________.

I (like/do not like) to play alone.

I help at home by______________________.

The thing I like to do at home is__________

____________________________________.

News About My Pets

I have a pet ___________________________.

I (do/do not) take care of my pet.

I do not have a pet because______________

____________________________________.

I would like to have a pet ______________.

News About My Books and My Reading

I like to read about ____________________

____________________________________.

The best book I ever read was____________

____________________________________.

I (do get/do not get) books from the library.

I (have/do not have) a library card.

I have________ books of my own at home.

I read aloud to_________________________.

My _______________________ reads to me.

News About My Friends

My best friend is_______________________.

I like (him/her) because ________________

____________________________________.

We play_______________________________.

I would rather play (at my house/at my friend's house) because______________

____________________________________.

News About Things I Like and Dislike

I do not like__________________________.

I like________________________________.

I am afraid of_________________________.

I am not afraid of______________________.

News About My Wishes

When I grow up, I want to be____________

____

____________________________________.

If I could have three wishes I would wish

(1) _________________________________

____________________________________.

(2) _________________________________

____________________________________.

(3) _________________________________

____

____________________________________.

page 1

News about me *(continued)*

News About My Travels and Adventures

I have traveled by:

____ bus ____ car

____ airplane ____ truck

____ boat ____ train

____ bicycle ____ van

I have visited these interesting places:

____ circus ____ zoo

____ farm ____ park

____ hotel ____ museum

____ bakery ____ library

____ airport ____ fire station

____ factory, and ____________________.

The best adventure I ever had was ________

____________________________________.

News About My School Subjects

My favorite subject is ________________.

The subject I dislike most is ____________.

I am best at ________________________.

I wish I was better in _________________.

News About My Hobbies and Collections

One of my best hobbies is ______________

____________________________________.

My other hobbies are ___________________

____________________________________.

I collect ____________________________.

I want to collect ______________________.

Media Favorites

I (have/do not have) a computer at home.

I (use/do not use) a computer at home.

I watch ________ videos/DVDs each week.

I (have/do not have) my own cell phone.

I see ________________ movies each week.

I like to listen to ____________ on the radio.

I see __________ television programs a day.

My favorite programs are _______________

____________________________________.

Write any other news about yourself below.

____

____

____

____

____

____

page 2

INVENTORY OF EXPERIENCES

Name ______________________________ Date ______________

Special Interests

1. Which outdoor sports do you like?

   ____

2. Which indoor games do you like?

   ____

3. What types of collections or hobbies do you have?

   ____

4. Have you had classes or lessons in music, dancing, or art? Describe.

   ____

5. Do you belong to any clubs or groups like 4-H or Scouts? Describe.

   ____

6. Do you have any pets? Describe.

   ____

7. What are your favorite TV programs? Movies? Videos?

   ____

8. What is your favorite subject at school?

   ____

9. What do you do with your free time?

   ____

10. About how much time do you spend on a computer each day?

    ____

11. Who are some of your best friends, and what do you enjoy doing with them? Describe.

    ____

    ____

    ____

page 1

Your Family

1. What are the names and ages of your brothers and sisters?

   ____

2. What are some things you do together?

   ____

3. Do you ever go places, play games, or watch videos/DVDs with your entire family? If yes, please describe.

   ____

4. What trips have you taken?

   ____

5. Do you receive an allowance or spending money?

   ____

6. Do you have some regular duties or chores to do at home?

   ____

You and Books

1. What books and magazines do you have at home?

   ____

2. Do you have a library card? __________ Do you use it? __________
3. What kinds of books or stories do you like?

   ____

4. Do you like to have someone read to you?

   ____

5. Do you like to read to others?

   ____

page 2

BOOK TALKS

1. One good way to interest students in books is by giving a book talk. A book talk is a brief talk about a book with the purpose of enticing others to read it. There are several formats for sharing books through book talks:
   - Schedule a regular book talk every few days during which you can share one book you have read.
   - Read books about a theme and share them with the class before you begin the unit.
   - Share several books written by the same author.
   - Share different versions of the same story (e.g., Cinderella).
2. Read the book and prepare a short talk that will motivate students to read the book. As you prepare a book talk, remember that you do not want to give away the end of the story. If you tell the end of the story, you will destroy the students' suspense as they read it. Second, try to get the attention of the students during the first sentence. Third, try to make the book talk as appealing to your students as possible. A book talk is not a report on a book, but a motivational technique to encourage students to read the book. Finally, make the book talk short; two to three minutes are best.
3. There are several ways you can organize your book talk. Different books require different methods. Use whichever organizational pattern fits you and the book.
   - **Relate the book to a personal experience.**

     Ruckman, Ivy. (1984). *Night of the Twisters.* New York: HarperCollins.

     I've always been afraid of tornadoes. Whenever the siren rings out, I run to the basement with my radio, a bottle of water, and a hammer. My fear stems from a tornado that hit without warning in a nearby town. As I read *Night of the Twisters,* I felt what it would really be like to be caught in a tornado and what I would hear and see. Now I run to the basement whenever there's a tornado watch!
   - **Use quotations or excerpts from the book.**

     Paulsen, Gary. (1987). *Hatchet.* New York: Puffin Books.

     Imagine flying in a small airplane over the vast north woods of Canada. You are on your way to visit your father when suddenly something happens to the pilot, and he slumps over in his seat. *[Read pages 9–12 where the pilot has a heart attack.]* You are the only one aboard to land the airplane, and when you land, you are all alone, far away from civilization, trying to survive with only a hatchet and your own wits.
   - **Use props whenever appropriate.**

     Hesse, Karen. (1992). *Letters from Rifka.* New York: Henry Holt.

     [Wear a scarf, apron, and/or shawl.]

     Have you ever been to a new school? Remember how you felt: new, different, lonely? Rifka left Russia during the height of the Russian Revolution in 1919. She arrived in America sick and not knowing English. This diary shows how she felt and how she coped with the newness of America.

- **Dramatize the book talk by telling the book in the first person, using the main character's speech and dialect when appropriate.**

  Gardiner, John Reynolds. (1980). *Stone Fox*. New York: Thomas Y. Crowell.

  If only I had enough money to save my granpappy's farm. It's only $500, that's all I need. But $500 is a heap of money, more than I could git in a lifetime. Thar's only one way I can be fixin' to git the money, and that's not goin' to be easy. My dog, Searchlight, is the onliest chance I got. If he kin jist beat that ole Stone Fox, my granpappy's farm might be saved.

- **Prepare a short interview with the main character or the author.**

  Paterson, Katherine. (1978). *The Great Gilly Hopkins*. New York: Thomas Y. Crowell.

  Interviewer: Gilly, how did it feel to be put in a foster home again?

  Gilly: Man, I get sick of all these new places. Here I'm with this crazy lady, name of Maime Trotter, and William Ernest.

  Interviewer: Why are you here?

  Gilly: Well, my mom has had some trouble and couldn't take care of me.

  Interviewer: What will you do?

  Gilly: I'm going to find my mom and get out of here.

- **Prepare a script for a scene from the book. Ask students to read it, practice it, then perform it for the class.**

  Lowry, Lois. (1989). *Number the Stars*. New York: Bantam Doubleday, Dell.

  Annemarie walks outside where Uncle Henry is milking the cow.

  Annemarie: Uncle Henry, you're lying to me.

  Uncle Henry: You're angry.

  Annemarie: Yes. Mama has never lied to me before. Never. Why now?

  Uncle Henry: How brave are you, Annemarie? Are you brave enough to know the truth?

  They return to the house together. Several people are gathered around a casket.

  Mama: Remember, Annemarie, this is Great-aunt Birte. If anyone asks you, you must convince them. It could mean the safety of our family and our friends!

  Pounding on the door, boots stomping in.

  Officer: Why are all of you gathered here?

  Annemarie: *(trembling)* My Great-aunt Birte has just died.

Strategy 3

USING POPULAR CULTURE

1. Tell students that you will be asking them for ideas that are of interest to them to use as reading topics (Alvermann, Moon, & Hagood, 1999). Explain to students that their interests are valued in your class.
2. Ask students to list their three favorite types of media. For example, you might say something like the following.

   I'd like you to list your three favorite media. If I were to list my favorite media, I'd list the radio, movies, and the Internet. What are your favorite media?

3. After students have listed their favorite media, probe deeper by asking them to list their favorite shows, websites, or stations. For example you might say what follows.

   I like listening to Prairie Home Companion *and* Car Talk *on National Public Radio. I also like to watch movies that are set in Ireland.*

4. Have students continue making lists of their popular culture by asking them to list favorite movie stars, sports heroes, television characters, radio personalities, video games, and/or online games.
5. Ask students to share their lists with class members. Divide the class into groups of three or four students and have students tell their classmates about their media interests. Allow enough time for all students to share.
6. Ask students to volunteer to share their interests with the entire class. As students discuss their media interests, create a list of the things that interest them. Post the list in a visible place in your classroom.
7. Collect books and magazine articles about the media interests of the students. Place the materials in an accessible place in the classroom. Tell students that they can also bring in reading material. Allow students time to browse the materials and suggest that they select this reading material for independent reading.

Are there reading materials available in classrooms that will be of interest to these students?

ITEM OF THE WEEK

1. When students have read a particularly good book, story, article, or other type of reading material, they may want to share it. Tell students that "Item of the Week" will provide an opportunity for some of them to share their reading with other students in the class.
2. Develop guidelines for sharing and take time to teach students how to share. Some possible considerations are listed below.
   - Your sharing should take only 60 to 90 seconds.
   - Include the title and author in your sharing.
   - Decide the best way to interest others in the reading material.
   - Avoid giving away the ending.
   - A few sentences might be read aloud to interest or entertain.
   - Pretend that you are on TV.

   Model a way to share something you have read and then discuss qualities of that sharing with the class.
3. Provide a place where students can write their names, the title, and the author of the materials they want to share. You could use part of the chalkboard, a poster, or a bulletin board. Emphasize that only best items should be considered for sharing.
4. Once three to five students have signed up to share, meet the students individually to monitor their sharing to provide constructive feedback. Later, give each student a minute or two to share and "sell" their material.
5. After sharing, invite the class to vote for one or two of their favorite items. A ballot box could be provided. Later, count the votes and write the favorites on a poster or bulletin board. You may say something like the following.

   > *Yesterday after school I counted your votes. Every item got votes. I have listed all the items on this chart and starred the one that got the most votes along with the name of the student who did the sharing. Some of you may like to read this item. I'd be interested in your reactions. You can fill out a reaction sheet and rate the material.*

6. Introduce the Reaction Sheet (see the next page for an example) and explain how it can be completed. Provide a notebook or folder for the completed Reaction Sheets. Use the Item of the Week and Reaction Sheet to help encourage and motivate reading.

REACTION SHEET

Title ____

Author ____

Directions:	For the above title, tell why you liked or did not like it. You can also share a favorite part of the story. Color in the number of stars at the bottom of the sheet to rate the item as excellent (5 stars), very good (4 stars), good (3 stars), not so good (2 stars), or poor (1 star). Be sure to sign your name as the reactor.

My Reaction

____

____

____

____

____

____

____

____

____

My Rating

☆ ☆ ☆ ☆ ☆

____

Student's Signature

Practice and Reinforcement Activities

1. Do your best to help students find books of interest. Sooner or later, interests will be directed toward related areas or completely new areas. When this occurs, be ready to help students find books and materials that will satisfy the emerging interest areas.
2. To help expand interests, invite community members to share their special interests, hobbies, or experiences. Try to link their sharing to books available in the school, classroom, or community library.
3. Provide plenty of reading material that varies in difficulty, content, and genre.
4. Poll students to determine their major interests and create numerous reading experiences in these areas.
5. Read to students daily. Select a wide variety of material from various genres. Assist students who would like other books similar in nature to the ones you have read to them. Perhaps they would like a different book by the same author. Encourage book-sharing ideas among classmates. Introduce a "book of the week" or an "author of the week" (or month).
6. Use movies, filmstrips, photographs, videotapes, DVDs, and concrete objects to help stimulate an interest in different subjects. Secure books or other reading materials that relate to these subjects and have the material available for the students to read.
7. If available, local authors can be invited to talk about books they have written. Family members can also be invited into the classroom to share the kinds of materials they like to read.
8. Develop a paperback book exchange in the classroom.
9. Encourage students to follow up on their natural curiosity by brainstorming a list of interests that students have. Then conduct a search of books at the students' grade level that would support the students' interests. Staple the lists inside the students' reading folders and invite students to read at least two books from each list.
10. Have students from other classes or schools at your grade level develop a list of their top 20 books. Share each class's list with other participating classes. Post the lists in a prominent place and encourage your students to read books from each list.
11. Decorate a box to place in your room that you can use as a Suggestion Box. Invite students to think about topics that interest them and have them list the ideas on an index card. Then have them drop the card in the Suggestion Box. Explain that any time students have ideas about books they would like to read, they should write the ideas on a card and drop it in the box. Use the suggestions students submit to guide your choices of read alouds and book talks.
12. When students self-select books, encourage them to ask themselves why they have chosen the book. Ask them occasionally to write about their book selections in their journals. You might ask some students to keep track of their reasons for choosing their books on a book choice chart.
13. In literature circles have students discuss self-selected readings and why they chose each book.
14. Encourage students to present their own book talks. Videotape them to play back when students are inside during recess or when you want to reinforce the idea of varying book selections.
15. Ask students to prepare a poster advertising a genre of books.
16. Ask the librarian to highlight new books and other materials in the library that would be appropriate for your grade level.
17. Prepare individual bingo sheets with the different genres printed in each block. As a motivational tool, ask students to keep track of their self-selected reading. When they get four down or across, award them with additional free reading time. The next page contains a sample bingo sheet.

(continued)

Book Genre Bingo

historical fiction	fantasy	"how-to"	folktales
realistic fiction	plays	biographies	science fiction
poetry	picture books	folktales	historical fiction
picture books	realistic fiction	fantasy	informational books

Section 1.4

Low Confidence in Reading Ability

Behavior Observed →
The student has a low level of confidence in his or her reading ability.

Anticipated Outcome
The student will gain greater confidence in reading.

Background

Confidence, or the belief that you can succeed, is an important factor in motivation (Ryan & Deci, 2000). Younger students may lack confidence in reading because there are many unknown words in their books. Older students, especially those who have experienced difficulty with reading, may have a fear of repeated failure. In both cases, students need to experience success with reading. Ruddell and Unran (2004) encourage teachers to "design an environment that intentionally builds student self-worth" (p. 971). The following strategies and activities may prove useful for students with low confidence in their reading ability.

READER SELF-PERCEPTION SCALE

1. Tell students that you will be giving them a survey to determine how they feel about reading. Explain to students that you are interested in their honest responses and that their responses on the survey will not affect their grade.
2. Duplicate and distribute the Reader Self-Perception Scale (Henk & Melnick, 1995) on pages 54–55. Have students write their names on the top of the survey.
3. Read the directions on the survey with the students. If students are able to read the survey, have them complete it independently. Allow ample time for students to complete the survey. For students experiencing difficulty with reading, read the statements aloud.
4. Collect the surveys and use the scoring sheet following the survey to determine each student's reading self-perception.
5. For students who have a low level of confidence in their reading ability, try several strategies and activities in this section and make a concerted effort to help them gain greater confidence in reading.

Reader Self-Perception Scale

William A. Henk and Steven A. Melnick

Purpose

The Reader Self-Perception Scale (RSPS) is intended to provide an assessment of how students feel about themselves as readers. The scale consists of 33 items that assess self-perceptions along four dimensions of self-efficacy (Progress, Observational Comparison, Social Feedback, and Physiological States). Students are asked to indicate how strongly they agree or disagree with each statement on a 5-point scale (5 = Strongly Agree, 1 = Strongly Disagree). The information gained from this scale can be used to devise ways to enhance students' self-esteem in reading and, ideally, to increase their motivation to read. The following directions explain specifically what you are to do.

Administration

1. For the results to be of any use, students must understand exactly what they are to do, have sufficient time to complete all items, and respond honestly and thoughtfully.
2. Briefly explain to students that they are being asked to complete a questionnaire about reading. Emphasize that this is not a *test* and that there are no *right* answers. Tell them that they should be as honest as possible because their responses will be confidential.
3. Ask students to fill in their names and the date.
4. Read the directions aloud and work through the example with the students as a group. Before moving on, discuss the response options and make sure that all students understand the rating scale. It is important that students know that they may raise their hands to ask questions about any words or ideas they do not understand.
5. Students should then read each item and circle their response for the item. They should work at their own pace. Remind students that they should be sure to respond to all items.
6. When all items are completed, students should stop, put their pencils down, and wait for further instructions.
7. Care should be taken that students who work more slowly are not disturbed by students who have already finished.

Scoring and Interpretation

1. To score the RSPS, enter the following point values for each response on the RSPS scoring sheet (Strongly Agree = 5, Agree = 4, Undecided = 3, Disagree = 2, Strongly Disagree = 1) for each item number under the appropriate scale. Add each column to obtain a raw score for each of the four specific scales.
2. Each scale is interpreted in relation to its total possible score. For example, because the RSPS uses a 5-point scale and the Progress scale consists of 9 items, the highest score for Progress is 45 ($9 \times 5 = 45$). Therefore, a score that would fall approximately in the middle of the range (22–23) would indicate a child's somewhat indifferent perception of herself or himself as a reader with respect to Progress. Note that each scale has a different possible total raw score (Progress = 45, Observational Comparison = 30, Social Feedback = 45, and Physiological States = 40) and should be interpreted accordingly.

Henk, W.A., & Melnick, S.A. (1995). The Reader Self-Perception Scale (RSPS): A new tool for measuring how children feel about themselves as readers. *The Reading Teacher, 48*, 470–482. Reprinted with permission.

READER SELF-PERCEPTION SCALE

Name ____ Date ____________________

Listed below are statements about reading. Please read each statement carefully. Then circle the letters that show how much you agree or disagree with the statement. Use the following scale.

SA = Strongly Agree		D = Disagree	
A = Agree		SD = Strongly Disagree	
U = Undecided			

Example: **I think pizza with pepperoni is best.** SA A U D SD

If you are *really positive* that pepperoni pizza is best, circle SA (Strongly Agree).
If you *think* that it is good but maybe not great, circle A (Agree).
If you *can't decide* whether or not it is best, circle U (Undecided).
If you *think* that pepperoni pizza is not all that good, circle D (Disagree).
If you are *really positive* that pepperoni pizza is not very good, circle SD (Strongly Disagree).

1. I think I am a good reader.	SA	A	U	D	SD
2. I can tell that my teacher likes to listen to me read.	SA	A	U	D	SD
3. My teacher thinks that my reading is fine.	SA	A	U	D	SD
4. I read faster than other kids.	SA	A	U	D	SD
5. I like to read aloud.	SA	A	U	D	SD
6. When I read, I can figure out words better than other kids.	SA	A	U	D	SD
7. My classmates like to listen to me read.	SA	A	U	D	SD
8. I feel good inside when I read.	SA	A	U	D	SD
9. My classmates think that I read pretty well.	SA	A	U	D	SD
10. When I read, I don't have to try as hard as I used to.	SA	A	U	D	SD
11. I seem to know more words than other kids when I read.	SA	A	U	D	SD
12. People in my family think I am a good reader.	SA	A	U	D	SD

Henk, W.A., & Melnick, S.A. (1995). The Reader Self-Perception Scale (RSPS): A new tool for measuring how children feel about themselves as readers. *The Reading Teacher, 48*, 470–482. Reprinted with permission.

READER SELF-PERCEPTION SCALE *(continued)*

13. I am getting better at reading.	SA	A	U	D	SD
14. I understand what I read as well as other kids do.	SA	A	U	D	SD
15. When I read, I need less help than I used to.	SA	A	U	D	SD
16. Reading makes me feel happy inside.	SA	A	U	D	SD
17. My teacher thinks I am a good reader.	SA	A	U	D	SD
18. Reading is easier for me than it used to be.	SA	A	U	D	SD
19. I read faster than I could before.	SA	A	U	D	SD
20. I read better than other kids in my class.	SA	A	U	D	SD
21. I feel calm when I read.	SA	A	U	D	SD
22. I read more than other kids.	SA	A	U	D	SD
23. I understand what I read better than I could before.	SA	A	U	D	SD
24. I can figure out words better than I could before.	SA	A	U	D	SD
25. I feel comfortable when I read.	SA	A	U	D	SD
26. I think reading is relaxing.	SA	A	U	D	SD
27. I read better now than I could before.	SA	A	U	D	SD
28. When I read, I recognize more words than I used to.	SA	A	U	D	SD
29. Reading makes me feel good.	SA	A	U	D	SD
30. Other kids think I'm a good reader.	SA	A	U	D	SD
31. People in my family think I read pretty well.	SA	A	U	D	SD
32. I enjoy reading.	SA	A	U	D	SD
33. People in my family like to listen to me read.	SA	A	U	D	SD

Henk, W.A., & Melnick, S.A. (1995). The Reader Self-Perception Scale (RSPS): A new tool for measuring how children feel about themselves as readers. *The Reading Teacher, 48*, 470–482. Reprinted with permission.

READER SELF-PERCEPTION SCALE SCORING SHEET

Student Name ______________________________

Teacher ______________________________

Grade ______________________ Date ______________________

Scoring key: 5 = Strongly Agree (SA)
4 = Agree (A)
3 = Undecided (U)
2 = Disagree (D)
1 = Strongly Disagree (SD)

Scales

General Perception	*Progress*	*Observational Comparison*	*Social Feedback*	*Physiological States*
1. ____	10. ____	4. ____	2. ____	5. ____
	13. ____	6. ____	3. ____	8. ____
	15. ____	11. ____	7. ____	16. ____
	18. ____	14. ____	9. ____	21. ____
	19. ____	20. ____	12. ____	25. ____
	23. ____	22. ____	17. ____	26. ____
	24. ____		30. ____	29. ____
	27. ____		31. ____	32. ____
	28. ____		33. ____	
Raw score	____ of 45	____ of 30	____ of 45	____ of 40
Score interpretation				
High	44+	26+	38+	37+
Average	39	21	33	31
Low	34	16	27	25

Henk, W.A., & Melnick, S.A. (1995). The Reader Self-Perception Scale (RSPS): A new tool for measuring how children feel about themselves as readers. *The Reading Teacher, 48*, 470–482. Reprinted with permission.

Strategy **2** SECTION 1.4

WE-CAN CHARTS

1. Determine specific reading skills and strategies to teach students over a three- or four-week period and list them on the We-Can Chart (Cleland, 1999). A sample chart is provided on page 58.
2. Read the list of reading skills and strategies with students. Have students contribute additional things they want to learn.
3. Make a copy of the We-Can Chart for each student. Have students place the chart in their reading folders.
4. Tell students that you will be working with them on the skills and strategies listed on the chart. Explain to students that they will learn each of these skills and strategies in the next few weeks. You might say something like the following.

   For the next few weeks we will be learning how to identify the setting of a story, how to decode compound words, and how to make predictions while reading. As we work on these skills and strategies, you will find that you are able to do them well. After a few weeks, we'll add them to the We-Can column of the chart and add more items to our list.

5. After you have taught a skill or strategy, have students write the sentence "We can __________ (name of skill or strategy)." Express your delight that the students are learning so well.
6. Remind students frequently of the many things they have learned how to do.

Strategy **3** SECTION 1.4

CUSHIONING

1. Tell students that no one can do everything, learn everything, and be the best at everything. Explain to students that people often *cushion* themselves when they are facing a difficult task (Harmin, 1995).
2. Describe the word *cushion* by having students visualize the bumper of a car. For example say something like what follows.

   Cars have front and rear bumpers to prevent damage if they are hit. The bumper absorbs the impact before it gets to the main car. When you cushion, you are putting a barrier like a car bumper in front of you.

3. Give students examples of statements that are meant to cushion their egos. For example, if you are introducing a difficult skill like syllabication, say something like the following.

   We are going to learn how to divide two-syllable words today. The rules are kind of difficult to learn, but if you try really hard, you'll learn the rules in time.

4. Provide students with examples of your own cushioning attempts. For example you might say something like what follows.

   I know I need to exercise, but I can't do it every day. I try to exercise three times a week.

continued on page 59

WE-CAN CHART

Name ______________________________________ Date ________________

Skill or Strategy	*We-Can Sentence*

5. Introduce a difficult skill and have students practice cushioning statements. Have them write their statements on an overhead transparency or on the chalkboard. Then have the class read the statements together.
6. Explain to students that cushioning is an important skill to learn in school and that they need to be in charge of building their own confidence by expecting just the right amount of effort from themselves.

Strategy 4 SECTION 1.4

STORY AMBASSADOR

1. Identify a student whose confidence in reading is low and invite him or her to become a Story Ambassador. Explain that a Story Ambassador prepares a story or book to be shared with a younger student or a small group of students that you have identified with the help of another teacher. That teacher may also be able to suggest a specific story or book to read. Adapt the following example as you talk to the student.

   I'd like to invite you to be a Story Ambassador. That's someone who will read a story to a younger student. Ms. Wright, who taught you in second grade, has given me this story that she would like you to read to Jason, one of her students. I'll help you practice so you can do a great job. Take a look at this story and then we'll talk. Okay?

2. Meet with the student after the story has been read for the first time to determine what needs to be done. It would also be helpful to have the student tape record the story, listen to it, and identify areas to strengthen. Some areas to consider are listed below.
   - Knows all the words
   - Reads with phrasing and expression
   - Sits near the other student so pictures can be seen
   - Has confidence
3. Once the student, with your guidance, feels comfortable and confident, have the student practice with one student in your classroom. Use additional students if more practice is needed or desired.
4. Make a badge or button with the words "Story Ambassador." When the student is fully prepared, arrange a time for the younger student to listen to the story read by the Story Ambassador.
5. After the story has been shared, meet with your student for a debriefing session. The other teacher may also share some input with you and provide a "thank-you" note for the Story Ambassador.
6. Give the student other opportunities to be a Story Ambassador. The student could also help you prepare other students from your class to become Story Ambassadors. You can initially focus on students who lack confidence as well as students who are struggling in reading. Practice leads to automaticity and automaticity, coupled with reinforcement from others, can help the student acquire more confidence in reading. The potential for Story Ambassadors is great, so use it to empower more of your students. Strive to include all of your students during the school year.

Strategy 5

READERS THEATER

1. Select a Readers Theater script that will appeal to a group of your reluctant readers. One source for free scripts on a range of grade levels is *www.aaronshep.com.*
2. Read the script yourself and decide which parts to assign to students. Parts can be assigned based on reading ability, length, or other criteria you deem important.
3. Read the script to students as they follow along. Discuss the plot, characters, events, and resolution. Then assign parts and guide students in marking their parts.
4. Encourage students to practice reading their parts alone or with a partner. Some students may be able to find easy-to-use props that can enhance meaning and promote engagement.
5. When students have practiced so they can read with expression and meaning, perform the script for other students in the class. Repeat the performance for a variety of audiences (e.g., other classes or groups, parents).
6. Provide additional opportunities for students to participate in reading and sharing scripts. Students could also assume greater responsibility for the entire process.

Practice and Reinforcement Activities

1. The best way to instill confidence in the student is to ensure that reading material is at the student's independent level. At this level the student should have no difficulty pronouncing words (1% error rate) or understanding the passage. In short, the independent level is that level at which the student can read fluently without teacher assistance.
2. Praise the student. Use positive reinforcement as much as possible. Encourage the student whenever he or she is reading.
3. Provide opportunities for the student to read and reread materials several times. Rereading materials often provides the practice needed to make reading more fluent. A description of Structured Repeated Reading is in Chapter 4 Resources (page 326).
4. If the student appears to be overwhelmed by books, provide phrases, sentences, or short paragraphs that the student can read prior to attempting full-length passages or books. In addition, some teachers have found that converting basal readers, anthologies, or longer stories into small "books" can help build a student's confidence.
5. Use progress charts or visuals that show the student's gains in areas such as words known, strategies mastered, passages read, or books completed. Construct the charts or visuals in such a way that small gains reveal progress. This approach can be especially motivating if the student is invited to select a theme or format for the activity. For example, a student can draw a jar shape on construction paper and then cut out jelly bean shapes from construction paper. When a new word is learned, the student can write it on a jelly bean and paste it to the jar. You can also use student-decorated boxes for words learned.
6. Have the student prepare a story or book to be read to another teacher, the school secretary, volunteers, or the principal. Encourage rereading of stories or books by having the student gather signatures from students, family members, or other adults (the principal, secretary, and so on) who have listened to the book being read.

7. Use pattern books to motivate students to write their own stories. A repeated phrase or theme can help students create stories. For example, a repeated pattern or sentence might be "Little dog, little dog, why do you dig?" Students write the question and create a response. Students should try to think of several different responses to the questions. Part C on the CD contains a list of pattern books that may be useful for developing students' stories.
8. Encourage family members to reinforce any reading that is done at home.
9. Use a taped version of a book or story and have students listen and follow along.
10. Employ choral reading activities to help students gain confidence in sharing a poem with the rest of the class.
11. Permit students to choose what they will read without coercion or encouragement from anyone.
12. Have a small microphone available for students to use when reading a book to the class. Have students practice reading a book several times and then give them the opportunity to go "on stage."
13. Remember the positive influence of the student's friends. "My friends were really the push I had for reading. My best friend read the encyclopedias for fun! She introduced me to many high-brow books and poetry. I imagine we were some of the few seventh graders that had read *Candide* twice" (Carlsen & Sherrill, 1988, p. 72).
14. Decorate a cardboard box as a book box. Put classroom-made books into the book box. Invite students to read these books to a selected audience such as the principal, the students' friends, or their families.
15. Try book stacking with students who have low confidence in their reading ability. Place a stack of five or six books that are very easy to read on each student's desk. When students come into the classroom, ask them to begin reading the stack of books in order. Allow time for students to read all of the books.

Section 1.5

Reluctant to Set Goals

Behavior Observed →

The student does not set reading goals.

Anticipated Outcome

The student will learn how to set goals to improve reading.

Background

An important component of motivation is the ability to set goals (Ames, 1992). When students set achievement goals, they make a determination to learn, feel a sense of accomplishment, and take control over their own learning. Students who are motivated to set learning goals have a better self-concept; the act of setting goals and completing a task gives students the belief that they can learn. As a result, students who set learning goals have a better self-concept about their abilities as students (Ames, 1992).

Students who set achievement goals
- are determined to learn,
- feel a sense of accomplishment, and
- take control over their own learning.

Learning goals are different from extrinsic rewards for learning. Students who set learning goals are internalizing and organizing their learning tasks; they are not merely receiving rewards for their accomplishments. The distinction between having students set learning goals and giving them rewards is in the outcome of the activity. Students who are setting learning goals are keeping track of their achievements, not for a reward but for their own advancement. Teachers can help their students become more goal oriented by using the strategies and activities that follow.

DAILY READING RECORD

1. Explain to students that some readers keep track of the number of pages that they read. Emphasize that readers keep track of their reading to accomplish learning goals, not for rewards.
2. Tell students that they can keep track of their reading with a Daily Reading Record. Explain to students that a Daily Reading Record is a system to record how many pages, chapters, stories, or books they have read each day.
3. Duplicate and distribute the copy of Juanita's Daily Reading Record at the bottom of this page or make a transparency and place it on the overhead projector. Explain how the graph was made by saying something like the following.

   This is a graph that shows Juanita's Daily Reading Record. On the left-hand side of the graph you will find the numbers 1 through 10+. The number 1 is at the bottom of the graph and the numbers ascend through 10+. These numbers indicate how many pages Juanita read. On the bottom of the page are the days of the week. For each day the bar is at the height of the number of pages Juanita read.

4. Ask students to practice reading the graph by choosing a day and then ask students how many pages Juanita read. Repeat this process until the students are comfortable reading the graph.
5. Duplicate and distribute to students the blank copy of the Daily Reading Record on page 64. Ask students to put their names in the blank at the top of the graph. Tell students that this copy will be their way of recording the number of pages they have read.
6. Ask students to record the number of pages they have read each day. Keep copies of the graphs in a folder for future reference. Encourage students to increase the number of pages they read with each graph.
7. After students have completed several weeks of Daily Reading Records, have them reflect on any improvements they have shown.
8. An alternative to charting the number of pages read is charting the amount of time students have read.

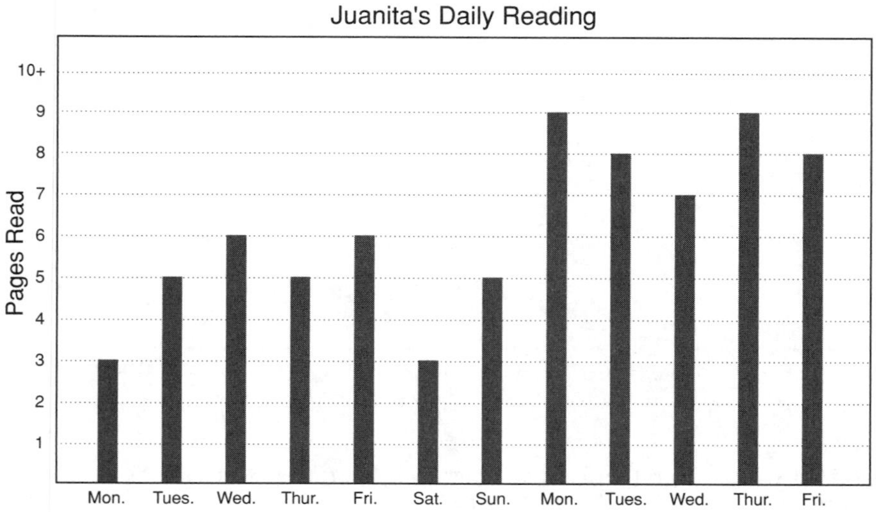

DAILY READING RECORD

Name ____ Date ____________________

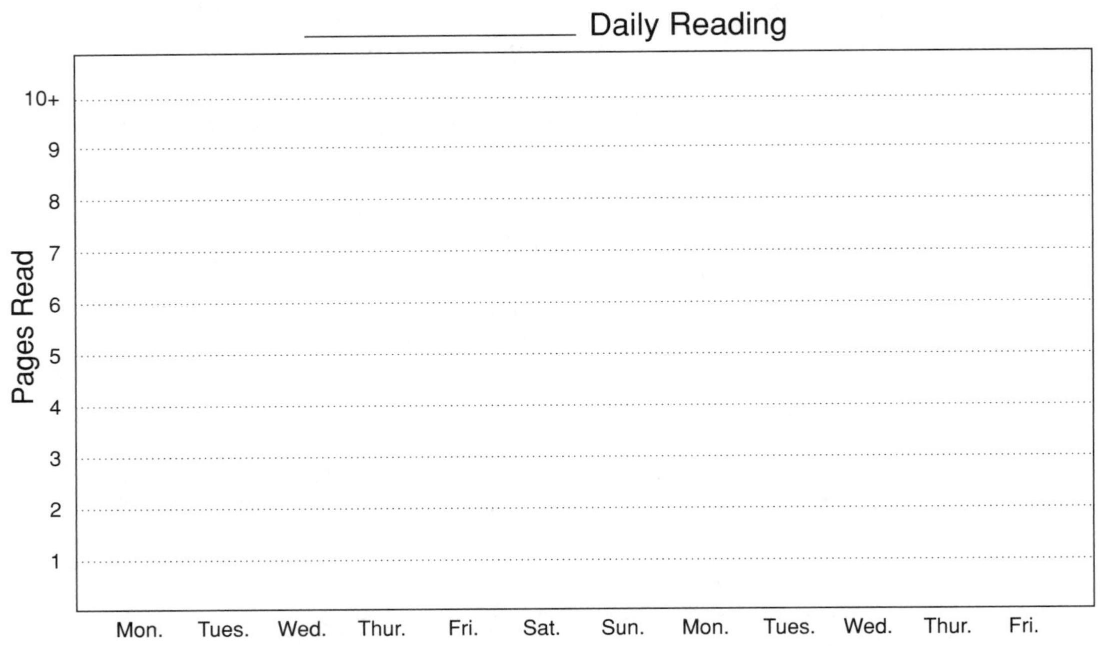

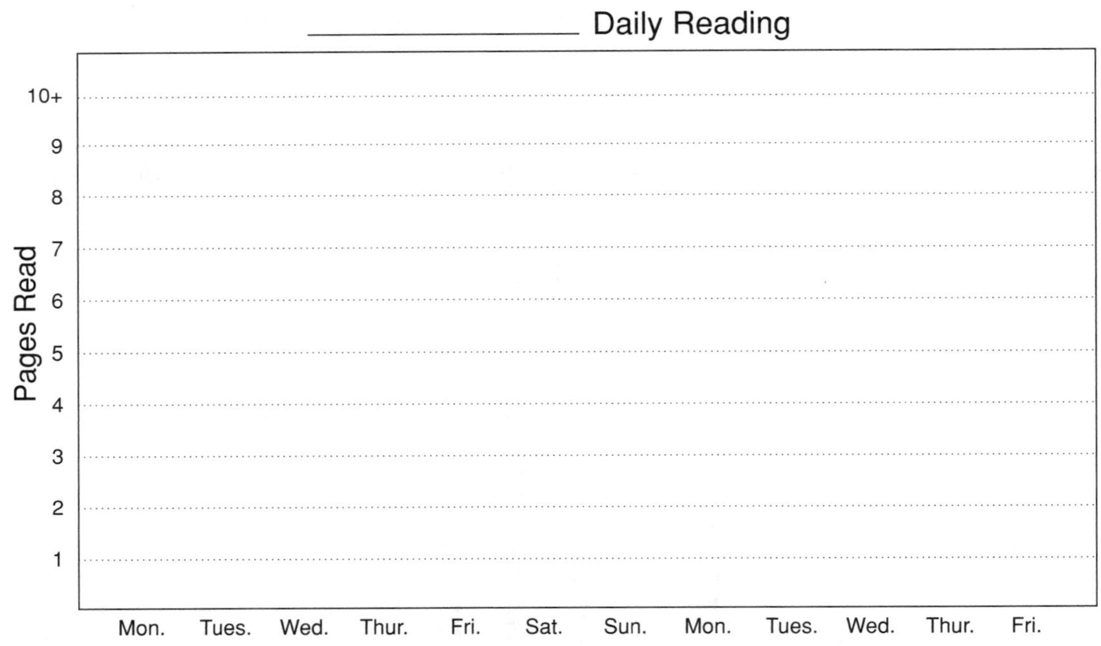

GENRE CHARTS

1. Tell students that good readers often keep track of the kinds of books they read in order to challenge themselves to read a variety of books. Say something like the following.

   Sometimes readers get in a rut. They keep reading the same type of books. It's not wrong to read the same kind of book week after week, but good readers know that they need variety to improve their reading. I usually read mysteries at home, but I try to read a different kind of book every two weeks. Last week I read a science fiction book, and I really liked it.

2. Duplicate and distribute copies of the Book Record Chart on page 66. Tell students that you want them to record the types of books they read during the next several weeks. Show students how to use the chart by making an overhead transparency of a sample Book Record Chart and putting it on an overhead projector. Show students where to place their names, the dates, the authors, the titles of the books, and the genres.
3. Keep track of your own independent reading in the same way.
4. Tell students that if they are unsure of the genre of the book that they should look on the spine of the book or ask a friend, a librarian, or you. Explain to students that books are classified by genre but that sometimes people can disagree about the name of the genre.
5. After several weeks of students keeping track of the books they have read, have them record their reading choices on the Reading Genre Chart on page 67.
6. Duplicate and distribute copies of the Reading Genre Chart. To explain how to use the chart, make an overhead transparency of a blank copy of the chart (or use a sample) and put it on the overhead projector. Use your own Book Record Chart to fill in your reading choices. To complete the Reading Genre Chart, color one grid per book next to the genre of each book read. For example, if you read two informational books, color two boxes next to the term informational books.
7. Have students complete their own Reading Genre Chart. Then have students reflect on their book choices and set personal goals for adding more variety to their reading.
8. You may also choose to compile a Reading Genre Chart for the entire class so students can see the range of genres read over a period of time.

BOOK RECORD CHART

Name ______________________________ Date ______________

Date	Author/Title	Genre

READING GENRE CHART

Name ______________________________ Date ______________

Genre	*Number of Completed Books*											
	1	*2*	*3*	*4*	*5*	*6*	*7*	*8*	*9*	*10*	*11*	*12*
Informational books												
Picture books												
Historical fiction												
Science fiction												
Biographies												
Fantasy												
Realistic fiction												
Folktales												
Plays												
"How-to" books												

Strategy 3

CHALLENGING BOOK CALENDAR

1. Explain to students that good readers try to challenge themselves by reading challenging books. Say something like the following.

   I like to read mysteries and informational books, but sometimes I read poetry to challenge myself. I try to read at least one challenging book every month. Last month, I read a book called War and Peace. *It's an extremely long book set in Russia. It was difficult for me because of the Russian names, but I kept with it and finished it. I felt really good about myself because I know that I am becoming a better reader by reading challenging books.*

2. Ask students to take out their independent reading books. Have students scan through the pages thinking about how challenging the books are for them. Tell students to decide whether the books are pretty easy, medium, or difficult. Have students who are reading books that are difficult raise their hands and tell the class why the book is challenging.
3. Discuss what makes a book challenging for students at your grade level. Probably the length of the book, the size of the print, the difficulty of the sentences, the words, and the content will be some reasons why a book is easy or difficult.
4. Help students identify books that are challenging for them. Have students write a list of books that they could read but that would not be easy.
5. Explain to students that good readers don't always read challenging books but that they make a point to read them occasionally. Duplicate and distribute the calendar on page 69. Have students write their names and the date on the calendar.
6. Ask students to place one or more stars on the calendar for the days when they predict they will finish a challenging book. Say something like the following.

   I'm going to read two challenging books this month so I will place two stars on the calendar two weeks apart. My goal is to have a challenging book read on the date by the star.

7. Remind students every few weeks to update their Challenging Book Calendar. Praise students for reading challenging books and encourage them to feel good about accomplishing a learning goal.

CHALLENGING BOOK CALENDAR

Name ______________________________ Date ______________

Place a star (★) on the days you predict you will finish reading a challenging book.

Sunday	*Monday*	*Tuesday*	*Wednesday*	*Thursday*	*Friday*	*Saturday*

Strategy 4 SECTION 1.5

PURPOSES OF LITERACY IN LIFE SURVEY

1. Intermediate-grade students may not see a purpose in reading. Use this activity to help them see how much reading is done in everyday life. Discuss with students the purposes for reading (i.e., instructions, communication, enjoyment, learning, and entertainment).
2. Share a list of reading you did in one day or on a weekend, at home and at school, on the Purposes of Literacy in Life Survey on page 71. Discuss the purpose you had for each reading.
3. Duplicate and give a copy of the survey on page 71 to each student.
4. Brainstorm other types of reading that might be done. Make a list of these and have students write them on the back of the survey as a reminder.
5. Have students fill out the survey at home over a weekend.

6. Have students share their individual surveys in small groups. Then combine the results of the surveys on chart paper together as a class.
7. Post the chart in the classroom for students to be reminded of the purposes for reading. Provide a variety of materials in the classroom and encourage students to share their purposes for reading particular materials. The sharing may be done orally or in writing. A list of possible texts you might include in your classroom is listed below (Worthy, 2001).

   - Reference books (e.g., thesaurus, dictionary, encyclopedia)
   - Informational books and magazines (e.g., *Discovery, Cobblestone*) on a number of interesting topics
   - A variety of current news and information sources (e.g., record books, almanacs, newspapers, news magazines, the Internet)
   - Song lyrics
   - Materials that encourage language play (e.g., jokes, riddles, secret codes, puns, palindromes, word games, mad-libs, or other fill-in-the-blank stories)
   - Poetry
   - Student-authored works
   - School publications
   - Bilingual materials
   - Manuals and how-to books including some on magic, yo-yo tricks, sports and games, simple science, and math activities
   - Cartoons and comics with appropriate language and concepts
   - Scripts and screenplays

PURPOSES OF LITERACY IN LIFE SURVEY

Name ____ Date ____________________

Time	*Person*	*Type of Material*	*Purpose*

Practice and Reinforcement Activities

1. Remind students that all sorts of people set goals. For example, sports figures often set goals such as improving a batting average, decreasing the amount of time to run a marathon, or climbing a higher mountain. Have students collect other examples of goal setting. Encourage students to ask their friends and family members to help them. Suggest that students use information from television and magazines. After students have collected and discussed a number of examples of goal setting, remind them that they should set goals for learning as well. Explain to students that learning is an activity similar to sports activities and that they need to continue to have learning goals throughout their lives.
2. Tell students that when people set goals they engage in self-talk. Provide an example for students such as the following.

   I am reading a very challenging book right now. It's a book about the formation of mountains. I don't know much about this subject, but I'm eager to learn, so I'll struggle through this book. I'm about halfway through the book, and I'm really enjoying the feeling of accomplishing something difficult.

   Remind students to talk to themselves about their goals during difficult learning tasks.

3. Explain to students that when they are working toward their goal they may enter what is called the "flow" state (Csikszentmihalyi, 1991). Tell students that when they are truly absorbed in what they are doing, they may forget about the task and just enjoy themselves. Tell students about a time when you felt that "flow" as in the following.

   I was sitting at the computer last night looking up sites on the Internet about travel in Alaska. I was fascinated with all of the wonderful things to see and do in Alaska, and I was entranced with the pictures of the wildlife. Before I knew it, it was already an hour past bedtime. I shut down the computer, but I knew that I had really become involved with what I was doing.

   Have students share examples of similar situations. Then tell students that they should also become aware of the "flow state" when they are learning. Explain to students that, as they work toward their learning goals, they also need to learn to become totally involved in learning.

4. Have students create daily learning goals on an index card for each day of the week. Take a few minutes at the end of the day to encourage students to reflect on ways they met that goal.
5. At the beginning of the school year or at the beginning of a unit of study, ask students what they would like to learn. Encourage students to discuss the process of learning rather than topics. For example, in a unit on penguins, the students may want to learn *how* to memorize the types of penguins and their habitats. Write the phrase *memorization of names and places* on a sheet of colored paper and post it on a bulletin board. From these ideas, create a bulletin board titled Class Learning Goals.
6. Have your students interview students in the next higher grade to determine what these students have been learning. For example, if you teach second grade, have your students interview third graders. Have students ask questions such as "What are you learning in reading? What have you learned about learning vocabulary words? and What have you learned about becoming a better reader?" Have your students create a list of next-grade learning goals. Post the list. Then explain to your students that they can work on next-grade goals any time they want. Encourage students to use next-grade goals as part of their own learning goals.

7. Praise students who have set learning goals and have achieved them. Without giving external rewards, let students know that you are aware of their hard work and their accomplishments. When a student has accomplished a learning goal, say something like the following.

   You've really worked hard on finishing that goal. You must feel very proud of yourself. I'm glad to see that you're becoming such a good learner.

   Also, encourage students to praise themselves for finishing their learning goals.

8. Write the word *contract* on the chalkboard or on an overhead transparency. Ask how many students know the meaning of the word *contract*. Have students share their meanings and write them below the word. Explain that one meaning for contract is "agreement." Tell students that as they set learning goals they should form contracts with a friend. Tell students that these "friendly contracts" can help them achieve their learning goals. Begin with an example using yourself as in the following.

   I'm going to enter into a friendly contract with my best friend, Pam. Pam knows that I want to improve my reading vocabulary in science so that I can read books about geology. I've been writing down words that I've come across in my reading that I want to learn. However, I sometimes forget to look them up in a dictionary. I'm going to use the idea of a "friendly contract" to have Pam periodically check in with me to see how I'm doing on my learning goal.

   After you have given students an example, have them think of examples of friendly contracts into which they could enter. Give students several minutes to think. Then divide the class into groups of three or four students and have students share their ideas. Encourage students to actually make these contracts. See the following page for an example of a Friendly Contract.

FRIENDLY CONTRACT

Name ______________________________ Date ______________

My friend ______________________________ will check with me from time to time to see how well I'm doing on ______________________

____

____

____

____

____

Date	*My Friend's Comments*
________	______________________________
________	______________________________
________	______________________________
________	______________________________
________	______________________________

Resources

1

Interest Inventories

Reading Attitude Inventories

Teacher Resource

Note: [student icon] indicates student reproducible. [apple icon] indicates teacher material.

ABOUT ME

Name ____ Date ____________________

1. My name is ____
____.
2. I like to ____
____.
3. I feel good when ____
____.
4. I feel happy when ____
____.
5. I feel important when ____
____.
6. I worry when ____
____.
7. I don't like to ____
____.
8. I don't like it when ____
____.
9. I think ____
____.
10. I would like to be ____
____.
11. Some of my favorite things are ____
____.
12. My favorite TV shows are ____
____.
13. Reading is ____
____.

SENTENCE COMPLETION

Name ______________________________ Date ______________

Directions: I am going to begin certain sentences for you. I want you to finish each sentence with the first idea that comes to your mind.

1. My idea of a good time is ______________________________.
2. When I have to read, I ______________________________.
3. I wish my family knew ______________________________.
4. I can't understand why ______________________________.
5. I wish teachers ______________________________.
6. People think I ______________________________.
7. I especially like to read about ______________________________.
8. To me, homework ______________________________.
9. I hope I'll never ______________________________.
10. I wish people wouldn't ______________________________.
11. When I finish school, ______________________________.
12. When I take my report card home, ______________________________.
13. Most brothers and sisters ______________________________.
14. I feel proud when ______________________________.
15. I like to read when ______________________________.
16. I am really interested in ______________________________.
17. I often worry about ______________________________.
18. I wish someone would help me ______________________________.

From Boning, T., & Boning, R. (1975). I'd rather read than. . . . *The Reading Teacher, 10*, 196–200.

INDEPENDENT READING ATTITUDE SURVEY 1

Name ______________________________ Date ______________

Directions: You read each statement silently as I read them aloud. After each statement, circle the word that best describes your reading behaviors.

1. I enjoy free reading time at school.	Always	Sometimes	Never
2. I feel that books are boring.	Always	Sometimes	Never
3. I like to recommend good books to my friends.	Always	Sometimes	Never
4. I read if the teacher assigns it as homework.	Always	Sometimes	Never
5. I think reading is hard.	Always	Sometimes	Never
6. I like to read when I have spare time.	Always	Sometimes	Never
7. If I start reading a book, I finish the book.	Always	Sometimes	Never
8. It takes me a long time to read a book.	Always	Sometimes	Never
9. I like to read when I'm not at school.	Always	Sometimes	Never
10. I try to find books by my favorite authors.	Always	Sometimes	Never
11. I'd rather watch TV than read a book.	Always	Sometimes	Never
12. I only like certain types of books.	Always	Sometimes	Never
13. I think I am a good reader.	Always	Sometimes	Never
14. I learn new things from free reading.	Always	Sometimes	Never

INDEPENDENT READING ATTITUDE SURVEY 2

Name ______________________________ Date ______________

Directions: Please respond to the following in writing.

1. What do you think is the easiest thing about reading when you are alone?

____

2. What do you think is the hardest thing about reading when you are alone?

____

3. What do you like about reading alone?

____

4. What do you dislike about reading alone?

____

5. Describe your favorite place to read and why you like to read there.

____

6. Who do you know who likes to read?

____

7. How do you know this person likes to read?

____

8. Who do you know who doesn't like to read?

____

9. How do you know this person doesn't like to read?

____

10. Are you more like the person who likes to read or the person who doesn't like to read? Why do you think so?

____

READING AND ME

Name ____ Date ____________________

Directions:	Ten statements will be read to you. After each statement is read, circle either yes or no, depending on what you believe.

Yes No 1. I can read as fast as good readers.

Yes No 2. I like to read.

Yes No 3. I like to read long stories.

Yes No 4. The books I read in school are too hard.

Yes No 5. I need more help in reading.

Yes No 6. I worry quite a bit about my reading in school.

Yes No 7. I read at home.

Yes No 8. I would rather read than watch television or use a computer.

Yes No 9. I am not a very good reader.

Yes No 10. I like my family to read to me.

Reading Survey

Name ______________________________ Date ______________

Directions: Six questions will be asked. After each question is asked, circle the face that best answers the question.

1. How does reading make you feel?

2. How well do you think you can read?

3. How much do you like reading at school?

4. How much do you like reading at home?

5. How do you feel when you get to check out a book at the library?

6. How do you feel about getting a book as a present?

MY FEELINGS ABOUT READING

Name ______________________________ Date ______________

Directions: Ten statements will be read to you. After each statement is read, circle the response that tells what you feel or believe.

Agree	?	Disagree	1. Reading is a good way to spend spare time.
Agree	?	Disagree	2. Most books are too long and dull.
Agree	?	Disagree	3. There should be more free reading in school.
Agree	?	Disagree	4. Reading is as important as watching television.
Agree	?	Disagree	5. Reading is boring.
Agree	?	Disagree	6. Reading is rewarding to me.
Agree	?	Disagree	7. I think reading is fun.
Agree	?	Disagree	8. Teachers ask me to read books that are too hard.
Agree	?	Disagree	9. I am not a very good reader.
Agree	?	Disagree	10. My family spends quite a bit of time reading.

CLASS SUMMARY SHEET FOR READING ATTITUDE SURVEY

Teacher ______________________________ Grade ____________ School ______________

Student	*Date Administered* ________		*Date Administered* ________	
	Score	*Comments*	*Score*	*Comments*

Self-Report Reading Scale

Beatrice Dubnow and Martin H. Jason

Purpose

To help measure elementary students' self-perceptions of their reading abilities.

Administration

1. Reproduce the scale on pages 85–86.
2. Explain how students should mark their answers. Because words above the third-grade reading level were not included in the items, most students should be able to complete the scale independently. For younger or less able readers, read the items aloud.

Scoring and Interpretation

1. Students are given one point for each item to which they give an answer representing a positive self-perception. Use the key that follows.

1.	No	12.	Yes
2.	No	13.	Yes
3.	Yes	14.	No
4.	No	15.	Yes
5.	Yes	16.	Yes
6.	No	17.	No
7.	Yes	18.	Yes
8.	No	19.	No
9.	Yes	20.	No
10.	Yes	21.	Yes
11.	No	22.	Yes

2. The student's total score is a qualitative self-perception of his or her reading abilities.
3. Teachers can use the results to help plan intervention strategies.

Jason, M.H., & Dubnow, B. (1973). The relationship between self-perceptions of reading abilities and reading achievement. In W.H. MacGinitie (Ed.), *Assessment problems in reading* (pp. 96–101). Newark, DE: International Reading Association.

SELF-REPORT READING SCALE

Please Print

Name ______________________________ Boy ☐ Girl ☐

School ______________________________

Room ______________ Grade ______________

Today's Date ______________________________
Year Month Day

Date of Birth ______________________________
Year Month Day

What to do:
1. These are sentences about reading.
2. Read each sentence and make an ☒ in the Yes or No box.
3. There are no right or wrong answers. Just mark the way you feel about each one.

1. I can do better in my other school work than I can in reading. Yes ☐ No ☐
2. There are too many hard words for me to learn in the stories I read. Yes ☐ No ☐
3. If I took a reading test, I would do all right on it. Yes ☐ No ☐
4. In school I wish I could be a much better reader than I am. Yes ☐ No ☐
5. I can help other pupils in my class to read because I'm a good reader. Yes ☐ No ☐
6. If reading gets too hard for me, I feel like not trying to read anymore. Yes ☐ No ☐
7. Most of the time I can read the same books as well as the good readers. Yes ☐ No ☐

(continued)

Jason, M.H., & Dubnow, B. (1973). The relationship between self-perceptions of reading abilities and reading achievement. In W.H. MacGinitie (Ed.), *Assessment problems in reading* (pp. 96–101). Newark, DE: International Reading Association.

8. When I read in school, I worry a lot about how well I'm doing. Yes ☐ No ☐
9. Most of the time when I see a new word, I can sound it out by myself. Yes ☐ No ☐
10. I can read as well as the best readers. Yes ☐ No ☐
11. Most of the time I feel I need help when I read in school. Yes ☐ No ☐
12. If my teacher called on me to read to the class, I would do well. Yes ☐ No ☐
13. I can read as fast as the good readers. Yes ☐ No ☐
14. Most of the things I read in school are too hard. Yes ☐ No ☐
15. Pupils in my class think I'm a good reader. Yes ☐ No ☐
16. Most of the time I can finish my reading work. Yes ☐ No ☐
17. Most of the time I feel afraid to read to the class. Yes ☐ No ☐
18. I can read a long story as well as a short one. Yes ☐ No ☐
19. It's hard for me to answer questions about the main idea of a story. Yes ☐ No ☐
20. Most of the time I feel I will never be a good reader in school. Yes ☐ No ☐
21. My teacher thinks I'm a good reader. Yes ☐ No ☐
22. I know what most of the hard words mean when I read them. Yes ☐ No ☐

Jason, M.H., & Dubnow, B. (1973). The relationship between self-perceptions of reading abilities and reading achievement. In W.H. MacGinitie (Ed.), *Assessment problems in reading* (pp. 96–101). Newark, DE: International Reading Association.

Motivation to Read Profile: Conversational Interview

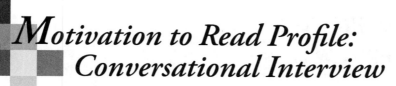

Linda B. Gambrell, Barbara Martin Palmer, Rose Marie Codling, and Susan Anders Mazzoni

Purpose

To qualitatively assess students' self-concepts as readers and the value they place on reading.

Administration

1. Reproduce the Conversational Interview that follows for each student.
2. Choose in advance the section(s) or specific questions you want to ask from the Conversational Interview. Reviewing the information on students' Reading Surveys may provide information about additional questions that could be added to the interview.
3. Familiarize yourself with the basic questions provided in the interview prior to the interview session in order to establish a more conversational setting.
4. Select a quiet corner of the room and a calm period of the day for the interview.
5. Allow ample time for conducting the Conversational Interview.
6. Follow up on interesting comments and responses to gain a fuller understanding of students' reading experiences.
7. Record students' responses in as much detail as possible. If time and resources permit, you may want to audiotape answers to A1 and B1 to be transcribed after the interview for more in-depth analysis.
8. Enjoy this special time with each student!

Scoring and Interpretation

1. The interview explores three areas: 1) motivational factors related to the reading of narrative text, 2) information about informational reading, and 3) general factors related to reading motivation.
2. Use the students' responses along with the MRP Reading Survey to gain greater depth into students' reading experiences.

Gambrell, L.B., Palmer, B.M., Codling, R.M., & Mazzoni, S.A. (1996). Assessing reading motivation. *The Reading Teacher, 49*, 518–533.

MOTIVATION TO READ PROFILE: CONVERSATIONAL INTERVIEW

Name ______________________________ Date ______________

A. Emphasis: Narrative text

Suggested prompt (designed to engage student in a natural conversation): I have been reading a good book . . . I was talking with . . . about it last night. I enjoy talking about good stories and books that I've been reading. Today I'd like to hear about what you have been reading.

1. Tell me about the most interesting story or book you have read this week (or even last week). Take a few minutes to think about it. (Wait time.) Now, tell me about the book or story.

   ____

   ____

   ____

   Probes: What else can you tell me? Is there anything else? ______________________________

   ____

   ____

2. How did you know or find out about this story? ______________________________

   ____

   ____

   ☐ assigned ☐ in school

   ☐ chosen ☐ out of school

3. Why was this story interesting to you? ______________________________

   ____

   ____

   ____

B. Emphasis: Informational text

Suggested prompt (designed to engage student in a natural conversation): Often we read to find out about something or to learn about something. We read for information. For example, I remember a student of mine . . . who read a lot of books about . . . to find out as much as he/she could about. . . . Now, I'd like to hear about some of the informational reading you have been doing.

(continued)

Gambrell, L.B., Palmer, B.M., Codling, R.M., & Mazzoni, S.A. (1996). Assessing reading motivation. *The Reading Teacher, 49*, 518–533.

1. Think about something important that you learned recently, not from your teacher and not from television, but from a book or some other reading material. What did you read about? (Wait time.) Tell me about what you learned.

   Probes: What else could you tell me? Is there anything else? ______________________

2. How did you know or find out about this book/article? ______________________

   ☐ assigned ☐ in school

   ☐ chosen ☐ out of school

3. Why was this book (or article) important to you? ______________________

C. Emphasis: General reading

1. Did you read anything at home yesterday? ______________ What? ______________

2. Do you have any books at school (in your desk/storage area/locker/book bag) today that you are reading? ______________ Tell me about them. ______________________

3. Tell me about your favorite author. ______________________

(continued)

Gambrell, L.B., Palmer, B.M., Codling, R.M., & Mazzoni, S.A. (1996). Assessing reading motivation. *The Reading Teacher, 49*, 518–533.

Motivation to Read Profile: Conversational Interview *(continued)*

4. What do you think you have to learn to be a better reader? ____________________

5. Do you know about any books right now that you'd like to read? Tell me about them. ____________________

6. How did you find out about these books? ____________________

7. What are some things that get you really excited about reading books? ____________________

   Tell me about . . .

8. Who gets you really interested and excited about reading books? ____________________

   Tell me more about what they do. ____________________

Gambrell, L.B., Palmer, B.M., Codling, R.M., & Mazzoni, S.A. (1996). Assessing reading motivation. *The Reading Teacher, 49*, 518–533.

What Are Some of Your Ideas About Reading?

Thomas H. Estes

Purpose

To acquire a quantitative idea of a student's attitude toward reading. The scale can be used with students in grades 3 through 12.

Administration

1. Reproduce the sheet titled "What Are Some of Your Ideas About Reading?"
2. Assure students that their responses will not affect their grades or standing in the course.
3. Explain how students should mark their answers.
4. Read each of the statements aloud and permit students ample time to circle their responses.

Scoring and Interpretation

1. Assign numerical values to each of the 20 items as follows:

Type and Number of Item		*Numerical Values*				
		SA	A	U	D	SD
Negative:	1, 3, 4, 6, 8, 9, 11, 12, 13, 16, 17, 20	1	2	3	4	5
Positive:	2, 5, 7, 10, 14, 15, 18, 19	5	4	3	2	1

2. Add the numerical values for the positive statements and the negative statements. The student's total score is a quantitative reflection of his or her attitude toward reading. Scores above 60 indicate varying degrees of positive attitudes, and scores below 60 indicate varying degrees of negative attitudes.
3. By administering the scale on a pretest and posttest (September and May) basis, the teacher can note changes in attitude toward reading by subtracting the early score from the later one.
4. Consult the original article for further information on the construction of the attitude scale. Further validation of the scale can be found in Dulin, K.L., & Chester, R.D. (1974). "A validation study of the Estes Attitude Scale," *Journal of Reading, 18*, 56–59.

Adapted from Estes, T.H. (1971). A scale to measure attitudes toward reading. *Journal of Reading, 15*, 135–138.

WHAT ARE SOME OF YOUR IDEAS ABOUT READING?

Name ______________________________ Date ______________

Directions: Twenty statements will be read to you. After each statement is read, circle the letter that best describes how you feel about that statement. Your answers to the statements will not be graded because there are no right or wrong answers. Your feeling about each statement is what's important.

SA	=	Strongly Agree	D	=	Disagree
A	=	Agree	SD	=	Strongly Disagree
U	=	Undecided			

SA	A	U	D	SD	1. Reading is for learning but not for enjoyment.
SA	A	U	D	SD	2. Money spent on books is well spent.
SA	A	U	D	SD	3. There is nothing to be gained from reading books.
SA	A	U	D	SD	4. Books are a bore.
SA	A	U	D	SD	5. Reading is a good way to spend spare time.
SA	A	U	D	SD	6. Sharing books in class is a waste of time.
SA	A	U	D	SD	7. Reading turns me on.
SA	A	U	D	SD	8. Reading is only for students seeking good grades.
SA	A	U	D	SD	9. Books aren't usually good enough to finish.
SA	A	U	D	SD	10. Reading is rewarding to me.
SA	A	U	D	SD	11. Reading becomes boring after about an hour.
SA	A	U	D	SD	12. Most books are too long and dull.
SA	A	U	D	SD	13. Free reading doesn't teach anything.
SA	A	U	D	SD	14. There should be more time for free reading during the school day.
SA	A	U	D	SD	15. There are many books that I hope to read.
SA	A	U	D	SD	16. Books should not be read except for class requirements.
SA	A	U	D	SD	17. Reading is something I can do without.
SA	A	U	D	SD	18. A certain amount of summer vacation should be set aside for reading.
SA	A	U	D	SD	19. Books make good presents.
SA	A	U	D	SD	20. Reading is dull.

Adapted from Estes, T.H. (1971). A scale to measure attitudes toward reading. *Journal of Reading, 15*, 135–138.

CHECKLIST FOR STUDENT'S ATTITUDES AND PERSONAL READING

Student ______________________________ Grade __________ Teacher ______________

	Seldom			*Sometimes*			*Often*		
	Oct.	*Feb.*	*May*	*Oct.*	*Feb.*	*May*	*Oct.*	*Feb.*	*May*
1. Possesses printed materials not assigned									
2. Uses classroom library									
3. Checks out books from school library									
4. Voluntarily shares outside reading									
5. Talks with other students about reading									
6. Seems to have a favorite author									
7. Requests more reading materials about topics									
8. Uses reading to satisfy personal interests									
9. Reads for recreation									
10. Chooses reading when choices are given									
11. Reading reflects interests in ______									
12. Applies ideas from reading to his or her life									
13. Seems to enjoy reading									
14. Participates in classroom book club									
15. Participates in book exchange club									
16. Family reports reading at home									

Adapted from Johns, J.L. (1991). Literacy portfolios: A primer. *Illinois Reading Council Journal, 19,* 4–10.

CHAPTER TWO

Oral Language, Phonemic Awareness, and Beginning Reading

With Regina Slattery Gursky

Overview

Many children gain knowledge about print from literacy experiences prior to entering school. Beginning readers may also be helped to unlock print by direct teaching. This chapter offers activities and strategies to teachers for helping students acquire or refine abilities related to the nature and purpose of reading, concepts about print and words, oral language, phonological awareness, story schema, auditory and visual discrimination, and rhyming. It is important to connect these activities and strategies to experiences with texts to help ensure transfer.

Beginning readers often have vague or limited concepts about the purpose and nature of reading. They also may not understand the terms used by teachers such as letters, words, sounds, context, and beginning. In addition, they may not know that reading is a process of constructing meaning from print.

In addition to vague concepts about reading, students frequently exhibit confusion regarding the terms teachers use in instruction. Younger students, for example, often confuse letters with words or vice versa. They may also show confusion with terms such as beginning, middle, and end. Teachers often assume that students understand these basic, instructional terms. Unfortunately, when this assumption is made, students may be at a great disadvantage for learning. In the box below are some basic concepts that students should understand. Teachers may choose to assess which concepts students know and which they do not yet understand.

Consider these concepts and the language you use during instruction. Be alert for other terms or concepts that your students may not understand. By looking at your instruction through the eyes of your students, you may discover that you take too much for granted when you teach. Plan appropriate instruction to help students develop concepts about print and the specialized terms used in instruction.

One of the most important areas related to emergent literacy and later success in reading is the ability to hear and manipulate phonemes (individual sounds) in words (Gillet & Temple, 1990) and understand how these sounds are connected to print (International Reading Association, 2000). This ability is called phonemic awareness (PA). PA and letter recognition are the two best predictors, upon school entry, of reading acquisition during the first two years of instruction (National Reading Panel, 2000). Letter recognition often results in an interest in letter sounds and spelling. It also plays an important role in helping students store printed words into memory, focusing on the ordered sequence of letters rather than a holistic pattern (Adams, 1990b). Moreover, letter recognition facilitates reading and spelling acquisition when letters are used during PA instruction (National Reading Panel, 2000).

Phonemic Awareness: The ability to hear and manipulate individual sounds in words.

Making connections between letters, PA, and print is important for reading and spelling acquisition. In fact, PA instruction is most effective when it involves an explicit connection to print and when

Basic Reading Concepts

- Reading is making sense of print.
- Reading is essentially making sense of language that has been written down.
- Words are made up of sounds.
- The individual sounds in words map onto letters and groups of letters.
- Most words are made up of more than one letter (*I* and *a* are the exceptions).
- Words can be different lengths. The number of letters determines whether a printed word is short, medium, or long. The number of sounds (phonemes) determines its spoken and aural length.
- There are white spaces between words.
- Words can be organized into sentences.
- Reading can be done for different reasons or purposes.
- There is usually a relationship between the words on a page and pictures or illustrations.
- Words are arranged in sentences, sentences into paragraphs, and paragraphs into stories or books.

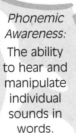

letters are used to help students make connections to reading and spelling (National Reading Panel, 2000; Slattery Gursky, 2003). PA enables students to use letter-sound relationships in spelling and reading. Students attend to the phonemes in words as they segment the individual sounds in words during invented spelling (Adams, 1990b), attend to phonetic (letter-sound) cues during early attempts to read, and later blend the individual sounds in words as they develop cipher reading (decoding skills) (Ehri & Wilce, 1985).

PA is part of a broad range of skills, called phonological awareness, that work together to help emergent readers hear phonemes in words (Treiman & Zukowski, 1996). Phonological awareness is the ability to hear and manipulate larger units of sound in spoken language, such as syllables, onsets, and rimes. It appears that phonological awareness progresses from whole to part. First, students are able to hear words in sentences and then progress to hear syllables in words, onsets in words, rimes in words, and phonemes in words (Anthony, Lonigan, Driscoll, Phillips, & Burgess, 2003; Treiman & Zukowski, 1991). Furthermore, evidence suggests that phonological awareness tasks have a hierarchical degree of difficulty (Yopp, 1988). Rhyming tasks appear to be the easiest, followed by blending and segmenting; the most difficult are phoneme deletion tasks. Sections 2.4 through 2.10 in this chapter relate directly or indirectly to the area of phonological awareness. We urge you to give careful attention to these sections as you teach emergent or struggling readers.

Literacy experiences prior to entering school promote knowledge about print and words.

Section **2.1**

Oral Language

Behavior Observed → **Anticipated Outcome**

The student has limited oral expression. → The student will orally communicate in an effective and appropriate manner.

Perspective and Strategies

Oral language is an important predictor of reading comprehension (National Association for the Education of Young Children, 2009). Successful readers draw upon what they know about language to interpret fine shades of meaning or to simply understand print. Students who do not have a rich, diverse language background may have difficulty understanding and interpreting text. Oral language, then, may be regarded as the basis for reading. Fostering oral expression provides students with the opportunity to learn language and its structures and to build vocabulary.

The following suggestions are helpful for increasing the quantity and quality of oral communication among students. Although these activities may be adapted for work with one student, language learning may be more successful in small groups because it increases interaction and provides more opportunity for authentic oral expression.

1. Provide a concrete experience and have students discuss the event. Opportunities for expression and interaction should be encouraged. During the discussion, list some key terms on the chalkboard. Next, write an experience story incorporating the key terms. Read chorally and take turns so that each student gets a chance to read alone or with a group.
2. Echo read to give students an opportunity to repeat sentences that use appropriate syntax. Read a line of a story or poem aloud. Students repeat exactly what has been said. Repeat and allow students to echo read line by line. Using the sentence patterns, students may more readily communicate their own material.
3. Use pictures from a story to have students retell the story. Select and tag, with sticky notes, pictures from the story that represent the story's grammar (setting, main characters, problem, and solution). Next, create a poster with pictures and words to illustrate the story grammar. For example, you can use a picture of a house and clock to represent the setting, stick figures

to represent the characters, wilted flower to represent the problem, and watering a flower to represent the solution. Model how to retell the story, including the setting, main characters, problem, and solution in the story. Then, explain the parts of story grammar, using the poster you created. The following day, review the story grammar poster and reread the story. Provide support as you have students take turns retelling the story using the pictures from the story and the story grammar poster. This activity works best after several readings of the story on subsequent days. After students are familiar with the story and how to retell stories, the story grammar poster and pictures from the story can be used as a retelling center activity for several students.

4. Provide students with pictures and encourage sharing. Ask questions where appropriate. Invite students to bring in interesting photographs for discussion.
5. Bring in objects and have students discuss what they know about them, especially those that relate to topics being studied or read.
6. Provide care for an animal to help foster a lively interchange of ideas.
7. Read a variety of books to students and discuss them. "The importance of storybook reading in early literacy success is undisputed" (Paratore, 2002, p. 57). Students who have had numerous and diverse experiences in storybook reading do well on school-based measures of literacy.
8. Encourage students to make up a story that goes along with wordless picture books. A listing of books without words can be found in Part A on the CD.
9. Use puppets to promote communication among students. Puppets often encourage the shy students to participate in discussions.
10. Plan and take interesting field trips around the school and the community. Write together about the experience, having students dictate the events of the field trip. See pages 103 and 104, #3 for details on shared writing.
11. Introduce concept words such as *same-different, in-out,* and *over-under.*
12. Have students speak into a tape recorder one at a time. For the first experience, students may say their name, age, and something that they like to do. Play the tape back after each student has had an opportunity to speak. Exercise caution with students who are hesitant to participate in this activity; do not force the activity upon them. The teacher may also participate in this activity and serve as a role model. Later, students can tape-record a story that they have made up or one to accompany a wordless picture book. Students will sometimes tell more elaborate stories when they speak into a tape recorder. The teacher or classroom volunteer may then transcribe the story and have students illustrate it.
13. Provide parents or caregivers with a list of suggestions for promoting rich oral language in the home. Some suggestions are in the box on the following page.
14. Classify objects or pictures in various ways: by color, shape, purpose, etc. Have students discuss why they grouped items together and how the groups and items in the groups are similar and different. Label each group of items.
15. Invite adults or older students into the classroom to listen to small groups of students share. Topics could include favorite play activities, television, or animals.
16. Create a picture file so students can choose a picture and talk about it with a partner or small group of classmates.
17. Provide play or real telephones so students can have conversations with each other.

Suggestions for Promoting Rich Oral Language

- Read stories and books. Ask questions about the content; talk about the illustrations; and discuss points of interest.
- Be open to what students want to talk about. Make encouraging comments to promote their language use. Listen carefully to what students say and try to spend 80% of your time listening.
- Take walks or excursions in the neighborhood or community. Talk about what you see. Point out things that students might miss. Give labels to these things and explain them in words appropriate for the students' level of maturity.
- Talk to your students. Encourage them to talk about friends, interests, and special events at school.
- Encourage conversation by asking questions that require more than a "yes-or-no" answer.
- Play card and board games that provide an opportunity for conversations about the game and other topics.
- Help students expand their statements. For example, if the student says, "The cat is black," the teacher may comment, "Yes, the cat is black except for the white markings on its paws."

18. Encourage small-group and one-on-one discussions. Some of the best conversations may be the natural, language-rich activities that are part of daily classroom routines.
19. Provide props, possibly in a drama center, for students to act out their favorite stories and books. Label a bag or box with the title of the story and include the book with one or more of the following props: character felt pieces and a felt board, puppets, articles of clothing, or artifacts from the story. For example, for the book *If You Give a Mouse a Cookie* (Numeroff, 1996), include items from the story such as a napkin, straw, and scissors for students to use when acting out the sequence of the story.

Strategy 1 SECTION 2.1

CREATING NEW VERSES TO SONGS

1. Invite students to write new verses of a song that is familiar to them. Choose a song with a predictable, repetitive pattern.
2. Write the pattern that repeats in black on chart paper, leaving blank lines for the words that change. For example, in Ella Jenkins' (1997) song titled "You'll Sing a Song and I'll Sing a Song," a line from the second verse, similar to the title, replaces *sing* and *song* with *play* and *tune* respectively. Prepare chart paper with a template verse, beginning with the line

   You'll ________ a ________ and I'll ________ a ________.
3. Sing the phrase together, placing the words *sing/song* and then *play/tune* into the blanks.
4. Record these word pairs on the chart below the template verse or on a separate piece of chart paper.

   You'll __________ a __________ and I'll __________ a __________.

sing	song	sing	song
play	tune	play	tune
jump	rope	jump	rope
read	book	read	book

5. Have students think of their own word pairs to create new verses and record the new word pairs.
6. Sing the new song together.
7. To extend this activity, create two or more class books by having each student fill in his or her own word pairs and illustrate the new verse(s). The class books can be used as a center for small groups of students to read and reread together with a partner.

Strategy 2 SECTION 2.1

THINK, DRAW/WRITE, PAIR, SHARE

1. Based on the work of Lyman (1981) and Fisher and Frey (2007), this strategy helps develop academic language and assess students' understanding.
2. Engage students in reading a passage, discussing a concept, viewing a video, or observing an activity.
3. Ask students a question based on your goal. For example, after reading a fictional story with hippos as the main characters and a nonfiction text about real hippos ask, "How are the hippo characters in our story different from real hippos?"
4. Provide students with some time to think about the question.
5. Have students draw/write their response to your question.
6. Instruct students to stand when they complete their response and then to pair up to share their responses with a partner.
7. Randomly call on students to share one of their ideas that they drew or wrote.

8. Record their ideas on chart paper, and have students check off, on their papers, the ideas shared by other students.
9. Continue calling on other students until all ideas are shared.
10. Discuss the ideas shared and have students help you clarify or revise ideas as needed.

Strategy 3 SECTION 2.1

MY IMPORTANT WORD(S) PLUS

1. In this strategy, based on Yopp and Yopp (2007), students identify words that are important to them. After a read aloud or a shared reading, have students identify one or several words that are important to them.
2. Explain that important words can be words that are new, interesting, or related to the big idea/topic. For example, in the story "The Surprise" from *George and Martha 'Round and 'Round* (Marshall, 1988), several important words for students might include *cross, wicked, observed, drenched, unmoved,* and *thoroughly.*
3. Have students write their words or illustrate them on a piece of paper.
4. Call on students to share their words. After you list them on chart paper (in writing or in pictures), ask if anyone has the same word. Then, make tallies next to the word to represent all who wrote or drew the same word. Examples of pictures could include an angry face for cross, a witch for wicked, and a pair of eyes for observed.
5. After all the words are shared and listed, read the charted words together.
6. Discuss students' word choices together: what they mean, why they think the words were chosen, and what the words contribute to the topic/text. Yopp and Yopp (2007) explain that discussing the words not only supports language development by promoting the use of the words and students' understanding of both the words and the topic/text, it also gives them insight into other students' thinking.
7. Extend this activity by selecting several charted words that have synonyms and antonyms (e.g., cross, observed, drenched, and wicked) and prepare color-coded response sheets for each word. For example, if you have 24 students, select four words and make three yellow sheets with the heading Synonym (Same) and three blue sheets with the heading Antonym (Opposite) for each word to total 24 sheets. (For an extra challenge, pink can be used for writing a sentence using the word as it is used in the text, and green can be used to write a sentence that is very different from the text.)
8. In a follow-up lesson, review the charted words. Then group students according to their color-coded response sheets and have them work in their group to write synonyms and antonyms for their words.
9. Have each group share their synonyms and antonyms with the class.

Section 2.2

Concepts About the Nature and Purpose of Reading

Behavior Observed → **Anticipated Outcome**

The student is unaware of the basic functions of print. → The student will understand that print conveys meaning.

Perspective and Strategies

Students at all ages must realize that reading is the process of making sense from print. They must learn that spoken language—their own and that of others—is made up of words that can also be written down. Later, they will understand that these words can be broken down into parts, or syllables, and further into sound units, or phonemes.

1. Introduce a picture book by reading it to an individual or a group of students more than once. Have students join in with the reading as they become more familiar with the story. Give the book to a student and encourage "reading" of the book. Provide all students opportunities for storybook reading on a daily basis. Some useful pattern books can be found in Part C on the CD.
2. Place a big book (two to three feet high) on a chart stand where it can readily be seen by a group of students. Read a familiar story and have the students read along. Point out features of print: where the text begins on a page, the left-to-right progression of reading, the return sweep, the white spaces between words, and punctuation.
3. Write together about classroom experiences or stories that have been read aloud together. For stories, choose a favorite part, retell the story, or provide a new ending. Draw a picture to provide focus for the writing. Ask students to tell you what to write, pro-

Reading to very young children leads them to understanding that reading is the process of making sense from print.

viding guiding questions as needed to elicit their responses. After writing each new sentence, invite the students to read the text from the beginning to make sure it makes sense, making any necessary changes. As you write, model and describe features of print during initial writings. When you think your students are able, have them tell you what they know by asking the following questions as you write.

- Where should we begin to write our first word?
- What do we need to do after this word?
- We wrote a great sentence. What do we need to put at the end of the sentence?
- Should we write a capital letter or lower-case letter when we start our new sentence?
- We are out of space on this line. Where should we write next?
- We are out of space on this paper. Where do we write next?

4. Help students create their own books, using their chosen vocabulary. Each page of these short books is student dictated and has one word, phrase, or sentence on it. The student reads the text on a page and then illustrates it. These books can be used to practice the vocabulary associated with directions such as *up, down, in,* and *out.* Repeated readings to classmates and family members should be encouraged. Building a collection of these books to share within the classroom will help improve sight vocabulary and develop print awareness.

5. Use familiar poems, songs, and text that have been committed to memory. Show the printed form, line by line. Read aloud, pointing to each word. The students then read aloud, pointing to each word, modeling the teacher's behavior. When the student appears to be familiar with the short text and points word by word while reading, the teacher may point to a single word and ask the student to say it. This technique may also be used with short, dictated experience stories as the text.

6. Write *kingcup* on the chalkboard. Ask a student to pronounce the word. Ask other students if they agree. Continue the process until the class agrees that the word is *kingcup.* Ask students whether they can *read* the word. Most students will respond that they can read the word because they view reading as a process of decoding. When this point is reached, ask the students, "How do you know that you can *read* the word?" Many students will respond by saying, "I can read the word because I can pronounce it." Sooner or later, a student is likely to ask what the word means. Lead students to the conclusion that reading involves understanding. Distinguish between being able to say a word and knowing what a word means. Invite students to suggest ways they might be able to find out what the word *kingcup* means. A common response is to have someone look it up in a dictionary. Have students look up the word and discuss its meaning (a plant with yellow flowers; the marsh marigold). Have students use the word in a sentence. Point out to students that they can now read the word *kingcup.* Tell them that readers are always concerned with meaning. Follow this activity with other words that students can probably pronounce even though the meaning is unknown. Some possible words include yegg, tutu, dingo, truffle, and eyelet.

7. The following example is designed to help students realize that 1) reading is a form of communication, 2) reading can be talk written down, and 3) reading is constructing meaning from print.

   Teacher: If you wanted to tell Eric a secret, how would you do it?

   Beth: I would just tell him.

   Teacher: You mean you would talk to him or whisper to him?

   Beth: Yes, that's what I'd do.

   Teacher: What would you do if Eric weren't here and you still wanted him to know?

Beth: I might write him a note.

Teacher: OK, and when Eric gets here, what should he do?

Beth: He should read what I wrote down.

Teacher: Good. Have you communicated with Eric?

Beth: Yes.

In this example, Eric has received a note that a student has written. But what did Beth write down? She wrote down what she would have said to Eric if he were here. In other words, her talk has been written down. Each printed word represents only one spoken word, and we can now say that a word is a verbal symbol. The following example demonstrates this concept.

Teacher: Suppose that you were going to tell Eric that you have some new baseball cards. Because you had to write it down, it probably looked like this: I have some new baseball cards. Eric took this note and began to say what you had written. He said to himself, "I-have-some-new-baseball-cards." If he were to say that out loud, would that sound like what you were going to say?

Beth: Yes, that's what I would have said.

Teacher: But Eric still has not read what you have written down. He has said the words out loud, but he has not read them. In order to be really reading, Eric must understand what you have said. He must make some meaning from those symbols called words. If he comes to you later and asks to see your hat you wrote about, he has not read anything. You told him about some new baseball cards, not a hat, so he did not read that note. He had not gotten meaning; therefore, no reading has taken place. Reading involves meaning, and if you do not know what something means, you have not read it! Now, what are some of the things in daily life that you read—some things you get meaning from?

Beth: We read road signs on the highways like SLOW and STOP. We read cereal boxes that say FREE TOY INSIDE.

8. Use *Hey! I'm Reading!* (Miles, 1995) as a fun and engaging way to help students learn about reading. This book would also be good for parents to share with their children.

Section 2.3

Alphabet Knowledge

Behavior Observed → **Anticipated Outcome**

The student does not know the letters of the alphabet. → The student will learn the alphabet.

Perspective and Strategies

There are three components to letter knowledge: letter recognition, letter production, and letter-sound correspondence. These three aspects of letter knowledge can help students learn how the alphabetic system works. Such knowledge can also help with spelling and associating certain sounds with certain letters. To help assess letter recognition and production, easy-to-use assessments are included in this section. Strategies for increasing students' letter-sound correspondence are included in Section 2.8, Alphabetic Principle. For students who could benefit from increasing their alphabet knowledge, the following strategies may be useful.

1. Try your best to use meaningful activities within the context of your classroom. As students begin to write their names, their attention is being directed to specific letters. Be direct and tell students that their names are made up of letters. Using students' names is a powerful way to focus on meaningful instruction. Teach students the names of the letters that comprise their names. Make name cards for all students and invite them to learn or generalize their knowledge by asking questions such as the following ones.

   - Does anyone have a name that begins with the same letter as Rosanna's name? Invite students to share and discuss their ideas. Compare the first letters of the names and comment appropriately.
   - Does anyone have a letter in their name that is the same as the first letter in Rosanna's name? Invite students to hold up their name cards and point to the letter in their name that is the same. Use the opportunity to discuss uppercase letters and lowercase letters.
   - Who has a name that begins with *N*?
   - Does your name have a lowercase letter that has the same name as the uppercase letter *O* that I'm writing on the chalkboard? If so, hold up your name card and point to the letter. Does anyone have two *Os*?

2. Make individual, laminated name puzzles (see sample) that are kept in separate envelopes with the name printed on the envelope. You can help students see the letters as tall (A), small (m), and fall (y) letters by writing the names on grids three squares high, with each being one inch square. Cut each letter on the vertical line separating each letter. To make the puzzles a multilevel learning manipulative, print the vowels and consonants in two different colors (Slattery, 2000b).

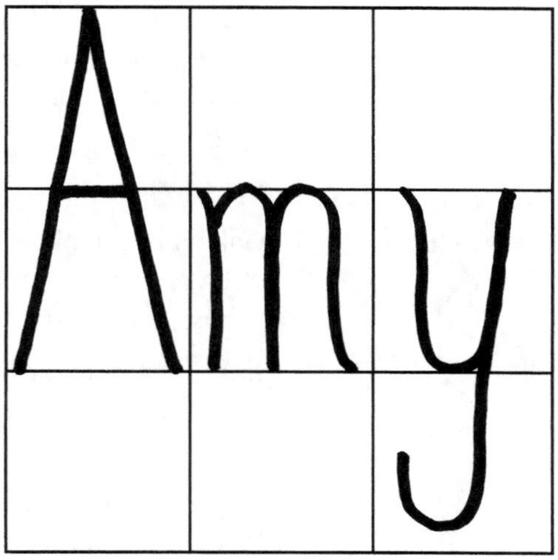

3. Because students learn letters by their distinctive features (open or closed, curved or slanted, above or below the line), introduce at least two different letters at a time. Talk about the letters and what makes them similar and/or different. Although you will probably begin with letters that have dissimilar features such as *i* and *b*, you will want to eventually contrast similar letters such as *b* and *d* and verbalize the reasons they are different. It is through such experiences that students will learn what makes the letters different. Dunn-Rankin (1968) noted the following groups of letters that tend to confuse students.
   - b, d, p, and o, g, h
   - f, l, t, k, i, and h when combined
   - e, a, s, c, o
   - n, m, u, and h and r
4. Refer to print on signs and posters in the room and talk about the letters that make up the words.
5. Invite students to bring in objects such as cereal boxes, toothpaste boxes, paper bags, and newspapers. Discuss the words and the letters that make up the words on these items.
6. Be sure a model alphabet is displayed in the room so students can see how the letters are formed. They should also be able to see the corresponding uppercase and lowercase letters.

Working with alphabet blocks can help a child learn letters.

7. Use a variety of hands-on activities to help students learn the names of the letters and to practice how they are written: alphabet cereal, finger painting, sandpaper letters, Play Doh letters, and so on.
8. Help students create their personalized alphabet books. Invite students to share them with one another.
9. Make a big book that contains the alphabet song. Have different students point to the letters and words as the students sing along. Take time to discuss the difference between letters and words. Invite students to ask each other questions about the letters and words.
10. Sing or play recordings of songs that spell out words or that use letters as part of the song (for example, "Bingo," "Old MacDonald Had a Farm"). Chart and display these songs.
11. Use a newspaper, poem, or song and invite students to find and circle as many examples (uppercase and lowercase) of a particular letter as they can within a specific time limit. Use the exercise to also encourage identification of known words.
12. Develop cards for alphabet bingo or dominoes. For bingo, have a student assist in calling the letters. Game cards can include uppercase letters, lowercase letters, or a combination of both.
13. Secure a keyboard and invite students to type and explore the alphabet. If a computer is available with speech capability, there are computer programs that will say the name of the letter when the key is depressed. Other programs have activities that will help students learn the letters.
14. Supply students with magnetic letters and stamp printing sets to stimulate involvement with the alphabet and making words.
15. Take time to point out the differences between the manuscript *a* and the typeset a. Do the same for the letter *g*.
16. Provide a print-rich environment in which students are encouraged to explore and talk about their literacy experiences. Encourage students to "read the room" at center time or free choice time.
17. Develop a writing center where students can compose and draw. Remember that writing is developmental and students may be making letter-like forms as they progress to conventional printing. Include pencils, colored pencils, markers, letter stamps, and various shapes and colors of paper.
18. Have students learn and sing the alphabet song. Point to the letters as they sing. After modeling this process, invite a student to point. Once students are able to sing the song, invite them to be the "alphabet" as they line up to go somewhere (Cunningham, 1995). Laminate a set of alphabet cards and mix them up. Pass them out randomly so each student has one. The teacher keeps any extras. Then have the class sing the alphabet song slowly as each student gets into line.
19. Read alphabet books (see Part B on the CD) as well as other books that students enjoy. Engage in natural and meaningful sharing about letters, words, and meaning. Some of the books listed in Chapter 2 Resources on page 180 will be especially appropriate.
20. Play Go Fish with alphabet letters written on index cards. Make two of each uppercase letter, lowercase letter, or uppercase and lowercase pairs. Play with two to four students.

21. Create letter-sequencing activities with several letters at a time. Write the letter pairs to be sequenced in boxes in mixed-up order. Provide each student with a strip of mixed-up letter pairs and a strip of construction paper on which to glue the letter pairs in correct order after cutting them apart.

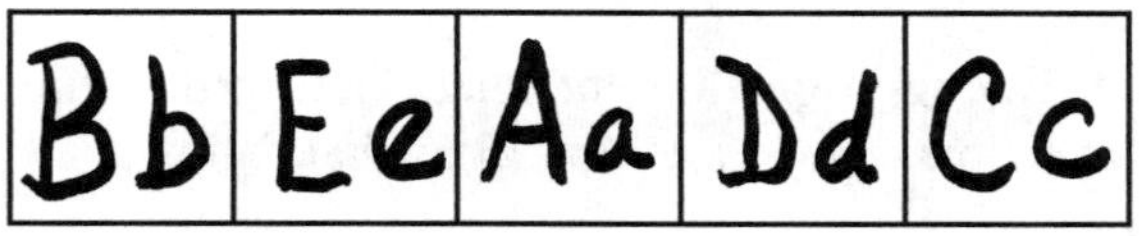

22. Make uppercase and lowercase letter-pair puzzles by purchasing and laminating an alphabet chart. These charts usually have pairs of letters and a picture of an object beginning with each letter. Cut out each letter pair and picture into a box and cut between the uppercase and lowercase letters. Have students match the uppercase and lowercase letters of the puzzle. These puzzles are self-correcting, with each half only matching its corresponding part.

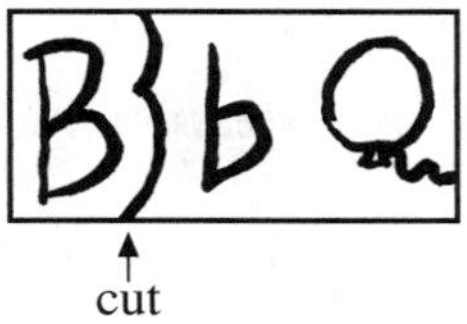

DETERMINING ALPHABET RECOGNITION

1. Duplicate the Alphabet Recognition Record Sheet on the next page and get two index cards.
2. Place the Alphabet Recognition Student Sheet before the student and ask him or her to identify any known letters. Say something like what follows.

   Here are some letters. I want to see how many you know.

   Have the student say "pass" or "skip it" if a particular letter is unknown.
3. Use the index cards to block off everything but the lines being read. If necessary, point to each letter with a finger.
4. As the student responds, use the Alphabet Recognition Record Sheet to note correct (+) and incorrect responses. When responses are incorrect, record the actual response or D.K. (student doesn't know) above the stimulus letter. If the student self-corrects, write ok; self-corrections can be made at any time.

Letter	**Meaning of Recording**
+ O	Identified correctly
D.K. H	Don't Know
C S	Said *C* for S
B ok E	Said *B* for E but self-corrected

5. Count the correct number of responses for the uppercase and lowercase letters. Based on the number of correct responses, make a judgment of the student's alphabet knowledge. Unknown letters or incorrect responses provide the basis for instructional interventions.

ALPHABET RECOGNITION RECORD SHEET

Name ______________________________ Date ______________

Directions: Present the Alphabet Recognition Record Sheet. Use two index cards to block off everything but the lines being read. If necessary, point to each letter with a finger. Then say, "Here are some letters. I want to see how many you know." Place + above correctly identified letters. The first row of letters is organized according to letters most recognized by kindergartners (Barr et al., 2004). If students are unable to identify the first row in uppercase and lowercase letters, have them scan the remaining letters to identify any remaining letters recognized. Record the student's responses for incorrect letters. Total correct responses and record the score in the box.

O	B	X	C	Z	S	E
P	V	I	M	J	K	
H	A	R	G	L	N	
Y	Q	W	D	U	T	F

Scores ☐

o	c	s	x	z	e	i
l	u	r	t	q	h	y
m	d	k	a	b	w	g
j	p	v	f	g	n	a

\+ ☐

Total Score ☐

ALPHABET RECOGNITION STUDENT SHEET

O	B	X	C	Z	S	E
P	V	I	M	J	K	
H	A	R	G	L	N	
Y	Q	W	D	U	T	F

o	c	s	x	z	e	i
l	u	r	t	q	h	y
m	d	k	a	b	w	g
j	p	v	f	g	n	a

DETERMINING ALPHABET PRODUCTION

1. Duplicate both the Alphabet Production Record Sheet and the Alphabet Production Student Sheet on pages 114–115.
2. Place the Alphabet Production Student Sheet before the student and ask him or her to print the letters. Say something like what follows.

   I am going to say the name of letters, and I want you to print the letters.

   If you do not know how to print a letter, say "pass" or "skip it," and you can leave the line blank.

3. Tell the student that first he or she will print the big (uppercase) letters and that when those are finished he or she will print the small (lowercase) letters.
4. As the student prints each letter, use the Alphabet Production Record Sheet to note correct (+) and incorrect responses. When responses are incorrect, record the actual response or D.K. (student doesn't know) next to the stimulus letter. If the student self-corrects, write ok; self-corrections can be made at any time.

Letter	**Meaning of Recording**
A +	Printed correctly
M *D.K.*	Don't Know
d *b*	Printed *b* for d
u *w ok*	Printed *w* for u but self-corrected

5. Count the number of both uppercase and lowercase letters that were produced correctly. Based on the number of correctly printed letters, make a judgment of the student's alphabet production. Unknown letters or incorrect responses provide the basis for instructional interventions.

Alphabet Production Record Sheet

Name ______________________________ Date ______________

Directions: Present the Alphabet Production Student Sheet. Say, "I am going to say the name of letters, and I want you to print the letters. First, you will print the big (uppercase) letters. When those are finished you will print the small (lowercase) letters." Place + for correctly printed letters. Record the student's responses for incorrect letters. Total correct responses and record the score in the box.

1. W ____	2. D ____	3. A ____	4. R ____
5. V ____	6. J ____	7. E ____	8. X ____
9. N ____	10. O ____	11. U ____	12. Z ____
13. T ____	14. P ____	15. H ____	16. Q ____
17. M ____	18. C ____	19. F ____	20. G ____
21. L ____	22. K ____	23. B ____	24. I ____
25. S ____	26. Y ____		

Scores

☐

1. p ____	2. e ____	3. x ____	4. c ____
5. h ____	6. j ____	7. d ____	8. a ____
9. f ____	10. o ____	11. g ____	12. i ____
13. t ____	14. w ____	15. v ____	16. m ____
17. q ____	18. r ____	19. n ____	20. u ____
21. b ____	22. l ____	23. y ____	24. z ____
25. k ____	26. s ____		

\+ ☐

Total Score ☐

ALPHABET PRODUCTION STUDENT SHEET

Name ______________________________ Date ______________

Uppercase Letters

1. ______	2. ______	3. ______	4. ______
5. ______	6. ______	7. ______	8. ______
9. ______	10. ______	11. ______	12. ______
13. ______	14. ______	15. ______	16. ______
17. ______	18. ______	19. ______	20. ______
21. ______	22. ______	23. ______	24. ______
25. ______	26. ______		

Scores

☐

Lowercase Letters

1. ______	2. ______	3. ______	4. ______
5. ______	6. ______	7. ______	8. ______
9. ______	10. ______	11. ______	12. ______
13. ______	14. ______	15. ______	16. ______
17. ______	18. ______	19. ______	20. ______
21. ______	22. ______	23. ______	24. ______
25. ______	26. ______		

+ ☐

Total Score ☐

Section **2.4**

Auditory Discrimination

Behavior Observed ⟶ **Anticipated Outcome**

The student has difficulty distinguishing fine differences in the sounds of spoken words. ⟶ The student will distinguish fine differences in the sounds of spoken words.

Perspective and Strategies

Auditory discrimination is the ability to distinguish between fine sound differences in language. Discriminatory ability is developmental and may not be fully achieved until a student is eight years old. Students who have problems with auditory discrimination may have trouble in beginning reading, especially if intensive phonics instruction is used.

An informal hierarchy of auditory discrimination abilities consists of four levels.

Level 1 Environmental sounds that are grossly different, such as a dog barking and a telephone ringing.
Level 2 Words that are grossly different, like *the* and *banana*.
Level 3 Words that are somewhat different, like *father* and *mother*.
Level 4 Words that differ in only one phoneme, such as *big* and *pig*.

> Auditory discrimination ability may not be fully achieved until a student is eight years old.

An Assessment of Auditory Discrimination can be found in this section. If an auditory discrimination problem is apparent, be sure to investigate possible physical causes through a hearing screening. The school nurse can often conduct the screening. Another physical aspect to check is whether the student has a cold or allergy. Students with allergies, as well as those who swim regularly, may experience temporary hearing difficulties.

Although a physical problem may be present, a more common finding is that the student has not been taught to recognize the fine differences between sounds and words. Also important to remember is that speech sounds may vary from one dialect to another. For example, the difference between standard English and students' everyday language may be great.

Before auditory discrimination instruction can actually begin, the student must be aware of the concepts of same and different. It is best to use actual concrete objects to develop these concepts. Next, progress to sounds. Commercial or teacher-made recordings can be used to practice environmental sounds. A piano can be used to help students differentiate sounds.

It is difficult to isolate auditory discrimination teaching from practice. The following ideas should be useful.

1. If students do not understand the concepts of same and different, begin with environmental sounds and move to words that are obviously different (such as *big–truck*). Some students find it easier to use the words *yes* for *same* and *no* for *different.*

2. Begin with word pairs whose initial sounds differ. Include words that are also the same (e.g., cat–cut). Pronounce the two words and have students indicate whether they are the same or different. Progress to words that differ in ending sounds and then to words that differ in medial sounds. Possible words for practice are listed here. Additional practice endings can be found in the Chapter 3 Resources.

Beginnings	Middles	Endings
take–make	cat–cut	cat–cap
car–far	sit–sat	fan–fat
dark–bark	log–leg	lad–lap
sod–rod	luck–lick	mom–mop
lit–mitt	pot–pit	rap–rat
dead–bed	Tim–Tom	lip–lit
rock–sock	pet–pat	hot–hop

3. Have students tell whether word pairs are different in the beginning, middle, or end. Be sure the students understand concepts of beginning, middle, and end. Students will also profit from a visual representation of the word pair. They may then develop the concept that words sounding differently usually contain at least one different letter. Homonyms are, of course, the exception.

4. Encourage students to discuss the meanings of words so that they can begin to understand that words that sound different usually do not mean the same thing. Synonyms are the exception.

5. Remember that speech sounds vary from dialect to dialect. For example, *pin* and *pen* may be pronounced the same by some speakers, whereas other speakers use different sounds for the *i* and *e*. See Oral Reading as Performance in Chapter 4 for helpful information on students' dialects.

6. Consult Section 2.6 on rhyming in this chapter for additional ideas.

Yes-No. Each student has two cards that contain the words *same* and *different* (or *yes* and *no*). The teacher pronounces two words and the students hold up a card that indicates whether the words are the same or different. Points may be given for correct answers.

Picture Pairs. Develop a series of picture pairs whose names differ in only one sound, as shown here.

Name both pairs and have students take turns pointing to the picture that was named a second time. A variation is to number the picture pairs and have students hold up cards or fingers to indicate the picture that was named a second time. The following words may make good picture pairs.

chair—hair	ham—lamb	man—pan	car—star
train—rain	mail—snail	plane—mane	gate—skate
nail—pail	cake—lake	cap—map	farm—arm
ball—wall	snake—rake	grape—cape	

Additional word pairs can be found in Chapter 4 Resources.

Funny Questions. Ask students questions where the correct answer is one of two words that differ in only one sound. Take turns or allow students to volunteer. Several possible questions are given here.

- Would you put your feet in fox or socks?
- Would you open a door with a bee or a key?
- Would you hit a ball with a bat or a cat?
- Would you sit on a mat or a map?

A variation of the game is to have students make up similar questions that could be posed to others in the group.

Pronounce a Word. Have students pronounce the same word after you. Using individual chalkboards or wipe-off cards divided into fourths, have students write each word you pronounce. After all four words are written, ask students to erase words one by one. Observe whether they erase each word as it is pronounced.

DETERMINING AUDITORY DISCRIMINATION ABILITY

1. Practice the words on the Auditory Discrimination Record Sheet: Forms A and B on pages 120–121. You should say the words in a clear, normal voice.
2. Do not rush the student during the testing. Darken the Same or Different box if the student responds correctly. Draw a line through the square if the student makes an incorrect response.
3. If the student asks for a pair of words to be repeated, return to them at the conclusion of the test.
4. Facing the student, say something like what follows.

   Listen to the two words I am about to say: FAIR–FAR.

   Do they sound exactly the same or are they different?

   Yes, they are different.

   Listen to these two words: CAP–CAP.

   Are they the same or different?

   Now I am going to read you pairs of words. I want you to tell me if they are the same or different. Do you understand what you are to do? Please turn your back to me and listen very carefully.

5. Say all the words distinctly but in a normal voice.
6. When finished, add up the incorrect Same and Different responses and enter the number in the error score boxes. The following error score indicates inadequate auditory ability.

   5-year-olds—errors in Different box greater than 6
   6-year-olds—errors in Different box greater than 5
   7-year-olds—errors in Different box greater than 4
   8-year-olds—errors in Different box greater than 3

7. More than three errors in the Same box indicates an invalid test. The alternate form of the test should be used.
8. Refer to the strategies on the previous pages in Section 2.4 for instructional interventions.

AUDITORY DISCRIMINATION RECORD SHEET: FORM A

			Same	Different
1.	though	– show		☐
2.	bad	– dad		☐
3.	sit	– sick		☐
4.	jump	– jump	☐	
5.	buff	– bus		☐
6.	mat	– gnat		☐
7.	dub	– dug		☐
8.	oath	– oaf		☐
9.	lag	– lad		☐
10.	judge	– judge	☐	
11.	set	– sit		☐
12.	watch	– watch	☐	
13.	ball	– bowl		☐
14.	sink	– think		☐
15.	luck	– lock		☐
16.	tot	– top		☐
17.	duck	– duck	☐	
18.	foam	– phone		☐
19.	mauve	– moth		☐
20.	seek	– sheik		☐
21.	fought	– thought		☐
22.	done	– gun		☐
23.	chop	– chop	☐	
24.	can	– tan		☐
25.	boat	– goat		☐
26.	lab	– lad		☐
27.	light	– sight		☐
28.	zinc	– zinc	☐	
29.	sing	– sing	☐	
30.	bed	– bad		☐
31.	moss	– moth		☐
32.	till	– pill		☐
33.	fall	– fall	☐	
34.	mass	– mash		☐
35.	vine	– thine		☐
36.	rode	– rode	☐	
37.	cot	– pot		☐
38.	rap	– rack		☐
39.	mash	– math		☐
40.	mar	– mar	☐	

	Same	Different
Error Score:	☐	☐

Inadequate auditory discrimination is indicated by more than:

6 errors in Different box for 5-year-olds
5 errors in Different box for 6-year-olds
4 errors in Different box for 7-year-olds
3 errors in Different box for 8-year-olds

An invalid test is indicated by more than 3 errors in Same box.

AUDITORY DISCRIMINATION RECORD SHEET: FORM B

		Same	**Different**
1. breathe	– brief		☐
2. grove	– growth		☐
3. fuss	– thus		☐
4. mall	– mall	☐	
5. fame	– feign		☐
6. mast	– mask		☐
7. thing	– thing	☐	
8. disk	– desk		☐
9. duck	– dock		☐
10. suit	– soup		☐
11. crab	– crag		☐
12. zig	– zig	☐	
13. brash	– brass		☐
14. sad	– said		☐
15. van	– than		☐
16. thin	– shin		☐
17. mud	– mug		☐
18. save	– shave		☐
19. bask	– bath		☐
20. age	– age	☐	

		Same	**Different**
21. froze	– froze	☐	
22. sew	– saw		☐
23. bib	– bid		☐
24. came	– tame		☐
25. cat	– pat		☐
26. busy	– dizzy		☐
27. debt	– get		☐
28. tank	– thank		☐
29. fought	– sought		☐
30. guessed	– best		☐
31. touch	– touch	☐	
32. tick	– tip		☐
33. tail	– pail		☐
34. jury	– jury	☐	
35. champ	– champ	☐	
36. lass	– laugh		☐
37. maze	– maze	☐	
38. math	– mass		☐
39. star	– star	☐	
40. nice	– mice		☐

	Same	Different
Error Score:	☐	☐

Inadequate auditory discrimination is indicated by more than:

6 errors in Different box for 5-year-olds
5 errors in Different box for 6-year-olds
4 errors in Different box for 7-year-olds
3 errors in Different box for 8-year-olds

An invalid test is indicated by more than 3 errors in Same box.

Section 2.5

Concept of a Word

Behavior Observed → **Anticipated Outcome**

The student does not seem to understand what words are.

The student will develop the concept of a word.

Perspective and Strategies

Words are critical in reading, yet many emergent and struggling readers have difficulty understanding what is meant by a "word." Johns (1980), for example, found that below-average first graders had significantly greater difficulty in locating one or two words than did average and above-average first graders. Even some struggling readers in third grade had difficulty consistently identifying one word or one letter (Johns, 1977). McGee and Richgels (1996) note that emergent readers and writers may use various ways to show words in their writing. One student used a dot between words, another wrote each word in a different color, and a third student circled each word.

Concept of a word in text is evident when the student is able to finger point to words when repeating a simple text read-aloud. Another indication is when the student is able to identify a target word immediately after the student rereads while pointing to each word. Concept of a word in text develops after the student becomes aware of beginning consonants in words. Only then is the student able to accurately track print (Morris, Bloodgood, Lomax, & Perney, 2003).

Because concept of a word is often a basis for instruction in rhyming, phonological awareness, and phonics, the following concepts may need to be taught explicitly to students.

- Most words are made up of more than one letter (*I* and *a* are the exceptions).
- Words can be different lengths. The number of phonemes determines whether a spoken word is short, medium, or long.
- The number of letters in a word determines its written length.
- There are spaces between words.
- Words can be organized into sentences.

Consider the following strategies and activities to help students develop the concept of a word and word boundaries. Remember, too, that an awareness of words develops over time with language use and can be enhanced by reading and writing (Roberts, 1992).

1. A student's name is extremely meaningful. Print it on a card and show it to the student. Point to the student's first name, say it, and then point to the student's last name and say it. Show the student the space that separates the first and last name by pointing to it. Tell the student there are two words on the card, framing each with your hands. In subsequent interactions, you may wish to talk about letters that make the name. Call attention to the initial letters and their sounds.
2. Refer to words in the room and ask students how many words are shown. Have them explain their answers. Provide explanations or clarifications as needed. Help students understand that words (except *I* and *a*) are made up of more than one letter.
3. Encourage students to show you words they can write or read. Have them frame a word with their hands. They can also name and talk about the number of letters that make up the word.
4. Provide ample opportunities for students to talk with each other, write, and read. Although their reading and writing may be in an emergent stage, promoting a risk-taking and supportive environment in the classroom will pay rich dividends in literacy acquisition.
5. Have students point to words as they read experience stories, big books, wall charts, poems, and books. Pointing helps students practice the match between printed words and spoken words.
6. Prepare a sentence on a one-inch strip of paper, based on a simple, predictable book. For example, write the following.

   My neighbor is ________________.

   Have students fill in the blank. Write the complete sentence on an envelope. With the sentence on the envelope as a guide, have students cut their sentences into words. Ask students to use their words to remake the sentence. Send these envelopes home for students to practice using words to build a sentence. This activity works best with individual students or with a small group.

COUNTING WORDS

1. For Counting Words (Cunningham, 2000) give each student 10 counters in a plastic cup. Manipulatives such as paper squares work best since they are quiet.
2. Count some familiar objects in the room: i.e., bulletin boards, doors, plants, pillows.
3. Ask students to place one of their counters on their desks as you point to each object. Be sure students return their counters to their cups at the end of each count.
4. Tell students they can also count words by putting down a counter for each word they say.
   - Model the process with manipulatives at the overhead projector for a large group or at the table for a small group. Use the sentence "I am your teacher."
   - First, say the sentence naturally.
   - Then say the sentence slowly, pausing after each word. Put down a marker as each word is said.
   - Ask the students to do it with you this time as you say the sentence slowly, pausing after each word. Have the students put down a marker with you as each word is said.
   - Ask the students how many words you said.
   - Proceed to other sentences, capitalizing on your students' experiences. Start with simple sentences. As students demonstrate competency, make the sentences longer. (Diana is sitting. Scott is wearing blue. Steven is wearing tan pants. Sandra has a new baby brother. Isabella is wearing a white blouse today. Julio will be six years old this month.) Follow the same sequence as above.
   - As students demonstrate that they understand the concept of sentences, invite them to offer sentences. They should say the sentence once naturally and then one word at a time.
5. Familiar nursery rhymes, poems, finger plays, and texts from books may also be used.
6. Extend this strategy by providing written sentence strips. Invite students to count words by placing a counter beneath each word. Place the sentence strips in a pocket chart and leave an empty pocket beneath each sentence strip for counters to be placed under each word.
7. Provide instruction and support by calling attention to the white spaces between each word or by cutting the sentence strips between words as the students watch.
8. Variations of this activity include clapping or moving a block forward for each spoken word.

SEQUENCING WORDS IN FAMILIAR TEXT

1. Choose a familiar book, nursery rhyme, short poem, song verse, or finger play. Finger plays and texts with predictable patterns are ideal because they help the students remember the text.
2. Write the text twice on sentence strips, using different colors for the title and each sentence or line. Then cut apart the words of one set. Next, place the cut apart word cards in envelopes marked with the sequential number of the title and sentences or lines.
3. After students are orally familiar with the text, place the sentence strips in order in a pocket chart, one line at a time. Read each line as it is placed in the pocket chart and reread again from the beginning until all the lines are placed in the pocket chart.
4. Provide the opportunity for all interested students to use a pointer and point to the words of the entire text as the others "read and reread" the text.
5. Tell students you are going to play a game with the words and that the game will be fixing the words after you mix them up.
   - First, ask them to close their eyes while you place the mixed-up word cards on top of the title.
   - Then ask, "What should the title say?"
   - Next, call on a student to place the word cards in the correct order as the other students say the correct words.
   - Reread the title to make sure it makes sense. If it does not make sense, lift up the word card and ask the student if he/she sees a difference between the two words. Discuss the differences, calling attention to the initial letter and its sound.
   - Repeat these steps for each line, calling on different students.
6. For an additional challenge, remove the sentence strips and play with only the word cards.
7. Once students demonstrate independence with this game, place in a bag the numbered envelopes filled with the word cards, with or without the sentence strips, depending on the ability of the students. Label the bag with the title and a picture clue. Teach students how to take turns with the envelopes. Then use this activity as a center for independent practice.
8. These familiar texts are ideal reader's theater scripts for emergent readers. Type text and label alternate lines with Reader 1, Reader 2, and so on. Further information for conducting reader's theater productions can be found in Johns and Berglund (2006).

Section 2.6

Rhyming

Behavior Observed → **Anticipated Outcome**

The student does not understand the concept of rhyming. → The student will demonstrate the concept of rhyming by identifying and supplying words that rhyme.

Perspective and Strategies

Rhyming is a valuable tool in the early stages of reading. Fox (2000) notes that rhyming activities will benefit reading ability regardless of the age or intelligence of the student. Rhymes help students develop an understanding that phonograms (letter clusters or families) can represent the same sound in different words. Phonograms that can be used to develop the concept of rhyming are given in Chapter 3 Resources on pages 267–274.

Rhyming activities are also important for emergent readers because they provide an entry to phonological awareness. Phonological awareness is the ability to hear and manipulate the different sound units in spoken language. Rhyming ability is developmentally easier than more complex phonological tasks (e.g., blending, segmenting, and deleting syllables) and can therefore be attempted without frustration (Adams, 1990b). The purpose of these rhyming activities is to provide opportunities for students to begin to develop their ability to attend to sounds in language.

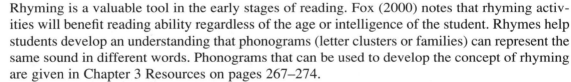

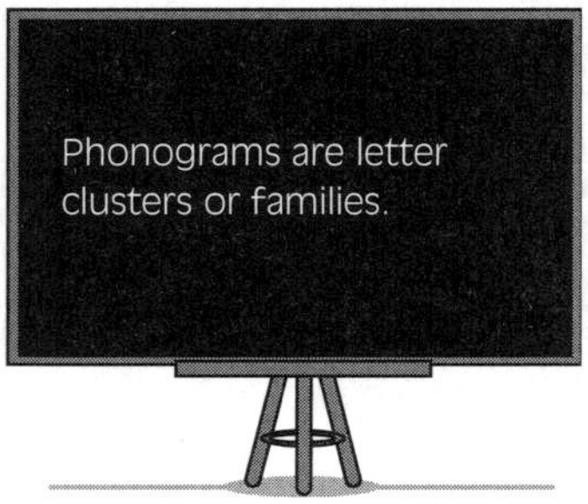
Phonograms are letter clusters or families.

The activities and strategies are organized in the following developmental sequence: listening, reciting, discriminating, and producing strategies. Students who are unable to identify rhymes need daily experiences hearing and reciting rhymes before they will be able to identify or produce rhymes. They will enjoy hearing the playful language and will need to have the rhyming words pointed out to them at this beginning stage.

Listening Strategies and Activities

1. Use nursery rhymes as a natural starting point for helping students develop an understanding of words as units of sound that can be manipulated independently of meaning. Students often enjoy nonsense words, catchy rhymes, and rhythms. Encourage students to experiment with familiar rhymes and words.

2. Read to students daily from books with rhyming elements.
3. Listen to rhyming books on tape to help solidify the concept of rhyme.
4. Listen to rhyming poetry. Reread poems, placing additional stress on the rhyming words. Point out words that rhyme.
5. Create rhyming names for students. Use rhyming names only for those who enjoy theirs. This is an excellent way to provide second language students, who may have minimal rhyming patterns in their first language, with rhyming background knowledge. Some examples include Bravo Gustavo, Okay Jose, and Carolina Ballerina. Be extremely careful not to create a negative name.

Reciting Strategies and Activities

6. Recite poems, finger plays, and chants. Write the poems, finger plays, or chants on chart paper, using rebus picture clues such as a 5 and a duck over the respective words in the finger play "Five Little Ducks." First, read the entire text. Then recite the first line, inviting all the students to echo back the line. Continue to add one more line as you start again from the beginning; each time you recite, they echo read until all lines are learned.
7. Sing rhyming songs. Chart these, following the steps described in number 6. Examples include *Five Little Pumpkins, I'm a Little Teapot, Mitten Song, Teddy Bear,* and *Going to the Zoo*.

Discriminating Strategies and Activities

8. Read or recite a nursery rhyme that has been written on chart paper. Chose several rhyming word pairs from the rhyme and draw pictures on index cards to represent the words. Have students match the rhyming pictures. For example, for the rhyme "One, Two, Buckle My Shoe," prepare these rhyming pair illustrations: 2 and shoe, 4 and door, 6 and sticks, 8 and straight (a straight line will do), and 10 and hen. This activity is also a good assessment to determine whether students are able to hear rhyming patterns. Those unable to hear the rhymes need additional experiences hearing and reciting rhymes.
9. Draw or cut out pictures of word pairs that rhyme. Mix the word pairs and have students take turns selecting word pairs that rhyme. Ask students to say the words aloud. Possible word pairs are listed below.

nest	box	ten	hat
chest	fox	hen	cat
car	can	green	top
jar	fan	queen	mop
log	pan	late	mice
dog	man	gate	rice
tree	duck	boat	bug
bee	truck	coat	rug
toad	bone	book	corn
road	cone	hook	horn
growl	fin	pen	mail
owl	chin	ten	pail

Children have fun with rhyming activities.

10. Present students with four cards containing illustrations. Three of the cards should rhyme; one of the cards should not rhyme with the other three. Invite students to select the picture that does not rhyme and explain their reasoning. Three sets of sample cards follow.

Set 1

Set 2

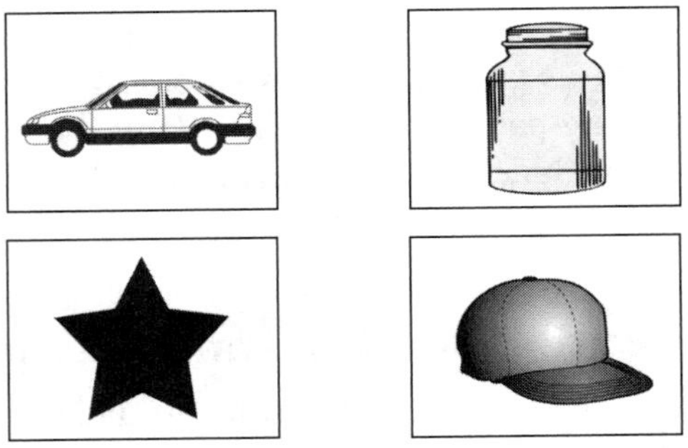

Set 3

11. Create a rhyming bulletin board. Put blank sheets of paper on the bulletin board where they can be readily reached by students. Invite students to search newspapers or magazines for pictures that rhyme and fasten them to the appropriate piece of paper. Pictures might also be drawn by students.

Producing Strategies and Activities

12. Begin with part of a familiar poem (perhaps "Jack and Jill") that contains a rhyming element. Say and print the first line on the chalkboard.

    Jack and Jill
    Went up the hill

    Tell students that two words rhyme: *Jill* and *hill*. Say, "Rhymes are words that sound alike at the ends." Have students inspect the words to find the common element (-ill). Tell them that *Jill* rhymes with *ill* and begins with */j-j-j/*. Ask them what word rhymes with *ill* and begins with */h-h-h/*. Practice other words that fit the same pattern (*pill, mill, bill, dill, kill, till, will*). Use the following format: What word rhymes with *ill* and begins with */p-p-p/*? Model when necessary and give students ample opportunities to respond individually. Have students use the words in sentences. Extend the preceding strategy to nursery rhymes or Dr. Seuss books. Have students listen for and locate rhyming words. They could also underline or circle the rhyming words.

13. Sing songs that have one or more rhyming words. Invite students to identify the rhyming words.

14. Use poetry that contains rhyming words. Help students to identify the words that rhyme. Then read the poem aloud and leave out selected words. Have students supply the rhyming word that was left out.

15. Do riddles with body parts. Fox (1996) offers the following riddles in which all the answers rhyme with *head*.

    - What can you toast? (bread)
    - What do you call something that's not living anymore? (dead)
    - What is the color of blood? (red)
    - What do you use to ride down snowy hills? (sled)
    - Where do you sleep? (bed)

    Encourage students to make up riddles and questions that rhyme with certain words.

16. Use magnetic letters or letter cards to help the students see how changing the initial letter can make a new word that rhymes with the original word. Help students understand that rhyming words have the same endings. An example follows. After teaching this activity to students, provide time for students to practice in small groups or centers, having them make the words and write and illustrate them in individual rhyming books for each phonogram taught.

b	at	b	ell
r		f	
h		s	
f		w	
s			

17. Encourage students to determine a rhyming word when you say: "What word rhymes with (use a phonogram) and begins with (use an initial sound)?" A few examples follow.

    oy: boy, joy, toy, Roy
    um: drum, thumb, gum
    op: crop, drop, pop, shop, stop, mop

    Rhymes are very generalizable. Nearly 500 primary grade words can be derived from the following set of only 37 phonograms (Whylie & Durrell, 1970, as cited in Adams, 1990b, pp. 321–322).

-ack	-ail	-ain	-ake	-ale	-ame
-an	-ank	-ap	-ash	-at	-ate
-aw	-ay	-eat	-ell	-est	-ice
-ick	-ide	-ight	-ill	-in	-ine
-ing	-ink	-ip	-ir	-ock	-oke
-op	-or	-ore	-uck	-ug	-ump
-unk					

18. Tell students, "I'm thinking of a word that begins with *b* and rhymes with *cat*." Have students make up other "I'm thinking of" riddles.

19. Secure a copy of the book *"Fire! Fire!" Said Mrs. Mc Guire* by Bill Martin (2006). In this version of the rhyme, the smoke is coming from birthday candles. Read the book several times to students. Then, before you read the book again, tell students that you will need their help to finish each rhyme. As you read each rhyming sentence, put additional stress on the first rhyming word and say only the onset of the second rhyming word, leaving off the rime.

For example say, "'Where? Where?' said Mrs. /B/____." In this example the students reply, "Bear." Other rhyming book titles can be found in Section 2.9 Onsets and Rimes and in Opitz (2000).

20. Encourage students to write rhyming words and explain how they are able to create the words.
21. Use poems, songs, and chants as ways to encourage students to create their own rhymes.
22. Make class-rhyming books. Read a poem together. Create a sentence, based on the topic of the poem, with two blanks that students will fill in with rhyming pairs. For example,

    In my house I have a ______ and a ______.

    This sentence could be used after reading "My House" by Jane W. Krows (1993). Have each student fill in a sentence and illustrate the page. These books make wonderful independent reading materials for emergent readers and can be reread in a center or with a reading partner. They enjoy reading their own books and become more familiar with the spelling features of rhymes.
23. Have students brainstorm as many rhyming words as they can in 30 seconds. Repeat this activity often to reinforce rhyming skills.
24. Have students create their own poem using words that rhyme.

Find a Rhyme. Make a pair of rhyming words for each two students. Put each word on a note card. Each student gets a card. The object of the game is to find the other person who has the word that rhymes. This game can be repeated several times by mixing the cards.

Remember and Rhyme. For oral practice with rhyming words, students can form small groups and play a game. One student in the group begins with a simple one-syllable word (for example, *nice, best,* or *stop*) and says the word aloud. The next player in the group has to say the first student's rhyming word and then add one of his or her own. This process continues until no other rhyming word can be given. Begin again and play with a new word.

Find These Rhyming Words. Try a rhyming word scavenger hunt with a small group of students. Begin with one word that has many others that rhyme with it (for instance, *cake, bug,* or *top*). Give the students 10 minutes to look for items that rhyme with the given word. Pictures from magazines can be included along with symbols that represent the word. For example, a twig may represent the word nest. Following the 10-minute word-hunting period, form a group and share items found. Write the rhyming words on the chalkboard.

Group Me. Use a deck of cards containing groups of rhyming words. Shuffle the cards and encourage the students to categorize the rhyming words into their appropriate groups after saying each word out loud.

Section **2.7**

Syllabic Awareness

Behavior Observed → **Anticipated Outcome**

The student is unable to segment words into syllables and blend syllables into words.

The student will successfully segment words into syllables and blend syllables into words.

Background

Once students have developed the concept of a word, they will be ready to learn that words are made up of strings of smaller units of speech called syllables. Research (Adams, 1990b) suggests that syllabic awareness is an essential link between the ability to rhyme and the developmentally harder-to-acquire ability to hear and manipulate phonemes, the individual sounds in spoken language. Developing students' ability to reflect on syllables as smaller units of sound in words is a useful step in preparing them to later develop phonemic awareness, found to be causally related to reading acquisition (Bradley & Bryant, 1983; Lundberg, Frost, & Petersen, 1988).

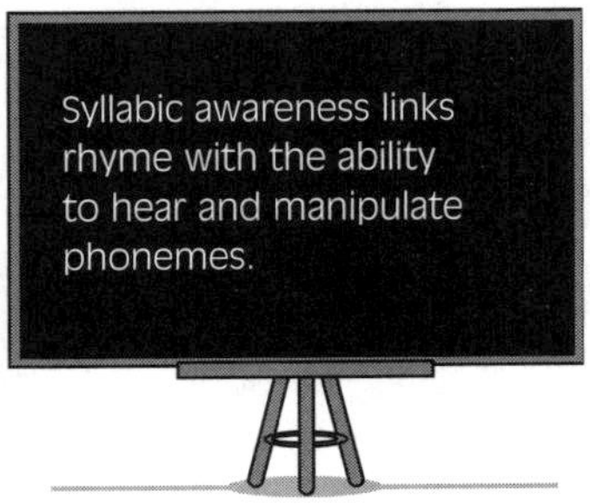

Syllabic awareness links rhyme with the ability to hear and manipulate phonemes.

We encourage you to use the following teaching strategies to develop students' syllabic awareness. Be careful to enunciate words clearly and to use only familiar words with your students.

SEGMENTING SYLLABLES

1. Begin teaching separation of words into syllables after students are proficient at separating an oral phrase or sentence into words. If students have difficulty with this task, refer to Section 2.5, Concept of a Word, for some useful strategies.
2. For Segmenting Syllables (Cunningham, 1995) use the names of your students for initial activities. Say the first name of one student; then say the name again and clap the syllables. Clap as you say each syllable.
3. Say the first names of other students and clap the syllables as you say them the second time. Encourage students to clap with you.
4. Continue with other names. As students become proficient, use some of their middle and/or last names. The word *beat* may be a more easily understood term than syllables for young students. By clapping, students should realize that *Bob* is a one-beat word, *Giti* is a two-beat word, *Natalie* is a three-beat word, and so on.
5. When students can clap beats easily, help them see that the length of the word is usually related to the number of claps it gets. Start with students' names that begin with the same letter. Then print the names on different strips of paper so that the short words have short strips and the long words have long strips, as in the following example.

Bob	Barbara

   Before showing the words, say *Bob* and *Barbara* and have students decide that *Bob* is a one-beat word and *Barbara* takes more claps and is a three-beat word. Ask them to predict which word is probably longer and has more letters. Then show them the words and develop the understanding that, because longer words (like *Barbara*) take several claps, they probably have more letters than shorter words. Use some of the other names of your students to further develop and practice this basic understanding.
6. Extend this activity by having students sort pictures of classmates or their names written on index cards according to the number of syllables in their names. Provide number cards as header cards to sort under. Make the activity self-correcting by writing the number of syllables on the back of the pictures or names. Use this activity to assess an individual student's syllabic segmentation ability and as an independent center activity.
7. Then use a similar procedure with word pairs (or triplets). Possible categories and words to use are shown below.

Toys		**Animals**	
ball	bicycle	canary	bobcat
crayons	paint	cat	bear
doll	puzzle	chimpanzee	beaver
dominoes	bingo	camel	bison
cards	computer	hippopotamus	giraffe
game	markers	horse	goat

8. A variation is to show students two words they probably can't read and ask, "Who can figure out which of the two words I'm holding is canary and which is cat?" The goal is to have students recognize that words requiring more claps probably contain more letters.
9. Moving blocks to represent each syllable or tapping a pencil or other object could be used instead of clapping syllables. Such variations may help sustain students' attention.

BLENDING SYLLABLES

1. For Blending Syllables (Lundberg, Frost, & Peterson, 1988) begin by reading *The Three Billy Goats Gruff* to help students gain an understanding of what a troll is. When the troll talks in the story, say the words syllable by syllable.
2. Then pretend to be a troll. Tell students you will say words and students must figure out the words being named. Provide and discuss several examples.
3. Use words like *paper, pencil, candy, marker, eraser, notebook, automobile, airplane, buggy, hamburger,* and *chalkboard.* If possible, have the actual objects so that students can make a visual association *after* they have identified the word.
4. Extend the lesson by having students use tokens (see Strategy 2 in Section 2.10) for each syllable heard or hold up a finger for each syllable.
5. Invite students to volunteer for the troll's role. Provide guidance and support as needed.
6. Create an audiotape of the troll words used in the lesson. Record each troll word and its normally spoken equivalent. Provide these directions.
   - Listen to the troll's word.
   - Push the pause button after you hear the troll's word.
   - Say the word normally.
   - Push the pause button again to listen to the word spoken normally.

Students can divide their friends' names into syllables.

Practice and Reinforcement Activities

1. Provide direct instruction in invented spelling by modeling for students and encouraging them to spell words by breaking words into syllables. This is easily done by students clapping out the syllables of words and then writing down the letters for the sounds they hear within each syllable. This process is very empowering for young students, providing confidence in "spelling" multisyllable words (Slattery Gursky, 2003).
2. Have students categorize the names of pictures according to the number of syllables. Photos of classmates are very engaging for students. Some other possible pictures to use follow.

3. Clap or tap to the beat (syllables) of songs.
4. Write a cloze sentence on the board, placing dashes to represent the number of syllables in the missing word. For example, write

   I like _____ _____ _____ chip cookies.

   Read the sentence aloud, clapping three times to represent the three syllables in the word choc-o-late. Have students think of possible word choices that make sense and have the correct number of syllables. Accept any reasonable response.

5. Practice blending action-word syllables. Perform an action, segmenting the spoken word into syllables while simultaneously segmenting the action to represent the number of syllables. For example, say *walk* taking one step and *ing* taking a second step. Have students blend the syllables into the action word *walking*. Other action words to say and act out in segmented syllables include *breathing, snapping, singing, batting, throwing, coloring,* and *following*.

Section **2.8**

Alphabetic Principle

Behavior Observed → **Anticipated Outcome**

The student lacks knowledge of sounds associated with letters of the alphabet. → The student will become aware of associating letters with their sounds.

Perspective and Strategies

Once beginning readers understand the language and concepts of printed materials, further progress is made by developing the alphabetic principle. The following activities focus on introducing the student to associate selected letters of the alphabet with their sounds.

1. See Chapter 3 for an expanded explanation of letter-sound correspondences.
2. Introduce the concept of beginning sounds by reading aloud alphabet books (see Part B on the CD) or pattern books (see Part C on the CD). Draw attention to words that begin with the same sound. *The Little Book of Big Tongue Twisters* by Foley Curtis (1977) contains alliterative pieces that could be used to introduce most of the beginning sounds.
3. Use graphic displays that combine the letter form with a picture of something that begins with that letter. Draw letters within the picture rather than next to the picture, as demonstrated below.

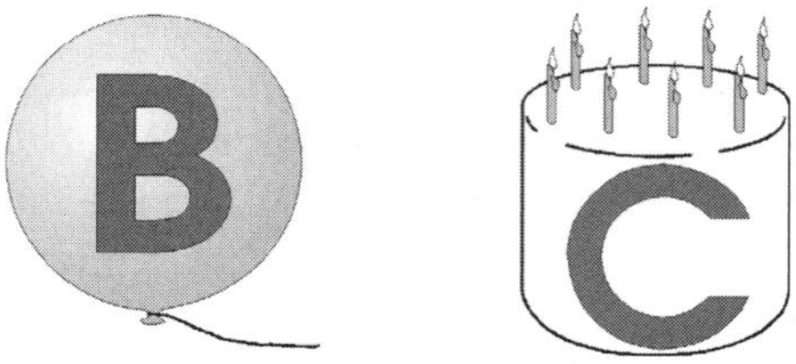

Give students lots of practice with the pictures, perhaps drawn on cards, until the letter drawn and its associated object become familiar. Large cards displayed around the classroom are a helpful reminder. Read alphabet books to your class and request that parents do the same at home. Immersion in the alphabetic principle will facilitate sound-symbol association. Part B on the CD lists some titles of alphabet books.

4. Make alphabet books with your students. At first, simply paste or draw pictures of objects beginning with a given letter on its letter page. For example, the *Ss* page might have a silly smile, a snake, scissors, and spinach. Upon completion of the first step, subsequent alphabet books might carry a theme, such as animals. In this case, the *Ss* page might have pictures of a squirrel, a snake, and a squid. Taken one step further, the alphabet book might include a combination of pictures and written words that begin with *s*.
5. Say a word and have students indicate whether their names begin with the same sound. Remember to stress sounds so names like *Cecil* and *Sam* begin with the same sound as *circus*. Clarify students' responses as necessary.
6. Play the game "I Spy." Tell students that you see or spy something in the room that begins with the same sound as *paper*. As students say words, note words with incorrect sounds ("I'm sorry, *box* does not begin like *paper*") or say, "The word *pen* begins like *paper* but it isn't the word I was thinking." A more advanced version of the game could involve an ending sound.
7. Make letter-sound puzzles by purchasing and laminating an alphabet chart with corresponding initial sound pictures. Cut out each letter and picture set and cut off the picture in a jigsaw fashion. Have students match the letters to the pictures that represent the initial sounds. These puzzles are self-correcting when each half only matches its corresponding part and make an ideal center activity for small groups.

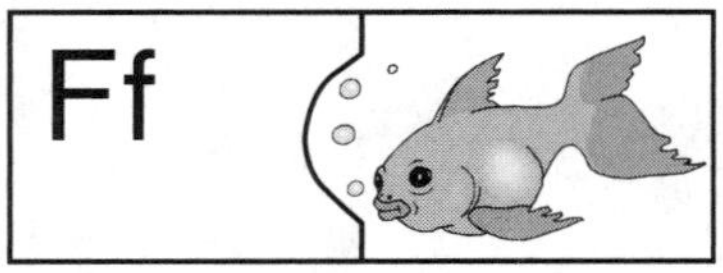

8. Establish mailboxes for each student (hanging file folders in a plastic crate works well) and encourage students to write to each other.
9. Provide plenty of opportunities for students to engage in writing and be supportive of their efforts.

CLOSED AND OPEN SORTS

1. Model a closed sort using pictures of students, pictures of objects, or toys/small objects. Sort them according to their initial letter sounds.
2. Provide four to five pictures and/or objects for each pair of initial letter sounds being sorted. Start by sorting pictures or objects that begin with different sounds. For example, avoid pairing soft *c* and *s* or hard *c* and *k*. Choose letters that also appear dissimilar. For example, avoid sorting *b* and *d* items or *p* and *q* items at the same time. The Letter-Sound Sorting Progress Monitoring Form found on the next page will assist in providing a systematic approach to closed sorting and a method for tracking students' sorting progress. For example, for the first pair of letters listed (*Bb* and *Ff*), you might include photos of students (e.g., Bobby and Frank), a button, and pictures of a ball, bacon, bat, foot, flower, finger, and the number 4.
3. Make a header card for each initial letter being sorted by writing the letters on index cards.
4. Review the two letters and their sounds. For example, while pointing to the *Bb* header card say, "What is this letter?" Then ask, "What sound does *B* make?" If the student does not know the sound, provide a sample object or picture. Say, "Ball begins with *Bb*. /B-B-B/all begins with */b-b-b/. Say the sound /b-b-b/* with me." Repeat this procedure for the other letter.
5. Mix up the sorting objects. Have the student pick an object and say its name while stretching out the initial sound (*/f-f-f-f/oot)*. Ask the student to place the object under the letter that has the same sound as the beginning sound of the object.
6. After all objects are sorted, repeat the name of each object placed under each letter. If a student placed an object or picture under the wrong letter, guide the student by asking whether the object has the same sound as the letter. (Does */b-b-b-b/all* start with the same sound as */f-f-f-f/*?)
7. When students are familiar with the concept of sorting, challenge them to figure out the common initial letters themselves (open sort). Have them sort the pictures/objects that go together and explain their sorts.
8. Extend the closed or open sort by having students glue pictures on a two-column sorting mat as a center activity. An example of a closed sort is shown below.

Bb Ff

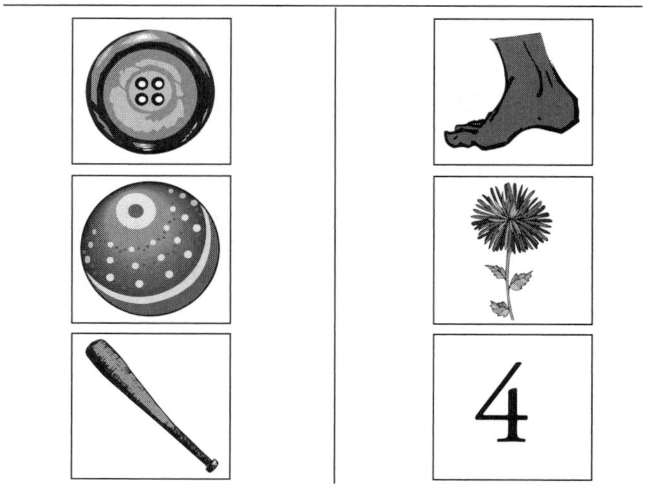

LETTER-SOUND SORTING PROGRESS MONITORING FORM

Directions: Fill in your students' names in the first column and record the date when each letter-sound pair is mastered.

Students	*Bb* *Ff*	*Ff* *Dd*	*Dd* *Cc*	*Cc* *Bb*	*Bb* *Gg*	*Gg* *Hh*	*Hh* *Jj*	*Jj* *Kk*	*Kk* *Ll*	*Ll* *Mm*	*Mm* *Pp*	*Pp* *Nn*	*Nn* *Rr*	*Rr* *Ss*	*Ss* *Tt*	*Tt* *Ww*	*Ww* *Zz*	*Zz* *Qq*

ALPHABET BOOK PARODIES

1. Secure a copy of *Poor Puppy* by Nick Bruel (2007). This book is about a puppy whose friend Kitty does not want to play. He tires himself out by playing with one airplane, two balls, three cars, and so on. When he takes a nap, he dreams about playing with Kitty all over the world, playing games such as Football in France, Golf in Greece, and Hopscotch in Hawaii.
2. After reading the story, engage students in creating a class alphabet book. Begin by brainstorming and listing possible titles. Ask the students, "What do you notice about the two words in the title *Poor Puppy*?" Guide them to notice that *poor* and *puppy* begin with the same letter. Have them think of an animal and describe the animal using a word that starts with the same letter. List the possible titles on chart paper. Some examples include Amazing Alligator, Busy Bird, Curious Cat, and so on. Read the charted titles. Then, ask students to vote for the title for their class book. You may wish to display the charted titles in a writing center for future independent writing ideas.
3. Engage students in creating a list, numbered from 1 to 26, of things the character will play with that represent letters of the alphabet, such as 1 apple, 2 books, 3 crayons, and 4 drums. Write this list on chart paper with simple pictures. Record the initials or number of each student next to their ideas, making sure all students get a turn.
4. Have students create a page. Leave the chart in clear view so students can see their ideas.
5. Share each page in alphabetical order and assemble the book.
6. Several versions of the alphabet book can be made by the class and placed in a center for small groups to read and reread with a partner.
7. Invite students to create their own alphabet books in a writing center.

Section **2.9**

Onsets and Rimes

Behavior Observed → **Anticipated Outcome**

Behavior Observed	Anticipated Outcome
The student is unable to segment, blend, and manipulate onsets and rimes.	The student will be able to segment, blend, and manipulate onsets and rimes.

Background

A rime is a vowel-consonant or consonant-vowel cluster combination at the end of a syllable. In the one-syllable word *string*, the rime is *ing*. The onset is the consonant or consonant cluster that precedes the rime. In the word *string*, the onset is *str* (Anthony et al., 2003; Slattery, 2000a). Teaching students onsets and rimes helps them to understand that phonograms (letter clusters or word families) can represent the same sound in different words. This knowledge enables students to decode words by analogy (National Reading Panel, 2000). Knowing how to read *cat* provides a basis for students to read *bat, fat, hat, mat, pat, rat, sat,* and *flat*.

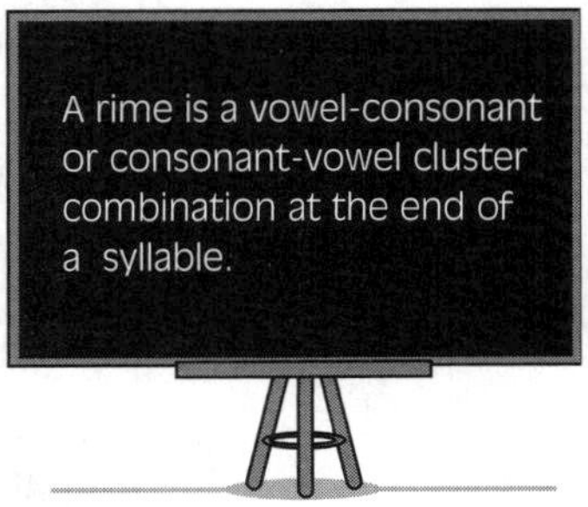
A rime is a vowel-consonant or consonant-vowel cluster combination at the end of a syllable.

Begin teaching segmenting and blending of onsets and rimes after students are able to separate words into syllables. After students are able to hear syllables in words, the next unit of sound they are able to hear is onset followed by rime (Treiman & Zukowski, 1991). Separating syllables into onsets and rimes is easier than separating them into other sound units. *Ran* is more easily divided into *r-an* than *ra-n* or *r-a-n* (Cunningham, 2000).

SEGMENTING ONSETS AND RIMES

1. Select or make illustrations of familiar rhyming words to make rhyming pairs that share the same initial letters (Slattery, 2000a). For example you can use *c* and *r* (*cake* and *rake* and *cat* and *rat*). See Word Patterns in Chapter 3 Resources on pages 267–274 for possible choices.

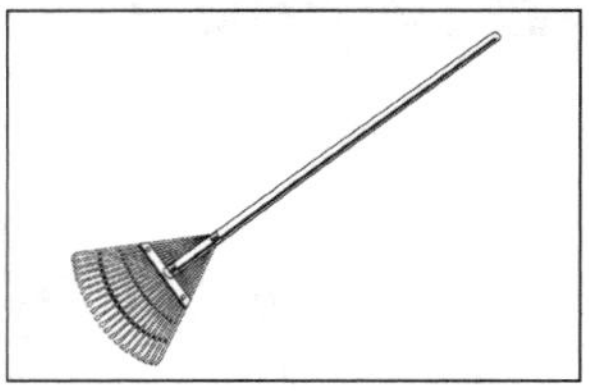

2. Mix up the pictures and have students sort the pictures by the onsets. If you would like to do this activity with blends, have students sort by the blends (onsets) that come before the rimes.
3. After students have sorted the pictures into two columns, one with c words and the other with r words, ask the students the question that follows.

   What ***sound*** *do you hear at the beginning of these words [pointing to those beginning with c]?*

   Similarly, ask the same question for those beginning with r.
4. Ask what **letter** makes the /c/ and /r/ sound respectively at the beginning of each group of sorted pictures. As the students tell you the letters, write a c and an r in black on index cards, placing the corresponding letter over the group of rhyming pictures.
5. Gather the picture cards. Have students sort them according to their rimes. Explain that this time you are going to listen to the part of the word that comes after the first sound. Hold up a picture, modeling the process by saying "*Cat* starts with /c/ and ends with /at/ c-at." Pick up the next picture, asking: "What sound do you hear at the beginning of *rake*?" and "What comes after the /r/ sound?" "Does /ake/ sound like /at/?" When pictures have the same rime, group them together.
6. After all the rime pairs have been grouped together, place index cards with the rimes written in red above each set.
7. Say each rime pair, segmenting the onset from the rime. Model this process by saying "c-at, r-at." This activity works best with small groups. You may want to use the illustrations from this activity to assess whether students are able to segment onsets and rimes.
8. Extend the activity by having students take turns blending the correct onset card with the rime header card to form the word for the picture.
9. Extend the activity further by mixing the red rime cards and having students make rhyming words by blending the onsets and rimes.

BLENDING ONSETS AND RIMES

1. Create and read rhyming words from a word students can read. Choose a word they can already read and write it on an index card. The word *fish* will be used for this example. Prepare individual consonants cut out from index cards.

fish	b	c	d	f	g	h	j	k	l	m
	n	p	q	r	s	t	v	w	y	z

2. Tell students, "We are going to make words that rhyme with a word we already know by using consonants."
3. Place the word *fish* in a pocket chart, asking the students to read the word.
4. Using the consonant letters in *consecutive* order, place one consonant at a time over the onset (f) in *fish,* asking the students to read the new "word" and asking whether you have made a real word. Write all the real words on the chalkboard.
5. Read all the words together that are written on the chalkboard.
6. Help students understand that all the words have the same rime by asking the question that follows.

   Do you notice any letters that are the same in all the words I wrote on the chalkboard?

   If students are unable to identify the entire *ish* phonogram (word family or letter clusters) and are only able to find one or two of the letters, ask a question like what follows.

   Are there any more letters that are the same in all the words?

7. Point out that knowing how to read and spell a rime like *ish* in *fish* helps students to read and spell other words with the same rime. In Strategy 3 (Show and Tell a Word) students will be taught to make this reading and spelling connection.

SHOW AND TELL A WORD

1. For Show and Tell a Word (Slattery, 2000a), read a book or poem with rhyme patterns. After students are familiar with the rhyme patterns, prepare for the activity by choosing one word family or rime pattern from the text. This activity is based on the *at* word pattern found in Dr. Seuss' *Hop on Pop* (1965). Consider the following in making your choice: rimes that begin with a short /a/ appear most frequently in children's books, those beginning with a short /u/ rarely occur, and short /e/ is difficult for children to hear (Johnson & Kaufman, 1999).

2. Make the student onset and rime manipulatives, teacher manipulatives, and rhyming word cards. Write the rime *at* on a strip of two connected one-inch squares, placing an *a* and *t* in each square, and duplicate enough copies for students (see example below). Also, make a four-inch high version in red. Prepare individual one-inch squares with the onsets *b, c, h, P,* and *s* (see example) and make four-inch versions of these same onsets. (Blends and diagraphs can be used after students are confident with single-letter onsets.) Write *at, bat, cat, hat, Pat,* and *sat* on index cards, writing the onset in black and the rime in red. Make two additional rhyming words, *mat* and *fat,* to be used in steps 12 and 13.

Rime
(Do not cut apart.)

a	t

Onset
(Cut apart.)

b	c	h	P	s

3. Place the four-inch high version of the rime in red in a pocket chart, with the onset letters in white above the rime. (Letter squares the same size as the students' letters can be used for small groups without a pocket chart.)

4. Provide each student with a set of onsets (*b, c, h, P,* and *s*) and the rime *at* on connected squares. These can be easily passed out as a strip of onsets that the students cut apart and a rime strip that the students are instructed to color red. Until they get used to this step, pass out the rime first and have them color it red like yours and then pass out the onset to be cut apart like yours. They quickly learn to look at the pocket chart for what needs to be colored and what needs to be cut apart.

5. Tell students the following.

   The red letters are called the rime. You will notice that all rimes begin with a vowel. The letter before the rime is called the onset.

6. After several readings of *Hop on Pop* (Seuss, 1965), model the activity by placing the onset *c* in front of the rime *at* to show a word that they know from the book. Tell them what the rime and onset are. Place the rhyming word card *cat* in the pocket chart.

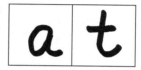

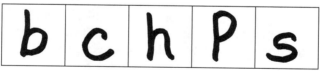

7. Invite a student to volunteer to show a word that can be made with the same rime and to tell the word and its onset and rime.
8. Have other students show the new word using their *at* rime strip and matching letter square.

   Ask them to tell the new word and its parts by pointing to each word part, stating, "The onset is ________, and the rime is ________." Place the new rhyming word card next to the word *cat* in the pocket chart.
9. Continue the activity repeating steps 7 and 8 until all of the rhyming words but two have been made, saving *mat* and *fat* for steps 12 and 13.
10. Read all the rhyming cards together and ask students to tell what they notice about the words. Some possible responses are:
    - All the words have an *a*.
    - All the words have a *t*.
    - All the words have an *a* and *t*.
    - All the words look the same except the first letter.
    - I hear /at/ in all the words.

    Encourage responses by asking if there is anything else that students notice.
11. Ask the following question.

    How do you think these words can help us?

    Try to elicit that knowing the rime pattern will help students pronounce and spell words.
12. Ask a student to **pronounce** *mat,* one of the remaining rhyming words in your hand, and ask the student how he or she was able to read the new word.
13. Invite another student to help you **spell** *fat,* the last rhyming word. Show the correctly spelled word, asking how the student knew how to spell the word.

    Making the connection to reading and spelling in steps 12 and 13 is extremely important. Without this explicit connection, many students will not be able to apply what is being taught in this activity to their own reading and spelling.
14. Extend this activity by including the onsets *ch* and *fl*, for the words *chat* and *flat*.
15. See Chapter 3 Resources (pages 267–274) for additional rhyming words to use with other books.

RESOURCES

Practice and Reinforcement Activities

1. Read a rhyming poem or book. Copy the poem or section of the book on chart paper or a transparency. Cover the rime of corresponding rhyming words. Have students use the onsets to help figure out the word. Uncover the rime and read it aloud. Following are examples of poems to use.
   - Ayres, K. *Up, down, and around*. Cambridge, MA: Candlewick Press, 2007.
   - Charao, K. *Jumpety-Bumpety Hop: A Parade of Animal Poems*. New York: Dutton, 1997.
   - Graham, J. "Steam." In *Splish Splash*. New York: Scholastic, 1994.
   - Harris, T. *Jenny found a penny*. Minneapolis, MN: Millbrook Press, 2008.
   - McCord, D. "Notice." In *One at a Time*. Boston: Little, Brown, 1952.
   - Rogers, S. *Earthsongs*. New York: Dutton, 1998.

- Ruelle, K. G. *Bark Park*. Atlanta: Peachtree, 2008.
- Schertle, A. *I Am the Cat*. New York: Lothrop, Lee & Shepard, 1999.
- Silverstein, S. "Ickle Me, Pickle Me, Tickle Me Too." In *Where the Sidewalk Ends*. New York: HarperCollins, 1974.
- Spires, E. *Riddle Road*. New York: Margaret K. McElderry/Simon & Schuster Children's Books, 1999.

Following are examples of books to use. Other titles can be found in Opitz (2000).

- Aylesworth, J. *Old Black Fly*. New York: Scholastic, 1992.
- Bunting, E. *Flower Garden*. New York: Harcourt Brace, 1994.
- Cain, J. *The Way I Feel*. New York: Scholastic, 2000.
- Couric, K. *The Brand New Kid*. New York: Scholastic, 2000.
- Deming, A. *Who Is Tapping At My Window?* New York: Penguin, 1994.
- Lear, E. *A Was Once an Apple Pie*. Cambridge, MA: Candlewick, 1997.
- Westcott, N. *The Lady with the Alligator Purse*. Boston: Little, Brown, 1988.
- Wood, A. *Silly Sally*. San Diego: Harcourt Brace, 1992.

2. Write a sentence using several words from a word family, leaving the rime off of one of the words. Tell students that the missing rime has the same rime pattern as the underlined rhyming words in the sentence. Have students use the rime clues and onset clue to figure out the missing word. For example write the following sentence:

   The big pig danced a j __ __.

3. Sort two sets of word families, adding one or two additional word families as students show readiness. Begin with short vowel word families in the following order: *a, i, o, e*. Short /a/ word families are most commonly found in children's books, short /e/ is harder for children to hear than short /i/ and /o/, and short /u/ word families are not commonly used in children's books (Johnson & Kaufman, 1999). See Word Patterns in Chapter 3 Resources for possible word families.
4. After students practice word sorts with a teacher, have students cut out and glue words, sorting them on paper.
5. Write rime patterns several times in large letters, providing a blank for students to fill in the onset. Duplicate these patterns for independent practice or laminate and use rime patterns for practice at a center.
6. After students have learned the word family, develop word wheels, sliders, or flip books where the various words can be made by turning a wheel, sliding a strip of paper, or flipping pages in a book. Possible words for this activity can be found in Word Patterns in Chapter 3 Resources.

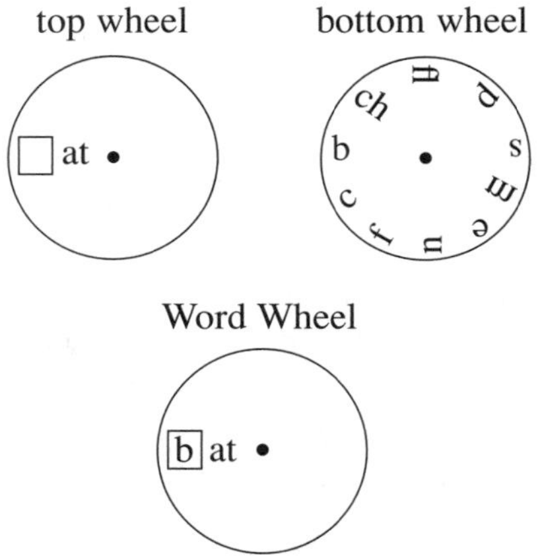

Word Wheel

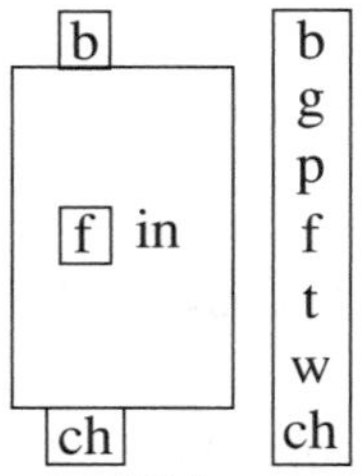

Slider

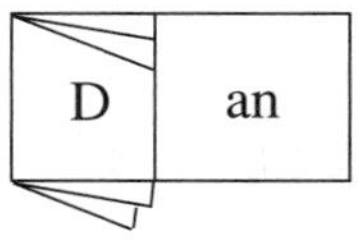

Flipbook

7. See rhyming section (2.6) for additional activities.

Section **2.10**

Phonemic Awareness

Behavior Observed →

The student is unable to segment, blend, and manipulate phonemes.

Anticipated Outcome

The student will successfully segment, blend, and manipulate phonemes.

Background

Phonemic awareness is "the ability to attend to and manipulate the smallest units of sound in spoken language" (Slattery Gursky, 2003, p. 1). It is strongly related to success in reading and spelling acquisition and is a powerful predictor of reading achievement (Yopp, 1995). In order to benefit from phonics instruction, students seem to require at least some basic level of phonemic awareness. Research reported by Bentin and Leshem (1993) and Tumner, Herriman, and Nesdale (1988) has led some to view phonemic awareness as a necessary prerequisite for success in learning to read. No matter how students are taught, they must grasp the abstract concepts that words are composed of separate sounds and that individual letters and combinations of letters are used to represent those sounds (Gunning, 1998).

For a number of students, the ability to segment and manipulate sounds in words does not come naturally; nevertheless, explicit instruction in phonological awareness can be given before and during reading instruction. Some examples (Stanovich, 1993/1994) of questions related to phonological awareness tasks follow.

- *Phoneme Deletion:* What would be left if the /h/ sound were taken away from *hat*?
- *Word-to-Word Matching:* Do *pen* and *paper* begin with the same sound?
- *Phoneme Blending:* What word would we have if you put these sounds together: /m/, /a/, /t/?
- *Phoneme Segmentation:* What sounds do you hear in the word *hot*?
- *Phoneme Counting:* How many sounds do you hear in the word *kite*?
- *Phoneme Deletion:* What sound do you hear in *seat* that is missing in *eat*?
- *Odd Word Out:* Which word starts with a different sound: *bag, nine, beach, bike*?
- *Sound to Word Matching:* Is there a /k/ in *Mike*?

The National Reading Panel (2000) conducted a meta-analysis of the experimental research on phonemic awareness and found that training students to segment and blend phonemes has a greater effect on students' reading than training them in multiple phonemic awareness skills. Segmenting phonemes helps students gain an awareness that speech consists of a series of sounds or phonemes (for example, *mat* is made up of three segments). The National Reading Panel (2000) also stated that invented spelling is equivalent to phoneme segmentation. In fact, invented spelling instruction may be more effective in developing phoneme segmentation than phoneme segmentation training (Slattery Gursky, 2003). The contextualized nature of invented spelling also provides additional literacy benefits beyond promoting phonemic awareness (e.g., function of print, alphabetic principle, and various writing skills) according to the work of Richgels (2002) and Slattery Gursky (2003). Principles for encouraging invented spelling appear in Strategy 1 of this section. The ability to blend phonemes helps students to sound out words, blending the sounds associated with letters into a meaningful whole. Although the ultimate goal for the reader is to construct meaning from print, knowledge of phonemic segmentation is an excellent predictor of success in reading (Gillet & Temple, 1990). Providing instruction in blending skills concurrently with segmentation training enhances phonological awareness skills in general. Assuming that a student knows the sounds associated with letters, the task then becomes one of blending the sounds into a word that is already in the student's listening or meaning vocabulary.

Instructional and practice activities are offered here and in other sections of this chapter. See the sections on auditory discrimination (2.4), concept of a word (2.5), rhyming (2.6), syllabic awareness (2.7), and onsets and rimes (2.9). The following strategies are most effective when used in small groups (National Reading Panel, 2000). Also, since students generally acquire phonological skills according to their linguistic complexity (Anthony, Lonigan, Driscoll, Phillips, & Burgess, 2003), the following strategies and activities for developing phoneme segmentation and blending will benefit students more after they have developed a concept for words, a concept for rhyme, the ability to rhyme words, the ability to segment syllables, and the ability to hear onsets and rimes (Treiman & Zukowski, 1991).

DEVELOPING PHONEME SEGMENTATION THROUGH INVENTED SPELLING

1. Provide time daily for writing using invented spelling, even if students are writing single words or short phrases to accompany illustrations. The process students go through listening to the sounds in words as they write using invented spelling helps them to attend to the individual sounds in words. Invented spellings provide information about students' development of letter-sound relationships. Writing using invented spelling also helps develop phonemic awareness (McCormick, 1995; National Reading Panel, 2000; Richgels, 2002; Slattery Gursky, 2003).
2. Some students lack confidence to attempt their own spellings, because they are afraid to make a mistake. Help them feel comfortable by modeling the use of invented spelling and by stressing that it is okay to make a mistake. For example, when writing a class story together, ask, "What sound do you hear at the beginning of *play*?" After they respond /p/, intentionally make a mistake by writing /g/, saying, "Oops! I made a mistake, but that's okay. I'll try again." Have a student show you what a /p/ looks like (Slattery, 2000b).
3. Some students will feel it necessary to ask the teacher to spell each word for them. Ask the students what sound the word begins with, what sound is heard next, and so on, until the word is spelled. With encouragement and practice, students should become willing to attempt spelling on their own and may need only an occasional sound spelled for them.
4. Spelling provides a clue as to the progress of phonemic segmentation. For example, *gowe* eventually becomes *going* in a student's writing development. The ability to write increasingly conventional spellings is a key to improved reading ability and should be encouraged through writing.

   Provide individual assistance, as you observe students writing, based on their developmental spellings. Some examples (Slattery, 2000b) of scaffolding strategies follow.

   - **Prephonemic Spellings:** Create a shared background of letter knowledge with students' names. Make a Picture Wall with pictures of students in the class. Label the pictures with their names. Use other familiar pictures to represent the letters that do not start students' names. Take time to study each student's name and discuss the letters and their sounds. Refer to the Picture Wall when students are unable to identify an initial or ending letter sound. If a student is trying to spell *boat* and you have spent time learning that Bobby's name starts with /B/, ask, "What **sound** do you hear in the beginning of *boat*?" After the student responds "/b/," focus on the letter sound, asking, "Is there anyone in our class whose name begins with the same sound?" When the student answers "Bobby's name begins with /b/. But I don't know what that letter is," go over to the Picture Wall and point to the letter at the beginning of Bobby's name.
   - **Phonemic Spellings:** Students' spellings at the phonemic stage represent beginning, middle, and ending letter sounds. Short vowels are represented by a vowel whose letter name sounds closest to the letter sound. Provide help identifying the short vowel by connecting the sound to something with which the student is familiar. For example, if the student is struggling with short *i*, bring him or her to a chart displaying the familiar finger play, "Itsy, Bitsy Spider." After reading and tracking the title together, ask, "Can you find a letter with the same sound as /i/?" Have the student track the words of the title again as you remind him or her that you are listening for the short *i* sound.

- **Transitional Spellings:** Students' spellings at this stage creatively represent long vowel sounds. Complement these students for the way they use what they know about long vowels. Also, provide small group time for these students to sort words with long vowel patterns. When they sort words like *team, read, meal, knee, feed,* and *feel,* have them practice picturing the word in the mind, since the /ea/ and /ee/ patterns both have the long e sound.

5. The following chart illustrates aspects of the developmental stages of students' spellings (Morris & Perney, 1984). The stages may be thought of as a continuum and, in most cases, are not hard and fast. As students gain knowledge of the English phonological system, they gain control of conventional spelling.

Developmental Spelling Stages

Prephonemic		Phonemic	Transitional	Correct
B	BC	BAC	BACK	back
S	SK	SEK	SINC	sink
M	ML	MAL	MALLE	mail
J	JS	JRAS	DRES	dress
C	CD	SID	SIED	side
F	FT	FET	FEAT	feet
B	BK	BIK	BICKE	bike
S	SK	SEK	STIK	stick

1. Prephonemic spellers perceive and represent initial and final consonants in one-syllable words, often using letter names to represent phonemes (*j, js,* or *jc* for *dress*).
2. Phonemic (letter name) spellers produce spellings that have short vowels produced as phonologically appropriate substitutions (*sek* for *sink*).
3. Transitional spellers begin to represent short vowels correctly, although long vowel markers are often incorrectly placed (*sied* for *side*).
4. Correct spelling is evidenced by spellers who nearly always spell words conventionally.

SOUND BOXES FOR SEGMENTING PHONEMES

1. For Sound Boxes for Segmenting Phonemes (Elkonin, 1973) prepare cards with a simple illustration along with a matrix that contains a box for each sound (phoneme) in the word. Note that the boxes represent each sound, not necessarily each letter. The words selected should be familiar to students. Secure sufficient tokens (plastic, pennies, cardboard squares) for each of your students. Additional cards are included on pages 153–159. They can be copied on heavy paper and cut out for use. An example of a sound box is shown below. Use empty boxes until letter recognition and letter-sound correspondence begin to develop (Ball & Blachman, 1991; Hohn & Ehri, 1983). After letter recognition and letter-sound correspondence begin to develop, place letters in the boxes (see duck), making sure to leave enough space in the boxes so tokens do not cover the letters.

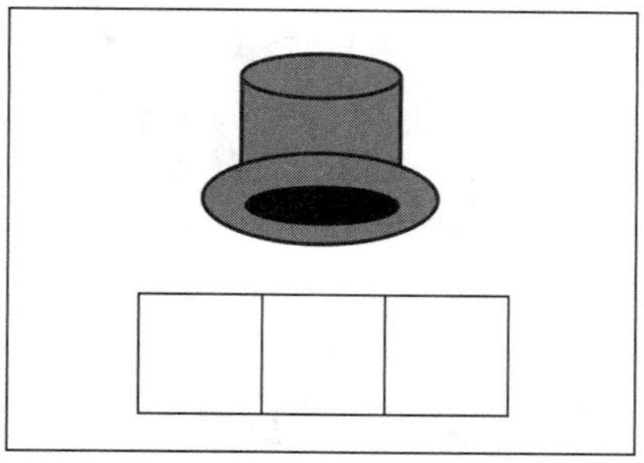

2. Instruct a small group so you can provide assistance as needed. Guide students through the task. Slowly say the word while pushing tokens into the boxes sound by sound. Model the process a second time. Then invite the students to say the word, perhaps stretching the sounds, so they can hear the separate sounds while you move the tokens. Invite students to push the tokens into the boxes while you say the word slowly.
3. Then provide another example and begin to transfer the responsibility to the students. Encourage a student to identify the picture and then pronounce the word very carefully and deliberately. The goal is to emphasize each sound without distorting the word and to put a token in each box while saying each sound.
4. Use other examples to help students catch on to the concept of segmenting. Some examples of sound boxes follow.
5. The following are useful variations that will solidify and expand students' abilities.
   - Eliminate the boxes below the pictures and have students just move their tokens to the bottom of the picture.
   - Say a word aloud and have students repeat it and count the number of sounds on their fingers. Ask, "How many sounds are in the word?" In the beginning, it may be beneficial to stretch out the sounds and repeat the process for each word two or three times.
   - Have students simply tell you how many sounds are in the word shown in the picture after they have pronounced it. The pictures used should contain no boxes.
   - Record a word's letters in boxes and have students put tokens in the box that represents the segmented sounds. Make sure there is enough space in the boxes so that the tokens do not cover the letters.

- Invite students to pronounce the word illustrated by the picture and then write letters or place plastic letters in the boxes instead of using tokens.
- After students are quite proficient at counting the number of sounds in a word, ask questions about the order of sounds, such as the following ones.
  - What is the first sound you hear in *duck*?
  - What sounds do you hear after /*d*/ in duck? After /*u*/?
- Let's write the letters in the boxes.

- Also, after students are proficient at counting the sounds in words, have students sort pictures of familiar one-syllable objects according to the number of phonemes (sounds) in the pictures' names. Begin with pictures of words with two phonemes and progress to three phoneme words. Introduce initial blends as students are developmentally ready. Provide number cards as header cards to sort under. Make the activity self-correcting by writing the number of phonemes on the back of each picture. Use this as an independent center activity or to assess an individual student's phoneme segmentation ability. For an additional challenge, have students sort pictures or names of classmates according to the number of phonemes in their names.

SOUND BOXES

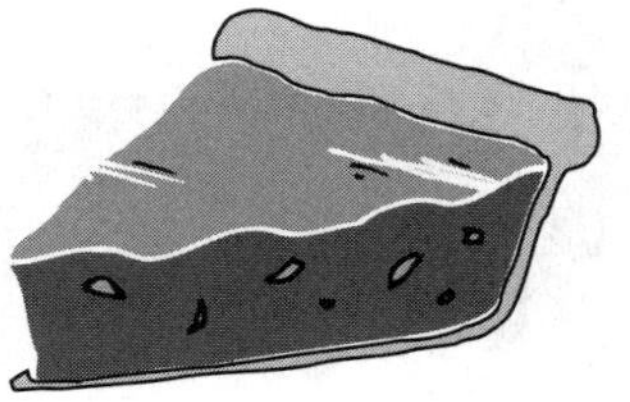

SOUND BOXES *(continued)*

SOUND BOXES *(continued)*

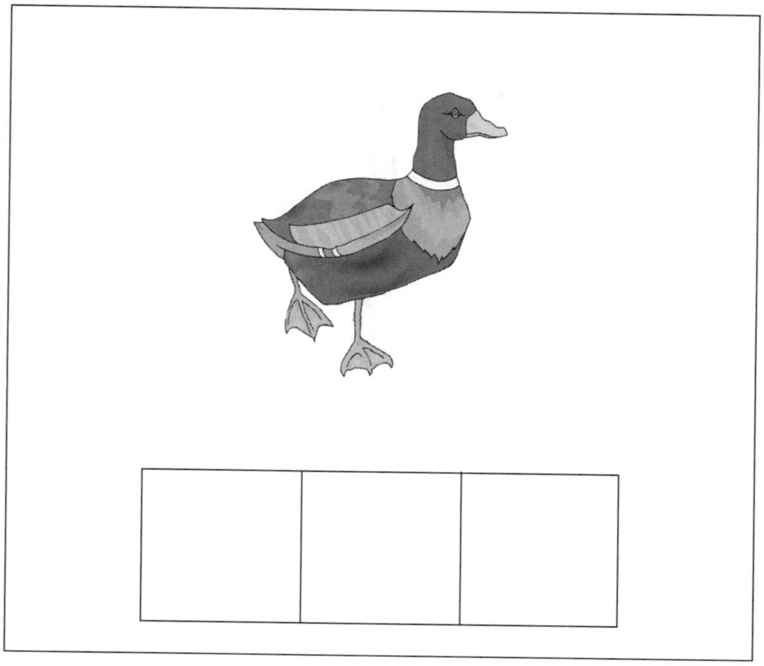

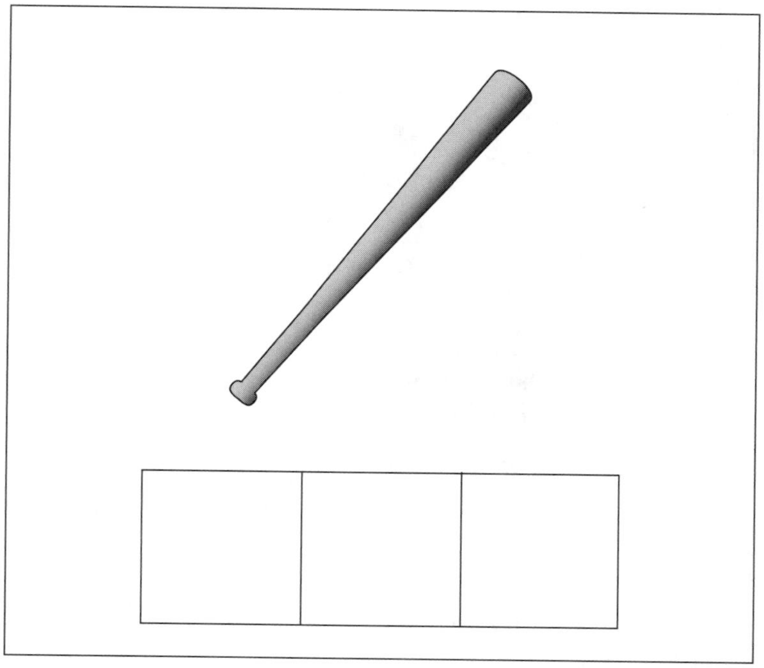

Sound Boxes *(continued)*

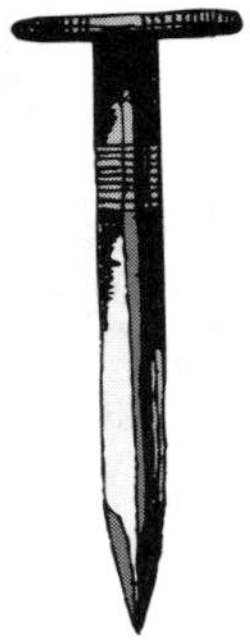

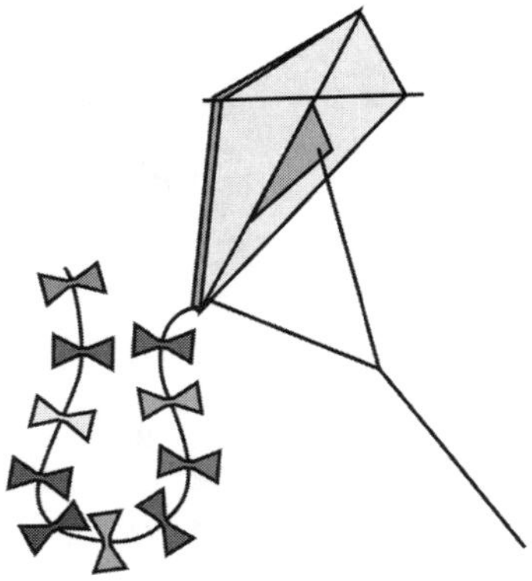

SOUND BOXES *(continued)*

SOUND BOXES *(continued)*

Sound boxes *(continued)*

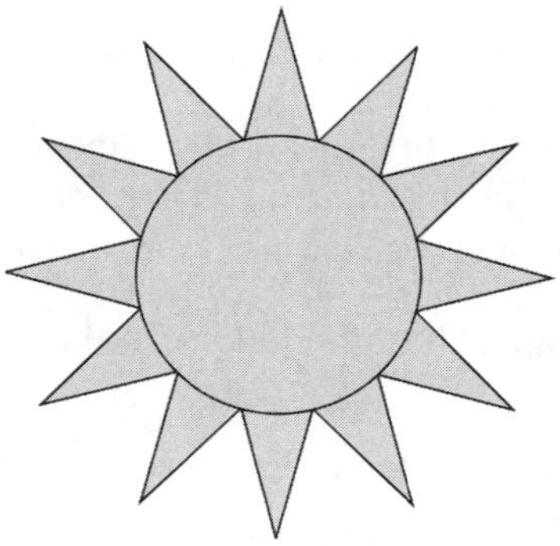

Strategy 3

WORD GAME ASSESSMENT FOR SEGMENTING PHONEMES

1. For this Word Game Assessment (Yopp, 1995) duplicate the Phoneme Segmentation Record Sheet on the next page.
2. With the student, say something like what follows.

   Today we're going to play a word game. I'm going to say a word, and I want you to break the word apart. You are going to tell me each sound in the word in order. For example, if I say "old," you should say "/o/-/l/-/d/."

   Be sure to say the sounds, not the letters, in the word.
3. Then say, "Let's try a few together." The practice items are *ride, go,* and *man.* If necessary, segment the word for the student. Encourage the student to repeat the segmented sounds.
4. During the test, feedback is provided to the student. You could nod or say, "right" or "that's right." If the student is incorrect, correct him or her. You should also provide the appropriate response.
5. Proceed through all 22 items. Circle those items that the student correctly segments. Incorrect responses may be recorded on the blank line following the item.
6. The student's score is the number of items he or she correctly segments into all constituent phonemes. No partial credit is given. For example, *she* (item 5) contains two phonemes /sh/-/e/; *grew* (item 7) contains three phonemes /g/-/r/-/ew/; and *three* (item 15) contains three phonemes /th/-/r/-/ee/. If the student notes letter names instead of sounds, the response is coded as incorrect, and the type of error is noted in the record sheet. Such notes are helpful in understanding the student. Some students may partially segment, simply repeat the stimulus item, provide nonsense responses, or give letter names. A wide range of scores is likely. Yopp (1995) reported that the two samples of kindergartners achieved mean scores of 11.78 and 11.39.
7. Refer to the strategies in this section for instructional interventions.

PHONEME SEGMENTATION RECORD SHEET

Directions: Today we're going to play a word game. I'm going to say a word and I want you to break the word apart. You are going to tell me each sound in the word in order. For example, if I say "old," you should say "/o/-/l/-/d/." **(Be sure to say the sounds, not the letters, in the word.)** Let's try a few together.

Practice items: (*Assist the child in segmenting these items as necessary.*) ride, go, man

Test items: (*Circle those items that the student correctly segments; incorrect responses may be recorded on the blank line following the item.*) The correct number of phonemes is indicated in parentheses.

1. dog (3) ______________________
2. keep (3) ______________________
3. fine (3) ______________________
4. no (2) ______________________
5. she (2) ______________________
6. wave (3) ______________________
7. grew (3) ______________________
8. that (3) ______________________
9. red (3) ______________________
10. me (2) ______________________
11. sat (3) ______________________
12. lay (2) ______________________
13. race (3) ______________________
14. zoo (2) ______________________
15. three (3) ______________________
16. job (3) ______________________
17. in (2) ______________________
18. ice (2) ______________________
19. at (2) ______________________
20. top (3) ______________________
21. by (2) ______________________
22. do (2) ______________________

Total Correct ☐

The author, Hallie Kay Yopp, California State University, Fullerton, grants permission for this test to be reproduced. The author acknowledges the contribution of the late Harry Singer to the development of this test. Adapted from Yopp, H.K. (1995). A test for assessing phonemic awareness in young children. *The Reading Teacher, 49,* 20–29.

BLENDING PHONEMES

1. Begin with a picture that has been cut into several pieces and show how the pieces, when put together properly, make a picture. Simple puzzles can be used. Tell the students that sometimes words can be identified by putting together the sounds associated with the letters or letter combinations.
2. Write several words on the chalkboard that the students may or may not know by sight (such as *sat, sit,* or *map*). Students should know, at an automatic level, the letter-sound relationships used in the blending exercises.
3. Have students watch while you blend the sounds associated with each letter into a whole word. Tell them that you will point to the next letter. Initially, sound the letters in *sat* for about a second (except for the final letter). When done with the sounding procedure, say the word as you would in normal pronunciation.
4. Next, have students sound out the word with you. Touch the letters and sound out the word with the students (for example, *sssaaat*). Repeat the process until students respond correctly. At the end of the sounding, always ask the students to say the word. Because of the limitations in short-term memory, the longer the pause between sounding and saying the word, the greater the possibility that students will have difficulty saying the word.
5. After students gain confidence with the process, have them sound out words together and individually. Gradually reduce the time during which they sound the individual letter.
6. Note that all vowels and some consonants can be given a continuous sound in blending. Other consonants rely on the following vowel (for example, *ham, cat*). To teach blending with such words, have students initially make the sound for the vowel, because they will need to move quickly from the sound associated with the consonant to the sound associated with the vowel.
7. Point out to students that this strategy is not usually the first method of word recognition they will try and that it does not always work. Blending is a useful skill; however, some students tend to have difficulty using it or overuse it even after careful teaching.
8. After numerous blending exercises, help students understand that the goal of blending is to be able to pronounce or say a word that they have already heard.
9. Once parts of a word have been blended into a whole, focus on meaning. For example, if the blended word is *map,* ask students, "What is a map?" or "How could you use map in a sentence?" Keep the focus on meaning, not merely pronunciation.

BLENDING PATHWAYS

1. The basic procedure for Blending Pathways (Fox, 2000) is for students to imagine the sounds of a word lined up on their shoulder to their hand. This is the blending pathway.
2. Demonstrate the procedure with a word like *kite*. Say the first sound as you place your right hand on your left shoulder, the second sound as you place your hand in the crook of your arm, and the third sound as you place your hand near your wrist. Then slide your right hand down your left arm from your shoulder to your wrist blending the sounds as your arm moves. For left-handed students, use your left hand on your right shoulder.
3. Model the process several times and have students join you.
4. Say the individual sounds in another word. Have students place their hands on their arms at the shoulder. Then have students blend the sounds together as they slide their hands down their arms. Ask students what the word is. Repeat the process with other words.
5. When students are comfortable with the technique, have them blend silently. Then ask a student to say the entire word.
6. One variation is to enlarge the drawing of a slide and place it on the chalkboard tray. Tape or print letters on the slide so they go from the top to the bottom. Pronounce each sound as you slide your hand under each letter. Then ask a student to say the word and write it at the bottom of the slide. Invite students to do the activity themselves. Provide guidance as necessary.

Practice and Reinforcement Activities

1. Use children's literature that playfully deals with sounds in language. In addition to the Dr. Seuss books, a list of other helpful books is in Chapter 2 Resources on page 180. Many additional titles have also been compiled by Opitz (2000) and Griffith and Olson (1992).
2. Use a variation of the troll activity presented in Strategy 2 in Section 2.7. In this case, the troll pronounces individual phonemes of a word instead of syllables, and students must combine the sounds to identify the word.
3. Say a sound and let students whose names include that sound line up. Be sure students respond to the **sound**. For example, if you say *"kkk,"* Ken, Cathy, and Nikki could all respond.
4. Place three or four familiar pictures on the chalkboard tray and invite a student to say each word, one sound at a time. Another student is asked to identify the picture. Gradually increase the number of pictures and possibly use some pictures whose sounds are similar.

Section **2.11**

Visual Discrimination

Behavior Observed →

The student has trouble visually discriminating differences among letters and words.

Anticipated Outcome

The student will visually discriminate differences among letters and words.

Background

Reading is more than a visual process; nevertheless, being able to discriminate letters and words accurately is crucial for efficient reading. A hierarchy of five levels for visual discrimination is shown below.

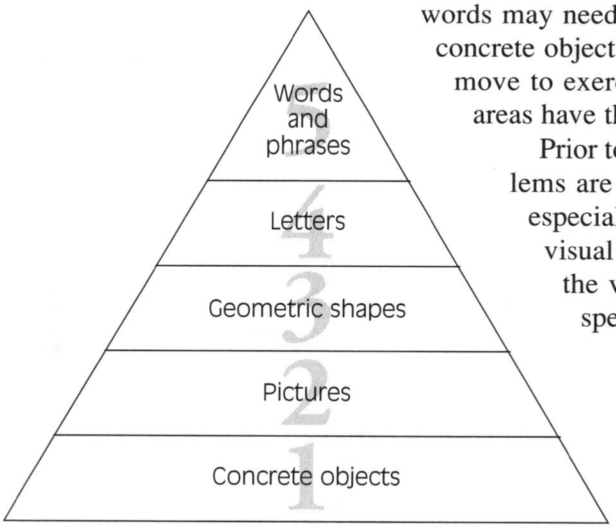

Visual Discrimination

A student experiencing difficulty in the visual discrimination of letters or words may need to begin by differentiating similarities and differences in concrete objects, pictures, or geometric shapes. The emphasis should then move to exercises related to letters, words, and phrases, because these areas have the closest relationship to reading.

Prior to visual discrimination training, ensure that any visual problems are checked through visual screening or testing. Sometimes, especially in the early stages of reading instruction, there may be a visual cause that is responsible for discrimination problems. Once the visual problem has been corrected by lenses or treatment, specific teaching and practice strategies may be undertaken.

Before beginning instruction in visual discrimination, be sure the student understands the concepts of same and different. Beginning readers, and some older students experiencing difficulty in reading, fail to understand the "same-different" concepts. Usually, with the aid of concrete objects, these concepts can be established.

Strategy **1** SECTION 2.11

LETTERS

1. For students who are having difficulty discriminating between letters, begin with unlike pairs that are grossly different (for example, *x–o, n–p*) and move to pairs that require finer discrimination (such as *c–o, r–n, m–n, p–q, b–d*).
2. Provide various tactile activities for students to draw, write, or form letter pairs. For example, use cornmeal, sand, shaving cream, chalk, clay, finger paint, or paint. Students also enjoy using a large brush with water on the sidewalk.
3. Encourage students to verbalize reasons why the letter pairs are different. Let the students know that some letter pairs are particularly difficult to tell apart and model appropriate types of comments (for example, the *m* and the *n* are different because one letter has two humps and the other has one hump).

Strategy **2** SECTION 2.11

WORDS

1. If students demonstrate the ability to discriminate between concrete objects, pictures, and geometric forms, proceed with words. On the chalkboard, write words that have gross structural or physical differences (such as *house, elephant*) and also words that are the same (for example, *run, run*). Discuss the similarities and differences in the word pairs.
2. Encourage students to express their thoughts on why the words are the same or different. Use questions such as the following:
   - Are these words the same or different?
   - How do you know?
   - Are you sure that the different words have a different number of letters? Count them.
   - Are you sure that the two words have exactly the same number of letters and kinds of letters?
   - Are the letters in exactly the same position?
3. As these and other questions are asked, it is often useful to place one word of a pair under the other to aid discussion and promote a clearer grasp of the concept. For example, the first word pair is different because the first letter in each word is different; the other word pair is the same because all the letters are identical and occur in the same position.

h o u s e	r u n
	↕ ↕ ↕
e l e p h a n t	r u n

4. Use a similar procedure when a certain part of the word is different from that of another word. Some examples follow.

[h] o p e	p [e] n	h o [t]
[r] o p e	p [i] n	h o [p]

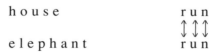

5. Use a variety of words and encourage students to discuss why the words are the same or different. Some possible word pairs are provided below.

grandfather	bang	boy	went
grandmother	banging	boys	want

6. Prepare a short passage, display a particular word (such as *cat*), and have students circle the word each time it occurs in the passage.

Practice and Reinforcement Activities

1. Most practice activities are variations of matching games. A common activity is to ask students to draw a circle around a letter or word that is the same as the example. The choices vary in difficulty. A variation of this activity is to have students put a line through the letter or word that does not match the sample.
2. Use two columns of words (or letters) and have students draw lines from words in the left column to the same words (or letters) in the right column.
3. Give students a set of cards containing words (or letters) and have them hold up the word (or letter) that matches your sample.
4. Prepare a page with a letter or word at the top of the page and have students circle the letter or word each time it appears.
5. Cut out a set of large uppercase and lowercase letters from construction paper. Have students find the same uppercase and lowercase letters in magazines or copies of duplicated text. Then glue the found letters to the appropriate construction paper letters. Hang these letters in the classroom, referring, for example, to the pink Pp letters.

Wordo. Word Name or Letter Bingo. Prepare cards containing words, students' names, or letters. Hold up a stimulus card and have students place a marker on the square that is the same as the stimulus. The first student who gets Wordo wins.

W	O	R	D	O
big	if	was	it	on
no	get	to	then	when
saw	where	got	too	there

W	O	R	D	O
no	where	to	too	there
saw	get	was	then	on
big	if	got	it	when

Match. Prepare two cards for each letter or word that tends to cause confusion. Students take turns matching the letters or words. The student who gets the most pairs wins. One variation of the game involves the use of a stopwatch or timer. Each student attempts to better his or her previous time.

Letters and Names. Prepare a large set of cards containing the letters of the alphabet (capital and lowercase letters). Give students their names on individual letter cards. Hold up one large card at a time. Students who have the same letter(s) turn over the appropriate card(s) in their names. Play the game until the students designated have turned over all the letters in their names. The games can be played with first names, last names, or entire names. One variation is to have students exchange names with a friend. Favorite words can also be used.

Go Fish. Prepare two sets of letter or word cards. Pass out four cards to each student. Students take turns asking another student if he or she has a match to a letter or word they have in their hand. If the other student does not have the matching card, he or she tells the other student "Go fish." The student then fishes for a card in the draw pile. When students get a match, they place the match in front of them and take another turn. The student with the most matches wins.

Section 2.12

Letter and Word Reversals

Behavior Observed → **Anticipated Outcome**

The student reverses letters or words. → The student will reduce the number of reversals.

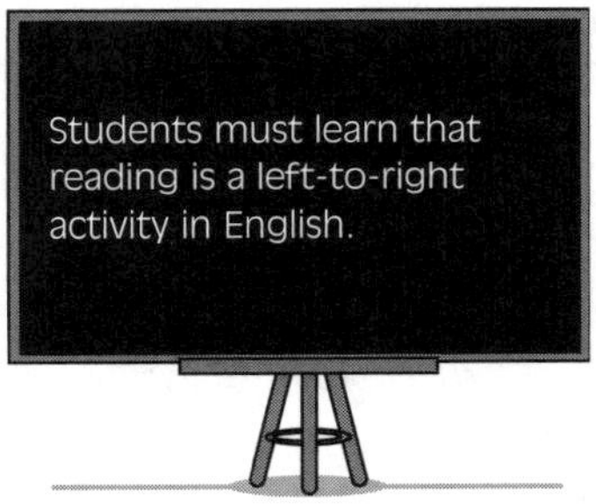
Students must learn that reading is a left-to-right activity in English.

Perspective and Strategies

It is not unusual for some beginning readers and for older students experiencing difficulty in reading to reverse letters or words. To succeed in reading, students must learn that reading is a left-to-right activity in English.

Researchers have hypothesized many causes to explain reversals. Among them are visual problems and mixed dominance as well as an unfamiliarity with directionality as it relates to letter and word discrimination. The recommended procedure is to provide direct instruction with letters or words that are causing the student difficulty. If the student is a beginning reader, some reversals may be developmental in nature; however, if they persist, referral for more intensive study may be warranted. The following strategies may be helpful.

1. Teach students the concepts of left and right by showing them the difference between their left hand and right hand. Give oral directions where students must use their left hand or right hand to touch a book, pick up a pencil, open the door, and so on. Other body parts may also be used.
2. Transfer the concepts of left and right to reading by demonstrating how names are read from left to right.
3. Develop brief stories that can be placed on the chalkboard. Choose one student to point to the words as they are read to the class. Stress that reading goes from left to right. The hand or pointer indicates the required direction in reading. A sample is shown here.

   Today is December 17.
   The weather is cold and snowy.
   Winter vacation begins after school today.
   Winter will soon be here.

4. Provide exercises where students draw lines to connect dots horizontally and obliquely and relate the activity to lines of print. An example follows.

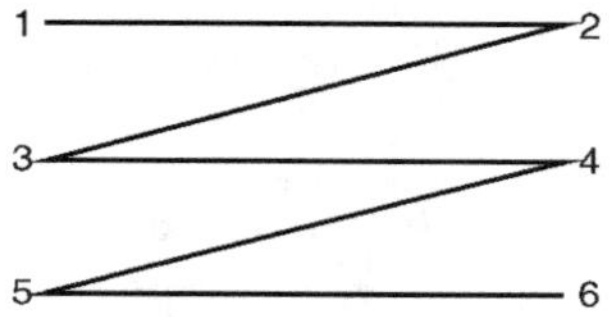

5. Have students draw an arrow, pointing to the right, under the first letter of a word or sentence.
6. Provide exercises to help eliminate common reversals (such as *was* and *saw, no* and *on*) by practicing on paper where the student is directed to trace over a word whenever it appears. An example follows.

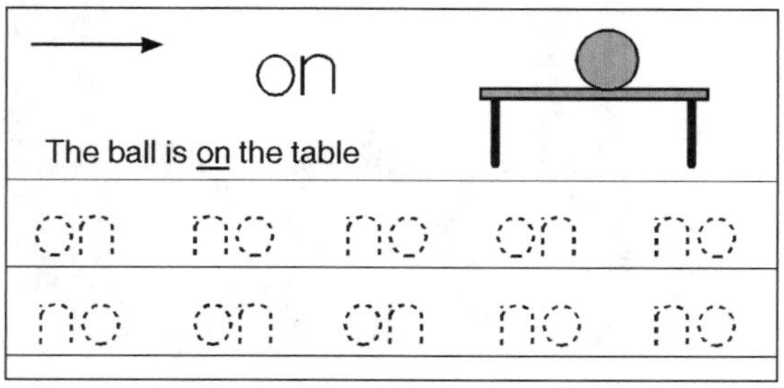

7. Provide sentences in which a reversal will result in a sentence that doesn't make sense. When students read each sentence ask, "Does it make sense?" Ask this question, even when sentences are read correctly, to promote thinking while reading. Several sample sentences follow.

   Was–Saw Confusion
   I *saw* a man.
   She *was* eating an apple.
   We *saw* the book.
   It *was* in the box.

   There–Three Confusion
   We have *three* cats.
   There is his dog.
   Put the book over *there*.
   The *three* boys are playing.

8. Place commonly reversed words so they can be closely compared. Discuss similarities and differences. An example follows.

was	Both have three letters.
	Both have the same three letters but in different positions.
saw	Both have an *a* in the middle.

9. Use a sentence that the student can read (or a word he or she can spell); make an elongated picture (snake, dragon, alligator); and write the sentence over the picture. Cut out the sentence and ask the student to put the sentence back together from left to right. Then have the student write the sentence. Words or stories can be substituted for sentences in this activity.

10. Provide lots of practice using a multisensory approach that involves forming the letter or word in sand, finger paint, or shaving cream. Pipe cleaners, Play Doh, or sandpaper can also be used to make letters or words.

11. Use the word *bed* to help the student learn *b* and *d*. Teach the student to spell *bed* and draw attention to the two "posts" on the bed to help with letter formation. Find and share a good illustration of a poster bed with the student or use the following illustration.

12. Provide the following mnemonic device to help students discriminate between *Bb* and *Dd*. *Bb*s have bumps. As you say this, cover the top bump in uppercase *B*. Then, ask for a student to volunteer to dance with you, pointing out that you face your partner when you dance just like the *D* and *d* face each other. Point out that *bump* begins with *b* and *Bb*s have bumps and that *dance* begins with *d* and the *Dd*s are dancing because they face each other. Have students print *Bb,* and ask them to cover the top bump in uppercase *B* to reveal the lowercase *b*. Next, have students print *Dd*, and have them draw legs, arms, and heads on the *Dd*s to have them resemble people dancing.

13. Use the word *pig* to help the student learn *p* and *g*. Teach the spelling and use the following graphic to help the student see that the *p* and *g* can help form the lines of a circle.

14. Provide letter or word activities where the student is asked to circle a particular letter or word. For example, circle every *n*.

n x o m n u m u n
w h n n v m n v h

GAMES

Fish. On paper fish write words that students frequently confuse. Attach a paper clip to each fish. Using a fishing pole made of a yardstick, string, and magnet, have the student fish for words. If the word can be pronounced correctly, the student keeps it; if not, he or she throws it back. Students having difficulty should play this game with students who already recognize the words. The words can also be used in sentences.

Tricky Words. Students who have some reading ability should be encouraged to read troublesome words or phrases in short sentences. Prepare a game board with phrases or sentences containing frequently confused words (for example, I *saw* the bear. He *was* here.). Students roll dice and proceed to the appropriate space. If the student can read the phrase, he or she can stay there. If the phrase or word is not read correctly, the student returns to his or her previous position. The student who first crosses the finish line wins.

Section 2.13

Sense of Story

Behavior Observed →
The student does not understand the parts of a story and may be unable to retell story events successfully.

Anticipated Outcome
The student will understand the parts of a story and will retell story events accurately.

Background

Good readers possess background for text structure that allows them to anticipate and understand how the details relate to the main theme of a written piece of discourse. For beginning readers, this sense of story must be developed sufficiently for comprehension to occur.

Simple stories include characters, a sequence of events, conflict, and resolution. In reading, a sense of what composes stories influences the student's prediction, comprehension, and recall of stories. In writing, students often create stories around their internal concept or understanding of those elements that compose a story.

Texts contain a variety of elements, or story structures, that relate characters and occur in a certain sequence. Most story structures include the following elements.

Story Structure

setting
initiating event
internal response
attempt
outcome
consequence
reaction

(attempt, outcome, consequence:) These elements make up episodes. There may be one or more per story.

STORY STRUCTURE FOR YOUNGER STUDENTS

1. Secure a copy of *Aunt Isabel Tells a Good One* by Kate Duke (1992). This book is about a mouse called Penelope who wants her Aunt Isabel to tell a story. Aunt Isabel asks Penelope to help with the story by asking questions such as "When does this story begin?" and "Who shall be in this story?" The book can help provide students with a literature-based introduction to story structure.
2. Preread the story and decide the best way to introduce it to your students. For example, you might say something like what follows.

   I'm going to read you a story about a little mouse that helps her aunt make up a story. Listen to the story. Then we'll talk about it and make up a story.

3. Read the story to students and share the colorful illustrations. Encourage students to react to the story and make predictions. For example, Penelope asks, "What are they going to do?" Invite students to predict what might be done.
4. Discuss the story with students. Then guide students to share some of the things that make up a good story. Some of the elements from the story include when, where, who, problem, solution. Refer, if necessary, to specific parts in the story to help students understand the story structure. Then write the story elements on the chalkboard.
5. Decide where it would be best to create a class story using some of the elements that students learned about in *Aunt Isabel Tells a Good One*. A new story could be created immediately following the discussion or at a later time, depending on your students' interest and engagement. When a story is being created, refer to the book and model some of the questions used by Aunt Isabel. A list of the questions could be written on the chalkboard to guide the development of the story.
6. Consider writing a draft of the story on large chart paper to model the writing, revising, and editing processes. When completed, the story could then be read and enjoyed by students.
7. Encourage students who are interested in writing their own stories to do so. See Lenski and Johns (2000) for five teaching strategies for writing fictional stories that use writing frames, graphic organizers, and character webs.
8. Remember that helping students understand story structure has several important benefits. First, it helps students understand that stories are made up of certain elements. Second, these elements appear in the stories students read and write. Third, knowing the elements should help students remember and retell stories. Take time to explicitly explain these fundamental benefits of story structure to students. Use vocabulary that students will understand.

PREDICTING STORY STRUCTURE

1. Using clues such as title and cover illustrations, encourage students to predict what the material or story will be about. Read a little of the text, perhaps one or two pages. Invite students to confirm or revise the prediction providing support from the text. Predict what will happen next by asking open-ended questions. Check out that prediction by asking students to defend their answers from material specific to the story or text. Continue the prediction-confirmation pattern until the passage has been completed. Daily practice with predictions will enhance knowledge of story structure and improve comprehension.

2. Begin with a well-known story such as *Goldilocks and the Three Bears* or *Little Red Riding Hood*. Encourage students to share what they remember about the story. Write their responses on the chalkboard. See the example that follows.

   There was a little girl named Goldilocks.
   There were three bears.
   Goldilocks went into the bears' house when they were gone.

3. After students have shared their responses, ask them to name some of the parts of a story. Responses might include where it takes place, people, animals, and things happening. Use words offered by the students and begin to develop the concept that stories are made up of places (settings), people and/or animals (characters), and things happening (actions or episodes). Also, tell students that stories have a beginning, middle, and end.

4. Write three major story elements on the chalkboard and have students that have previously shared information classify their responses under the proper elements, as in the following example.

Goldilocks and the Three Bears

Places	People and Animals	Things That Happen
in the woods	Goldilocks	She went into the
house	Papa Bear	bears' house.

5. Then read the story to the class and encourage students to listen carefully so they can confirm or enlarge upon their earlier contributions. After the story has been read, have students share story elements. Write them on the chalkboard. Encourage a discussion that emphasizes and expands major story elements.

Goldilocks and the Three Bears

Places	People and Animals	Things That Happen
a house in the woods	Goldilocks	The bears went for a walk in the woods.
kitchen	three bears	Goldilocks went into their house while they were away.
living room	Papa Bear	She found three bowls of porridge.
bedroom	Mama Bear	She ate Baby Bear's porridge.
	Baby Bear	She sat in the three bears' chairs.
		She broke Baby Bear's chair.
		She went into the bedroom and tried out the beds.
		She fell asleep in Baby Bear's bed.
		The three bears returned.

6. Repeat this basic procedure with other stories. Emphasize how students can use their knowledge of story structure to better understand or remember a story. Knowledge of story structure may also aid in predicting what might happen next in new stories.

STORY STRUCTURE

1. It is possible to develop the elements of story structure in greater depth through character analysis, details of the setting, and a discussion of theme and plot. Also, some variations of well-known stories can be analyzed. For example, five versions of Cinderella are provided below.

   - Climo, S. *The Egyptian Cinderella.* New York: HarperCollins, 1989.
   - Huck, C. *Princess Furball.* New York: Greenwillow, 1989.
   - Martin, R. *The Rough-Face Girl.* New York: Putnam, 1992.
   - Steel, F.A. *Tattercoats,* New York: Bradbury, 1976.
   - Steptoe, J. *Mufaro's Beautiful Daughters.* New York: Lathrop, Lee & Shepárdi, 1993.

2. Use a visual representation of story structure to help students understand major story elements. Discuss them. Students should understand that the setting is the place or location of the story and the time (present, past, or future) when the story takes place. The characters are the people or animals that the story focuses on. There can be major or minor characters. The plot is the general plan of the story, which is composed of actions or episodes. The episodes lead to a climax, which is the high point of the story.

3. After the story elements have been presented and discussed, read a well-known story (for example, *The City Mouse and the Country Mouse* or *The Three Billy Goats Gruff*) and have students form small groups to construct a visual representation of the story. Have the various groups discuss their representations. Encourage the use of proper terminology (setting, character, episodes) presented earlier. Repeat this basic procedure with other stories. The use of key questions can be used to help students uncover the major story elements. See the following example.

Setting
- Where does the story take place?
- When does the story take place?
- Does the action of this story occur in different places? If so, where?

Characters
- Who are the people or animals in this story?
- Are some people more important than others? If so, which ones?
- What words does the author use to describe the characters or animals?
- What other words can also be used to describe the characters?

Plot
- What happens in this story?
- What problems or difficulties are there?
- How are the problems or difficulties solved?
- In what order do the major events happen?
- Who or what started the events in the story?

Practice and Reinforcement Activities

1. Encourage family members to read to the child. Reading aloud often helps the listener to internalize the story structure. Discussions with the child can also help in developing a sense of story structure.
2. Provide many opportunities for students to hear and read many different kinds of literature. Discuss the major story elements with them. Storytelling can also be used.
3. When appropriate, have students role play or dramatize stories. If an entire story does not lend itself to dramatization, select one or more episodes and have several groups of students present scenes to the class.
4. Have students make drawings or illustrations of the major events in a story. These drawings can serve as a basis for retelling the story.
5. Retell a familiar story by changing certain key elements (settings, characters, and events). Then have students correct the retelling. Depending on the students involved, you may want to change "obvious" characters, events, or settings. Later, brief written summaries of stories can be used. After students read the summaries, they correct the erroneous information. An excellent story of this type is *The True Story of the 3 Pigs by A. Wolf* (Scieszka, 1989).
6. Help students learn to use semantic webbing. According to Freeman and Reynolds (1980), semantic webbing contains the following elements:
   - a core question—focus of the web, which is initially chosen by the teacher;
   - web strands—answers that students give to the core questions;
   - strand supports—facts, inferences, and generalizations that students give to differentiate one strand from another; and
   - strand ties—the relationships that strands have with one another.
7. As students become more comfortable with semantic webbing, they can show relationships among characters and events (adapted from Freeman & Reynolds, 1980) as is shown here.

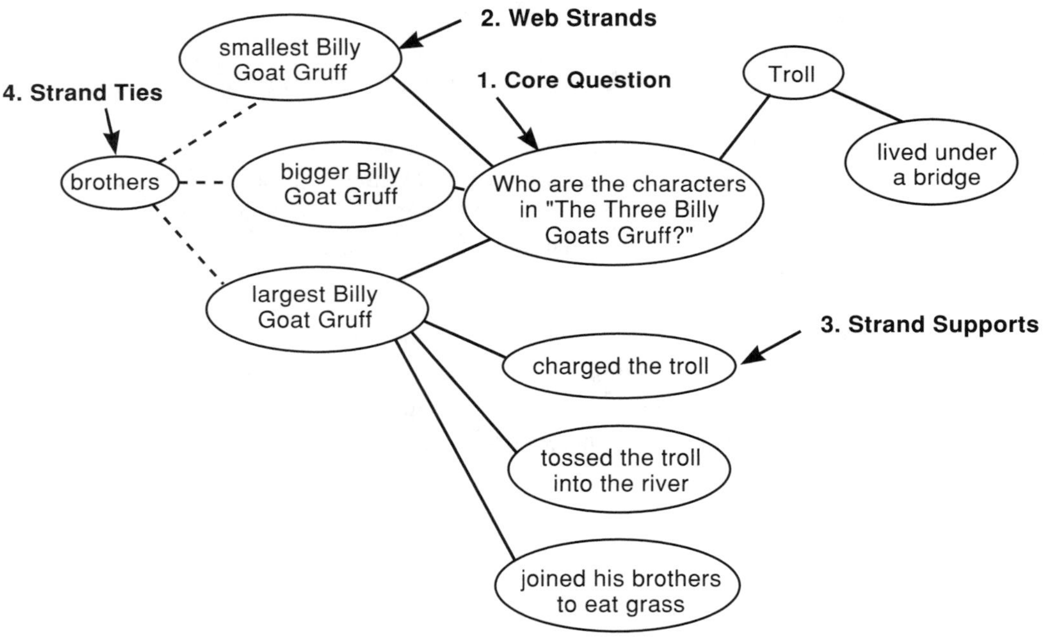

8. Semantic webbing is especially useful for helping students to identify story elements related to characters and events. Possible core questions of a generic nature are listed below.
    - Who are the characters?
    - What words describe the characters?
    - What are the major events?
    - What happens in each major event?
9. The example below, based on "Little Miss Muffet," may be used to help students visualize the major elements in the story. The terminology can be changed to match the words used in lessons. Acting out nursery rhymes with logical sequences can help students identify story elements. Change the order of events so students will see how the new order destroys the story line.

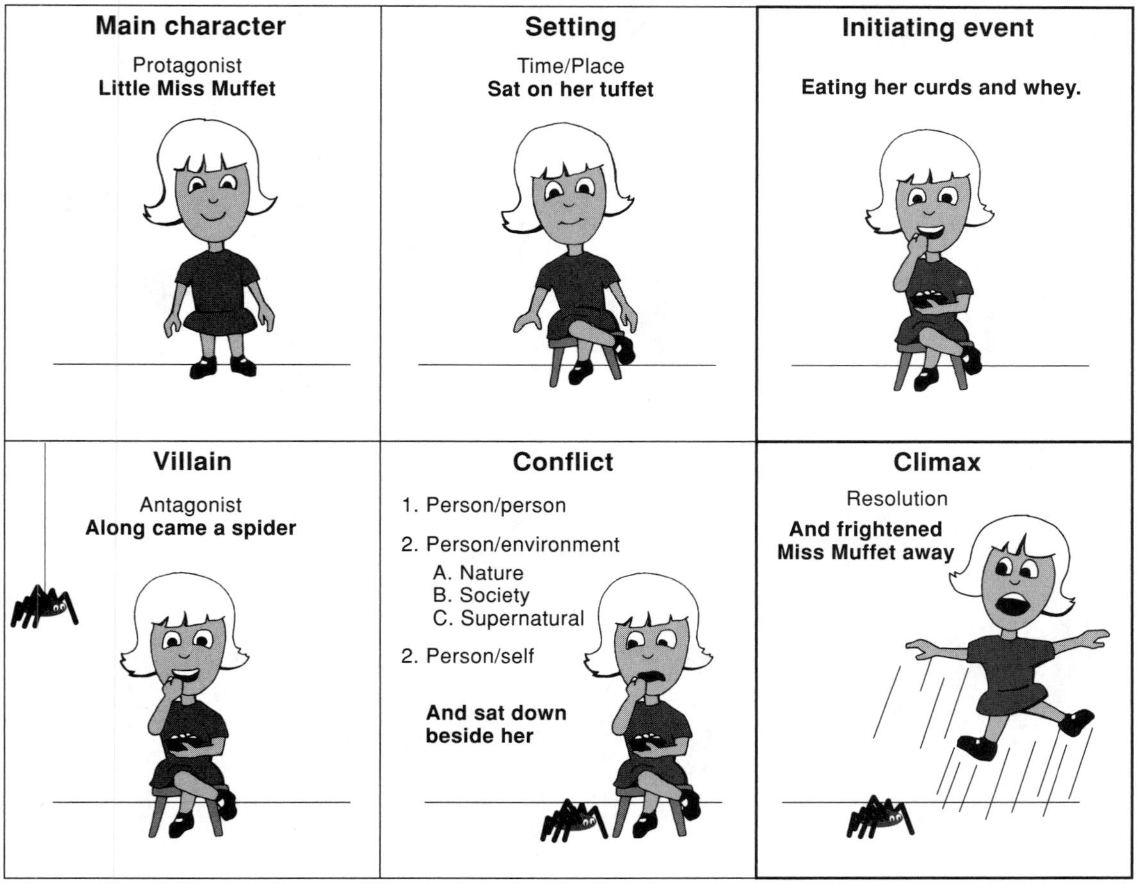

10. Have older students begin a story by writing the setting. Then have students exchange papers and write about characters. Repeat the process with problem/conflict and solution/resolution. Then return the story to the student who began it. After giving time for independent reading, invite students to share in small groups.
11. Write or dictate stories based on wordless picture books. A list of such books can be found in Part A on the CD.

2

Resources

Teacher Resource

Note: indicates teacher material.

PHONEMIC AWARENESS: BOOKS TO READ ALOUD

Aylesworth, J. *Old Black Fly.* New York: Scholastic, 1993.

This alphabet book uses rhythm and rhyme as it describes a bothersome fly that lands on things beginning with each letter of the alphabet.

Brown, M.W. *Four Fur Feet.* New York: Doubleday, 1993.

In this book, the student is drawn to the /f/ sound as the phrase "four fur feet" is repeated in every sentence as a furry animal walks around the world. The same pattern is used throughout the story.

Carter, D. *More Bugs in Boxes.* New York: Simon and Schuster, 1990.

This pop-up book contains a series of questions and answers about make-believe bugs that are found inside a variety of boxes. Both the questions and answers make use of alliteration: "What kind of bug is in the rosy red rectangle box? A bright blue big mouth bug."

Deming, A.G. *Who is Tapping at My Window?* New York: Penguin, 1994.

A young girl hears a tapping at her window and asks, "Who is there?" The farm animals each respond, "It's not I," and she discovers that it is the rain. The book is predictable in that each pair of animals rhymes (for example, dog/frog).

Geraghty, P. *Stop That Noise!* New York: Crown, 1992.

A mouse is annoyed with the many sounds of the forest. The animal and machine sounds make the book useful in drawing students' attention to the sounds in language.

Gordon, J. *Six Sleepy Sheep.* New York: Puffin Books, 1991.

The use of the /s/ sound throughout the book is useful for developing a letter-sound association.

Graham-Barber, L. *Say Boo!* Cambridge, MA: Candlewick, 1996.

A young ghost has difficulty learning to say boo. As he tries to say boo, he says different onsets instead of /b/ for boo.

Kuskin, K. *Roar and More.* New York: HarperTrophy, 1990.

This book contains many poems and pictures that portray the sounds that animals make. Both the use of rhyme and presentation of animal sounds draw students' attention to sounds.

Lear, E. *A Was Once an Apple Pie.* Cambridge, MA: Candlewick, 1997.

This alphabet book has nonsense rhymes that accompany silly pictures of words that begin with each letter of the alphabet. For example, "D was once a little doll, Dolly, Molly, Polly, Nolly, Nursy dolly."

Lewison, W. *Buzz Said the Bee.* New York: Scholastic, 1992.

A series of animals sit on top of one another in this story. Before each animal climbs on top of the next, it does something that rhymes with the animal it approaches. For example, "the pig takes a bow before sitting on the cow."

Most, B. *Cock-A-Doodle-Moo.* New York: Harcourt Brace, 1996.

A rooster loses his voice and asks the cow for help to wake all the animals in the barnyard. The cow's inability to crow like a rooster results in him saying different onsets instead of /c/ for cock, as well as moo for doo.

Otto, C. *Dinosaur Chase.* New York: HarperTrophy, 1991.

Both alliteration and rhyme are present in this simple, colorful book.

Parry, C. *Zoomerang-a-Boomerang: Poems to Make Your Belly Laugh.* New York: Puffin Books, 1991.

Practically all of the poems in this collection play with language, particularly through the use of predictable and humorous rhyme patterns.

Pomerantz, C. *If I Had a Paka.* New York: Mulberry, 1993.

Eleven languages are represented among the 12 poems included in this book. Attention is drawn to phonemes (sounds) when languages other than English are introduced. Rhyme and repetition are also included.

Sendak, M. *Alligators All Around: An Alphabet.* New York: HarperTrophy, 1990.

This book uses alliteration for each letter of the alphabet.

Westcott, N. *The Lady with the Alligator Purse.* Boston: Little, Brown, 1998.

This highly engaging book tells the story of Tim, whose mother put him in the bathtub to see if he could swim. The silly rhyme and rhythm have made it a well-loved children's song and book.

Winters, K. *Whoo's Haunting the Teeny Tiny Ghost?* New York: Scholastic, 1999.

This Halloween story uses alliteration and rhyme to tell the bold, brave story of the teeny, tiny ghost who searches his home for things that go bump and thump.

Adapted from Yopp, H.K. (1995). Read-aloud books for developing phonemic awareness: An annotated bibliography. *The Reading Teacher, 48,* 538–542.

CHAPTER THREE

Phonics, Decoding, and Word Identification

Overview

Estimates of the number of words in the English language range from 600,000 to over one million. The sheer volume of words that students are expected to read quickly and accurately is daunting: 25,000 distinct words in third grade and over 80,000 different words by the end of eighth grade (Juel & Minden-Cupp, 2004). The ability to identify words, then, is a critical foundation of the reading process (Stanovich, 1991). Although we realize that the meaning of text is much larger than the sum of the meanings of each word, it is important for students to have strategies to identify words that they do not recognize at sight (Hampton & Resnick, 2009).

There are several strategies students use as they encounter words. One strategy is to read words by sight. That means that students see the word and pronounce it correctly. There are many words students read by sight. They don't need to try to figure out the words because they are *sight words*. All proficient readers have a large number of words they can read by sight.

> Identifying words is only part of reading.

No reader knows all words by sight. When students come to words they don't know by sight, they can figure out the words by one or more of these five ways: 1) decoding, 2) analogy to known spelling patterns, 3) using context clues, 4) using structural analysis, and 5) using a dictionary or glossary.

When students encounter a word they can't pronounce, they could try to figure it out initially by using the sounds symbolized by the letters or letter combinations and then blending those sounds together. For example, if the word *enigmatic* is unknown, the student can give each letter one or more sounds from the variety of sounds the letters symbolize to decode the word, trying various pronunciations in an effort to have the word sound like one that has been heard before.

Not all words can be read using their letter sounds. The word *tough,* for example, cannot be pronounced by its letter sounds. Many words that do not have phonetic spelling have syllables that can be read by analogy to a known spelling pattern. For example, students who have never seen the word *tough* can use what they know about the sound of word part *ough* in the known word *rough* to figure out the word. Many words have at least one part that can be read by analogy.

Phonological recoding and analogy can give students a good sense of an unfamiliar word; however, they need to test the words within the context of the text to see whether they make sense. If students use what they know about letter sounds and spelling patterns and the word makes sense in the context of the text, it is probably correct. Context can help students test words, and it is also useful to assist students in identifying unknown words. Context clues, therefore, can be an additional way for students to identify words.

Identifying words is only part of reading. We all have encountered students who can identify words without understanding them. That's because words are actually symbols for concepts. Words don't have a single meaning. They have a range of meanings that are unique to each individual. Everyone has had experience with the word *picnic*. Students may each have a different picture in their minds when they read that word. One may picture an idyllic scene by a lake; another one may picture eating fried chicken on a stoop of an apartment building. No one has the exact same concept of any word because all people's experiences are different.

This chapter is about identifying words using phonics, word patterns, structural analysis, sight, context, and the dictionary. Many sections in Chapter 2 contain ideas that will also be helpful in developing or strengthening students' word identification (see Sections 2.5, 2.8, 2.9, and 2.10).

Section 3.1

Phonics: Consonants

Behavior Observed → **Anticipated Outcome**

The student has difficulty associating the sounds that consonants symbolize.

The student will be able to use the sounds of consonants to phonologically recode unknown words.

Background

The essence of phonics is to give students a means to associate sounds with letters and letter combinations so students can pronounce a word that is not known at sight. If the pronounciation can be related to a word in the students' experiences, there is a connection with meaning. Phonics only helps students read (understand) words for which they already have meaning. For example, if the student sounds *yyy-eeeg* and says *yegg,* but has no meaning for the word, phonics is of little value. Fortunately, however, students have meanings for many words, and if they can decode a word, they are often able to associate meaning with the word, especially in the first few years of school.

Using phonics, or the sounds people assign to letters and letter combinations, is one way students can pronounce unfamiliar words. The value of phonics should not be underestimated. Phonics is one of the cueing systems readers use for words that are not in their sight vocabulary. Unfortunately, the teaching of phonics has been the topic of controversy for decades. An examination of the research literature concerning phonics instruction by the National Reading Panel (2000) led to the finding that "systematic phonics instruction enhances children's success in learning to read and . . . is significantly more effective than instruction that teaches little or no phonics" (p. 9). It is our belief that phonics should be an important foundation of a quality reading program, and it should be taught as one of the strategies readers can use when they want to identify an unfamiliar word. In short, phonics is a vital component (along with context and structural analysis) of balanced word identification.

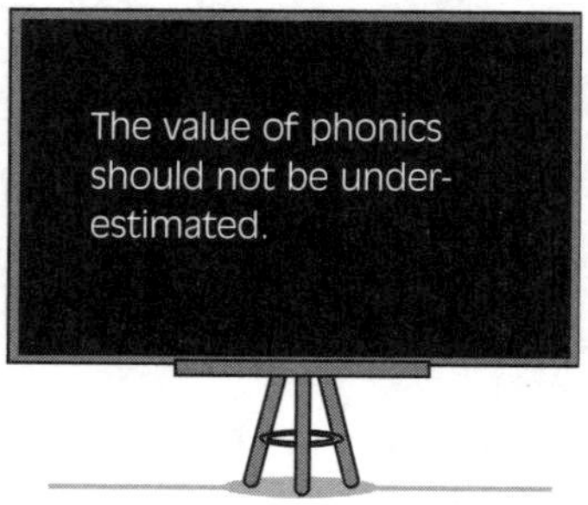
The value of phonics should not be underestimated.

Although there are 26 letters (graphemes) in the English alphabet, there are (depending on the dialect) forty or more sounds (phonemes). Because the consonants are more regular than the vowels, they are often introduced first. For the 25 consonant sounds listed in the box on the following page (adapted from Gunning, 2008), begin teaching sounds that occur with the highest frequency and that are quite easy for students to say (e.g., sounds for *m, r,* and *s*).

The basic teaching strategies and practice and reinforcement activities used for initial consonants can be used with final consonants, consonant diagraphs (e.g., *ch, gh, kn, ph, sc, si, th, ti, wh, wr*), consonant blends in the initial position (e.g., *bl, cl, fl, gl, pl, sl, br, cr, dr, fr, sch, sm, sl*), and blends in the final position (e.g., *ld, lf, lk, nce, nk, nt*). Gunning (2001) has developed a useful resource manual for teaching a wide variety of word analysis strategies.

Letter-Sound Correspondences for Consonants

Sound (Phoneme)	Letter (Grapheme)	Initial/Final	Final	Key Words
/b/	*b*, bb	*b*arn	e*bb*, ca*b*, ro*b*e	bell, ball
/d/	d, dd, ed	*d*eer	ba*d*	dog
/f/	f, ff, ph, lf, gh	*f*un, *ph*oto	ha*lf*, lau*gh*	fish
/g/	g, gg, gh	*g*ate, *gh*ost, *gu*ide	ra*g*	goat
/h/	h, wh	*h*ouse, *wh*o		horse, hat
/hw/	wh	*wh*ale		whale
/j/	g, j, dg	*j*ug, *g*ym, sol*d*ier	a*g*e, ju*dg*e	jar
/k/	c, ch, k, ck, q	*c*an, *k*ite, *q*uick, *ch*aos	ba*ck*, a*ch*e	cat, key
/l/	l, ll	*l*ion	mai*l*	leaf
/m/	m, mm, mb, mn	*m*e	hi*m*, co*mb*, autu*mn*	monkey, man
/n/	n, nn, kn, gn	*n*ow, *kn*ow, *gn*u, *pn*eumonia	pa*n*	nest, nail
/p/	p, pn, pp	*p*ot	to*p*	pencil, pen
/r/	r, rr, wr	*r*ide, *wr*ite		rabbit, ring
/s/	s, c, sc, ss	*s*ight, *c*ity, *sc*ience	bu*s*, mi*ss*, fa*c*e	sun, Santa
/t/	t, tt, ed	*t*ime	ra*t*, wa*tt*, jump*ed*	table
/v/	v [f in *of*]	*v*ase	lo*v*e	valentine, vest
/w/	w	*w*e		wagon
/y/	y, i	*y*acht, on*i*on		yo-yo
/z/	z, zz, s	*z*ipper	ha*s*, bu*zz*	zebra
/ch/	ch, c, ti	*ch*ip, *c*ello, ques*ti*on	mat*ch*	chair
/zh/	z, si, g	a*z*ure, ver*si*on	bei*g*e, gara*g*e	garage
/th/	th	*th*in	brea*th*	thumb
/th/	th	*th*is	brea*th*e	the
/sh/	sh, ti, ssi, s, si, sci	*sh*ip, *s*ure, *ch*ef, ac*ti*on, con*sc*ience	pu*sh*, spe*ci*al, mi*ssi*on	sheep
/ŋ/	ng		si*ng*	ring

EXPLICIT PHONICS

1. Younger students may need to be told directly that letters have a name and that a sound can also be associated with the letter. Sometimes teachers say that letters make sounds, but that is not correct. Letters do not say anything; however, sounds can be associated with the letters. Begin by teaching letter-sound correspondences in the initial position of the word.
2. Print an uppercase and a lowercase *d* on the chalkboard and name words that begin with a *d*. Encourage students to think of names of students in the class or friends whose names begin with a *d*. Pictures and concrete objects can also be used.
3. Record the responses on the chalkboard as in the example shown below.

D	d
Don	dad
Dave	duck
Donna	dog
Debbi	door
Dan	down
Dion	deer

4. Ask students to examine each list and note similarities and differences between the words. As the discussion continues, develop the concept that the *d* represents the same sound at the beginning of each word listed on the chalkboard. Be direct in connecting a sound with the letter.
5. Say each word on the list while you move your hand under the word. Emphasize the *d* sound distinctly so students can hear it. Have students pronounce each word after you. Help students see that all the words begin with the same letter and that the letter *d* stands for the sound /*d-d-d*/ heard at the beginning of each word.
6. Invite students to think of other words that begin with the sound associated with *d*. Add these words to the list.
7. Conclude the lesson by asking students to listen while you say some words. If a word begins with the sound associated with *d*, have them raise their hand. If the word begins with a different sound, they should not raise their hand. Use words from the list on the chalkboard as well as new words (for instance, *Dave, Tom, door, Marie, zoo, down*).
8. Refer to the Practice and Reinforcement Activities (page 189) for additional ideas.

EAR TO EYE PHONICS

1. Say five or six words and have students listen carefully to hear how each word begins. When you say the sounds, elongate but do not separate the sound associated with the initial consonant, for example, *bbball, bbbat,* and *bbboy.*
2. Ask students what they noticed about the beginning sounds of all the words that you pronounced. The expected response is that they all begin with the same sound.
3. Encourage students to give other words with the same sound that is heard at the beginning of *ball, bat,* and *boy.*
4. To provide auditory training, say three words (two that have the same beginning sound and one that is different) and have students say the words that begin alike. Elongate the initial consonant sound in each word. Repeat this procedure several times. Pictures and concrete objects can also be used (box, bear, badge, banana, balloon, beaver). The purpose of this activity is to provide ear training for the sound being taught.
5. Write the letter *b* on the chalkboard and make a list of words that begin with *b.* Encourage students to suggest additional words. Explore what all the words have in common. Guide students to realize that words all begin alike when you see them and sound alike at the beginning when you hear them.
6. Use a picture or concrete object to help students associate the sound with the letter. Sometimes the pictures can be put together or arranged to make the shape of the letter that is associated with a particular sound being learned, as shown below.

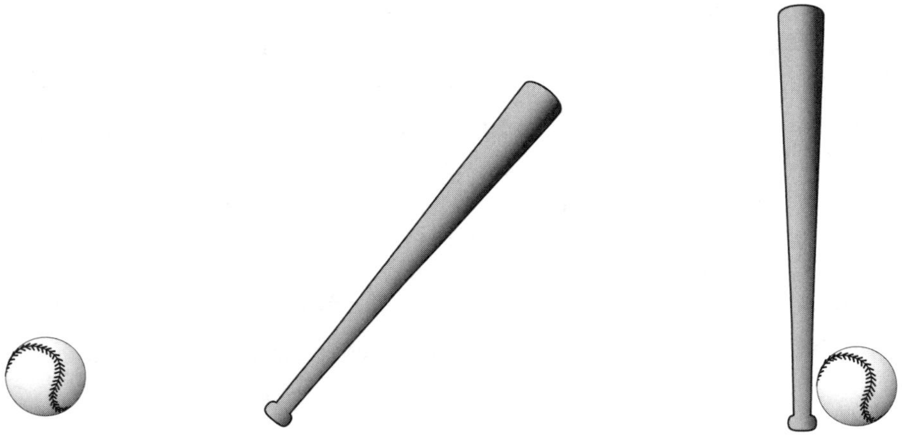

Strategy 3

USING ALPHABET BOOKS

1. Secure an alphabet book. Various publishers have colorful, small books for each letter of the alphabet. Part B on the CD contains a listing of alphabet books that may be useful. Choose the page dealing with the consonant being taught (for example, *t*).
2. Read the *T* page aloud: "Tiny Tom told Tim to take a toy." Tell students that many of the words begin the same way. Then read the page again pointing to each word that begins with *t*.
3. Help students realize that *t* spells the sound heard at the beginning of almost all the words.
4. Secure another alphabet book and read the sentence. Invite students to help identify the *t* words. Relate the words in the two books by writing them on the chalkboard or a poster. Then show students that the words begin with *t* and have the *ttt* sound.
5. Invite students to practice by providing cards with words from the alphabet books as well as new words (for example, *tag*). Show the word, cover the *t*, point to the remaining part of the word, and say, "This part of the word says *ag*. Now I'll uncover the *t*. What is the word? Guide students as needed and provide additional practice using words such as those below.

tail	tall	take	talk
tape	tank	team	ten
tent	tooth	tongue	toot

Refer to the pictures in the alphabet books whenever possible to keep the focus on the word's meaning. In addition, use students' names to help practice the letter-sound relationship being taught.

Strategy 4

USING WHOLE TEXT

1. Read a story to the class that has words with the consonant sound (or other sound) you wish to emphasize. Part C on the CD has pattern books that may be used with this strategy.
2. Write several sentences from the story on sentence strips.
3. Read the sentences to the class and have students echo read each sentence after you.
4. Point to the target words and ask students to read them after you.
5. Ask students to identify the letters in the target words. Then ask them which sound is the same in each word. Have the students make the sound with you.
6. Reread the sentences emphasizing the targeted sound.
7. Encourage the students to read the sentences and to use the letter sound in their writing.

Strategy 5

WRITE IT

1. In beginning reading instruction, Heron (2008) has recommended teaching students to write words before reading them. Rather than a focus on decoding, attention is given to encoding or constructing words. Over the course of numerous lessons, use letter cards, letter tiles, magic slates, or a pencil to help students learn to write consonant-vowel-consonant words so that the letters and diagraphs that represent the 40 or so sounds (phonemes) in English are mastered. Depending on your class, introduce three or four phonemes a week.
2. Begin by building phoneme (sound) awareness using lessons, strategies, and activities in Chapter 2, Sections 2.6, 2.7, 2.8, 2.9, and 2.10. Do not focus on counting phonemes but on students' mouth movements in saying words.
3. You might begin the initial lesson by saying something like the following.

    We have been saying words and paying attention to different sounds and the way our mouths move as we say different words. Today we will learn to write some words using paper and pencil. Listen as I say the word sip. [Say the word and have students repeat it, paying attention to their mouth movements.] *Have you ever taken a* sip *of water?* [Demonstrate what it looks like to sip water.] *Let's see if we can write the word. Who has an idea of how I might begin writing* sip*?*

4. Guide students through the process as needed, writing the word on the chalkboard. Then segment the word orally and have students repeat after you. Invite a few students to share what they have written.
5. Ask if anyone can think of a word that rhymes with *sip*. If the given word rhymes with *sip* (e.g., *tip*), use it. You might say what follows.

    Yes, you're right. Tip *rhymes with* sip. *Because the words rhyme, they are the same at the end. Only the beginning is different. Let's say the words together. Did you hear a different sound in the beginning?* [Clarify and explain as needed.] *Let's see if we can write* tip. *Pay attention to your mouth movement as you begin to say the word. How might we write that sound?* [Guide and model as necessary. Have students write the word.]

6. Depending on student knowledge, other words that rhyme with *tip* and *sip* could also be written by students. See page 269 in Section 3 Resources for other words that rhyme with the two written words.
7. Remember that letter tiles, magic slates, and white boards can be used for the lesson to add variety.

Practice and Reinforcement Activities

The following activities are exemplified with the letter *d* but can be adapted to other consonants.

1. Have students look through magazines and stories to find pictures that can be associated with the sound *d*. The pictures can be arranged on a bulletin board or on individual letter sheets. Include the capital and lowercase letters on the display.
2. Use oral sentences where the missing word begins with the letter-sound association being learned. After students share responses that might make sense, have them choose the words that make sense and begin with the correct sound. For *d*, possible sentences might include the examples that follow.

   I brush my teeth every________. (day)

   I gave my ____________________ a bone. (dog)

   I saw a ____________________ at the farm. (duck, dog)

   The toy cost me a ____________________. (dime, dollar)

3. Provide a group of pictures and have students take turns sorting those pictures whose names begin with the sound being studied. Pictures can also be sorted according to whether the sound at the beginning, middle, or end of the words is different or the same.
4. Invite students to bring in objects whose names begin with the sound being studied.
5. Place pictures and/or objects in a box. Some of the items should begin with the sound being studied; a few should not. Have a student reach into the box, take out an item, name it, and indicate whether the initial sound of the object is the same as or different from the sound being studied. Then have the student use the word in a sentence.
6. List words on the chalkboard that begin with consonants not being studied which can be erased and replaced with the consonant that is being practiced. Have a student pronounce the word. Then erase the first letter of the word and put a *d* in its place to make a new word. Have students use their knowledge of the letter-sound association for *d* to pronounce the new word. Repeat this procedure with each of the other words listed here. Have students use the new words in sentences. Chapter 3 Resources (pages 267–274) include a list of pattern words that should be helpful for this activity.

   RESOURCES

hot	dot
tip	dip
tog	dog
sent	dent
pig	dig
kid	did
him	dim

7. When students are reading and come across an unfamiliar word that contains the letter being studied, encourage them to use the context along with their knowledge of the letter sound to pronounce the word.
8. Orally read sentences where students give a word beginning with the sound being learned. The word must make sense in the sentence. Some examples follow.

   Jim's pet is a ____________________. (dog)

   Another name for a plate is a ____________________. (dish)

   At night it is ____________________. (dark)

   It's about time to eat ____________________. (dinner)

9. Have students name objects in the classroom that begin with the sound associated with the letter being learned. A variation is to have students find objects in the classroom with the same beginning sounds as their names.

10. Read words that begin with different sounds on a tape recorder. Play the tape for the students asking them to stand up if they hear a word that begins with the letter *d*.
11. Place 10 or more word cards in a pocket chart, each beginning with a different sound. Ask a student to think of another word that begins with one of the beginning sounds of the words. For example, if one of the word cards contained *little,* the student might say the word *like*. Play until all 10 sounds are used. The meanings of the words in the pocket chart should be known to students.
12. Use the sounds of consonants during your regular school routine. For example, when the class is dismissed for the day, ask students whose last names begin or end with *D* to leave first.
13. Have teams of students create tongue twisters with the letter *d*. A sample sentence follows: Dan drove to the downtown Dairy Dream for diet drinks.
14. Have students think of words beginning with the letter *d*. Students take turns saying a new word without repeating any words. When a student is unable to add a new word, ask another student to suggest one.
15. Place pictures in an envelope and have students sort the pictures according to initial, medial, or final sound.
16. Prepare a list of sentences that have a missing word. Sketch or cut out pictures that complete each sentence. Put them on cards and ask students to select the appropriate card or cards to complete each sentence that begins with a particular sound.

    I saw a ______________________.

17. Connect an action with each consonant sound. For example, when you teach the sound *d,* ask the students to dance. You can make a game of this activity after you have taught several of the letter sounds. Make a card with each letter. Show one letter to the class and call on a student to show the class the action you learned for that letter. Examples of actions for consonants, digraphs, and blends follow (Cunningham, 1993).

b	bounce	n	nod	sh	shiver	gr	grab
c	catch	p	paint	th	think	pl	plant
d	dance	r	run	wh	whistle	sw	swim
f	fall	s	sit	br	breathe	sk	skip
g	gallop	t	talk	bl	blink	sl	sleep
h	hop	v	vacuum	cr	crawl	sm	smile
j	jump	w	wiggle	cl	climb	sp	spin
k	kick	y	yawn	dr	drive	st	stand
l	laugh	z	zip	fl	fly	tr	track
m	march	ch	cheer	fr	frown	tw	twist

18. When students have learned several consonant sounds, provide sentences or stories with a word missing and invite students to use the context and their knowledge of certain sounds to predict the word. As an example you could say, We ran ___ the stairs. Remind students that the word begins with the sound that begins like *dog*. If a word is given that makes sense but does not begin with *d* (for example, up), discuss why it is not the right answer. Invite students to share their thinking about particular responses and guide them as necessary.
19. Cunningham and Hall (1997b) have prepared an excellent book to provide systematic, multilevel instruction in phonics for students in first grade using a month-by-month approach.

Pick Up. Give each student 10 cards with a different consonant on each card. Lay out the 10 cards on the table in front of each student. Students may have different consonants. As you read a list of words, ask the student to pick up the card corresponding to the initial, medial, or final sound of the word.

Consonant Rummy. Use a deck of cards with a consonant on each card. Each player is dealt eight cards. The first player asks another player for the consonant that begins a certain word. For example, "I'd like Jen to give me a letter that begins like the word down." If the player does not have the letter *d*, the caller picks a card from the deck and the next student takes a turn. The first student to have four cards of the same letter is the winner.

Section 3.2

Phonics: Vowels

Behavior Observed →

The student has difficulty associating the sounds that vowels symbolize.

Anticipated Outcome

The student will be able to use the sounds of vowels to help decode unknown words.

Background

Vowels are much more difficult for students to learn than consonants. Unlike most consonants, vowels can represent more than one sound. Gunning (2008) notes that English contains approximately 16 vowel sounds. Most vowels have two or three common sounds, but there are also many exceptions for certain vowels. For example, the long *e* sound can be spelled 16 different ways: *see, team, equal, he, key, Caesar, deceive, receipt, people, demesne, machine, field, debris, amoeba, quay,* and *pity* (May, 1990). Although it is not necessary to teach students rules for each of these vowel sounds, there are some vowel generalizations that can help students as they learn to decode words.

Emergent readers need to begin to learn the sounds for long and short vowels, and as students progress in reading, they can also learn about some of the less frequently occurring vowel sounds in the English language. As you teach your students vowel sounds, however, you need to remember that having students learn the sounds of vowels is not useful in itself. The purpose of teaching vowel sounds is for students to be able to make better predictions about unfamiliar words. If you find that you are spending more time teaching the sounds associated with the letters than your students spend reading text, you should probably balance the proportion of time you are spending teaching phonics with opportunities for students to read printed materials.

Teaching the various sounds of the vowels will probably span at least two grade levels. Generally, "short" vowels are taught first because they have fewer spellings. Some "long" vowels, however, are quite easy to learn, especially when they are the final letter in two-letter words (e.g., *me, he, we*). Even though vowels can be taught in a manner similar to consonants (see Section 3.1), we have provided teaching strategies for two different vowels.

The following are some of the more common sounds associated with vowels.

Long/Short Vowels

a as in *age*
a as in *an*
e as in *ease*
e as in *end*
i as in *ice*
i as in *inch*
o as in *old*
o as in *odd*
u as in *use*
u as in *up*

Vowel Digraphs

ee, ea	*e* as in *ease*
ai, ay	*a* as in *age*
oa, ow	*o* as in *old*
oo	*oo* as in *too*
oo	*oo* as in *good*
ou, ow	*ou* as in *out*
oi	*oi* as in *oil*
au	*o* as in *off*

Teachers need to balance time spent teaching letter sounds with the time students spend reading.
© 2010 JupiterImages Corporation.

Strategy **1**

SECTION 3.2

SHORT I

1. For short *i*, students may need to be reminded that our alphabet contains vowels and consonants and that sounds can be associated with both vowels and consonants.

2. Write the vowels on the chalkboard and circle the vowel that will be the focus of the lesson. Tell students that there are two common sounds (long and short) associated with *i* and that they will be taught to associate the short sound with *i*.

3. If possible, select some objects and pictures whose names exemplify the short sound associated with *i* (for example, baseball *mitt*, fish's *fin*, jar *lid*). Appropriate names of class members may also be used (for example, *Bill, Jill*). Say the words and have students listen for the sound of the vowel.

4. Place the words on the chalkboard in a single column. Point to each word and pronounce it, emphasizing the sound associated with *i*. Have the students say each word as you move your hand from left to right under the word.

5. Ask students to inspect the words and note their similarities and differences. When students note that all the words have an *i,* emphasize that the sound associated with this letter is called the short sound of *i.*

6. Pronounce pairs of words orally (one containing the short sound of *i*) and have students identify the word containing the short *i.* By using some words with the long sound of *i,* students should be able to note how this sound differs from the short sound of *i.* An alternative is to pronounce a word and have students show a card with a short *i* if the word contains that sound. Some possible words follow.

fit–fat	rim–ram	mitt–met
line–lit	ham–him	jam–Jim
rid–ride	dig–dog	did-doll

7. Encourage students to think of additional words with the short *i* vowel sound. List those words on the chalkboard. Have students use the words in sentences.

8. If desired, help students understand the generalization that the vowel *i* in the middle of a word and surrounded by consonants usually has a short sound. This generalization can also be applied to other vowels in a similar position.

9. After students have learned the vowel sounds, develop word wheels where various words can be made by turning the wheel. Possible words for this activity can be found in Chapter 3 Resources (pages 267–274).

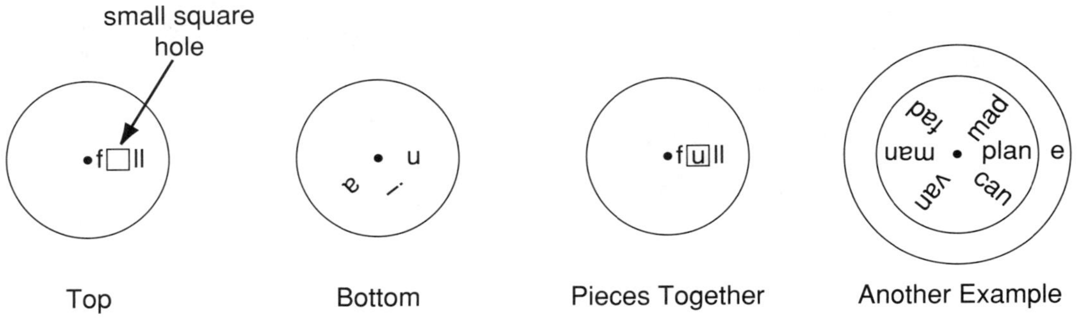

Strategy 2 SECTION 3.2

LONG E

1. Tell students that you will help them learn the long sound for *e.* Print *e* on the chalkboard and ask students to tell you the name of the letter.

2. Help students realize that the name of the letter and the long sound are the same. You might say something like what follows.

   Notice that the name of the letter and the long sound of the vowel are the same.

   Have the students say the sound together.

3. Then say, "Watch as I put a letter in front of the e and make a word." Print an *m* and say, "I know the sound *mmm* and when I put it with the *e* it makes *me.*" Have the students repeat the sounds and make the word by blending the sounds.

4. Guide students in creating other words that end with *e* (*be, he, we*).

Practice and Reinforcement Activities

1. Provide cards with the vowel, a key word for that vowel, and a picture for that word. For example, you may want to remember the sound for *i* with the word *twins*. The card should have a picture of twins with the word and the letter.
2. Place on the chalkboard a column of words that contains the short vowel sounds. Show students that adding a final *e* to the words often changes the vowel sound from short to long. Begin a second column where an *e* is added to each word. Have a student pronounce these words and use each of them in a sentence. Emphasize the change in vowel sound when the final *e* is added. Sample words are shown below.

can	cane	hid	hide	bit	bite	not	note
man	mane	rid	ride	hop	hope	mad	made
tub	tube	rob	robe	cut	cute	kit	kite

3. Have students read a short passage and circle words with long vowel sounds. Then copy the words on a separate sheet of paper and have students attempt to categorize them. Each category should then be labeled with a description of what the long-vowel words have in common.
4. Create cards that have long vowel sounds, short vowel sounds, and r-controlled vowel sounds. Have students sort each card into the categories by vowel sounds. Chapter 3 Resources (pages 252; 267–274) contain possible words to use.
5. Teach students the importance of vowels by placing the cards with the consonants on a table. Ask a volunteer to make a word with the letter cards. The students should quickly see that it is impossible to write words without vowels. Then include vowel cards and ask the students to make words (DeGenaro, 1993).
6. Write basic sight (high-frequency) words using two colors of crayons—one color for vowels and another color for consonants. The Revised Dolch List in Chapter 3 Resources (page 254) contains basic sight words.
7. Provide students with letter tiles and have them engage in word-building activities. Fox (1996) provides many helpful suggestions for word building.
8. Use Venn diagrams, such as those below, to help students explore letters that represent more than one sound in words.

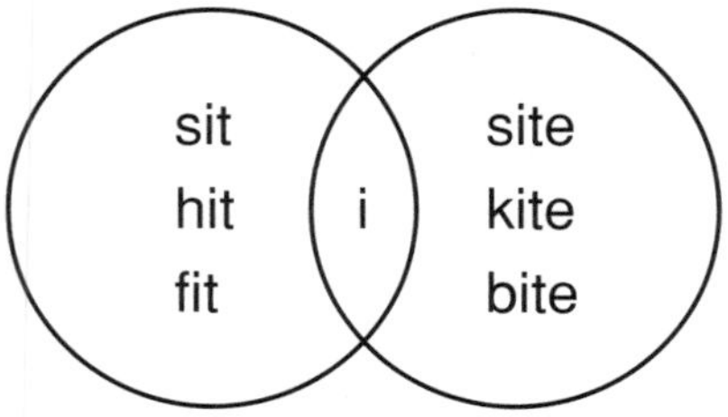

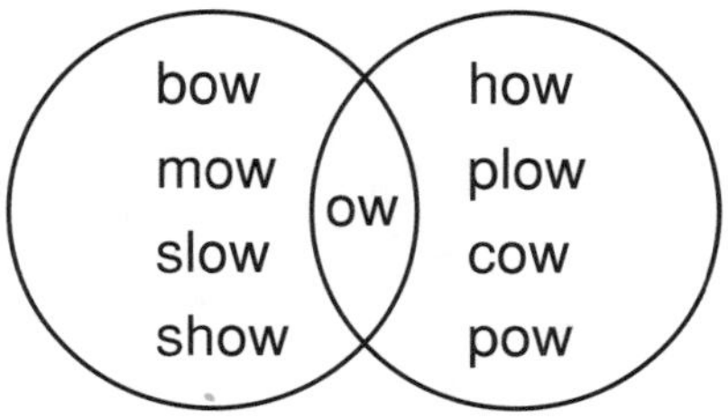

9. Help students experience printed materials that contain specific phonic elements or rhymes. If some of the books are too difficult for independent reading, they can be shared aloud and discussed. Some books that contain phonic elements or rhymes follow.

Oppenheim, J. (1990). *Wake, Up Baby!* New York: Bantam. (long *a*)
Ziefert, H. (1990). *Follow Me!* New York: Puffin. (long *e*)
Hoff, S. (1988). *Mrs. Brice's Mice.* New York: Harper. (long *i*)
Schade, S. (1992). *Toad on the Road.* New York: Random House. (long *o*)
Demarest, C. (1998). *Farmer Nat.* San Diego: Red Wagon/Harcourt. (rhyme)
Hague, K. (1999). *Ten Little Bears: A Counting Rhyme.* New York: Morrow. (rhyme)

10. Provide letter tiles and encourage students to build words with onsets and rimes (see Section 3.3). Letters can be written on bathroom tiles (1") with a permanent marker. Velcro can be attached to a small plywood board. After using the letter tiles, they can be secured on the plywood board for easy storage.
11. Encourage students to write sentences with rhymes being learned.
12. Use books that contain patterns being studied. In addition, some of the older linguistic readers (The cat sat on a mat, etc.) could be used for practice with certain onsets and rimes.
13. Use pocket charts so students can manipulate various letters to create words.

Section 3.3

Word Patterns and Word Building

Behavior Observed → **Anticipated Outcome**

The student is unable to use knowledge about word patterns to identify unfamiliar words. → The student will be able to identify unfamiliar words by using common word patterns.

Background

Proficient readers rarely sound out words letter by letter. Instead, they use what they know about common spelling patterns to figure out the word. This means that readers will make the association between spelling patterns they know and unfamiliar words. For example, if students encounter the word *hobbit* in reading, they may know that the word pattern *ob* may sound like *rob* or *mob* and that the pattern *it* may sound like *mit* or *bit*. Using what they know about consonant sounds, then, students can figure out a word that they do not know by sight.

Word patterns is another strategy that students should use as they read. Cunningham (2003) notes that as students learn more words, they use patterns and analogy to decode. Like phonics and context clues, using word patterns is not a panacea; not all unfamiliar words will have familiar word patterns in them. For instructional purposes, however, you should help your students use this strategy as one more way to read unfamiliar words.

A word pattern has two components: an onset and a rime (Adams, 1990a).

- The onset is the initial part of a word that precedes a vowel (for example, the *h* in *hat* or the *sh* in *ship*).
- The rime is the part of the word that rhymes (for example, the *at* in *hat* or the *ip* in *ship*).

Rimes are also known as word families or phonograms. A list of word patterns is included in Chapter 3 Resources (pages 267–274). The list will be helpful for teaching.

RESOURCES

An innovative developmental approach that helps students explore letter patterns, letter-sound correspondences, and words has been developed by Cunningham and Cunningham (1992). The approach involves students in making words, and over 300 lessons have been developed for students in elementary school (Cunningham & Hall, 1994a, 1994b, 1997a, 1997b). The steps for making word lessons are shown on the next page (adapted from Cunningham and Cunningham, 1992).

Planning Lessons to Make Words

1. Choose the word that will be made last in the lesson (for example, *stand*). Consider your students' interests and word knowledge when selecting words.
2. Make a list of other words that can be made from *stand* (*at, sat, as, Stan, Dan, tan, Tad, an, and, sand*). Arrange these words in order from the shortest to the longest.
3. Decide on the words you will use based on patterns, words of various sizes, words that can be made by rearranging the letters (for example, *and, Dan*), and proper names to show the use of capital letters. When making your final selections, keep in mind that most students should have *heard* the words and know what they mean.
4. Make big letter cards to use in a pocket chart or on the ledge of the chalkboard. Then prepare an envelope that contains the order of the words and the patterns that will be stressed. Finally, print the words on cards.

Strategy 1 SECTION 3.3

MAKING WORDS

1. Use the above box to plan the lesson or consult Cunningham and Hall (1994a, 1994b, 1997a, 1997b) for ready-made lessons. Distribute the necessary letters to each student. Keep the letters in reclosable bags and have individual students pass out the different letters. Each card should contain an uppercase letter on one side and a lowercase letter on the other. At the end of the lesson, the same students pick up the letters they originally distributed. Finally, you should have large letter cards that you can use with a pocket chart or on the chalkboard ledge to model as necessary. Below is a sample lesson.
2. Distribute the letters *a, d, n, s*, and *t*. If necessary, hold up the large letter cards and have students hold up their small letter cards that match your card.
3. Say, "Use two letters to make *at*." Use the word in a sentence.
4. Invite a student to assemble the correct response using the large letter cards in the pocket chart or on the chalkboard ledge. Have the student read the word and have students correct their individual responses as necessary. Students should be able to fix their words by comparing their words to the large letter cards.
5. Continue steps 3 and 4 with other word-making directions such as those shown below.
   - Add a letter to make *sat*.
   - Remove a letter to make *at*.
   - Change a letter to make *an*.
   - Add a letter to make *tan*.
   - Add a letter to make *Stan*.
   - See what word you can make with all the letters (*stand*).
6. When all the words have been made, take words you previously printed on index cards and put them in the pocket chart or on the ledge of the chalkboard. Keep these guidelines in mind.
   - Do one word at a time.
   - Present the words in the order they were made.
   - Have students say and spell the words with you.
   - Use the words for sorting and pointing out patterns (for example, find the word that has the same pattern as *tan*). Align the words so students can see the patterns.
   - Transfer word learning to writing by asking students to spell a few of the words you say.
7. Remember that word building can be used with upper-grade students and students of all ages who are struggling with reading (Cunningham & Hall, 1994a).
8. Consider using the *Word Wizard* (Falwell, 1998) to introduce Making Words.

Strategy 2 SECTION 3.3

PHONOGRAM -AY

1. Write the word *day* on the chalkboard or on a sentence strip.
2. Read the word to students, drawing attention to the *-ay* sound.
3. Substitute a different initial consonant such as *m* for *may*. Say, "If d-a-y spells *day*, what do you think m-a-y spells?" Repeat this activity with three or four different consonants. Write each word on the chalkboard or a sentence strip. Chapter 3 Resources (pages 267–274) contain lists of phonograms.
4. Ask students to pronounce each of the words. Although this may seem like an easy activity, many young students have difficulty reading rhyming words.
5. Write a sentence for each word or have students write sentences for the words. Ask students to read the sentences aloud and to pay close attention to the word pattern that is being studied.
6. For students who are able to progress to the next step, write an unfamiliar word on the chalkboard that contains the word pattern. An example for *-ay* could be to*day* or *may*be.

Strategy 3 SECTION 3.3

PHONOGRAM -IG (younger students)

1. Write the word *pig* on the chalkboard. Ask for a volunteer to pronounce the word. Then have students explain how they know that the word is *pig*. Guide and question students as necessary.
2. Tell students that the letters *-ig* make the */ig/* sound. Putting a *p* in front of *-ig* spells *pig*. Then tell students that if a different letter is put in front of the *-ig*, words that rhyme with *pig* can be made. Explain, if necessary, what it means to rhyme words.
3. Then invite students to try to think of other words that rhyme with *pig*. To model the process, you might say something like what follows.

   Let me see if I can think of a word that rhymes with pig. *If I put a* b *in front of the* -ig, *I get the word* big. Big, pig. *Yes, the words rhyme.* [Write *big* under *pig* and underline the *-ig*.] *I can hear the rhyme, and I can also tell that the word rhymes because of the letters.*

4. Challenge students to work with a partner or in small groups to think of other words that rhyme with *pig*. Have students write their words on paper.
5. When most students have finished, have them share possible words. Write the words on the chalkboard and then guide students in determining whether each word rhymes with *pig*. If the word is correct, underline the *-ig*. If the word does not fit the pattern, erase or cross out that word.
6. When the list is complete based on students' words, have students echo read each word after you say it. If there are any words students did not include (see a list of possible words on page 269), you could ask the question that follows.

   How about ___________ *? Does it rhyme with* pig*?* [Include a few non-examples as well.]

7. Be sure to discuss the meanings of any unknown words. Encourage students to use the words in sentences.
8. To extend the lesson, invite students to write sentences using one or more of the *-ig* words. The sentences can be true or fanciful.

Strategy 4 SECTION 3.3

PHONOGRAM -ILL

1. Write *-ill* on the chalkboard and ask students what letter would need to be added to *ill* to make the word *hill.*
2. Add the *h* to *ill*, pronounce the sounds, and then blend the sounds as you say the whole word. Have students repeat the blending.
3. Then write *ill* underneath *hill* and ask students what letter should be added to *ill* to make the word *Bill.* Ask a student to blend the sounds to form the word.
4. Invite students to examine the two words and note how they are the same and how they are different. Guide students to understand that the words end with the letters *i, l, l* which make the sounds heard in *ill*; the words are different in the initial sounds and that accounts for the two different words.
5. Continue with other examples and model words like *Jill* and *fill.* Invite students to suggest other onsets that could be used to make a new word.
6. Use the words in oral sentences and written sentences and possibly create stories. Some examples follow.

   Jill climbed a *hill.* She looked for *Bill.* She saw *Bill fill* a bucket.

Strategy 5 SECTION 3.3

MAKING YOUR OWN WORDS

1. Pick a word from the book you are currently reading that has a variety of letters or that has a particular word chunk you want to emphasize. You may also choose a holiday word. Write the letters in alphabetical order without telling students the word.
2. Have students use letter tiles from the word to create a list of words using those letters. (This strategy would be the opposite of the making words activity described in Strategy 1. Students are asked to come up with the word instead of the teacher supplying the words to make.)
3. Have students compare their lists in small groups and then come up with a final list with the entire class. Post the list in the classroom. The list might be titled Words We Made from ________________ (write the word that was used for the activity).
4. Other activities that use this basic idea include the games Scrabble, Scrabble Jr., and Boggle.

Section **3.4**

Structural Analysis

Behavior Observed → **Anticipated Outcome**

The student is unable to use word structure to help decode unfamiliar words.

The student will use word structure to help decode unfamiliar words.

Background

When students come to an unknown word that is made up of more than one syllable, they can use structural analysis skills to divide that word into pronounceable units. Structural analysis skills can allow students to focus on the larger units of letter patterns within words. Such letter patterns typically include inflectional endings, prefixes, suffixes, contractions, compound words, and syllabication. You can teach students how to figure out longer words by using their background knowledge about words and word parts, focusing on that knowledge, applying what students know to a new reading situation, and extending what students already know by imparting additional knowledge about words.

INFLECTIONAL ENDINGS (younger students)

1. For younger students, draw one of the four figures on the chalkboard without the tail. Print the word inside the figure and have students pronounce it. Then ask students to look at the figure and tell you what is missing (the tail).

2. Tell students the missing tail contains an ending that can be put on the word. Draw the tail and put one of the endings in it. Have a student pronounce the new word. Ask another student to use the word in a sentence. Then write the word on the chalkboard.

3. Repeat the process with the other endings. Be sure to write the new words under one another as in the example below.

   jumps
   jumping
   jumped

4. Draw students' attention to what is the same (*jump*) and different (the ending) in the words. Help students realize that some words have endings. Have students apply this knowledge to a known word with different endings in sentences. Provide some sentences and invite students to locate the common root word in the sentences. See the following examples.

I want some food.	They were playing ball.
She wants to play.	He played a board game.
He wanted to go home.	She plays with her friend.

5. Use some of the other illustrations for additional practice or independent activities. Encourage students to try some different endings on common words to build new words. Use words that do not involve spelling changes. Some examples follow.

look	walk	bark	work
play	talk	laugh	record
pack	fill	help	end

6. Conclude the lesson by reminding students that some words have endings. By covering the ending, they may recognize the root word. Then they can add the ending and pronounce the word.

Strategy **2** SECTION 3.4

INFLECTIONAL ENDINGS

1. Tell students that inflectional endings are the endings that can form a plural noun (dogs, quizzes), show the present tense of a verb (barks, wishes), are the present participle of a verb (walking), show past tense (talked), show possession (Jerry's), and show comparisons in adjectives and adverbs (bigger, biggest).
2. Present a root word that your students know from previous lessons. Write the word on a sentence strip or on the chalkboard. Have students pronounce the word and use it in a sentence.
3. Then have students watch carefully while you add an ending to the word. Have different students pronounce each derived word. If a student makes an error, cover the ending and have the student pronounce the root word. Then have the student try the word with the ending.
4. Once the words are pronounced correctly, have students use each new word in a sentence. Discuss the change in meaning that occurred when the ending was added. Students should understand that adding an ending to words may change the way the word is used in a sentence.
5. Conclude the lesson by helping students realize that some long words are really root words with inflected endings added. Encourage them to look for such endings when they are unable to pronounce a word at sight.

Strategy **3** SECTION 3.4

THE NIFTY THRIFTY FIFTY

1. The Nifty Thrifty Fifty (Cunningham, 2000, p. 165) is a list of 50 words containing "all the most useful prefixes, suffixes, and spelling changes" that should be understood by most fourth graders. Helping students learn to spell and build words using the affixes and spelling changes will require sustained instruction throughout the school year. Your efforts will be rewarded by students who gain confidence in decoding longer words. The 50 words can be found in Chapter 3 Resources (see pages 277–278).
2. Teach students to spell the words gradually over time and look for ways in daily instruction to share how the words can help students decode other words. Begin by explaining that many big words are smaller words with prefixes and suffixes added to them. Choose five or six words from The Nifty Thrifty Fifty to teach. Write them on the chalkboard or an overhead transparency.
3. Chant each word several times. Then help students analyze the words by noting prefixes, suffixes, and any spelling changes. Word meanings should also be discussed. For example, you might model by saying what follows.

> Dishonest *means not honest. The root word is* honest *and the prefix is* dis. *In many words, the prefix* dis *changes the word to an opposite. An example of another word using* dis *is* disobey.

4. Invite students to suggest other words with the same prefix. Some possible words are presented below.

discourage	discredit	discolor	disarm
disengage	disappear	disconnect	disassemble
disappoint	disadvantage	disappear	disclaim
disarmament	disapprove	disjointed	discomfort
disband	disarray	disagree	discontinue
disclose	disbelief		

5. Use a similar procedure for the other words in the lesson and then have students write each of the five or six words you have presented. Give clues to the word to be written. Several examples are provided below using words from The Nifty Thrifty Fifty.

dishonest	For number 1, write the word that is the opposite of honest.
employee	Number 2 could be used to describe someone who works for a business owner.
swimming	Number 3 is an activity that takes place in a lake.

6. Have students check their work by "chanting the letters aloud, underlining each as they say it" (Cunningham, 2000, p. 169).

7. Teach another five or six words the next week and then show students how parts of the words can be combined to spell other words. In addition, because the same word parts can be found in different words, the parts can be used to help pronounce many long words. You might use a think-aloud like the following:

> *I know the word* dishonest. *If I see the word* displease [write it on the chalkboard] *in my reading, I can remove the* dis *and then see the word* please. *I can then put the two parts together to pronounce the word. If I look for patterns or chunks in the big words in my reading, I can probably use what I know to help pronounce words.*

8. The Nifty Thrifty Fifty list can be found in the Chapter 3 Resources (pages 277–278). Lessons based on this list can be found in Cunningham and Hall (1998). Presenting quality lessons to your students will pay rich dividends in helping them pronounce longer words.

Strategy 4 SECTION 3.4

AFFIXES

1. Affixes are prefixes and suffixes that are attached to a base word. Chapter 5 Resources (pages 408–411) contain prefixes and suffixes that can be used for teaching and practice. "If students learn just the four most common prefixes in English (un-, re-, in-, dis-), they will have important clues about the meaning of about two-thirds of all English words that have prefixes" (Armbruster, Lehr, & Osborn, 2001, p. 38).

2. Explain to students that prefixes and suffixes form syllables because they are a pronunciation unit. They can be added to root words to change their meanings or part of speech. Provide examples.

reread	*re* is a prefix; *read* is a root word
painless	*pain* is a root word; *less* is a suffix

3. Have students offer some words that contain affixes. Write them on the chalkboard. Then ask students how they think knowing prefixes and suffixes can help them in reading. Through discussion, lead students to the following conclusions about prefixes and suffixes:

- Knowing them can help me recognize words more rapidly; I don't have to sound out an unknown word letter by letter.
- They can help me figure out some of the longer words in reading.
- Sometimes I can use affixes to help determine the meaning of the word.

4. Model how to figure out unfamiliar words with prefixes and suffixes. Think aloud as you read. For example, if the word is *unicycle*, the following might be shared.

> *I can't recognize the word immediately, so I look for the root word. It is* cycle, *and I know what a cycle is. I can see that the prefix is* uni-. *I know that the word is* unicycle, *but what does it mean? Because I know that* uni- *often means one, I have a pretty good idea that unicycle means a one-wheeled cycle. I may need to look up the word in a dictionary to be sure of its meaning, but I now have an idea of the word and can ask myself whether the meaning makes sense in the sentence.*

Strategy 5 — SECTION 3.4

CONTRACTIONS

1. Tell students that some words in our language, called contractions, are really two words joined together so that not all of the sounds are heard. Give students an example of a contraction such as *didn't*. Explain that *didn't* is a contraction for *did not*.
2. Show students how to write the contraction *didn't* by writing both *did* and *not* on the chalkboard. Explain that when forming a contraction, the letters that are not written are replaced by an apostrophe. Show students how to write an apostrophe in the word *didn't*.
3. Have students write a sentence that uses *did not*. Then ask them to replace *did not* with the contraction *didn't*.
4. Repeat these steps with other contractions that are found in the Chapter 3 Resources (page 275).

Strategy 6 — SECTION 3.4

COMPOUND WORDS

1. Explain to students that two words are sometimes put together to make a longer word. These words are called *compound words*.
2. Write several compound words on sentence strips. Ask students to pronounce the words and to use each one in a sentence. Write the sentences on strips and find the two words that make up each compound word.
3. Stress that looking for compound words in longer words may help students pronounce such words. Make it clear that some seemingly difficult words are actually compound words.
4. Provide sentences and help students identify the compound word and the two words that comprise it. Sample sentences follow.

> I saw a footprint in the snow.
> There was an earthquake in California.
> Please put the dishes in the dishwasher.

5. Conclude the lesson by helping students realize that they can sometimes recognize a longer word by identifying the two words that comprise it.
6. Repeat these steps with other compound words that are found in the Chapter 3 Resources (page 276).

Strategy 7 SECTION 3.4

DECODING POLYSYLLABIC WORDS

1. Help students realize how you might go about decoding polysyllabic words by modeling (i.e., showing and talking about what you do).
2. Select a word and write it on the chalkboard or an overhead transparency. Be sure that the word is presented in a sentence. An example follows.

   Her *unexpected* arrival caused a change in our plans.

3. Model by saying something like the following.

   I'm going to tell you how I might say or decode the word in italics. I will think aloud to help you understand what's going on in my brain. If you already know the word, please don't say anything. In a moment, I'll give you a chance to model what you do when you come across a polysyllabic word that you can't pronounce.

4. Read the sentence aloud, skipping over the unknown word. Then say something like what follows.

   I've read the entire sentence and skipped the word I don't know. I think I'll look for parts I know. The first part is the prefix un. *The next part is the word* expect *and there is an* ed *at the end. The word has three parts:* un-expect-ed. *The* un *is like the beginning of* uncover *and the* ed *is like the end of* wanted. *I can put the parts together and get* un-expect-ed. *I have heard that word before. In the sentence it makes sense. Her arrival was not expected and plans were changed.*

5. Present sentences to students that contain one or more polysyllabic words. Ask students to select a partner and think aloud while trying to pronounce the italicized words. Stress that it is best to think aloud only for words that cannot already be pronounced. Develop sentences based on what you know about your students. Several of the following sentences might be used or adapted.

   The *seaport* is now *unimportant*, and it is used for *recreational purposes*.
   Can you name some *important* products that are *exported* from the *shipyard*?
   The *manager* of the *convenience* store *expressed* his *appreciation* for my *assistance*.
   I *corrected* the *subtraction problem* in *mathematics*.
   The *unfriendly canine barked loudly* at the *mail carrier*.

6. Have students volunteer to share some of their think-alouds. For any words that students are unable to decode, model the process for them.
7. Gather additional polysyllabic words and devote a few minutes to modeling think-alouds from time to time. Invite students to share polysyllabic words from their reading and explain how they were able to pronounce them.

MATCHING WORD PARTS TO BUILD AND DECODE WORDS

1. Tell students that longer words can often be segmented into smaller parts to help pronounce the words. Then say something like the following.

   Instead of giving you some longer words to pronounce, I'm going to give you some words or word parts and ask you to make some longer words. I want to see how many different words you can make by joining different parts. Then when you come across longer words while reading, you may be able to see some smaller parts that will help you to pronounce words that you don't recognize immediately.

2. Reproduce the Matching Word Parts to Build Words on page 208 so each student has a copy. Mountain (2005) is the source for the word parts.
3. Give students a few minutes to work independently to form longer words. Then have students work with a partner to share unique words thereby expanding their lists.
4. Invite the entire class to share their words as you write them on the chalkboard. Invite students to add additional words that may not be on their lists. If necessary, discuss word meanings and invite students to use the words in sentences.
5. Help students realize that they should look for word parts when they encounter difficult words in their reading.
6. To extend learning, invite students to become a master word builder using one of the words or word parts with word parts not on the list to make longer words. You might say the following.

   If I take re *and put it at the beginning of* view, *I can make* review. *You can try your hand at building new words in your spare time. We'll see how many different words are created in a day or two.*

7. Remind students to look for and use word parts when they come upon difficult words while reading.

MATCHING WORD PARTS TO BUILD WORDS

Name ______________________________ Date ______________

Directions: Use the word parts below to make longer words. Write the words on the lines.

Words/Word Parts	*My Words*	
phone	______	______
scope	______	______
auto	______	______
way	______	______
tele	______	______
micro	______	______
sub	______	______
scribe	______	______
vision	______	______
graph	______	______
mobile	______	______

Master Builder

Directions: Use the words or word parts from the list above with other words or word parts **not** on the list to make new words. Write your words below. If you need more space, use the back of this sheet.

______ ______ ______

______ ______ ______

______ ______ ______

SYLLABICATION

1. Tell students that long words can be divided into smaller parts or syllables. By knowing how to divide words into syllables, students have another strategy to figure out words as they read.
2. Say a multisyllabic word such as *bicycle*. Have students say *bicycle* several times.
3. Tell students that you will clap your hands one time for each syllable in the word *bicycle*. As you say the word, clapping for each syllable, stretch out the word such as *bi—cy—cle*.
4. Say several more words that have more than one syllable, clapping one time for each syllable. Have students clap with you.
5. Explain that there are generalizations for the different ways words are divided into syllables. Spend time teaching the syllables in words that follow the syllable generalizations in the box below. Numerous lessons will be needed.

Syllable Generalizations*

1. When there are two like consonants, divide between them as in *pup/py*.
2. When there are two unlike consonants, divide between them as in *wal/rus*.
3. When a consonant is between two vowels, divide after the first vowel as in *si/lent*.
4. Prefixes, suffixes, and inflectional endings are their own syllables as in *pre/heat*.
5. When a syllable ends in a vowel, the vowel is long as in *o/pen*.
6. When a syllable ends in a consonant, the vowel is short as in *cab/in*.

*McCormick, 2003.

6. Encourage students to use their new knowledge to separate longer words into units that can be pronounced. By trying various pronunciations, students may recognize the word as one they have heard before.

Practice and Reinforcement Activities

1. Provide sentences containing root words that have the inflected ending omitted. Students read each sentence and add the appropriate ending. Consider the following examples.

   Bill was look ______ for his mother.

   The cat jump ______ over the branch.

   I miss ______ the school bus.

2. Prepare one set of cards that has root words and another set that contains different inflected endings (such as *s, ed, ing, er, est*). The root words for this activity should be those that remain unchanged when an inflected ending is added. Students draw a card from each set and try to match the root-word card with an inflected-ending card to make a new word. Have students write the new word and use it in a sentence. Possible root words for this activity are listed below.

ask	play	warm
call	thank	deep
help	new	hard
jump	small	walk

3. Ask students to circle the inflected endings in one of their pieces of writing. After finding endings in their own writing, they may want to read a story written by a classmate and find endings in a classmate's writing. This activity helps create an awareness of endings.
4. Write two columns of root words on the chalkboard, one that requires no change in spelling before adding an *ed*, and the other that requires doubling the final consonant before the *ed* is added. Try to use words that are in the students' sight vocabularies. Pronounce the words in the first group, add *ed* to the words, and have the students pronounce the new words. If students have difficulty, cover the ending, have them pronounce the root word, and then try the word with the *ed*. Ask students to use the words in sentences before and after adding *ed*.
5. Invite students to bring personal possessions to the front of the classroom. Tell students that they will be learning different ways of saying the same thing. For example, take Annette's barrette and say the following sentences.

   This is the barrette of Annette.
   The barrette belongs to Annette.
   This is Annette's barrette.

   Emphasize that each of the sentences means the same thing. Then write the sentences on sentence strips and direct the attention of the students to the last sentence. Identify the apostrophe and say that the *'s* on the end of the word *Annette* shows that the noun following her name belongs to her. Encourage the class to suggest phrases or sentences in which *'s* is used to show possession. Write the sentences on sentence strips.
6. Print prefixes and suffixes on tagboard or file cards. Pass out the cards to students. Write root words on sentence strips. Hold one root word card in front of the class. A student who has a prefix or suffix that would make a new word comes up to the front of the class and places the card in front of or behind the root word card. The student pronounces the word, and, if correct, the student may take the root word. Invite students to use the word in a sentence and, if necessary, have them discuss the meaning of the word.
7. As you introduce a new suffix, prepare several flip strips. To create a flip strip, print root words on the front left-hand side of colored strips of construction paper. On the back, print suffixes so that when the paper is folded a new word appears. Give the flip strips to students to practice making words with suffixes. Examples of flip strips are found on the following page.

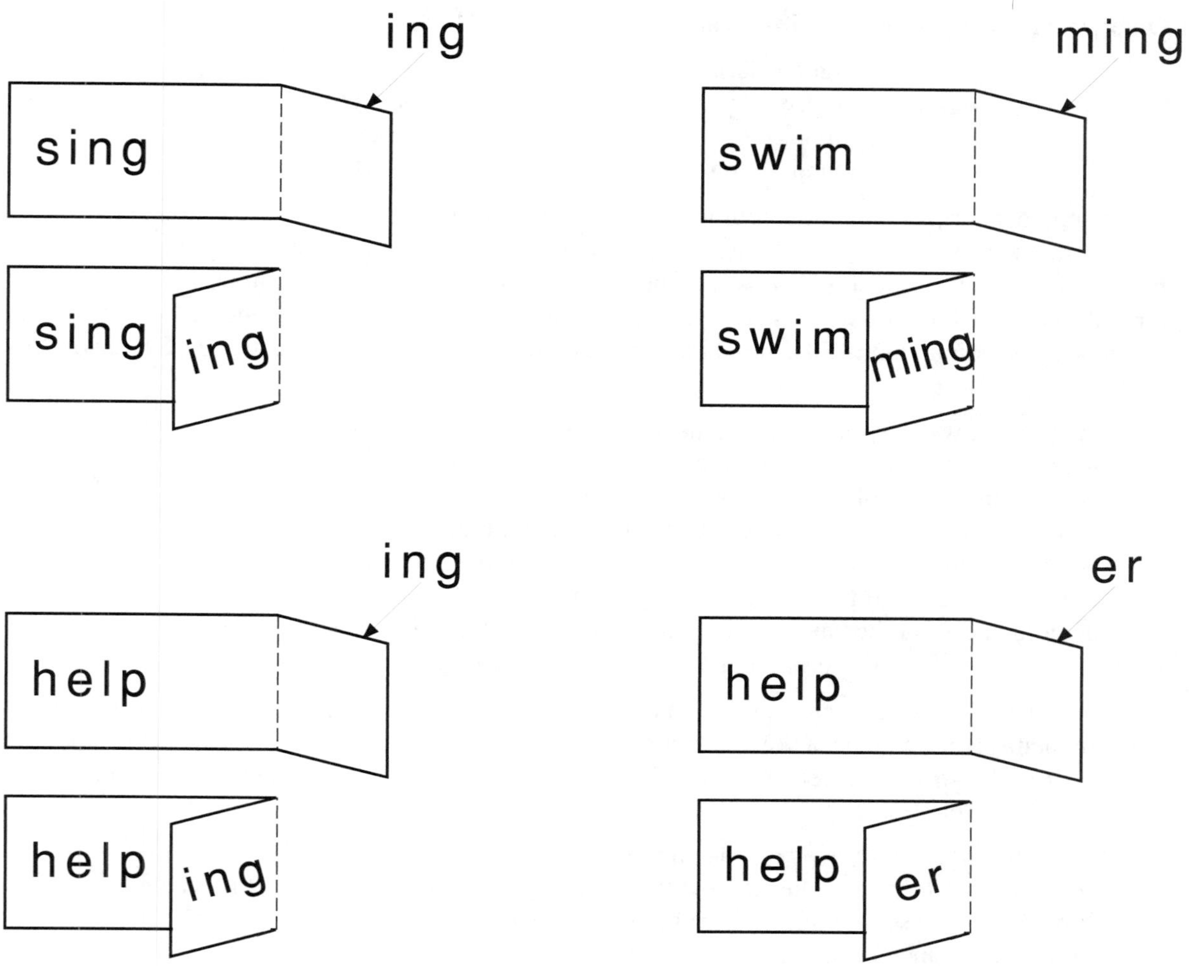

8. For compound words, make two lists. Write half of the compound words in List A and the other half of the compound words in List B. The words should not be in the correct order. Have students draw a line from a word in List A to a word in List B to form a complete compound word. Invite students to use the compound word in an oral or written sentence.

List A	List B
break	out
day	day
birth	fast
sell	light

9. Place several headings on the chalkboard (for example, places, people, rides, things, times). Have students write compound words that will fit under each heading.
10. Provide a series of words and invite students to write the antonym of each word and then combine the words to make a compound word. A completed example is given below.

rest + in
work + out = workout

Other words to use include the following.

night + dark	adult + stand
empty + front	death + night
tall + go	over + sky
mend + slow	laugh + adult

11. Make sentence strips containing compound words. The sentences should be constructed so they can be illustrated easily. Each student chooses a sentence strip. Have the student copy the sentence on the bottom of a sheet of paper and illustrate the sentence. The picture of the compound word should be circled in red. Display the papers so that students can read each other's sentences, look at the circled pictures of the compound words, and then find the compound words in the sentences. See the following sample sentences.

    - The goldfish was swimming in a tank with a red fish and a green fish.
    - There was a hammer, a box of nails, and a piece of wood on the workbench.
    - The blue and red airplane flew above the trees and houses.
    - The typewriter is on the desk next to the lamp and a picture of a family.
    - The big, brown bear climbed the hill to get closer to the beehive.
    - Three boats were sailing near the shore by the lighthouse.
    - The golden dog sat between the doghouse and a big, tall tree.
    - I have a sandwich, popcorn, an apple, and carrots for lunch.

12. Prepare a list of sentences with a blank space for a compound word. Invite students to read the sentence to themselves and have a volunteer suggest a compound word that makes sense. Have the student explain how the word was selected, and, if it is correct, write it in the blank space. Some possible sentences are given here.

    - At my *(birthday)* party we had cake and ice cream.
    - There was not a cloud in the sky and the *(sunshine)* streamed in through the windows.
    - We did not go to school in the morning, but we did go in the *(afternoon).*
    - The jets and planes flew in and out of the *(airport).*
    - At the movies we had buttered *(popcorn).*
    - The man's boots left deep *(footprints)* in the snow.
    - My sister's chore is to put the dishes into the *(dishwasher).*
    - The woman told me to walk on the *(sidewalk)* and not on the grass.
    - The dog ran into the *(doghouse).*
    - The football player threw the *(football).*
    - I put stamps on the letters and dropped them into the *(mailbox).*
    - At recess, the boys and girls played on the *(playground).*
    - Because it was raining, I wore my *(raincoat).*
    - When the lights went out, my father got a *(flashlight)* so we could see.
    - When Tom was sick, he had to stay *(inside)* the house.
    - Frosty is a famous *(snowman).*
    - The train moves on the *(railroad)* track.
    - I squeezed toothpaste on my *(toothbrush).*

13. Give students several endings (e.g., *-it*, *-ed*, *-ip*, *-et*). Have students select one or more endings and then think of a beginning letter or blend that they could add at the beginning to make different words. Students could make words by themselves, with a partner, or in small groups. After several minutes, review the lists, have students use the words in sentences, and clarify or explain word meanings as necessary.

Group Ball Toss. Draw a target on a piece of felt with a marker and write in root words. Glue a strip of velcro around a lightweight ball. Mount the target on the chalkboard and beside the target write word endings. Divide students into teams and let them take turns throwing the ball at the target. When the ball hits the target, the student reads the word closest to the ball and then writes the word on the chalkboard with one of the inflectional endings. If the word is correct, the team scores one point. The students can play until one team gets 20 points (McCormick, 1995).

Compound Word Dominoes. Write two compound words on tagboard or index cards cut in half. Write the words facing the short sides and draw a line down the center. Distribute the cards to four students. Have students take turns making compound words by matching the words with two different cards. A list of compound words that might be useful can be found in Chapter 3 Resources (page 276).

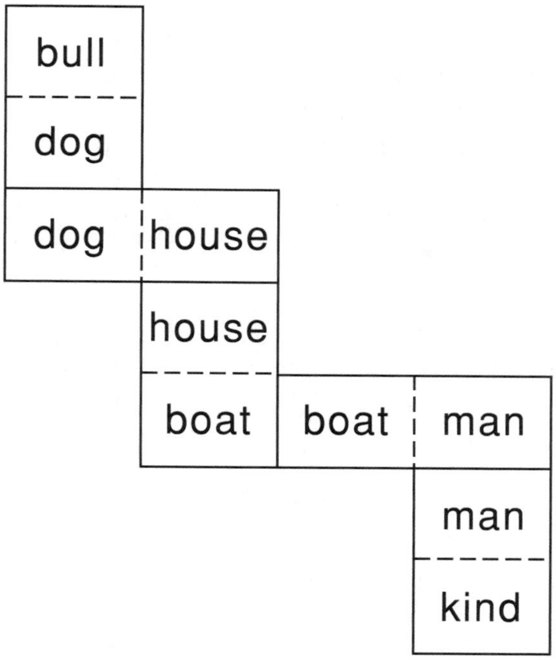

Twister. Draw 20 large circles on a 4' x 6' oilcloth and attach words written on cards in the center of these circles. Using two teams, have students from team 1 put a hand on one word and a foot on a second word of a compound word. Then the student places a second hand on a word and a second foot on another word that would make sense as a compound word. If the words are correct, a student from team 2 tries the same activity. The team 2 student, however, needs to manipulate around the student from team 1. Then another student from team 1 joins the two students on the Twister board and so on until no more words can be formed.

The Affix Stopped Me. Make a set of 50 game cards. (See Chapter 3 Resources on page 276 for a list of compound words.) On 40 of the cards, write compound words. On the remaining 10 cards, write words with affixes. Shuffle the cards and place the deck on the table. Each student takes a turn flipping the cards over one at a time. As each card is turned, the student reads the card and determines if it is a compound word or a word with affixes. If the student correctly identifies the word as a compound word, the student pronounces the word and, if correct, keeps the card and turns the next card over. The turn continues until the student incorrectly identifies a card or when a word with an affix is uncovered. Continue until the cards are gone. The winner is the student with the most cards. This game is intended for a small group of four or five students. If more students want to play, the number of cards must be increased. Variations of the game include pronouncing the word correctly and using it in a sentence.

One, Two, or Three. Make a deck of 20 cards with each card containing three sentences. One sentence will contain a compound word. Two sentences will not have compound words. Number the sentences 1, 2, and 3. Vary the cards so that the compound word sentences appear in all three locations. To play the game, shuffle the cards and place the deck on the table. The first student takes the top card, reads the sentences, and decides which sentence contains a compound word. If the student correctly identifies the first sentence as containing the compound word, the student receives one marker: a button or a bean. If the second sentence contains the compound word, the student receives two markers for correctly identifying it. If it is in the third sentence, the student receives three markers, and the turn ends. If the student is incorrect, no markers are earned and the turn is over. The winner is the student with the most markers when all the cards have been used. Variations of the game could include sentences with affixes.

Four in a Row. Choose 20 compound words and write them on the chalkboard. Each student divides a piece of paper into 16 squares. Then have students choose 16 of the 20 words and write them in the boxes. A box of markers will be needed. To play the game, say one of the words in a sentence. Have students listen for the compound word in the sentence and look for it on their paper. If they find it, they should cover the space with a marker. Continue creating sentences for the compound words until a student has four marked squares in a row. A variation of the game could involve a student creating the sentences.

Wheel Spin. Construct two circles of tagboard, one smaller than the other, and fasten them in the center with a brad. Print a verb on the smaller circle and print the endings *s, er, ed,* and *ing* on the larger circle. Several examples are illustrated below.

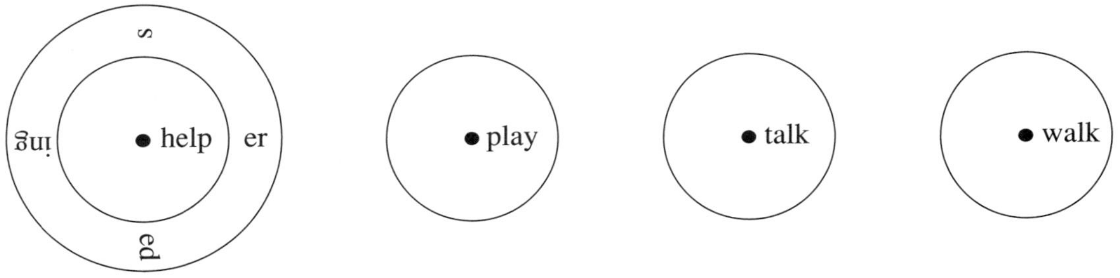

Two students can play. One student spins the top circle and pronounces the word that is made. The other student uses the word in a sentence. Students can change the top wheel to gain practice with other words.

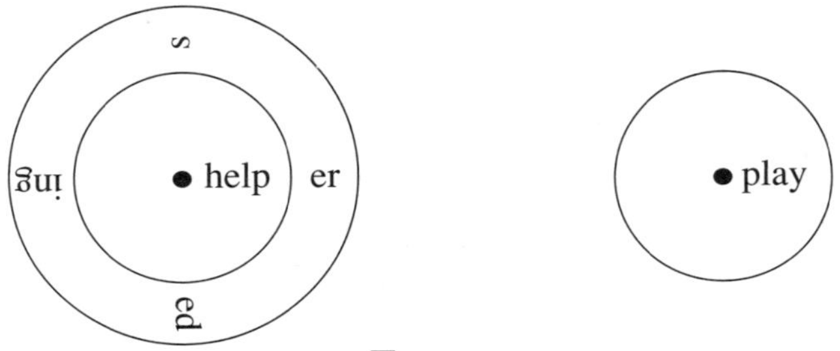

Section 3.5

Basic Sight (High-Frequency) Words

Behavior Observed → **Anticipated Outcome**

The student cannot identify basic sight (high-frequency) words automatically.

The student will be able to identify basic sight (high-frequency) words without hesitation.

Background

There are certain words in the English language that occur regularly in text. Look at the thirteen words below.

a and for he in is it of that the to was you

These words account for approximately 25% of all of the words in school texts. Because they occur so frequently, they are called *basic sight words* or *high-frequency words*. You probably noticed that the words are difficult to define or describe. That's because they are *function words*—words that are used to connect other words. They have little meaning themselves. Obviously, students who can read basic sight words automatically will have a much easier time reading text, but because basic sight words are abstract, they can be difficult to teach and learn.

The 13 words listed above are not the only high-frequency words in the English language. In fact, 109 words make up over 50% of the words used in school texts, and only 5,000 words make up 90% of the words in texts (Adams, 1990b). Although that may seem like a lot of words, remember that a typical high school senior will have a vocabulary of approximately 40,000 words and that students generally learn 3,000 words per year. Knowing how quickly students learn words makes the task of teaching sight words much more manageable. You may be wondering what words make up the high frequency list of words. There are several word lists in the Chapter 3 Resources (pages 253–254; 265; 279) for you to use in selecting sight words to teach.

Because more and more teachers fuse instruction in reading and writing, you might also be interested in the most frequent words students use in their writing. Look at these 10 words.

I and the a to was in it of my

According to a research study conducted by Hillerich (1978), these 10 words account for over 25% of the words used by approximately 3,000 students in grades one through six. These

Thirteen words make up approximately 25% of all words used in school texts.

words have great overlap with the 13 most frequently occurring words in the English language. Students should be taught to recognize and spell these words in the beginning stages of the instructional program. In addition, the words in the Revised Dolch List and the Alphabetized List of the 100 Words Used Most Frequently by Students in Their Writing in Chapter 3 Resources (pages 254; 279) comprise over half the words students read and write. These lists may be useful for instruction. It is important that students learn to read and spell these words as soon as possible. The reason is clear: these high-frequency words are a critical, though not sufficient, component for efficient and effective literacy.

WORD WALL

1. Decide which words to include on your Word Wall (Cunningham, 2000). Your Word Wall should include about 100 to 120 words by the end of the school year that students use frequently in their reading and writing. A Word Wall begins with five words, and you should add about five words each week. Consider words from two lists included in the Chapter 3 Resources: Revised Dolch List (page 254) and Alphabetized List of the 100 Words Used Most Frequently by Students in Their Writing (page 279). Teachers in the primary grades often begin with students' names and then add common words students need for reading and writing.
2. Write the words in big, black letters on different colored paper. Be sure to use a variety of colors for words that are frequently confused (*then, when*) or words that are pronounced the same (*to, two, too*). Some teachers cut around the shape of the word to provide another clue for students. Place the words in alphabetical order where all students can see them easily.
3. Begin the activity by having students number a sheet of paper from 1 to 5. Pronounce each word, use it in a sentence, and have a student locate and point to the word on the Word Wall. Then have students clap and chant the spelling of the word before they write the word. Repeat this basic process for each of the remaining four words.
4. Lead students in checking the accuracy of the words they have written and make corrections as needed. The charting, writing, and checking can take about 10 minutes. As the school year progresses, students become more proficient in this basic activity, and a few minutes can be spent on an activity (see number 5) using the back of the paper on which the five words were written.
5. Consider some of these activities that Cunningham (2000, p. 64) identifies as the "most popular and productive."
   - **Easy Rhyming:** Teach students how Word-Wall words that rhyme help them pronounce and spell words (for example, *be, he, she, we*). Use the words in context and have students write the words.
   - **Easy Ending Activity:** Help students add an ending to five Word-Wall words (for example, *s* to *boy, car, girl, school, tree; ed* to *ask, want, need, play, walk*). Other related activities include *ing* or *er.*
   - **Harder Ending Activity:** Work on how to spell five Word-Wall words when different endings are needed. Provide a sentence and have students find the word on the Word Wall, identify the end, decide how the word is spelled, and write it on their papers *(wanted, playing, walks).*
   - **Combine Rhyme and Endings:** Say a sentence containing a word that rhymes with a Word-Wall word (for example, My bicycle *brakes* are broken). Model how you can find *make* on the Word Wall, change the beginning to make *brake*, and add an *s* to make *brakes*. Have students spell the word aloud before writing it.
   - **Mind Reader:** Think of a word on the Word Wall, write it on a piece of paper without students seeing it, and give students five clues to the word. Have students write a word after each clue. By the fifth clue, all students should have read your mind. An example follows.
     1. It's one of the words on our Word Wall.
     2. It has five letters.
     3. It begins with *n*.
     4. Both vowels are *e*.

5. It makes sense in this sentence: I ____________________ walked on the moon.

Then show students the word (*never*) and find out which students read your mind and wrote *never* next to numeral 4, 3, 2, or 1.

6. Refer to Cunningham's (2000) book for many additional ideas. Remember that the real power in a Word Wall comes from **using it**—not just having it. That means using Word-Wall activities on a daily basis for about 10 minutes. Remember that Word-Wall words should be spelled correctly in students' writing.

Strategy 2 SECTION 3.5

EXPLICIT INSTRUCTION

1. Select a word that students want to learn to read by sight. The word may be one that is in a story the class is reading, or it may be one that students need for writing.
2. Write the word on the chalkboard and ask students to write the word on a card. If a student is unable to copy the word correctly, you may want to write it for him or her. Chant the word.
3. Locate a story or create a language experience story that uses the word several times.
4. Read the story to the class. Each time you say the sight word, ask students to raise their cards.
5. Ask students to read the word on their cards, saying the word and then each letter.
6. Cut the word into letters and ask students to arrange them to make up the word. Place the letters in envelopes so that students can practice arranging the letters at other times during the day.
7. Write several sentences on the chalkboard with a blank space for the word. Ask students to write the word in the blank and then read the sentences out loud.
8. Give students text in which the word under study occurs frequently. Ask students to carefully notice the word while reading.

Strategy 3 SECTION 3.5

PATTERN BOOKS

1. Select a pattern book that emphasizes the word you want students to learn. An extensive list of pattern books can be found in Part C on the CD.
2. Read the book aloud to the students. If possible, secure a big book version so students can follow along.
3. Read the book again, asking students to join in whenever they can. Point to each word as it is being read.
4. Ask students to take turns reading the book with you and to each other.
5. Write the text of the book on sentence strips or ask students to write it for you. Then ask students to read the text from sentence strips.

6. Write the word being studied on word cards. Ask students to match the word to the sentence strips.
7. Cut the sentence strips into words. Mix up the words and ask students to arrange them in order.
8. Take out the word being studied from the sentence and ask students to write the word from memory.
9. Ask students to create a sentence using the targeted word.
10. Create a rebus story using the word under study. Draw pictures for the nouns so that students must read the high frequency words.

Strategy 4 SECTION 3.5

LEARNING THROUGH REPETITION

1. Use one of the word lists from the Revised Dolch List (pages 254–264) from the Chapter 3 Resources and have the student read the words. While the student reads, record miscues. Encourage the student to say "skip" or "pass" whenever he or she finds a word too difficult. The object is to recognize the basic sight words immediately.
2. Make a set of flash cards for the student with the words that were missed. (The list of words can be printed on card stock and cut out.) You might include words that the student hesitated on and the ones missed. Generally, one second or less means the basic sight word is known. Select three to five missed words for initial teaching.
3. Present three to five words to the student, saying the word as you place the card on the table facing the student. After the student seems to recognize the words in that position, move the cards around until automaticity is achieved with these words. Keep these words separate from the rest of the deck.
4. Begin the next session with a review of the words learned in the previous session. Any missed words will be reviewed again in this session. Place known cards to the side. Add new cards for any missed words and review these using the same procedure as stated above. Keep these cards separate from the known and unknown piles. (An envelope can be a great way to keep the cards organized. Clip the words that are missed or newly learned on the outside of the envelope. Keep the new cards clipped together inside with the learned ones in another clip.)
5. In subsequent sessions, review the three to five words first, add them to the known pile, and then have the student pronounce all the words. Unknown words are taken out each time and reviewed. If there are still new words to learn, enough are added to make three to five words that are taught to the student.
6. After the student has learned the whole set, review them until the student can automatically recognize the words three times in a row. Send the cards home for continued practice and review.
7. Retest the student with the word list again to check mastery in another print form. Words that are missed can be added to a new set of cards from the next level of sight words after they are tested. Follow the same procedure with the new word list.

8. Other activities that can be done with the cards are listed below.
   - Do word sorts (number of letters, beginning sounds, vowel sounds, etc.).
   - Put the words in alphabetical order, saying the words as they are moved around.
   - Play concentration with a student at the same level. Make two sets of word cards for the student.
   - Find the words in a poem or book, on a Word Wall, or around print in the room.
   - Learn to spell the words.
   - Use one or more words in a sentence.
9. As words are mastered, use the words in phrases so the student is given an opportunity to recognize and practice the words in context. Later, short sentences containing high-frequency words and nouns can be read by the student to help promote confidence and automaticity. Create phrases and sentences from the Revised Dolch List (page 254) and High-Frequency Nouns (page 265) found in Chapter 3 Resources. A few phrases and sentences are provided below.

   a long day   their old dog   going home   over the top

   Will you help me?   She saw him.   The book is in my hand.

Practice and Reinforcement Activities

Basic sight (high-frequency) words need to be practiced many times to become automatic. The following activities are designed to reinforce sight words.

1. Place the sight words on a Word Wall as explained in Section 3.5, Strategy 1.
2. Have students put selected sight word cards in alphabetical order.
3. Have students sort the words by categories. They may make up imaginative categories for the words, because most of them have little concrete meaning. Sample categories for some of the words on the Revised Dolch List (page 254) in Chapter 3 Resources are shown in the box.

Category	Examples
Numbers	one, two, three
Other People	he, her, him, she, them
Talk Words	call, say, tell, ask
Action Words	run, leave, put, walk
Question Words	who, what, when, would
Size/Shape Words	big, little, long, round
Color Words	black, blue, white, red
Temperature Words	cold, hot, warm

4. Ask students to find the words in texts around the room. For example, the word *and* may be on a "Friends and Neighbors" bulletin board.
5. Use word games such as Bingo, Hangman, Word Dominoes, Word Checkers, or Go Fish.
6. Have students use the buddy system to practice word cards.
7. Place word cards in a file box to use as a word bank of known words for writing.
8. Prepare cards that contain an illustrated sentence with the basic sight word underlined. Cards containing words and phrases may also be used.
9. Develop line searches. Be sure that the words only go from left to right. Ask students to circle the hidden word among each line of letters. Students can also be asked to use the word in an oral or a written sentence. Following are examples of line searches.

m f d(b i g)k d d s a(b l u e)d s d e(t h a t)d s d e s d(w h e n)d s

10. Use familiar rhymes to help students learn basic sight words in a meaningful context. Write a rhyme on the chalkboard or on sentence strips. Write the basic sight words in a color that is different from the color of the rest of the rhyme. In the following example, the basic sight words are in italics.

    Humpty Dumpty
    Sat *on a* wall.
    Humpty Dumpty
    Had a great fall.

11. Chant the spelling of words. Clap together as the class spells a word out loud.
12. Have students write words. Writing provides a kinesthetic mode to help students learn and remember words.
13. Have students unscramble words they are learning as in the following example.

tge	flul	mrfo	egno	tgo	og	dogo
get	*full*	_____	_____	_____	_____	_____

14. Use a tachistoscope (a quick-exposure device) or cards to briefly expose a word, phrase, or sentence. Give students repeated practice over several days.
15. Provide sentences where the student writes the correct word in the blank. Provide choices for the answer.

    I like ______ that ______ one.
    not that came

    He ____________________ do his work.
    any didn't about

    The night seemed ____________________ long.
    must very no

    He ____________________ many nice things.
    such when does

16. Have students locate the most common basic sight words (*a, and, for, he, in, is, it, of, that, the, to, was, you*) in newspapers or magazines. This activity will help students realize how frequently such words occur. Use a selection about 100 words in length.
17. Create "flexible" sentences using words from the Revised Dolch List (page 254) and the list of High-Frequency Nouns (page 265). Students can read the many different sentences with a partner when the words and phrases in the boxes are inserted. Two examples are shown below.

Example 1 The ^ dog liked fish. ←

little black
good
best big blue
small kind

in the morning
but never got enough
of any kind

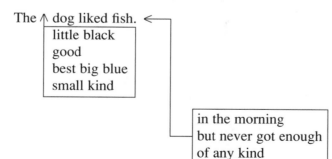

Example 2 The ↑ boy found ↓ ↑ short tables at school.

big	six	new
small	two	white
fast	many	other
first	four	round
little	both	short

18. To aid in the practice of words such as *in, on, under, over, behind,* get a cup and straw. Place the straw in various positions and ask students to use a word that answers the question, "Where is the straw?" Alternative ideas include a stuffed animal and a cardboard box.
19. Give students plenty of opportunities to read lots of easy materials.

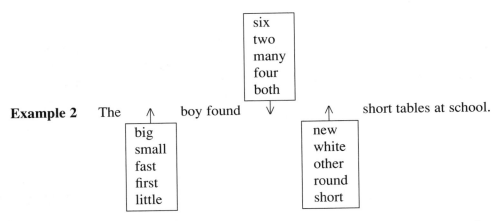

Section **3.6**

Sight Vocabulary

Behavior Observed → **Anticipated Outcome**

The student's sight vocabulary is so limited that it interferes with reading fluency. → The student will increase his or her sight vocabulary.

Background

Students who know words by sight are able to pronounce them automatically. A large sight vocabulary enables students to read fluently and to focus their attention on making sense of the passage. It also helps students use other reading strategies, such as context clues, more effectively.

A student's sight vocabulary, then, is composed of all of the words recognized in an instant. Some words recognized on sight occur very frequently in printed materials and are often referred to as basic sight or high-frequency words (for example, *when, then, the*). These words are a vital part of the student's sight vocabulary but are a subset of the total number of sight words a student may recognize. The partial example to the right shows some high-frequency words in relation to the student's sight vocabulary.

Total Sight Vocabulary*

when	elephant	bookmark
big	Illinois	Bryan
there	Ms. Grant	grandma
so	Garfield	library
was	baseball	chocolate
where	video	Hannah

*High-frequency words are in bold print.

Basic sight or high-frequency words tend to be abstract words. The other words that comprise sight vocabulary usually refer to real things or are adjectives or adverbs. This difference generally permits greater variety in teaching and practicing words that are not basic sight words.

When selecting words to teach as sight words, remember that many repetitions of the word may be necessary before the word becomes part of the student's sight vocabulary. Gates (1931) found that average students may need 35 repetitions of a word before recognition becomes automatic. The crucial variable is often the meaningfulness of the word to the student. The word *sled,* for example, might become a sight word quickly for a student who uses a sled frequently. A student who has never used a sled may have greater difficulty learning the word.

Strategy 1 SECTION 3.6

SIGHT WORDS

1. When possible, use the actual object or a picture of the word being taught. Have a student identify the object. If you have no access to a visual representation of the word, begin with the next step.
2. Pronounce the word and write it on the chalkboard. Have students pronounce it. If necessary, discuss the meaning of the word with the students. Have students try to think of synonyms for the word. Students should also be encouraged to relate the word to their experiences.
3. Encourage students to use the word in different sentences. Write some of these sentences on the chalkboard and underline the word being taught. If a word has more than one meaning, be sure sentences are provided that exemplify these meanings.
4. If students are confusing two or more words (for example, *chair* and *chew*), compare the words by having students point out similarities and differences between the words. Students might also close their eyes and picture the word that is being taught.

Strategy 2 SECTION 3.6

STUDENT-DICTATED STORIES

1. The language experience approach (Hall, 1981; Stauffer, 1980) uses student-dictated stories to create reading materials. It is based on an experience and can be used with individuals or groups.

2. Share a photo, illustration, or experience with an individual student or a group of students. For example, you might use a picture of children playing in a park. In this example, a group of students will create the story.
3. Elicit comments from students relating to the picture. Following discussion, invite the students to dictate sentences that could form the story. As sentences are shared by students, write them on chart paper. Below is a possible story.

    There are children in the park. (Troy)
    The children are having fun. (Angel)
    Some children are swinging. (Mati)
    Some children are playing tag. (Eric)
    A girl is kicking a ball. (Coty)
    A boy is sitting under a tree. (Reann)
    I wonder if they will have a picnic. (Kyle)

4. Read each sentence and ask students if any changes are needed. As students share ideas, make agreed-upon changes directly on the chart paper.
5. When the story is complete, read each sentence to the students and have them read it after you. Use a pointer so students can focus on each word as they read it.
6. Recopy the story at a later time. In the next session, read the story with students. Some possible areas of focus are listed below.
    - reading the story together
    - focusing on particular words or phrases
    - using the story to help teach or reinforce a particular phonic element
    - asking comprehension questions (e.g., Who can read the sentence that tells what the girl did?)

7. In subsequent lessons, the story can be written on individual sentence strips and placed in a logical order. Sentences can also be cut apart in phrases and/or individual words so students can put the words and/or phrases in proper order.
8. Individual word banks can be prepared by using two envelopes for each student: Words I Know and Words I'm Learning.
9. Student-dictated stories can also be made into books and placed in the class library. The books can be taken home by students to share with family members.
10. Informational student-dictated stories can also be developed on a wide variety of topics that support the ongoing curriculum or class routines (e.g., steps to follow in a fire drill, how to check out books, proper care for our class animal).

Strategy 3 SECTION 3.6

RHYMES, POEMS, AND SONGS

1. Select a rhyme, poem, or song that most of your students know. You can also choose something that is likely to be of interest to them. Begin with something easy to learn because of the rhyme or rhythm. The example for this lesson is "Jack and Jill."
2. Help students learn the rhyme by oral repetition over a period of several days.
3. When the rhyme is known orally, write it on chart paper or on an overhead transparency. Tell students that the rhyme they know is now printed for their closer inspection.
4. Read a line or sentence, pointing to each word. Then have students echo it back. Repeat the process again, followed by having the class or group read it together.
5. Take time to discuss the content and vocabulary. For example, in "Jack and Jill," discussion will probably be needed to clarify or explain the meanings of *fetch*, *pail*, and *crown*.
6. If appropriate, focus on a word that can be the basis for further word study and vocabulary development (e.g., *pail*). For example you might say something like what follows.

   Let's see if you can use your knowledge of other sounds and change the first letter of pail *to make other words. For example, if I erase the* p *in* pail *and add an* n, *I will make the word* nail*—something you can pound with a hammer. What ideas do you have? Look at the alphabet at the front of the room to get ideas for letters to try.*

7. Elicit student ideas, guiding and clarifying as needed. Write the new words on the chalkboard. Then have volunteers use the words in sentences. Possible words that can be made by students are listed below.

pail	tail	sail
rail	nail	jail
Gail	mail	fail

8. Words that are judged to be of greater frequency and usefulness can be written on index cards for further practice. If a word can be represented by a picture or illustration, place it on the other side of the card to aid recognition. Be sure to provide ample practice opportunities in other contexts (e.g., phrases and sentences).

Practice and Reinforcement Activities

1. See Section 3.5 for additional teaching strategies and activities.
2. Students should read many books that are easy for them. There are many books appropriate for students who have limited sight vocabularies. See Part C on the CD for a list of pattern books.
3. For words that can be represented by a picture, print the word on the front of a card under the picture. The back of the card should contain the printed word. You can use logos from stores and businesses for some sight words.
4. A list of leveled books for students in the early stages of reading has been provided by Gunning (1998). Several titles recommended for emerging to beginning readers are listed below.

   Avery, M. W., & Avery, D.M. (1995). *What is Beautiful?* Berkeley, CA: Tricycle.
   Cocca-Leffler, M. (1994). *What a Pest!* New York: Grosset and Dunlap.
   dePaola, T. (1994). *Kit and Kat.* New York: Grosset and Dunlap.
   Farjeon, E. (1996). *Cats Sleep Anywhere.* Scranton, PA: HarperCollins.
   Ziefert, H. (1995). *Nicky, 1-2-3.* New York: Puffin.

   Gunning (2000) has also compiled a list of "best books" for grades one through six.

5. Provide many varied opportunities for students to interact with print. Use some of the following techniques.
   - sustained silent reading
   - read-along stories and books
   - repeated readings
   - shared reading
   - poems, songs, and rhymes

How Many? Have students write the words they need to practice on cards. Each word should have at least four cards. The students can then play the card game "How Many?" The word cards are shuffled and the deck is placed face down. Students take turns rolling a die to determine how many words are drawn from the deck. Each word is pronounced, placed on the table, and used in a sentence. Any words pronounced incorrectly are returned to the bottom of the deck. The student with the most words wins.

Word Sort. Prepare 10 word cards relating to each of the categories appropriate for the words. Shuffle the cards and deal them to each of the players. Players take turns rolling a die and placing one or two words under the correct category.

Around the World. Using sight word flash cards, show a card to a pair of students. The student who responds correctly first can move on to another student. The object is for a student to make it around the class, or around the world. The winning student can then hold the cards for you while the class resumes play.

Word Hunt. Place several sight word cards around the room. Ask the students to hunt for the cards, reading them aloud when they find one. The student with the most cards wins.

Concentration. Place several pairs of sight word cards face down on a table. Have students take turns uncovering and pronouncing two cards, looking for pairs. When a student finds a pair, he or she pronounces the word and takes the cards. The student with the most pairs of cards wins the game.

Section 3.7

Using Context to Predict Known Words

Behavior Observed →
The student has difficulty using context clues to anticipate a familiar word.

Anticipated Outcome
The student will use context as one reading strategy to anticipate known words.

Background

The context of a word can be the words surrounding it. One of the ways to identify words is to use the other words in the sentence and to make a prediction about what word would make sense. Using context clues to anticipate known words can make reading a more efficient process.

To make a good prediction about a word, the student's prior knowledge and experiences play an important role. For example, consider these sentences.

The dog was chewing on a ____________.

Peaches grow on ____________________.

The baby began to ___________________.

Students with prior knowledge about dogs, peaches, and babies should have little difficulty supplying a word that would make sense in the sentences. These students are able to draw upon their existing knowledge to make a logical prediction about the missing words.

Unfortunately, some students' reading comes to an abrupt halt when they come across a word they don't recognize on sight, even if only one word would make sense in the sentence. For example, peaches only grow on trees. No other response would make sense in the sentence. For the other sentences, however, the student would also need to consider at least the initial sound in the unknown word. For example, the baby began to *sm-* or the baby began to *cr-* would elicit two different responses, each correct in the context. Context clues, therefore, are helpful but should not be considered the only strategy to use when students try to pronounce unfamiliar words.

WORD PREDICTION

1. Before students arrive in the classroom, write several words on the chalkboard and cover them. Develop a sentence containing each word that should be helpful in predicting the covered word. These sentences will be part of the lesson. Some examples are listed below.

Covered Words	Sample Sentence
bark	I heard the dog ________________.
book	I was reading chapter 2 of the ____________.
tree	The squirrel climbed a ____________.
rings	School begins when the bell ____________.
laughed	The joke was funny and I ____________.

2. Tell students that they can sometimes use the other words in a sentence to predict or guess a word they have heard before. Stress that the sentence may contain helpful clues.

3. Point to the card covering the word *bark* and ask students if they know the word behind the card. They may have many ideas, but they are only guessing. Tell students that if that word were in a sentence, they might be able to use sentence clues to make a better guess or prediction. Ask students to be word detectives and focus on the clues in a sentence you are going to write on the chalkboard.

4. Place a line for each word in the sentence and begin to write the sentence as shown below.

   __I__ __heard__ ________ ________ ________.

   After writing *heard,* invite students to predict things they might hear. Write these words on the chalkboard and stress that the words are things that can be heard. Suggest a few additional words (*thunder, smoke, light*) and have students evaluate whether they would be good choices. Model as needed. For example, "*Smoke* would probably not be a good choice, because I don't hear *smoke*. I see *smoke*."

5. Continue writing the sentence on the lines but do not include the last word.

   __I__ __heard__ __the__ __dog__ ________.

   Most students will say the word *bark* after you have written *dog*. Take a moment to have a student explain why the word makes sense. Then uncover the word to confirm it. Invite students to suggest other words that would also make sense (*cry, run, growl*). Confirm such words as good choices. Note that authors can sometimes use several words, but the author decides which words to use.

6. Use some of the other examples as needed. Invite a student to assist you and model as necessary. Be sure to help students realize that they may not always predict the exact word, but they should at least predict words that make sense.

7. Take time to have students create oral or written sentences and omit a specific word in each sentence. Give students an opportunity to share sentences with a partner and make predictions about the missing word.

8. Conclude the lesson by telling students that they can sometimes predict a word in their reading by using the other words in the sentence. Then share a few preselected sentences from books in your classroom and have students listen carefully and try to predict the missing word. An example from *A Prairie Year* (Bannatyne-Cugnet, 1994, p. 4) follows.

   "For Matthew, January means no sleeping in and no Saturday morning cartoons on ________________."

Strategy 2

ADVANCED WORD PREDICTION

1. Consider adapting the approach used in Strategy 1 with younger students by using specific examples from instructional materials. Extend the lesson by including initial letter clues to help students refine their predictions.
2. Be sure students understand that context refers to words around a particular word. Help them realize that sometimes they can use their background knowledge and sense of language to predict a word—even before seeing it in print.
3. Provide an example and guide the process for students. A sample sentence from *The Giver* (Lowry, 1993, p. 78) that might be used follows.

   "The man paused, seeming to search his mind for the right words of ________."
   (description)

4. Write the sentence on the chalkboard or an overhead transparency, replacing the last word with a line. Have students read the sentence silently and think of words that might make sense in the blank. Students should write their ideas on a piece of paper.
5. Ask students to form small groups and share their words. Encourage each group to decide on its best word choices. Take time for students to share their words and reasons for their choices. Write these words on the chalkboard or an overhead transparency.
6. Compliment students on their predictions and then say something like the following.

   You have suggested some good possibilities that fit the context of the sentence. I'm now going to provide a further clue to help you eliminate some of your words and help you refine your predictions. The first letter of the word is d. *Which words can we eliminate? Which words are still possible? Are there any new words you want to suggest?*

7. Continue providing additional letters in *description* until students identify the word. Invite students to share their thinking. Guide the process as necessary.
8. Tell students that the sense of the sentence and letter clues can sometimes be used to help pronounce a word that they have heard before. Repeat the core lesson using other sentences. Include at least one sentence where the context will probably not help predict the word because it is not a known word in students' listening vocabularies. For example, I took a walk near the *quay.* Other sentences for possible use include the following.
   - The job was very *dangerous.*
   - I ran so far that I was *exhausted.*
   - The camper needed to *filter* the liquid.
   - *Fingerprints* can be used to identify a specific person.
   - The sun helped the water *evaporate.*
   - *Flippers* help seals and whales swim.

Practice and Reinforcement Activities

1. Daily routine activities will help students use oral context skills to predict words. Some examples follow.

   Today is ____________________.
   The two students absent are ____________________ and ____________________.

2. Read familiar pattern books to students, pausing at appropriate places so students can predict the missing word. A list of pattern books can be found in Part C on the CD.
3. Make tape recordings of books and omit several words. Give students a copy of the text to underline the words omitted on the tape.
4. Use a book at the students' independent level and mask selected words with removable tape. (Post-it® notes also work well.) Have the students make predictions for the words before the tape is removed. Then remove the tape to see what the author has written. Discuss different responses to determine overall appropriateness.
5. Create or provide a passage from a text in which selected words have been replaced with lines. Instruct students to read the passage and write in their choices of words. Stress that their words should make sense. Later, discuss their choices in conjunction with the words used by the author.
6. Using a text the students will be reading, read several sentences while omitting several words and have students predict the words that have been omitted. Then tell students the words used by the author and develop the idea that it is sometimes possible to predict a word the author will use.
7. Select a text that the students will need to read. Preview the text and determine which words might give the students difficulty. Model how you would use the context to help figure out the words. Think aloud so the students can hear your strategies. Choose at least one example where context is not particularly helpful.
8. List some common topics that students might be asked to read about and encourage them to list words that are likely to appear in the stories. Develop the notion that certain words might be expected to be associated with a particular topic.
9. Present incomplete sentences orally and have students suggest words that would make sense. Begin with sentences in which a large number of meaningful responses are possible and conclude with a sentence in which only a few choices make sense. Help students understand that if they listen to a sentence they can usually think of a word that makes sense. Some possible sentences follow.

   I like to eat ____________________.
   One day of the week is ____________________.
   There is no school on ____________________.

10. Write sentences with a missing word on the chalkboard and have students suggest words that make sense. Supply additional words, including some that do not make sense, and ask students why a particular word is or is not appropriate. Discuss clues within the sentence that may help students make decisions. Underline such clues. For example, in "I like to eat ____________________," the words *like* and *eat* are important clues; *eat* is probably the most important clue. Some additional examples are shown below.

    I was listening to the ____________________. (radio, iPod, music, etc.)
    The old ____________________ was shiny and beautiful. (car, ring, etc.)
    The weather was ____________________. (cool, sunny, rainy, etc.)

Section 3.8

Dictionary: Word Pronunciation

Behavior Observed →
The student is unable to use the dictionary to help pronounce unknown words.

Anticipated Outcome
The student will be able to use the dictionary as one strategy to help pronounce unknown words.

Background

We know that using the dictionary to help pronounce unknown words is a difficult undertaking for many students. There are numerous skills that the students must possess: knowledge of the alphabet and alphabetical sequence, how to use guide words and the pronunciation key, and how to actually apply these skills to arrive at the pronunciation of an unknown word.

The focus of dictionary use in this section is to help students pronounce unknown words. Section 5.6 offers strategies for using the dictionary to help determine the meanings of an unknown word. Sections 3.8 and 5.6 may be taught together.

Dictionary use should be purposeful and meaningful to students. It is seldom the strategy of choice when a word is unknown in either pronunciation or meaning. Other strategies (context, phonics, structural analysis, morphemic analysis) that were taught are the logical and efficient places to begin. When the word is still unknown, a dictionary should be a viable resource. Using a dictionary for pronunciation can be difficult, even for adults. The pronunciation key seems to work well when we can already pronounce the word. When the word is unknown, however, the pronunciation key often becomes very challenging. The goal in using the pronunciation key is to enable students to associate various sounds with letters and letter combinations in an effort to try to say the word and hopefully recognize the word because it has been heard before. If the word is unfamiliar, students will be unable to decide whether it was pronounced correctly. An expert source (you or another student) would be needed to confirm the correct pronunciation.

The use of a pronunciation key, pronunciation symbols, or phonetic respellings to help pronounce unknown words is a complex skill that requires good instruction, guided practice opportunities, and plenty of encouragement to students as they apply what was taught. The teaching strategies in this section represent some useful beginnings. Be sure to adapt and extend the strategies so they are meaningful and useful to your students.

ARRANGEMENT OF ALPHABET IN DICTIONARIES

1. Be sure students know the alphabet in sequence. If the alphabet is above the chalkboard, use it to visually demonstrate what alphabetical sequence means. Then tell students that the words in a dictionary are arranged in alphabetical sequence or order. Have students survey their dictionaries to confirm this arrangement.

2. Take time to develop the understanding that not all letters encompass the same number of words. For example, help students locate the number of pages devoted to words beginning with *s* and *x*. They will see that there are more *s* words. Use other examples as needed. Tell students that approximately one-fourth of all the words are covered by the letters a through d; the remaining three-fourths of the words are covered by the following groups of letters: e through l, m through r, and s through z. Present this information in a chart like that shown below.

a-d	e-l	m-r	s-z
a b c d	e f g h i j k l	m n o p q r	s t u v w x y z

3. Model how this information can be used to find where a word is located. You might say the following.

   If I want to look up the word language, *I can see that* l *words are near the middle of the dictionary* (point to the l in the chart). *I can then open my dictionary to about the middle to find the* l *words.*

4. Invite students to use their dictionaries and try to open them to the middle to see if *l* words are there. Show students what to do if they open to a different set of words. Model as needed. For example, you might say the following.

   When I opened my dictionary to find the l words for language, I was in the n *section, because I see words beginning with* n *at the top of the page. By looking at the chart, I see I need to turn the pages toward the front of the dictionary.* (Turn more to the front.) *Yes, now I've found the* l *section.*

5. Use numerous examples with students to practice finding the general place in a dictionary where specific words could be found. The goal of this activity is to locate the general area, not the specific word. Invite students to suggest words and locate the general area of the dictionary where the words can be found. Some possible words to use are listed below.

ball	run	noon	infest	pot
energy	contest	unicorn	solar	fortify

6. Conclude the lesson by asking students where their names could be found if they were listed in a dictionary. Refer to the chart and have students gather in one of four groups (a-d, e-l, m-r, or s-z). Students could group themselves in three different ways for practice: first names, last names, and middle names.

ALPHABETICAL ORDER

1. Tell students that words in a dictionary are arranged in alphabetical order (*a* to *z*) by first letter and then second letter, and so on. Then tell students that you are going to help them learn how to find words in a dictionary.
2. Use the names of two students whose names begin with the same first letter and write their names on the chalkboard. The following names will serve as examples.

   Jerry
   Jana

3. Explain that because both names begin with the same letter, you go to the second letter and ask, "Which letter comes first in the alphabet—*e* or *a*?" Point to the two letters on an alphabet wall chart so students can see which letter comes first. Because *a* comes before *e* in the alphabet, *Jana* would come before *Jerry* if the words were to be placed in alphabetical order. Place these two words in alphabetical order on the chalkboard.
4. Ask for volunteers whose names begin with the same letter to come forward and print their names on the chalkboard. Repeat the above process and, if needed, show how you would go to the third or fourth letter of the names. Several examples follow.

   Jane
   Jana
   Jamall

   Have students make a name card and practice with classmates whose names begin with the same first letter. Name cards for both first and last names can be used.

5. Then have about one-half of the students arrange themselves in alphabetical order by first name. Invite classmates at their seats to help verify the order and ask questions when needed. Using last names, repeat the activity with the remaining group of students.
6. Transfer this knowledge to the dictionary by supplying several words on cards and having students put the words in alphabetical order. Once correct alphabetical order is achieved, tell students the page numbers in their dictionaries where each word can be found and have students check the page to find the word to confirm alphabetical order. Consider using only guide words from students' dictionaries in the initial practice exercises. Two sets of examples are shown below, but you should select words from your students' dictionaries.

crown, p. 173	dachshund, p. 179
crutch, p. 174	dahlia, p. 180
cyclist, p. 179	dapper, p. 181

7. Provide students with more practice but increase the difficulty as appropriate. Include three or four words that appear on the same page of the students' dictionaries and have students put them in alphabetical order. When they are finished, tell students the page numbers where the words are found so they can check whether the words were alphabetized correctly.

daisy	daffodil	daddy-longlegs	(p. 180)
example	exact	excellent	(p. 246)
fossil	foul	forty	(p. 281)

   Keep the focus on understanding alphabetical order, not actually looking up words. The next lesson will help students use guide words in a dictionary to help locate words.

8. To provide practice in using guide words, give students the actual guide words and page numbers from several pages of their dictionaries. In a second column, provide words and have students indicate on what page the word would be found. After completing the exercise, students can self-check their work by consulting dictionaries and noting whether they were correct. A sample is shown below.

Guide Words and Page	Word	Page	Were You Correct?
close-club, 134	collect	______	______ yes ______ no
collar-colon, 139	compass	______	______ yes ______ no
compare-complain, 145	cloth	______	______ yes ______ no
compost-concern, 147	concept	______	______ yes ______ no
	complain	______	______ yes ______ no
	collier	______	______ yes ______ no
	cloud	______	______ yes ______ no
	compete	______	______ yes ______ no
	cologne	______	______ yes ______ no
	compress	______	______ yes ______ no
	clover	______	______ yes ______ no

Practice and Reinforcement Activities

1. Use daily opportunities in the classroom, such as the following activities, to help students practice alphabetical order.
   - Have students put three spelling words beginning with the same letter in alphabetical order.
   - Ask students who are wearing a particular color of clothing to line up in alphabetical order.
   - Invite students to offer short lists of words (states, birds, games) that classmates could put in alphabetical order.
2. Make a chart like the following example.

a-d	e-l	m-r	s-z
a b c d	e f g h i j k l	m n o p q r	s t u v w x y z

Have students tab (using Post-it® notes) these areas in their dictionaries: the beginning of the *e, m,* and *s* words. Tell them the page numbers where to place the tabs. Then have them use the chart along with their dictionary tabs to locate the general **area** of the dictionary where words could be found. Begin with areas in the dictionary that are easier to find and remind students to use their tabs. Some possible words to use are listed below.

accordion	mailbox	reel
zebra	scooter	dimple
equator	bicycle	quill

GAMES

Envelope Alphabet. Prepare a group of envelopes, each with 10 to 15 index cards to be arranged in alphabetical order. Have the students take an envelope, remove the cards, and place them in correct alphabetical order. The game can be made self-checking by numbering the cards on the back or putting an answer sheet inside the envelope. Number the envelopes and make the higher numbers increasingly difficult to arrange. Three increasingly difficult lists are given below in alphabetical order.

List 1	List 5	List 10
1. almost	1. about	1. hinge
2. for	2. after	2. hint
3. happy	3. back	3. hip
4. just	4. because	4. hippopotamus
5. pretty	5. day	5. hire
6. red	6. did	6. his
7. street	7. do	7. hiss
8. then	8. we	8. history
9. where	9. will	9. hit
10. yellow	10. would	10. hive

Strategy 3 SECTION 3.8

GUIDE WORDS

1. Ask students to open their dictionaries to a predetermined page. Direct their attention to the top of the page where the two guide words are found (for example, *cook* and *copra*).
2. Tell students that guide words will help them determine whether a particular word can be found on that page just by using the guide words. Show students that *cook* is the first word or entry on that page and *copra* is the last word or entry. Have students turn to other pages in their dictionaries to confirm this basic information about guide words.
3. Then tell students that you will help them learn to use guide words. Use the example provided or preselect several students' names that begin with the same letter and choose two names as guide words. Add additional names if needed. Then write the two names on the chalkboard or an overhead transparency as guide words (Hayes and Hull, for example).

Hayes	Hull

4. Model for students how you would determine if Hernandez would be found on this page. For example, say something like what follows.

   I begin with the first letter (h) and know I'm in the right area of the dictionary. Then I look at the second letter in Hernandez (e) and the second letter in Hayes (a). Because the e *comes after the* a, *I know Hernandez comes in the alphabet after Hayes. Next, I look at the second letter in Hull (u) and ask myself whether the second letter in Hernandez (e) comes before or after* u. *Because* e *comes before* u *in the alphabet, I know that Hernandez comes before Hull. Because Hernandez comes after Hayes and before Hull, I know that word will be found on the page with those guide words.*

5. Model several additional examples to help students see how some words would be found on earlier pages or later pages. Then invite students to share their thought processes with additional words. Some possible names to use are listed below.

Earlier Page	**On Page**	**Later Page**
Harris	Henry	Humphry
Harty	Hill	Hurley
Hanson	Holt	Hynd
Hall	Hoover	Hynes

6. Invite students to play detective by deducing whether a list of words would be found on a particular page of their dictionaries. Choose a page from their dictionaries and develop a list of words. Use examples that reflect students' general level of understanding. Some words can be very easy to assign to one of the three categories below. Write the list of words on the chalkboard or an overhead transparency and have students work in pairs to assign the words to the appropriate category. A completed example is shown below for the guide words *cook* and *copra*.

Earlier Page	**On Page**	**Later Page**
brain	cool	copse
archer	coop	corn
convey	coot	cork
control	copilot	delta
continue	copper	fawn

7. Discuss the completed chart and clarify as needed. Encourage students to share their thinking and reinforce students who were able to explain and show why their answers were correct or incorrect.

8. Challenge students to apply their learning by completing a sheet where you present two guide words from their dictionaries and a group of four words. Have students complete the sheet before looking in their dictionaries. Check their work. For further practice, students could actually write the page numbers for those words on an earlier or later page. A reproducible is included on the next page for this activity.

DICTIONARY DETECTIVE

Name ______________________________ Date ______________

Words ____

____

Where would the four words printed above be found in your dictionary? Use your detective skills, knowledge of guide words, and alphabetical order to put the words where they belong. For the words that come before and after the guide words, look up the words in your dictionary and write the page numbers where they are found.

Guide Words

Earlier Page ______________ ______________ Later Page

page __________ ____________________ page __________
word

page __________ ____________________ page __________
word

page __________ ____________________ page __________
word

page __________ ____________________ page __________
word

PRONUNCIATION SYMBOLS

1. Be sensitive to your students' dialects and the region of the country in which you live. Dictionaries show how words are pronounced by people who speak what is called General American. Canadian dictionaries will have a number of pronunciation differences when compared to dictionaries published for the United States. Keep this information in mind when you teach the pronunciation symbols—they may not be entirely appropriate for the area where you live. Remember also that this lesson is an introduction. Students will need numerous opportunities to learn and use pronunciation symbols in their dictionaries.

2. Introduce pronunciation symbols by having students find them at the bottom of one of their dictionary pages. Tell students that the special symbols in parentheses after the entry word, when used with the pronunciation key at the bottom of the page, are intended to help with word pronunciation. Take time to teach or review the long mark (macron) for the vowels (ā, ē, ī, ō, ū), no marks for the short sounds of the vowels, and perhaps some of the special marks shown below. Refer to the pronunciation key as needed.

Some Special Pronunciation Symbols

Name	Symbol	Example	Name	Symbol	Example
Two-dot a	ä	cär	Tilde u	ũ	fũr
Circumflex o	ô	hôrn	Schwa	ə	a in ago

3. Give students an opportunity to look at the special symbols in parenthesis in their dictionaries, especially for words they can pronounce. Then have them look up a word they can pronounce (for example, *be*). Write the pronunciation symbols for *be* on the chalkboard or an overhead transparency (bē). Help students see how this information, while easy to use with a word they know, can be used with a word that might be unknown. You could use a think-aloud by saying what follows.

> *The word* be *is easy for me to pronounce, but I can remember that the long mark over the vowel means that I say the name of the vowel when trying to pronounce a vowel. I can use that sound along with other sounds in the word and try different pronunciations. If I say a word I've heard before, I've probably pronounced the word correctly.*

4. Present only the pronunciation symbols for *bias* (bī´əs). Cover everything but the *bi* and ask for a volunteer to pronounce that part of the word. Then present the remaining pronunciation symbols and point out the accent mark and the spacing that indicates that the word has two syllables. Invite students to refer to the pronunciation key to try to pronounce the word. Encourage different pronunciations and stress to students that they are probably right if they say a word with those sounds that they have heard before. Confirm the pronunciation and take time to find the word and examine the meanings for *bias.*

5. Write (kē) on the chalkboard or an overhead transparency. Ask students what word it represents. Most students should say *key.* Have them confirm the word by locating it in their dictionaries and looking at the pronunciation symbols. You might also take time to explore the meanings that can be associated with *key.*

6. Use similar activities with the pronunciation symbols for other words. Invite students to try to pronounce the words. Confirm the correct pronunciation and, if necessary, refer to the dictionary for meanings. Be sure to try to build on the students' existing knowledge. Some possible words to use are given below along with the pronunciation symbols from a dictionary. Be sure to use symbols that are in your students' dictionaries.

Pronunciation Symbols	Words
(kik)	kick
(kil or kiln)	kiln
(kid′ nē)	kidney
(kip′ər)	kipper
(kin)	kin
(joor′ē)	jury
(jōō lī)	July
(sit′ē)	city
(sũr′ kəs)	circus

7. Conclude the lesson by stressing that pronunciation symbols can be useful aids to help pronounce unknown words. Remind students that they need to be willing to try different pronunciations until they say a word they have heard before.

Strategy 5 SECTION 3.8

PRONOUNCING UNKNOWN WORDS

1. Begin by helping students realize that pronouncing words is not the same as reading words. When a word is read, one or more meanings are associated with the word. Remind students that a dictionary can be a resource for both meanings and pronunciations.

2. Select a few words from upcoming lessons that students may be unable to pronounce. Adapt the procedure used with the word *quay.* Remember, however, that the real power of such lessons comes from using words students have encountered or will encounter in their reading.

3. Tell students you will show them how to use a dictionary to help pronounce an unknown word. Write the word *quay* on the chalkboard or an overhead transparency. Then write the sentence that follows.

   The dog was near the quay.

   Have students read the sentence to themselves and then offer possible pronunciations for *quay.* It is possible that most students will agree that the word is pronounced (kwā) to rhyme with *way.*

4. Explore students' ideas about the meaning of the word. List their ideas on the chalkboard or an overhead transparency. Then ask students how they could find out the pronunciation and meaning. Common responses include asking someone and using a dictionary.

5. Place the following information on the chalkboard or overhead transparency or have students use their dictionaries.

    quay (kē, kā) a wharf for loading or unloading ships, usually made of stone or concrete

6. Have students use the pronunciation symbols to pronounce the word and compare it with their initial ideas. Help students realize there are two pronunciations given in this dictionary entry. You might model word pronunciation by using the following think-aloud.

    When I saw the word in the sentence, I thought it was pronounced (kwā). Now that I've looked at the pronunciation symbols, I see I was wrong. The word is pronounced as key *(kē) or* kay *(kā). I can see that some words can be pronounced more than one way. I also see that the meaning of quay is a wharf. That means that the dog was near a wharf which is near a body of water. The dictionary helped me with both pronunciation and meaning.*

7. Present several additional words that are difficult for most students to pronounce. Give them the dictionary pages on which the words are found and have small groups work together using the pronunciation symbols to say the words. Any student who already knows how to pronounce any of the words should not participate for that particular word. Instead, the student can be the expert source when the correct pronunciation is needed. Spend time with the meanings of the words and encourage students to relate the words to their experiences.

8. For additional practice, use words that are pronounced in different ways. Have groups of students use their dictionaries to find or confirm the different pronunciations. Help students realize that some of these differences are due to the part of speech. Other pronunciations are due to regional differences. Some possible words to use for this activity are given below.

either	data	object	read
route	creek	wind	bow
tear	house	minute	lead
dove	wound	live	idea

9. Conclude the lesson by telling students that a dictionary is a source to use to help pronounce unknown words. Have students offer other strategies that can also be used (e.g., context, phonics, structural analysis). Remind students that they should be flexible in their approach and remember that a dictionary should be used if the other strategies have not been helpful and the pronunciation or meaning of the word is needed.

Practice and Reinforcement Activities

1. Invite students to use the pronunciation symbols from their dictionaries and answer the following questions.

   Which is part of a building?
   (ruf) (flou´ər) (sē´ling)

   Which is an insect?
   (flī) (bēd) (spē´dar)

   Which one crawls?
   (snak) (wôm) (kat´ər pil´ər)

2. Provide pronunciation symbols for some words and have students use these symbols to try to pronounce the words. Then provide a helpful context where the pronunciation is likely to be confirmed. Remember that different publishers use different pronunciation symbols. Some examples of words and sentences are presented below.

(kwit)	I *quit* playing the game.
(māt)	Where is the *mate* to my sock?
(sit´ē)	Do you live in a large *city*?
(sũr kəs)	I saw a clown at the *circus*.
(rēd)	I will *read* the exciting story.

3. Use electronic dictionaries for students who have not yet learned how to use pronunciation symbols. Such dictionaries can also be useful for readers who struggle because these dictionaries pronounce the word and read the definition. Remember, however, that the definition spoken may not fit the context of the sentence being read.
4. Choose some particularly interesting words in terms of spelling and pronunciation and have students look up the words and use the pronunciation symbols to try to pronounce the words. Some possible words are listed below.

   aviary   axis   calyx   czar   depot

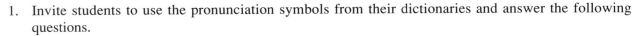

Section **3.9**

Lack of Flexible Word-Identification Strategies

Behavior Observed → **Anticipated Outcome**

The student does not use a variety of word-identification strategies. → The student will use various strategies for identifying unknown words.

Background

Students experiencing difficulty in reading often do not apply all of the word-identification strategies they have learned. They may, for example, use decoding, but they rarely use the context of the sentence when they encounter an unknown word. Good readers, however, recognize that the most efficient method of figuring out unknown words varies with the reading situation. Therefore, teachers need to emphasize that students use reading strategies most appropriate for the situation.

The following ideas are meant to help teachers begin to refine the process of teaching students to develop a set of flexible word-identification strategies.

Strategy 1 SECTION 3.9

WORD WIZARDS

RESOURCES

1. Use the Word Wizards on page 245 or in the Resources for Chapter 3 (page 266) as a visual for this lesson. You have several options:
   - Display them on an overhead transparency.
   - Enlarge them and make posters.
   - Make a copy for each student.
   - White out the faces so students can put in their facial features.
2. Tell students that you want them to become better Word Wizards. Explain that Word Wizards have a variety of ways to try to figure out unknown words. Invite students to name some of the things they do when words are unknown and write their ideas on the chalkboard. Guide students as necessary. The list may look something like the one presented below, but remember to be sensitive to the specific skills you have taught.

Sound it out.
Chunk the word.
Skip it.
Say blank and read to the end of the sentence.
Look it up.
Use the pictures.
Look for parts you know.
Ask someone.
Look at the beginning letter and try to think of a word that makes sense.
See if the word has prefixes and/or suffixes.

3. Commend students for their suggestions. Then say something like the following.

   When we read and come upon an unknown word, our Word Wizards know different things that they can try. There is not just one thing to do. And if something doesn't work, we can try another thing on the list. That's called being flexible, and our Word Wizards are flexible. Over the next several days, we'll learn more about some of the best things to try when words are unknown.

4. Then choose one or two of the items from the list and model how a good Word Wizard would use that strategy. Be sure to combine strategies when appropriate and help students realize that the same strategy is not used all the time. The Word Wizard is flexible and tries various strategies.

5. Below are some ideas for using three major strategies: context, phonics, and word parts. Be sure to use examples with each of the ideas. The examples should be appropriate for the students you are teaching.

   Context
   - I can try to think of a word that would make sense.
   - I can say *blank* in the place of an unknown word and read to the end of the sentence. Then my Word Wizard could ask, *What word would make sense in the sentence?* (Later show students how the context and initial letter or word parts can be used along with context.)
   - I can read the sentence with the word I put in, and my Word Wizard could ask, *Does that word sound right?* (If the word doesn't sound right, I could try to think of another word.)
   - I can look at any pictures or illustrations for an idea of what the word might be.

   Phonics
   - I can look at the beginning of the word. Then my Word Wizard could ask, *What word begins with that sound that makes sense in the sentence?*
   - I can say the sounds in the word slowly and then faster. My Word Wizard could ask, "*What word has those sounds that I have heard before? If that doesn't work, I can say the word differently to come up with a word that I have heard before. I might have to try this a few times.*"

   Word Parts
   - I can look for parts in the word that I know.
   - I can see if the word has endings like *-ed, -ing, -ly, -ness, -tion,* and so on. My Word Wizard can ask, "*If I take off the ending, will I recognize the word? If yes, let me add the ending and try to say the word.*"
   - I can see if the unknown word is similar to other words that I know. My Word Wizard can then ask, "*Can I use the sound in the part I know along with sounds for the unknown part and say a real word?*"

- I can look for two smaller words that make up the larger word. My Word Wizard can ask, *"Do I see two smaller words in the bigger words? If so, let me say each of the two smaller words and then say the larger word."*
- I can look for prefixes, suffixes, and root words to help break the larger word into parts. My Word Wizard could ask, *"Does this longer word have a prefix and/or suffix along with a root word? Let me say the root word and then add the prefix and/or suffix to try to pronounce the word."*

6. Systematically teach each of the above items using helpful examples from your curriculum and students' daily reading. Then show how the Word Wizard combines strategies and is flexible in the use of strategies when trying to pronounce unknown words. Several brief examples follow.

- Mike saw *everyone* at the *party*.
  I didn't recognize *everyone*, but I saw the two smaller words (*every* and *one*), and the word was then easy to say. If I hadn't known *party*, I would have said *part* (a word I know) and then try an ending sound for the *y*.
- The *buses* were on the road.
  I didn't immediately recognize *buses*, so I read to the end of the sentence and asked myself, "What can be on the road that begins with *bbb*?" I knew the word *cars* made sense, but that was not the right beginning sound. I then noted the *-es* at the end and quickly saw *bus*. I then added the ending and said the word. It made sense in the sentence.
- A group of people was *preparing* dinner.
  I saw the prefix *pre-* and the ending *-ing*. I then said the word *păr* and then added the *pre-* and *-ing* The word *pre-păr-ing* did not make sense, so I tried another way to say *par*. I tried *pear* and when I added the prefix and ending, the word made sense. It's like the group was making dinner.

7. Create a Word Wizard bulletin board where students can add examples similar to those above to show how their Word Wizards help figure out unknown words.

Strategy 2 SECTION 3.9

CSSR: CONTEXT, STRUCTURE, SOUND, REFERENCE

Ruddell's (1993) four-step strategy is described briefly and linked to other sections in this book. An example for modeling is also provided.

1. **C** **Context.** Tell students that when they come to a word they don't know, they should read to the end of the sentence to see whether the rest of the sentence defines the word. Students needing practice in figuring out unfamiliar words from context should be taught the strategies in Sections 3.7 and 5.2.
2. **S** **Structure.** If the word cannot be identified by the context, students should look at the parts of the words. They should look for any familiar word parts that can help them understand the new word. For teaching strategies using the structure of words, see Sections 3.3, 3.4, and 5.3.
3. **S** **Sound.** If the word has familiar word parts, students should try to pronounce the word using their knowledge of the sounds of consonants and vowels. After trying to give some of the letters the sounds they represent, students should reread the sentence, thinking about the way the word is used. Often students will be able to read the word using these three steps. For teaching strategies using the sounds associated with letters, see Sections 3.1 and 3.2.
4. **R** **Reference.** If students are unable to identify the word, they may use reference materials such as a glossary or a dictionary. After finding a word in the dictionary, however, students still need to determine how it is used in the context of the sentence. For teaching strategies using a dictionary, see Sections 3.8 and 5.4.
5. You may want to model the CSSR with your students. For example, consider the unknown word *amicable* in the sentence "The family came to an amicable agreement about vacation plans." You might say what follows.

   I don't know the word a-m-i-c-a-b-l-e, so I would first read to the end of the sentence. I know that the word describes agreement, but nothing in the sentence tells me what kind of agreement they had. It might have been friendly, but it might not have been. After reading to the end of the sentence, I look for word parts that I know. The word has parts I can pronounce, but it doesn't have a base word or affixes that will help me understand the word. Next, I try to read the word by giving the letters the sounds that I know (sound out word). I know the sounds in the word, so I can pronounce it. After pronouncing amicable, *I reread the sentence. Yes, I've heard the word before, and it makes sense in the sentence. Just to be sure, however, I check the dictionary and find that* amicable *means 'friendly or peaceable.' I think I'll remember the word the next time I see it.*

Section 3.10

Ineffective Use of Word-Identification Strategies

Behavior Observed → **Anticipated Outcome**

The student knows word-identification strategies but does not use them effectively.

The student will become more effective in using word-identification strategies.

Background

One student always seems to sound out unknown words. Another student substitutes a word that makes sense but changes the author's meaning. A third student stops reading completely when confronted with an unfamiliar word. These and other reading behaviors, when observed consistently, can work against students becoming proficient readers.

The basic problem is that often the student has not learned why a particular strategy works and/or when to use it for figuring out unfamiliar words. It is also possible that the student does not know when to abandon one strategy and move to another. Usually, the student is overreliant on one word-identification strategy even though he or she may have learned other strategies. This situation usually occurs because the student has not been taught how to use a *combination* of strategies flexibly when confronted with an unknown word. Your primary responsibility in such a situation is to help the student use word-identification strategies in combination with one another to produce a word that makes sense in the sentence and has graphic characteristics similar to the word printed in the text. Students might be told that this is the "sound-sense strategy." If a specific strategy like context or phonics needs to be taught, refer to the ideas presented in Chapter 3. The following strategy should help you begin to refine the process of teaching students to develop a set of flexible word-identification strategies.

Could this student be pondering which strategy will help him figure out a word?
Photo by S. Johns

Strategy 1

BE FLEXIBLE

1. Invite students to share some of the strategies they use when they come across an unknown word. Typical responses may include sounding it out (phonics), skipping it, trying to figure it out from the other words in the sentence (context), breaking it into parts (syllabication), looking it up in a dictionary, and asking someone. Acknowledge that all these strategies may be used at one time or another and encourage students to provide examples of times when they have used each of them. List all of them on the chalkboard.

2. Tell students that strategic readers are flexible in terms of how they try to recognize unfamiliar words. This means that they know several strategies and use the most efficient and/or effective one(s) to figure out unknown words. Provide several examples where context can be used to figure out the unknown word. Have them identify the strategy that is used.

   The man put a ________________ on his head. (hat)

   The color of milk is ________________. (white)

3. Help students recognize that there are times when context can be used; moreover, stress that skilled readers also rely on context clues. Guide students to realize that context clues are used to help answer the question "What word would make sense in the sentence?"

4. Provide another sentence for which context clues can be used to predict more than one word that may sound right or make sense in the sentence.

   Jake climbed a tree and picked a red ________________.
   (for instance, apple, cherry)

   After the words have been given by students, list them on the chalkboard and ask, "Does *apple* make sense in this sentence? Why?" Repeat this question for each word listed on the chalkboard. Then use a word that does not make sense and have students explain why the word would not be a good choice.

5. Ask students whether the word the author used in step 4 can be correctly predicted from its context. Because it cannot, provide an initial letter clue.

   Jake climbed a tree and picked a red a__________.

   Students should now be able to determine that the word is *apple*. If additional clues are necessary, supply another letter or two. Once the correct word is supplied, help students realize that they used context and some letter clues to figure out the word. Stress that context and phonics were used in combination. Use other examples, such as those included below, and have students think aloud.

   I like ________________.

   The game lasted more than ________________ hours.

   In the first example, a student might say, "I like. . . . Let's see. There are many words that make sense here: *soccer, candy,* and *music*. From the context or words provided, I can't really know the word so I need some letters in the word (teacher writes in a *b*). The word could be *bears,* a girl's name like *Brenda* or *Barb,* or. . . . No, wait, it can't be *Brenda* or *Barb,* because a small *b* is there and people's names begin with capital letters. It must be *bears* or *beans* or something like that. I still need more information (teacher writes *ban*). Well, I guess it can't be *bears* or *beans* because they are not spelled that way. Perhaps the word is *bands*. I need more letters (teacher writes *banan*). No, it isn't *bands*; *ban-na, ba-nan* (student tries different pronunciations). Oh, *banana* could be the word; I mean *bananas,* because it makes sense, and I think that's the way the word is spelled."

6. After several similar examples, remind students that in reading all the words are always there. It is easier to make predictions because both context and letter clues are readily available in natural text.
7. Provide another example in which the missing word is difficult for students to pronounce and have them try to predict the unknown word. With context clues, many words are possible.

   The story was ________________________. (unbelievable)

   Supply the initial letter and the student may still not know the word. Sometimes it is possible to find prefixes, suffixes, endings, and a root word. Write the word in the sentence and encourage students to use this knowledge. Draw lines between the major word parts and have students try to pronounce the word. Encourage discussion about how affixes can be used to determine the word's meaning. Then ask whether it sounds like a word they know and whether it makes sense in the sentence.
8. When numerous activities such as the foregoing have been completed, help students develop a flexible approach to use when figuring out unknown words. Two charts that might be adapted follow.

Strategies to Figure Out Unknown Words

1. Use the words around the unknown word to help think of a word that makes sense in the sentence.
2. Use the letters, the sounds associated with the letters, and the words around the unknown word to say a word that makes sense in the sentence.
3. Look for root words, prefixes, suffixes, and endings. Try to pronounce the various word parts to see whether you have heard it before. Try various pronunciations, especially for the vowels.
4. Continue reading. Later sentences may help you figure out the unfamiliar word.
5. As a last resort, use the dictionary, ask someone, or skip the unknown word.

Questions for Figuring Out Unknown Words

1. What makes sense here?
2. What sound does it start with?
3. Are there root words, prefixes, suffixes, or endings that I know?
4. Should I skip the word and keep reading?
5. Can a dictionary help me?
6. Should I ask someone?

9. Help students realize that *flexibility* is essential to identifying unknown words. Good readers don't keep trying something that doesn't work; they move to another strategy. Strategy 3 in Section 7.5, where the notion of a critter is developed, may be useful in helping students monitor the effectiveness of the strategies they use to identify unknown words.

Practice and Reinforcement Activities

1. Have students share a word they are unable to figure out, along with the context in which it is found. If the student is unable to share his or her strategies, model how a combination of strategies might be used to figure out the unknown word. Help students refine the effectiveness of their strategies.
2. Encourage students to record and share their successful attempts at figuring out unknown words by verbalizing the various strategies they used.
3. Develop exercises where a modified cloze procedure is used to refine students' ability to use context and letter clues. Discuss the word choices with the students, as in the following example.

   She left a ____________ on the table.

   She left a p ____________ on the table.

   She left a p ___ ___ on the table.

   She left a p ___ n on the table.

   Students may request another letter to determine whether the word is *pin, pen,* or *pan.*
4. Younger students may profit from picture clues in cloze exercises, as illustrated below.

   There is a ____________.

   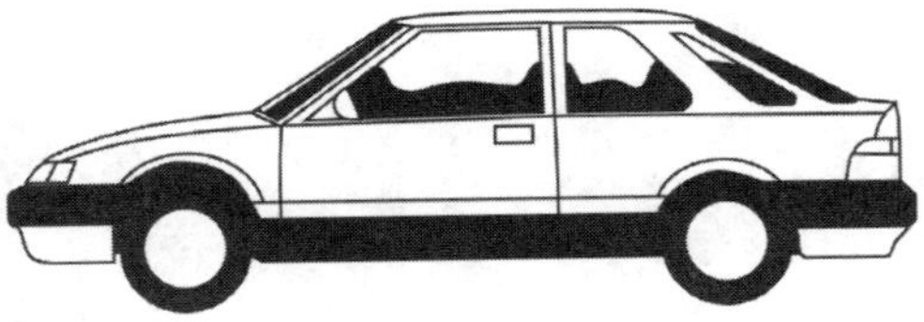

5. Have students write sentences with space for a word that is missing. Students can exchange papers with one another and attempt to fill in the missing word. Papers are returned to the authors for verification. If students have difficulty, the authors can supply the first letter or two of the missing word. This activity may also lead students to an understanding of synonyms.
6. Have students keep a log in which they record unfamiliar, unknown words, the context (a phrase or sentence), and the strategies used to pronounce the words and determine their meanings. Provide opportunities for small group sharing. Be sure especially useful efforts are shared with the entire class. Be sure to acknowledge that strategy use is not always successful.

Date	Book/Page	Underlined Word in Sentence	What Was Done
3-12-01	Sitting Bull, p. 1	But inside the cone-shaped, buffalo-hide <u>tipi</u> on the south bank of the river . . .	From the words buffalo hide and cone-shaped, I decided it was a tepee. When I looked up the word tipi, I was correct.

7. Apply strategies for identifying unknown words within the ongoing instructional program.

Resources

3

Note: indicates student reproducible. indicates teacher material.

WORDS FOR USE IN TEACHING VOWEL SOUNDS

Short Sounds

a		e		i		o		u	
and	fat	bell	beg	is	it	sock	clock	rug	us
can	apple	red	slept	twin	dig	frog	stop	run	up
add	last	rest	sled	slid	hip	hog	pop	dug	dust
at	mad	pet	met	hill	tin	odd	hot	rut	rub
cat	fast	bed	help	brick	hit	mop	log	must	but
hand	glad	step	sell	his	big	hop	cot	sun	bus
dad	am	men	hen	did	will	pond	not	fun	bum
flag	bad	send	wet	milk	in	fog	dot	drum	duck
bag	had	pen	egg	rib	trip	pot	doll	tug	bug
fact	tan	bet	chest	drill	ill	lot	ox	struck	mud

Long Sounds

a		e		i		o		u	
fade	may	Pete	east	Mike	like	hose	note	use	flute
say	bake	three	see	hide	time	hope	poke	music	plume
tape	pay	eat	eve	bike	ripe	rose	open	cue	cute
same	rain	peep	free	pike	pile	note	over	mule	rule
pain	Jane	feed	jeep	dime	mice	boat	slope	tube	blue
take	tame	be	team	die	fine	robe	rode	fuel	rude
way	save	mean	beet	dine	light	home	row	clue	unit
wave	age	green	bean	five	ride	joke	nose	fuse	cube
ate	day	weed	she	side	pine	bone	rope	suit	brute
take	make	keep	seat	nice	pie	cone	stove	dual	tune

RANK ORDER OF THE 300 MOST COMMON WORDS

the	up	make	right	food	body	money
of	said	now	should	under	end	become
and	out	way	small	always	hand	group
to	if	each	old	however	head	government
a	some	called	think	men	read	later
in	would	did	take	air	others	living
is	so	just	still	asked	year	change
that	people	after	place	both	since	days
it	them	water	find	being	against	animals
was	other	through	off	does	young	word
for	more	get	different	going	give	let
you	will	because	part	big	set	wanted
he	into	back	found	without	kind	across
on	your	where	us	looked	room	American
as	which	know	world	say	eyes	early
are	do	little	away	left	number	though
they	then	such	life	began	far	four
with	many	even	three	mother	person	face
be	these	much	went	during	city	best
his	no	our	those	tell	better	became
at	time	must	own	land	white	seen
or	been	before	help	next	side	himself
from	who	good	every	once	family	sure
had	like	too	here	need	night	energy
I	could	long	house	high	didn't	sun
not	has	me	might	last	country	second
have	him	years	between	until	name	feet
this	how	day	never	children	it's	really
but	than	used	home	along	ever	certain
by	two	work	thought	took	form	turned
were	may	any	put	together	usually	toward
one	only	go	again	sometimes	hard	parts
all	most	use	important	saw	knew	black
she	its	things	while	enough	today	ways
when	made	well	something	light	times	show
an	over	look	states	got	soon	means
their	see	another	don't	example	told	door
there	first	around	why	words	several	special
her	new	man	large	united	system	course
can	very	great	want	almost	state	known
we	my	same	few	father	upon	move
what	also	came	school	live	thing	yet
about	down	come	often	keep	earth	

Reprinted with permission from Zeno, S.M., Ivens, S.H., Millard, R.T., & Duvvuri, R. (1995). *The Educator's Word Frequency Guide*. Brewster, NY: Touchstone Applied Science. Copyright © 1995 by Touchstone Applied Science Associates (TASA), Inc.

REVISED DOLCH LIST

a	could	he	might	same	told
about	cut	heard	more	saw	too
across	did	help	most	say	took
after	didn't	her	much	see	toward
again	do	here	must	she	try
all	does	high	my	short	turn
always	done	him	near	should	two
am	don't	his	need	show	under
an	down	hold	never	six	up
and	draw	hot	next	small	upon
another	eat	how	new	so	us
any	enough	I	no	some	use
are	even	I'm	not	soon	very
around	every	if	now	start	walk
as	far	in	of	still	want
ask	fast	into	off	stop	warm
at	find	is	oh	take	was
away	first	it	old	tell	we
be	five	its	on	ten	well
because	for	just	once	than	went
been	found	keep	one	that	were
before	four	kind	only	the	what
began	from	know	open	their	when
best	full	last	or	them	where
better	gave	leave	other	then	which
big	get	left	our	there	while
black	give	let	out	these	white
blue	go	light	over	they	who
both	going	like	own	think	why
bring	gone	little	play	this	will
but	good	long	put	those	with
by	got	look	ran	thought	work
call	green	made	read	three	would
came	grow	make	red	through	yes
can	had	many	right	to	yet
close	hard	may	round	today	you
cold	has	me	run	together	your
come	have	mean	said		

The rationale and research for this list are described in Johns, J.L. (1981). The development of the revised Dolch list. *Illinois School Research and Development, 17,* 15–24.

From Jerry L. Johns and Susan Davis Lenski, *Improving Reading: Interventions, Strategies, and Resources* (5th ed.). Copyright © 2010 Kendall Hunt Publishing Company (800-247-3458, ext. 4). May be reproduced for noncommercial educational purposes.

REVISED DOLCH LIST 1 CARDS

a	and	are
at	big	blue
call	can	come
did	do	down
for	get	go
green	have	he
help	here	I
in	is	it
little	look	make

(continued)

Revised Dolch List 1 Cards *(continued)*

me	my	no
not	play	ran
red	said	see
stop	that	the
this	to	up
want	we	what
who	will	with
work	you	

REVISED DOLCH LIST 2 CARDS

about	all	around
ask	away	but
eat	fast	from
good	has	him
his	into	know
let	like	may
new	now	of
on	one	out
put	run	saw

(continued)

say	she	show
so	some	soon
take	then	they
too	two	us
went	yes	your

REVISED DOLCH LIST 3 CARDS

after	again	am
an	another	any
as	be	before
began	better	black
bring	by	came
cold	could	cut
didn't	does	don't
far	find	first
five	found	four

(continued)

gave	give	going
gone	got	had
hard	her	hold
how	if	its
just	kind	last

REVISED DOLCH LIST 4 CARDS

light	long	made
many	more	much
must	never	next
off	oh	old
or	other	our
over	own	read
right	should	still
tell	than	their
them	there	these

(continued)

REVISED DOLCH LIST 4 CARDS *(continued)*

think	those	three
told	took	try
under	very	walk
was	were	when
where	which	white
why	would	

REVISED DOLCH LIST 5 CARDS

across	always	because
been	best	both
close	done	draw
enough	even	every
full	grow	heard
high	hot	I’m
leave	left	mean
might	most	near
need	once	only

(continued)

Revised Dolch List 5 Cards *(continued)*

open	round	same
short	six	small
start	ten	thought
through	today	together
toward	turn	upon
use	warm	well
while	yet	keep

HIGH-FREQUENCY NOUNS

air
back
book
boy
car
children
city
day
dog
door
eye
face
father
feet
friend
girl
group
hand
head
home
house
man
men
money
morning
mother
Mr.
Mrs.
name
night
nothing
people
place
road
room
school
side
table
thing
time
top
town
tree
water
way
year

The development of this list is described in Johns, J.L. (1975). Dolch list of common nouns—A comparison. *The Reading Teacher, 28,* 338–340.

Word Wizards

WORD PATTERNS

Short *a* Sounds

-ab	**-ack**	**-ad**	**-ag**	**-am**	**-amp**	**-an**
cab	back	ad	bag	am	camp	an
dab	hack	bad	gag	bam	damp	ban
gab	jack	cad	hag	dam	lamp	can
jab	pack	dad	tag	ham	champ	fan
lab	rack	fad	lag	jam	clamp	man
nab	sack	had	rag	clam	cramp	pan
tab	tack	lad	sag	cram	stamp	ran
blab	black	mad	tag	dram	tramp	tan
crab	slack	pad	wag	slam		van
drab	crack	sad	brag	swam		clan
grab	track	clad	crag			plan
scab	shack	glad	drag			scan
slab	whack	shad	flag			span
stab	smack		shag			than
	snack		snag			
	stack		stag			

-and	**-ang**	**-ank**	**-ap**	**-ash**	**-ast**	**-at**
and	bang	bank	cap	ash	cast	at
band	fang	rank	gap	bash	fast	bat
hand	gang	sank	lap	cash	last	cat
land	hang	tank	map	dash	mast	fat
sand	rang	yank	nap	gash	past	hat
bland	sang	blank	rap	hash	vast	mat
gland	tang	clank	sap	lash	blast	pat
grand	clang	plank	tap	mash		sat
stand	slang	prank	zap	rash		vat
strand		crank	chap	sash		brat
		drank	clap	clash		chat
		flank	flap	crash		flat
		frank	slap	smash		scat
		shank	snap	stash		slat
		spank	trap	trash		that
		thank				
		swank				

-atch
catch
hatch
latch
match
patch
thatch

(continued)

Short *e* Sounds

-eck	-ed	-eg	-ell	-en	-end	-ent
deck	bed	beg	bell	den	end	bent
heck	fed	egg	dell	hen	bend	dent
neck	led	keg	fell	men	lend	lent
peck	red	leg	sell	pen	mend	rent
check	wed	peg	tell	ten	send	sent
speck	bled		well	glen	blend	tent
	fled		yell	then	spend	went
	sled		quell	when	trend	spent
	shed		shell			
	sped		smell			
			spell			
			swell			

-ess	-est	-et
less	best	bet
mess	nest	get
bless	pest	jet
chess	rest	let
dress	test	met
	vest	net
	west	pet
	chest	set
	crest	wet
	quest	vet
		yet
		fret

Short *o* Sounds

-ob	-ock	-od	-og	-ong	-op	-ot
cob	cock	cod	bog	bong	cop	cot
fob	dock	hod	cog	gong	hop	dot
gob	hock	nod	dog	long	lop	got
job	lock	pod	fog	song	mop	hot
rob	mock	rod	hog	tong	pop	jot
mob	pock	sod	jog	wrong	sop	lot
sob	rock	clod	log	strong	top	not
blob	sock	plod	clog		crop	pot
slob	tock	shod	frog		drop	rot
snob	block		smog		shop	blot
	clock				stop	clot
	knock					plot
	flock					slot
	crock					shot
	frock					spot
	shock					trot
	smock					
	stock					

(continued)

Short *i* Sounds

-ib	-ick	-id	-ift	-ig	-ill	-im
bib	kick	bid	gift	big	bill	dim
fib	lick	did	lift	dig	dill	him
jib	nick	hid	rift	fig	fill	rim
rib	pick	kid	sift	jig	gill	brim
crib	sick	lid	drift	pig	hill	skim
	tick	rid	shift	rig	kill	slim
	wick	grid	swift	wig	mill	swim
	brick	skid		brig	pill	trim
	trick	slid		swig	rill	whim
	chick				sill	
	thick				till	
	click				will	
	flick				chill	
	slick				drill	
	quick				frill	
	stick				grill	
					trill	
					quill	
					spill	
					still	

-in	-ing	-ink	-ip	-ish	-it	-itch
in	bing	ink	dip	dish	it	itch
bin	ring	fink	hip	fish	bit	ditch
din	sing	kink	lip	wish	fit	pitch
fin	wing	link	nip	swish	hit	witch
kin	bring	mink	rip		kit	stitch
pin	fling	pink	sip		lit	switch
sin	sting	rink	tip		pit	
tin	string	sink	zip		sit	
win	swing	wink	yip		wit	
chin	thing	drink	chip		grit	
shin		blink	ship		mitt	
thin		slink	whip		quit	
grin		stink	flip		slit	
skin		think	slip		skit	
spin			grip		spit	
twin			trip		twit	
			quip			
			skip			
			snip			

(continued)

Short *u* Sounds

-ub	-uck	-ud	-uff	-ug	-ull	-um
cub	buck	bud	buff	bug	cull	bum
dub	duck	cud	cuff	dug	dull	gum
hub	luck	mud	huff	hug	gull	hum
nub	muck	stud	muff	jug	hull	mum
pub	puck	thud	puff	lug	lull	rum
rub	suck		bluff	mug	mull	sum
sub	tuck		gruff	pug	null	glum
tub	chuck		stuff	rug	skull	slum
club	shuck			tug		drum
grub	cluck			chug		scum
stub	pluck			thug		chum
	stuck			plug		
				shrug		
				slug		
				smug		

-ump	-un	-unch	-ung	-unk	-up	-ush
bump	bun	bunch	dung	bunk	up	gush
dump	fun	lunch	hung	dunk	cup	hush
hump	gun	punch	lung	hunk	pup	lush
jump	nun	brunch	rung	junk	sup	mush
lump	pun	crunch	sung	sunk		rush
pump	run		clung	chunk		blush
clump	sun		flung	drunk		flush
plump	shun		stung	flunk		plush
slump	spun		swung	skunk		slush
stump	stun					brush
thump						crush
						shush

-ust	-ut
bust	but
dust	cut
just	gut
lust	hut
must	jut
rust	nut
crust	rut
	shut

(continued)

Long *a* Sounds

-ace	**-ade**	**-age**	**-aid**	**-ail**	**-ain**	**-ale**
ace	fade	age	aid	ail	gain	ale
face	jade	cage	laid	bail	main	bale
lace	lade	page	maid	fail	pain	dale
mace	made	rage	paid	hail	rain	gale
pace	wade	sage	raid	jail	vain	hale
race	blade	wage	braid	mail	brain	kale
brace	glade	stage		nail	drain	male
place	grade			pail	grain	pale
space	trade			rail	train	sale
	shade			sail	chain	tale
	spade			tail	plain	vale
				vail	slain	scale
				wail	stain	shale
				frail		stale
				quail		whale
				snail		
				trail		

-ame	**-ane**	**-ape**	**-aste**	**-ate**	**-ave**	**-ay**
came	cane	ape	baste	ate	cave	bay
dame	lane	cape	haste	date	gave	day
fame	mane	gape	paste	fate	nave	gay
game	pane	nape	taste	gate	pave	hay
lame	sane	rape	chaste	hate	rave	jay
name	vane	tape		late	save	lay
same	wane	drape		rate	brave	nay
tame	crane	grape		sate	crave	pay
blame		shape		crate	grave	ray
flame				grate	shave	say
frame				plate	slave	way
shame				skate		clay
				slate		play
				state		fray
						tray
						stay
						sway

-aze
daze
gaze
haze
maze
blaze
glaze
graze

(continued)

Long *e* Sounds

-e	-ea	-each	-ead	-eak	-eal	-eam
be	pea	each	bead	beak	deal	beam
he	sea	beach	lead	leak	heal	ream
me	tea	peach	read	peak	meal	seam
we	flea	reach	plead	weak	peal	team
she	plea	teach		bleak	real	cream
		bleach		freak	seal	dream
				speak	veal	gleam
					zeal	
					steal	

-ean	-eat	-ee	-eed	-eek	-eel	-een
bean	eat	bee	deed	leek	eel	keen
dean	beat	fee	feed	meek	feel	seen
lean	feat	see	heed	peek	heel	teen
mean	heat	tee	need	reek	keel	green
wean	meat	wee	seed	seek	peel	queen
clean	neat	free	weed	week	reel	sheen
glean	peat	tree	bleed	cheek		
	seat	glee	breed	creek		
	cheat	thee	creed	sleek		
	cleat	three	freed			
	pleat		greed			
	treat		speed			
	wheat		steed			
			tweed			

-eep	-eet
beep	beet
deep	feet
jeep	meet
keep	fleet
peep	greet
seep	sheet
weep	sleet
creep	sweet
sheep	tweet
steep	
sweep	

(continued)

Long *o* Sounds

-o	-oad	-oam	-oan	-oast	-oat	-obe
go	goad	foam	loan	boast	oat	lobe
no	load	loam	moan	coast	boat	robe
so	road	roam	roan	roast	coat	globe
	toad		groan	toast	goat	
					moat	
					bloat	
					float	
					gloat	

-ode	-oe	-oke	-old	-ole	-olt	-ome
ode	doe	coke	old	dole	bolt	dome
bode	foe	joke	bold	hole	colt	home
code	hoe	poke	cold	mole	dolt	Nome
mode	toe	woke	fold	pole	jolt	
rode	woe	yoke	gold	role	volt	
		bloke	hold	stole		
		choke	mold			
		smoke	sold			
		spoke	told			

-one	-ope	-ose	-ost	-ote	-ow
bone	cope	hose	ghost	note	bow
cone	dope	nose	host	rote	low
lone	hope	pose	most	tote	mow
pone	mope	rose	post	vote	row
tone	rope	chose		quote	sow
zone	scope	those			tow
shone	slope	close			blow
stone					flow
					glow
					slow
					crow
					grow
					show
					snow

Long *u* Sounds

-use	-ute
use	cute
fuse	mute
muse	flute

(continued)

Long *i* Sounds

-ice	-ide	-ie	-ife	-igh	-ight	-ike
lice	bide	die	knife	high	fight	bike
mice	hide	lie	life	nigh	light	dike
nice	ride	pie	rife	sigh	might	hike
rice	side	tie	wife	thigh	night	like
vice	tide	vie			right	mike
slice	wide				sight	pike
spice	bride				tight	spike
twice	glide				bright	
	slide				flight	
					fright	
					plight	
					slight	

-ild	-ile	-ime	-ind	-ine	-ipe	-ire
mild	file	dime	bind	dine	pipe	ire
wild	mile	lime	find	fine	ripe	dire
child	pile	time	hind	line	wipe	fire
	rile	chime	kind	mine	gripe	hire
	tile	crime	mind	nine	swipe	mire
	vile	grime	rind	pine		sire
	smile	slime	wind	sine		tire
	while		blind	tine		wire
			grind	vine		
				wine		
				shine		
				spine		
				swine		
				thine		
				twine		
				whine		

-ite	-ive
bite	dive
kite	five
mite	hive
site	live
quite	chive
spite	drive
white	

COMMONLY OCCURRING CONTRACTIONS

let's	haven't	they'd
didn't	aren't	you'll
it's	I'm	she'd
won't	he's	weren't
that's	we're	I'd
can't	you're	you've
wasn't	what's	you'd
isn't	there's	we'd
hadn't	she's	they'll
don't	wouldn't	we've
I'll	she'll	who'll
we'll	here's	he'd
I've	ain't	doesn't
he'll	couldn't	where's
hasn't	they're	they've

COMPOUND WORDS

afternoon
airplane
anybody
anyone
applesauce
backbone
backseat
barefoot
barnyard
baseball
basketball
bathtub
bedroom
beehive
billboard
birthday
birthplace
bookcase
bookmark
campfire
chalkboard
checkerboard
classroom
cookbook
copyright
cowboy
cupcake
daydream
deadline
doghouse
downhill
downtown
downstairs
dragonfly
driveway
drugstore
earthquake
everyone
everything
eyebrows
farmland
firecracker
firefly
firehouse
fireplace
fishhook
flashlight
football
fullback
goldfish
grandmother
grasshopper
hallway
headlight
headset
highchair
highway
homesick
horseshoe
jellybean
jellyfish
keyboard
mailbox
mailman
maybe
motorcycle
necktie
neighborhood
newspaper
notebook
oatmeal
outlaw
outside
overboard
pancake
peanut
pinball
playground
playhouse
quarterback
quicksand
railroad
rainbow
raincoat
rattlesnake
rollerblade
rowboat
sailboat
sandpaper
skyscraper
snowball
snowflake
sometimes
starfish
strawberry
sunrise
sunset
sunshine
teenager
thunderstorm
toothbrush
underline
uphill
volleyball
waterfall
watermelon
whirlpool
wildlife
without
wristband
wristwatch

THE NIFTY THRIFTY FIFTY

Word	*Prefix*	*Suffix or Ending*
antifreeze	anti	
beautiful		ful (y-i)
classify		ify
communities	com	es (y-i)
community	com	
composer	com	er
continuous	con	ous
conversation	con	tion
deodorize	de	ize
different		ent
discovery	dis	y
dishonest	dis	
electricity		ity
employee	em	ee
encouragement	en	ment
expensive	ex	ive
forecast	fore	
forgotten		en (double t)
governor		or
happiness		ness (y-i)
hopeless		less
illegal	il	
impossible	im	
impression	im	sion
independence	in	ence
international	inter	al
invasion	in	sion
irresponsible	ir	ible
midnight	mid	

(continued)

The nifty thrifty fifty *(continued)*

Word	*Prefix*	*Suffix or Ending*
misunderstand	mis	
musician		ian
nonliving	non	ing (drop e)
overpower	over	
performance	per	ance
prehistoric	pre	ic
prettier		er (y-i)
rearrange	re	
replacement	re	ment
richest		est
semifinal	semi	
signature		ture
submarine	sub	
supermarkets	super	s
swimming		ing (double m)
transportation	trans	tion
underweight	under	
unfinished	un	ed
unfriendly	un	ly
unpleasant	un	ant
valuable		able (drop e)

Alphabetical List of the 100 Words Used Most Frequently by Students in Their Writing

a
about
after
all
an
am
and
are
around
as
at
back
be
because
but
by
came
can
could
day
did
didn't
do
don't
down
for
from
get
go
got
had
have
he
her
him
his
home
house
I
if
in
into
is
it
just
know
like
little
man
me
mother
my
no
not
now
of
on
one
or
our
out
over
people
put
said
saw
school
see
she
so
some
that
the
them
then
there
they
things
think
this
time
to
too
two
up
us
very
was
we
well
went
were
what
when
who
will
with
would
you
your

From Hillerich, R.L. (1978). *A Writing Vocabulary of Elementary Children*. Springfield, IL: Charles C Thomas.

Rank Order of the 100 Words Most Frequently Used by Students in Their Writing

I	there	go	around
and	with	do	see
the	one	about	think
a	be	some	down
to	so	her	over
was	all	him	by
in	said	could	did
it	were	as	mother
of	then	get	our
my	like	got	don't
he	went	came	school
is	them	time	little
you	she	back	into
that	out	will	who
we	at	can	after
when	are	people	no
they	just	from	am
on	because	saw	well
would	what	now	two
me	if	or	put
for	day	know	man
but	his	your	didn't
have	this	home	us
up	not	house	things
had	very	an	too

From Hillerich, R.L. (1978). *A Writing Vocabulary of Elementary Children.* Springfield, IL: Charles C Thomas.

CHAPTER FOUR

Fluency and Effective Oral Reading

Overview

Reading fluency is the ability to read text with speed, accuracy, and expression to construct meaning (Johns & Berglund, 2006). Students who read fluently have developed automaticity (Samuels, 1994). Automaticity means that students do not have to devote their attention to the task of decoding words; they can focus on constructing the meaning of what they are reading. Suppose Maria is able to read each of the words in a passage correctly, but pauses after each word. She may have difficulty understanding the passage because of her lack of fluency.

Good readers read fluently without much thought about how they are reading. On the other hand, readers who lack fluency may read word by word in a monotone or spend so much time trying to pronounce words that they have little or no attention focused on comprehension. Samuels (2006) notes that assessments of fluency should require the student "to decode and comprehend at the same time" (p. 343).

Related to fluency are various oral reading behaviors. Although oral reading has traditionally been misused, effective teachers understand that both silent reading and oral reading are valuable tools for instructional decisions. Just as silent reading tends to be a better method for assessing reading comprehension, oral reading provides important information about the reader's proficiency in applying reading strategies and possible needs in word identification and/or fluency (Allington, 2009).

> Good teachers understand that both silent reading and oral reading are valuable tools for instructional decisions.

Oral reading can serve two primary purposes: assessment and performance. When used as assessment, oral reading should be private. Teachers should listen to students individually to assess reading miscues, comprehension, and to identify problems with reading fluency. On the other hand, oral reading can be an end in itself, a public performance. If students are reading aloud for the purpose of performing, they should read for an appropriate audience.

This chapter begins by examining oral reading as assessment with a rationale for using oral reading as a diagnostic tool. The heart of the chapter considers fluency and many common difficulties students may have when reading aloud. Resources for Chapter 4 begin with a rationale for oral reading as performance and then provides appropriate suggestions for using oral reading in the classroom. Other resources include information on dialects, norms for oral reading, and a fluency rubric.

Oral Reading as Assessment

Oral reading can provide teachers with useful diagnostic information about the strategies students employ as they read. Imagine a second-grade student, Maria, who has just silently read a grade-appropriate book. Maria is unable to retell any part of the story. Is Maria's comprehension problem the result of insufficient background knowledge, a weak understanding of story structure, very slow rate, or the result of too many miscues? Of course, the answer is impossible to determine without listening to Maria read aloud.

Suppose you ask Maria to read her favorite part of the story. Using picture clues, Maria turns to her chosen chapter, but, as she reads, you notice she makes several miscues per page. These miscues, or deviations from the text, signal to you that Maria's lack of comprehension may be attributed, at least in part, to oral reading miscues. You can then pinpoint Maria's problems and use some of the recommendations in this chapter to create lessons for Maria and other students with the same problem.

You may also have students who read all of the words in a passage correctly but still do not understand because they are not reading the words in natural phrases. Word-by-word reading can hinder comprehension. If you have students who are not fluent readers, refer to Sections 4.1, 4.2, 4.3, 4.4, and 4.5 for strategies to help build reading fluency.

You should not use oral reading as a diagnostic tool in a public setting or in the traditional round-robin reading situation. Round-robin reading is asking one student to read aloud while a group of students listens. Think back to your own days in school. Most likely you had at least one teacher who used round-robin reading. Were you uncomfortable when it was your turn to read? Many students who are asked to read aloud in front of a group are acutely embarrassed. What did you do when other students were reading? Students often read ahead, lose their place, speak out to correct the student reading, or simply tune out. None of these behaviors promote

Working one-on-one with students enables teachers to identify fluency weaknesses.
Photo by S. Johns

good reading or a stimulating reading discussion, yet some teachers persist in round-robin reading in their classes. Round-robin reading is not a good use of class time. See Chapter 4 Resources (page 331) for Oral Reading Alternatives to Round-Robin Reading. Additional ideas can be found in Opitz and Rasinski (2008).

How, then, should you listen to students read aloud if you don't have them read in front of the class? Remember, listening to oral reading is a private performance between you and the student. Instead of wasting time with round-robin reading, make a commitment to listen to each student read every two or three weeks. That means you should listen to two or three students read aloud to you every day.

Reading with three students individually should take only a total of 10 minutes out of your daily schedule. While the class is completing reading-writing activities, simply ask one student at a time to read with you. Make this a personal time between you and the student. Don't sit at your desk, but move to the student's desk or to another table. During the session, alternate between choosing the selection for the student and letting the student make the decision about what to read. The passage you select may be from a reading book, trade book, or graded reading passage. When you select material for oral reading, choose a passage the student has not yet read. Remember, your purpose is to listen for the strategies the student uses while reading rather than to hear a practiced piece of prose.

When the student reads to you, note the kinds of miscues he or she makes. You may jot down the miscues while you are tape-recording the student and record them on a chart. See Chapter 4 Resources (pages 324–325) for a way to record and summarize a student's miscues. This procedure will help you assess the student's fluency. As the student reads, you can also assess the use of comprehension strategies by asking the student to retell the story.

At the end of two or three weeks, you should have information about the oral reading strategies of each student. You can group the students for instruction by their reading needs. For example, students who are word-by-word readers can meet with you for a lesson on reading fluency. Students who tend to omit words can be grouped together for that lesson. It's important to remember that one of the purposes of listening to your students read aloud is to make instructional decisions. Listening to oral reading can be the basis for much of what you teach.

Listening to oral reading can also be the basis for retrospective miscue analysis. Retrospective miscue analysis invites and engages students to reflect upon and evaluate the reading process by analyzing their oral reading miscues (Goodman & Marek, 1996). In essence, students can use retrospective miscue analysis to realize the predicting, confirming, and correcting behaviors that characterize good readers; moreover, such analysis "can help them come to revalue themselves as readers" (Goodman & Marek, 1996, p. ix). We urge you, when appropriate, to use students' reading miscues for instructional purposes in the various situations we describe. For each situation, the behaviors are listed with the outcome you should anticipate after you have designed appropriate intervention. Please remember that you need not use every strategy listed in each part. Use only the ones that best complement the needs of your students.

Section **4.1**

General Lack of Fluency

Behavior Observed →
The student's oral reading lacks fluency.

Anticipated Outcome
The student will read more fluently.

Perspective and Strategies

Most emergent readers lack fluency as they begin reading. They may be *choppy readers,* reading with many stops, starts, and hesitations. They may be *monotonous readers* and read with little or no expression, or they may be inappropriately *hasty readers* and race through the passage ignoring phrasing and punctuation (Wilson, 1988). The cause of fluency problems for beginning readers is that they are processing many new things at the same time. They are just beginning to expand their sight vocabulary and are learning word-identification strategies. For beginning readers, fluency may be considered a developmental process. As they learn more reading strategies and read a variety of materials, they should become more fluent. Such is the case for most beginning readers, whatever their age.

Older readers may also have difficulty reading fluently. These students probably lack a sight vocabulary and effective word-identification strategies. They may also be asked to read books that are too difficult for them.

Clay (1967) has noted that average readers typically move through the four stages of reading described in the chart on the following page. Teachers who see students *remaining* at the second or third stages have cause for concern and may need to use intervention strategies.

Stage	Characteristics/Behaviors
1	■ Reading sounds fluent, but students make many miscues. ■ Students are unaware or unconcerned that their reading does not accurately represent the passage or text.
2	■ Students are conscious of matching their speech to words in the passage or text. ■ Students may point to individual words. ■ Students may read in a staccato fashion.
3	■ Students continue reading word by word, but finger-pointing disappears. ■ Students are still conscious of matching their oral responses to each word.
4	■ Students no longer read word by word. ■ Meaningful phrase units characterize reading.

Additional ways to assess fluency can be found in Chapter 4 Resources. These resources contain, among other items, a Procedure for Determining Words Per Minute (page 332), Oral Reading Norms for Students in Grades One through Eight (pages 333–334), and a Four-Point Fluency Rubric (page 335). These three resources will be especially helpful in determining and assessing fluency in reading.

Numerous strategies for developing sight vocabulary and word identification are presented in Chapter 3, and they should be considered in tandem with the following strategies. Note that there are two major classifications of strategies—one for emergent readers and another for readers who are struggling.

For Emergent Readers

1. Recognize that reading is a developmental process and fluency is likely to develop as students increase their sight vocabularies, acquire a repertoire of word-identification strategies, and have plenty of reading opportunities with materials at their instructional level—a level where students make five or fewer miscues per each one hundred words (Johns, 2008). A lack of fluency may be expected with beginning readers.
2. Encourage the repeated readings of pattern books. See Part C on the CD for a listing of pattern books and related activities. Plenty of practice will help students learn words automatically and will build their confidence. Students can read to each other, to their favorite stuffed animal, to family members, and so on. In addition, encourage multiple rereadings of students' favorite stories, books, and poems.
3. Use daily class experience stories and guide students in the reading. A story could be as simple as the following one.
   - Today is _______.
   - The date is November _____, ________.
   - The weather is _______.
   - It is _______ days until our field trip.

   Begin by inviting volunteers to supply missing words. Then read the story to the class. Encourage students to join you. Point to words and phrases. Use your hand to indicate phrases and have individuals and the whole class read and reread the story. Comment positively on the smoothness of the reading.
4. Provide opportunities for students to listen to talking books on audiotapes or computer programs. Capitalize on their interests when a particularly popular audiotape or computer program is identified by staying out of the way while students enjoy the same experience over and over.

5. Fasten a sheet of paper in the front of books that students can read to others at home or school. The sheet is signed by the person who has listened to the book. The person may also comment about the student's reading.
6. Use echo reading where you read a phrase or sentence and the student repeats it after you and tries to "echo" your phrasing and expression.
7. Identify poems, songs, and rhymes that are enjoyed by students. Print the words on chart paper, the overhead projector, or the chalkboard. Engage in repeated readings or singings.
8. Read a short passage to students, explaining that you are reading with expression. Tell students to pay attention to *how* you read the passage. Then ask students to read the passage with you. Ask students to try to read with the same expression that you use. Reread the passage together until students seem comfortable with the text. Next, fade out of the reading by lowering your voice or stopping reading while students continue. Then have students practice with a partner. Finally, ask a student to read the passage alone and give praise for appropriate expression.
9. Make a video or audio recording of yourself reading an easy book. Send the book and recording home with the student to practice reading at home.
10. Use the Fluency Development Lesson developed by Rasinski, Padak, Linek, and Sturtevant (1994). The lesson was designed for teachers of students in the primary grades who struggle to achieve even initial stages of fluency.
    - Make copies of a 50 to 150 word passage for each student and distribute them. Choose passages that will be enjoyable for students.
    - Read the passage to students while they follow along silently on their copies. You may want to reread the passage several times.
    - Discuss the content of the passage and the quality of your reading with students.
    - Guide students in choral readings of the passage. Vary the readings by using echo reading and responsive reading.
    - Have students select a partner and then practice reading the passage three times with the partner. The partner follows the passage, provides help if needed, and gives affirmations. Then the students reverse roles.
    - Invite students to read the text to the class. Individuals, partners, and groups up to four can read to the class. Seek additional opportunities for students to share the passage with others in the school (e.g., principal, specialists, other teachers) and to receive positive reinforcement.
    - Have students take the passage home to share with as many family members as possible. Be sure students are praised for their efforts.
    - Maintain a file of short, interesting passages used in the lessons and encourage students to read them on their own. These passages could also be used in a classroom learning center.
11. Use a big book in a shared book experience. After the book is introduced, read, and discussed, it can be reread several times. Encourage students to read along. Provide regular-sized versions of the big book that students can access for additional readings at school. Encourage the books to be taken home and shared.
12. Locate short, enjoyable selections of poetry and make them available to students. In addition, read such selections to students daily.
13. Encourage the reading and rereading of a variety of books and other printed materials.

For Older Readers Who Struggle

1. Be sure students are not asked to read books that are too difficult. A student who makes 10 or more miscues in 100 words is probably being asked to read material that is too difficult (Johns, 2008). Seek easier materials where the student will make fewer than seven miscues in every 100 words. Remember that word recognition must be accurate before reading can become automatic.
2. The method of Structured Repeated Reading found in Chapter 4 Resources (pages 326–329) is an excellent strategy. It motivates struggling readers and provides a visible means for them to see their progress.
3. Encourage wide reading and the rereading of easy books and other printed materials.
4. Invite students to prepare a story to read orally to younger readers. Have the students practice with a tape recorder and also share the story with you before it is shared with the group of younger students. Ensure that the experience will be a positive one. The books could also be recorded and shared with younger students.
5. Secure scripts for readers theater (www.aaronshep.com/rt) and have students practice their parts and then perform for an appropriate audience.
6. Try the Neurological Impress Method (NIM). The basic NIM procedure is described in the box below.

Procedure for the Neurological Impress Method (NIM)*

1. The student sits slightly in front of the teacher so that the teacher's voice is close to the student's ear.
2. The student is told not to think about reading; the teacher is helping him or her to slide the eyes across the paper. Another explanation is that we practice swimming in order to become good swimmers, so we need to practice reading to become good readers.
3. The teacher and student read the same material out loud *together*; the teacher reads a *little* louder and faster than the student.
4. *Reread* the initial lines or paragraph several times together before going on to new material (i.e., wait until the student is confident in reading that section). The teacher should drop his or her voice back behind the student's when the student is gaining fluency.
5. In the *initial* sessions, two to three minutes of reading lines is sufficient. The aim is to establish a fluent reading pattern with the student; appropriate *intonation* and *expression* in reading the lines are vital.
6. At *no* time correct the student or test the student in any way. The major concern is with the style of reading rather than with reading accuracy.
7. The teacher runs his or her finger under the words *simultaneously* with the words being read. The student should take over this function when he or she is confident enough. The teacher can help the student by placing his or her hand over the student's and guiding it smoothly. *Make sure finger and voice* are operating together.
8. *Echoing* is used as a supplementary technique to NIM if a student has extreme difficulty with saying a phrase or word. The student must repeat the phrase *after* the teacher several times; when he or she has satisfactorily repeated the phrase, the teacher then goes back to the *written* version.
9. Periodically, the pace *must* be speeded up just for a few minutes.
10. Start with reading material at the student's independent level.
11. Do 15 minutes a day to a total of 8 to 12 hours over several weeks.

*Heckelman, 1969.

7. Remember that the lack of fluency may be a symptom of an inadequate sight vocabulary and/or word-identification strategies. Refer to appropriate sections in Chapter 3 for strategies to strengthen these areas.

Evidence-Based Strategies for Building Fluency

Thirty easy-to-use lessons and activities for building fluency along with sixteen assessment passages can be found in Jerry L. Johns and Roberta L. Berglund (2006), *Fluency: Strategies & Assessments* (3rd ed.). Dubuque, IA: Kendall Hunt. www.kendallhunt.com/readingresources.html 800-247-3458, ext. 4.

Section 4.2

Lack of Fluency: Poor Phrasing

Behavior Observed → **Anticipated Outcome**

The student uses poor or inappropriate phrasing.

The student will read text with more appropriate phrasing.

Perspective and Strategies

Inappropriate phrasing beyond the initial stages of reading may be the result of poor reading habits, a lack of fluency, or an overreliance on phonics. It may also be related to the failure to follow the author's flow of ideas. You need to hypothesize why the student is using incorrect phrasing and then select an approach to the situation. The following strategies may help.

1. Read pattern books with the student. (See Part C on the CD for a list of pattern books.) Each time the pattern is repeated, ask the student to read it. Stress that the pattern should sound like speech.
2. Write experience stories with the student. Ask the student to read the story back to you and to pay close attention to the natural phrasing of the words. Refer to Chapter 3 (Section 3.6, Strategy 2) for student-dictated stories.
3. Enlarge a portion of text that you read to students. Have students follow along as you model appropriate phrasing. Highlight text cues that assist with appropriate phrasing.
4. List common phrases on cards and place them in a pocket chart. Ask the student to read the phrases so they sound natural. Some possible phrases are listed below.

in the lake	on the road
out of sight	near the school
over the hill	on the table
before the bell	in my room
in the closet	by my house
on the playground	by the river

Words for phrase building can be found on pages 254 and 265 in Chapter 3 Resources (Revised Dolch List and High-Frequency Nouns).

5. Use phrase markers. On a page of copied text, place slash marks at each natural break. Have the student try to read fluently to each slash mark before pausing. Model phrases as needed.

   My friend and I / decided to / ride our bikes / to school today.//

   Tomorrow / our class / will go / on a field trip.//

   We had pens, / pencils, / and markers for creating a large, / informative poster.//

6. Give the student ample opportunities to read with correct phrasing and punctuation by reading along with him or her. First, read an easy text to the student. Then ask the student to read along with you. Finally, ask the student to read the text independently as you support the effort by softly reading in the background.
7. Use echo reading to encourage reading fluency. Choose an easy text, read one phrase, and ask the student to read the same phrase with the same intonation that you used.
8. Often, students experiencing difficulty with reading hear only other novice readers reading aloud. Model good reading fluency to the entire class by reading to students each day. Also, model good reading with small groups of students who have difficulty with inappropriate phrasing. Alternate reading pages or paragraphs with the students.
9. Use repeated readings with partners as a technique to build fluency. Ask two students to choose short selections and read them until they know them well. Have each student read the selection to the other. See Johns and Berglund (2006) for a paired reading strategy.
10. Model phrasing by first reading a sentence word for word and asking the student to comment. Then use different phrasing to help the student grasp the idea that certain words go together.

    The/little/puppy/began/to/bark.
    The little/puppy/began/to bark.
    The little puppy/began to bark.

11. Select natural, meaningful ways for students to share their reading using appropriate phrasing. See Chapter 4 Resources (pages 320-321; 331)

Section 4.3

Lack of Fluency: Ignoring Punctuation

Behavior Observed →
The student ignores punctuation, adds punctuation, or uses inappropriate intonation.

Anticipated Outcome
The student will pay more attention to punctuation in order to read the text more fluently.

Perspective and Strategies

A student who ignores or adds punctuation is also likely to make some significant miscues when reading. Sometimes the student is anticipating a word or phrase that differs from that of the author. At other times, the student experiences difficulties with words, and these difficulties may influence whether punctuation is added or omitted. It is also possible that the student has not been taught about the role punctuation plays in constructing meaning from text. The following strategies may be helpful.

1. It may be most helpful to teach the most basic marks of punctuation and demonstrate how they function in text. Begin with the period and comma and then move to the question and exclamation marks. More advanced punctuation marks include the semicolon, colon, and dashes. It may be helpful to make a simple chart for teaching and display in the classroom. A partial chart is shown below.

Punctuation Chart

Type of Punctuation	Symbol	What It Means	Example
Period	.	Stop briefly	I ran around the track.
Comma	,	Pause	I had to feed my dog, so I got the dog food.
		Cluster words between two commas	I met Cody, my best friend, at the school fun fair.
		Words in a series	There were pens, pencils, paper, and notebooks for sale.
Exclamation Mark	!	Excitement	What a great race!

Explain one mark, provide a written example, model by reading the example aloud, and then have the student echo your reading. Then provide another example and have the student read it appropriately. Provide guidance as needed. Use a similar procedure for the other marks of punctuation in subsequent lessons. Invite students to point out punctuation marks in their reading and explain how the mark can influence how the sentence is read. Refer to the Punctuation Chart as necessary.

2. Write language experience stories with the student. Then have the student read the story, paying special attention to the punctuation.
3. Highlight particular sentences in the student's reading materials where different punctuation marks are found and have the student read the sentences with the appropriate pauses and emphasis. Provide support as needed.
4. Show the student examples where punctuation is ignored, substituted, or added. Discuss with the student whether the readers should have paid closer attention to the punctuation. Be sure to consider possible impact on meaning. Invite the student to offer ideas or hypotheses that may help explain the miscue. The examples below may be useful.

    Reader: Sharon Kay is my best friend.
    Text: Sharon, Kay is my best friend.

    Reader: Jake, my puppy is sick.
    Text: Jake, my puppy, is sick.

    Reader: John Allen, Mark, and Wayne are friends.
    Text: John, Allen, Mark, and Wayne are friends.

    Reader: I went to the store. Last Sunday . . .
    Text: I went to the store last Sunday.

    Reader: She said, "Use your head and think."
    Text: She said, "Use your head and think!"

5. When students do not pause at periods and commas, have them point to the marks of punctuation and reread the sentence with a pause. Model as appropriate.
6. When a student fails to use the proper expression for question and exclamation marks, draw attention to the specific mark, ask what the mark signifies, and invite the student to reread the text with the proper emphasis. Model as needed.
7. Segment a group of numbers or the alphabet into several segments that include different marks of punctuation. Invite students to silently look at the sequence, paying particular attention to the marks of punctuation which signal particular intonations. Then have selected students read the sequence. Other students should listen carefully and comment on how the sequence was read. Several different sequences are shown below.

    123! 4—56. 7.8.9. 10? 11,12—13,14. 15! 16.17—18? 19,20!
    1! 234? 56! 789,10. 11,12. 13? 14,15—16! 17? 18,19,20!

    ABCD! EFG? HIJ. K? LMNOP! QR—ST UV. W! XYZ.
    AB. CD. EF,GH. I! JKL? M? NOP. QR? S—TUV. W, X, Y! Z?

8. Read a selection of text as students follow along. Omit and/or add punctuation. Have students point out how the reading could be improved. Then reread the selection making some of the same errors. Invite students to comment. Finally, reread the selection with appropriate punctuation and then have students comment on improvements noted.
9. Remind students that good readers pay attention to punctuation marks so that they can read fluently and construct meaning from the text.

10. Have students mark or note places in their readings where they have ignored punctuation, added unnecessary punctuation, or used inappropriate intonation. Then invite students to talk about these instances with you. Later, small groups of students could share their notes with each other. The goal is for students to learn from their miscues. Some guiding questions follow.

    - Why did I read the sentence that way?
    - What was I thinking about as I read?
    - Did I decide something didn't make sense? Why?
    - If it didn't make sense, what did I do (if anything)?
    - Did I repeat to confirm or correct what I was reading?
    - What have I learned about my reading from these examples?

Section **4.4**

Lack of Fluency: Repetitions of Words or Phrases

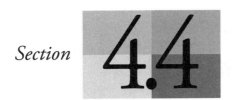

Behavior Observed → **Anticipated Outcome**

The student repeats words, phrases, or sentences. → The student will be able to read the text with fewer repetitions.

Perspective and Strategies

Repetition may help the student understand what he or she has read. The teacher must decide whether the student is analyzing the repeated word, anticipating a difficult word, making a legitimate effort to have the reading make sense, repeating from habit, or striving for word-perfect oral reading. Consider the following.

1. If the student's repetitions are frequent attempts to correct or to try to correct numerous miscues, it is possible that the reading material is too difficult. If this is the case, provide the student with reading material at a level that is easy to read.
2. Repetitions characterized as "stalls" provide the student with extra time to try to figure out an unknown word. This may be a normal part of the reading process. Excessive use of the stall technique, however, may indicate that the reading material is too difficult and/or more effective reading strategies are needed. It may also indicate a need to teach how language clues can be used to anticipate words.
3. Praise the student when a word, phrase, or sentence is repeated to correct (or to try to correct) a miscue and preserve ongoing meaning.

   Below are three examples. The © means that the miscue was corrected; the underline signifies words repeated.

   They ©
   He <u>also saw</u> a library book.

   from ©
   The bear <u>had come</u> for the honey.

   was ©
   <u>Ken</u> had solved the mystery.

Tell the student that this behavior is fully acceptable in order to make sense of what is read. Too many repetitions of this sort, however, can impact rate of reading.

4. If repetitions are merely a habit, it may be helpful to have the student record a passage on audiotape and discuss it with you. The student should be guided to note which repetitions are habitual, resulting in less efficient reading. Encourage rereadings to promote greater fluency. Two such examples are shown below.

   The underlines indicate words repeated.

   Elwood <u>looked</u> <u>like</u> Mr. Wilson.

   Ken <u>saw</u> the <u>skateboarder</u> slide <u>down</u> the library railing.

5. Sometimes a student repeatedly overcorrects to ensure word-for-word accuracy. The student should be encouraged not to break the meaning flow of the text when the reading makes sense.

6. Invite students to share and discuss instances when they repeated words, phrases, or sentences in their reading. Help them see how their repetitions may contribute to or detract from efficient reading. For example, repeating to confirm meaning would be an effective use. Some repetitions may make reading less efficient because they are not done to correct a miscue or to help make sense of the passage.

Section 4.5

Lack of Expression

Behavior Observed → **Anticipated Outcome**

The student's oral reading lacks expression. → The student will read orally with improved expression.

Perspective and Strategies

Appropriate expression is typically characterized by using phrasing, punctuation, tone, emphasis, intonation, and pitch to help convey the author's message and to facilitate comprehension. Prosody (Cecil, 2007; Dowhower, 1991) is the term often used for these elements. Several other sections of this chapter deal with some of these elements, and you might refer to them (see 4.1, 4.2, 4.3, and 4.4) for additional ideas. Expression can be influenced by the student's automaticity (immediate recognition of words), understanding of punctuation, use of typographic signals (e.g., bold print, type size, italics), and the quality of instruction in prosodic cues. It is also important to ensure that the student is given reading materials that are at an appropriate level. Some strategies to use are presented below.

1. If the student's sight vocabulary is limited, refer to Chapter 3 for ideas to build greater automaticity with words.
2. Take time to teach the various elements of prosody within the ongoing instructional program. Many of these elements can be modeled and discussed when you read orally to students. Comment on relevant elements before or after you read a particular sentence or passage. It is often helpful for students to see the passage when you are using it instructionally. Consider the sentence that follows from a novel by Sansom (2005).

> "Yeeees," she said, drawing out the "yes" as though stretching a balloon.

You might display this sentence to students and say the following.

> *You can see that the first word looks strange, but the rest of the sentence gives us a clue as to how it should be read. Listen as I read the sentence and pay particular attention to how I stretch out the word* yes. [Read the sentence and then have students echo your reading. Pointing out that the way the word was stretched out gives the reader a cue as to how it should be read.]

3. Use sentences or short passages from students' reading materials to teach, model, and practice other aspects of prosody in a manner similar to the first example. Some examples (Sansom, 2005) for possible use are also provided below.

   "Don't go. Sit down. Come on. Come on! Sit!"
   "Take. The keys," said Ted insistently.
   "I'm delighted, delighted, delighted. Wonderful!"
   "Oh, that's great! That's great," exclaimed Linda.
   It was his *head* that hit the tree first.
   "Ah, right. I'm afraid . . . actually I lost all that stuff, I'm afraid."

4. Encourage students to be alert for interesting sentences in their reading that can be shared with other students. Be sure to have the student highlight the particular prosodic element. You might also share some of the following sentences.

   Very quietly Cote said, "I don't think I can go."
   He looked both ways—and then he ran across the street.
   The swing went higher and higher and HIGHER!
   Jose, a very friendly person, was chosen to greet the guests.
   I want *more*!
   Wait—I forgot my gift.

5. Promote expressive reading by using plays and reader's theater scripts (see page 320 for sources of scripts).
6. Select a portion of text that contains prosodic features you want to help students understand. Enlarge the passage for use on an overhead projector. Read the selection aloud using no expression, pauses, or changes in pitch. Ignore punctuation. Invite reactions from students and then have them listen as you read the passage with expression. Discuss cues in the passage that helped you read it appropriately. Then have students practice the passage with a partner. You can also provide a new passage containing features you just modeled, have students read it silently, and then read it with their partners. Finally, ask several students to read the passage to the class using good expression. Provide guidance as needed.
7. Have students listen to recorded texts that model good expression. Students should have a copy of the text so they can follow along. Later, provide opportunities for students to read portions of the text to model the recording.
8. Encourage students to read poems in an expressive manner with partners. Share some of your favorite poems and make them available for students to read along with you.
9. Older students can be encouraged to read famous speeches and select portions of them to share with an audience. Actual recordings of some famous speeches (e.g., FDR, Martin Luther King, Jr.) can be found on the Internet so students can listen to the speech as they read along and prepare for their performance.

10. Prepare a sheet containing character dialogue from your curriculum or develop some. Share the segments with students and have them practice aloud the way the character(s) might have spoken. Encourage students to look for typographic signals or other cues for phrasing, emphasis, and so on. Model a sample. Some possible items to use or adapt are listed below.

    Eyeballs for sale!
    This is my *first* time.
    Where do you want me to put the **biggest** box?
    Watch your head!
    Mr. West, our teacher, is also a great singer.
    Do you want chocolate or vanilla ice cream?
    I think Montana is the best state.
    Where did you put my gift?
    It's hot, so you don't need a sweater.

Section **4.6**

Overemphasis on Speed and Accuracy

Behavior Observed ⟶ **Anticipated Outcome**

The student is concerned primarily with speed and accuracy when reading.

The student will realize that factors in addition to speed and accuracy are important when reading.

Perspective and Strategies

In recent years, educators have witnessed a great increase of progress monitoring in fluency, and much of the monitoring (or assessment) has focused primarily on the timing of reading (often one minute) and the determination of accuracy of word identification. Hence, speed and accuracy may be perceived by students as the primary purpose of reading. Teachers need to realize that their progress monitoring may unintentionally lead to students becoming word-callers instead of meaning seekers (Marcell, 2007). The first and most important action to remedy this situation is for the teacher to help students realize, develop, and maintain a concept of fluency that involves four components: comprehension, expression, speed, and accuracy. This more comprehensive concept should also be integrated into progress monitoring (i.e., use retelling and/or questions for comprehension). Other strategies that may be useful with students are listed below.

1. Develop the concept that fluency involves more than speed and accuracy. Make a diamond on a poster and write the four components of fluency on the outside of the diamond. Take time to discuss each of these components and display the poster in a prominent place. Encourage students to keep these components in mind as they read.

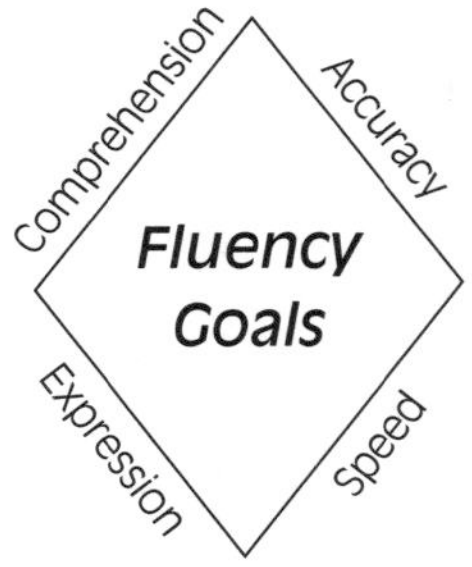

2. Model each of these aspects of fluency during teacher read alouds and draw students' attention to times when expression was used. Also, discuss the content so students realize that the primary purpose for reading is to construct meaning (comprehension). Some examples follow.
   - Did you notice how I made my voice sad when I read the last sentence? Why do you think I did that?
   - In the next section I read, you will notice that my voice changes to help capture the mood of the two characters. Listen carefully and then we'll discuss that section.
   - You probably noticed that I read the last few sentences very slowly. What do you think I was trying to help you understand? Did you notice that when I was reading?
   - Notice that I read that last sentence in an exciting way. I wanted to enhance the idea that the character was quite excited.
   - Why do you think the two characters had such a heated exchange? How might you have acted if you were in a similar situation?
3. Look for natural opportunities in the instructional program and small group activities to highlight and stress an appropriate concept of fluency.
4. Have students listen to multiple readings of a portion of text and compare and contrast the readings. Encourage discussion. Some suggested ways to read the selection are listed below.
   - Read the selection in a word-by-word manner.
   - Read the selection very slowly.
   - Read the selection with inappropriate phrasing.
   - Read the selection without expression.
   - Make many meaning-changing miscues as you read the selection.
   - Use many repetitions in the selection.
   - Ignore punctuation as you read.
   - Read the selection very fast.
5. If the student makes many miscues in an effort to increase speed, stop the student and say that accuracy is also an important part of reading. Encourage the student to practice the selection so that it can be read accurately with appropriate expression.
6. For the student who races through the selection and does not understand what was read, help the student realize that the reasons to read are to construct meaning, gain information, and make sense of what was read. Provide examples of various types of reading that can be done and have the student offer ideas as to why the reading was likely to be done in a particular way. Some examples to use or adapt are listed below.

   the directions to a picnic
   a favorite poem
   a list for a scavenger hunt
   a list of school supplies
   directions for a new game
   a note your teacher gives you
   a menu
   a note on the kitchen table
   a cereal box
   a new comic book
   a letter from a friend
   a grocery list
   a postcard received in the mail
   a book about famous people
   a new poster in the school hall
   a book of jokes and riddles
   comics in the newspaper
   directions with a new purchase

7. Have students prepare written "conversations" between two classmates. Tell students that some oral reading involving characters should sound a lot like conversations they have. Then invite students to choose a partner and practice the "conversations" using appropriate expression, phrasing, emphasis, and rate. Students should be encouraged to extend the conversation by predicting what would likely be said next.
8. Use reader's theater scripts to help students practice appropriate rate and expression to convey meaning to the audience. Model as needed and then have students echo the lines using the same emphasis, tone, and expression.
9. Provide plenty of opportunities for meaningful oral reading in audience situations where students can practice communicating the intended message to listeners.

Section 4.7

Failure to Attempt Unknown Words

Behavior Observed →

The student waits to be told unknown words and does not attempt them independently.

Anticipated Outcome

The student will use appropriate strategies to decode unknown words.

Perspective and Strategies

The failure of some students to attempt unknown words may be due to several factors. First, students may be asked to read materials that are too difficult, so they come upon many unknown words and feel overwhelmed. Second, students may not have been taught a functional strategy for word identification, and they do not have a variety of strategies to use when confronted with an unknown word in reading (see Sections 3.9 and 3.10). Although students may have been taught phonics and the use of context, they do not realize that these strategies may be used during reading. Third, the teacher may tell students unknown words, thereby reducing their need to acquire internal strategies for word identification. Fourth, students who are usually struggling may be reluctant to take risks. Instead, they manipulate the teacher or other students to tell them words they don't know. The following strategies may be useful.

1. Determine the suitability of the reading materials. Choose easier materials if the student makes nine or more miscues in one hundred words. In appropriate materials, the student may miss, on average, about one word in twenty (the instructional level).
2. When the student hesitates at an unknown word, wait ten seconds before saying anything. If there is no response, ask the student to try the word using the known sounds. Praise the student for any attempt at the word.
3. Discuss what the student thinks should be done when confronted with an unknown word.

   For example, ask the student to think about a time when he or she was reading and came to an unknown word. Ask the student what strategies were used to figure out the word. If the student is unable to suggest any strategies, guide the student in expressing strategies that emphasize the sound-symbol correspondence of the word (see Sections 3.1 and 3.2), strategies that use the meaning of the sentence, and strategies that use knowledge about the English language (see Section 3.7).

4. Have the student give the word some sounds and take a guess at the word. Then have the student read to the end of the phrase or sentence and decide whether the word makes sense.
5. Ask the student to go back a line and see if the preceding sentence and the words around the unknown word suggest a possibility. Read the sentence aloud for the student, skipping the unknown word, and ask what word might make sense in the blank.
6. Ask the student to reread the sentence and try to guess a word that begins with the initial sound of the unknown word and makes sense in the sentence.
7. Provide oral examples where the student uses context to anticipate the missing word. Stress that context clues can be used while reading.

    I really like to watch ___________.

    I would like to see the ___________ game.

    It's time to go to ___________.

    I found ___________ in my backpack.

8. Use easy cloze exercises where students are asked to predict a word that makes sense. Discuss various choices offered by the students and invite them to share how and why they made their specific predictions. Gradually include graphic information about the exact word the author used. Use examples like the following ones.

    I like ___________.

    I like to go to ___________.

    I like to go to s _ _ _ _ l.

9. If the student encounters several unknown words in a line of print, the reading material is probably too difficult. Provide reading material that is easy for the student to read.
10. Invite other students to share their experiences with unknown words by using a chart like the one on the next page.

    Have students complete the chart during a reading assignment by filling in the various categories. Then have students share their strategies by focusing on predicting, confirming, and correcting strategies. Be sure to reinforce the strategies that are especially good—even if they did not result in success. Help students also realize that sometimes the strategies used will not result in the correct pronunciation of the word.
11. Be alert for instances in your reading where you encounter a difficult word. Bring in the passage and model for students what you did to deal with the word. Thinking aloud can be especially helpful to show students some of what goes on in your head while reading.

What strategy can be used when this student hesitates to attempt an unknown word?

MY WORD CHALLENGES

Name ______________________________ Date ______________

Page	*Difficult Word/Phrase/Sentence*	*What I Did*	*How It Worked*

Section 4.8

Meaning-Changing Substitutions

Behavior Observed → **Anticipated Outcome**

The student substitutes a word or words, and the text does not make sense. → The student will read the text with fewer substitutions that change the meaning.

Perspective and Strategies

Remind the student that reading is a process of constructing meaning from print. When reading, the student should ask, "Does this make sense?" This question serves as one way for the student to monitor his or her comprehension. The student should be taught to use semantic (meaning) cues in reading. Try the following strategies.

1. Remind the student to think while reading and encourage the student to stop and reread the material if it does not make sense. The student may be viewing reading as "saying words" rather than reading to construct meaning.
2. Give the student oral exercises to identify words that do not make sense in the context of the sentence. Some examples follow.

   - The mail carrier delivered the groceries.
   - Helen set her calendar so it would ring at seven o'clock.
   - Bill went to the store to buy some candy for her sister.

   Have the student explain why a particular word does not make sense and invite a substitute word or phrase. For example, if the student identifies *groceries* in the first sentence, have the student explain why the word doesn't make sense and offer a word that would make sense. The student might say what follows.

   > *Mail carriers do not deliver groceries, but they do deliver mail, letters, and packages. Any of those words would make sense.*

   You might also ask the student what word or words wouldn't make sense if *groceries* was the correct word (i.e., mail carrier) and what word or words might be substituted for mail carrier (e.g., employee, store, woman, girl, man, boy).

3. Give the student oral and written exercises containing cloze tasks and instruct the student to anticipate omitted words that make sense. Develop the idea that language dictates that only certain types of words can be placed after certain language structures.

   - After playing, the children ________ inside.
   - I will see you after ________.
   - He was reading a ________.
   - "I lost my money," ________ Carlos.

   For example, in the sentence, "I saw an ______ in the tree," the word *an* signals that a word beginning with a vowel (e.g., apple) would be required. Provide another example where the preceding part of the sentence may signal an adjective or noun (e.g., The _____ frog jumped in the pond; The little ______ began to bark).

4. Use small-group activities in which certain key words in a story are covered. Ask for responses from the group and have students evaluate each response. The ultimate criterion is "Does the word make sense?" Invite students to explain how the words in the story help the reader to predict other words. Then uncover the word letter by letter and encourage students to refine their predictions and ultimately confirm the word.

5. Keep track of substitutions to see whether certain words are habitually associated with other words. Write selections where the grammatical structures make it highly unlikely for the habitual associations to occur. Consider the following examples.

   was and *saw*

   Once upon a time there *was* a girl named Jennifer. Her hair *was* long and brown. Jennifer liked to wear headbands in her hair. One day, while she *was* walking downtown, she *saw* some headbands in a store window. She *saw* blue, yellow, and pink headbands. The blue headband *was* the prettiest, so she bought it.

   in and *on*

   Vanessa liked to collect insects. She kept the spiders *in* a jar *on* top of her dresser. One Friday, her family invited some friends to come over for coffee. They were talking *in* the kitchen. Vanessa took her jar of spiders into the kitchen and set it *on* the table. When one woman reached for a cup *on* the table, she bumped the jar. It landed *on* the floor. What do you think happened next?

   when and *then*

   Adam and his mother had some errands to do. His mother said, "I will get my coat; *then* I will be ready to go. *When* you find your jacket, come out to the car. First, we will go to the supermarket; *then* we can go to the pet shop to find out *when* the puppy will be ready to come home. *When* we bring the puppy home, you will get the basket out of the closet. *Then* the puppy will have a nice place to sleep."

6. Provide sentences from students' reading that contain a substituted word written above the text. Have students discuss whether the substituted word makes sense. Use the examples provided below or construct your own.

   they
   They went to the zoo because there were many things to see.

   like
   It sounded as if someone were trying to break into my cabin.

   from
   The bear had come for the honey.

hat
He hit the ball out of the park.

saw
She was the first one to finish the race.

7. Provide exercises that contain substitutions two different readers made in the same sentence. Discuss which substitution appears to be closer to the author's meaning. Be sure students understand why one particular substitution may be better than another substitution. See the following examples.

the
Michael decided to ride along a little road.

walk
Michael decided to ride along a little road.

body
No one knew who the talented person was.

had
No one knew who the talented person was.

8. Tape-record the student's reading. Give the student a copy of what was read and have the student listen to the reading and underline the substitutions that occur. Ask the student if the substituted word would make sense in the sentence. Then check the letters in the word to determine the actual word the author used.
9. If there are many substitutions that distort the author's intended meaning, the book may be too difficult. Choose materials that are easy for the student to read. Generally, materials are appropriate for instruction if the student misses fewer than 7 of 100 running words in text.
10. Have students keep track of their reading and report instances where a word that did not make sense was substituted for a word in the text. Invite students to share how they dealt with the substitution. Help them realize and verbalize the predicting, confirming, and correcting behaviors that they may have used.
11. Use actual examples from students' reading to model how they can monitor their reading. Such examples could be used in minilessons. You can also use examples from your own reading.

Section 4.9

Nonmeaning-Changing Substitutions

Behavior Observed → **Anticipated Outcome**

Behavior Observed	Anticipated Outcome
The student substitutes a word or words, and the phrase or sentence still makes sense.	The student will read the text with fewer substitutions.

Perspective and Strategies

Substitutions in reading may occur for several reasons. First, the student may be ignoring graphophonic cues in reading. Second, the student may be relying too heavily on context clues to predict words that make sense in the sentence. Third, the student's oral language may be different from the author's written language, and the student produces a response that makes sense. For example, the student may say "can't" for "cannot."

Because the basic meaning of the text is not adversely affected, there may be no need for the teacher to take any action. A student who continues to substitute words that differ from the text, however, may not be willing to take the time to identify unknown words. For students who habitually make these kinds of substitutions, you may want to try some of the following strategies.

1. Commend the student by noting that his or her substitution miscues rarely change the author's meaning. Show the student a few examples and give the student an opportunity to offer an explanation. Use the experience to help the student reflect on his or her reading behavior.
2. After the student has completed the passage, point out the words that differ from the text. Ask the student to reread the sentence paying close attention to these words. If the student rereads the word correctly, mention the change. Tell the student that, although the first attempt may not have changed the author's meaning, misreading words can lead to difficulty understanding the text. If the student repeats the miscue, draw attention to the sounds in the word. Ask the student to think of another word that uses the sounds represented by the letters in the word.

3. Some students make substitutions in reading because they are not given enough time to decode unknown words. As the student is reading, encourage all attempts at identifying unfamiliar words. Be patient and use wait time.
4. For a student who makes many substitutions, tape-record the student reading an easy passage. Give the student a copy of the text and play back the audiotape. Ask the student to underline any words from the audiotape that do not match the printed text. Ask the student to use the sounds associated with a letter or letter combination to help figure out the underlined word. If the student is unable to correct the miscue, model an effective strategy by thinking aloud.
5. Students who make many miscues in reading may be reading from a passage that is too difficult. Give the students easier reading material and stress the point that reading means understanding the printed text.

Section **4.10**

Nonword Substitutions

Behavior Observed → **Anticipated Outcome**

The student produces a nonword instead of a real word.

The student will say more real words that make sense in the text.

Perspective and Strategies

The student must be helped to realize that reading is a meaningful process and words pronounced should make sense. Use or adapt Section 2.1. Reading should sound like oral language.

1. Ask the student what the nonword means. It is possible that the student knows the meaning but has mispronounced the word.
2. Provide oral and written examples in which the student attempts to predict the appropriate word that has been omitted. Stress that some words can be predicted from context and have the student use background knowledge to make predictions. The goal should be to say a real word, not a nonword.

   Guide the student with questions and model as necessary. For the first sentence below you might say:

   > *What are some things you can play?* [Student says ball.] *I also think chess could fit. What other words make sense?*

   - After school, we went to play ___________.
   - I will mail the ___________.
   - The horse ___________ over the fence.
3. Provide examples that contain a nonword and ask the student to tell what real word could replace the nonword. Have the student explain why he or she was able to give a real word. Praise the student for saying that the other words in the sentence provided cues, and highlight the words. Some examples follow.

- He drank a glass of fex. (e.g., milk, water, juice)
- One day Ken tassed a skateboard. (e.g., saw, noticed, rode, dropped)
- The zop bought some candy. (e.g., girl, boy, woman, person)

4. Place removable opaque tape over certain words in the student's reading materials that can be easily predicted. Encourage the student to supply a real word or words that make sense. Then remove the tape and compare the prediction to the actual word. Help the student to transfer this same strategy to identifying unknown words when they appear in text.
5. Five or more nonwords per 100 words probably indicate that the reading material is too difficult. Provide materials that are easy for the student to read aloud.
6. Tape-record the student reading. Play back the audiotape while the student follows the text. Pause the tape recorder at each nonword. Ask the student,

   Does this make sense? What word would make sense in that spot?

   Then discuss the student's response. If necessary, guide the student in suggesting a real word.

   To avoid the student forming a mental set, ask the same question from time to time when the student's reading does make sense.
7. Model how you can use context and phonic knowledge to pronounce a word. For example, you could read *mansion* as *mīnsīn* in the following sentence.

   The big old mansion in the neighborhood had several broken windows.

   Then you could model by saying something like what follows.

   I know mīnsīn *doesn't make sense. Let me take another look at the word and think of words that could have broken windows. A* house, garage, *and* car *can have broken windows, but none of those words begin with the same beginning sound as the word. Let me try the word again. I see the word* man *but* mansin *doesn't sound like a word I know. Perhaps it's* mānsin. *No, that doesn't make sense. Let me try again:* mānshun, mănshun. *I've heard of a mansion. Let me try that word in the sentence to see if it makes sense. Yes, the word* mansion *makes sense. It is another name for a house that is big. I think that's it.*

   Be sure students understand the predicting, correcting, and confirming behaviors that characterized your reading.

Section 4.11

Meaning-Changing Omissions

Behavior Observed → **Anticipated Outcome**

The student omits one or more words, and the text does not make sense or distorts the author's intended meaning.

The student will read text with fewer omissions.

Perspective and Strategies

Because this type of omission changes the meaning or does not make sense of the text, the student needs to understand that reading is the process of constructing meaning from print (see Section 2.2). Suggested strategies follow.

1. Frequent omissions may mean that the reading material is too difficult. Supply reading material at a lower level.
2. Provide exercises that contain omissions made by a reader. In a pocket chart, make sentences from word cards that have a word that can be omitted without losing the grammatical sense of the sentence. Have students discuss whether (or how much) the omission changes the author's intended meaning and how they arrived at that conclusion. Use sentences like those below.
   - The large horse ate lots of oats. (large)
   - Jeff walked to the toy store. (toy)
   - I have twenty-five dollars. (five)
   - The bear had come for the honey. (the)
3. Remind students that reading is supposed to make sense and convey the author's meaning. Ask students the question that follows.

   Did that make sense?

   Use this same question from time to time when the omission also makes sense. Help students reflect on their reading so they come to realize that some miscues may change the meaning and not be corrected—especially if they make sense in the context of the passage. At other times, students will correct miscues that do not make sense. Encourage students to explain their various behaviors so they gain greater insight into monitoring their reading.

4. Some students who omit text are reading too fast. Ask the student to follow the line of print with his or her finger or a marker. Following text with a marker or finger may slow the reading down and increase concentration on the text.
5. Place the student in a group for choral reading. Choral reading is reading text aloud in a group. By reading in a group, the student may pay closer attention to the text.

6. Have the student tape-record his or her reading. Using a printed copy of the selection, help the student mark the omissions. Then discuss the omissions with the student, seeking the student's insights about the omissions and their impact on meaning. Help the student realize the importance of monitoring his or her reading to construct meaning. Reinforce important observations the student makes.

   Some examples are provided below. The crossed out word was initially omitted. The © indicates that the student "corrected" the omitted word. Underlined words were repeated during the "correction."

©
The summer was ~~a~~ dry one.

©
Their objective ~~was~~ to reach the fort.

Section **4.12**

Nonmeaning-Changing Omissions

Behavior Observed → **Anticipated Outcome**

The student omits one or more words, and the text still makes sense. → The student will read text with fewer omissions.

Perspective and Strategies

Note this important point: Omissions that result in little or no change in meaning should not require any direct action from you unless the student habitually omits words. If the omissions occur frequently, consider the following strategies.

1. Ask the student to slow down when reading aloud. Younger students may wish to follow the line of print with a marker or their finger to make sure they do not omit text. Even expert readers occasionally use this strategy with challenging text, so do not discourage its use with young students.
2. Give the student several opportunities to read along with a taped story. Encourage the student to keep up with the reader without omitting words.
3. Older students develop an eye-voice span where their eyes are "ahead" of their voice. Omissions may occur when the student's eyes are reading faster than his or her voice. When this type of behavior is observed, discuss it with the student to gain insight.
4. Tape-record the student's reading and have him or her listen to the tape while following with the text, paying particular attention to omissions. Then ask the student to evaluate the quality of the omissions and offer reasons why they occurred. During the discussion, help the student realize that, although the overall meaning is retained, some omitted words probably would have provided greater detail or a richer meaning.
5. Provide examples where one or more words are omitted. Guide the student in evaluating the reading to determine the degree to which meaning is impacted. Three possible examples to use are presented below.

He had a ~~blue~~ box.
I climbed the hill to get a ~~better~~ view.
We had a big test ~~the~~ next day.

Section **4.13**

Excessive Use of Phonics

Behavior Observed → **Anticipated Outcome**

Behavior Observed	Anticipated Outcome
The student habitually tries to sound out words when confronted with an unknown word in text.	The student will use phonics, context, word chunks, and other strategies to try to identify unknown words.

Perspective and Strategies

Some students may have been taught that the appropriate strategy to figure out unknown words is to sound them out. These students may not have been taught other strategies that can be used with unknown words. In either case, teachers must instruct students to use their knowledge of language (syntax) and context (meaning) cues. The following strategies may be useful.

1. Ask the student why he or she uses phonics frequently. Use the student's response to make instructional decisions. For example, if phonics is the student's basic or first word-identification strategy, refer to Sections 3.4, 3.5, 3.7, 3.9, and 3.10.
2. Show students that they can sometimes correctly predict a word in oral language before hearing it. Help them transfer this same knowledge in reading. Use the examples provided below.
   - He gave the kitten some ____________.
   - Put a stamp on the ____________.
   - Ten dimes make a ____________.
3. Provide examples where two readers made different miscues on the same unknown word. Discuss the responses of the two readers in an attempt to decide which reader has been most effective and the reasons for the effectiveness. Be sure students give reasons for their decisions. Model appropriate responses as needed.

   Text: The car went down the old street.
   Reader 1: The car went down the old road.
   Reader 2: The car went down the old stream.

4. Provide words that students are unable to pronounce. The difficult words can then be placed in a context that builds meaning for the words. Through these exercises, the students should realize that they can understand without always sounding out words.

   guerdon
   After finding a purse, Jason returned it to the owner. The owner of the purse gave a *guerdon* to Jason, who bought a model car kit with it.

   engrossed
   Dana was *engrossed* in an adventure story. Her mom and dad both had to call her for dinner. Finally, she put the book down and came to the kitchen table.

5. Help students build fluency by using Structured Repeated Reading (pages 326–330) in Chapter 4 Resources.
6. Consult Chapter 3 for ways to help develop a variety of word-identification strategies and how to use them. Sections 3.9 and 3.10 may be especially helpful.

Section 4.14

Excessive Use of Experience

© 2010 Stephen Coburn. Used under license from Shutterstock, Inc.

Behavior Observed ⟶ **Anticipated Outcome**

The student overrelies on experience and context while reading.

The student will use phonic information and word chunks with context while reading.

Perspective and Strategies

You may have some students who "read" quite fluently; however, a number of the words students read may not have been written by the author. The students seem to rely heavily on their background knowledge to the partial exclusion of graphophonic knowledge. The result is often an interesting story that is quite different from the one in print. Effective reading requires the use of context, language, and graphophonic cues. The following strategies may be useful.

1. Tell the student that experience and background knowledge is important to help predict words while reading, but other cues can also be used. Model how initial sounds along with context can be used to pronounce words. The following examples may be useful.
   - The tree is l______. (large)
   - My f______ is older than I am. (friend, father)
2. Tape-record the student's reading, listen to it, and mark miscues. Then review selected miscues with the student and discuss how meaning has been disrupted even though a particular miscue may make sense. Model how some graphic information can be used to arrive at the word used by the author. Consider these examples.

   cat
   My pet dog is very friendly.

   pleasant
   She was very pleased.
3. Present a few sentences where the student can make initial predictions of the word.

   Milk is perhaps a favorite drink of __________ throughout the world.
   (children, men, women, boys, girls, people)

Then present some graphic information (e.g., the initial letter) and have the student explain why some words may or may not be good choices based on the available information. For example, help the student see that, while all the words make sense, the beginning letter of the word used by the author will narrow the choices to only one of the words. Add the initial letter and have the student predict a word beginning with that letter that makes sense. Add additional letters if necessary. Help the student realize that the context and graphic information provide cues to help pronounce the word the author wrote. Use some other examples and then supply graphic information for the beginning, middle, or end of the word. Use examples from the student's reading or adapt the examples below.

- The northern deserts of Mexico have lizards, (*rattlesnakes*), and prairie dogs. (Perhaps use *r* and *snakes* as graphic cues.)
- The early Indians used (*seashells*) for music and dances. (Perhaps use *sea* and then *sh* as graphic cues.)
- Popular sports in Mexico include baseball, soccer, and (*volleyball*). (Perhaps use *v* and *ball* as graphic cues.)

4. Acknowledge that all readers make miscues but stress the importance of trying to pronounce the words written by the author. Relate the situation to a piece of writing that the student has written. When it is read by someone else, the expectation is that the student's words will be read. You might be able to model how you could change words from the student's piece of writing and still have it make sense even though the student had a different message in mind. Below is a partial sample from a student's writing (Lenski & Johns, 2004) with miscues that change the meaning although the sentence still makes sense.

Sam *baseball*
One day Sean bought a basketball at the sports department.

Resources

4

Note: indicates teacher material.

Oral Reading as Performance

Teachers should give their students a wide range of opportunities to practice oral language. Students who read aloud for an audience are subtly learning several things. They are learning how language is used in written text; they are learning how to communicate to an audience; and they are learning how to interpret text. Students reading aloud can also stimulate interest in stories and encourage other students to read. Oral reading, therefore, is a beneficial practice when students have adequately prepared and are sharing their reading with an appropriate audience.

Teachers can provide different kinds of experiences with reading aloud. Some may be more time-consuming and rather formal, such as reader's theater and storytelling. Others may be more spontaneous, such as reading an exciting part of a story. With both types of reading, however, students should always have sufficient opportunities to practice before performing and should rehearse their part before reading to their audience. The following are some examples of ways to use oral reading as performance.

Students Create Reader's Theater

To create a reader's theater script, ask students to:

1. Choose a piece of literature with a strong story line or a chapter from a content area book that could be read in parts.
2. Read the piece silently. Discuss the contents of the story and ask the students to read it again.
3. Develop a script from the literature. Students may use the entire story, or they may decide to create a scene from the story.
4. Assign parts and rehearse the play.
5. Present the play to an appropriate audience.

Reader's Theater Scripts

Teachers may prefer to use commercially available scripts for reader's theater. Johns and Berglund (2006) have provided various sources for scripts that can be used with students in primary grades through middle school. Selected websites follow.

http://www.aaronshep.com/rt
http://www.geocities.com/EnchantedForest/Tower/3235
http://www.lisablau.com/scriptomonth.html
http://www.loiswalker.com/catalog/guidesamples.html
http://www.readers-theatre.com
http://www.stemnet.nf.ca/CITE/langrt.htm#Gander
http://www.storycart.com

(continued)

Storytelling

Ask students to:

1. Choose a favorite piece of literature.
2. Read the story several times, thinking about the sequence of action in the plot.
3. Think or write the entire story without the text. Include the story line and the main point of the story.
4. Retell the story to a friend, a group, or for a tape recording.

Functional Situations for Oral Reading

- Poetry and rhymes
- Student-written advertisements
- Announcements from the office
- Riddles and jokes
- Letters from pen pals
- Student stories

Oral Reading Opportunities

- Read the part that tells when the event happened.
- Read the part that describes one of the problems encountered.
- Read what a certain character said.
- Read the most exciting part of the story.
- Read a funny part of the story.
- Read the part you like best.
- Read the part that tells you the most about a character.
- Read the part that makes you see the setting most clearly.
- Read the most surprising part of the story.
- Read the part that explains the goal or problem of the main character.
- Read the part that explains the outcome or solution of the story.
- Read the part that you think your best friend would like.
- Read the part that supports your answer.
- Read the part that tells you what to do next.
- Read the part that explains why ___________.

Taking Account of Dialects

Changes of sounds and endings in some words may be a result of the student's dialect (adapted from Kress, 1993 and Rubin, 1993). A dialect of English is a variation of standard English, which is the language most widely used in print and by the media. When students read aloud, they may pronounce standard written English with their own dialect and may even change grammatical structures. Because reading in dialect rarely affects comprehension, you should not consider dialect differences to be significant miscues.

Spanish

A student with a Spanish-language background might exhibit the following dialect differences when he or she reads standard English.

- The vowel sounds in the following words may be difficult for the Spanish-speaking student to pronounce: *i* in *bit, a* in *bat,* schwa sound in *but,* and *u* in *full.*
- There are several sounds in English that are not found in Spanish: *v* in *vote, th* in *then, z* in *zoo, zh* in *measure,* and *j* in *jump*. The Spanish-speaking student will probably replace these sounds with similar sounds from the Spanish language.
- English words that end in *r* plus the final consonants *d, t, l, p,* or *s* are usually pronounced without the consonant (*car* for *card, car* for *cart*).
- English has many words that blend an *s* with a consonant, which does not occur in Spanish. Spanish-speaking students may have difficulty with words that end with an *s*-consonant blend: *wasp, last, disk.*
- In Spanish, no words begin with an *s*-consonant blend; a vowel always precedes the consonant. Spanish-speaking students may have difficulty beginning a word with an *s* sound and may even pronounce a vowel before the *s* (*es-tar* for *star*).
- There are also several grammatical differences between Spanish and English. Spanish-speaking students may have the following difficulties with standard English.

  Subject-verb agreement: The cars runs.
  Verb tense: I need help yesterday.
  Use of negatives: He no go to school.
  Omission of noun determiners: He is farmer.
  Omission of pronouns: Is farmer?
  Word order of adjectives: The hat red is pretty.
  Comparative forms: My car is more big.

- Some problem English sounds for native speakers of Spanish are *b, d, dg, h, j, m, n, ng, r, sh, t, th, v, w, y, z, s*-clusters, and end clusters.

African-American English

African-American students who speak with a nonstandard English dialect may read aloud using their dialect. Unless the changes interfere with meaning, they should not be considered significant miscues. The following differences exist between the African-American dialect and standard English.

- In African-American English, the *r* sound becomes a schwa or is not pronounced before vowels or consonants: *pass* for *Paris, cat* for *carrot.*
- The *l* sound is also dropped and may be replaced by a *u* sound: *hep* for *help, too* for *tool, awe* for *all, fought* for *fault.*
- Consonant clusters at the ends of words are often simplified to single consonants: *pass* for *past, men* for *meant, wine* for *wind, hole* for *hold, sick* for *six.*
- Endings of words may be dropped or changed: *boo* for *boot, row* for *road, feet* for *feed, see* for *seed.*
- The possessive forms of words may be deleted: *John cousin* for *John's cousin, they book* for *their book, you* or *you-all* for *your.*
- Speakers of the African-American dialect may make changes in verb forms as they read: *I be happy* for *I am happy. He goin'* for *He is going.*
- In African-American English, there is no third person singular marker. Students may read: *He don't* for *He doesn't, He do* for *He does,* or *He have* for *He has.*
- The past tense for regular verbs may be dropped, such as *miss* for *missed, fine* for *fined, raise* for *raised.*
- In African-American English, the word *ain't* is used as a past negative as in *I ain't neither.*
- African-American speakers may also use negatives differently than do standard American speakers: *Nobody had no bloody nose. She didn't play with none of us. Nobody don't know about no club.*

Chinese

Among the many Chinese dialects, Mandarin is spoken by the majority of the people in China, but most of the Chinese students in schools speak the Cantonese dialect. There are several difficulties speakers of Cantonese may have as they read standard English.

- English has many more vowel sounds than Chinese, so students may have difficulty with the vowel sounds in *buy, bough, bought, beat,* and *bait.*
- English also has consonant sounds not found in Chinese: *th* in *that, sh* in *she, n* in *need,* and *r* in *rice.*
- In Chinese, many consonants are not used to end words as they are in English. Students may add an extra syllable to a final sound, such as *day offu* for *day off.*
- Because consonant clusters do not exist in Cantonese, students may have difficulty with words such as the following: *wished, dogs, laughed.*
- In Chinese, most grammatical relationships are indicated by word order rather than by changes in form as in English. The Chinese student may say *Yesterday he give I two book* for *Yesterday he gave me two books.*
- The Chinese-speaking student may not use the plural form of nouns, because plurality is indicated by the word preceding the noun in their language. The student may read *three book* for *three books.*
- The word order for questions is not inverted in Chinese as it is in English. The Chinese-speaking student may have difficulty reading questions because of that difference.
- Some problem English sounds for native speakers of Chinese are *b, ch, d, dg, f, g, j, l, m, n, ng, ō, sh, s, th, TH, v, z, l*-clusters, and *r*-clusters.

Recording a Student's Oral Reading Miscues

Substitutions

Jim saw ^a^ the boy.

Omissions

Poor little ~~Baby~~ Bear could not move from the tall tree.

Insertions

He strolled along the path and soon ^he^ was deep in the forest

Reversals

Are they twins?

Repetitions

A. Plain repetition

Jim saw <u>a bear</u>.

B. Correcting a miscue

Baby Bear (c) | did not know | ^see^ where he was.

C. Abandoning a correct word initially pronounced correctly

He stayed (ac) | ^along^ alone in the pine tree all night

D. Unsuccessfully attempting to correct an initial miscue (attempts are numbered)

He had slept (uc) | hard ^2. ha-^ ^1. heavy^ all night.

Additional Markings

A. Partial Words

The hunters ^res –^ rescued the boys.

B. Nonword substitutions

People on the ^$ frontmer^ frontier had shooting contests.

C. Punctuation ignored

. . . from some maple and oak trees⌐ As Bill

D. Intonation

He played a record⸴ that was his favorite.

E. Word pronounced by examiner

Men on the ^P^ frontier often had shooting contests.

F. Dialect

He (d) | ^goed^ went home

G. Lip movement place LM in margin

H. Finger pointing place FP above word

I. Vocalization place V in text

QUALITATIVE SUMMARY OF MISCUES

Jerry L. Johns

MISCUE	TEXT	GRAPHIC SIMILARITY: Beginning	GRAPHIC SIMILARITY: Middle	GRAPHIC SIMILARITY: End	CONTEXT: Acceptable	CONTEXT: Unacceptable	Self-Correction of Unacceptable Miscues
	Column Total						
	Number of Miscues Analyzed						
	Percentage						

PREDICTION STRATEGY

	Graphic Similarity: B	Graphic Similarity: M	Graphic Similarity: E		Miscues Acceptable in Context
100%				100%	
90				90	
80				80	
70				70	
60				60	
50				50	
40				40	
30				30	
20				20	
10				10	

____% ____% ____% ____%

CORRECTION STRATEGY

Unacceptable Miscues Self-Corrected

100%	
90	
80	
70	
60	
50	
40	
30	
20	
10	

____%

From Johns, J.L. (2008). *Basic Reading Inventory* (10th ed.). Dubuque, IA: Kendall Hunt Publishing Company (800-247-3458, ext. 4).

Structured Repeated Reading

The structured repeated reading strategy is useful with students who:

- need to develop greater fluency.
- read word by word.
- experience little success in reading.
- lack motivation.
- read very slowly.
- lack conversational qualities in oral reading.
- show little confidence in reading.
- say they can't read well.

Using Structured Repeated Reading

Follow these steps to apply the strategy.

1. Select a passage or story of 50 to 200 words at an appropriate level of difficulty for the student.
2. Have the student read the selection orally. Keep track of the time (in seconds) and miscues.
3. Record the time in seconds and number of miscues on a chart.
4. Ask the student to reread the same material silently.
5. Then have the student reread the selection orally to the teacher or aide. Chart the time and the number of miscues again.
6. Continue the procedure over a period of time until a rate of about 85 words per minute is achieved.
7. Repeat the strategy with a new selection.

Example

This is how the structured repeated reading strategy worked with Tracy, a student experiencing difficulty in reading. The following six steps correspond to those in the original explanation.

1. The teacher chose a selection for Tracy to read. The selection contained 132 words.
2. Tracy read the selection orally to the teacher. She made 6 miscues and it took her 124 seconds. To convert seconds into rate, multiply the number of words in the selection by 60 and then divide by the time (in seconds) it takes the student to read the passage. For Tracy, the rate is 64 words per minute (wpm).

number of word in selection		constant		seconds required for reading		rate
(132	$\times$	60)	$\div$	124	=	64 wpm

3. With Tracy's help, the teacher recorded the scores (6 miscues and 124 seconds) on the accompanying Reading Progress Chart.
4. Tracy practiced the same selection silently several times by herself.
5. Later, Tracy read the same selection to her teacher a second time. On this reading she made 5 miscues and took 100 seconds—quite an improvement over her first reading.
6. The procedure was repeated over a period of several days. By the third reading, Tracy achieved a rate of about 88 words per minute:

$$(132 \times 60) \div 90 = 88$$

$$7{,}920 \div 90 = 88$$

At this point, the teacher could have introduced a new passage, but Tracy wanted to try to improve her reading of the first passage even more. After some independent practice and three more readings, the result was a rate of 132 wpm ($7{,}920 \div 60 = 132$) with no miscues. Then Tracy felt she was ready to move on to a new passage.

Reading Progress Chart for Tracy

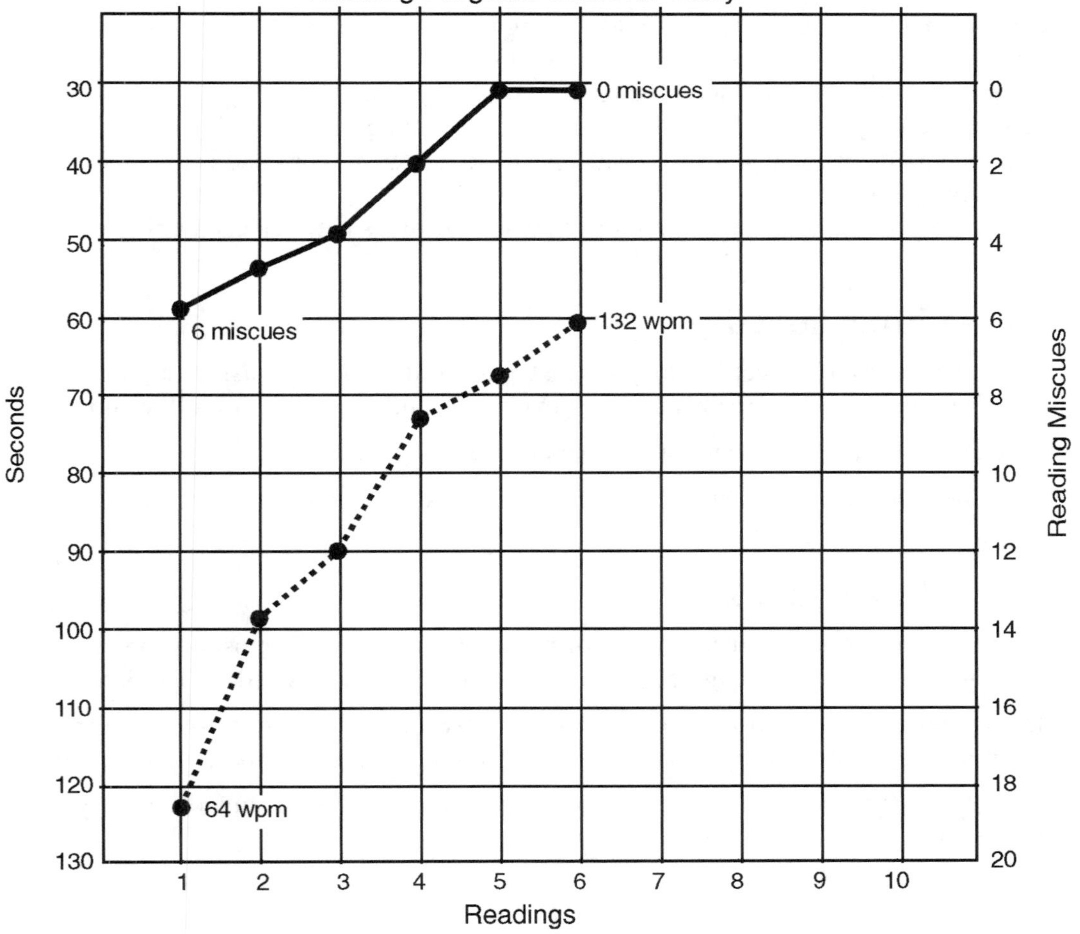

(continued)

Additional Comments

Notice that the Reading Progress Chart was set up to show visible evidence of gain. A blank chart is provided on page 330 to duplicate and use with students for whom the procedure is appropriate. The chart is a real motivational device for most students. They enjoy watching their progress. The chart, however, should not be posted in the classroom without students' permission. Some students are private about their reading and may not wish for others to see their chart. It is recommended that the chart not be displayed in the classroom.

Comprehension is not the main focus of this strategy, but the National Reading Panel (2000) reported that repeated reading did help comprehension. In addition, comprehension questions can be asked or retellings completed after the initial and final readings to help assess improvement, or a different comprehension question can be posed after each rereading. As less attention is needed for decoding, more attention becomes available for comprehension. With greater speed and accuracy, the student can concentrate on the meaning of the selection.

Often the question of counting miscues arises. Should all miscues be recorded or only those significant ones that change meaning? Some teachers begin by counting all miscues and then move to discussing miscues with the student to determine those that are significant. In addition, counting all miscues will result in more dramatic gains, because fewer miscues are usually made on subsequent readings.

Remember the following guidelines.

- Repeated readings are a supplement to reading instruction.
- Some students respond more readily than others.
- The 85 wpm criterion isn't an absolute; use your judgment.
- Repeated readings focus on accuracy and speed of reading.
- With increased accuracy and speed, students make fewer miscues and can focus more on comprehension.
- Encourage students to engage in multiple practice readings between each timed reading.

Alternate Procedure 1

1. The student reads the selection along with a tape-recorded narration using earphones. (Caution: The rate of reading on the tape must match the student's ability to follow along.)
2. The student repeats step 1 until audio support is no longer needed.
3. The student begins the process outlined in the original procedure.

Alternate Procedure 2

Samuels (2002) offers a simplified method of repeated reading that is most appropriately used with students in first and second grade who are not yet automatic in word recognition.

1. Help students understand that one becomes skilled in any activity through practice and repetition. Use examples that relate to students and then make a connection to reading.
2. Select appropriate materials for students and read the passage to students as they follow along silently.

3. Assign each student to a partner. It is recommended that a better reader be paired with a struggling reader.
4. Have one student read the passage orally while the other student listens to the oral reading and follows along with the words in the passage. Model the process with a student if necessary.
5. Have students reverse roles. After the reading, the process is reversed again and repeated until each student has read and listened to the passage four times.
6. Use the same procedure with other passages in subsequent sessions.

Research Note

Samuels (1979) initially developed the repeated reading method. Over the years, more than 100 studies have tested the repeated reading method. "A consistent finding from these studies is that repeated reading practice produces statistically significant improvement in reading speed, word recognition, and oral reading expression on the practiced passages" (Samuels, 2002, p. 179). Later, Samuels (2006) noted that findings from the National Reading Panel (2000) indicated that repeated reading helped comprehension "even though the method was not designed to affect comprehension" (p. 338). In addition, O'Shea, Sindelar, and O'Shea (1985) have found that most of the gains in word recognition, error reduction, reading speed, and expression in oral reading are acquired by the fourth reading.

READING PROGRESS CHART FOR ____________________

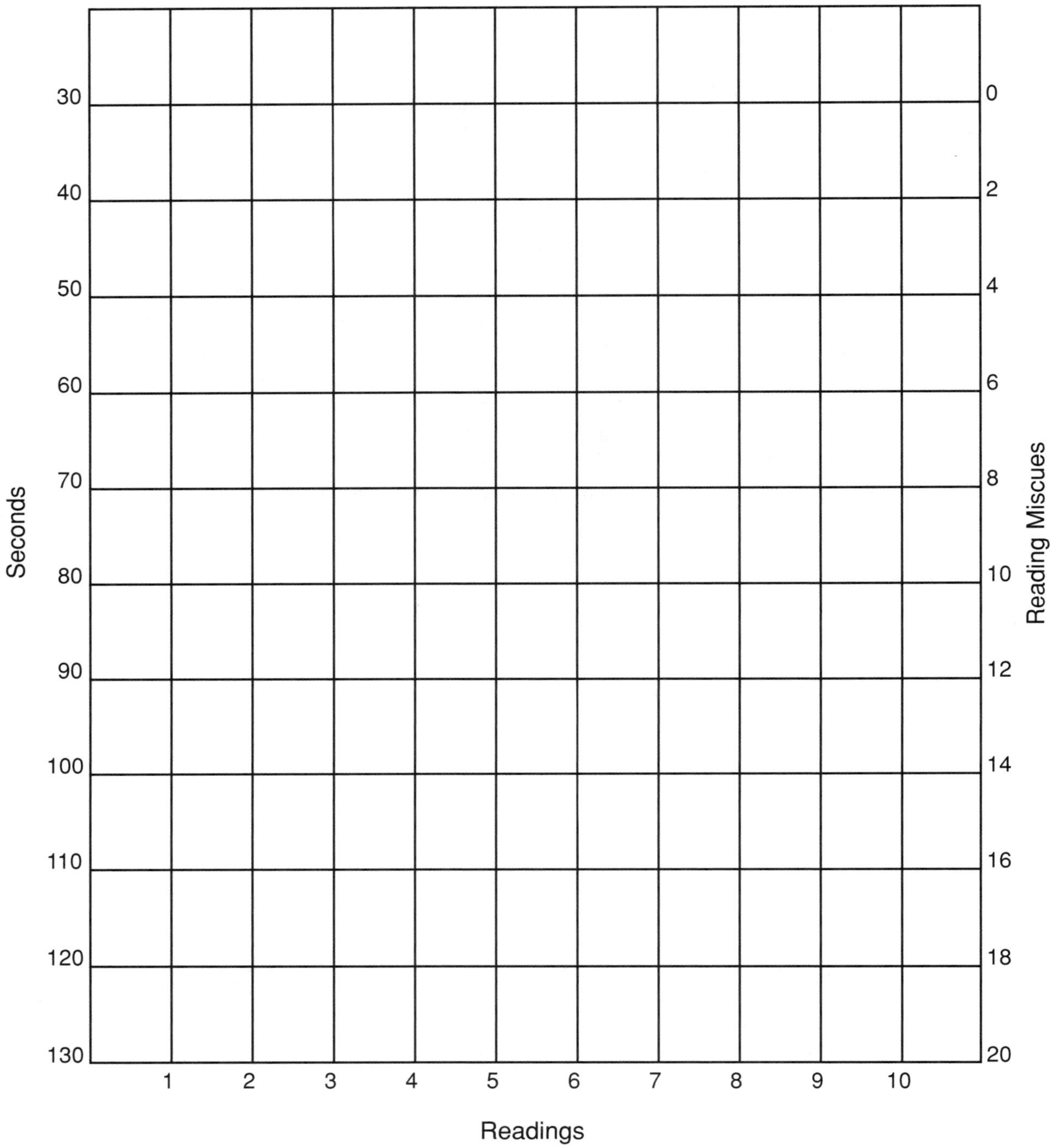

Oral Reading Alternatives to Round-Robin Reading

Choral Reading. All students read text aloud together.

Glossing. The teacher models reading fluency by reading a selection slowly with expression. The teacher "glosses" by stopping to explain a word or phrase. Students listen, or listen and follow along with the printed text.

Official Announcer. Give each student the opportunity to be the official announcer by assigning a student each day to read announcements, students' writings, and memos. Students may ask the teacher for assistance with the text before reading to the class.

Radio Program. A small group of students reads a play or radio script into a tape recorder for class presentations.

Overviewer. A student reads aloud titles, subheads, and vocabulary words before the class reads a selection.

Flash Cards. Using sight words, or vocabulary words on cards, students try to read the group of cards as rapidly and accurately as possible. Phrases can also be used.

Play Reading. Students practice and read plays for class performances.

Singing. Students read lyrics of a song before singing it.

Games. Many board games require students to read text as they play.

Formal Speech. Students write and read a persuasive or informational speech for the class.

Find the Answer. The teacher asks a question about a text. Students read the part of the text that includes the answer.

Joke of the Day. Students read aloud a joke or riddle for the class.

Adapted from Fry, E.B., Kress, J.E., & Fountoukidis, D.L. (1993). *The Reading Teacher's Book of Lists* (3rd ed.). Englewood Cliffs, NJ: Prentice-Hall.

PROCEDURE FOR DETERMINING WORDS PER MINUTE

		Example
1.	Count or estimate words in selection.	150
2.	Multiply by 60.	9000
3.	This numeral becomes the dividend.	$\overline{)9000}$
4.	Time the student's reading in seconds.	100
5.	This numeral becomes the divisor.	$100\overline{)9000}$
6.	Do the division.	$\begin{array}{r} 90 \\ 100\overline{)9000} \end{array}$
7.	The resulting numeral is the quotient, which is words per minute.	90

$$\begin{array}{r} 90 \\ 100\overline{)9000} \\ \underline{900} \end{array}$$ words per minute

ORAL READING NORMS FOR STUDENTS IN GRADES ONE THROUGH FOUR

Grade (N)	Percentile	*Fall*		*Winter*		*Spring*	
		N	*WCPM*	*N*	*WCPM*	*N*	*WCPM*
	90		32		75		105
	75		14		43		78
1 (74,623)	50	2,847	7	33,366	22	38,410	50
	25		2		11		27
	10		1		6		14
	90		102		124		141
	75		77		99		116
2 (99,699)	50	29,634	50	33,683	72	36,382	89
	25		24		44		62
	10		12		19		34
	90		128		145		161
	75		100		119		137
3 (96,460)	50	29,832	72	32,371	91	34,257	107
	25		46		60		78
	10		24		36		47
	90		144		165		180
	75		119		139		152
4 (87,436)	50	29,609	94	27,373	111	30,454	124
	25		69		86		99
	10		42		60		72

N = number of student scores
WCPM = words correct per minute

Note: The reading rates for grades one through four are based on over 350,000 student scores.

ORAL READING NORMS FOR STUDENTS IN GRADES FIVE THROUGH EIGHT

Grade (N)	Percentile	*Fall*		*Winter*		*Spring*	
		N	*WCPM*	*N*	*WCPM*	*N*	*WCPM*
	90		165		181		194
	75		137		155		167
5 (82,073)	50	28,510	109	25,229	126	28,334	138
	25		85		98		108
	10		60		73		81
	90		177		194		204
	75		153		166		178
6 (57,575)	50	18,923	127	17,668	140	20,984	150
	25		98		111		122
	10		67		81		93
	90		176		188		200
	75		154		162		176
7 (29,135)	50	10,687	127	7,313	134	11,135	150
	25		102		108		122
	10		79		86		97
	90		183		193		198
	75		160		168		176
8 (24,105)	50	8,674	130	5,986	142	9,445	151
	25		104		112		124
	10		79		84		97

N = number of student scores
WCPM = words correct per minute

Note: The reading rates for grades five through eight are based on over 135,000 student scores.

FOUR-POINT FLUENCY RUBRIC*

	1	*2*	*3*	*4*
Comprehension	Questions—less than 60% Retelling—few major ideas, poor accuracy, poor ordering.	Questions—60%–74% Retelling includes some ideas, not fully accurate or well-ordered.	Questions—75%–89% Retelling is mostly complete, accurate, and well-ordered.	Questions—90% or more Retelling is fully complete, accurate, and well-ordered.
Accuracy	90% or less	91% to 94%	95% to 98%	99% to 100%
Speed (rate)	Slow and laborious; struggles with words.	Rate varies; some hesitations.	Generally conversational; rate varies as appropriate.	Reads at conversational pace throughout.
Expression	Reads with monotone; does not sound like natural speech; little or no use of punctuation.	Mostly monotone; sometimes voice matches interpretation of the passage; some use of punctuation.	Reads with expression and uses punctuation most of the time; voice matches interpretation of the passage.	Reads with varied volume and expression; voice matches interpretation of the passage and punctuation is used consistently.

*Jerry L. Johns, Roberta L. Berglund, and Susan K. L'Allier. *Fluency at a Glance*. Copyright © 2007 Kendall Hunt Publishing Company.

CHAPTER FIVE

Vocabulary Development and Extension

© 2010 carlosseller. Used under license from Shutterstock, Inc.

Overview

English has the largest vocabulary of all the languages in the world—600,000 to 1,000,000 words (Gillet & Temple, 2000). Although no reader knows all those words, Graves (2008) estimates that students have a reading vocabulary of approximately 25,000 words by eighth grade. It has been estimated that students learn 3,000 to 4,000 words each school year. That's a lot of words! And it is clear from this estimate that only a portion of these words is taught. You would need to teach 16 to 22 words every school day for students to learn 3,000 to 4,000 words a year. What all this means is that students acquire vocabulary on their own as well as through systematic instruction. You play an important role in creating a classroom environment that promotes an interest in words. You also need to provide systematic instruction to help students develop, extend, and refine their knowledge of words.

Students have four vocabularies: listening, speaking, reading, and writing. The listening vocabulary is the first to develop. Chall (1987) estimated that the average first grader knows 5,000 to 6,000 words (estimates vary from 2,500 to over 20,000 words). The student's listening vocabulary remains the student's largest vocabulary through the middle school years. Ultimately, the student's reading vocabulary may become the largest.

Learning words and expanding vocabulary knowledge have a strong influence on comprehension (Baumann, 2009). Developing and extending vocabulary is a complex process that requires multiple and varied encounters with words. We can tell you that *kingcup* is a flower, but that definition, while helpful, does not clarify the color of the flower, its size, or where you are likely to find it. "Knowing a word cannot be identified with knowing a definition" (Nagy & Scott, 2000, p. 273). When a word is known, the student can recognize it and use "knowledge of the word, in combination with other types of knowledge, to construct a meaning for a text" (Nagy & Scott, 2000, p. 273).

Students must learn over 88,000 words by ninth grade.

To help develop vocabulary within the context of a quality reading program, we suggest the following principles and practices. Use these basic ideas to provide a structure for students' learning.

1. Provide opportunities for students to read many types of materials that are of interest to them. Supply books and other types of printed materials at a range of reading levels.
2. Build students' experiential backgrounds. A rich variety of direct experiences in school, at home, and in the community can help build and expand what we like to call students' mental museums. Indirect experiences gained from listening to stories and informational books, watching films and videotapes, and viewing computer simulations can also build students' backgrounds.
3. Talk about experiences and relate vocabulary to students' backgrounds. Encourage students to be active learners. Word meanings have a greater likelihood of becoming working concepts through discussion and relating the word to other words. Numerous strategies are included in this chapter to assist students in establishing relationships between and among words.
4. Teach words to students and help them gain a depth of meaning. A common word like *run* has over 20 meanings in an elementary dictionary. Some of those meanings could be explored in a systematic manner through discussion, examples, and inviting students to relate particular meanings to their prior experiences. Other words may be important, specialized vocabulary particular to understanding a story or section in a content area text. Words such as *deceitful* and *treacherous* may lead to word study (e.g., the meaning of *ful*), dictionary use, and using examples with which students are familiar. Learning words generally requires numerous exposures in a variety of situations.

5. Create word consciousness by using a variety of means to help students develop and extend their vocabularies. Context clues, morphemic analysis, and effective dictionary use are some of the strategies that can be taught to students to help them engage in independent word learning while reading. Inviting students to share words of interest can help foster engagement in word study. Encouraging students' active sharing using materials they are reading will help promote vocabulary growth within a meaningful context.

According to Farstrup and Samuels (2008), vocabulary has become an increasingly important focus in reading instruction. With this renewed interest, our hope is that teachers will use the ideas and strategies presented in this chapter in an authentic, meaningful, and integrated manner to engage students in expanding their vocabulary knowledge to better construct meaning from texts.

Section **5.1**

Extending Meaning Vocabulary

Behavior Observed →
The student's knowledge of word meanings is limited.

Anticipated Outcome
The student will increase the number of known words and expand the range of meanings for words encountered in text.

Background

Helping students expand and enrich their meaning vocabulary is not easily accomplished. You need to do far more than provide your students with a list of vocabulary words to study for a test on Friday. Students learn new vocabulary words in four ways (Manzo & Manzo, 1993).

- The first way is incidentally, through their own reading and conversation. Children come to school knowing approximately 5,000 words and acquire approximately 3,000 words each year during elementary school, middle school, and high school (Snow, Burns, & Griffin, 1998). Many of these words are learned without teacher intervention; they are learned through students' exposure to language.

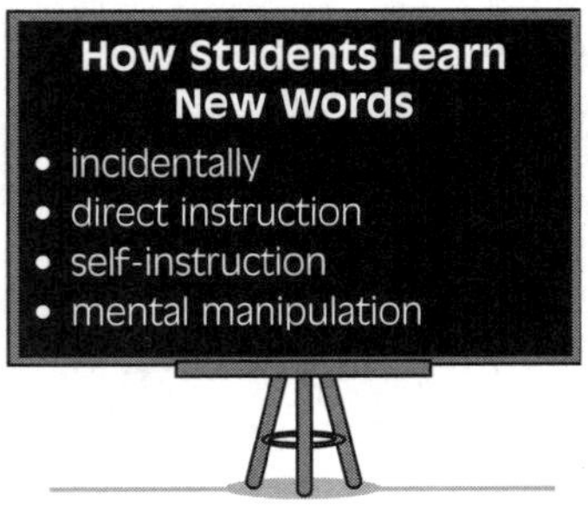
How Students Learn New Words
• incidentally
• direct instruction
• self-instruction
• mental manipulation

- The second way students learn new vocabulary is through direct instruction. Teachers can have an impact on students' learning vocabulary through well-thought-out vocabulary instruction. Giving students the definitions for new words, however, usually does not ensure that those words will become part of their vocabulary. That is because giving definitions for words merely provides students with the denotation, or general meaning, of a word. Each word, however, also has a connotation. The connotation of a word is the range of meanings it has and the specific context in which it occurs (Readence, Bean, & Baldwin, 1998).
- The third way students learn new vocabulary is through self-instruction. As students read, they can consciously try to learn new words. Teachers can help instill in students a desire to learn words, and they can provide students with strategies that help them make the new words part of their expressive vocabulary.

- Finally, students learn vocabulary through mental manipulation of words while thinking, speaking, and writing. Students are constantly exposed to new words in school, at home, and in books. As they use these new words, they begin to extend their knowledge of the words' meanings. Students learn new words to different degrees. With every word, students may be anywhere on a continuum from not knowing the word at all, having heard the word but being unsure about its meaning, having a general sense of the meaning of the word, to having the word in their expressive vocabulary (Beck, McKeown, & Kucan, 2002). Even if they know more meanings for a word, they often initially lack the understanding of a word's richness.

Teaching the various meanings of a word, however, is not sufficient. Word knowledge should be constantly changing as new information is added to students' existing schemata (background knowledge) and as new schemata are developed. That means teachers need to encourage students to continue to expand their meanings of words on their own as well as to provide instruction on new words. Blachowicz and Fisher (2004) suggest that, to assist students in enriching their meaning vocabulary, teachers need to provide students with experiences that will build their background knowledge, help them relate new words to that background, assist them in building relationships between words, help them develop depth of meaning of new words, present several exposures to each word to students, help students become interested in words, and help students transfer words to their own vocabulary. The following strategies will help students enrich their meaning vocabularies.

Direct instruction is one way teachers help students learn new words.

TEXT TALK

Text Talk (Beck & McKeown, 2001) uses oral language about carefully selected words from read alouds to help build and expand primary students' listening and speaking vocabularies. Beck, McKeown, and Kucan (2003, 2008) use direct instruction in this powerful strategy. The steps below provide the general framework for lessons.

1. Select a children's book to read aloud. It should contain several words unknown to students that have applicability across various subject areas. The words selected are called Tier 2 words. Tier 1 words are basic words such as *when, there,* and *what* that occur frequently in English (see Section 3.5). Tier 3 words are specific to a particular subject area, or they may occur rarely in text. They lack general application. Examples of such words are *longhorn beetle, entomologist,* and *metamorphosed* (Beck, McKeown, & Kucan, 2002). The Tier 2 words in *Amazing Grace* (Hoffman & Binch, 1991) that could be used are *trusty, fantastic,* and *stunning*. What is important is the instruction that occurs with the words.
2. After reading, the word is first contextualized for its role in the story. You might say the following about *trusty* when you have finished reading *Amazing Grace*.

   In the story, Grace's trusty *cat was always with her when she acted out stories and fairy tales.*

   Then have students repeat the word so that they create a phonological representation of the word.
3. Explain the meaning of the word in language that will be readily understood by students. An example may also be embedded in the explanation. You could say the following.

   Trusty *means someone or something you can count on. For example, if you are always there when your friend needs you, you could be called a* trusty *friend.*
4. Extend the meaning by providing contexts beyond the story that are likely to be meaningful to your students. You could say the following.

   If your dog always waits for you by the front door when you come home from school, you could say that you have a trusty *dog. You can always count on him to be there for you. You are SURE he will be there for you. If your bicycle always gets you where you want to go without breaking down, it could be called a* trusty *bicycle.*
5. Have students interact with examples of the word's use and have them provide their own examples. You might say the following.

   If you wanted to show your friend that you are a trusty *friend, what would you do? Try to use the new word when you tell us. You could start by saying,* I would show that I was a trusty friend by . . .
6. Students are then asked to say the word again to help reinforce its phonological representation. Some of the wording you could use is noted below.

   - What's the word we've been talking about?
   - What's the word we are learning?
   - Let's all say the word together.

7. Use a similar approach to present the other two words. Then bring all three words together. One way is to use choices by saying the following.

   > *We talked about three words today after we read our story. The words were* trusty, fantastic, *and* stunning. *What would you find* fantastic *and* stunning, *seeing a full moon in the sky or seeing a full moon and a satellite in the sky at the same time? When would you say you have a* trusty *radio, if it works every time you turn it on or if it works only once in awhile?*

   You can also use questions, reasons, and examples. Helpful resources for this type of direct instruction can be found in *Bringing Words to Life: Robust Vocabulary Instruction* (Beck, McKeown, & Kucan, 2002) and *Creating Robust Vocabulary Instruction: Frequently Asked Questions & Extended Examples* (Beck, McKeown, & Kucan, 2008).

8. Be patient with yourself as you begin to use this strategy. It will take time to create the lessons initially, but you will soon become more facile with the process and reap the rewards of students who take delight in learning and using words—a critical foundation for comprehension.

Strategy 2 SECTION 5.1

KNOWLEDGE RATING GUIDE

A Knowledge Rating Guide (Blachowicz, 1986) can help students understand to what degree they initially know a specific word and can provide a vehicle for a class discussion that allows students to expand their background knowledge of the words. To prepare and use a Knowledge Rating Guide, use the following steps.

1. Prepare a list of words that you want students to learn.
2. Next to each word, draw three columns similar to the example.

	Can define	**Have seen/heard**	**Unknown**
glacier	________	________	________
avalanche	________	________	________

3. Ask students to place a check in the column that best describes what they know about the new word. If they are unclear about the directions, model the procedure for them. For example, you could say the following.

   > *The first word on this list is glacier. I know that a glacier is made of ice, and I have heard the word many times, but I'm not exactly sure if I could define the word. I think I'll place a check under the column* Have seen/heard. *On the other hand, I do know what an avalanche is. It's falling rock or snow. I'll check* Can define *for that word.*

4. After students have filled out the Knowledge Rating Guide, discuss the words with them. Ask which words were difficult, which were easy, which most of the students knew, and which words few students knew. As you discuss the words, ask students to share their background knowledge and experience with the words.
5. From the class discussion, ask students to make predictions about further meanings of the words and how they would be used in a text.

Strategy 3 VOCABULARY SELF-COLLECTION

Haggard's (1982) Vocabulary Self-Collection (VSC) is a strategy that encourages students to find words from their environment to learn. VSC helps students understand that learning new words needs to be a consciously active process that should be part of their lives.

1. Ask students to look for unknown words in their reading, conversations, and environment. As they find words, ask students to write them down on an index card.
2. Have five students who have found new words write the words on the chalkboard.
3. At an appropriate time, ask the students who submitted the words to define them.
4. After each definition, ask the class to try to add to the word's definition or to further clarify its meaning.
5. All students should record the words with their meanings in a vocabulary notebook for reference during reading and writing.

Strategy 4 FOUR-SQUARE

1. The Four-Square strategy can help students expand their understanding of a new vocabulary word by having them review a word's definition and think of examples and non-examples of the word. Students are better able to remember the meaning of new vocabulary words when they use this strategy.
2. Select a word that you want students to learn and remember. This word should be one of the Tier 2 words (see page 342) or a word that students will see in other situations both in school and outside of school.
3. Draw a square with four quadrants on the chalkboard, the computer, or on an overhead transparency. In the top left quadrant, write the vocabulary word. In this case the word is *spring*. Since this word has multiple meanings, provide students with a sentence that uses the word in context such as the following: The pioneers got their water from a *spring*.
4. Invite students to predict a definition for the word *spring*. Some possible predictions that students might share could include a pool of water, a creek, a river, or a pond.
5. Scaffold student learning by using the students' ideas and adding more information to correct any misconceptions. You can also add information about the definition as in the following.

   You are right when you say that a spring *is water. It's not a pond or a river, though. A* spring *is a source of water that comes from underground. It can become a pond or a river, but the important thing to remember is that a* spring *does not come from rain or snow melt, but it comes from underground.*

6. Give students a short phrase defining *spring*, and write it in the lower-right quadrant of the square. Explain to students that they can use this definition for the word.
7. Tell students that when they learn new words, they should think of other words and phrases that are similar to the new word. Use the sentence starter, "A spring is like a ____________________." For example, students might answer any of the following.

A *spring* is like a water faucet turned on low.
A *spring* is like a garden hose with the water running.

8. Write one or more of the examples in the upper-right hand quadrant of the square.
9. Explain to students that when they learn new words they also need to think of non-examples so they can differentiate between the meanings of similar words. You can use the sentence starter, "A spring is not like a _______________," to help students think of non-examples. Have students keep to the general topic of the word's meaning and discourage students from non-examples that stray from the topic. Some appropriate examples follow.

A *spring* is not like a waterfall.
A *spring* is not like an ocean.
A *spring* is not like a puddle.

10. Write some of the non-examples in the lower right-quadrant of the square. Your completed square might look something like the example below.

Vocabulary Word	**Like a . . .**
Spring	Garden hose with the water on low.
The pioneers got their water from a *spring*.	Water faucet turned on.
Definition	**Not like a . . .**
Water that flows from underground.	Waterfall
Springs can be hot or cold.	Ocean
	Puddle

11. Invite students to draw a picture of the vocabulary word under the definition to help them remember the word.
12. Have students use Four-Square to write definitions of new words in vocabulary notebooks or on index cards. Remind students to review the words frequently and encourage their use in conversations.

Strategy 5 SECTION 5.1

THREE-DIMENSIONAL WORDS

1. When students are able to connect word definitions to real objects, they remember word meanings better. Therefore, Bromley (2007) suggests that students develop Three-Dimensional Word displays to better learn word meanings.
2. To use Three-Dimensional Words, select a Tier 2 (see page 342) vocabulary word for students to learn. This word should be one that most students do not already know but will need to know throughout their school years. For example, the word *volcano* is one that many young students will not know.
3. Write the word *volcano* on the chalkboard. Tell students that they will be learning the word *volcano* and that they will need to add it to the words they know and remember.
4. Develop a sentence using *volcano* that fits the context of what students will be learning. For example, you could write, "Mt. St. Helens is a *volcano* in the United States that erupted in 1980."

5. Ask students to brainstorm possible definitions for the word *volcano*. Scaffold student answers to develop a definition that is accurate and that students can remember. For example, you might write the definition for volcano as "an opening in the earth's surface that ejects molten material. Some mountains are still active volcanoes."
6. Show students pictures of volcanoes. Check that students understand the meaning of the word *volcano* by asking them to draw pictures of their own.
7. Ask students to select a vocabulary word that you have already taught to develop a display of the word. Give students a large piece of construction paper. Have students fold the paper in thirds. On the left-hand section of the paper, have students write the vocabulary word and a definition. In the middle section have students draw a picture. On the right-hand section have students write two or more sentences using the word.
8. Ask students to bring in something from home that would represent the vocabulary word. In the example of the word *volcano*, students could bring in a small model of a volcano, rocks, or even sand that reminds them of lava dust.
9. Have students set up their posters of the words on their desks or on a counter and set the objects in the center.
10. Have students teach the word to their classmates by showing them their display and explaining the objects of their Three-Dimensional Words.
11. Place the Three-Dimensional Word displays in an area of the classroom that students can use to review the meanings of the words.

Strategy 6 SECTION 5.1

LIST-GROUP-LABEL

One of the ways students develop the concepts for words is to learn the relationship of that word to other words. Classification strategies such as List-Group-Label (Taba, 1967) help students learn how words fit in relation to other words. These strategies also engage students in the content of the text they are reading.

1. Select one or more related topics about a passage the students have read. Make sure there are several subtopics for the topic you have chosen. For example, if the students read a chapter about animals, you might think of the subtopics farm animals, pets, wild animals, and characteristics of animals.
2. Write the name of the topic on the chalkboard. Ask students to think of all of the terms that are associated with the topic. List them on the chalkboard. The following list is an example of possible terms students might give for the topic *animals*.

dog	cat	lion	elephant
cow	hen	gerbil	warm-blooded
horse	hamster	giraffe	breathing
born alive	white mouse	cheetah	goat

3. Ask students to organize the list into groups and give each group a label. Students can work in small groups or alone. Be prepared for a variety of answers. Because the object of the lesson is for students to interact with the concepts, you can allow them to differ on some decisions about where an item would fit in a list. For example, *white mouse* in this list would probably be considered a pet, but some students may argue that the term would belong in a different category.

FEATURE ANALYSIS

Feature Analysis (Pittelman, Heimlich, Berglund, & French, 1991) helps students realize that several words may have certain features in common. It also helps them learn the distinguishing concepts behind different words.

1. Select a general category and list some words within the category. One example is the term *transportation*. Of that general category, car, bicycle, and airplane are all examples of modes of transportation.
2. List some features common to each word and one or more unique features for each word. For transportation, some of the features include two wheels, wings, uses fuel, has an engine, and carries passengers. You may suggest a feature or two and ask the students to think of other features. Students may not be able to think of features unless the teacher first provides some examples.
3. Ask students to determine which features fit with which words. Have them make an x for features that fit and a — if the features don't describe the word. The following is an example for the category *transportation*.

Transportation	two wheels	wings	uses fuel	engine	passengers
car	—	—	x	x	x
bicycle	x	—	—	—	x
airplane	—	x	x	x	x

4. Ask students to explain their rationale for each word. Then ask students how the terms are similar and how they are different.
5. Another way to introduce Feature Analysis is to ask students to use their own names as words to describe. For features, they might use such ideas as "has a brother," "owns a pet," or "has freckles." Students can have fun using Feature Analysis and can get to know each other as well. A blank Feature Analysis Chart is on the following page.

FEATURE ANALYSIS CHART

Name ____ Date ____________________

SEMANTIC MAPPING

Semantic Mapping (Heimlich & Pittelman, 1986) is a graphic representation of related concepts. Semantic Mapping is another way students can learn the relationships among words.

1. Select a topic from the text you have been reading. For example, if students were reading a text about band music, the key word might be *musical instruments*.
2. Write the word on the chalkboard.
3. Ask students to brainstorm as many related words as they can. Examples for musical instruments might be *cornet, clarinet, snare drum, cymbal, xylophone, oboe, flute, trumpet, French horn, saxophone*.
4. Organize the words into a diagram similar to the example.

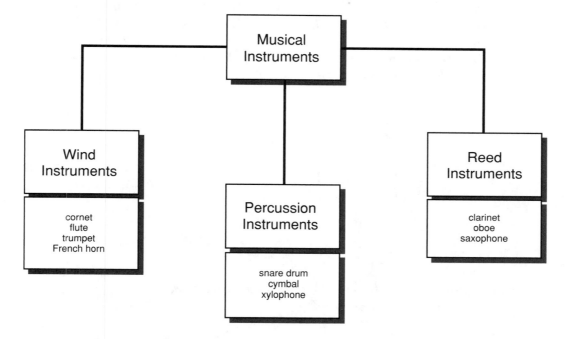

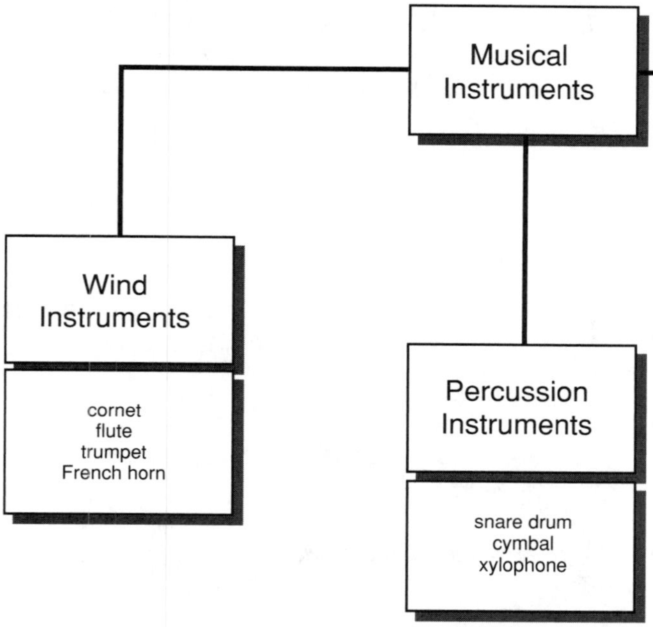

5. Students can add words to the diagram as they think of them.
6. Ask students to give names to the categories represented on the diagram. In this example, the category names are in larger type.
7. Discuss why the words fit into the categories. Ask students to give the salient features that separate the categories.

WORD MAP

A Word Map (Readence, Bean, & Baldwin, 1998) helps students develop a framework for a word. A Word Map gives the category of the word, the ways it's different from other similar words, and examples.

1. Discuss the Word Map with the students, explaining how it helps students think about a variety of aspects of a concept.
2. Model an example such as the one that follows.

> *The term we have been studying is* emu. [Write emu in the middle box.] *Let's think about what an* emu *is. We've learned that an* emu *is a bird, so that goes in the top box that represents the class or category of the term. On the right we will write properties or characteristics of the* emu. *We know that the* emu *is an Australian bird, that it is tall, and that it can't fly. At the bottom of the word map, we write examples or illustrations of the* emu. *In this case, we'll write that it is smaller than the ostrich and that it is like the rhea. That completes our word map.*

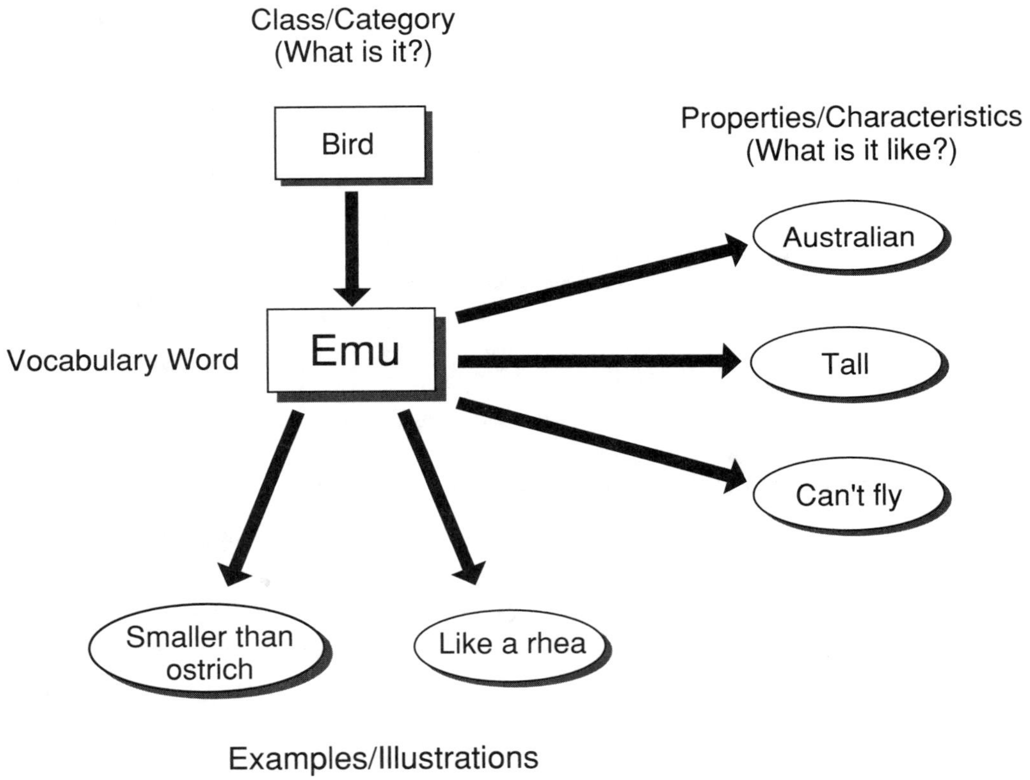

3. After the students have listened to you complete a Word Map, give them a blank map like the one below, and suggest a term to describe. You might suggest that students work in small groups.

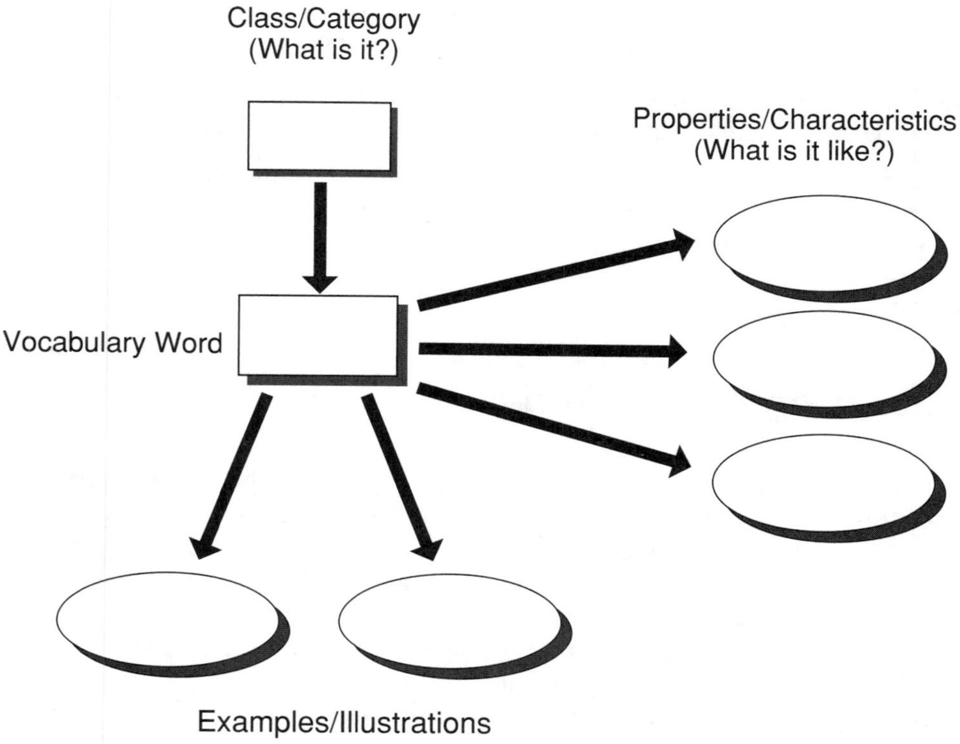

Strategy **10** SECTION 5.1

VOCABULARY FLOOD

1. Vocabulary words need to be reviewed frequently so that students remember them. Labbo, Loe, and Ryan (2007) suggest that teachers can make word meanings "stick" by using a variety of word learning strategies combined with computer activities.
2. Select a book to read aloud to students. For example, you could read the book *Coolies* by Yin (2001).
3. Ask students to volunteer some vocabulary words from the story for the class to learn. Write the words on index cards or a digital whiteboard. Display the words in a place that students will see. Examples from *Coolies* could include:

incense	rebellion	laborers
frantic	voyage	fragile
calligraphy	harsh	dynamite
trestle	tunnel	feast

4. On Day 2, read the book again, highlighting the words that students have selected. You might guide students to focus on Tier 2 words (see page 342), or words that will have high usability for students in other reading. Help students understand word meanings through the context of the story by explaining each word or term.

5. On Day 3, review the words on the chart and ask several true/false questions that use the words. Some examples follow.

   Incense can be fragrant and spicy. (True)
   The trestle was under the ground. (False)
   The family had little to eat at the feast. (False)
   His calligraphy was beautiful but difficult to read. (True)

6. On Day 4, have small groups of students retell the story using the vocabulary terms that they learned earlier. Take digital pictures or short videos of students retelling the story.
7. Later in the month, show the digital pictures and/or show the videos to the class. Have students retell the story with you as you show them the pictures. Remind students to use the new vocabulary words they learned as they retell the story.

Practice and Reinforcement Activities

1. Students need to discuss how words are used in a variety of ways before the words can become part of their reading and writing vocabularies. Francis and Simpson (2003) suggest that teachers use Concept Cards to help students remember the words they have learned. Concept Cards are index cards with appropriate information about words on the card. For example, students can write several sentences using the new word, a variety of definitions, synonyms, antonyms, and/or examples. Young students might include pictures that illustrate the meanings of the word. Students can store Concept Cards in recipe boxes and should add information to their cards periodically.
2. Vocabulary Bingo is a good review for new vocabulary words. Write new vocabulary words with definitions on cards, one to each card. Use these cards to play bingo. Give students papers that have been divided into nine squares. Read the new vocabulary words and have students write one word in each space and then trade papers with a classmate. Distribute nine markers to each student. Read one definition of a new word from the vocabulary cards and instruct students to place a marker on the space of the word that you have defined. When a student has three words marked in a row, have students clear their cards and continue playing.

enormous	numerous	frantic
tiny	companion	jovial
ridiculous	swift	clumsy

3. Students can learn vocabulary words in a specific content area when you create a Content Area Word Wall (Boehle, Darrow, Lovin, & White, 2001). To develop a Content Area Word Wall, obtain poster boards for each content area. At the top, write the title of the subject. Write letters of the alphabet on the poster, saving room to the side of each letter for vocabulary words. Fasten the posters together so that the posters can be turned like a book. As you introduce vocabulary words in a specific content area, write the words on that subject's poster. Have students practice saying the meanings of the words frequently.

Science Word Wall

A *air*	J	R *root*
B	K	S *soil, stem, sun*
C	L *leaves*	T
D	M	U
E	N	V
F *flower, fruit*	O	W
G	P *petal*	X
H	Q	Y
I		Z

4. Students need to practice the words they have learned so that they remember them. One of the most effective methods of practice is to have students talk about the words with each other. Lenski and Ehlers-Zavala (2004) suggest that students practice words by using the activity Vocabulary People Search. Prepare a list of words that students have already learned and add two blanks next to the words: one for the words' definitions and one for class members' signatures. Have students walk around the room asking their peers if they know the meanings of the words on the list. If a student knows one of the words, that student will sign his or her name on the blank marked signature. The students should develop a definition together and write it on the blank marked definition. An example follows.

Vocabulary Words

Puffin — *Katie* ____ Signature

Definition *a black and white diving bird* ____

Mukluk — ____ Signature

Definition ____

Umiak — ____ Signature

Definition ____

Section **5.2**

Differentiating Between Word Meanings

Behavior Observed → **Anticipated Outcome**

The student is unable to use a word's connotation to select the right meaning for the context.

The student will be able to differentiate between word meanings to select the right meaning for the context.

Background

As you teach new vocabulary words, it is important that you teach not only word definitions, or denotations, but that you also focus on the connotation of words. Connotations are the range of meanings a word may have and how the word is used in the context of a sentence. Words have multiple associations connected to them. These connotations are the implied feelings and ideas associated with the word. Since connotations are subtle, they often have a positive or negative feeling or attribute associated with them.

Connotations go beyond literal definitions. For example, the definition of the word *drop* is to *let go or cause to fall*. Synonyms of the word *drop* when it is used as a verb are *fall*, *go down*, *plunge*, *plummet*, *crash*, *jump down*, *dive*, *fumble*, *slump*, *decline*, and *release*. If you were describing how a football player dropped a ball, you could not substitute just any word for drop. You could say, the player *dropped* the ball. However, a more common word to use is a synonym for *drop*—the word *fumble*. The word *fumble*, however, is not a neutral word. It has a negative feeling associated with it. So, it would be entirely different to say, the player *dropped* the ball, and the player *fumbled* the ball.

The example of synonyms for the word *drop* illustrates how important it is for students to learn not only the denotations but the connotations of vocabulary words. After students are comfortable with a word's definition and use in context, you can teach students the subtle variations of the word by exploring the synonyms and antonyms associated with that word's definition. By teaching how synonyms are associated with each other, you are helping students learn how to differentiate between word meanings and how to select the right meaning for the context.

Strategy 1 SECTION 5.2

SYNONYMS AND ANTONYMS

1. Write *synonym* and *antonym* on the chalkboard and ask students if anyone can give the meanings of the words. Develop the notion that synonyms refer to words having a meaning similar to that of another word. Antonyms are words of opposite meaning.
2. Have students form small groups to brainstorm some synonyms and antonyms. After students have had several minutes to develop their lists, they can write their words on the chalkboard. Select a few words for closer study. Develop the understanding that, although two words mean about the same, there are still some differences. For example, *big* and *large* are synonyms whose meanings differ slightly. Have students check the dictionary definitions and note the subtle differences in meaning.
3. Using *big* and *large,* ask students to identify some antonyms (*small, tiny, minute*). Help students realize some of the differences in the words. For example, a dime could be small but it is not minute.
4. Create a synonym web (Blachowicz & Fisher, 2000) for a word of focus. For example, if the unit of study in science is inventors, you might choose the word *invent*. Place the word in a circle and invite students to suggest synonyms for the word. Draw lines from the circle and add those words. Have students refer to a dictionary or thesaurus to find additional words. Add these to the synonym web. See the example below.

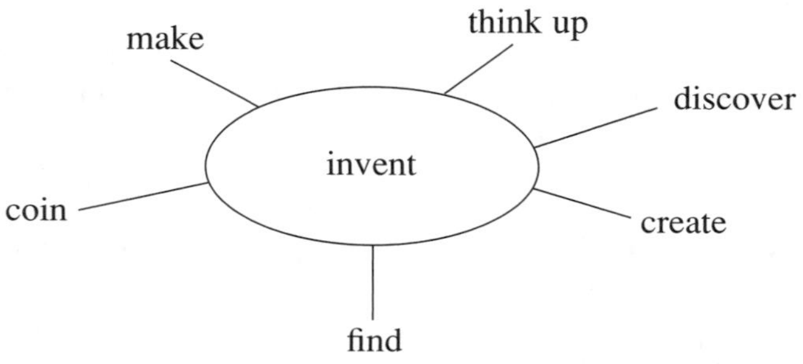

5. Ask students to consider if some of the synonyms are related to each other. For example, *make* and *create* may be more similar than *find* and *discover.* Explore the meanings of the words with students and help them revise their general synonym web to one that shows how the words may be related in meaning. See the example below.

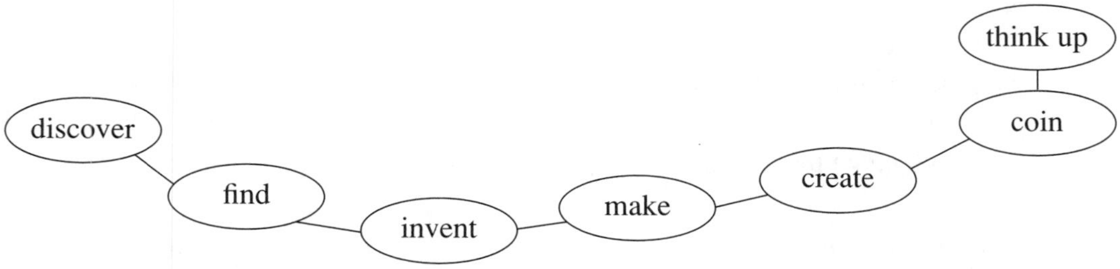

6. Think of other creative ways to teach synonyms. Gandy (2003) suggests using different shaped webs such as ice cream cones and flowers. Encourage students to color the webs; display them in the classroom so that students remember to enrich their vocabularies through synonyms.

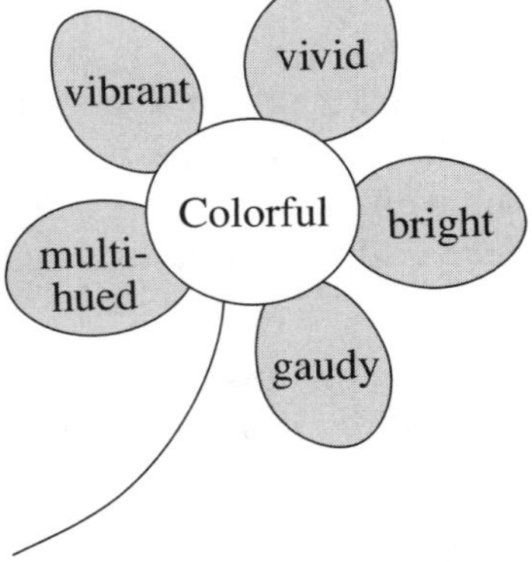

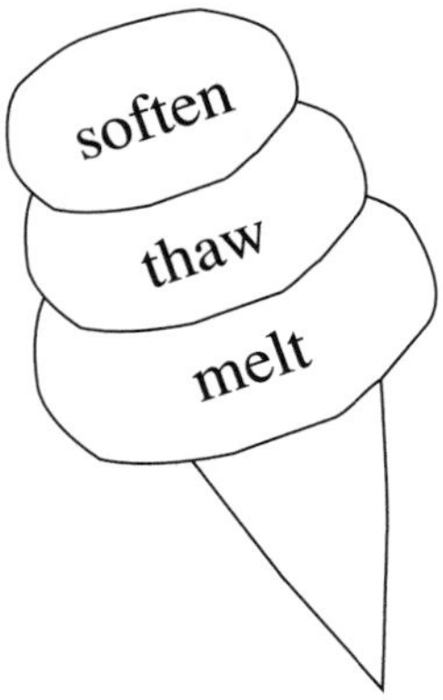

Strategy 2 SECTION 5.2

HOMOGRAPHS

1. Ask students if they can think of any words with the same spellings that have different meanings and possibly different pronunciations. List them on the chalkboard. Tell students that such words are called homographs.
2. Help students classify the words into two groups as shown below.

Same Pronunciations Different Meanings	**Different Pronunciations Different Meanings**
bay	wind
palm	tear
bat	dove

3. For the first column, explore the different meanings for each word. Refer to a dictionary as needed. Learning new meanings for a known word can be difficult for students.

bay	**palm**	**bat**
1. part of a sea	1. part of the hand	1. a flying mammal
2. long, deep barking by a dog	2. a type of tree	2. a wooden stick
3. reddish-brown		3. to wink or flutter

   Make the point that the words have different meanings even though they are pronounced the same.

4. Focus on the second group of words and ask students to give two pronunciations for each word. Have students use each word in a sentence. Write sentences on the chalkboard and help students see that the context clarifies how the word should be pronounced. Two examples follow.
   - My uncle has an old clock he must wind by hand.
   - I couldn't fly my kite, because there was no wind.

Invite a student to explain which clues in the sentence were helpful to get the proper pronunciation of the word.

5. Encourage students to be alert for homographs in their readings. They could add the words to a bulletin board along with new meanings and provide examples of how the context can reveal the pronunciation of a word.

tribune
- an official of ancient Rome
- a raised platform (He spoke to the crowd from a tribune.)

row

I will row the boat.
The plants were in a row.
The students were in a row about the game.

Older students might use a dictionary to explore the origins or etymologies of words. Such explorations may help students understand the basis for words' meanings.

6. Provide sentences to students that contain examples of how the same word can have different pronunciations. Have students determine the different pronunciations using the context or a dictionary (especially if the meaning is not clear). Some possible sentences are provided below.

- The bandage was wound around the wound.
- The farm was used to produce produce.
- The dump was so full that it had to refuse more refuse.
- He could lead if he would get the lead out.
- The soldier decided to desert his dessert in the desert.
- Since there is no time like the present, he thought it was time to present the present.
- A bass was painted on the head of the bass drum.
- The dove dove into the bushes.
- I did not object to the object.
- The insurance was invalid for the invalid.
- There was a row among the oarsmen about how to row.
- They were too close to the door to close it.
- A seamstress and sewer fell down into a sewer line.
- Can a farmer teach a sow to sow?
- The wind was too strong to wind the sail.
- After a number of injections my jaw got number.
- Upon seeing the tear in the painting I shed a tear.
- I had to subject the subject to a series of tests.
- How can I intimate this to my most intimate friend?

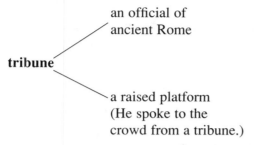

Strategy 3 WORD LADDERS

1. Students can differentiate between words when they understand how the words relate to each other. One strategy that can help students understand relationships between related words is a word ladder.
2. Draw a word ladder on the chalkboard like the one that follows. Tell students that you will give them a word at one extreme on the top and a word at the other extreme at the bottom.

Hottest

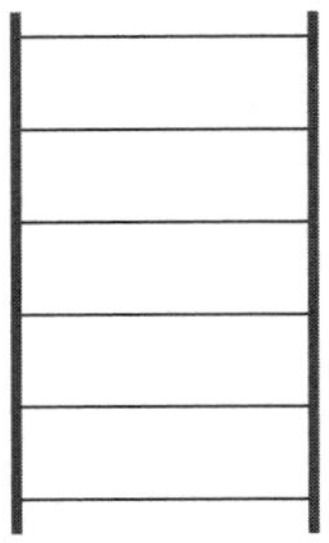

Coldest

3. Provide students with words that come between the two extremes, such as *warm*, *chilly*, *frigid*, *lukewarm*, *scalding*, and *cool*. Have students place the words in order between the two ends of the ladder. Provide a think-aloud that illustrates how to think about word placement.

    I'm thinking about the hottest of the words. I know it's not lukewarm *or* warm. *The only other word on the list is* scalding. *I think scalding is the word that is the hottest. I'll put that one on the top of the word ladder.*

4. When students are comfortable with arranging words in order on a word ladder, try a more interactive activity. Write a group of eight related words on large index cards, such as *sunny*, *partly sunny*, *overcast*, *drizzle*, *mist*, *raining*, and *thundershowers*. Give one word card to each of eight students. Invite students to come to the front of the room and arrange themselves from one extreme to the other. When students have finished putting themselves in order, have them explain why they placed their card in the order they did.
5. A Word Ladder reproducible can be found on the next page.

WORD LADDER

Name ________________________ Date ____________

Directions: Arrange the words in order on the ladder.

Words

WORD PAIR CHART

1. Students can think about how words relate to each other by deciding whether pairs of words are similar or opposite and whether they go together or have no relationship.
2. Draw a Word Pair Chart on the chalkboard like the one that follows.

Word Pair	Same	Opposite	Go Together	No Relationship

3. Develop a list of word pairs to use as a teaching demonstration. Have at least one word pair for each category, such as *stem-flower*, *fantastic-terrific*, *rapid-slowly*, *tunnel-lake*.
4. Write one of the word pairs on the chalkboard, such as *stem-flower*. Tell students that they will be deciding how the words relate to each other. Ask students how *stem* and *flower* relate to each other. Ask students whether the words are the same. [The answer should be no.] Then ask students whether the words are opposite. [The answer should be no.] Finally, ask students whether the words go together or have no relationship to each other. [The answer should be that they go together because flowers grow on stems.]
5. Repeat the process with the other word pairs that you have developed. Place an x or a checkmark in the column that represents how the words fit together as in the example that follows.

Word Pair	Same	Opposite	Go Together	No Relationship
Stem-flower			X	
Fantastic-terrific	X			
Rapid-slowly		X		
Tunnel-lake				X

6. Invite students to get into small groups. Have each small group brainstorm word pairs that fit the four categories of the Word Pair Chart. List the word pairs on the chalkboard. Have students place an x or a checkmark under the appropriate category for each word pair. A Word Pair reproducible is on the following page.

Word Pair Chart

Name ______________________________ Date ______________

Word Pair	*Same*	*Opposite*	*Go Together*	*No Relationship*

SYNONYM MATRIX

1. The connotations of words can be positive or negative. For example, the word house is relatively neutral, but the word *mansion* has a positive connotation and the word *hovel* has a negative connotation. Words can also be formal or informal. The word *shack*, for example, is an informal word, and the word *abode* is a formal word. Crovitz and Miller (2008) suggest that having students arrange synonyms on a matrix helps them understand a word's connotations.
2. Draw a line on the chalkboard with arrows on both ends. On the left side of the arrow write the word *informal*, and on the right side of the word write the word *formal* similar to the example that follows.

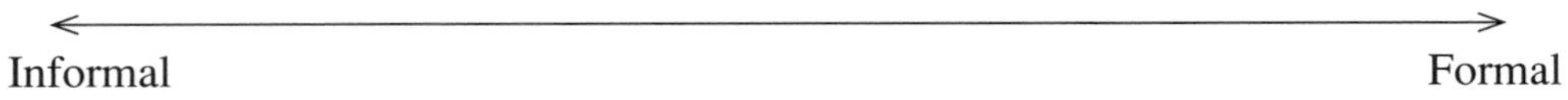

3. Explain to students that some synonyms are often used in formal settings and some words are used more informally. Provide examples of words and phrases that students would use in situations where they are talking informally. Provide additional examples of language that would be used in very formal settings. Make sure students understand the differences between formal and informal language situations.
4. Provide students with a list of words that range from formal to informal, such as *eat*, *gobble*, *consume*, *scarf*, *dine*, *chow down*, and *devour*. Place the word *eat* in the center of the arrow.
5. Read each one of the words aloud. As you read the words, ask students whether it is more formal than *eat* or more informal. You might say something like the following.

   > *Let's look at the word* consume. *If someone said, "Let's* consume *lunch," does that seem more formal than the word* eat*?* [Guide students as needed.] *In what situations would someone use the word* consume *for* eat*?* [Invite students to provide examples.]

6. Repeat the process with the additional words until all of them are placed along the continuum.
7. After students are comfortable placing the words on the arrow between formal or informal, add another arrow to the Synonym Matrix. Draw a horizontal arrow with the word *informal* on the left-hand side and the word *formal* on the right-hand side. Then draw a vertical arrow. At the top of the arrow, draw a plus sign (+). At the bottom of the arrow draw a minus (–) sign.

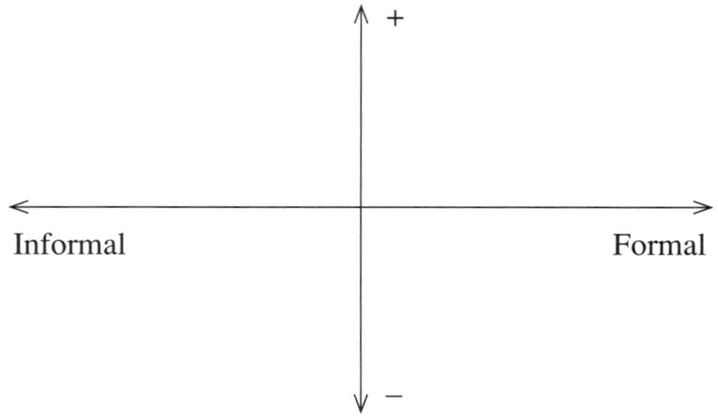

8. Tell students that some words have a positive connotation and some words have a negative connotation. Ask students whether the term *pig out* has a negative or positive connotation. Have students discuss where *pig out* would fit best on the positive and negative continuum. Most students would place the term near the bottom of the arrow, in the negative range.
9. Place remaining words along the vertical continuum.
10. After students are comfortable placing words along both continuums, have them think of the connotation of words from both perspectives: whether the word is formal or informal and whether the word has a positive or negative connotation. Explain to students that there is a range of correct answers and that everyone will place words in a slightly different place.
11. Place the words on a Synonym Matrix similar to the following example.

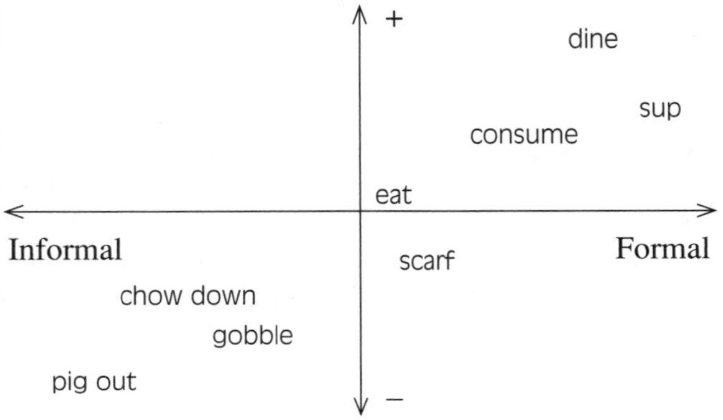

Strategy 6 SECTION 5.2

TRUE AND PARTIAL SYNONYMS

1. After students have learned about synonyms, they can begin to use a thesaurus to find synonyms of their own. Mountain (2007/2008) suggests that when students use a thesaurus they need to learn that there are different types of synonyms.
2. Explain to students that they have learned about true synonyms, or words that are very similar. Develop a chart that has two column headings: True Synonyms and Partial Synonyms such as the one that follows.

True Synonyms	Partial Synonyms

3. Give several examples of true synonyms, such as *car* and *automobile*. Have students volunteer additional true synonyms that they have learned. Record the true synonyms on the chart.
4. Then explain to students that some synonyms are close but are only partial synonyms, such as *picture* and *photograph*. List several vocabulary words that students have recently learned. Use a thesaurus or think of your own partial synonyms for the words. List the partial synonyms on the chart. Ask students if they can think of additional partial synonyms as in the example that follows.

True Synonyms	Partial Synonyms
Car—Automobile	Picture—Photograph

5. Post the True and Partial Synonym chart on a bulletin board. Invite students to add word pairs to the chart as they find examples from their reading and writing.

Practice and Reinforcement Activities

1. Students need to practice the synonyms they learn through a variety of activities. One activity that students can participate in is Synonym Bingo. Provide students with a list of words that you have already taught and ask them to think of synonyms for each one. Prepare a sheet of paper with 16 squares. Have students write a synonym for the listed words by writing one synonym on each square. Then have students trade papers so that they have a bingo sheet prepared by a classmate. Call out the vocabulary words and have students check off the synonyms on their bingo sheet. When a student gets four words across or four words down, have them call out, "Bingo." To play another game, have students use a different colored pen or marker to check off the synonyms.
2. Synonym Webs are another way students can practice the synonyms they have learned. Tell students that some synonyms are partial synonyms and that they may not mean exactly the same thing. Have students write a word in the center of the web such as the word *cold*. Provide a sentence using the word such as, "I felt *cold* when I went outside." Have students think of words that could be used instead of *cold* in the sentence, or have them use a thesaurus to find synonyms for the word. Students can write the synonyms in a web similar to that shown below.

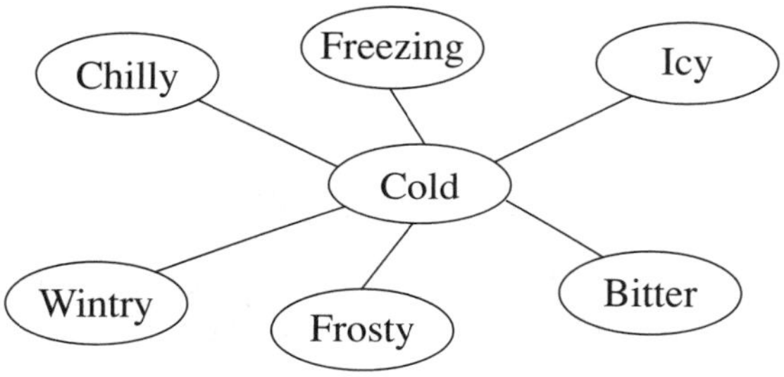

3. Selecting just the right word in speaking or writing is challenging. Lenski and Johns (2004) suggest using Million Dollar Word posters to reinforce the new words that you have taught. A Million Dollar Word poster contains all of the synonyms and partial synonyms for a commonly used word. Create several of these posters to display in the room so students have easy access to Million Dollar words. Explain to students that each word on the list has a slightly different connotation of the word and that the words cannot necessarily be used interchangeably. Instead, the Million Dollar Word posters list words that have different shades of meaning for the targeted word. Once students are familiar with using the posters, have groups of students create their own lists of words. The Chapter 5 Resources section (page 415) has a list of Million Dollar Words for *said*. You might also have students list words for other overused words such as *nice*, *good*, *went*, and *fun*.

Section **5.3**

Speaking and Writing Vocabulary

Behavior Observed → **Anticipated Outcome**

The student does not use new vocabulary words in speaking and writing. → The student will correctly use new vocabulary words in both speaking and writing.

Background

Knowing words involves four different vocabularies: reading, listening, speaking, and writing (Baumann, Kame'enui, & Ash, 2003). Reading and listening are receptive vocabularies. When you teach word meanings, your first goal is for students to be able to understand new words when they read. You do this by having students associate word meanings with the word itself. Teaching word meanings helps to build reading comprehension. After you teach and review vocabulary words, you should expect students to be able to understand sentences that contain these new words.

Being able to use words in speaking and writing represents an entirely different goal. Speaking and writing are part of expressive vocabularies. In order for students to be able to use words that they have learned in their expressive vocabulary, they need to learn the word deeply so that the word is retained in memory and easily retrieved. It is unreasonable to expect students to use every word that you teach in their speaking and writing.

You can, however, focus on specific words that have high usability for students to learn deeply. We have discussed Tier 1, Tier 2, and Tier 3 words (Beck, McKeown, & Kucan, 2002) earlier in this chapter. To review, Tier 1 words are those words that students already know and are most likely in both their receptive and expressive vocabularies. Tier 2 words are the words that many students do not already know but that they need to learn to be able to read with comprehension at their grade level and beyond. Tier 3 words are those words that you may want to teach so that students are able to understand a particular unit of study but that will be rarely used again. If you want students to build their speaking and writing vocabularies, you will want to focus on Tier 2 words.

Many teachers ask how they will know which words are Tier 2 words. To answer that question, you should consider whether deep knowledge of the word is critical for students to learn and understand grade level material. You should also think about whether students will most likely hear this word again in the future. For example, the word *gauntlet* (a glove with a long cuff, commonly used in the phrase *to throw down the gauntlet* which means to issue a challenge) might be a word that is fun to teach but that students will probably have little use for in school or life. *Gauntlet*, therefore, might be a word that you teach just enough so students understand it in a lesson, but you may not want to spend the time and effort to teach the word so that students use it in their speaking and writing.

The strategies and activities in this section are designed for Tier 2 words. You will want students to learn them so well that they are in memory and can be retrieved for speaking and writing.

Strategy 1 SECTION 5.3

INTERACTIVE READ ALOUDS

1. Interactive Read Alouds can help students use new vocabulary terms in their speaking vocabularies because they illustrate how a word is used in real text.
2. Select a picture book to read to students, such as *Stellaluna* (Cannon, 1993). Skim through the book looking for vocabulary words that students already know but that they do not use in speaking or writing. The list could contain the following words.

   search   scent   escape   limp

3. Write the words on the chalkboard and ask students the meanings of the words. Remind students where they have seen the words in the past and scaffold student responses to fit the way the word is used in the context. For example, you might say something like what follows.

   > *Remember, we learned the word* scent *in science class when we were learning about the five senses. Who remembers what the word* scent *means? Yes, it means a smell and is usually used in a positive way such as a sweet smell.*

4. Read the story, emphasizing the vocabulary words that you have written on the chalkboard. In *Stellaluna*, for example, the sentence that contains the word scent is, "One night, as Mother Bat followed the heavy *scent* of ripe fruit, an owl spied her."
5. After you have read the entire book, return to the sentences containing the key words. Write the sentences on the chalkboard if necessary. Invite students to read the sentence with you, again emphasizing the key words.
6. Ask students to create their own sentences using key words from the story. To scaffold this activity, you might give them sentence frames based on the story, such as the following.

   One night, ________________ followed the *scent* of ________________________.

   The ________________ followed the *scent* of ____________________________.

   The *scent* of ____________________________ was noticed by Mother Bat.

7. Invite students to use the key words in their own sentences.
8. Write the key words on a word wall and invite students to look for meaningful opportunities to use the words in their conversations and written work. Students can also be asked to generate sentences using the key words during the next several weeks.

USE IT OR LOSE IT

1. When students use new vocabulary words in their speaking or writing, they are more likely to remember them and use them automatically. The Use It or Lose It strategy capitalizes on students' ability to think of multiple sentences using vocabulary words, thereby, extending the words to a variety of contexts.
2. Develop a list of five to seven words that you have taught and that you are certain most students remember. Write the words on the chalkboard.
3. Read the words aloud to the class and review the word meanings. If students have questions about word meanings, answer them at this time. Be sure to use student-friendly definitions.
4. Tell students that you want the words on the list to become part of their speaking and writing vocabularies by saying something like the following.

   We have talked about each of these words several times. A few weeks ago, I introduced the words and provided you with common definitions. We also found the words in our reading and developed sentences for the words. The words are on our word wall and you have practiced saying the words, defining them, and using them in sentences several times. I now expect you to know the words well and to begin using them in your speaking and writing. I have already heard several of you use some of the words, and that's exactly what I want for each of you.

5. Divide the class into groups of four or five students. Give each group the list of words.
6. Tell students that you want them to generate sentences with the words one student and one word at a time. Give the directions as follows.

   I'm going to give you five minutes to generate as many sentences as you can using the words on the list. I'd like one of you to be the recorder for the group. The recorder will not participate but will write down the sentences that you generate. Beginning with the student on the left of the recorder, say a sentence that uses one of the words on the list. Then move to the next student who also says a sentence. Go around the group in turn, saying sentences with one of the words. You can repeat the words on the list. The purpose of this strategy is to generate as many sentences as you can in a short time.

7. Give the students a set amount of time to generate sentences. Five to seven minutes should be adequate considering that the purpose is for students to think of sentences very quickly.
8. After the time is up, ask the recorder in each group to read the sentences that the group generated. If sentences do not make sense, have the recorder delete those sentences. Take time to explain why the sentence is deleted. It may also be possible for students to change the sentence so that it makes sense.
9. Encourage students to create oral and written sentences using the words on the chalkboard through the week. Reinforce and praise students when they think of a sentence.
10. Rotate the words after a week or so. Replace words that students were able to use frequently in sentences with other vocabulary words. Keep words on the list that students had difficulty using automatically in sentences in their speaking and writing.

Strategy 3 SECTION 5.3

CONNECT TWO

1. Connect Two (Blachowicz & Lee, 1991) is an excellent strategy for encouraging students to generate vocabulary words in sentences. It also has the benefit of having students think about how new words fit together.
2. Select 10 to 12 vocabulary words from the words you have taught to students. The words can be from one unit of study or from a variety of topics. In this example, all of the words are taken from the book, *The Nez Perce* (Nelson & Nelson, 2003), which is about the Native American nation that helped Lewis and Clark in their expedition.
3. Divide the words into two columns and write them on the chalkboard as in the following example.

List 1	List 2
ancestors	tributaries
dwellings	disputes
explore	elders
gristmill	trappers
emigrants	treaty
reservation	extinction

4. Divide the class into groups of two or three students. Ask students to develop a sentence that uses a word from List 1 and List 2. After students have written a sentence, have them reflect on the reasons why they connected the two words. Demonstrate Connect Two with a sentence and reflection of your own such as the following.

   I'm going to try and connect the two words, gristmill *and* tributary*, because I know that gristmills are found near water. Here is the sentence that I wrote: The* gristmill *ground flour for the settlers who lived near a* tributary *of the Snake River.*

5. Once students are familiar with Connect Two, have them work independently writing sentences using words from each list. Depending on the skill level of your students, you could ask students to develop two sentences. You might ask students to write sentences that connect as many of the words as possible.

Strategy 4 SECTION 5.3

POSSIBLE SENTENCES

1. Possible Sentences (Moore & Moore, 1992) is a strategy that helps students see how new vocabulary words fit together in authentic texts.
2. Select 10 to 12 words that will be found in a book that you will read to the class or in a text that students will read silently. Select words that are Tier 2 words or words that are important to know for the story and that also have usability in other contexts. Try to choose some words that are familiar to students as well as some words that are new but that students need to learn. As an example, the following words are a list that could be used from the book, *Through My Eyes* (Bridges, 1999).

swept	whirlwind	struggle
racism	integrated	federal
deadline	limited	broiling
rented	comfortable	protect

3. Write the words on the chalkboard and read the words aloud to students. Divide students into groups of two or three and have students talk about each of the words, sharing what they know about the word meanings.
4. Ask students to volunteer definitions for each of the words. If students do not know one of the words, provide them with a student-friendly definition and example of how the word could be used.
5. Show students the cover of the book and provide a brief overview of the story. In the example of *Through My Eyes* (Bridges, 1999), you could say the following.

   > *This is a true story of Ruby Bridges who was the first black student to integrate an elementary school in New Orleans. We've learned about the civil rights era in social studies and have talked about the words* segregation *and* integration. *We also know about the term* racism *and how that term has been talked about in our country's history. We've also drawn a timeline of the events of the 1960s so we're very familiar with the context of the story.*

6. Before reading the book, ask students, who are still in groups of two or three, to select two words from the vocabulary list and to predict a sentence that could possibly be in the book. As students are writing the sentences, they are not only making a prediction about the story, but they are considering how the author used the vocabulary words in sentences. Examples of sentences could include the following.
   - *Racism swept* through the South during the 1960s.
   - *Federal* marshals had to *protect* the children.
   - They lived in a *rented* house that was very *comfortable*.
   - There was a *deadline* for *integrated* schools.
7. Invite students to volunteer to read their sentences to the class. Write the sentences on the chalkboard.
8. Read the story to students or have them read them independently. Ask students to look for the vocabulary words during their reading to determine whether the "possible sentences" were in the text.
9. After reading and using the story as a reference, discuss each of the sentences. Ask whether the sentences (or a similar sentence) was written in the story. You could have students vote whether they think the sentence or basic idea was present.
10. Have students generate new sentences to replace those that were not found in the text.
11. Discuss how the author used the vocabulary words and how students can use these words in speaking and in writing.

Practice and Reinforcement Activities

1. Select books that students have read or heard with vocabulary words that students have probably learned. Read the sentences that contain the vocabulary words highlighting how the word is used. Tell students that authors try to select just the right word for the context of the story. Have students substitute a different word for the vocabulary word. Discuss how a different word changes the meaning of the sentence. Repeat for several different sentences from the story and for other familiar books.
2. Use vocabulary words as sentence starters. Select two or three of the vocabulary words that you have taught. Write a sentence for each one, using the vocabulary word and leaving the rest of the sentence blank for students to complete. For example, you could use the examples that follow.

   If I lived in a *cabin*, I would ______________________________.

   Tony was *livid* when he learned ______________________________.

   Her description was *implausible* because ______________________________.

3. Encourage the use of vocabulary words that are listed on the word wall. Several times during the day, point to a word and ask students to create at least three different sentences using the words. If students have difficulty thinking of a sentence, give them one yourself. On some days you might want to have a race with students to create sentences by pointing to a word and giving students three seconds to come up with a sentence before you do.
4. Encourage students to watch for how vocabulary sentences are used in classroom conversation through Vocabulary Bingo. Select a list of 15 vocabulary words that you want students to use in their speaking and writing. List the words on the chalkboard. Have students fold a piece of paper into nine squares and write one of the 15 vocabulary words from the list on each of the squares. Each student should have a slightly different card. Tell students that you will be looking for them to use the words in sentences during class discussions. When a student uses a word correctly, check the word on your master list and have students check the word on their Vocabulary Bingo sheet. You can also use vocabulary words in sentences as you teach. Encourage students to fill up their Vocabulary Bingo card, or you could give students a point or a reward when they have three squares crossed out either down or across. An example of a Vocabulary Bingo card follows.

Trace	Incredible	Legal
Slippery	Unite	Enclose
Counter	Jaded	Squirm

Section **5.4**

Using Context Clues to Predict Meanings of Unknown Words

Behavior Observed → **Anticipated Outcome**

The student has difficulty using context clues to predict meanings of unknown words.

The student will use context as one reading strategy to predict meanings of unknown words.

Background

The words surrounding an unknown word can sometimes be used by the student to predict its meaning. When this process occurs, the student is using context clues. Such clues help students associate meaning with words that they may not be able to pronounce and can aid students in constructing the meaning of a sentence or passage.

For example, suppose a student comes across the word *yegg* in a passage. It is probable that the student will be able to pronounce the word but will not know what it means. Depending on the context, the student may or may not be able to make a reasonable guess at the meaning of the word. If the only context is "Two people saw the *yegg,*" it is unlikely that the student could use the context to figure out the meaning of *yegg*. The student could determine that a *yegg* is something that can be seen, but such information is not very helpful in determining the meaning, because millions of things can be seen.

A different context might be more helpful. For example, "The *yegg,* a burglar, was seen by two people." In this sentence, the meaning is given in an appositive phrase, and the student may be able to associate the meaning with the word.

Many teachers encourage students to use context to figure out meanings for unfamiliar words. Unfortunately, such advice often has two limitations. First, little direct instruction is given. Second, teachers need to be aware that not many words are actually defined by their context (Johnson, 2001). Some words, however, can be determined solely by their context. These words will probably be found in one of the following types of sentences (two examples of each type follow the description).

- **Definition or Description:** Words are directly defined by the sentence.
  - A *kingcup* is a yellow flower.
  - The *commencement* or beginning of the journey was exciting.

- **Appositive Phrase:** The definition of the unknown word or the word itself is in a phrase set off by commas.
  - The *kithara,* a musical instrument, was played in ancient Greece.
  - The *kinglet,* a tiny bird, eats insects.
- **Linked Synonyms:** The unknown word is in a series of known words.
  - His *barbarous,* cruel actions were unexpected.
  - Her aim, goal, and *inclination* was to finish the book.
- **Comparisons and Contrasts:** The word can be defined by its opposite in the sentence.
  - Rather than his usual lively self, today William appeared to be *ponderous.*
  - Unlike the *dowdy* customer, the salesperson was neat and clean.
- **Examples:** The word can be defined by examples in the following sentences.
  - My family is very *musical.* My sister plays the violin; my father plays the piano; and my mother sings.
  - His *machinations* to get a promotion were obvious. He bragged about his accomplishments and told his boss his colleagues were inept.
- **Classification:** The word can be defined by its relationship to known words.
  - The water *molecule* is comprised of two parts hydrogen and one part oxygen.
  - Mike was an important player on the *offensive* football team. His skills at passing the ball to any player within reach were stunning.
- **Experience:** The word can be defined by applying previous experience to the unknown word.
  - As I stepped onto the diving platform, I felt *paralyzing* fear. The water surface appeared unforgiving. If I landed any way other than vertical, I could end up with a serious injury.
  - He looked *deliriously* happy. As he held his new son in his arms, his eyes glowed with emotion, and his lips slowly spread into the widest grin of his life.

Strategy 1 SECTION 5.4

WHAT'S THE MEANING?

1. Develop a series of passages in which context can be used easily to help to reveal the meaning of an unfamiliar word. Use a hierarchy in which context clues can be ranked informally from easy to hard.
2. Write a word on the chalkboard that students may or may not be able to pronounce. Ask whether anyone knows the meaning of the word. If the word is carefully selected, few, if any, students should know its meaning. Suppose the word is *kingcup* and a few students think they know what it means. Those students could be asked to remain quiet while the lesson continues.
3. Ask students how they might make a good prediction for the meaning of *kingcup.* Common responses include looking in the dictionary, asking someone, and seeing the word in a sentence. Stress that seeing a word in a sentence is using context.
4. Now write the unfamiliar word in a sentence where the meaning is made clear by definition or description.

A kingcup is a yellow flower.

5. Have students read the sentence and then identify the word or words that reveal the meaning of the unfamiliar word. Circle or underline these words.
6. Repeat this procedure with additional words. In subsequent lessons, teach other types of context clues in a similar manner. Occasionally, use an unfamiliar word in a context in which the meaning is not clear. These instances will help students realize that there are limitations to using context to determine word meanings.

Strategy 2 SECTION 5.4

PREDICT AND CHECK

1. Explain to students that context clues can be important in understanding the meaning of unknown words (Gunning, 2008). From a passage the students are reading, select four or five words that can be defined by their context. Write the words on the chalkboard.
2. For each word, have students apply the following questions (Sternberg & Powell, 1983).
   - What information in the passage will help me figure out the meaning of the word?
   - When I put together all the information that I know about the word, what word makes sense in the sentence?
   - What do I know that will help me figure out this word?
3. Write down the students' guesses for each word on the chalkboard. Explain that if a word does not make sense, a different word should be tried. Try several words in the passage until students read the unknown words correctly. Discuss the meanings of the words.
4. Reflect on the strategies students used as they applied context clues to their reading. Discuss the strategies they used and suggest other strategies students could use as they try to understand the meanings of unknown words.

Strategy 3 SECTION 5.4

CONTEXT CHART

1. Tell students that they can learn the meanings of some new words from the context of the sentence. Explain to students that they can remember the words they have learned from a Context Chart.
2. Duplicate and distribute the Context Chart reproducible on page 375. Give an example of a word in context to learn or use the example adapted from Zwiers (2004).

Word or phrase in context	Word parts, related words	Prediction of meaning	Meaning from discussion or dictionary	Image to remember meaning
She *circumvented* the barrier by driving around it.	Circum-	Went around	Avoided	Circumference is round = go around

3. Identify a vocabulary word that can be understood by the context of the sentence. Write the sentence in the first column.

4. Ask students whether there are any word parts that they already know. If they do, write that in the second column. In the case of the word *circumvented*, some students might know the word part *circum-*. Discuss the meaning of the word part and remind students that word parts can help them figure out the meanings of unknown words.

5. Have students predict the meaning of the word *circumvented*. Remind students to use the context of the sentence and also what they know about word parts. Have students share their predictions with a classmate and then write their predictions in the third column.

6. Discuss students' predictions. If several students have predicted the actual meaning of the word as it is used in the sentence, have those students replay their thinking for the class. If few or no students were able to generate the meaning of the word, model how you would think about the word's meaning as in the following example.

   > *As I read the sentence, I realized that I didn't know the meaning of the word* circumvented. *As I read the sentence, however, I noticed that the word seemed to be defined later in the sentence when it said she drove around the barrier. I thought that* circumvented *must mean to get around in some way. As I further thought about the word, I remembered that I had learned that* circum- *means* circle. *I thought maybe she circled the barrier, but that didn't fit with the rest of the sentence. Therefore, I thought the word means* went around.

7. Discuss the meaning of the word and, if needed, look the word up in the dictionary. Have students write the meaning of the word in the fourth column.

8. Tell students that they need to remember the new word so that they know its meaning when they see it again. Encourage students to think of an image that helps them remember the word. In the case of *circumvented*, students can remember its meaning if they know that the word *circumference* means round. They can then remember that *circumvented* means to go around. Explain to students that remembering an image or key word will help them remember the new word.

9. Have students practice figuring out words in context frequently. Remind students, however, that many new words cannot be understood by the context of the sentence and that they will need to know a variety of ways to figure out new words during reading.

CONTEXT CHART

Name ____ Date __________________

Word or phrase in context	*Word parts, related words*	*Prediction of meaning*	*Meaning from discussion or dictionary*	*Image to remember meaning*

From Zwiers, J. (2004). *Building Reading Comprehension Habits in Grades 6–12: A Toolkit of Classroom Activities*. Newark, DE: International Reading Association.

Strategy 4

CONTEXTUAL REDEFINITION

Contextual Redefinition (Readence, Bean, & Baldwin, 1998) can give students a better understanding of how to learn words in the context of text as well as helping them discover the meanings of new words on their own.

1. Select unfamiliar words from the students' text that could be considered key to understanding the text.
2. Write sentences using words that give their meanings in context.
3. Ask students to define the new words aloud. Discuss how the context helped the students understand the meanings of the words.
4. Then ask students to verify their definitions by checking a dictionary. The dictionary can also help them learn other ways the words are used.

For example, try to define the following words using your background knowledge.

jejune ____

convivial ____

Now read the following sentences that contain the words *jejune* and *convivial.*

The teacher was surprised by his *jejune,* immature answer to the problem.

Her *convivial* personality was appealing to friends who enjoyed parties.

If you didn't know the words before, you probably know now that one of the definitions for *jejune* is immature and one of the definitions for *convivial* is sociable. Remember that words are symbols for concepts, so you can't understand the connotations for either word by reading one sentence. You do, however, get a sense of the meaning of each word, and if you would read either word in a text, you would probably know enough about the word to comprehend the phrase it was in.

Contextual Redefinition is a useful strategy for a variety of reasons. First, the strategy illustrates how difficult it is to identify definitions of words in isolation. Second, students tap into their background knowledge by making a prediction about the word. Some students may have a tentative knowledge of the word before you teach its definition. This strategy helps them bring what they know to the teaching situation. Third, contextual redefinition helps students become engaged in the lesson rather than having them list sterile definitions. Finally, the strategy encourages students to use the dictionary to confirm predictions rather than being the first strategy they use when they come to an unknown word.

PREVIEW IN CONTEXT

Preview in Context (Readence, Bean, & Baldwin, 1998) is a strategy that has students look for words in the context of their text to give them a better understanding of which definition of the word will be used. Discussing key words before reading also helps students begin to develop schemata (background knowledge) for the topic of the text selection.

1. Select words from a text that you think will be unfamiliar to your students. Make sure you choose words that are key to the understanding of the text and don't make your list too long. It's better to have an effective lesson with 4 or 5 words than to have a lesson of 10 words that students forget.
2. Show students where the words are in the text and read the context of the new word. You may read the passage aloud or have the students read it silently. If you are using a content area text, you might also want to spend some time explaining the concepts in the text.
3. Help students learn the word's meaning by discussing it in its context. You might want to ask the students questions leading them to the definition, as in the following example.

   The protective coloring of the horned viper helps *camouflage* him by hiding him from his enemies and by helping him blend into his background.

   Teacher: What do you know about the word *camouflage* from this sentence?
   Student: The horned viper is hiding from his enemies.
   Teacher: How does being camouflaged help him?
   Student: He blends into his background.
   Teacher: What else does the sentence tell us about being camouflaged?
   Student: I think the part where it says *protective coloring* is another way of saying *camouflage*.

4. Expand word meanings. After students learn the initial meaning of the word, provide additional contexts for the same word. That way students who come across the word in different contexts will make predictions about what they know about the word's meaning to another situation.

   Teacher: How many of you have seen *camouflage* shirts or pants?
   Student: I have some on my GI Joe.
   Teacher: What are they like?
   Student: They're all different colors, but mostly brown and green.
   Teacher: Why do you think they are those particular colors?
   Student: So he can hide from the bad guys.
   Teacher: How are the GI Joe camouflage clothes similar to the snake's skin?
   Student: Both the clothes and the skin help them blend into the background.

Practice and Reinforcement Activities

1. Watch for examples in instructional materials in which context can be used to build meanings for unfamiliar words and use these examples to help reinforce students' use of context.
2. Encourage students to consult dictionaries to find words whose meanings are likely to be unfamiliar to other students in the class. Then have students write sentences or brief passages that could be shared with other students who would attempt to identify the meanings of the words.
3. Provide brief passages that contain unfamiliar words and have students select or write the meanings of the underlined words based on the context.
4. To encourage students to use self-monitoring strategies as they read, print the following questions on a brightly-colored bookmark.

    - Did what I just read make sense to me?
    - Can I retell this passage in my own words?
    - Are there any words I don't understand?
    - Are there any sentences that confuse me?

    Remind students to ask themselves these questions as they read (Richek, Caldwell, Jennings, & Lerner, 1996).

Section 5.5

Compound Words and Affixes

Behavior Observed → **Anticipated Outcome**

Behavior Observed	Anticipated Outcome
The student does not use knowledge about word parts to help determine meanings of unknown words.	The student will use knowledge about compound words and affixes as an aid to help determine word meanings.

Background

Compound words and affixes (prefixes and suffixes) are part of structural or morphemic analysis. In Chapter 3 (see Section 3.4) strategies were given to help students use compound words and affixes to help pronounce or decode words not known at sight. In this section, the focus is on the meanings of words, and the teaching strategies are designed to help students use compound words and affixes to make informed predictions about words' meanings.

Strategy 1 SECTION 5.5

COMPOUND WORDS

1. Refer to Chapter 3 (see Strategy 6 in Section 3.4) for ideas to develop knowledge about compound words so students can use that knowledge as an aid to pronounce words of more than one syllable.
2. Review the meaning of compound words so students understand their essential characteristic: a compound word is made up of two smaller words. In addition, the meaning of each smaller word may be retained in the compound word (*bluebird*), may be somewhat changed (*softball*), or have practically nothing to do with the meaning of the individual words (*dragonfly*).

3. Invite students to form small groups and brainstorm a list of compound words. Students could write their words on an overhead transparency or a sheet of paper. After a few minutes, invite a student from one group to share some of the words.
4. As the words are given, be sure they are written on the chalkboard or shared using an overhead projector. Then identify each word that makes up the compound word, have a student use the compound word in a sentence, and make sure students understand the word's meaning.
5. Note that the meaning of each smaller word can sometimes contribute to the meaning of a compound word. Invite students to model this process for some of their compound words or select from the following list.

doghouse	notebook	crossroads
blueberry	cornbread	schoolwork
suppertime	blackbird	homework

6. Share some compound words whose separate meanings are unlikely to contribute to an accurate meaning for the compound word. Model for students by saying something like the following.

> *I can see that two small words,* goose *and* berry *make the word* gooseberry. *I know a berry is something that could be eaten, but some berries are not edible and others are poisonous. A goose is an animal that is bigger than a duck. What I don't know is whether a* gooseberry *looks a bit like a* goose. *That meaning just doesn't make sense to me. I'm pretty sure this is some type of berry, but I don't know much more. I'd better consult my dictionary.* (Look up the word and share the meaning: a spring shrub having greenish flowers and edible greenish berries.) Then say: *I was right about* gooseberry *being a type of berry that can be eaten, but it does not look like a goose. I also found out the color of the berries.*

7. Present some compound words in sentences. Have students underline the compound words and draw a line between the two words. If the meaning of the word is not known, have students consult their dictionaries. Then discuss the meanings of the compound words. Some sample sentences are provided below.
   - He brought homemade cookies to the lunchroom.
   - My grandparents gave me a notebook.
   - The radio broadcast was about a breakthrough in medicine.
   - The artwork and paintbrushes were in the workroom.
   - My dad's workshop has many tools.
   - My mom's workday is eight hours.
   - The blueberry plants were invaded by birds.
8. Conclude the lesson by encouraging students to use their knowledge of compound words when they come across longer words in their reading. This knowledge can be used to help separate the word into pronounceable chunks and possibly help with the word's meaning. Remind students that a dictionary can also be used if the meaning is not clear or if additional clarification is desired.
9. Consult Chapter 3 Resources (page 276) for a list of compound words.

Strategy 2 PREFIXES

1. Explain to students that prefixes can be attached to a root word and the meanings of a particular prefix can sometimes give clues to the meaning of the word. Two lists of prefixes can be found in Chapter 5 Resources (pages 408–409). A prefix is a separate syllable that can change the meaning of a root word completely or make meanings more specific (Fox, 2000). Provide an example of each and invite students to suggest words of each type. Several examples are provided below.

Changes meaning of root word completely	Makes meaning of root word more specific
uncover	review
disembark	repay
invisible	preview
irregular	foreground
overlook	midweek
unhappy	semicircle

2. Tell students that there are a few prefixes that account for over half of all prefixed words (White, Sowell, & Yanagihara, 1989). List the following prefixes on the chalkboard or an overhead transparency. Encourage students to provide examples, use those given below, or select examples from your instructional materials.

Prefix	Meaning	Example
dis	opposite	disappear
un	opposite	uncover
re	back/again	return
in (im, ir, il)	opposite	impossible

3. Help students understand that prefixes have predictable spellings and pronunciations. They can be used to help pronounce the word. Then direct students to each word and ask them if they know the meaning of the prefix as it is used in each sentence. They are likely to identify the *re* in *rewrite* to mean to write again. The *re* in *return* means to give back. The *re* in *record,* however, is just the first syllable in the word and does not mean *back* or *again.* Help students understand the three ways the prefix *re* can be used.

4. Develop a bulletin board or sheet of paper that looks like the following chart.

re		
re (means back)	re (means again)	re (just the first syllable)

Share some additional words that can be formed from the *re* prefix and have students place the words in the column where they fit best. Encourage students to use the words in sentences and, if necessary, consult a dictionary to clarify their meanings. Many possible words to select from are listed below.

react	rebellion	rebuild	recap
readjust	rebirth	rebuke	recapture
reaffirm	rebound	recall	recast
realign	rebuff	recant	recede
receipt	receive	recent	reception
recess	recharge	recital	recite
reclaim	recline	recoil	recollect
recompose	reconfirm	reconstruct	reconvert
recount	recoup	recourse	recover
recreate	recruit	recuperate	recur
recurve	recycle	redemption	redesign
redirect	rediscount	redistribute	redistrict
reduce	refect	refer	refill
refine	refit	reflect	reflex
reforest	reform	refract	refrain
refresh	refrigerator	refuel	refund
refuse	refute	regain	regard

5. After categorizing enough of the words so that students understand the three categories, have students be alert for *re* words as they read and complete assignments over the next several days. When they find a word, have them decide in which category it fits and write it on their sheet of paper or write it on a card and attach it to the bulletin board.

6. Review the words from time to time and be sure the new words are placed in the appropriate categories. Provide additional practice so students will learn the two meanings of the prefix *re*. Help them understand that prefixes can sometimes reveal a word's meaning, but students should always ask if the meaning makes sense in context. Model this strategy for students from time to time and also have students share instances when their knowledge of prefixes has helped them understand the meaning of a word.

7. See the two lists of prefixes in Chapter 5 Resources (pages 408–409). One of the lists suggests grade levels for introducing specific prefixes.

SUFFIXES AND ENDINGS

1. Suffixes and endings are generally more complex than prefixes. Gunning (2003) suggests that *er* can be introduced in second grade and Cunningham (2000) notes that *er* is appropriate for an initial lesson. Some suffixes change the function of the word or the part of speech (*act, actor*). Two lists of suffixes can be found in Chapter 5 Resources (pages 410–411).
2. Introduce the suffix *er* by writing it on the chalkboard. Tell students that adding this suffix to the end of certain words can change their meanings. For older students, you could say that some verbs or actions can be changed to a person who performs an action by adding *er* or *or*.
3. Write *teach* on the chalkboard and ask for a volunteer to pronounce the word. Then tell students that *teach* is an action. Next ask what you are that relates to the word *teach*. When students say *teacher*, write it under *teach* and point out that both words are related: one is an action and the other is a person who does the action.
4. Invite students to offer other words that end in *er* or *or*. The words can be placed in one of four categories. Write these categories on the chalkboard and help students place their words in the appropriate category. Some words, such as lighter, might fit in more than one category. An example is provided below.

People (who do something)	Things (that do something)	More (compares)	Leftovers (just end in er/or)
teacher	calculator	prettier	never
preacher	computer	smaller	winter
actor	radiator	greater	
reporter	washer	taller	
painter		shorter	
investigator		happier	
		faster	

5. Discuss the meanings of the words, have students use them in sentences, and model how students might use this knowledge to help determine words' meanings. For example, you might say something like what follows.

> *When you read, sometimes a word will have a suffix that will give you a clue to the meaning of a word. If you know the meaning of the word* paint, *the word* painter *would probably mean a person who paints. Other words that end in* er *may be a clue that things are being compared (a dime is* smaller *than a quarter).*

6. Design other lessons using the lists of suffixes in Chapter 5 Resources (pages 410–411).

ROOT WORDS

1. Begin with a simple word like *work* that students are able to pronounce. Tell students that additions can be made to words to make new words.
2. Invite students to suggest additions to the beginning and/or end of *work*. Write each word on the chalkboard and talk about how the meaning of each word changes. Some words that are possible are listed below.

works	overworked	workbag
worked	underworked	workbench
working	homework	workbook
workers	workable	workbox
workfare	workhouse	workload
workmanship	workout	workshop
workweek	schoolwork	groundwork
woodwork	woodworking	rework
teamwork	workmen	workable

3. Do similar exercises from time to time with other common words (*agree, play, form*). Then direct the focus of the lesson to what are called combining forms (*tri-, tele-, astro-, bi-, semi-,* and so on).
4. Select one of the forms (*bi-*) and tell students that *bi-* usually means two. Knowing the meaning of *bi-* can sometimes help determine a word's meaning.
5. Write the word *bicycle* on the chalkboard. Students will probably know that it has two wheels. Tell students that *bi-* can mean two and ask if anyone knows what a bike with one wheel and one with three wheels are called (*unicycle* and *tricycle*). Develop meanings for *uni-* and *tri-*.
6. Write *uni-, bi-,* and *tri-* on the chalkboard and give students the opportunity to suggest or find words whose meanings are likely to fit each category. Encourage students to add words to the list; then develop a chart like the one that follows.

uni-	bi-	tri-	other
unicycle	bicycle	tricycle	bias
unicorn	bicentennial	triacid	biological
unidirectional	biceps	triangle	trial
unify	bicolor	triazine	tribunal
unilateral	bicorn	tribasic	trifle
unilingual	bicuspid	triceps	triumph
	biennial	tricolor	
	bilingual	tricuspid	
	bimodal	trifold	
	binary	trilogy	
	binominal	trimonthly	
		triple	
		triplet	
		tripod	

RESOURCES

7. Refer to Chapter 5 Resources (pages 408–411) for other affixes to teach or use some of the following root words for students at and above the third grade.

Root	Meaning	Example
graph	writing	autograph
tele	distance	telemetry
port	carry	export
phone	sound	telephone
duct	lead	conduct
auto	self	autopilot
ology	study of	biology
mid	middle	midsummer
hemi	half	hemisphere
bio	life	biography

Practice and Reinforcement Activities

1. Help students review the prefixes and suffixes they have learned by creating a Morpheme Word Wall. After teaching a prefix, such as *re-*, add it to the Word Wall. Invite students to think of words that begin with *re-* when reviewing Word Wall words. Have students think of as many words as they can, such as *renew*, *review*, *return*, and so on. Remind students as they think of words that the prefix *re-* means to "come back" and that it often changes the meaning of root words. Asking students to use a Morpheme Word Wall helps students become more comfortable with prefixes and suffixes.
2. You may have already had students develop word webs using prefixes or suffixes. Gill (2007), however, suggests that you have students create these types of word webs using the popular computer program Kidspiration. Give students a prefix such as *bi-* and ask them to place it in the middle of the web. Then have students find representative pictures of words that begin with *bi-*, such as *bicycle*, *bilingual*, *bi-monthly*, *bicolor*, and so on. If students are unable to find a picture that represents one of the words, have them write a sentence with the word highlighted. See the example that follows.

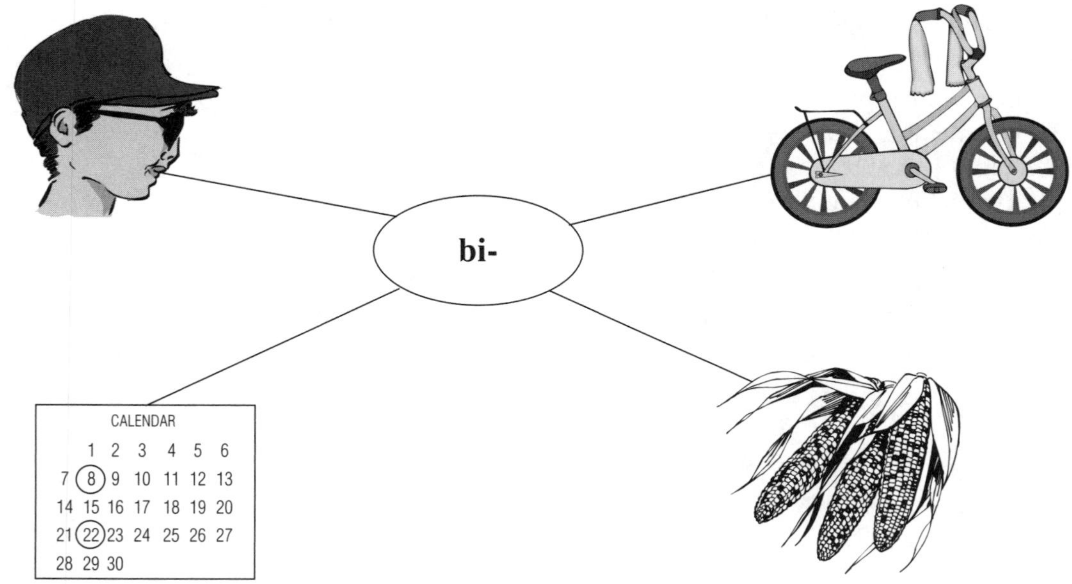

3. Have students draw a word tree. Have students select a word part that they have studied, such as *geo-*. Ask students to draw a tree and write the word part on the trunk of the tree. Then have small groups of students brainstorm lists of words that have the selected word part in it. For example, students could think of *geography*, *geometry*, *geothermal*, and so on. Ask students to write the words that begin with *geo-* on the branches of the tree. Remind students that they can learn new words by knowing word parts and that their trees illustrate that. See the example that follows.

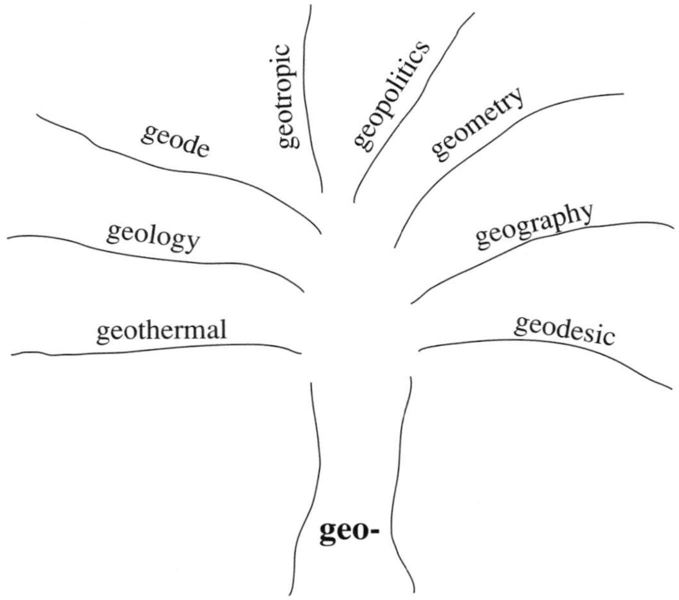

4. Students can practice word parts by using the strategy Twenty Questions (Newton, Padak, & Rasinski, 2008). Develop a list of word and word parts that you have taught. Tell students that one of them will be asked to select one of the words. The other students should ask questions about the word that can be answered by "yes" or "no." Scaffold student questioning by giving them examples of questions they could ask. For example, if the word was "triangle," some examples of questions that could be asked follow.

   - Is it an animal?
   - Is it something that people have in their houses?
   - Would it be in the classroom?
   - Is it something that we could make?
   - Did we learn about it in school?

   Once students have begun developing questions, they are quickly able to learn to be more strategic in their questioning. After students have become capable questioners, limit them to 20 questions. You might eventually have students try to decrease the number of questions they ask each time.

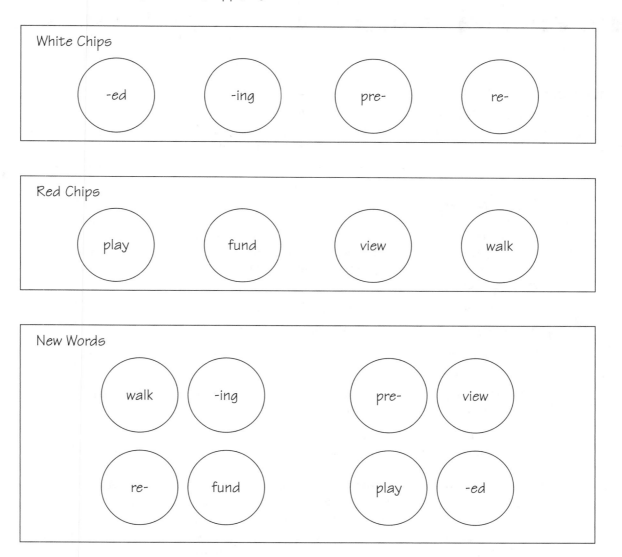

Students who are learning how to apply prefixes and suffixes to root words can benefit from added practice using Flip-a-Chip (Mountain, 2002). To play the game, write the names of common prefixes and suffixes on both sides of 15 or more white game chips. (See Chapter 5 Resources, pages 408–411 for lists of prefixes and suffixes.) Write root words on 15 or more red game chips. Give students both red and white game chips and have them make as many words as they can by adding a white chip (suffix or prefix) to a red chip (root word). As students play, remind them that they can learn more vocabulary words by applying affixes and root words.

White Chips

-ed | -ing | pre- | re-

Red Chips

play | fund | view | walk

New Words

walk -ing | pre- view

re- fund | play -ed

Section **5.6**

Dictionary: Word Meanings

Behavior Observed → **Anticipated Outcome**

The student does not use a dictionary to help determine, verify, or clarify the meanings of words in context.

The student will be able to use a dictionary to help determine, verify, or clarify the meanings of words in context.

Background

Look it up! Those words have been used by teachers for years—often without providing students with the skills needed to use a dictionary. In order to use a dictionary to look up the meaning of an unknown word, students need to acquire a number of prerequisite skills. Some of these skills are listed below.

1. knowing the letters of the alphabet in sequence,
2. arranging several words in alphabetical order by their initial letters,
3. arranging several words in alphabetical order to the second, third, and, if necessary, all the letters of a word, and
4. being able to locate a word in an efficient manner by knowing the general organization of a dictionary and how to use guide words.

Section 3.8 presents introductory lessons for alphabetical order and guide words. Once these skills are learned, students can be taught to determine, verify, or clarify the meanings of unknown words in their reading.

The focus of dictionary use in this section is to help students locate word meanings that may be helpful in understanding words in their reading whose meanings are unknown or uncertain. Students may begin using picture dictionaries in kindergarten through second grade. Such experiences, if carefully developed by teachers, help students learn alphabetical order and how to locate words. These dictionaries often use attractive colors, drawings, and photographs. While helpful to all students, such dictionaries may be especially useful for students of all ages who are learning to speak English. The attractive drawings and photographs may help students better understand particular words and possibly form a visual link with their experiences.

Gunning (2008) notes that students with average reading achievement are ready to use real dictionaries by third grade. The availability of hand-held electronic and CD dictionaries may be easier for students who struggle with reading. Such dictionaries may be motivational and may also pronounce the word and read its definition. Because most classrooms contain traditional dictionaries, teaching and practice strategies are given to help students use these resources to determine meanings of unknown words.

Dictionary use should not be the primary strategy students use when word meanings are unknown. Students should be encouraged to continue reading the paragraph in which the word appears and try to determine if the context is helpful in predicting the word's meaning. Morphemic analysis (prefixes, suffixes, etc.) may also be used to construct meaning of the unknown word. If the context and morphemic analysis are not helpful, the student must then decide the importance of that particular word in constructing the overall understanding of the paragraph or passage. If the word is judged to be important, a dictionary could be consulted. Finally, if the student encounters quite a few unknown words, it is a strong indicator that the reading material is too difficult. Dictionaries should be used selectively to help students achieve their purposes while reading.

Strategy 1 SECTION 5.6

INTRODUCTORY LESSON FOR UNKNOWN WORDS

1. Remember to ensure that students know how to locate words in a dictionary or glossary. Check your classroom dictionaries for instructional ideas and practice activities. Effective dictionary use depends upon students being able to locate words efficiently. If the prerequisite skills are lacking, take the time to teach them. See Section 3.8.

2. Invite students to share what they do when they come across a word in their reading whose meaning is unknown. Write some of their responses on the chalkboard (e.g., "I skip the word." "I ask someone." "I look it up." "I try to figure out the meaning by reading the sentence.").

3. Stress that many different strategies can be used when a word's meaning is unknown. Help students realize that there is not one best method to figure out an unknown word; a flexible approach is needed. For example, context and morphemic analysis may be useful to predict a word's meaning. See Sections 3.9 and 3.10 for encouraging ways to use a variety of word-identification strategies effectively.

4. Identify a dictionary as one way to help determine a word's meaning. Invite students to share their experiences with a dictionary. Note both positive and negative comments. Then help students understand that a dictionary or a glossary is one way to locate meanings of unknown words.

5. Model how you use a dictionary from time to time while you are reading. Use an example from your own reading or the following think-aloud.

   I was reading a picture book for fun, and I came across the phrase "the fronts of their tuques." I didn't know what the word tuques *meant, so I looked it up in my dictionary.*

6. Ask students if they know what the word means. Then explain the meaning (a kind of knitted cap originally worn by French-Canadian trappers and farmers, but now worn by skaters and others involved in winter sports) or have students look up the word in their dictionaries. Be sure to discuss the word's meaning.

7. Conclude the lesson by inviting small groups of students to look up the meanings of several words in sentences from their current reading that they don't know. Have students share their findings with others. You might also use the following sentences.
   - She saw the biffins on the table.
   - He was in a ditty.
   - I like the dobbin.
8. Invite students to use the dictionary when they come across unknown words in their reading. A chart like the one on the next page could be given to students for their record keeping. Later, students could share the results of using the dictionary to help them understand unknown words.

USING THE DICTIONARY FOR UNKNOWN WORDS

Book: ____

Page: ____

Sentence containing unknown word: ______________________________

____

____

Word's meaning from dictionary (a phrase): ______________________

My new understanding of the word is now rated:

_______ very good _______ good _______ fair _______ poor _______ very poor

Book: ____

Page: ____

Sentence containing unknown word: ______________________________

____

____

Word's meaning from dictionary (a phrase): ______________________

My new understanding of the word is now rated:

_______ very good _______ good _______ fair _______ poor _______ very poor

Strategy 2

LOCATING WORD MEANINGS PRIOR TO READING

1. Preview a selection students have not read to identify important, difficult words. The selection may be a story, a section from a content area text, or some other genre. Materials from guided reading may also be used.
2. Select several difficult words whose meanings students are unlikely to know or are unable to determine through morphemic analysis (e.g., prefixes, suffixes) or context clues. Choose only a few words that are the most important to understand the reading selection.
3. Tell students that you have selected a few words from the selection they are about to read that they may not know. Be sure to distinguish between pronouncing words and reading or understanding words. Write the sentence containing the difficult word on the chalkboard. Underline the word and invite students to share their ideas about the meaning of the word. Remain neutral if a student shares an appropriate meaning.
4. Ask students to look up the word in their dictionaries or glossaries. Guide students through the definition(s) and invite them to share ideas about the word's meaning(s). Relate the discussion to students' earlier ideas and have them evaluate their ideas in light of the dictionary's definition. For words with multiple meanings, model how each meaning may or may not fit the context. Use a think-aloud procedure similar to the following one.

   > *I see that the word* quarter *has two meanings in our dictionary. The sentence in the passage is talking about the third quarter of the game. I can see that one definition is a piece of money. That definition doesn't make sense unless the game involves quarters. The other definition says that many games are divided into four parts. That meaning seems to fit the passage. I guess the third quarter is the third part of the game. I'll try to keep that meaning in mind as I read.*

5. Proceed to the next word using a similar procedure. You might invite a student to guide the discussion and the exploration of the word's meaning. Ask guiding questions as needed but work toward having students take greater responsibility for the task.
6. Invite students to write a phrase on the chalkboard that defines each unknown word. These brief definitions can be referred to as students read the selection.
7. Refer, as needed, to the words initially selected in students' discussions of the reading selection. Invite students to share their insights as well as any additional words that were unknown in the selection. Some of these words, if important to the selection, might be explored as part of the lesson or used for independent work.

Strategy 3 SECTION 5.6

BEST MEANING FOR THE CONTEXT

1. Tell students that many words have more than one meaning. Explain that the word *roll* has a different meaning in each of the two sentences on the chalkboard.
2. Write these two sentences on the chalkboard.
   - When Mr. Johnson called the **roll**, he learned that two students were absent.
   - My friend Beth eats one **roll** for lunch every day.

3. Ask students to read the sentences and try to determine the appropriate meaning for *roll* in each sentence.

4. Invite students to share the clues that helped them figure out the appropriate meanings for *roll*. For example, in the second sentence, Beth is eating something, and a roll is something that can be eaten.

5. Tell students that the dictionary contains the different meanings a word can have. Have everyone in the group look up the word *roll* in their dictionaries. Ask someone to read the definition that pertains to sentence one (roll: a list of names, especially of group members). Then ask a student to read the definition that pertains to sentence two (roll: a soft, round portion of bread). Ask students to read a third definition of roll (to tumble or turn over and over) to themselves. Then ask for volunteers to use it in a sentence.

6. Select an actual excerpt from students' dictionaries or use one of the examples below to help provide additional practice. Review the definitions and then provide sample sentences to match the appropriate definition. Help students see the connections. Some sample sentences follow.

   rope

   1. a strong heavy cord
   2. to catch by throwing

   Rosa tried to rope a calf.
   I tied a rope to my bicycle.

   elevator

   1. a platform or cage for carrying people and things up and down a building, mine, etc.
   2. a building for storing grain
   3. a part of the tail of an airplane that can be moved to make the airplane go up or down

   The pilot asked the mechanic to check the elevator of the plane.
   I take an elevator to my apartment.
   The farmer took a load of corn to the elevator.

   Finally, encourage students to create their own sentences using the words.

7. Invite students to suggest other multiple-meaning words. Write them on the chalkboard. Have students work in small groups to make sentences containing some of the words and then have students look up the words in their dictionaries to check the meanings. It is possible that some words may have additional meanings that could be placed in sentences. Have students share their work.

8. Tell students that when they are reading, a word may not make sense because they may be associating a particular meaning that does not fit the context. Remind students that looking up the word in a dictionary could be one strategy to consider when a word in their reading does not seem to make sense.

9. Extend the lesson by having students note other multiple-meaning words in their daily reading. These words can be discussed from time to time. You could also highlight multiple-meaning words in materials being read and discuss the meanings when appropriate. Use think-alouds when appropriate. Some possible multiple-meaning words to use are listed below.

dock	dive	ditch	dolly	dot	down
draft	draw	drawer	drop	duck	dump

Practice and Reinforcement Activities

1. To help students understand and work with multiple-meaning words, select a word with multiple meanings and write sentences on the chalkboard that exemplify various meanings. Then have students find the word in a dictionary and match the appropriate definition with the appropriate sentence. An example is given below.

Sentences		Corresponding Definitions	
1.	It is really light outside.	1.	that by which we see
2.	There is a light in the garage.	2.	thing that gives light; cause to give light
3.	I have a very light-colored dress for the party.	3.	pale in color
4.	That box is pretty light.	4.	not heavy

Help students realize that you can get quite a different meaning from what the author intended if an inappropriate meaning is associated with the word.

2. Provide a column of words and definitions. Have students match the words with the definitions, using a dictionary when necessary. Use important words related to units or themes being studied. A general example is provided below.

________	1.	calculate	a.	a special job
________	2.	literal	b.	a narrow crack or opening
________	3.	routine	c.	the money paid to a person for work performed
________	4.	assignment	d.	beautiful in movement
________	5.	crevice	e.	to inform
________	6.	murky	f.	the regular act of a performer
________	7.	notify	g.	exact, true, usual
________	8.	graceful	h.	to answer a problem
			i.	muddy, cloudy

3. Provide several sentences and definitions. Have students write the letter of the definition in the blank that matches the meaning of the word in a sentence. Similar exercises could be done with a dictionary where the number of the dictionary definition is written in the blank.

		Sentences		**Definitions**
______	1.	I have to go to the *store* to buy some milk.	a.	supply or stock
______	2.	I have quite a *store* of candy.	b.	put away for future use
______	3.	I have to find a place to *store* my clothes.	c.	place where goods are kept for sale

4. Create an interest in word study by inviting students to share words whose meanings are probably unknown to their peers. The words can be placed in a container. You can select a word several times during the week and provide guided practice in looking up the word's meaning(s) and engaging students in discussion. Students could also choose a word for independent exploration when time allows.
5. Prepare lists of words that are probably unknown to students. Invite them to answer a basic question about the words. Some sample questions without words are given below.

- Which of the following words are trees?
- Which of the following words are animals?
- Which of the following words are sports?

6. Provide sentences with words that students are unlikely to know. Have students look up the words so that the questions can be answered correctly. Sample questions follow.
   - Can you eat a pierogi?
   - What would you do with a tuque?
   - Could a borscht be ridden?
   - Is a gilt a tree?
   - Where would a windrow be found?
7. Invite students to explore their dictionaries and create questions that can be answered by determining the meanings of words. The question can be placed on one side of a card and the answer on the back. The cards can be placed in a Word Explorer box. Students can create questions and answers or select questions to answer. A sample card is shown below.

What is a common word for calyx? by Jen	*leaves* that are growing at the base of the flower
Front of Card	**Back of Card**

8. Provide dictionary entries and sentences. Have students read the sentences and write on the lines the number of the entry word and the number of the appropriate definition. An example is provided below.

page[1] (pāj), **1** one side of a sheet or piece of paper: *a page in this book.* **2** record: *the pages of history. noun.*
page[2] (pāj), **1** person who runs errands or delivers messages. Pages at hotels usually wear uniforms. **2** try to find (a person) at a hotel or club by having his or her name called out. **3** a youth who was preparing to be a knight. 1,3, *noun,* 2 *verb.*

palm[1] (päm), **1** the inside of the hand between the wrist and the fingers. **2** conceal in the hand: *The magician palmed the nickel.* **1** *noun,* 2 *verb.*
palm[2] (päm), **1** any of many kinds of trees growing in warm climates. Most palms have tall trunks, no branches, and many large leaves at the top. **2** leaf or stalk of leaves of a palm tree as a symbol of victory or triumph. *noun.*

   1. The breeze moved the leaves of the tall *palms*.
      Entry Word 2 Definition 1
   2. What *page* in the book are you reading?
      Entry Word 1 Definition 1
   3. Please *page* my friend.
      Entry Word 2 Definition 2

   A variation of this activity is to invite students to find words of interest and write sentences exemplifying the various definitions.

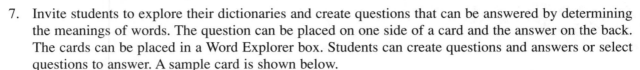

Tour the Zoo. Check students' dictionaries for unusual animals that might be found at a zoo. Write the name of the animal on the chalkboard. Have students look up the word in their dictionaries and read the definition. Then choose one student to be the guide who describes the animal to the other students. Some time also may need to be spent on using the pronunciation symbols so the word is pronounced correctly.

A variation of this activity might be the Museum of Interesting Things. Consider choosing words that have an illustration. Possible words for Tour the Zoo and Museum of Interesting Things are provided below.

Tour the Zoo	
aardvark	guanaco
caracal	hyrax
cassowary	margay
civet	okapi
coot	serval
dingo	siamang
egret	skink
eland	sloth
fisher	springbok
genet	wallaroo

Museum of Interesting Things	
abacus	breeches
adz	brooch
andiron	buoy
ankh	burnoose
anvil	calliope
aquaplane	cameo
arbor	capstan
aviary	catapult
awl	churn
beret	clavicle

Section 5.7

Interest in Words

© 2010 carlosseller. Used under license from Shutterstock, Inc.

Behavior Observed → **Anticipated Outcome**

The student lacks an interest in words. → The student will develop an interest in words and word study.

Background

When students have an interest in something, they will seek ways to engage in that activity. Some students enjoy games on the computer, sports, hobbies, playing with friends, and reading. Although few teachers would say many of their students have an interest in words, some of those teachers have witnessed students in the primary grades engaged in rhyming activities and even making nonsense words. As students jump rope on the playground, they often exhibit a playfulness with words. And there are some students who enjoy word games, crossword puzzles, jokes, and riddles. Finally, a few students actually spend some of their time using a dictionary or thesaurus to explore the meanings, origins, and uses of words.

We know that an interest in words can help students add words to their vocabulary in fun and meaningful ways (Blachowicz & Fisher, 2008). The strategies and ideas in this section are intended to serve as a source of activities to begin the process of helping students add to their vocabularies in more direct ways.

These students appear to be having fun with words.
© 2010 Jacek Chabraszewski.
Used under license from Shutterstock, Inc.

WORD OF THE DAY

1. Prepare a piece of sturdy cardboard with a rubber band around each end to hold a word you or students select for special focus that day. Place the card where it can be seen easily by students.

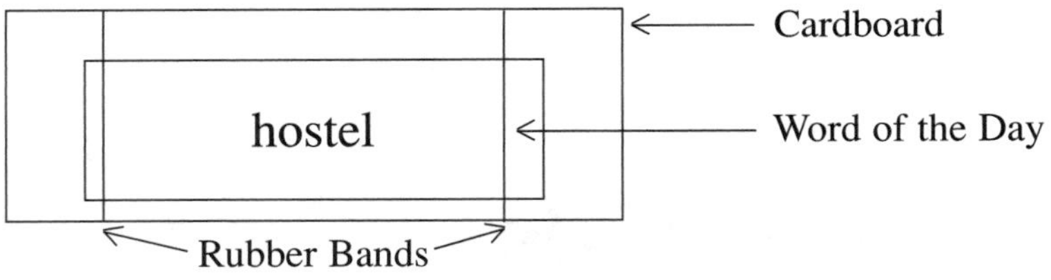

2. Introduce the Word of the Day to students. The word would relate to a unit or theme or just be a word of special interest to you or a student. Point to the word and tell students you will help them pronounce it, learn its meaning, spell it, and use it in a sentence.
3. Invite students to study the word and ask if anyone can pronounce it. Ask a volunteer to try the word. Provide assistance as necessary and point out how the word has parts similar to other words. (The word begins like hos*pital* and ends like *ho*tel.) Once the word is pronounced, have students say the word and chant the spelling.
4. Help students understand the meaning of the word (a place where travelers can stay that is not expensive; an inn). Use the word in a sentence like the following one.

   The youthful bicyclists stayed overnight at a hostel in an Italian village.

   Invite students to talk about the word and, if possible, relate it to their experiences. Contrast the meaning to other places for lodging (hotel, motel) and what would make a hostel different (hostels are mainly for youthful travelers).
5. Relate, if appropriate, the word's connection to a unit or theme of study. Encourage students to try to learn to spell, pronounce, and use the word throughout the day. You can also model the word for students. For example, you might say what follows.

   I am too old to stay at a hostel meant for youthful travelers. I would prefer to stay at a bed and breakfast or a hotel.

6. Develop a bulletin board for the words and invite students to write sentences, draw illustrations, or provide clues for pronouncing the words. Review the words when there are a few minutes left at the end of your lesson before recess, lunch, a special activity, or the end of the school day.
7. Invite students to suggest words for Word of the Day. Students could write the word on strips of card stock with their names on the back of the word strips. The words can be placed in a box or folder. When a student's word is selected, that student may be able to help teach the word.

SESQUIPEDALIAN WORDS

1. Use the Word of the Day approach to introduce the word *sesquipedalian* (Dale & O'Rourke, 1971). The word contains the Latin *sesqui* which means one and one-half and *ped* which means foot. The word means foot and a half or very long words. Students are often asked to learn long, distinctive, and difficult words.
2. Challenge students to locate words for the Sesquipedalian Words bulletin board. Students can be given index cards or sturdy paper for any words that might qualify for the bulletin board.
3. Model how a word card can be created. Be sure to provide the correct spelling, where the word was found, and a definition or illustration for the word.

Tyrannosaurus Rex

This is the name of the largest dinosaur in the world.

I saw a Tyrannosaurus Rex named Sue on our field trip to the Field Museum.

4. Remember that students will have their own ideas about what a very long word is. The goal should be to stimulate and encourage students to find out about words. Encourage their explorations.
5. You might be interested in the longest word (45 letters) found in *Webster's Third New International Dictionary*:

   pneumonoultramicroscopicsilicovolcanoconiosis

   If you look at its component parts and use your knowledge of Greek, Latin, and English word parts, you may be able to pronounce the word and determine its meaning.

   pneumono/ultra/micro/scopic/silico/volcano/con/iosis
   pneumono: related to the lung (as in pneumonia)
   ultra: beyond, exceedingly, super
   micro: very small
   scopic: related to sight
   (ultramicroscopic: exceedingly small to the sight)
   silico: related to hard stone or quartz; a mineral
   volcano: related to volcanic dust; very fine particles of rock powder
   con: dust (from Greek konis)
   iosis: disease

   If you are unable to determine the meaning, you might want to look it up in an unabridged dictionary.
6. A few words that might be of interest to students are listed below.

encyclopedia	convertiplane	diamondiferous
independence	conversazione	foretopmast
iconography	ichneumon	leatherback

Strategy 3 HOMOPHONES

1. Write *homophones* on the chalkboard. Underline *homo* and tell students that it means *same.* Underline *phones* and indicate that it means *sounds.* Then tell students that homophones are words that are pronounced the same but differ in spelling and meaning.

   homo + phones = homophones
   (same) (sounds)

2. Invite students to suggest some words that are homophones. Write them on the chalkboard. Students will need to provide a sentence so the meaning is clear. Some sample sentences are provided below.

   - She went *to* the store.
   - I have *two* pencils in my desk.
   - He wants to go *too.*

   Some homophones (*to, too, two, their, there, they're*) might be placed on a class Word Wall because they are used often by students in writing and occur frequently in printed materials. Other homophones (*carrot, carat*; *ruff, rough*; *pier, peer*) can be used for word study. There is a List of Homophones in Chapter 5 Resources (pages 412–414).

3. Tell students that some riddles use a play on words and orally ask this riddle:

   What's black and white and read all over?

   Have a student volunteer to identify the word that is a homophone (*read*). Take time to explain the riddle and compare the meanings of *red* and *read.* Help students realize that such riddles are usually asked orally because the spelling would give important clues. Write the riddle on the chalkboard with *read* so students can see that the word is not a color (*red*) but an action (*read* a book).

4. Help students realize that spelling and use in a sentence are important clues to the meaning of a homophone. Say two sentences and have students share the correct spelling. See the examples below.

   1. The wind *blew.*
   2. The sky is *blue.*

   Invite students to suggest other sentences containing homophones. Remember that dialect differences may influence the pronunciation of certain words in the List of Homophones in Chapter 5 Resources.

5. Consider using books that use homophones such as those that follow.

   - Gwynne, F. *Chocolate Moose for Dinner.* New York: Simon & Schuster, 1988.
   - Gwynne, F. *The King Who Rained.* New York: Simon & Schuster, 1970.

   The books can be read and the sentences corrected by using the appropriate word.

6. Invite students to use their knowledge of homophones to create sentences with crazy spellings. Sentences will vary depending upon students' knowledge of homophones. The sentences with crazy spellings can be placed on the front of an index card; the back of the card should have the sentence with conventional spelling. The cards can be placed on a bulletin board, and students could be challenged to read the front of the card and then write the sentence correctly on a separate sheet of paper. What was written could be checked by comparing it to the correct spelling on the back of the card. An example card is shown on the following page.

Aye gnu ewe wood bee hear.	I knew you would be here.
Front of Card	**Back of Card**

Strategy 4 SECTION 5.7

FIGURATIVE LANGUAGE

1. Write *Look out!* on the chalkboard and ask students to explain the meaning. It should quickly become clear that the meaning is not literal. Many students, especially those whose native language is not English, will profit from some discussion of idiomatic expressions.
2. Help students realize that for some phrases in our language the meaning cannot be understood by the meanings of the individual words. Return to the sentence on the chalkboard and model for students by saying something like the following.

   The word look *can mean to see and* out *can mean the opposite of* in *or away from the inside. These meanings will not help me understand the sentence because the words have a special meaning. They are used to indicate a warning. I might say,* Look out! *if something was falling toward you, and I wanted you to get out of the way quickly. When words are used in this way, they are called idiomatic expressions.*

3. Have students share any idiomatic expressions they may know and discuss the meanings of the expressions. A few expressions are included below.

don't be a sour puss	heads up
down in the dumps	mad as a wet hen
take a bath	take a walk
piece of cake	save face
laugh my head off	bored to tears
she won hands down	lighten up

4. Be alert for idiomatic expressions in materials students are asked to read and be sure to discuss their meanings, especially if the expressions are important to understanding.
5. Help students learn and appreciate figurative language by sharing and discussing with them Amelia Bedelia books by Peggy Parish as well as other related titles. Such books will help students learn and appreciate expressions that should not be taken literally. Two books for possible use are listed below.

   📖 Parish, P. *Amelia Bedelia.* New York: Harper & Row, 1963.
   📖 Terban, M. *Mad as a Wet Hen.* Boston: Clarion, 1987.

6. Create a bulletin board titled "Don't Be Fooled" and have students post strips of paper containing idiomatic expressions and other examples of figurative language. Have students write the meaning below the phrase, as in the following example.

"That's a piece of cake."

This has nothing to do with cake.
It means that something is easy to do.

7. Additional phrases for possible use are listed below.

led by the nose
in the pink
eat humble pie
turn a phrase
lose face
wet behind the ears
foot loose and fancy free
shut up
shot down
a shot in the dark
hit the books
a drop in the bucket
hit the hay
bit the dust
taken to the cleaners

step up
down and out
turn a new leaf
penny pincher
in the doghouse
going to the dogs
feeling dog tired
as pleased as punch
eat crow
put your foot in your mouth
getting up on the wrong side of the bed
hand to mouth
stuck up
cold feet

give up
a long shot
fiddle around
hit the road
kicked the bucket
hit the sack
turn in (go to bed)
got it for a song
mixed up
in a fog
face the music
stretch a dollar
treated like a dog
hounded by someone
puppy love

Strategy 5 SECTION 5.7

ALPHABET-ANTONYM TABLE

1. To use the Alphabet-Antonym Table (Powell, 1986), select five or six words that begin with the same letter such as *Save, Successful, Some, Silly, Sick,* and *Seldom.*
2. Write an antonym next to each word. Since many words have multiple meanings, select an antonym for the word meaning that would be most familiar to students. See the example that follows.

Words beginning with S	Antonyms
Save	Lose
Successful	Failure
Some	None
Silly	Serious
Sick	Well
Seldom	Often

3. Develop a chart similar to the one that follows for students to complete. Invite students to think of the target words based on the antonyms. You can have students work in groups or independently to complete the chart.

Antonyms	Words beginning with S
Lose	
Failure	
None	
Serious	
Well	
Often	

4. Once students are familiar with the Alphabet-Antonym Table, make the strategy more challenging by giving them the antonyms without the letter that begins the target words. You can also have students develop Alphabet-Antonym Tables for other class members. Provide students with dictionaries and thesauruses as resources if needed. According to Blachowicz and Fisher (2008), spending class time with motivational activities that are fun for students can increase their interest in learning new words. An Alphabet-Antonym Table reproducible is on the following page.

ALPHABET-ANTONYM TABLE

Name ______________________________ Date ______________

Words beginning with ____________	*Antonym(s)*

Practice and Reinforcement Activities

1. Students should be encouraged to develop a keen interest in words and the meanings of words. Through independent word study, students can enlarge their vocabularies. One way for students to develop their word awareness is by keeping a list of words in a journal. They may want to write down where they found the word, how the word was used, and an explanation of the word's definition.
2. Provide several common words and have students try to use each word in a few sentences where it has a different meaning each time. Have students share their sentences and discuss the various meanings of the words. Possible words for such exercises are given below.

tip	part	run	cast	center
dress	circle	fly	slip	

3. Select a group of words from a content area. Divide the students into groups and ask them to find pictures of the words or objects that are associated with the words.
4. Help students learn words through their own reading by providing them with time to read. You might use one of the independent silent reading strategies found in Chapter 1. When you give students silent reading time, try to do some reading of your own. This might be a good time to catch up on reading professional journals or that mystery that you've been trying to finish. Your students will learn that you too like to read. That positive reading model will encourage them to read for pleasure themselves.
5. Develop a portion of your classroom library for books and games that use words in fun ways. Have a group of books that describe figures of speech and books that have riddles, jokes, and puns. These types of books show students that words can be fun. Some examples of books that you might consider are listed below.

   - Clark, E.C. (1991). *I Never Saw a Purple Cow and Other Nonsense Rhymes.* Boston: Little, Brown.
   - Cole, J. (1989). *Anna Banana: 101 Jump-Rope Rhymes.* New York: Morrow.
   - Rosenbloom, J. (1988). *The World's Best Sports Riddles and Jokes.* New York: Sterling.
   - Terban, M. (1989). *Superdupers: Really Funny Real Words.* New York: Clarion.

6. Ask students to keep a pencil and paper handy when they read. As they come to a word they don't know, ask them to write down the word to look up at a later date or ask someone for the word's meaning. Then they can add the word to a Word Wall or a bulletin board.

When students are given class time to read, you can model and catch up on your reading as well.

7. Read to your students, no matter what their ages. Reading interesting novels, short stories, or poems to students helps them expand their listening vocabulary. As you read, ask students to write on an index card any word that they hear that they do not know. After you have finished reading, collect the index cards. At a time convenient for you, look through the words and determine which ones you want to review with the class. The best time to review these new words is right after you have finished reading the selection. As you describe the meaning of the new word, find it in the context from which you read it. Explain the meaning of the word, read the word in its context, and then explain the meaning of the word again. Finally, have students use the new word in another sentence. After you have provided the students with this range of meanings, ask them if they can share any other meanings of the word or sentences using the word. Then add the word to a compilation of new words in a class book.
8. Once a week, write a new word on the chalkboard. Without telling students the meaning of the word, use the word in your discussions, in directions, in conversations, and in handouts. Use the word as often as possible. Ask students to try to guess the word's meaning by your use of the word. At the end of the day, ask students to write down what they think the new word means. You may decide to tell them the meaning of the word at this point, or you might decide to keep the students in suspense by waiting until the next day to tell them the meaning of the word. After spending so much time on one word, however, make sure the students continue hearing and reading it. Place the word on the Word Wall and encourage students to use the word in their speaking and writing.
9. If one of the words that you want your students to learn can be dramatized, ask students to create brief scenes that use the word either in conversation or in action. For example, when asked to dramatize the word *amiable,* some sixth-grade students developed this scenario.

   Diana: Jean, I would like you to meet my good friend, Carmel. Carmel is one of the most good-natured, kindest girls I know.

   Jean: It's good to meet you, Carmel.

   Carmel: Thank you, Diana, for describing me as *amiable.* That's one of the nicest compliments I've ever received.

10. Students, especially readers who struggle, can benefit from computer-displayed stories where unknown words can be highlighted. Explanations and pronunciations of such words may help foster vocabulary growth. The motivational aspect of computer use is another benefit that can lead to increased student engagement in reading.
11. Reading stories to students can help foster vocabulary acquisition among students in the elementary and middle schools (Elley, 1988; Layne, 1996).
12. Many students increase their interest in words if they are "word experts" (Tompkins & Blanchfield, 2004). To encourage students to be word experts, have each student select a new vocabulary word to learn. Tell students that they will be the class expert on that word even though everyone in the class will be learning all of the words. Have students write the selected vocabulary word on a page in a notebook. Under the word, have students write the word's meanings, several sentences, antonyms, synonyms, and examples. Students can draw pictures as well. Tell students that they will have the opportunity to share their expert information during class to help other students learn the new words.

Resources

5

Note: indicates teacher material.

COMMON PREFIXES: GRADE LEVEL RECOMMENDATIONS

Prefix	*Meaning*	*Example*	*Grade to Introduce +*
un*	opposite	uncover	3
under	below	underdog	3
dis*	opposite	disapprove	4
re*	again	rewrite	4
re*	back	return	4
de	remove	defog	4
in (il, im, ir)*	opposite	inability illogical improper irregular	5
in (im)*	in	invasion	5
pre	before	predawn	5
sub	under	submerge	5
inter	between	intercept	6
mis	bad or wrong	misapply	6
trans	across	transoceanic	7
en	in	encompass	7
super	very big, large	superhighway	8
anti	against	antisocial	8
fore	in front of, before	foretell	—
mid	middle	midday	—
non	opposite	nondirective	—
over	too much	overachieve	—
semi	half	semipro	—

* These prefixes account for 58% of all prefixed words.

+ The recommended grade level to initiate instruction is from Gunning (2000).

From White, T., Sowell, J., & Yanagihara, A. (1989). Teaching elementary students to use word-part clues. *The Reading Teacher, 42,* 302–308.

FIFTEEN FREQUENTLY OCCURRING PREFIXES

Prefix	*Meaning(s)*
ab-	away, from, off
ad-	at, to, toward
be-	make, against, to a great degree
com-	with, together, in association
de-	separation, away, opposite of, reduce, from
dis-	opposite of, apart, away, not
en-	cause to be, put in or on
ex-	from, out of, former, apart, away
in-	into, in, within
in-	not
in-	the opposite of, reversal
pre-	before in place, time, rank, order
pro-	before, forward, for, in favor of
re-	again, back
sub-	under, beneath, subordinate

From Stauffer, R.G. (1969b). *Teaching Reading as a Thinking Process*. New York: Harper & Row.

SUFFIXES AND ENDINGS

Suffix	*Examples*
ed*	protected, acted
ing*	vanishing, painting
s/es*	authors, washes
al	national, informational
er/or	smaller, janitor
ible/able	possible, affordable
ion/tion	region, generation
ity	infinity, popularity
ly	slowly, friendly
ment	fulfillment, government
ness	likeness, kindness
y	rainy, discovery

*These suffixes or endings account for 65% of all suffixed words.

TWENTY-FOUR USEFUL SUFFIXES

Suffix	*Meaning(s)*	*Example*
-able	capable of being	allowable
-age	act of	marriage
-al	have the nature of	causal
-an (-n, -ian)	one who, relating to	librarian
-ance	state of being	brilliance
-ant	person or thing that acts	claimant
-ary	of or pertaining to	alimentary
-ate	cause to be	activate
-ence	state or quality of being	congruence
-ent	one who	recipient
-er	relating to	beater
-ful	having much, tending to	colorful
-ic (-etic)	pertaining to, resembling	heroic
-ical	of, like, pertaining to	monarchical
-ion (-tion, -ation)	act of, state, or condition	affirmation
-ish	having the nature of	dragonish
-ity (-ty)	quality, state, or condition of being	adaptability
-ive	tending or disposed to	meditative
-less	without, having no	aimless
-ment	state of being, act of	admonishment
-ness	quality, state, or condition of being	fairness
-or	person or thing that does	conqueror
-ous	having, abounding in	delirious
-y	pertaining to, causing	loamy

From Thorndike, E.L. (1941). *The Teaching of English Suffixes.* New York: Teachers College.

HOMOPHONES

air
heir

aisle
isle

all
awl

ant
aunt

arc
ark

assent
ascent

ate
eight

auger
augur

aye
eye

bail
bale

ball
bawl

base
bass

bate
bait

bazaar
bizarre

bear
bare

beat
beet

bell
belle

bin
been

birth
berth

blew
bleu

bore
boar

born
borne

bow
beau

bow
bough

bowl
boll

boy
buoy

brake
break

braze
braise

bred
bread

bridal
bridle

broach
brooch

bury
berry

but
butt

by
buy

cannon
canon

carrot
carat

caret
karat

cask
casque

cellar
seller

cheap
cheep

chews
choose

choir
quire

clime
climb

close
clothes

colonel
kernel

core
corps

course
coarse

creek
creak

crews
cruise

cue
queue

current
currant

dam
damn

dear
deer

desert
dessert

die
dye

do
dew

doe
dough

dun
done

earn
urn

ewe
yew

eyelet
islet

faint
feint

fair
fare

faker
fakir

fate
fete

feet
feat

feign
fain

ferule
ferrule

fir
fur

flee
flea

flew
flue
flu

flour
flower

fold
foaled

fore
four

foul
fowl

(continued)

fourth
forth

frieze
frees
freeze

gate
gait

gauge
gage

gnu
knew
new

great
grate

grown
groan

guild
gild

guilt
gilt

hail
hale

hare
hair

haul
hall

heart
hart

heel
heal
he'll

here
hear

him
hymn

hoard
horde

holy
wholly
holey

horse
hoarse

hour
our

hue
hew

idle
idol

knows
nose

leaf
lief

leak
leek

lee
lea

led
lead

lesson
lessen

liar
lyre

liken
lichen

lo
low

load
lode

lone
loan

loot
lute

maid
made

male
mail

mane
main

marry
merry

maul
mall

maze
maize

meet
meat
mete

mein
mean

metal
mettle

might
mite

minor
miner

moat
mote

morn
mourn

muse
mews

need
knead
kneed

night
knight

no
know

none
nun

not
knot

oar
ore
o'er

one
won

oral
aural

pair
pear
pare

pale
pail

palate
pallet

pane
pain

patients
patience

paws
pause

peak
pique

pearl
purl

peddle
pedal

peel
peal

piece
peace

pier
peer

plane
plain

plum
plumb

pole
poll

pray
prey

rack
wrack

racket
racquet

rain
rein
reign

raise
raze

(continued)

HOMOPHONES *(continued)*

rap
wrap

read
reed

real
reel

reck
wreck

red
read

right
write

rime
rhyme

ring
wring

rock
roc

rode
road

roe
row

roll
role

root
route

rows
rose

rude
rood

ruff
rough

rung
wrung

rye
wry

sale
sail

seam
seem

sear
seer
sere

see
sea

seed
cede

seen
scene

sell
cell

sense
cense

sent
cent
scent

serial
cereal

sight
site
cite

sign
sine

signet
cygnet

shoe
shoo

skull
scull

slay
sleigh

slight
sleight

so
sew
sow

soar
sore

son
sun

soul
sole

stare
stair

stationery
stationary

steak
stake

steal
steel

step
steppe

stoup
stoop

strait
straight

sunny
sonny

surf
serf

surge
serge

tale
tail

taught
taut

tax
tacks

tea
tee

team
teem

tear
tare

there
they're
their

the
thee

threw
through

throws
throes

time
thyme

toe
tow

two
to
too

vale
veil

vein
vain
vane

wait
weight

waste
waist

wave
waive

way
weigh

we
wee

wear
ware

week
weak

whole
hole

wood
would

wreak
reek

MILLION DOLLAR WORDS FOR "SAID"

added
admitted
agreed
announced
answered
asked

badgered
barked
begged
bellowed
blabbered
broadcasted

cackled
chattered
chuckled
coaxed
commented
complained
confessed
congratulated
cried

declared
decreed
demanded

echoed
exclaimed

gasped
giggled
grinned
groaned
grumbled

hectored
hinted
hollered
howled

informed
inquired
intimated

jabbered

laughed

mentioned
moaned
mumbled
murmured
muttered

nagged

ordered

persuaded
pleaded
proclaimed
prompted
proposed
protested

questioned

recited
remarked
reminded
repeated
replied
responded

screamed
shouted
shrieked
sighed
snarled
sniveled
stated
stormed
stuttered
suggested

taunted
teased
told

urged
uttered

wheedled
whined
whispered

yelled
yelped

CHAPTER SIX

Comprehension Skills

Overview

Reading is the process of making sense from print, and comprehension is the goal of all reading. Comprehension, or an understanding of the text, varies with every reader. Just think how different each of your students is. Each one has a unique set of life experiences, different experiences with print, and different abilities to process text. Since all of your students are different from each other, and they are all different from you, each one of you will understand a piece of text in a slightly different way (Fox & Alexander, 2009).

Comprehension is the goal of all reading.

Comprehension of text, or what a reader understands, is constructed by the individual reader. No two readers will produce the exact same meaning from a text, and no reader's understanding of a text will exactly match what the author had in mind while writing (Snow & Sweet, 2003). Your students, therefore, will construct different meanings from the text, some with a rich understanding of what the text could mean and some with a more superficial understanding of the text. How readers apply various strategies as they process text, however, will influence the depth of their understanding.

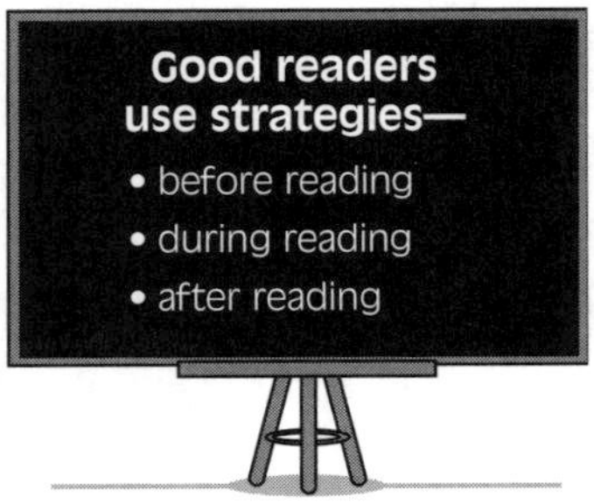
Good readers use strategies—
• before reading
• during reading
• after reading

Wharton-McDonald and Swiger (2009) suggest that there are lower-order and higher-order processes that readers use to comprehend text. Examples of lower-order processes are the skills and strategies of attending to words. Higher-order processes are activating prior knowledge, having a purpose for reading, predicting outcomes, and so on. The strategies good readers use occur before reading, during reading, and after reading (Rand Study Group, 2002). This chapter contains ideas for higher-order processes during the reading experience.

Students who use few comprehension strategies while reading need instruction in ways to comprehend text (Dole, Nokes, & Drits, 2009). For example, students may not be making inferences while reading, or they may not be able to identify the main point. As teachers, we want our students to be able to use a variety of strategies as they read so they can construct meaning from the text. We can help them construct meaning by teaching comprehension strategies for students to use during the entire reading process.

Section **6.1**

Previewing Text

Behavior Observed → **Anticipated Outcome**

The student does not preview text material before reading. → The student will preview text material as an aid to studying and reading.

Background

When students are assigned texts to read, many think they should begin reading with the first sentence and continue reading until the chapter is finished. Students who proceed in this manner usually are not using the most efficient means of reading. If students preview the text before reading, they can gain a better idea of the organization of the text, and they can begin to activate their prior knowledge about the subject. Understanding the text organization and making connections to what is known can help facilitate readers' comprehension as they read (Pressley, 2002). You should, therefore, encourage your students to preview text material before they read.

Strategy 1 SECTION 6.1

PICTURE AND TEXT SURVEY

1. Ask students to preview the pictures and text (Lamberg & Lamb, 1980) to get a general idea of the subject. For example, if students are going to read a chapter on insects, ask them to read the title of the chapter, the subtitles, the first sentence, and then look at each picture. As students look at the pictures, tell them to read any captions under the pictures and think about why the picture is included.
2. Tell students they should organize the information in their minds by writing a sentence describing the topic. In the case of a chapter on insects, students might write a sentence similar to the following.

   This chapter will discuss the life cycle of insects.

3. After students organize the information, ask them to predict questions they think the text will answer. The pictures will give them a clue. The following questions could be asked about the insect chapter.

   What are the stages of the life cycle of an insect? What happens to an insect in the egg cycle? What is larva and what does the insect look like in the larva stage? What is a pupa and what is happening to the insect in the pupa stage? How long does it take for the insect to become an adult?

4. Before students begin reading, ask them to try to answer their questions. Doing so will help them access their background knowledge. As they read, then, students will be better able to comprehend the information. In the example of the life cycle of insects, students can discuss the times they have seen insect larvae. They may know something about the stages of development of frogs, and the teacher can relate this knowledge to the life cycle of insects.
5. Ask students to read the text to locate answers to their questions. If they have carefully formulated questions for the text, they will be able to find answers to their questions. Many times, however, students will not be able to find answers to their questions because they did not ask good questions. If students were not able to find answers, help them revise their questions. If students are able to locate information, tell them to think about their predictions of the questions and to revise the answers.

Strategy 2 SECTION 6.1

TAG: TEXTBOOK ACTIVITY GUIDE

1. Decide on your objectives for the lesson. Then choose chapters from the text that relate to those objectives.
2. Decide which text features you want to include in the preview. Students may not need to read each passage of a chapter. Choose the ones that meet your objectives to emphasize in the Textbook Activity Guide (TAG) (Davey, 1986).
3. Choose a different task for each chapter of the guide. Even though students will be interacting with each chapter of the text, you should recommend a different strategy for each one. This will encourage students to use a variety of strategies as they read. Some strategies you might consider are predicting, reading and discussing in a small group, skimming the text (looking for the main ideas only), reading and retelling (explaining the gist of the text to a partner), and writing. Writing can take the form of a summary, a response that explains how the passage made the student feel, a fictional account of the passage, or comments on the passage in a journal.
4. Design TAGs so that students learn to interact with their texts in a variety of ways. A sample TAG follows so you can see what one looks like.

Sample Textbook Activity Guide (TAG)

1. Predict: With a partner, survey the headings on pages 20–24. Discuss what you think you will learn from the chapter.
2. Read and Discuss: Read the introduction on page 20 and discuss what you already know about the topic with your partner.
3. Skim: Skim pages 21 and 22.
4. Read and Retell: Read pages 23 and 24 and retell what you have learned to your partner.
5. Write: Write the gist of the chapter in your journal.

5. After students complete their TAGs, spend time discussing each part of the guide. Encourage students to share problems or difficulties they encountered as well as insights gained from using the guide.

Strategy 3 SECTION 6.1

SCROL

1. **S = Survey the headings.** To use SCROL (Grant, 1993), have students read the headings in the chapter and ask themselves what they already know about the topic. For example, if students are reading a text on the Civil War with the headings battles and generals, they may bring to mind all they already know about the topic. You might ask students to share some of their ideas. Write them on the chalkboard. List everything they say whether it is correct or not. Examples might include Grant, Sherman, Meade, Shiloh, Antietam, Gettysburg, and Vicksburg.
2. **C = Connect.** Direct students to ask themselves how the headings connect to one another. They may use key words in the headings to help them make the connections. In the example on the Civil War, students most likely will predict that the battles were battles of the Civil War and the generals were famous leaders in that conflict.
3. **R = Read the text.** Ask students to read the text, looking for words and phrases that explain the headings. As students read about the battles of the Civil War, for example, have them put the battles in order and understand their relative importance to the war as a whole.
4. **O = Outline.** Explain to your students that they should then write the headings and details under the headings that they remember from their reading. An example follows.

Battles

Gettysburg	July 1–3, 1863
	Under General Meade
	Lee retreated
	Both sides lost about 25% of their soldiers.

5. **L = Look back.** Finally, direct students to look back at the text to determine the accuracy of their outlines or notes. If they have incorrect information, they should revise what they have written. In looking at the outline for the Battle of Gettysburg, it would seem unlikely that each side lost so many men. Checking the text, however, confirms that the outline is correct.

Practice and Reinforcement Activities

1. Talk to students about movie previews such as "Coming Attractions" that appear before videos and movies begin. Tell students that these short clips are a preview of the movie. Discuss what previews are intended to do, such as interest people in the movie. Then have students select a book they have read. Create a poster or a PowerPoint™ presentation preview. Display three or four of these "Coming Attractions" each week.
2. Have students from high school or college come to your class with two or three of their textbooks. Have the older students show your class how the textbooks are organized and have them preview the books for students. Tell students that reading becomes more complex through the school years and strategies like previewing become increasingly important.
3. Display a website on a projector so that all students can see. Preview the website by scrolling through the options. Discuss the site's options with students. Ask students how many of them have spent time reading website information that they didn't want. Tell students that they should also preview websites to maximize their computer time.
4. Take the time to preview the books, magazines, and journals that you read. Occasionally tell students about your reading and model your previewing techniques.

Section 6.2

Activating Prior Knowledge

Behavior Observed → **Anticipated Outcome**

The student does not activate prior knowledge before reading. → The student will activate prior knowledge before reading to enhance comprehension of text.

Perspective and Strategies

The ability to access what you know about a subject before reading can help you understand the text with richer comprehension. Using what you know to help you connect your existing knowledge with the new knowledge from the text is called accessing prior knowledge. What students know is structured in their minds in schema, or abstract frameworks around which memory is stored. If students have knowledge about frogs and toads, for example, they will better understand the *Frog and Toad* stories by Arnold Lobel.

Since all students have limited background knowledge to a certain extent, because of the number of years they have lived and the experiences they have had, teachers need to help students both activate their prior knowledge and develop their knowledge before they read.

This section contains several strategies that can help students access their prior knowledge before reading.

Strategy 1

FILE FOLDERS

1. Get some file folders and ask students to share what they know about their use. Help students realize that each file folder contains information about a topic or subject and that the file folders could be related to each other. For example, if you use portfolios in file folders, students would know that each student has his or her own file folder. Discuss how the information in a file folder can be used to help understand the student or topic.
2. Relate the concept of file folders to the way the human brain holds information. Stress that the brain is efficient at "filing" large amounts of information in an organized fashion and that this information is vital if we are to understand what we are reading. The important point is to use this information before, during, and after reading.
3. Use an actual file folder or have students make one and write in the folder what they know about a particular topic. Choose a topic about which practically all students have knowledge. Some possible topics include a particular animal (dog or cat), an area in the community, a sport, a game, or a famous person.
4. Give students sufficient time to write what they know about the selected topic. Emphasize that words or phrases, not complete sentences, can be written. Charts and/or drawings may also be used.
5. Invite students to share their knowledge; then create a master file folder on the chalkboard. As some students share, other students may say, "I knew that but I didn't write it down." These students can add the information to their file folders. Encourage all students to share their knowledge.
6. Ask students how the information in their file folders could be used if they were asked to read a story, chapter, or book about the topic. Guide students to understand that such knowledge can help them link what they already know about a topic to what they are reading. It can help them make predictions about what might be in a book or story. It can help them make sense of and raise questions about what they are reading. And it can help them evaluate, within the context of their existing knowledge, what they have read.
7. To encourage students to use their background knowledge, have them pretend to take out their file folders prior to reading about a particular topic.

SECTION 6.2

Strategy 2

BRAINSTORMING

1. Tell students that before they read they should think about what they know about the topic. Explain how you activate your own background knowledge before reading. For example, say the following.

   > *Yesterday, I picked up a book about a group of British mountain climbers who climbed Mt. Everest. I thought about what I already knew: Mt. Everest is the highest mountain in the world, many people have died climbing it, and British climbers are known for their skill. I remembered the books and films I had already seen about Mt. Everest. Then I previewed the book and began reading.*

2. Select a book that students will be reading, such as *Owl Babies* (Waddell, 1975). Show students the book and say the following.

> Owl Babies *is a book about owls. Since the book is about owls, I'll write the word* owls *on the chalkboard. I'll draw a circle around the word so that I remember that my topic is* owls.

Have students also write the word *owls* on their paper and draw a circle around it.

3. Tell students that to activate their prior knowledge they should brainstorm all the things they know about owls before reading. You can ask for ideas from the entire class or have students discuss their ideas in small groups.
4. Write the students' ideas on the chalkboard with their ideas radiating out from the center circle. Have students do the same on their own paper. An example follows.

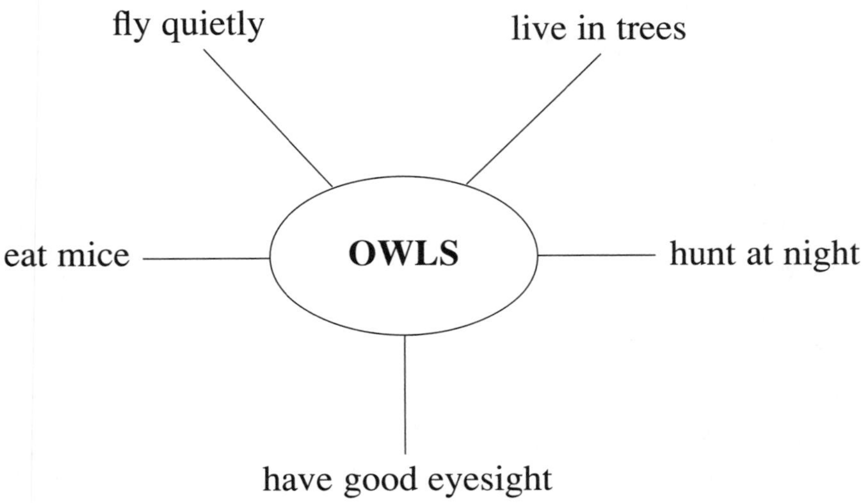

5. Encourage students to brainstorm before reading to activate their prior knowledge.

Strategy 3 SECTION 6.2

K-W-L

1. Before beginning a topic of study or before beginning a story or book, have students complete a K-W-L (Ogle, 1989) chart. Tell students that before they read they should think about what they already know. Explain that a K-W-L chart prompts them to think about what they already know, what they want to know, and, after reading, what they have learned.
2. Duplicate and distribute the K-W-L chart on page 427. Make a transparency of the K-W-L chart to model the strategy.
3. Identify a topic or story that students will be experiencing. Divide the class into groups of three or four students. Ask students to think about what they already know about the topic. Provide ample time for students to think and discuss.
4. Have students share their lists with the class. Write students' ideas on the K section of the K-W-L chart. An example follows.

Planets		
K	W	L
(what I already know)	(what I want to find out)	(what I have learned)
Earth is a planet. *There are nine planets.* *Planets are in space.* *Moons go around them.* *The sun is not one.*		

5. Ask students what they want to learn about the topic. Have them discuss in groups, share with the class, and list the ideas on the W section of the chart.
6. After students have read the book or the unit is complete, have students list what they have learned in the L section of the K-W-L chart. Provide additional charts so that you can include all of the things students have learned.

K-W-L CHART

Donna Ogle

Name ______________________________ Date ______________

	(title)	
K	*W*	*L*
(what I already know)	*(what I want to find out)*	*(what I have learned)*

From Ogle, D.M. (1989). The know, want to know, learn strategy. In K.D. Muth (Ed.), *Children's Comprehension of Text* (pp. 205–223). Newark, DE: International Reading Association.

ANTICIPATION GUIDE

1. Students can access or activate their background knowledge by participating in an Anticipation Guide (Herber, 1978).
2. Select a text to demonstrate the Anticipation Guide or use the article, "Chomping Champs" on page 431.
3. Read the text and identify between five and eight statements or ideas that you want students to consider. Make sure each of the statements can be answered with a *yes* or *no*. List the statements on the chalkboard or, if you are using "Chomping Champs," duplicate the Anticipation Guide on page 430.
4. Write the words *anticipation* and *anticipate* on the chalkboard. Say the words aloud running your finger under the word's syllables. Ask students if they know the words or if they have heard the words before. Give students a chance to explain what they think *anticipation* means.
5. Reinforce the correct meaning of *anticipation* by restating its definition and using it in a sentence. You might say the following.

> *The word* anticipation *means "eagerly looking forward to something that is going to happen." You might say you were looking forward to your baseball game with* anticipation *or you* anticipate *getting a good grade in reading.*

6. Invite students to generate additional sentences using either the word *anticipation* or *anticipate*.
7. Write the words *Anticipation Guide* on the chalkboard. Tell students that you will be demonstrating a strategy that has students anticipating what will be coming in the text they will read.
8. Distribute the Anticipation Guide that you prepared in advance or the one for "Chomping Champs." Invite students to read the directions at the top of the page. Have students retell the directions and determine whether students understand what to do. If students do not understand the directions, say the following.

> *Today you are going to anticipate what will be in the article that you will be reading. You have a list of statements. Discuss each statement in your group and decide individually whether the statement is true or false. If you think it is true, place a checkmark in the box. If you think it is false, leave the box unchecked.*

9. Divide the class into groups of two or three. Tell students to read the statements on the Anticipation Guide and to decide whether each statement is true or false. If you are using "Chomping Champs," remind students that they should be putting themselves in the place of a beetle.
10. After students have completed their Anticipation Guide, ask them to share with the class how they responded. Discuss each of the statements.
11. Have students read the text you have selected or the article "Chomping Champs" on page 431. Have students read independently or in pairs. Say something like the following.

Read the article "Chomping Champs." As you read, pay close attention to the ideas in the statements in your Anticipation Guide. After you read, you'll have the opportunity to review the statements you checked before reading.

12. After students have read the text, have them take out their Anticipation Guide. Ask students to look at the statements once again. Draw students' attention to the boxes at the end of the statements under the column titled *After You Read.* Tell students to place a checkmark in the boxes with which they agree. Encourage students to refer to the text as necessary.
13. Remind students that they can change their minds after reading and that often they learn something from reading that will alter their opinions. Give a specific example from the Anticipation Guide or say the following.

    I did not check the statement My house is made of metal. *I had never heard of a beetle that lived in a metal box. Before I read the article, I was picturing the kinds of beetles that I find outside. When I read the article, I was surprised that these dermestid beetles eat flesh and need to be kept in a metal box. I checked the box for the statement after reading. I changed my mind because I learned something as I read the article.*

14. Invite students to discuss the items for which they changed their minds after reading. Explain to students that they will not always change their minds and that sometimes their first response will be the correct one.
15. Reinforce the reading processes that students use while they engage in an Anticipation Guide by saying the following.

    Before you read something, anticipate what the text will be about. Ask yourself what you know about the topic and make predictions about what you will find. Remind yourself of any opinions you hold about the topic as well. As you read, check in with yourself to see if you need to change your mind about something you were thinking.

16. Demonstrate how to use an Anticipation Guide until students understand the strategy. After students are familiar with Anticipation Guides, you can have students complete them independently or in small groups without teacher guidance. Use Anticipation Guides regularly so that students learn how to anticipate texts.

CHOMPING CHAMPS

Name ______________________________ Date ______________

Directions: The article you will be reading is about fuzzy little insects called dermestid (dur-MES-tid) beetles. Pretend you are one of these tiny beetles. Read the statements below and check the items you think are true about yourself. After reading the article go back and check those items that the author agrees with.

Before You Read		After You Read
☐	1. I help museums save money by cleaning the bones of dead animals for their exhibits.	☐
☐	2. My favorite food is raw flesh.	☐
☐	3. I work for my room and board in museums all around the world.	☐
☐	4. My house is made of metal.	☐
☐	5. I can eat and eat and never get full.	☐
☐	6. After three days of eating, I spin a cocoon and turn into a butterfly.	☐
☐	7. Baby dermestid beetles are called dermies.	☐

Chomping Champs*

In a dark room in a museum lie the bodies of a monkey, a fox, a deer, and fifty bats. The skeletons of these animals soon will be used for studies and displays. But first the bones must be perfectly cleaned by a team of the museum's hardest workers.

These workers, fuzzy little insects called *dermestid* (dur-MES-tid) beetles, keep busy at their job nearly 24 hours a day. Dermestids are smaller than your thumbnail, but they have mighty appetites. They can scurry in and out of a skeleton's every nook and cranny—no matter how small—leaving no flesh on the bones. Just 60 larvae can make a small bird's bones spotless in only three days.

It would take loads of time and hard work for a person to do the same job by hand. By using hungry beetles, museums save money—and get spanking-clean skeletons.

Most of the eager eaters are the beetles' young, or *larvae*. They love to feast on dried flesh and almost anything else! That's why they always must be kept in boxes made of metal.

Scientists cut most of the extra meat off an animal's body, then let the remaining meat dry. As soon as they put the body into a beetle box, the chompers get busy. Adult females lay their eggs in the dried flesh right away, providing a steady supply of food from the moment the larvae hatch. After stuffing themselves for many days, they burrow into a layer of cotton on the bottom of their box, change into adults, and come out ready to lay their own eggs. (Dermestids live only about a month.)

One museum put its beetles to work on elephants and whales. Even though it will take years, they know they can count on the chomping champs.

*Adapted from Johnson, F. (1982). Chomping champs. *Ranger Rick's Nature Magazine*.

Practice and Reinforcement Activities

1. Invite students to use their background knowledge (file folders) to make predictions before reading. Remind them to use the title, pictures, chapter headings, and so on.
2. Model the think-aloud strategy to show students how you use your background knowledge to make predictions about a selection to be read. For example, say something like the following.

   The title of this story is "All About Fish." Because we are studying science, I think this is not really a story but a selection that will present some information and facts about fish. I know that fish [you give known knowledge] . . . *and I wonder if this passage will talk about goldfish. I have two at home and* [share knowledge]. . . . *I wonder if the passage will talk about sharks. I really would like to know more about them.*

   Use similar think-alouds to help students learn how you link knowledge in your head with the passage while reading and after reading. Remind students to use a similar strategy while they read.
3. Develop lessons that model what you do when the information in your head is different from what you are reading or have read in the text. Sometimes you may need to go back and reread to clarify something that does not match your existing knowledge. You may have to consider whether what you know is, in fact, accurate. You may also need to go to another source (person or text) for additional information that will help clarify the conflicting information. Try to provide actual examples from your experiences for each situation.
4. Use a variety of cloze activities in which students can use their background knowledge to make reasonable predictions about the missing word(s). Help students come to understand that predictions are possible because of their background knowledge and that it is useful in reading. Discuss the various words predicted and their appropriateness. Some possible items to use follow.

   Jack and Jill ____________________.
   Last ____________________, I went to the movies.
   Yesterday ____________________, I saw a racoon.
   The ____________________ had nearly finished building the house.
   The older person walked ____________________ to the car with a ____________________ in hand.
5. Based on the title of a book, chapter, or selection, have students brainstorm possible words that students might encounter. Discuss the reasons behind certain choices that may appear strange.
6. As you help students activate prior knowledge, you need to consider whether students have background in the figurative language in the text (Palmer & Brooks, 2004). Figurative language encompasses similes, metaphors, proverbs, allusions, and idioms. When students do not know an idiom in the text, comprehension can be affected. Therefore, identify any figurative language before reading and make sure students are familiar with the meanings of these terms.

Section **6.3**

Lack of Clear Purpose(s) for Reading

Behavior Observed → **Anticipated Outcome**

The student appears to approach reading tasks without purposes or goals. → The student will develop purposes or goals to guide his or her reading.

Background

When students have a clear purpose for reading, comprehension is enhanced. The trouble is that many students' purposes for reading may be dominated by thinking such as "the teacher said to read this," "so I can answer the questions," or a surprising "I don't know." Although external purposes are a reality of classroom instruction, students should also learn how to set their own purposes for reading.

Recognizing that there are externally imposed purposes for reading as well as internally generated purposes in both school and life, two principles should guide your actions when asking students to read.

- First, be sure you set clear purposes and expectations for students when making reading assignments.
- Second, model how to read to fulfill purposes.

Strategies such as taking notes, summarizing, outlining, answering questions, and mapping may need to be taught, preferably within the context of your lessons. Students sometimes may be able to fuse your expectations with their purposes. The following ideas should help students develop purposes for reading. Keep in mind that students can have more than one purpose for reading even though we generally use the singular form.

Could this student be interested in a book about fashion?

Strategy 1 WHAT'S THE PURPOSE?

1. Choose one or more sports (for example, soccer and softball) and encourage students to share reasons why players participate in that sport. Students could write their responses individually or in groups. If groups are used, be sure someone serves as a recorder.
2. Invite students to share their ideas. Write their responses on the chalkboard. Some possible responses are provided below.

for fun	to be with friends	to improve skills
to win	to stay fit	to be outside

3. Help students realize that players participate in sports for different reasons. Then make the connection to reading and suggest that there are different purposes for reading.
4. Have students share purposes for reading. It may be helpful to have them think of different types of reading materials (books, stories, magazines, recipes, road signs, newspapers, television guides, and so on) when they are suggesting purposes.
5. Spend time discussing some of the advantages for setting purposes for reading. Be sure that students realize that reading can be done for different purposes and that their purposes should guide their reading.
6. Model a few situations in which you set a purpose, read, and then evaluate whether your purpose was achieved. Here is one example.

   I want to find out which movies are playing in town. I'll use today's newspaper to help me. Let's see . . . from the index on the front page, I know that the movies are in section 2, page 6. Okay, I've found the page in that section, and I can see that the following movies are playing [read movies]. *I think I might like to see ________________ because I read a good review of it a few days ago. My purpose was to find out which movies were playing, and I was successful in achieving my purpose. I know I was successful because I found the movies.*

   Other situations to model are listed below.

   - beginning a short story
   - reading a textbook
   - finding a TV show
   - looking up a word
   - using an encyclopedia
   - reading an email
   - finding a telephone number
   - browsing a newspaper
   - reading a magazine
   - following a recipe

7. Encourage students to think aloud and model some of the purposes they have for reading. Be sure they also explain how they went about achieving their purposes and whether they were successful.
8. Transfer purpose setting to ongoing reading activities taking place in the classroom.

DIFFERENT BOOKS, DIFFERENT PURPOSES

1. Select a narrative book and an expository book on the same general topic (like *The Egypt Game* and *Mummies, Tombs, and Treasures*) to model setting purposes, activating background knowledge, and previewing.
2. Tell students which strategies you will be modeling and how they can help students become better readers. For example, say something like what follows.

> *I always have a purpose when I read. It helps me focus my attention, and I know why I'm reading. While reading, I can ask myself whether my purpose is being achieved. I also try to ask myself what I already know about the topic. Some of what I know will probably help me understand. I may also be able to link what I already know to what I'm reading. Before actually reading, I often preview the book or selection. That helps me see how the book is organized and how long the reading may take me.*

3. Model a preview for a narrative book (for example, *The Egypt Game*) by saying the following.

> *The teacher said I have to read a book for sharing with my literature circle, so I guess that's my major purpose for reading. Of course, I did have lots of books to choose from, and I chose* The Egypt Game *because the title sounded interesting. I suppose I want to know what this Egypt game is. I can see that I have at least two purposes for reading, and I'll probably have more once I start reading the book. I've got to keep in mind that I'll be sharing the book in a literature circle so I need to learn about the characters and have a good idea about the major events that happened in the book. I don't really know much about Egypt, but I do know how books like this are organized.*
>
> *Now, I'll preview the book. Wow! It's more than 200 pages long, so reading it will take me some time. I can see from the contents page in the front of the book that there are quite a few chapters, and the chapters are about 10 pages long. Perhaps I'll read a chapter or two at a time. The first chapter is called "The Discovery of Egypt." From the illustration on the cover of the book, I don't think the characters will discover the real country of Egypt. I think they may discover something that will eventually lead to the Egypt game. I'd better get started reading.*

4. Encourage students to react to your think-aloud by writing the words *setting purposes, using background,* and *previewing* to form column heads across the chalkboard. Have students recall what you did and write key words or phrases in the appropriate column. Ask students to share some of their relevant experiences and add them to the list within each column. Remember to ask questions such as, "Why is that useful?" and "How does that help you become a better reader?"
5. Model a preview for an expository selection (for example, *Mummies, Tombs, and Treasures*).

I'm choosing this book because I want to know about some of the secrets of ancient Egypt. That's part of the title, and I want to know more, so that's my main purpose. I know some things about mummies and tombs [describe]. *As I page through the book, I see a lot of interesting illustrations and photographs. On page 40 is a photograph of a real mummy without the cloth wrappings. Under the photograph, it says that the mummy's face and shoulders are packed with sawdust. The eyes are painted stone. I'll certainly want to know more about why and how those things were done. It sure sounds strange to me. The contents page shows seven chapters. I can see from the chapter titles that the book is mostly about mummies.*

6. Elicit responses from students using a procedure similar to the one in step 5 and encourage students to relate their experiences with expository materials.
7. Guide students in using these strategies in their classroom reading assignments. Invite students to confer with you to share their successes and problems using the strategies you have taught. When appropriate, offer advice, ask questions, and help solidify the strategies taught. Remember to give recognition for effort.

Practice and Reinforcement Activities

1. Use classroom events such as daily attendance lists, lunch counts, and families' letters to illustrate the different purposes people have for reading (Duke & Stewart, 1997).
2. Discuss the different purposes for reading. For example, you might read for pleasure, to gain information, to escape, and so on. Create a *Why Read?* chart that lists reading materials on one side and several purposes for reading on the other side as in the following example. Display the list in the classroom and add to the list when appropriate.

Why Read?

Reading Materials	Purposes for Reading
Picture books	Enjoyment
Magazines	Information
Mysteries	Escape

3. Have students record their purposes for reading their self-selected reading material. After several entries, have students reflect on their most frequent purposes for reading. Encourage students to read for a variety of purposes. Have students compare lists to find their classmates' purposes for reading.

Section 6.4

Main Point or Idea

Behavior Observed →
The student has difficulty understanding the main point of a reading selection.

Anticipated Outcome
The student will understand the main point of a reading selection.

Background

The identification of the main idea or central thought of what is read usually involves several processes. Students must distinguish between essential elements, make inferences, and make judgments—all higher-level thinking skills. Although the main idea may be stated somewhere in a passage (text explicit), it is also likely that the main idea may not be explicitly expressed, and students will need to infer it (text implicit).

Years ago, the identification of main ideas was "taught" with workbooks and skill sheets. Educators know now that these materials have limitations. Workbook exercises rarely teach main ideas or transfer to other reading materials. Such exercises may only provide practice in the task of identifying main ideas. In order for students to learn how to select or infer the main idea, the teacher should use the following teaching strategies.

FINDING THE MAIN IDEA

1. Tell students that this lesson will help them learn how to figure out the main idea of a passage. Begin by presenting lists of words (without headings) on the chalkboard. Ask students to think of a word or phrase that could be used to describe what the words are mostly about. Several lists are shown here. Be sure to select words that are appropriate for your students.

Animals	Clothes	Cars	Places to Stay
dog	shirt	Firebird	house
cat	pants	Mustang	apartment
hamster	dress	Corvette	duplex
guinea pig	shoes	RX7	trailer
horse	jeans	Ferrari	hotel

2. Discuss the words or phrases offered by the students. Stress that the words or phrases describe the topic; they tell what the words are mostly about. Relate the discussion to reading. Ask students to think of favorite books or stories and tell what the topics are. Indicate that the main idea is the most important idea given about a topic. Other pieces of information that support the main idea are called details.
3. Draw a wheel with spokes on the chalkboard and tell students that the center of the wheel represents the main idea and the spokes represent the supporting details.

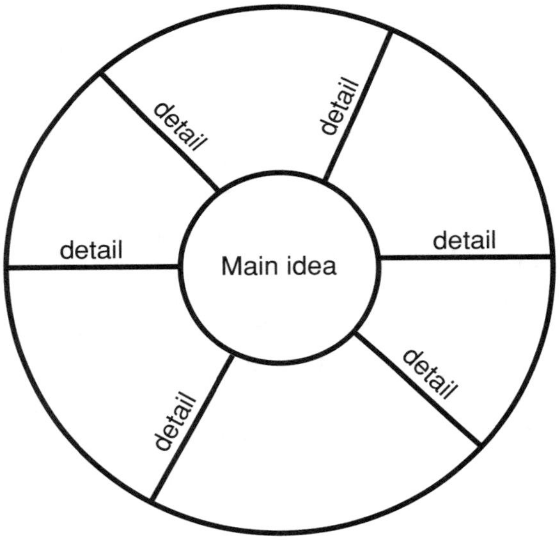

Then present a short passage and help students model how to go about finding the main idea, as in the following example.

> *Do you know how long it takes the planets to go around the sun? Our planet, Earth, takes 365 days. Mercury, the smallest planet, only takes 88 days to go around the sun. All of the planets in our solar system take a different number of days or years to go around the sun.*

After reading the paragraph aloud with students, think aloud to determine the main idea.

> *At first I thought the paragraph was going to be about all the planets. In fact, one sentence says something about all the planets . . . , so I think the paragraph is about planets, but what about planets? Each sentence gives some information about how long it takes some planets to go around the sun . . . , so I'm sure the paragraph is mostly about how long it takes planets to go around the sun.*

4. Then use another passage. Think aloud and explain why certain details are eliminated as the main idea. Encourage students to share their thoughts and also to think aloud as they process information in making their decisions to find the main idea. Choose a sample passage like the following one for this activity. Guide students as needed by saying what follows.

> *Owls are one kind of bird that you can see at night. That's because owls are nocturnal. They hunt at night, usually looking for small animals to eat. Owls can hunt at night because they have large eyes that can see in the dark. Their eyes are 50 times more powerful than are the eyes of humans. Owls also have extremely sensitive hearing and can hear the rustling of a mouse from high in a tree.*

5. Make the point that in some passages the main idea is directly stated. In others, it is not. Also, some paragraphs may not contain a main idea, because they may be transitional paragraphs.
6. Use additional paragraphs or passages to help students learn how to figure out the main idea. Perhaps you could develop a wall chart that contains the following reminders.

Finding the Main Idea

1. What is the paragraph mostly about?
2. What is the most important idea given about the topic?
3. Look for details that tell about the main idea. If you can't locate any details, you probably don't have the main idea.
4. Remember that the main idea is sometimes right in the passage. Other times you have to use the details to figure out the main idea.

Strategy 2 SECTION 6.4

MAIN IDEA T

1. Identify a piece of text that has a clear main idea with details or use the article on Pyramids from Chapter 7 on page 581. Remember that some informational text is written without clear main ideas so be sure to identify the main ideas before beginning this strategy.
2. Duplicate and distribute copies of the text to students. Tell students that you will be asking them to identify the main ideas and details.
3. Write the terms *main idea* and *details* on the chalkboard. Ask students if they know what the terms mean. Give students an opportunity to brainstorm ideas. Clarify as needed.
4. Draw the Main Idea T on the chalkboard. Point out that the main idea line is horizontal and the detail area is vertical. Ask students how the graphic helps them understand the meanings of the terms *main idea* and *details*.

Main idea

____

Supporting details

1. ____________

2. ____________

3. ____________

4. ____________

5. ____________

5. Scaffold students' understandings of *main idea* and *detail* by saying something like the following.

   The graphic shows a long line for the main idea. This line indicates that the main idea is the big idea of the text. We can write the big idea on the long line at the top. There are other ideas in the text that support the big idea. These are called details. We can list the details underneath the long line to show that they explain or support the big idea. You'll hear the words main idea *and* details *throughout your schooling so you need to really understand these terms.*

6. Draw students' attention to the text that you selected for the demonstration. Read the text out loud. You might need to read it more than once. Explain to students that they should be listening for the main idea by saying something like the following.

   I am going to read this text out loud. I know you could read it by yourself, but I want you to concentrate on thinking about the main idea and details. As I read, ask yourself, "What is this entire paragraph or passage about, or to what does most of this paragraph or passage seem to refer?" The answer to these questions will give you the topic.

7. Invite students to share the main ideas they generated. Scaffold students' contributions so that you have an accurate main idea statement. Once you have identified a main idea, ask students to list it on the top line of the Main Idea T.

8. Read the selection one more time. Tell students to listen for the details that support the main idea by saying something like the following.

   We have identified the main idea. Now let's find details that support this idea. While I am reading, ask yourself, "What ideas help us understand the main idea? What am I hearing that tells me something more about the main idea?" As you hear details, list them on the Main Idea T.

9. Divide the class into groups of two or three students. Have students share the details they heard from the passage. Tell students that they can change their answers as they talk in their groups.

10. Invite students to share the details they listed with the entire class. Write the details on the Main Idea T that you drew on the chalkboard. Have students check to see if they were able to identify the details of the passage.
11. Repeat the process with additional passages until students have a good understanding of main idea and details. Once students understand how to use the Main Idea T, have them use it independently.
12. Remind students that they should look for main ideas as they read. Tell students that not all passages will have the main idea at the beginning of the paragraph and that some paragraphs have main ideas at the end or that are unstated. Reassure students that you will teach them how to identify those types of main ideas at a later time.
13. A reproducible Main Idea T can be found on the next page.

MAIN IDEA T

Name ______________________________ Date ____________

Title of passage ______________________________

Author ______________________________ Paragraph Number ____________

Main idea

____

____

Supporting details

1. ______________________________

2. ______________________________

3. ______________________________

4. ______________________________

5. ______________________________

FINDING THE MAIN IDEA

1. Remind students that they may have learned that the main idea is often the first sentence of an informational passage. Tell students that at times the main idea will not be the first sentence but will be the last sentence or will not be stated at all.
2. Draw a triangle with the point on the bottom on the chalkboard. Tell students that some passages have the main idea at the beginning of the passages. Remind students that they are probably familiar with this type of main idea-detail passage.

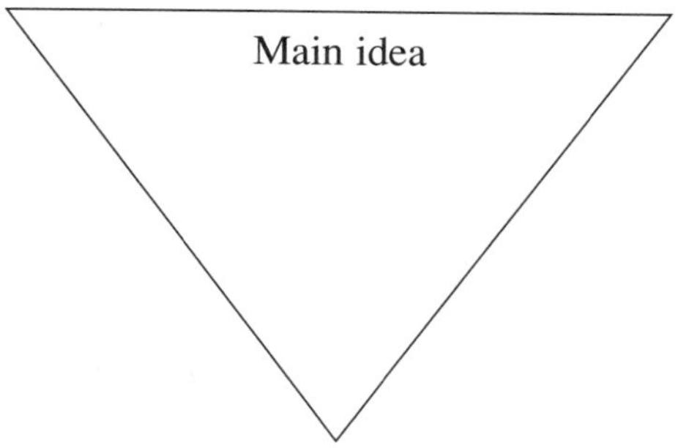

3. Draw a triangle with the point at the top on the chalkboard. Tell students that some passages have the main idea at the end of the paragraph and that it can also be illustrated with a triangle by saying something like the following.

> *Many passages have the main idea stated at the beginning of the paragraph. Some paragraphs, however, begin with the details and end with the main idea. In these cases, the main idea is the last sentence of the paragraph. When you read a paragraph, ask yourself whether the first sentence gives you the topic of the paragraph or whether it's one of the details. If the first sentence doesn't introduce the topic of the paragraph, read the paragraph and pay close attention to the last sentence. The last sentence is sometimes the main idea.*

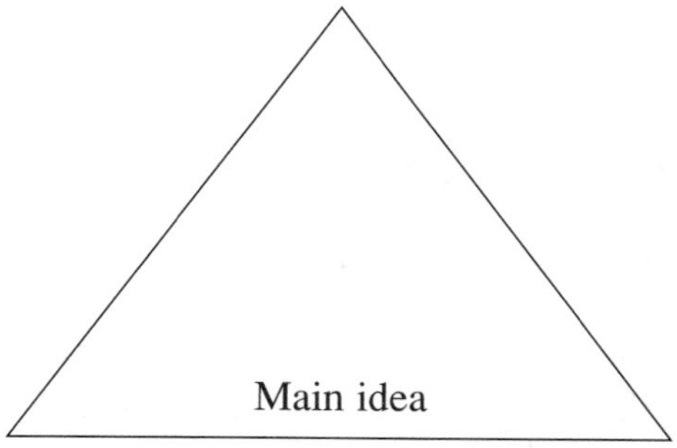

4. Draw a square on the chalkboard. Tell students that some passages do not state the main idea but that it is implied. Explain that when a main idea is implied readers can figure it out by saying something like the following.

When you read a paragraph, look at the first and last sentences for the main idea. Sometimes, however, the main idea is not stated. Ask yourself whether you understand what the main idea is without reading it in one of the sentences. If you know the main idea without finding it in one of the sentences, it is unstated. You can know the topic of a paragraph without it being written.

Main idea
(not stated)

5. Give each student a triangle that has the term *main idea* at the top, a triangle with the term *main idea* at the bottom, and a square.
6. Identify a variety of passages that have main ideas in the first sentence, the last sentence, and are not stated. Read a passage to students. Ask students to figure out whether the main idea is the first sentence, the last sentence, or not stated. Have students raise one of their figures to indicate their choice.
7. Check to see how many students were able to identify the main idea correctly. Repeat with the same type of text if several students had difficulty. If the students were able to correctly identify where the main idea was located, read a different type of passage.
8. Repeat this activity several times during the next weeks until students are able to identify the type of main idea in a passage.
9. Remind students that knowing the main idea of a passage will help them better understand the text.

Strategy 4 SECTION 6.4

THE REST OF THE STORY

1. When students generate their own main idea, they are more likely to understand how to find main ideas in reading. Manyak (2008) suggests that students develop their own news stories to help them understand how to structure texts and to understand how main ideas are developed by authors. You can think of this as having students tell The Rest of the Story. Explain by saying something like the following.

   Have you ever had someone begin telling a story and then have them stop before the ending? You might ask, "What's the 'rest of the story?'" This phrase was made famous by a broadcaster named Paul Harvey. When you get home, ask your parents or grandparents if they have heard the phrase "the rest of the story." It will probably be familiar to them.

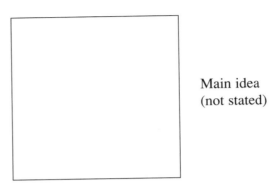

We're going to use that well-known phrase to help us learn how to find main ideas in informational text. Say it with me: The Rest of the Story. [Students should repeat the phrase with you.]

2. Select several short items from a local newspaper or use a newspaper written specifically for students, such as *Scholastic News*. Make sure each article has a clearly visible main idea statement.
3. Divide the class into groups of three or four students. Give a copy of a news article to each group. Have one student read the article to the group.
4. Tell students that main ideas are typically the first sentences in newspaper articles. Ask students to read the first sentence and decide whether it fits that pattern. Explain by saying the following.

   Read the first sentence of your passage aloud. Ask yourself whether the sentence gives you a big idea or a topic. Sometimes it's hard to tell right away. When I think about main ideas, I think about a bowl and pieces of fruit. The main idea is like the bowl. You can put pieces of fruit in the bowl but you can't put the bowl in the pieces of fruit. Read the first sentence and think about whether it's like a bowl or like pieces of fruit.

5. Invite students to read the main idea sentences from the articles. Write them on the chalkboard. Tell students that these sentences preface the details that follow.
6. Tell students that they can also write news articles about things they have experienced. Help students think of things they could write by giving them the following prompts.
   - What did you do last evening?
   - Did your family do something together last weekend?
   - What do you do in your free time?
   - Are you involved with any sports?
   - Did you watch television or a movie?
7. Have students write one sentence about their experiences on index cards. Collect the cards and read them to determine whether the sentences are broad enough for a main idea.
8. Select two or three of the cards. Ask students who wrote the sentences if they would like to tell their story to the class.
9. Write one of the main idea statements on the chalkboard. Invite the student who authored the statement to tell you the Rest of the Story. Write the dictated story on the chalkboard as the student tells it.
10. Read the entire story to the class and invite the class to read it along with you.
11. Explain how the details fit the story and how the first sentence tells the reader what the story will be about.
12. Remind students to think about main ideas when they read. Tell students that knowing the main idea can help strengthen their comprehension.

Practice and Reinforcement Activities

1. Pictures may be used to help students develop the notion of topic and to answer the question: What is this picture mostly about? Discussions can be used to develop an understanding of main idea and important supporting details.
2. Have students read a short passage. Select the best title from several given. Students could also create their own title or write a phrase or sentence that best describes the main idea of the passage.
3. Provide several passages, each followed by four sentences. One sentence states the main idea of the passage, another is too broad, one is too detailed, and the last contains information not stated in the paragraph. After students have selected their main idea for each passage, discuss their choices as well as why other statements were not appropriate for the main idea. Guided discussion is particularly important, because it will help students clarify their thinking.
4. Read a short passage to students and have them relate, in one sentence, the main idea. Write some of their sentences on the board as a basis for discussion.
5. Cut out passages from old books or articles that are at a variety of reading levels. Fasten the passages to 5" x 8" cards. On the back of each card write several possible phrases or sentences that describe the main idea. Students should read the passage, write their answers on a separate sheet of paper, and then compare them with the answers on the back of the cards.
6. Use newspaper articles and have students underline the main idea if stated, or write it if an inference is necessary. With a different colored pencil, marker, or pen, the student can underline the supporting details.
7. To help develop the inclusive nature of a main idea, provide lists where students can practice understanding the difference between general and specific ideas. Be sure to relate the lists to the study of main ideas and discuss reasons for the best answer. Several exercises follow.

    Pennies, nickels, and dimes are all ____________.

    Robins, sparrows, and hawks are all ____________.

    Circle the word that includes the others.

snow	stamps	Earth	games
rain	coins	Saturn	bingo
weather	stickers	planets	checkers
fog	collections	Jupiter	hopscotch

8. Use students' knowledge of familiar stories (such as *The Three Little Pigs, Hansel and Gretel,* and *The Gingerbread Boy*) and have students discuss their perceptions of the major thoughts in the stories.
9. Have students look through various types of reading materials to find examples of the main idea (the "point") or topic sentence. Students can also write their own paragraphs using these two different types of paragraph structures.

10. Have students read a selection and draw the outline of their hand on a sheet of paper. The main idea can be written on the hand and the supporting details on the fingers.
11. List and number a series of statements on cards. Have students read the sentences. Select the one that best describes the main idea. Place the number and the main idea on the back of the card so the activity is self-correcting.

Front of Card	Back of Card
1. Bats can fly. 2. Bats are found in caves. 3. Bats are unusual animals. 4. Bats are clumsy on the ground. 5. Bats can scare people.	The main idea is 3. Bats are unusual animals.

12. Use illustrations from a story or have students draw pictures to help them understand main ideas. Begin with familiar stories. Discuss the illustrations or pictures.
13. Practice naming lists of things that are arranged in categories. Students or the teacher list four or five items, such as paper, pencils, notebooks, pens, journals. Then invite a student to offer the title of the category—how these things fit together. Give several students a chance to offer the category title. Sometimes more than one answer is acceptable.

Match. Provide students with sets of six pictures and a title for them on individual strips of tagboard. Include a few additional titles that do not match the picture with the appropriate title. By writing the same number on the back of the title strip and picture, students can check their work.

Categories. Use pictures or objects from five categories (such as farm, jobs, food, colors, outdoors). Mix up the pictures or objects from the categories and have students sort them according to a logical scheme or attribute. Discuss the resulting categories and have students provide reasons for each category. Possible categories are provided below.

animals	clothing	shelters
foods	energy	musical instruments
flowers	fruits	tools
school supplies	shapes	vehicles
games	drinks	books

Section 6.5

Facts or Details

Behavior Observed → **Anticipated Outcome**

The student has difficulty recalling important facts or details from a passage.

The student will recall important facts or details from a passage.

Background

Important facts or details often can be taught along with main ideas. Facts and details are frequently at the factual level of comprehension (text explicit) but can also be interpretive or applicative (text implicit) (Duffy, 2002). For example, consider the following passage and question.

- Jerry saw Beth. She was wearing a red dress.
- What color was her dress?

Most teachers would consider the question to be at the factual or literal level. The correct answer (red) is certainly explicitly contained in the passage. However, to get the answer, the student has to do a bit of inferencing and infer that the word *her* in the question refers to Beth. Although such an inference might be considered to be lower level, it is, nevertheless, an inference that is text implicit. When teachers work with facts and details, they should be alert for the higher-level comprehension strategies (interpretive and applicative) that are sometimes demanded of the student.

Strategy 1

IDENTIFYING DETAILS

1. List several different topics on the chalkboard (for example, birds, animals, airplanes, or colors). Select one that seems to interest most of the students.
2. Write the topic on the chalkboard and have students share information they know about the topic. As students share, write sentences containing their thoughts. An example follows.

   Airplanes

   Airplanes can fly.
   Pilots fly airplanes.
   There are many different kinds of airplanes.
   Airplanes can carry people.

3. Tell students that you will ask them questions that can be answered by understanding the sentences. For example, What can airplanes carry? As the questions are answered, have students indicate which sentence provided the answer to the question. If students give correct answers that are not contained in the sentences, acknowledge the responses as correct. Then ask the students to find the answer that is given in a sentence that is written on the chalkboard. For example, if you ask "What can airplanes carry?" and the student says "Cargo," indicate that the response is correct. Then ask whether the student can also provide an answer that is contained in one of the sentences written on the chalkboard.
4. After several similar exercises, tell students they are learning how to answer questions that ask them to locate facts and details.
5. Develop another topic with sentences and encourage students to ask questions that other students who read the sentences can answer. Discuss various answers as appropriate.
6. Indicate that such questions can also be asked about the information and ideas contained in their reading. On the chalkboard, write a brief passage from a literature selection or content textbook and ask factual questions. Use a procedure similar to the one already described. A sample passage follows.

   It was the sweetest, most mysterious place anyone could imagine. The high walls which shut it in were covered with the leafless stems of climbing roses which were so thick that they were matted together. Mary Lennox knew they were roses because she had seen a great many roses in India. All the ground was covered with grass of a wintry brown and out of it grew clumps of bushes which were surely roses if they were alive. There were numbers of standard roses which had so spread their branches that they were like little trees (Burnett, 1990, p. 80).

Strategy 2

4 Ws

1. Write a sentence on the chalkboard. Have students read it silently and then have someone read it out loud.

   Early that morning, Brittany packed her lunch in the kitchen.

2. Tell students to use the information in the sentence to answer the questions you ask. Ask several questions (who, what, when, where) and remind students to use the information in the sentence for their answers. Tell students that the questions are checking the students' ability to identify facts and details. Remind students to ask who, what, when, and where as they read.
3. Continue this procedure with another sentence and then move to several sentences and brief passages. Encourage discussion and think aloud as necessary.
4. Use concrete objects and have students demonstrate the meaning of a sentence. For example, use several plastic animals and a small box. Have students read a sentence and manipulate or arrange objects to answer the question. Sample ideas are provided below.

   Sentence: The cat and dog are near the box.
   Question: Where are the cat and dog? (Show me.)
   Sentence: The horse is near the box and the cat is in the box.
   Question: Where are the cat and the horse? (Show me.)

Practice and Reinforcement Activities

1. During regular instructional periods ask students factual questions about the materials they are reading. Have students locate the sentences or phrases in the passage that support their answers.
2. Select a brief passage at an appropriate instructional level for your students and number each sentence. Write the passage on the chalkboard, use it on an overhead projector, or reproduce it so each student has a copy. Then have each student make individual response cards with a number that corresponds to each numbered sentence in the passage. Ask factual questions and have students hold up the card that corresponds to the sentence containing the correct answer. Discuss answers where appropriate. A sample passage with questions appears here.

Passage	Possible Questions
[1]Dennis helped his family load the minivan. [2]It took quite a while. [3]They put in sleeping bags, a small tent, fishing rods, a pocket radio, and sacks of food, so there was enough for several days. [4]They were going camping.	1. Who is this story about? (1) 2. Where are they going? (4) 3. How much food did they take? (3) 4. What did they load? (3) 5. How long did it take? (2)

3. Provide sentences for students to read that will enable them to answer who, what, when, and where questions. Here is an example.

   Last evening, Michael left his book at the library.
   Who? ____________________
   What? ____________________
   When? ____________________
   Where? ____________________

4. Encourage students to write brief passages along with questions that can be answered by using information in the passages. Have students exchange their papers and answer the questions.

Get the Facts. Use a world almanac, book of facts, *Guinness Book of World Records*, or another source to develop a series of sentences or short passages. Put this information on the front of a note card and put one question (with the answer) on the back of the card. Place the cards sentence-side up in front of the students.

After one student reads the sentence silently, the card is given to another student who reads the question. If it is answered correctly, the student who answered the question gets the card. Incorrectly answered questions are placed at the bottom of the pile. The correct answer should not be revealed. Questions can be developed around various themes: sports, people, movies, silly facts, celebrities, cars, TV shows, and so on. A possible list of sentences and questions related to silly facts (Sobol, 1981) follows.

Sentences	**Questions**
Green-yellow is the safest color for a car.	What is the safest color for a car?
The hair and skin on your body is dead.	What is dead?
Your heart weighs less than a pound, but it pumps 2,000 gallons of blood every day.	How much blood does your heart pump every day?
Cats and gorillas need 14 hours of sleep out of every 24 hours.	How many hours a day do most cats and gorillas sleep?
An elephant generally drinks about 50 gallons of water a day.	What drinks 50 gallons of water a day?
A mole can tunnel through nearly 300 feet of earth each day.	How far can a mole tunnel each day?
A bee has 5,000 nostrils and can smell an apple tree two miles away.	How many nostrils does a bee have?
The eyes of a giant squid are as large as a basketball.	How large are a giant squid's eyes?
A pig has 44 teeth.	What animal has 44 teeth?

Section 6.6

Sequence

Behavior Observed →
The student has difficulty sequencing events.

Anticipated Outcome
The student will sequence events correctly.

Background

Students who have difficulty retelling the events from a story in the proper order may be experiencing problems with understanding sequence. The same is true for students who have trouble following multistep directions.

Students who possess the ability to recognize or recall the sequence in a passage are often able to infer what occurred between two stated events or incidents. They can also make predictions about what might happen next in a passage based on the previous sequence of events. Sequencing demands that students use at least the literal level of comprehension. More often, however, the interpretive level as well as the applicative level must be used. In order to correctly sequence events, the students must interpret a passage of print or a series of pictures and then anticipate which event must come next (and also which cannot).

To teach sequence of events, begin with concrete experiences and then move to printed materials. In addition, consider the importance of sequence relative to the particular type of reading material and the students' purposes for reading. The following strategies are helpful in teaching sequence.

Strategy 1

SEQUENCING

1. Gather a series of objects that can be put in order. Some examples follow.

pencils of varying lengths	paper of different sizes
straws of different lengths	books of different sizes
balls of various sizes	chalk of varying lengths

2. Use a series of objects (such as three pencils of varying lengths) and have students arrange them from shortest to longest. Tell students that they are arranging the pencils in a particular order or sequence. Repeat this process with other objects (nested dolls or other toys also work well). Have students give directions for ordering or arranging the objects in a particular sequence.

3. Transfer the notion of sequence by using a series of three pictures. Have a student arrange the pictures in sequence. Then discuss the reasons for a particular sequence. Have students make up a brief story that explains the sequence and have them share it aloud. Two possible sets of pictures are given here.

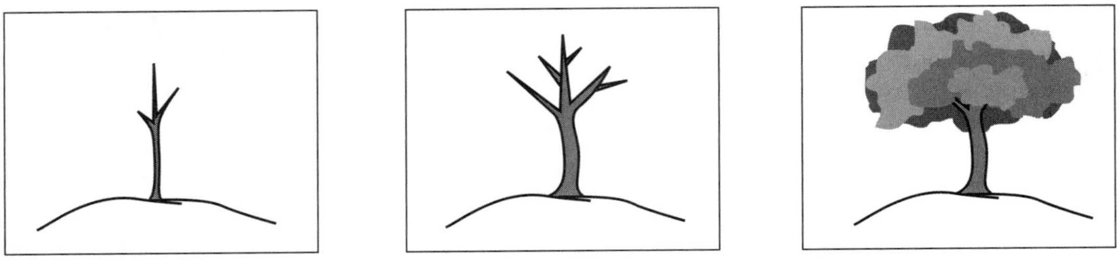

4. Help students become aware of sequences in their daily activities by discussing the order of the letters in their names, how a book is read (left to right and top to bottom), eating (breakfast, lunch, and dinner), getting dressed (socks before shoes, shirt before coat), and coming to school. Stress that the sequence or order observed in these activities also occurs in reading.

5. Use an activity like brushing teeth and have students list the major steps in the sequence. Write these steps on the chalkboard and encourage discussion.

6. To begin the transfer to reading, present sentence strips that relate to a particular sequence and have a student arrange them in proper order. Vary the number and complexity of the sentences for the group being taught. Think aloud and discuss the arrangement. Tell the students that during reading there is often a sequence or order to the story, as in the following example.

__________ Mario and Mike raked the leaves.

__________ The neighbor asked if the two boys wanted to earn some money.

__________ They put the piles into large brown bags.

__________ The neighbor looked out the window and saw the lawn covered with leaves.

__________ The boys counted the money they had earned.

Read the sentences with students and demonstrate how to choose the correct sequence by thinking aloud.

> *I wonder which thing happened first. Well, Mario and Mike didn't rake the leaves first because I think someone asked them to do that job. It was the neighbor who asked the boys to rake the leaves so the boys could earn some money. That's right, but something came before that. . . . Oh, the neighbor must have seen a lot of leaves first and maybe he didn't have time to rake. So, the fourth sentence down is the first thing that happened. Next, the neighbor must have asked the two boys if they wanted to earn some money. That's the second one down. Then the boys raked and put the leaves into the brown recyclable bags. Then they got paid for their work and counted their money . . . , so the sentences are numbered 3, 2, 4, 1, 5.*

Read the sentences in order with the students and ask them whether they agree. Encourage suggestions.

ACTIVITY LIST

1. Tell students that in stories they read events usually happen in a particular order or sequence. Invite their sharing based on books they have read, TV programs, or movies they have seen. Emphasize that a series of events can often show the progression of time.
2. Ask students to think about events in their daily lives like getting up, dressing, eating, going to school, going home, playing, doing homework, and going to bed.

   Encourage discussion and then provide a chart on which the day's activities in school can be listed. An example is provided below.

Time	Events/Activities
8:40	Arrive at school
8:50	School begins
8:50–9:00	Attendance, lunch count
9:00–9:30	Science

3. After activities at school have been listed, encourage students to share events that take place before and after school. Distribute the chart on page 457 that they can complete with events in their daily routines.
4. After students have completed their charts, help them to get a sense of events over a 24-hour period. A circle should help students see the sequence and repeated events in their daily routines.

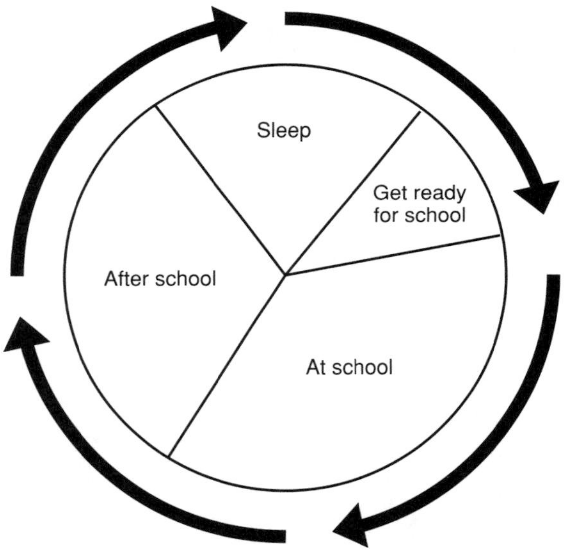

MY DAILY ACTIVITIES

Name ______________________________ Date ______________

When	*Time*	*Events/Activities*
Before school		
At school		
After school		
At bedtime		

Strategy 3

STORY GRAPH

1. Tell students that they can learn sequencing by reading stories and thinking about how and when the events in the story occur. For example, you could say something like the following.

   When you read a story, you know that it will have a beginning, a middle, and an end. As you read, you should also notice that the story has events that happen one after the other. Think about the sequence *of the events. Sequence means the order in which the events take place. As you think about the events, also think about how the events make an impact on the characters.*

2. Introduce the concept of a story graph to students. Tell students that a story graph lists the sequence of events and also ways those events are significant. Provide students with an example of your own or use the following example from *Diary of a Wombat* (French, 2003).
3. Think of a question or theme that runs throughout the book and write it at the top of the chalkboard. Tell students that they should consider this question or theme as they read the book.
4. Divide the class into groups of three or four students. Ask students to read the story and have them write the events that occurred in the story under the main theme. As students write the events, ask them to respond to the question or theme and graph each event as in the example that follows.

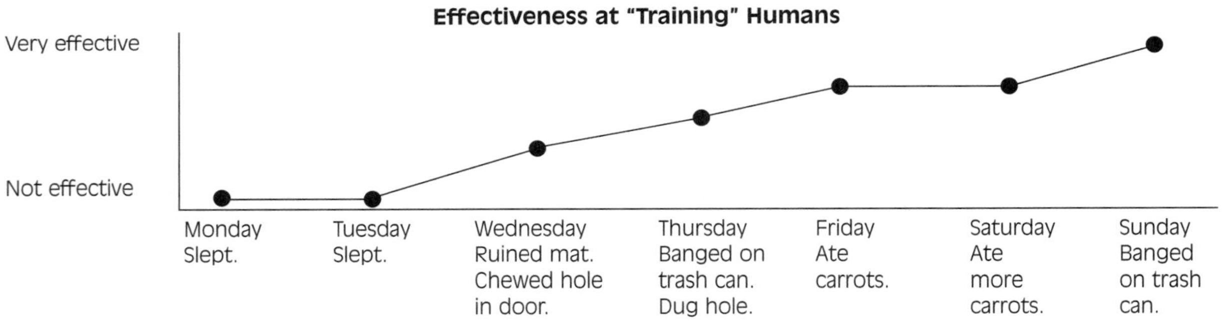

5. Have students share their story graphs with others in the class. Discuss the differences of opinions. Tell students that everyone does not need to have the same answers.
6. Remind students to think of the sequence of events in a story as they read and to apply the sequence to questions they have generated from the story or the main theme.

Practice and Reinforcement Activities

1. Students who need practice in acquiring the concept of sequence should be given various concrete objects and instructed to order them according to size, length, shape, and so forth.
2. Provide comic strips or stories told through pictures that are presented in a mixed-up order. Have students arrange the pictures in the order in which they happened and retell the story. Use the following example or create your own pictorial story.

3. Give students three or four letters of the alphabet and have them place the letters in correct sequence.
4. Provide an oral set of directions with several specific actions for students to carry out. Use words to help signal sequence (*first, then, last*). Other signal words include *yesterday, today,* and *tomorrow.*
5. After students have read a selection, ask them questions about the order of events.
6. List the major events of a selection in a scrambled order on the chalkboard. Instruct students to rewrite the list in the correct order or number the events in the order in which they happened. Have students discuss their answers.
7. After a selection has been read, students can draw pictures to illustrate the order of major events or write sentences that describe them.
8. Scrambled sentences can be arranged in proper order and discussed. An example follows.

    ___________ Thomas Edison worked hard and invented electric lights.

    ___________ Once there were no electric lights.

    ___________ Today we have electric lights in our homes.

9. Have students arrange sentence strips that go with pictures to tell the story in the proper sequence.
10. Prepare paragraphs that have a sentence missing and provide two to four alternative sentences that could be the missing sentence. Ask students to select the sentence that best fits within the sequence of the paragraph. Discuss why the other sentences are less likely choices.

    ___________________________. Use strong twine, sticks, and paper for the kite. Tie rags together for the tail. Wait for a windy day to try to fly your kite.

    1. You can buy a kite at the store.
    2. You need several things to make a kite.
    3. Flying a kite is not easy.

11. Provide activities where students can practice the correct sequence of events. See the example below.

1. noon	1. fruit	1. get dressed
2. sunrise	2. flower	2. get up
3. sunset	3. bud	3. go to school
123 132 (213)	312 123 (321)	231 (213) 312

12. Prepare sentences or brief passages that have a sequence of events or activities. Have students answer the questions posed and then discuss how they arrived at their answers.

    Bill took out the garbage after he cleaned his room.
    - What did Bill do first? ____________________
    - What did Bill do next? ____________________
    - What helped you decide on the sequence?

    Jessica left home before Katie.
    - Who left last? ____________________
    - What helped you decide on the sequence?

13. Have students develop lists of words that may give clues to sequence (such as *later, soon, tomorrow, yesterday, in the future, in the evening*). Discuss these words and have students write short selections that include some of them. Students can also write or ask questions that focus on sequence.
14. Have students list important times or events in their lives. Then help them arrange the events in order by years. Stress the notion that the events have been placed in a time sequence.
15. Have students list step-by-step instructions for cooking, making something, doing a magic trick, and so on. Other students can follow the directions as written in sequence.
16. Read stories to your students that have a clear sequence of events. Create story cards of the events and place them in random order on the table. Ask students to place the events in the order of the story. An example of story cards from *If You Give A Moose A Muffin* (Numeroff, 1991) appears on the following page.

Scramble. Prepare several sets of the same five sentence strips that can be formed into a paragraph. Divide the group into several teams and give each an envelope containing the sentence strips. The first team that arranges the sentence strips into a logical paragraph wins. One variation of the game uses a sentence that has been cut into words or phrases. A sequence of pictures also can be used.

How Is It Ordered? Develop a series of paragraphs that vary in how the reading is sequenced, such as time, events, directions, actions of the main character, or which ingredient comes next. Make note cards with the various sequences as headings. Place the paragraphs on note cards and have students draw a card, read it, and place it under the correct heading.

time	events	directions
sdkflas;df slkj did o odi osd pq0f df 0ad kfgiow owe o owir asvcna er dso osdo aa sdf s sdf jso pe w pwer pw as;f oe owe f o osdf so od sdf sdoi sod os osd oo o sd sdkflas;df slkj did o odi osd pq0f df 0ad kfgiow owe o owir asvcna er dso osdo aa sdf s sdf jso pe w pwer pw as;f oe owe f o osdf so od sdf sdoi sod os osd oo o sd	sdkflas;df slkj did o odi osd pq0f df 0ad kfgiow owe o owir asvcna er dso osdo aa sdf s sdf jso pe w pwer pw as;f oe owe f o osdf so od sdf sdoi sod os osd oo o sd sdkflas;df slkj did o odi osd pq0f df 0ad kfgiow owe o owir asvcna er dso osdo aa sdf s sdf jso pe w pwer pw as;f oe owe f o osdf so od sdf sdoi sod os osd oo o sd	sdkflas;df slkj did o odi osd pq0f df 0ad kfgiow owe o owir asvcna er dso osdo aa sdf s sdf jso pe w pwer pw as;f oe owe f o osdf so od sdf sdoi sod os osd oo o sd sdkflas;df slkj did o odi osd pq0f df 0ad kfgiow owe o owir asvcna er dso osdo aa sdf s sdf jso pe w pwer pw as;f oe owe f o osdf so od sdf sdoi sod os osd oo o sd

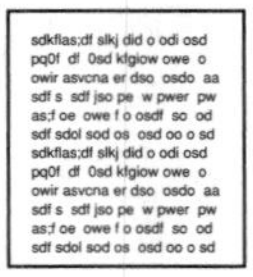

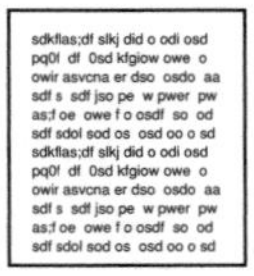

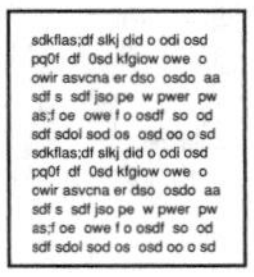

Going to New York. The first student says "I went to New York and took my _____." The next student repeats the object named and adds another. Subsequent students do the same, naming the objects in the proper order. The game can be played by a single group of students or by several students taking alternate turns. Help transfer the game to reading by telling students that there is a sequence in reading selections that needs to be remembered. Alternate names for the game can be used. (I went for a walk and saw a (an) _____.)

Directions: Enlarge the story squares and label them on the back with the title of the story, *If You Give a Moose a Muffin* (Numeroff, 1991). Read the book to your students and then place the story cards in random order. Ask students to place the story cards in the order of the story.

a muffin	blackberry bush	cardboard and paints
jam	needle and thread	a sweater
socks	a sheet	soap
Muffin Mix

Section 6.7

Making Predictions

Behavior Observed →
The student has difficulty predicting outcomes while reading.

Anticipated Outcome
The student will learn to make predictions before and during reading to improve comprehension.

Background

Prediction strategies help increase students' comprehension of text (Block & Pressley, 2002). When students predict before reading a story, they activate their prior knowledge and form purposes for reading. During reading, prediction strategies allow students to generate many possibilities for meaning they can confirm or discard as they find more information (Stahl, 2008). The teaching strategies and activities that follow were developed to encourage students to predict before and/or during reading. Teaching students a variety of prediction strategies can eventually help students become better comprehenders of text.

DIRECTED READING-THINKING ACTIVITY

1. For the Directed Reading-Thinking Activity (Stauffer, 1969a) select a story or a passage that students have not read. Show students the title of the story and ask "What do you think this story will be about?" Encourage students to draw upon their background knowledge to make predictions about the story. Write the students' predictions on the chalkboard or on chart paper.
2. Select a portion of text for students to read. Choose a stopping point after students have read enough of the story to have a sense of the problem but before the climax. Have students silently read the first portion of text. Tell students to stop at the predetermined point. Encourage students who finish early to think about the story thus far. (You can also copy the text on overhead transparencies to prevent students from reading ahead.)
3. Write the following questions on the chalkboard.
   - What has happened thus far in the story?
   - What do you think will happen next?
   - Why do you think so?
4. Duplicate and distribute the Thinking Chart that follows. Have students discuss what has happened in the story up to the point they have read and write their ideas on the chart.
5. Then have students generate ideas about what they think will happen next in the story. Encourage students to think of as many possibilities as they can. Have students list their ideas on the Thinking Chart.
6. Tell students that their predictions should be based on evidence from the story thus far. Have students justify their predictions with evidence from the story. Then have groups of students share their predictions with justifications.
7. Repeat the DR-TA procedures one or two more times during the story. Have students use the Thinking Chart for their ideas.
8. Encourage students to use the DR-TA thinking process as they read independently.

THINKING CHART

Name ______________________________ Date ______________

Story Title ____

What has happened?	*What will happen next?*	*Why do I think so?*

Strategy 2 STORY IMPRESSIONS

1. For Story Impressions (McGinley & Denner, 1987), develop a list of key ideas from a story that the students have not read. Write the words in a vertical list with arrows connecting the words. A partial list from the first chapter of *Little House in the Big Woods* (Wilder, 1932) follows.

girl
↓
Wisconsin
↓
deer
↓
moon
↓
Pa
↓
swift
↓
hinges
↓
chopping
↓
smoke
↓
coming
↓
venison

2. Write the list on the chalkboard, chart paper, or an overhead transparency. Have students read the list of words in order.
3. Divide the class into groups of three or four students. Have students look for relationships and connecting concepts between the words to develop a story from the words. Tell students that they are predicting the chapter or passage by creating their own story.
4. After students have created a story, have them write the story down or tell it to their classmates.
5. Have students read the chapter or passage. Tell them to think about the ways in which their predicted story is like or unlike the actual story.

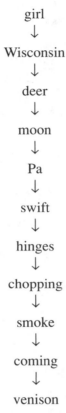

PREDICT-O-GRAM

1. Select a story that the students haven't heard or read. Choose several key words from the story.
2. List the words on the chalkboard, chart paper, or an overhead transparency.
3. Duplicate and distribute the Predict-O-Gram (Blachowicz, 1986) chart on the next page. Make a transparency and use it to model the strategy for students.
4. Tell students to predict what will happen in the story by placing the words from the list in the boxes of the chart. Model how to use the Predict-O-Gram by writing two or three words on the chart and telling students why you have made these decisions. An example of a partially filled Predict-O-Gram for *Clean Your Room, Harvey Moon* (Cummings, 1991) follows.

Saturday Harvey doom clean broom marched
dirty lunch creature dripping found sticky

Setting	*Characters*	*Goal or Problem*
Saturday	*creature* *Harvey*	*clean*
Action	*Resolution*	*Other Things*

5. Give students time to write all the words on their Predict-O-Gram. Take a few minutes to have students discuss reasons for their choices. Then have students read the story.
6. Following reading, have students refer to their Predict-O-Grams to find out how their predictions compare with the text. Tell students they may move words to the correct places on their charts.

PREDICT-O-GRAM

Camille L.Z. Blachowicz

Name ____ Date ____________________

Directions: What do you think these words will be used to tell about? Write them on a square on the Predict-O-Gram. You may have more than one word on a square.

____

____

____

____

Predict-O-Gram for ______________________________

Setting	Characters	Goal or Problem
Action	**Resolution**	**Other Things**

From Blachowicz, C.L.Z. (1986). Making connections: Alternatives to the vocabulary notebook. *Journal of Reading, 29,* 643–649.

Practice and Reinforcement Activities

1. Select a picture book with a text that has a plot and characters. Cover the text of the picture book and display the book on a table. Have students look at the illustrations and predict the contents of the text.
2. Ask students to choose one piece of writing from their writing folders. Then divide the class into pairs. Have each student tell the other student the title of the piece of writing. Then have the student predict the other student's story. After the student has made predictions, he or she should begin reading the piece of writing.
3. When students participate in paired reading, have them stop after each page or section and make predictions to share with their reading buddy.
4. Select an object, photograph, or picture that is connected to a story or book that students will be reading. Tell them that this object has "mysterious possibilities" (Stephens & Brown, 2000). Have students predict what those mysterious possibilities could be. Write the students' ideas on the chalkboard, on chart paper, or on an overhead transparency. After students have listed many ideas, show students the book that they will be reading.

Section **6.8**

Making Inferences

Behavior Observed → **Anticipated Outcome**

The student has difficulty making inferences during reading.

The student will learn to make inferences during reading to improve comprehension.

Background

Much of the meaning that readers construct is based on their own prior knowledge combined with the text. Using textual information along with prior knowledge is called drawing inferences. Drawing inferences is required when part of the knowledge necessary to understand a passage is found in the text but some is not. That's what we know as reading between the lines.

Another type of inference readers make is about characters in fiction. When students read stories, they pay attention to the plot, setting, characters, and theme. Writers do not tell readers everything about characters in stories, so readers need to draw inferences about them.

Many students have trouble drawing inferences (Allington & McGill-Franzen, 2009). The following strategies and activities can help students learn how to draw inferences in general and also to draw inferences about characters in fiction. Learning how to draw inferences can help students improve their reading comprehension.

Strategy 1 SECTION 6.8

WRITER AND ME QUESTIONS

1. Explain to students that there are two kinds of information: information in books and information in their heads. Explain that at times students will have to combine the information from the text with their own knowledge to understand a story.
2. Select a story or passage that has some subtlety—that doesn't explicitly explain everything that happens. Read the story or passage with students or have them read it independently.
3. Have students develop Writer and Me Questions (Raphael, 1984) and write them on index cards. These questions should not be able to be answered from information in the text alone. An example of questions from *The Magic School Bus Lost in the Solar System* (Cole, 1990) follows.
   - What do you think Ms. Frizzles' class was studying in science class?
   - Had the children been on the bus before? How do you know?
4. Collect the questions and ask the appropriate ones to the class. Encourage students to use the story as well as their own information to answer the questions.
5. Encourage students to ask and answer Writer and Me Questions as they read.

Strategy 2 SECTION 6.8

MAKING INFERENCES FROM PICTURES

1. Select a book that has pictures with which students can identify. You might select a picture book or a content area book that has pictures of people or animals in it.
2. Tell students that you will be asking them to pose like the picture in the book and think about what the characters are thinking and feeling by commenting as follows.

   When you read, you should try to understand the story. You can also put yourself in the place of the characters in the story by imagining what they think and feel. When you give words to characters, you are making inferences, which means you are trying to understand the story's meanings on a different level.

3. Identify a picture in the book you have selected that has multiple roles for students. For example, a picture in the book *Orphan Train* by Verla Kay (2003) shows a group of orphan children who have just arrived in town and another group of children who are with families who are selecting orphans to help with the farmwork.
4. Identify several students to strike the pose of the picture. Arrange the students so that they are standing exactly like the picture. Invite students who are not in the picture to help you set the stage.
5. Read the portion of the text from which the picture was taken. Tell the students who are posed like the picture to *become* the children in the picture and to think the way those children are thinking.
6. Ask students to say what they are thinking. Remind students that what they are thinking should represent the children in the picture rather than their own thoughts. Also tell students that they can say things that are not discussed in the story. An example of some of the conversation follows.

Older boy:	Take that one. He can do most of my chores for me.
Father:	I need someone strong to plow for me. None of these boys looks strong enough to me.
Mother:	I wish we could get a girl to help me in the kitchen.
Orphan boy:	I don't want to go with this family. I hope they don't choose me.
Orphan girl:	I want to go home. I don't like it here.

7. After students have said one or two lines, remind students that they are making inferences about the characters. Explain once more that inferences are the kinds of things that aren't stated in the story but that readers imagine based on information from the story.
8. Select another picture from the book and have different students pose for the picture and make inferences about what the characters are thinking and feeling. Tell students that each reader makes different inferences, so they should expect their ideas to be different from the ideas of the other students.
9. Encourage students to make inferences when they read independently.

Strategy 3 SECTION 6.8

OBSERVATION/INFERENCE CHART

1. Guiding students to make inferences about texts is one of the most challenging comprehension goals that teachers have. To help students think deeply about a text and make inferences, Nokes (2008) suggests using an Observation/Inference Chart.
2. Provide students with an informational text that you want them to read. You could use a book, a short article, a section of your textbook, or use the example *Theodore* (Keating, 2006), a retelling of Theodore Roosevelt's life in the first person.
3. Ask students to draw a line down the center of a piece of paper or make copies of the reproducible on page 473 and distribute it to students. On the left-hand side of the paper, have students write the word *Observations*. On the right-hand side ask students to write the label *Inferences*.
4. Tell students that you are going to read the book aloud and that you want students to record observations that they make from the text. For example, students could write something like the following from observations they made from the first few pages of *Theodore*.

Observations	Inferences
Born October 27, 1858	
Frail health when young	
Spent time reading about heroes	
Kept a diary	
Traveled around the world	
Soldier	
Hunted and rode horses	

5. Invite students to share their lists of observations with a classmate. As students discuss their lists and compare the observations they made, give students the opportunity to make revisions to their lists of observations.

6. Develop a class list of the observations students made by writing the most common observations on the chalkboard.
7. Tell students that they will be making inferences from the observations. You might say something like the following.

> *We've made observations from reading "Theodore" and they are listed on the chalkboard. Now we need to consider what they could mean. An important part of reading is making inferences. You make inferences when you "read between the lines." That means that you think of logical things that the observations could mean. Let's try it.*

8. Ask students to reread their observations and consider what they could infer from some of the observations. Remind students that the list of observations is actually a representation of all of the ideas that they have read and that they have ideas in their heads that they can also use.
9. Have students record some of their inferences on the lines on the right-hand side of the Observation/Inference Chart. Tell students that the inferences do not have to be a one-to-one relationship from the observation list. An example follows.

Observations	Inferences
Born October 27, 1858	
Frail health when young	Had extra time to read and learn.
Spent time reading about heroes	
Kept a diary	Was curious
Traveled around the world	
Soldier	Likes hard work
Hunted and rode horses	

10. Students may need several opportunities to think about and practice inferences before they can use the Observation/Inference Chart independently. Once students are comfortable drawing inferences from their observations, have them use the reproducible that follows.
11. If you wish to use an assessment rubric for this strategy, see Nokes (2008).

OBSERVATION/INFERENCE CHART

Name ____ Date ____________________

Directions: As you read, list your observations in the left-hand column of the chart. After you have finished reading, reread the observations and list inferences in the right-hand column.

Observations	*Inferences*

GETTING TO KNOW MY CHARACTER

1. Explain to students that Getting to Know My Character (Richards & Gipe, 1993) will help them comprehend fictional stories more easily.
2. Display the following summary of *The Balancing Girl* by Bernice Rabe (1981) on an overhead projector or write it on the chalkboard. Read the passage aloud and ask students to follow along.

> *Margaret was good at balancing. She could balance a book on her head while gliding along in her wheelchair. She could balance herself on her crutches too. One day Margaret went to a quiet corner in the classroom. She worked hard all morning and made a big domino castle. When Margaret came back to the classroom after lunch, she saw that her castle had been knocked down. "I DIDN'T DO IT!" shouted Tommy. Margaret yelled, "Yes, you did Tommy, and you better never knock down anything I balance again, or YOU'LL BE SORRY!" Later, Margaret made a new domino castle. When she finished, six dominoes fell down. "Oh no!" she thought, but just then, the dominoes stopped falling. "Thank goodness," Margaret thought to herself.*

3. Tell students that the author provides some important facts about Margaret in the story. Ask students to identify some of these facts. As students identify important facts, highlight the appropriate portions of the passage on the overhead projector. Ask questions as needed to help students identify facts.
4. After the important facts have been identified, place a transparency of the Getting to Know My Character chart (see page 475) on an overhead projector. Fill out the facts section of the chart. Guide students to make inferences about Margaret based on the facts presented in the summary. You can do this by asking questions such as "Why do you think Margaret balances books on her head?" or "Why might Margaret be in a wheelchair?"
5. Tell students that the author also helps the reader learn about Margaret by describing her actions. Guide students through locating portions of the passage that provide descriptions of Margaret's actions. Highlight these portions on an overhead transparency.
6. Record on an overhead transparency the information that describes Margaret's actions. Guide students to make inferences about Margaret by considering her actions. Model how you make inferences to aid students in making their own inferences. For example, you might say something like what follows.

   > *The story says that Margaret "worked hard all morning and made a big domino castle." That makes me think that Margaret was a careful, hard worker who had a lot of patience. I know that making something from dominoes can be very hard and take a lot of concentration and patience.*

   Encourage students to make other inferences by using information about Margaret.
7. Discuss how authors also tell readers about a character by use of the character's words and thoughts. Tell students that you can also draw inferences about the character by examining these words and thoughts.
8. Duplicate and distribute the Getting to Know My Character chart that follows after students have read fictional selections to help them make inferences.

GETTING TO KNOW MY CHARACTER

Name ______________________________ Date ______________

Story ____

My Character ______________________________________

Facts about my character	My character's actions
My character's conversations	My character's thoughts and feelings

Adapted from Richards, J.C., & Gipe, J.P. (1993). Getting to know story characters: A strategy for young and at-risk readers. *The Reading Teacher, 47*, 78–79.

Strategy 5 CHARACTER INTERVIEWS

1. To use Character Interviews (Swindall & Cantrell, 1999), select a novel or section of text that students will be reading. The text should involve a number of people, including a strong, central character.
2. Divide the class into groups of three or four students. Have each group read the novel or passage from the text. Because the novel will take much longer to read, you may want to have the students read it prior to meeting as a group. During their first meeting, students could skim back through the book to review the characters and story line.
3. After the selection or novel has been read, have students develop a list of main characters. An example for *Where the Red Fern Grows* (Rawls, 1961) follows.

Characters Identified

Billy Coleman   Mama   Papa   Grandpa

4. Have students generate questions for each of the people identified. If this strategy is being used with a novel, several characters could be identified. Groups of students should develop a set of questions for each character. The questions should require thoughtful responses, not merely yes-no answers. Explain to students that these are the interview questions. Then have students write the questions on colored strips of paper. Sample questions for Billy Coleman follow.
   - You worked to save your money for your dogs for two years. How did you feel each time you added coins to the can?
   - Were you ever tempted to give up and spend the money on other things for your family?
   - What role did your grandfather play during your childhood?
   - How would you describe your relationship with your dogs?
5. Have groups of students share their interview questions with the entire class. Provide extra colored strips for questions that are generated during discussion. Set aside duplicate questions. Have students add any new questions to their original list.
6. Within each group, have students assume the role of the different characters or people involved. Students can choose a character to portray for the interview by selecting a "prop" that represents the person. For example, a pair of empty eyeglass frames, costumes, or hats may be used. You will need to consider ahead of time what props to provide.
7. Tell students to take turns being interviewed as the character or person of their choice. Other students from the group should take turns as the interviewer and ask the "character" two or three questions. If enough characters are identified, each student in the group can assume a different role.
8. Tell students who are being interviewed to consider the character's actions, traits, and motives to evaluate how they think the character would respond to a question.
9. Upon completion of the interview process, have students discuss the responses different characters provided. Students should discuss whether they agree or disagree with how the characters answered the questions.

CHARACTER CIRCLES

1. When readers are making inferences about characters, they need to think of several types of attributes. Roser, Martinez, Fuhrken, and McDonnald (2007) suggest that students can make those inferences by organizing a character's qualities in three concentric circles. The outer circle should represent the external attributes; the middle circle should list the internal characteristics or qualities; and the insider circle should list core qualities.
2. Tell students that they will be making inferences about characters in a new way using three circles. Take the time to ensure that students understand what inferences are.
3. Draw three circles on the chalkboard one inside the other. Tell students that they should think about external attributes for the outer circles. For example, they should consider the character's age, gender, physical appearance, race, and behavior. Use an example of a book that students have read, such as *The Three Little Javelinas* (Lowell, 1992) which is an adaptation of the three little pigs. Say something like the following.

   > *You know the story of the* Three Little Javelinas. *Today we're going to think about one of the main characters: the coyote. When we think about characters, we first need to think about their external attributes, or how they look. Let's think about how the coyote looks and list some words and draw some pictures in the outside circle.* [See example.]

4. Draw students' attention to the middle circle. Tell students that readers have characteristics or qualities. Have students discuss the characteristics of the coyote in *The Three Little Javelinas*. Some qualities that students could list may be *impatient*, *deceitful*, *sneaky*, *persistent*, and *clever*. List the characteristics in the second circle.
5. After students have considered the external characteristics, ask students to think about the coyote in a different way. Tell students that characters in stories often have core qualities, motivations, and relationships that go deeper than their characteristics. Ask students to think about the coyote's core qualities. Provide students with some ideas if necessary. For example, he is a loner; he can be fooled quite easily; he is motivated by hunger. Have students write these ideas in the center circle.

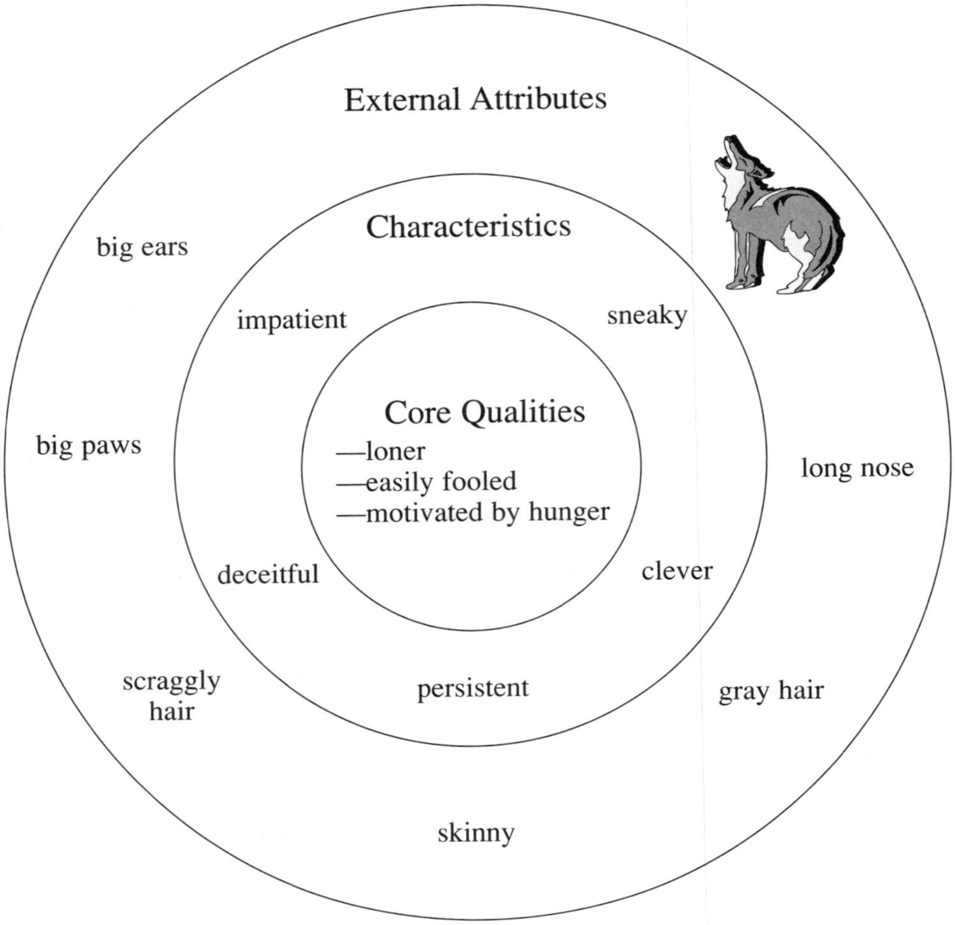

6. Tell students that they are developing inferences about characters when they list character traits in the Character Circle. Explain by saying something like the following.

   When you read, you are learning about the characters as you think about their characteristics. You take ideas from the story and "read between the lines" to make judgments about the character. For example, you might have learned that the coyote kept coming back to the javelina's huts. The story didn't say the coyote was persistent, but you made that inference based on facts from the story. As you read, you should be making inferences about characters all of the time.

7. After students have worked with the entire class to develop Character Circles and feel comfortable drawing inferences about characters, have students develop Character Circles in small groups or independently.
8. Tell students that drawing inferences about characters when reading independently can make characters come alive.
9. A Character Circle reproducible can be found on the following page.

CHARACTER CIRCLES

Name ______________________________ Date ______________

Title ____

Author ____

Character ____

Directions: List the external attributes of the character in the outer circle, the characteristics of the character in the next circle, and the core qualities of the character in the center circle.

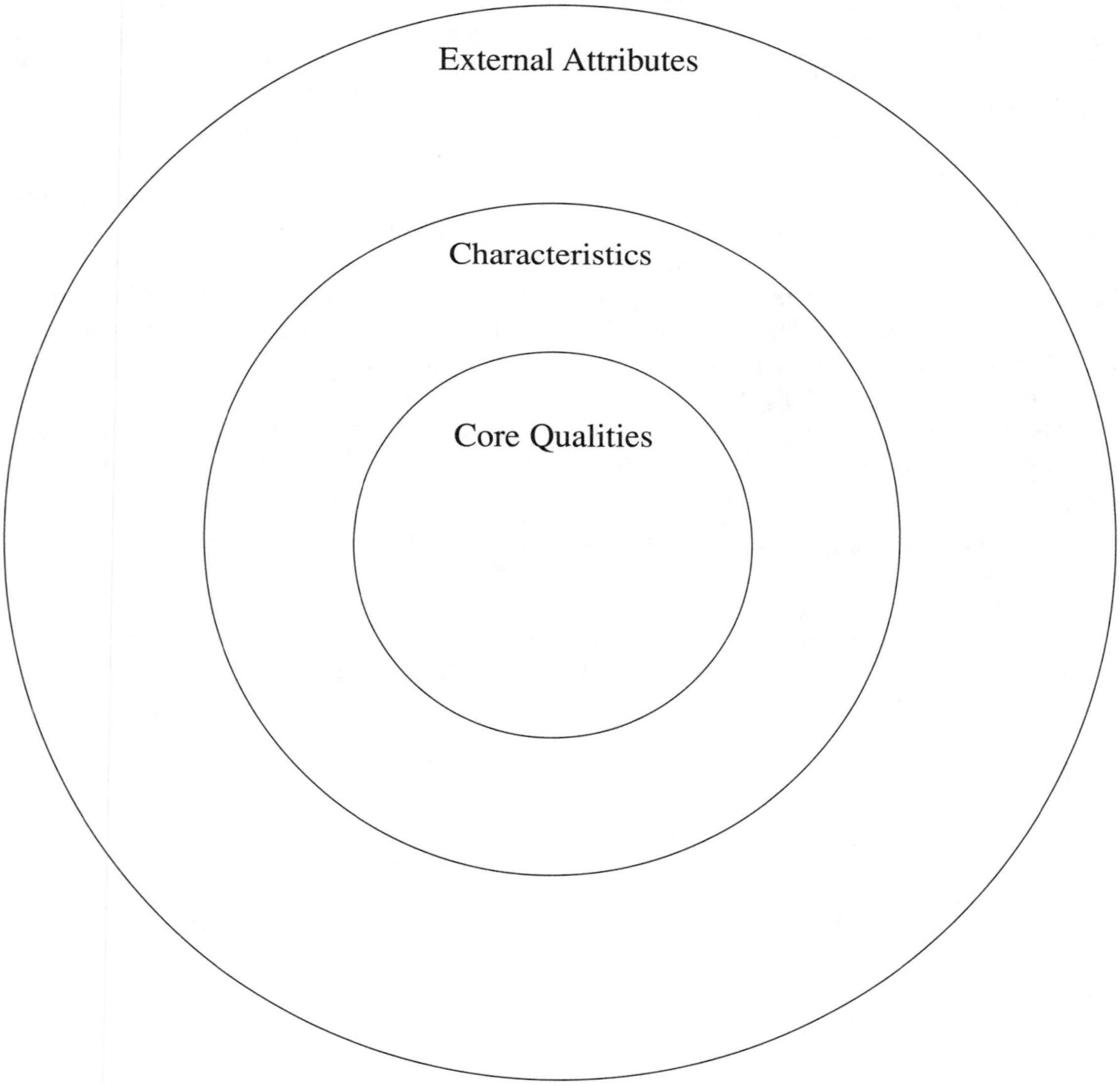

Practice and Reinforcement Activities

1. Write down on index cards several well-known sayings, such as

   "A penny saved is a penny earned."

   Divide the class into groups of two or three students. Have students choose a card. Tell students that they will be pantomiming the saying for the rest of the class. Provide students with time to practice. Then have them pantomime the saying and have the other students guess the saying.
2. Select a wordless picture book to show to students. Read the title and show students the illustrations. Then have students make up a story based on the illustrations.
3. Collect a variety of advertisements. Display the advertisements on chart paper. Read the advertisements with students and help students read between the lines of the ads.
4. Make sure that you vary your questions during discussions and on tests so that some questions encourage students to draw inferences.
5. Have students make a character doll (Hughey & Slack, 2001). Character dolls are pictures of the main character of a story with an explanation of the character's qualities. To have students make a character doll, have them draw an image of the character's face on a piece of paper and draw a circle for the body. On the circle place lined paper for students to write about the character's qualities. Encourage students to draw clothes on the character that are representative of the time period and place in which the character lived.
6. When you are conducting discussions about books in small or large groups, you can help students build inferences by asking them "How do you know?" According to Richards and Anderson (2003), asking this simple question encourages students to think beyond the surface level of comprehension to the deeper level of making inferences. You may need to model answers to this question before students are able to conduct discussions that facilitate inferences. For example, when you ask students to tell the class "how they know," you can first provide answers for those students. Through modeling, students will develop the habit of asking questions of each other and of themselves.
7. Students can draw inferences while reading by writing about the main characters in the story (Bluestein, 2002). The following ideas help students improve their understanding of a character in the story through writing.

   - Decide whether you agree with the character's actions. Write what you would do in the same circumstances.
   - Think about the character's problem. Write whether you would react the same way.
   - Think about the character's feelings. Write about the times you have had similar feelings.
   - Design a plan of action for the character. Write what the character should do.

Section 6.9

Visualizing

Behavior Observed → **Anticipated Outcome**

The student does not visualize while reading. → The student will visualize while reading to improve comprehension.

Background

Look for opportunities to model visualization for students.

In recent years, educators have renewed their interest in mental pictures and how they can be used to aid comprehension (Zeigler & Johns, 2005). Making mental pictures can facilitate the ongoing comprehension of text. Hibbing and Rankin-Erickson (2003) suggest using mental imagery along with text-relevant illustrations as complementary reading comprehension strategies. They also can be used by the strategic reader when comprehending is difficult, and the student activates the "read, picture; read, picture" strategy.

Students may not use imagery on their own, so you will need to help them create pictures in their minds. To do this, you will need to look for opportunities to model visualization for students. For example, as you read a book to your class, you can demonstrate ways that you create images in your mind through a think-aloud. You can also remind students occasionally to form mental images. In addition to these ongoing teaching strategies, you should try some of the activities or lessons in books about imagery (see Zeigler & Johns, 2005).

Strategy 1 SECTION 6.9

FORMING MENTAL PICTURES

1. Introduce the concept of forming mental pictures by telling students that mental pictures can help them comprehend what they read. Be sure they understand that the lesson is focused on how mental pictures can aid comprehension.

2. Explain why making pictures is useful.

   When we read, we can sometimes make pictures in our minds about what we're reading. Pictures of characters, where the story takes place, or what's happening can help us understand and remember what we read.

3. Model the strategy by thinking aloud and telling how you would use the strategy.

   I am going to read two sentences and try to make pictures in my mind about what I read. The air was warm and fragrant with the perfume of flowers. There were roses of various colors and fire bush. *In my mind, I am picturing some red, pink, and white roses. The name* fire bush *makes me think of fire, and I picture a bush that is red or yellow.*

4. Use some brief passages (see Practice and Reinforcement Activities) with students and encourage them to describe their pictures. Discuss how their pictures of the same material are similar and different.
5. Introduce other brief passages and give students opportunities to use mental pictures independently. Encourage students to help locate passages that are good for using mental pictures.
6. Several good guidelines for using mental pictures have been suggested by Cramer (1992).
   - Expect wide variation in students' pictures.
   - Explain that pictures are likely to be "hints and flashes." Rarely will students' pictures be as complete as motion pictures or TV.
   - Foster appreciation and tolerance for students' unique pictures.

Strategy 2 SECTION 6.9

MAKING A PICTURE

1. Tell students that good readers may picture what they are reading in order to understand and remember text. You may want to use the idea of taking pictures with a camera or camcorder. Picturing or visualizing is probably best done with books rich in description.
2. Invite students to share some of the things that they have pictured in their minds. Make the point that recalling pictures can help students remember something that may have taken place long ago.
3. Write a short, evocative passage on the chalkboard that is likely to foster discussion and create pictures in the students' minds. Use the following example or write your own passage.

   It was noon and the sun was at its hottest. The sand was scorching my bare feet. I could see nothing but dust and glaring sand for miles and miles. I was all alone.

4. After students have read the passage, have them elaborate on the scene using their five senses. Ask questions such as the following ones.
   - How do you feel?
   - What do you smell?
   - Where are you?
   - What are you going to do next?

After each response, have the students expand on it. If Barbara says she feels thirsty, have the class focus on thirst and how it feels. The idea is to help students physically experience being in the setting. You may want to use other selections such as an experience at a beach, in the middle of a deep forest, a musty barn, or a crowded city street, or attempting to climb a rocky cliff.

5. Tell students that you are going to read them a passage and you want them to try to picture the scene in their minds. They should be told that this is a strategy they can use during reading. Have students listen carefully as you read.

   I slept late again today. My family was doing errands, so the house was quiet—so quiet that I could hear the refrigerator humming. I was just about to roll over and get a few more hours of sleep when I heard a soft whining noise. I sat up on my elbow and tried to listen, but I didn't hear it again. Then I heard a scratching sound. I thought of mice and winced, burrowing my head under the covers. Finally, I heard the whining noise again and a short bark. I remembered. I was supposed to let the new puppy outside this morning.

6. Engage students in a discussion to share all that they can remember about the passage. Write their thoughts on the chalkboard. Then discuss how creating a picture of what you read can aid comprehension. Remember that not all students organize, store, and retrieve information in the same way.
7. Conclude the lesson by discussing the types of material for which thinking of pictures may work best and encourage students to consider creating pictures in their minds during reading to help them understand and remember. Tell students that there are no "correct" answers and that pictures vary depending on prior knowledge and experience.

Strategy 3 SECTION 6.9

CREATING COMIC STRIPS

1. To create comic strips (Sherman & Wright, 1999), identify an excerpt from a text or story for students to read. The section should include events or ideas that are new to students. A math story example follows.
   - Seven children are on the swings.
   - Two children got off.
   - How many children are left?
2. Model how to visualize the story by saying the following.

   As I was thinking about this story problem, I visualized a teacher watching students on swings at recess. I named the teacher Marty Math. As the teacher was watching the children, a beautiful butterfly flew by the swings. Two of the children got off the swings to look at the butterfly. Five children were left on the swings. They continued swinging.

3. Present three frames or panels using the chalkboard, an overhead transparency, or chart paper. Explain that you have invented a comic character who is watching the action and telling the story. Draw a simple face for students.

4. Show students how to place the comic figure in each frame with a "talking bubble" above its head. Also, show students how to leave room in the frame to illustrate the action. An example follows.

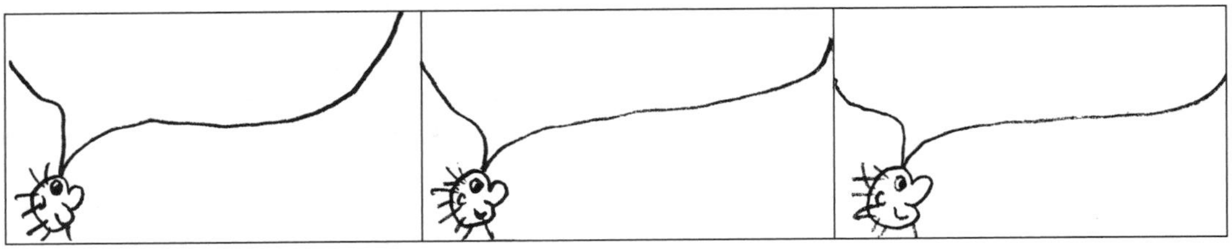

5. Fill in the "talking bubbles" with comments by the comic figure as in the following example.

6. Show students how to fill in the rest of the action of the picture. Think of ways to add a little humor as in the following example.

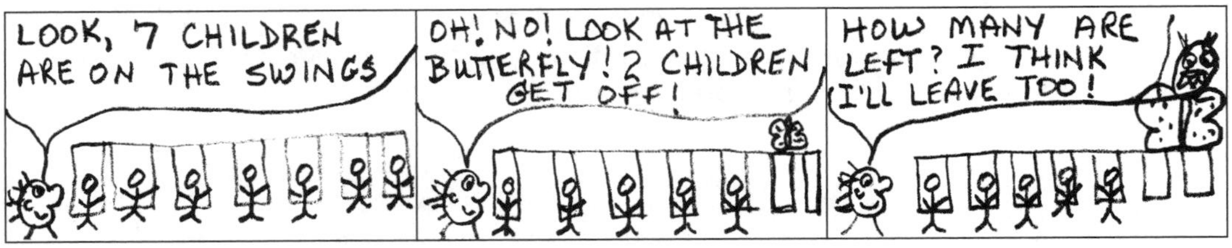

7. Have students read the text that you selected for them. While students are reading, have them visualize the information presented.

8. Explain that there are several ways to visualize material after reading a passage. Have students think of mental images that represent the information in the text.

9. Divide the class into groups of two or three students. Have students discuss the text that they just read including their mental pictures.

10. Duplicate and distribute the comic strips that follow. Have students create a comic strip that expresses the ideas from the reading.

11. Conclude the activity by having groups share comic strips with at least two other groups. Then discuss different approaches to the comic strips. Emphasize the visualization that occurred to help students understand the text that was read.

12. Extend the comic strip activity by having students create comics about their lives (Bitz, 2004). When students create their own comics, they begin to make connections between their lives and the books they have read. These connections can in turn help students form richer mental images as they read.

COMIC STRIPS

By

OPEN-MIND PORTRAITS

1. Select a story or a passage from a novel that has a well-described main character.
2. Have students read the story or passage. Ask students to identify the main character in the text.
3. After students have identified the main character, tell them that they can understand the story better by visualizing the main character. Explain to students that the strategy Open-Mind Portraits (Tompkins, 1998) can help them visualize the main character and understand the main character's actions.
4. Tell students that to create an Open-Mind Portrait they need to draw and color a portrait of the head and neck of a main character. Give students time to finish their portraits.
5. Then have students cut out the portraits and attach them with brads or staples on top of other sheets of drawing paper.
6. Have students lift the portraits and draw and write about the character's thoughts on the second page. Students can add several extra sheets of paper to show the character's thoughts at key points in the story. An example of an Open-Mind Portrait of Leigh from *Strider* (1991) follows.
7. Have students share their portraits with classmates and talk about the words and pictures they have chosen to include in the mind of the character.

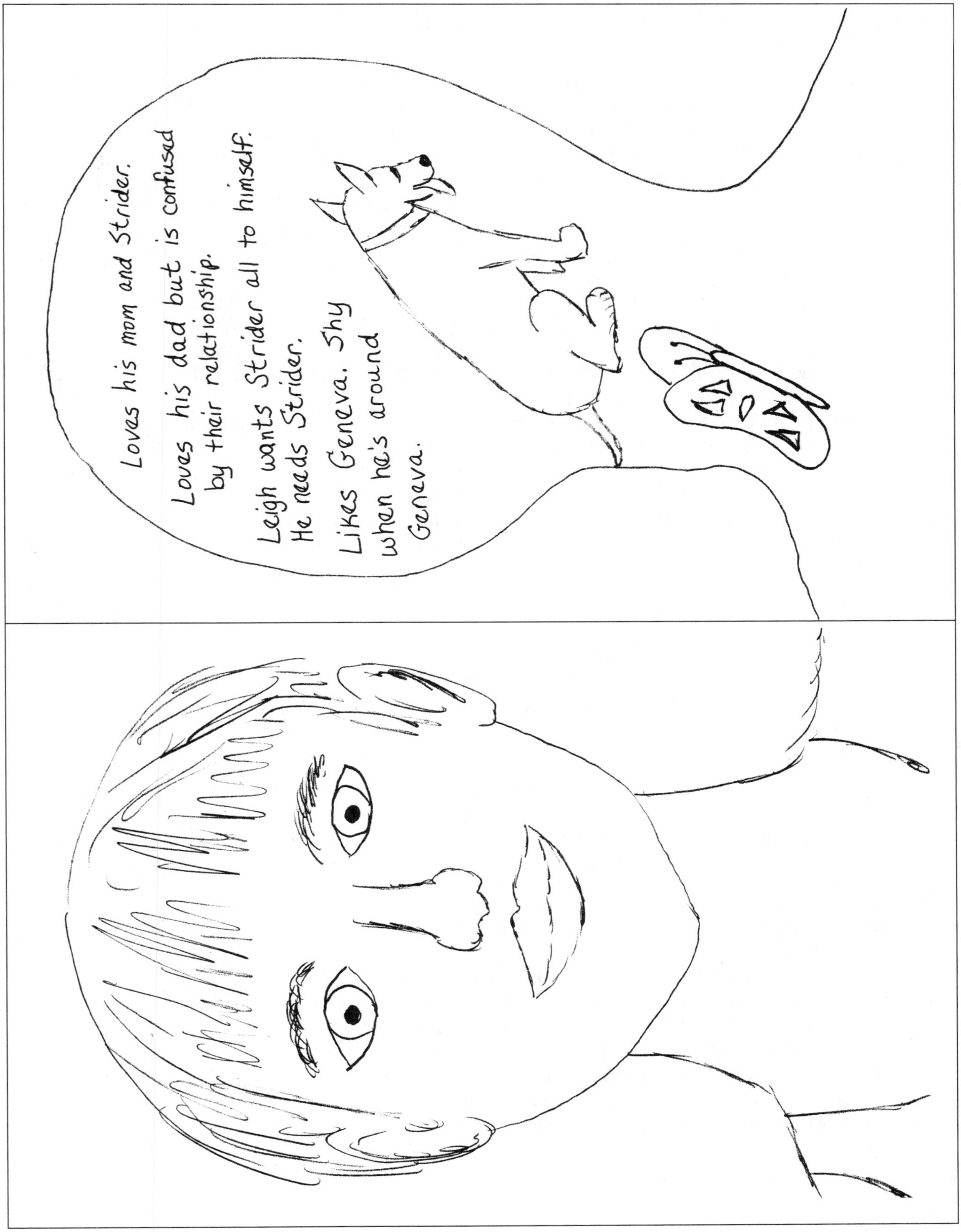
Loves his mom and Strider.
Loves his dad but is confused by their relationship.
Leigh wants Strider all to himself. He needs Strider.
Likes Geneva. Shy when he's around Geneva.

Practice and Reinforcement Activities

1. From a catalog, cut out the pictures and descriptions of various sets of articles (bikes, games, jewelry, clothes, and so on). Pass out the descriptions of one particular set of items (for example, bikes) to a group of students. Each student should have a different description of some similar item. Instruct students to read the description and to form a picture of the article in their minds. After they have fixed the description firmly in their minds, ask students to go to a table containing cutout pictures of similar articles. Their task is to match their picture of the item with the appropriate cutout picture.
2. Take advantage of what may be on your students' minds. For example, 10 minutes before lunch, have them read about food. Tear out food articles from magazines accompanied by pictures. Have students discuss their favorite menu selections from the assortment of articles. The rationale for this activity is that because students are hungry it will be easy for them to imagine food. Associating reading with their already-present pictures may help reinforce the habit of using mental pictures during reading.
3. Be prepared for unusual days by having an appropriate story or poem on hand. If it is a rainy, windy day, read your students a relevant story or poem. Try to take advantage of whatever may be on their minds by reinforcing it with a complementary reading passage. If a field trip is planned, be sure to read something related to the trip both before and after the excursion.
4. Use selected passages from literature to give students an opportunity to practice forming mental pictures. For example, *Charlotte's Web* (White, 1952) contains an excellent description of a barn, and *A Wrinkle in Time* (L'Engle, 1962) offers a rich description of a kitchen. Share with students parts of your reading that are appropriate for mental pictures. Here are two examples we have used with students (sources unknown).

   > *I allowed myself to walk out back yesterday afternoon when I returned to the farm. The air was warm and fragrant with the perfume of flowers, and I hoped that I wasn't too late to see the blooming of what Ozarkers call fire bush. All over these hills there are foundations of long-gone cabins—overgrown stone walls that show where families lived back in the days when the big timber was cut in this part of the country. Beside most of them, like the one at the back of my place, there are also flowers. Iris, bridal bush, and fire bush were planted, I think, by women who put them there to brighten their harsh homesteading lives.*
   >
   > *Early in the morning, after making a fire in the wood stove, I step outside my cabin while the bacon is frying to get a feel for the day in the darkness before dawn. There are no clouds in the sky, and the last stars are shining brightly. The day promises to be fair. It is too cool to have my breakfast outside and watch the sun rise, so I sit near the wood stove on an old rocking chair and watch the eastern sky through the large, inviting kitchen window.*

5. Have students draw pictures from the pictures they formed in their minds as you read. Students can talk about their pictures in small groups. You can also have students draw pictures of a scene from a book or story they have read recently.
6. Have students imagine that they are involved in a particular activity and describe it (e.g., reading a book in a comfortable location, flying a kite, swinging in the park).
7. Ask one student to leave the classroom. Ask the remaining students to describe the student in writing (clothes, physical attributes, interesting details like rings, and so on). When the student comes back into the classroom, the other students should compare their descriptions to the actual student.
8. Remember to have students use text-relevant illustrations along with mental pictures as complementary strategies.

Section **6.10**

Drawing Conclusions

Behavior Observed → **Anticipated Outcome**

The student has difficulty drawing conclusions after reading. → The student will draw conclusions about the text.

Background

Drawing conclusions and making inferences may be thought of as predicting outcomes and involves using material that is implicit or not directly stated in the text. This level of comprehension—interpretive—requires more reasoning skill on the part of the reader than factual recall. When a student draws a conclusion, the main idea, supporting details, and sequence of events in a passage often are used as the basis for the conclusion. A conclusion can be regarded as a reasoned deduction or inference. Although fine distinctions can be made between the two terms, teachers may assume that the terms describe students' attempts to infer a reasonable prediction of outcomes or conclusions based on the available information.

Strategy 1 SECTION 6.10

PREDICTING CONCLUSIONS

1. Explain to students that in much of their reading they are able to use the information presented to predict conclusions. Tell students that conclusions are based on what is stated in the story or text as well as what they already know.
2. Give students an opportunity to predict a conclusion after several facts are given. See the following example.

Fact 1: The sun did not shine on Saturday.
Fact 2: There were many clouds in the sky.
Fact 3: The grass, houses, roads, and sidewalks were wet.
Fact 4: Our picnic was canceled.

Then ask students to predict a conclusion or make an inference. Discuss the basis on which the conclusion or inference is made.

3. Present a series of events and several possible conclusions, as in the following example.

   Event: It snowed all night, and by Friday morning there was more than a foot of snow on the ground.

   Possible Outcomes: We went swimming in our outdoor pool.
   We shoveled the sidewalk and driveway.
   We didn't have school.
   We put the top down on our convertible.

   Be sure to discuss the reasons why some conclusions are more probable than others.

4. Give students part of a selection to read. At the end of the reading, have students consider the facts and events that have been presented in order to infer what will happen next. After listing the students' predictions on the chalkboard, read students the remainder of the selection and then discuss whether any of their predictions were right.

5. Help students realize that they draw conclusions based on the information they have gained by reading and from their own personal experiences that may relate to the passage they are reading.

Strategy 2 SECTION 6.10

PROBLEM-SOLUTION CHART

1. Duplicate and distribute copies of the Problem-Solution Chart that follows. You may also want to make a transparency of the chart to place on an overhead projector.

2. Present the class with a problem that needs to be solved. The problem could be one facing our country, your community, school, or classroom. It could also be a problem from a story the class is reading. For example, a problem facing your class might be that your class gerbil is not eating.

3. Write the problem on the chart in the section labeled *Problem.* Discuss the problem with students.

4. Tell students that you also want them to generate possible solutions to the problem. Guide students through a discussion of possible solutions. Have students vote on three of the most promising solutions. Record the solutions on the chart.

5. Divide the class into three groups. Have each group select one of the possible solutions. Ask group members to evaluate each possible solution by listing the pros and cons. (Explain the meanings of the words *pro* and *con* if necessary.)

6. Have groups share their evaluations of the solutions with the class. Have the class discuss each of the solutions and choose one solution for the problem.

7. Record the solution to the problem on the chart and give the reasons for the decision.

8. Tell students that when they read they are often faced with a problem with many possible solutions. Explain to students that to draw conclusions they need to entertain many potential ideas. Encourage students to think of many options as they draw conclusions during reading.

PROBLEM-SOLUTION CHART

Problem

Possible Solutions

1.

2.

3.

Pros	Cons

Pros	Cons

Pros	Cons

We chose ______________________________

because ______________________________.

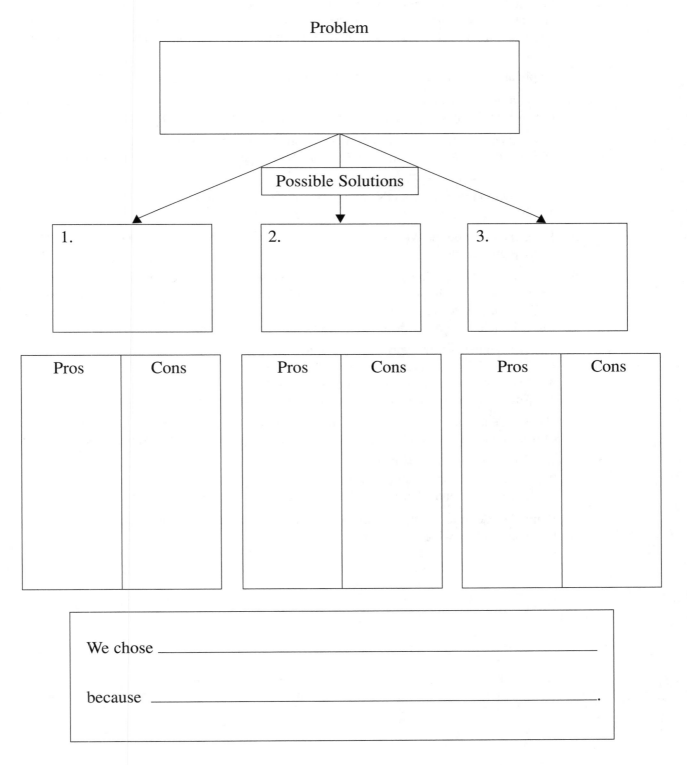

Strategy 3

CONCLUSION HIERARCHY

1. Tell students that they can draw conclusions from their reading by participating in a Conclusion Hierarchy (Barton & Sawyer, 2004). Explain to students that a Conclusion Hierarchy has students look for clues that answer an important question about the story they are reading.
2. Duplicate and distribute copies of the Conclusion Hierarchy on page 493 to students.
3. Select a story to read to students that you could use to demonstrate the Conclusion Hierarchy or use *Hey, Little Ant* (Hoose & Hoose, 1998). Read the story to students.
4. Ask students to think of an important question that could be answered by the story. Tell students that several questions could apply. Some questions for *Hey, Little Ant* follow.
   - Why do people step on ants?
   - Why did the boy's friends and family encourage him to kill the ant?
   - Was the ant persuasive in making the case to live?
5. Write the question that you want to answer on the appropriate line on the Conclusion Hierarchy reproducible.
6. Reread the story, having students identify clues that could answer their question. Look for clues at the beginning of the story, the middle, and the end. Remember to use pictures as well as the text for clues. Write the clues on the Conclusion Hierarchy reproducible. The following clues apply to the question Why do people step on ants?
   - The mother is frantically swatting at ants during a picnic.
   - The boy's friends are urging him to kill the ant.
   - The boy is annoyed by ants when he's outside.
   - The book shows how much bigger the boy is than the ant.
7. Have students answer the question using the clues that they found. Have students write some of these conclusions on the Conclusion Hierarchy reproducible. An example follows.
   - Ants are a nuisance at picnics.
   - It's culturally acceptable to kill ants.
   - The boy's friends don't think there's anything wrong with killing ants.
8. Remind students to use this strategy independently as they read by asking questions, looking for clues, and drawing conclusions.

CONCLUSION HIERARCHY

Name ______________________________ Date ______________

Important Question ______________________________

Beginning Clues ______________________________

Middle Clues ______________________________

Ending Clues ______________________________

Our Conclusion ______________________________

Adapted from Barton, J., & Sawyer, D.M. (2004). Our students *are* ready for this: Comprehension instruction in the elementary school. *The Reading Teacher*, *57*, 334–347.

Practice and Reinforcement Activities

1. Students who have difficulty seeing relationships may also have trouble drawing conclusions, making inferences, and predicting outcomes. These students often can be helped to see relationships through classification exercises. Present objects (concrete objects, pictures, or words) and have students identify the one that does not belong as well as explain why the others do belong. See the examples provided below.

bed	mountain	cow	black	book
table	river	robin	blue	pencil
apple	lake	horse	green	magazine
chair	ocean	pig	one	pamphlet

2. Provide reading materials at the students' instructional level and ask questions that encourage the students to use information in the passage to draw conclusions. Take time to discuss the basis for the conclusions that were drawn.
3. Provide questions for which students are asked to give logical conclusions. An example follows.

   What would happen if you—

   . . . didn't sleep for two days?

   . . . had to stay in bed for a week?

   . . . had a birthday every month?

   . . . ate a pound of candy?

   . . . crashed into a tree on your bicycle?

4. Give students brief passages where a conclusion must be drawn.

   Bill was reading about the sun, the moon, and Mars.
   It was a book about the ________________ (planets, solar system).

5. Provide pictures or illustrations and have students classify them under one or more of the following categories.

   Animals: Large, Small

   Sports: Football, Golf, Soccer

   Seasons: Summer, Fall, Winter, Spring

6. When students are reading a selection that lends itself to inference making, stop them at the appropriate point and ask them to write their predictions about what will happen next or how they think the story will end. Discuss their predictions, the basis for their judgment, and the supporting evidence in the story. Then let students read to the end of the story to see whether their predictions were right.
7. Provide students with pictures, illustrations, or verbal descriptions of events. Encourage them to list possible causes of the event and then select those that seem most appropriate. Sample events are listed below.

   - a soccer player being congratulated near the opponent's goal
   - a child who has just blown out the candles on a cake
   - a boy and girl with sad expressions on their faces looking out their front window and seeing that it's raining
   - a patient sitting in a doctor's office

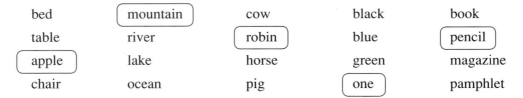

8. Provide sentences where students use the information given to answer a question. Stress that the answer isn't stated, so students must infer it. Discuss students' answers.

   - At recess the students got their gloves, bats, and balls. What were they likely to do?
   - During a very severe storm, the electricity went off. My grandfather lit a match. What did he probably want to find?
   - Maria had a day off school. She looked in the newspaper to find the best sales. Then she left the house. Where did she probably go?

   A variation of this activity is to provide possible answers and have students select the best one.

   - Jesse and his cousin went walking on a warm spring day. There was a nice breeze in the air. What might Jesse and his cousin do to have fun?

     __________ rake leaves   __________ fly a kite   __________ watch TV

   Be sure to discuss students' answers and their reasons for choosing them.

Resources

6

Note: indicates teacher material.

Using Multiple Intelligences

As you provide students with strategies to elaborate on text, you need to keep in mind that not all students think in the same ways. Each of us has preferred ways of thinking. Gardner (1993) has identified eight types of thinking which he calls intelligences. As you ask students to process text, try to give them a variety of options. You may have a strong verbal/linguistic intelligence and give assignments that fit that strength; your students may have other strengths. It is important, therefore, that you vary the types of activities you ask your students to accomplish. A general description for the intelligences follows (Eanes, 1997).

Learners with strong **verbal/linguistic** intelligence often:

- enjoy reading, writing, and speaking.
- enjoy research and report writing.
- recall names, places, dates, and details.
- prefer typing to writing.
- like books, periodicals, and recordings.
- enjoy storytelling and oral reading to share stories.
- enjoy creative writing, poetry, and joke telling.

Learners with strong **logical/mathematical** intelligence often:

- have good problem-solving and reasoning skills.
- like to formulate and answer logical questions.
- enjoy sorting, categorizing, and classifying.
- like to explore and analyze.
- like puzzles, mysteries, and riddles.
- like technology.
- are strong in math.

Learners with strong **visual/spatial** intelligence often:

- need visuals to understand new concepts.
- use a great deal of mental imagery.
- like to make and read maps, charts, and diagrams.
- enjoy mazes and puzzles.
- have a strong imagination.
- are good at designing, drawing, creating, and constructing.
- enjoy videos, photographs, slides, and multimedia.
- enjoy giving media presentations.

Learners with strong **body/kinesthetic** intelligence often:

- are good at physical activities.
- like to move around.
- like to touch things.
- use lots of gestures for communicating.
- enjoy hands-on learning.
- like to communicate through drama, dance, and movement.

Learners with strong **musical/rhythmic** intelligence often:

- enjoy listening and responding to music.
- recall melodies easily.
- notice things like pitch and rhythm.
- are highly aware of sounds in the environment.
- are fascinated by computerized sound systems.
- learn better while listening to certain types of music.
- love stories about music.

Learners with strong **interpersonal** intelligence often:

- have strong leadership skills.
- are very sociable and have good interpersonal skills.
- are good at organizing people.
- are good communicators.
- are good mediators and listeners.
- solve problems by talking through them.
- like discussion.
- enjoy interviewing and debating.
- learn best by talking to others.
- enjoy cooperative learning.

Learners with strong **intrapersonal** intelligence often:

- have a strong sense of self.
- are very self-confident.
- prefer working alone.
- have good instincts about strengths and abilities.
- pursue interests, dreams, and goals.
- seek help to pursue or achieve goals.
- like independent research projects.
- like cumulative writing projects.
- like to sit quietly.

Learners with strong **naturalistic** intelligence often:

- enjoy learning from nature.
- notice naturally occurring patterns.
- like ecological issues.
- analyze natural situations.
- work in natural settings.
- learn from living things.

Elaborative Strategies Using the Multiple Intelligences

As you prepare reading instruction for your students, try to provide a variety of strategies that will appeal to students who have different strengths. You might want to vary your assignments over several weeks, or give students a choice of assignments. The following ideas would be appropriate for each of the eight different intelligences. Additional ideas are presented by Freed and Moon (1999).

Verbal/Linguistic Intelligence

1. Tell or retell the story.
2. Respond to the story by drawing or writing.
3. Read related stories.
4. Write a story to go with a wordless picture book.
5. Model a new story on the one just read.
6. Create a compare/contrast chart with another story by the same author.
7. Write a script for Readers' Theater.
8. Read with a partner, emphasizing fluency and expression.
9. Read along with recorded text.

Logical/Mathematical Intelligence

1. Sort objects related to the story.
2. Measure or graph distances related to the story.
3. Make a matrix using the characters in the story.
4. Create a map showing the setting.
5. Discuss the character's motivations and decide whether they are reasonable.
6. Plan an itinerary for places a character visited.

Visual/Spatial Intelligence

1. Visualize your favorite part of the story and draw it.
2. Design a cover for the book.
3. Recreate several illustrations.
4. Make a newspaper, magazine, or video ad for the story.
5. Imagine you are part of the plot and draw an image that portrays how you are feeling.
6. Use hand gestures to help emphasize expression.

(continued)

ELABORATIVE STRATEGIES USING THE MULTIPLE INTELLIGENCES *(continued)*

Body/Kinesthetic Intelligence

1. Role play the story.
2. Create a puppet show for the story.
3. Have a special day relating to the book. Dress like the characters.
4. Act out a sequence of events from the plot.
5. Invent a game from the story.

Musical/Rhythmic Intelligence

1. Write a jingle or rap having to do with something in the story.
2. During a shared reading, create actions to fit the plot.
3. Sing a song related to the story and add verses that fit the plot.
4. Put words relating to the story to an existing tune.
5. March in a parade while singing a song related to the story.

Interpersonal Intelligence

1. In groups, design something relating to a character in the story.
2. Work with a partner and write a different version of the story.
3. In literature groups, discuss the plot, setting, character, and problem for the story.
4. Discuss the problem of the story and decide in groups how to solve the problem in ways the character did not use.
5. Discuss a character in the story and try to convince group members that the character would or would not be a good friend to have.

Intrapersonal Intelligence

1. Have students write down all they want to know about the topic of the story.
2. Designate a day for students to wear or bring something related to the story.
3. Ask students to tell about something similar that happened to them.
4. Write about how students would feel and what they would do if they were a character in the story.
5. Ask students to write their memories of an event from the story as a diary entry.

Naturalistic Intelligence

1. Have students read about the natural environment.
2. Take students outside for silent reading.
3. Use examples from nature for word study.
4. Discuss ecological issues from books or novels.
5. Write class stories using settings in the natural world.

CHAPTER SEVEN

Comprehension Strategies

© 2010 JupiterImages Corporation.

Overview

Readers who achieve a deep comprehension of text apply a variety of strategies as they construct meaning. First, active readers use their knowledge of organization of texts to identify relationships between ideas. Fictional texts are organized in different ways from informational texts. Readers who want to expand their ability to understand texts will apply what they know about text organization as they construct meaning from the text. Good readers also are able to monitor their comprehension, interpret charts and graphs, summarize as they read, make connections while reading, process text after reading, evaluate the ideas in the text, and remember what was read. All of these strategies help readers comprehend text (Almasi, 2003).

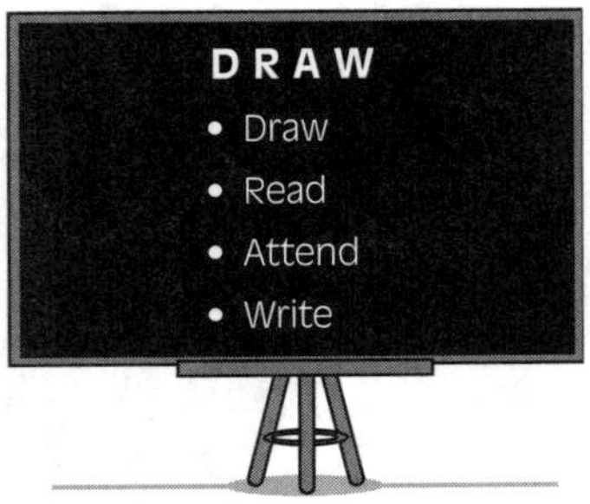

Many factors influence the use of strategies. Some factors include the teacher's theory of learning, the teacher's theory of the student, the student's response history, and the demands of the text (Lenski & Nierstheimer, 2004). Choosing which of the strategies to teach students is the first step. Let's say your students are having difficulty remembering what they have read. You might choose the strategy DRAW (Agnew, 2000). To teach students how to use DRAW, you should first model the strategy. After modeling, provide students with opportunities to use the strategy with support. After students have several experiences with DRAW, you can expect them to use their mental processes to remember what they have read. Students need to see how strategies are applied, and modeling gives them a verbal picture of the processes that occur in the mind.

> The goal of teaching comprehension strategies is to have students become self-regulated readers.

Teaching comprehension strategies tends to help students become better comprehenders. However, the modeling of teaching strategies is just the beginning. The goal of teaching comprehension strategies is to have students become self-regulated readers (Pressley, 2000). Self-regulated readers have a repertoire of skills and strategies that they use flexibly and appropriately as they approach printed materials. Therefore, it's also important that you give students the feeling of ownership when teaching comprehension strategies. Students need to understand that these strategies must have a prominent place in their reading routines (Trabasso & Bouchard, 2002).

Another way for students to improve comprehension is to make sure they read a lot. You can teach reading strategies every day, but if students do not have an opportunity to apply them independently, they will not incorporate them into their own reading repertoire. The research base for independent reading seems to indicate that just giving students books to read without any teacher guidance is not helping enough of your struggling readers. However, Lanier and Lenski (2008) found that when you give students access to books, match books with student's interests and abilities, and monitor their progress during independent reading, many students experience reading growth.

Helping students expand comprehension is challenging. The teaching of the strategies and the use of the activities provided in this chapter will help students become better comprehenders of text.

Section 7.1

Understanding Fictional Text Structure

Behavior Observed → **Anticipated Outcome**

The student does not understand how fictional texts are organized. → The student will apply knowledge of fictional text structure during studying.

Background

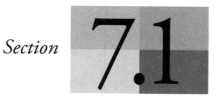

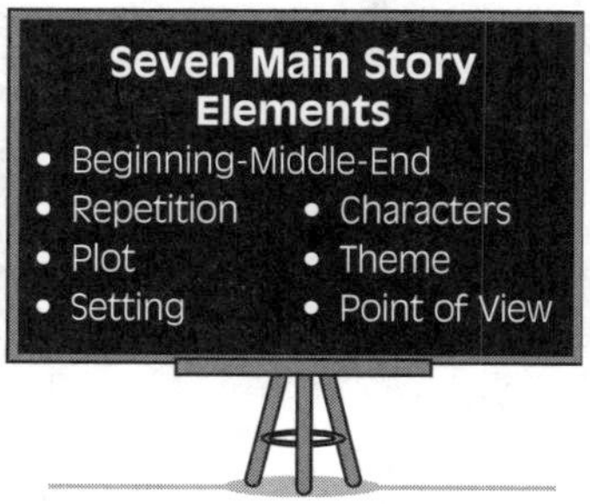
Seven Main Story Elements
• Beginning-Middle-End
• Repetition
• Plot
• Setting
• Characters
• Theme
• Point of View

Texts are written in a variety of organizational patterns, depending on the author's purpose. Authors may write a fictional story that is narrative (a sequence of events leading to a solution of a problem). Readers who can identify the elements in narrative text and who can discern the organizational pattern in expository text will have an easier time comprehending the selection and studying it.

When you teach text structure, first review the information yourself. Then model how you identify text organization and help students recognize organizational patterns. Finally, ask students to write text with different organizational structures. Only after students have had instruction and practice with different text structures can you expect students to use text structure as a tool for comprehension.

Narrative text is a more formal name for a story. Stories have seven main elements: beginning-middle-end, repetition, plot, setting, characters, theme, and point of view (Tompkins, 2001).

- **Beginning-middle-end.** All stories have a beginning, a middle, and an end. Often the beginning contains information about the characters and the setting. A problem or a conflict is also introduced in the beginning. In the middle of the story, events are described that advance the conflict until it is finally resolved at the end of the story.
- **Repetition.** Repetition is a writing device to make stories more interesting. Books for young children often use repetition to advance the plot. See Part C on the CD for a list of pattern books.
- **Plot.** The plot is the sequence of events that happen in the story. The characters in the story have a conflict (problem), and that conflict is explained by a series of events. The plot includes all of the events that take the characters through the conflict to the resolution.

- **Setting.** The setting is the story's time and place. The time may be past, present, or future. The setting can be real or imaginary.
- **Characters.** The characters are the people or animals in the story.
- **Theme.** The theme is the main point of the story, the idea the author wants to get across to the reader.
- **Point of View.** Stories are written from various points of view. Two common points of view authors use are first person and the omniscient. First-person viewpoint tells the story through the eyes of the author. In the omniscient viewpoint, the author knows everything about the characters and action.

Strategy 1 SECTION 7.1

STORY MAP

1. Tell students that they can map the events in pieces of fiction by completing a story map. Explain that a Story Map is an outline of the elements of the story. Tell students that when they map a story they are identifying key elements of the story.
2. Review the elements of fiction with students if necessary. Remind students of the definitions of the terms *title, setting, characters, problem, events,* and *solution.*
3. Select a piece of literature that clearly illustrates the elements of fiction. Read the selection with students or have students read the story independently.
4. Divide the class into groups of three or four students. Ask students to identify fictional elements: *title, setting, characters, problem, events,* and *solution.*
5. Select one of the Story Maps reproduced in Chapter 7 Resources (pages 586–589) that best fits the events of the story.
6. Duplicate and distribute the Story Map that you have selected.
7. Model for students how to complete the Story Map by filling in the sections listed on the map. Tell students that the map you have selected for this story may be used for different information from other stories.
8. Have students independently complete the Story Map for the piece of literature you have selected.
9. Use other types of Story Maps as you reinforce the organizational pattern of fictional text. Model how to use each map before having students complete it.

Strategy 2 SECTION 7.1

STORY FRAMES

1. Select a Story Frame from the Chapter 7 Resources (pages 590–592) in this chapter that fits a piece of literature students have read.
2. Duplicate and distribute the Story Frame. Make a transparency of the Story Frame to use on an overhead projector.
3. Read the Story Frame with students. Tell students that they can learn about the organizational pattern of fiction by focusing on a specific story element.
4. Divide the class into groups of three or four students. Tell them the title of the Story Frame and have them brainstorm ideas that they think will apply.

5. After students have discussed ideas, have them complete the story frame independently.
6. Use other Story Frames when you want students to think about specific elements of fiction. Model how to use each Story Frame before students complete it.

Strategy 3 SECTION 7.1

STORY PYRAMID

1. Select a fictional story that has a clear plot outline. Read the story to students or have them read it independently.
2. Divide the class into groups of three or four students. Have students identify a character, the setting, and the events in the story.
3. Duplicate and distribute the blank Story Pyramid on page 507. Make a transparency copy to use on an overhead projector.
4. Tell students to think of one word that names a character in the story. Have them write the name of that character on the first line.
5. Then have students think of two words that describe the setting. Tell students that they must use two words, no more and no fewer. Ask students to write the two words on the next two lines.
6. Complete the directions on the Story Pyramid by having students write three words that describe the character, four words in a sentence that describe one event, and five words in a sentence that describe another event.
7. After students have completed the Story Pyramid, have them share their work with class-mates.
8. Modify the Story Pyramid by adding additional lines and have students write six words describing the resolution and seven words that describe the theme.
9. Duplicate additional copies of the Story Pyramid (page 507) for students to use after reading fictional texts.
10. A sample Story Pyramid can be found on the next page.

STORY PYRAMID

1. Phoebe
2. Confused, guilty
3. Present, small, town
4. Mick's sudden unexpected death
5. The fight over a tattoo
6. Zoe says Mick can be everywhere.
7. Phoebe speaks at the assembly about Mick.
8. Phoebe writes **Mick Harte Was Here** in cement.
9. Phoebe realizes that Mick's accident was no one's fault.

Directions:

1. Name of the main character
2. Two words describing the main character
3. Three words describing the setting
4. Four words stating the problem
5. Five words describing one event
6. Six words describing a second event
7. Seven words describing a third event
8. Eight words describing a final event
9. Nine words stating the solution to the problem

Based on Park, B. (1996). *Mick Harte Was Here.* New York: Scholastic.

STORY PYRAMID

Name ______________________________ Date ______________

Directions:

1. Insert 1 word that names a character.
2. Insert 2 words that describe a character.
3. Insert 3 words that describe the setting.
4. Insert 4 words in a sentence that describe the problem.
5. Insert 5 words in a sentence that describe one event.

You can also adapt the Story Pyramid by adding more lines such as the resolution or conclusion.

1. __________

2. __________ __________

3. __________ __________ __________

4. __________ __________ __________ __________

5. __________ __________ __________ __________ __________

Strategy 4

ZIGZAG THE STORY

1. Tell students that they will be learning a new way to identify text structure through Zigzagging the Story (Wisendanger, 2001). Remind students that they may have used a variety of graphic organizers to identify story elements and that this is a different kind of graphic organizer.
2. Write the term *zigzag* on the chalkboard. Have students pronounce the word with you while you move your finger under the word. Point out the letter *z* in the word and tell students that very few words in the English language have two *z*'s.
3. Draw several zigzags on the chalkboard of various lengths and widths as in the example that follows. Explain to students that you are moving the chalk first one way and then changing directions and moving a different way. Have students practice drawing zigzags on paper.

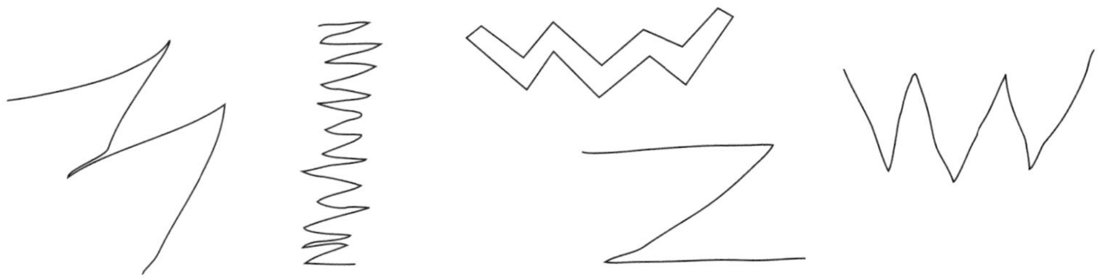

4. Tell students that you will be listing or illustrating story elements using the zigzag graphic. Erase the drawings of the various zigzags. If students are familiar with the terms plot, setting, conflict, resolution, and theme, draw a zigzag with five lines of equal length. If you have not taught one of these terms, draw a zigzag with the number of lines corresponding to the number of terms you have taught. List the terms under the lines as in the following example.

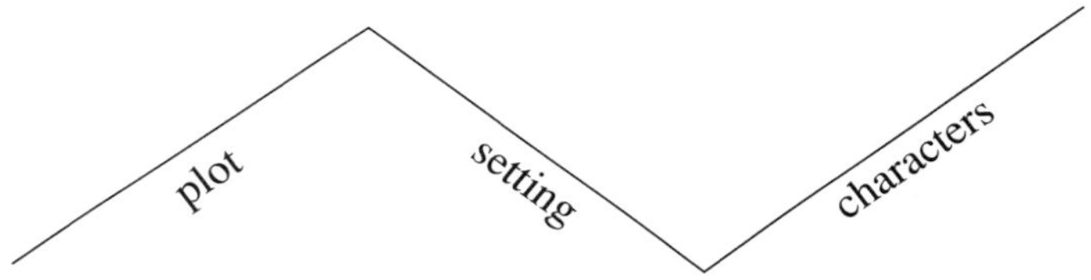

5. Select a story that students already know. Tell students that they will be thinking about story elements and use them to Zigzag the Story as in the example that follows.

> *We all know the story of the* Three Little Pigs. *Let's think about the setting of the story. Remember the setting is the time and place.* [Answers could include in the country and present time.] *List the time and place on the line that says setting. If you want to illustrate the terms, you may. Then think about the plot. Let's state the plot in just a few words.* [Answer: three pigs outsmart a wolf who is trying to eat them.] *Write the plot on the next line. Now we need to think about the conflict. Remember the conflict of a story is the idea that moves the plot forward and is often between the characters. The conflict in this story is that the wolf wants to eat one of the pigs. Write or draw that on the line above the term conflict. Next, we need to think about the resolution. The resolution is how the plot ends. In this case the*

wolf falls into a pot of boiling water. Write or draw that on the line about the term resolution. Finally, we need to think about the theme of the story. What lesson does the story teach us? [Answers could include being prepared, helping your friends, and so on.] *Write or draw your idea of the theme on the final line.*

6. After students have successfully Zigzagged the Story, have them share their work with a classmate. Tell students that some of their answers may be the same and that others may be different.
7. Provide students with the option of Zigzagging the Story when you have them identify story elements. Tell students that some of them will like this strategy and others will prefer different types of graphic organizers for identifying story elements.
8. Check students' work for accuracy. If students have missed some of the basic ideas from the story, have them revise their work. Post students' finished zigzags on a bulletin board.

Practice and Reinforcement Activities

1. Encourage students to read widely. Provide a classroom library with books and stories representing a variety of genres and levels.
2. When planning stories, have students draw storyboards to show the major story elements. For example, students can draw the main character, the setting, the problem situation, important events, and the solution. Older students can write phrases and details on their storyboards to prepare for writing the story. Once students have prepared their storyboards, they can tell their story to a partner to confirm effective use of story elements, clarity, and details. Students can then write a draft of their story.
3. Prepare a set of cards that contain information about story elements. Have students tell a story using the elements presented on the cards. Encourage them to add details and consider the sequence of events. Students can then write stories using the story line they have created from the cards. To show students how story elements are related to each other within a story, substitute one of the cards. Ask students how the story will be changed. Sample story element cards are shown below.

Setting: A small town in the United States	**Main Character:** A shy, quiet boy named Billy
Problem: Billy's best friend has moved away, and Billy is very lonely.	**Solution:** Billy learns he has a special talent that helps him make new friends.

4. Use wordless picture books to help students "read" pictures to discover the story line and identify the main story elements. Wordless books with clear, familiar patterns and story lines such as *Deep in the Forest* (Turkle, 1976), a modification of the "Three Little Bears," work well with younger or struggling students. After identifying the elements, younger students may dictate the story. Older students may write their own stories based on the pictures. Students can then analyze their stories and their peers' stories to determine if major story elements are present and used effectively in the story. A list of wordless picture books is provided in Part A on the CD.
5. Ask students to retell a story, emphasizing one of the story elements. You may choose a story that you have read to the entire class or one that students have read independently.

6. Ask students to dramatize stories with puppets or by acting out a play. They may want to focus on making the characters believable, on making the setting realistic, or on any combination of story elements.
7. Have students compare the beginning, middle, and end of different versions of the same story. Fairy tales are especially appropriate.
8. Some students learn how stories are organized by drawing class murals (McKenzie & Danielson, 2003). Mural lessons help students see how the various elements of the story are connected and how these connections make up a plot. To develop a mural lesson, first determine the type of story organization. If the story is an orderly sequence of events, draw a road. As students read the story, have them draw the events in order down the road. If the story is a cycle, draw a circle and have students draw the events around the perimeter of the circle. If the story is neither a sequence of events nor a cycle, consider drawing a scene. Draw the elements of the story around a central topic and add details as the story unfolds. Students find that mural lessons help them understand and remember the content of the story as well as the story's organization.
9. Students who struggle with reading may benefit from a story outline as they try to remember the plot of a story (Arthaud & Goracke, 2006). A story outline provides students with the basic story written with important words left out. Prepare a story outline that is easy enough for students to complete independently. For example, you could write the following sentence for *Sarah, Plain and Tall* (MacLachlan, 1987).

    Sarah tells Anna that she enjoys ______________________, ______________________,

    and ______________________.

    Sarah said that she would come for ______________________ months.

    After students have read the story, have them read the story outline independently and try to complete the sentences. If students have difficulty, give them a list of words to use. After students have completed the story outline, have them read it orally so that they can have a better understanding of the plot.

Section 7.2

Understanding Informational Text Structure

Behavior Observed → **Anticipated Outcome**

The student does not understand how informational texts are organized. → The student will learn how informational texts are organized.

Background

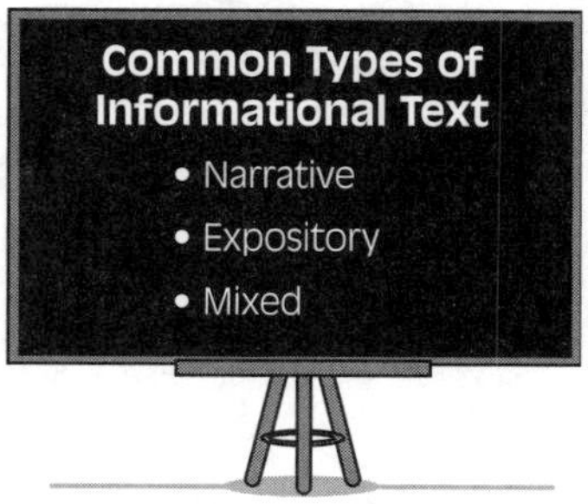
Common Types of Informational Text
• Narrative
• Expository
• Mixed

Informational texts are sometimes confused with expository texts. Informational texts, however, can be narrative, expository, or a combination (Kletzien & Dreher, 2004). The common types of informational texts are narrative-informational text, expository-informational text, and mixed texts. Narrative-informational texts are texts that are in story format, such as biographies and autobiographies. There are also many other examples of stories whose primary purpose is to share information, which they do through story. A second type of informational text is expository-informational which are the kinds of books often thought of when the term "informational text" is used. These books inform readers through expository text structures such as compare-contrast, problem-solution, and cause-effect. Many of the books about animals, places, and events are expository-informational texts. The third type of text is the mixed text, those texts that combine expository and informational material such as *Magic School Bus* books.

Informational texts have not been used very often in primary-grade classrooms. Duke (2000) found, for example, that primary teachers average approximately 3.6 minutes per day teaching from informational texts, and Moss (2003) found that middle-grade boys enjoyed reading informational texts. Duke, Bennett-Armistead, and Roberts (2002) believe that students can increase their motivation to read and can improve reading comprehension by reading a mixture of narrative and informational texts. This makes sense when you remember that many tests have both types of passages included in them. Beyond testing, however, students will have more opportunities to read informational texts as older students and adults than narrative texts. Older students typically spend more time reading textbooks, which are informational texts, than they do stories. Many adults find themselves reading manuals, directions, websites, and other informational texts frequently. Therefore, teachers should spend more time teaching students how to read informational texts (Fisher, Frey, & Lapp, 2009).

Strategy 1

GRAPHIC ORGANIZERS

1. Tell students that there are five types of informational organizational patterns: description, sequence, comparison, cause-effect, and problem-solution. Explain to students that knowing the types of informational organizational patterns can help them comprehend texts better.
2. Duplicate and distribute the Graphic Organizers that follow. Tell students that the Graphic Organizer depicts how information could be organized in informational texts.
3. Have students read the descriptions of the organizational patterns that accompany the Graphic Organizers. Help them note the differences between the types of informational writing patterns.
4. Locate five short passages that fit the five types of organizational patterns. Divide the class into groups of three or four students. Have students match the passages with the text organizations.
5. Encourage students to think about how texts are organized as they read. Refer, as appropriate, to a particular Graphic Organizer when it is demonstrated in a particular informational text.

   Description. The author of descriptive writing lists characteristics, features, and examples to describe a subject. Clue words for description include *for example* and *characteristics*. To map a descriptive passage, you might use the following Graphic Organizer.

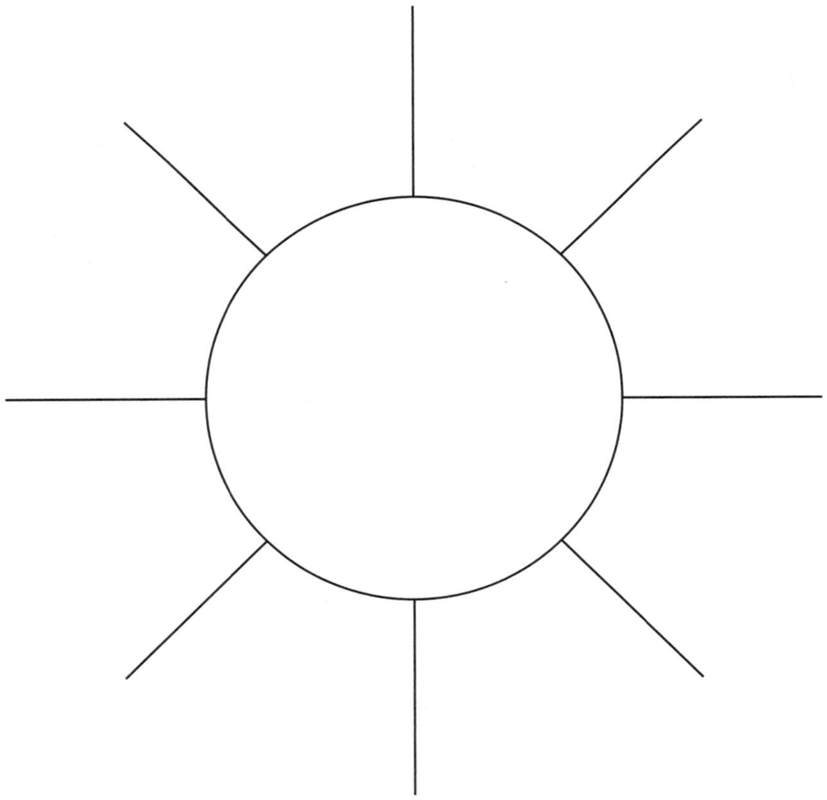

Sequence. Writers who use sequence in a text list events in chronological or numerical order. Some clue words are *first, second, third* or *next, then,* and *finally.* To map a sequential passage, you might use the following Graphic Organizer.

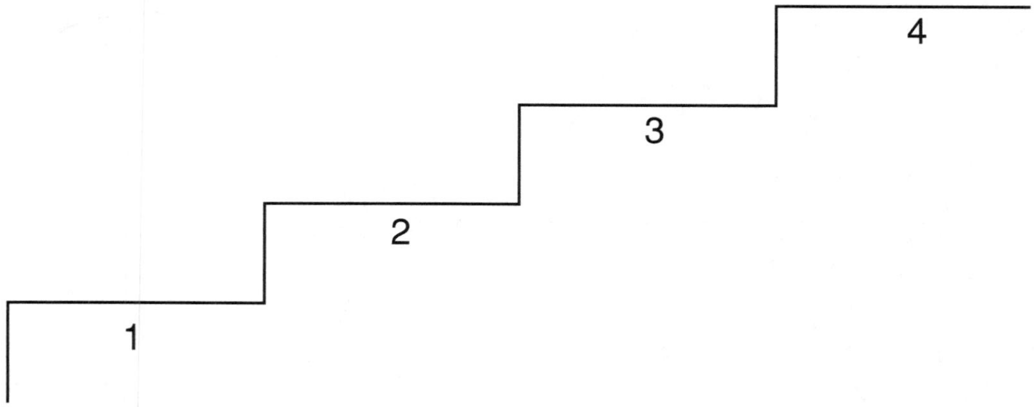

Comparison. In comparison text, the writer is explaining how things are alike or different. Clue words include *different, in contrast, alike, same as,* or *on the other hand.* The following Graphic Organizer best depicts a comparison passage.

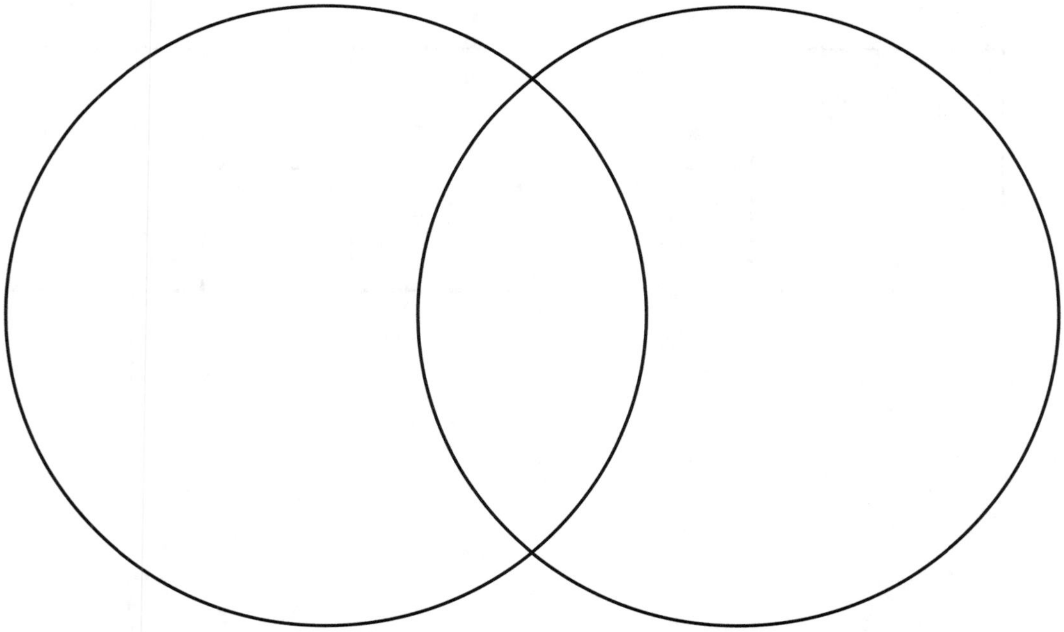

Cause and Effect. The author describes a cause and the resulting effect. Clue words are *reasons why, if . . . then, as a result, therefore,* and *because*. The following is the most common Graphic Organizer used in cause and effect writing.

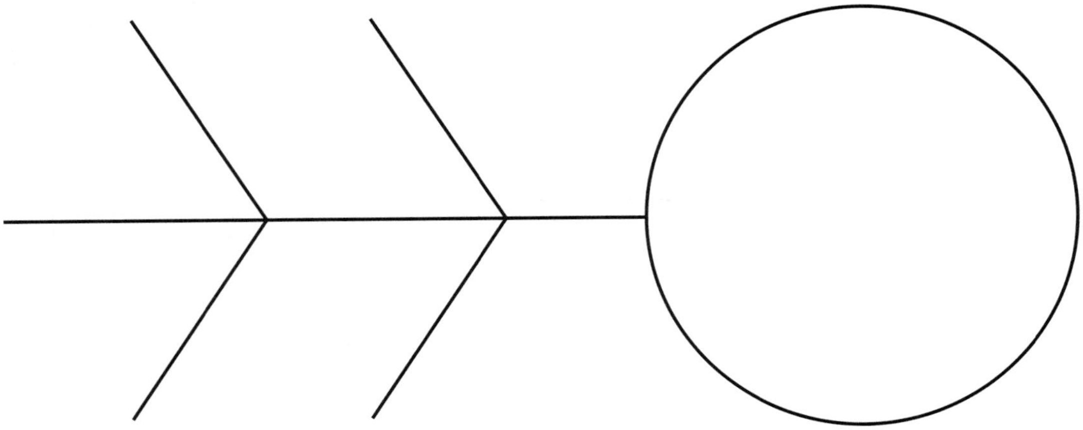

Problem and Solution. The author describes a problem and lists solutions for that problem. Some clue words are *the problem is, the dilemma is,* and *solved.* A Graphic Organizer used for problem and solution texts follows.

Strategy 2 SECTION 7.2

PROBABLE PASSAGES

1. For Probable Passages (Wood, 1984), select an informational text that students have not yet read. Identify the text organizational pattern.
2. Locate words in the passage that are important for text comprehension. Write the words on the chalkboard under their text categories. An example using a problem/solution text follows.

Problem	→	Solution
scurvy		nutrients
beriberi		diet
pellagra		carbohydrates
disease		vitamins
		minerals
		balanced diet
		thiamine
		niacin

3. Explain how the terms are used and what the problem and solution mean in this situation. Then ask students to write a Probable Passage, or a passage that makes sense, that contains the text structure and the identified words.
4. After students have completed their Probable Passage, have them read the original text.
5. After students have read the text, have them edit their own passage to reflect missing or contradictory information they learned from the passage.

Strategy 3 SECTION 7.2

IDEA-MAPPING

1. To use Idea-Mapping (Armbruster, 1986), select a passage that you want students to read. Determine the organizational pattern of the text. Select the appropriate Idea-Map for the text. Examples of Idea-Maps can be found in the Chapter 7 Resources (pages 593–596).
2. Tell students that you will be demonstrating how to use a strategy called Idea-Maps to help them understand how informational texts are organized.
3. Explain that there are five main patterns for organizing informational texts: description, sequence, comparison, cause-effect, and problem-solution. Write these words on the chalkboard or an overhead transparency.
4. Model the Idea-Map strategy using the following example. You might find it useful to make a transparency of the example to show students.

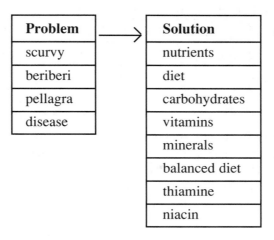

Topic: **Moving Ice Changes the Land**
Details:
Glaciers are snow piles that melt and refreeze.
Glaciers become mounds of ice.
Rocks become frozen to the bottom of the ice.
Weight of ice makes glaciers move.
Rocks on the bottom of the glacier cut into other rocks.
Glaciers can pick up rocks and carry them away.
Main Idea: **A glacier is a sheet of moving ice.**

5. Have students identify the main points of other passages using the appropriate Idea-Map. You may need to identify the text structure for your students initially and provide them with the appropriate Idea-Map to use as they read. After students have used Idea-Maps for a while, they should be able to identify the structure of each text themselves.

Strategy 4 SECTION 7.2

EXPOSITORY TEXT INVESTIGATION (ETI)

1. Students can learn about the structure of texts by using the Expository Text Investigation (ETI) (Kelly & Clausen-Grace, 2007).
2. Tell students that there are a variety of ways that writers organize information in nonfiction texts. Show students an example of an alphabet book such as *B is for Beaver: An Oregon Alphabet* (Smith & Smith, 2002). (Alphabet books are available for many states.) Show students the inside cover of the book and a sample page to demonstrate how the texts are organized. Explain that these authors have written a short poem that illustrates each letter of the alphabet and also some text to describe it. Discuss the characteristics of the book.
3. Reproduce and distribute copies of the Expository Text Investigation (ETI) chart on page 518. Have students write the title of the book in the left-hand column. In the middle column have students list the structure or genre of the book. In the right-hand column, have students write characteristics of that type of text as in the example that follows.

Title of Book	Structure/Genre	Characteristics
B is for Beaver	ABC book	The book has a page for every letter of the alphabet. Each page has a picture on it, a poem, and a longer explanation.

4. After students understand how to use the ETI, select a variety of informational materials and place them on a large table. Some materials you might choose are in the list that follows.

- Question-and-answer books
- Textbooks
- Encyclopedias
- Newspapers

- Magazines
- Brochures
- Invitations
- Menus
- Alphabet books

5. Have students work in small groups or independently to complete the ETI. Have each group of students select four or five books. Ask students to think of the materials by their structure or genre as they complete the ETI chart.
6. Tell students that knowing how texts are organized can help them become better comprehenders by saying the following.

   Understanding how a book is organized can help you become a better reader. When you look at a brochure, for example, you know to look for information, and you know that information will be divided into sections. You can read the different sections looking for main ideas and details. When you are reading a newspaper, you'll also be looking for sections to read. You'll have headlines to help you figure out what to read. Knowing about the different kinds of texts helps you know how to read it.

7. Remind students to ask themselves about the structure or genre of informational materials as they read independently.

EXPOSITORY TEXT INVESTIGATION (ETI)

Name ______________________________ Date ______________

Directions: List the title of the text in the left-hand column. In the center column, list the type of text it is, and in the right-hand column explain the characteristics of the book.

Title of Book	*Structure/Genre*	*Characteristics*

TEXT FEATURE CHART

1. Students can understand how to read informational text more easily if they can use the text features to guide them. Tell students that informational texts often have features that are not found in fiction.
2. Select a text that has several of the features commonly found in informational texts. Some of the features that you should look for are on the following list.
   - Boldface text
   - Italics
   - Unusual spacing
   - Titles and subtitles
   - Charts and graphs
   - Inserts
   - Captions
3. Write two or three of the names of text features on the chalkboard. For example, you might select *boldface text*, *italics*, and *subtitles*. Define each of these terms for students and then show them examples in the text.
4. When students indicate that they know the definitions of the texts, provide them with a Text Feature Chart and a text.

Text Feature	Where in book	Explain the importance

5. Tell students to look through the book, looking for text features. When students find a feature that is familiar to them, have them write the text feature in the left-hand column. Then have students list where they found the feature in the book. Ask students to be specific by putting the page number if they can and to also give additional information. In the right-hand column, have students write a short reason why this text feature can help them as they read the text.

Text Feature	Where in book	Explain the importance
Title and subtitles	At beginning of chapters and all through the book	The titles and subtitles let me know the topic that will be explained.
Words in italics	Several words in each chapter	These words are new to me and have a definition in the glossary.

6. A Text Feature Chart reproducible can be found on the following page.

TEXT FEATURE CHART

Name ______________________________ Date ______________

Directions: List the names of the text features in the left-hand column. Write where in the book you found the text feature in the middle column. In the right-hand column, explain why this text feature is important and how it can help you be a better reader.

The text features you should look for are listed below.

Text Feature	*Where in book*	*Explain its importance*

Practice and Reinforcement Activities

1. Have students write text passages using the different organizational patterns of informational text.
2. Have students work in groups to find out the text structure of a selected passage. Ask them to underline words or phrases that give them clues about the pattern.
3. Give students a blank Graphic Organizer and ask them to organize other information they know into the same pattern. Then ask them to write a passage similar to the passage they had read.
4. Have students diagram a passage using the Graphic Organizer suggested for the specific text pattern. A partial example from a passage on gold follows.

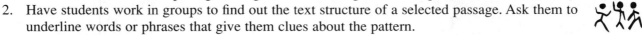

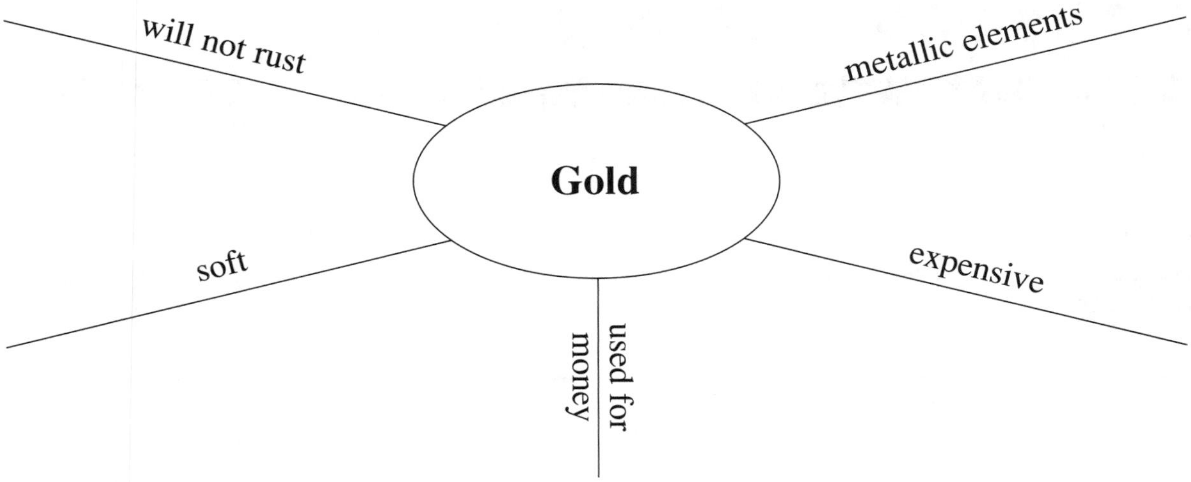

5. Many teachers do not have enough informational books in their classrooms to teach text structure. Teachers in one state solved this problem by creating Traveling Literacy Trunks (Fromherz, 2003). A Traveling Literacy Trunk is a group of materials in a box or suitcase that teachers from different schools can use. Traveling Literacy Trunks are usually housed in a common location such as a university or a regional office and are loaned out to teachers for a predetermined amount of time. Traveling Literacy Trunks also contain teaching materials as well as books so that teachers can benefit from the ideas of their colleagues. Traveling Literacy Trunks are ideal for housing informational texts.
6. One way to help students understand how informational texts are organized is for students to participate in a text retelling (Moss, 2004). Retelling texts is different from summarizing texts; students should tell you everything they can recall rather than simply remembering the main points. To have students retell an informational text, have them read the text and then either tell you or write down everything they can remember. As you listen to students retell informational texts, determine whether they have included the pertinent information in the structure that the text was organized. For example, if the text has a compare-contrast organization, look for both elements in the retelling.
7. Remind students about the text features of informational texts by developing a bulletin board with text features. The bulletin board could be called Text Feature Wall. After you have introduced and reviewed a number of text features, find examples such as titles, captions, charts, graphs, photos, italics, and so on. Make a copy of those text features and post them on the Text Feature Wall. Include a caption below the text feature to reinforce the name of the feature. Invite students to add features to the bulletin board that they have found in other texts. Have students give you the text with the feature bookmarked. Make a copy of the page of text so that students can post the feature and add a caption with the feature's name and how it can help readers.

Section 7.3

Charts and Graphs

Behavior Observed → **Anticipated Outcome**

The student has difficulty interpreting charts and graphs. → The student will use graphic aids to study.

Background

Graphs and charts are an integral feature of most texts because they can communicate information quickly, effectively, and persuasively. For some students, graphs and charts are a mystery rather than a source of information. Teachers need to be certain that students have the proper background in the interpretation of graphs and charts. The following strategies may provide some assistance.

Strategy 1 SECTION 7.3

INTERPRETING CHARTS

1. Explain that charts are ways of simplifying data to make it easy to read at a glance. Then hand out individual-size bags of M&M candies to each student. Let them open the bags and put the candy on their desks. Ask them to think about the aspects of the candies (weight, color, number).
2. Hand out a blank chart and ask students to record their data for the different colors and the number of each. An example is provided on the following page.

blue candies	3
green candies	5
brown candies	6
yellow candies	4
orange candies	7
red candies	4
Total	29

3. Discuss the importance of developing a descriptive title for the chart. Ask students to suggest titles for the M&M chart. Some students' responses might include M&Ms, Number of M&M candies, and Colors of M&M candies. Explain that someone reading the chart needs to know exactly what information is listed. Then ask students to write titles for their charts (perhaps Number of Colors in a Bag of M&Ms).
4. Ask students to compare their charts with each other, noting similarities and differences.
5. Synthesize the individual charts into a class chart. Discuss the information that the class found.
6. Explain that information listed on a chart can also be expressed in a pictorial form using a graph. Show students an example of a bar graph and ask them whether they are able to understand the information given more readily than by using a chart. Explain that many people find graphs a quick method of understanding information.
7. Create a bar graph on the chalkboard or an overhead transparency from the information gathered from the class chart on M&M candies. As you write, explain the different features of the graph.

   From the example that follows, for instance, you could say something like what follows.

   > *This bar graph has its title at the top. The title tells me exactly what I can find on the graph. I see that this graph compares the numbers of individual colors of M&M candies that were gathered from our class project. I see the numbers of candies is on the left side of the graph and the colors are listed at the bottom. Looking at the graph, I can see that the most colors found in the class were brown. We had a total of 56 brown candies. The next highest number was 50 orange. We had 45 green candies, 44 yellow candies, 40 red candies, and 35 blue candies.*

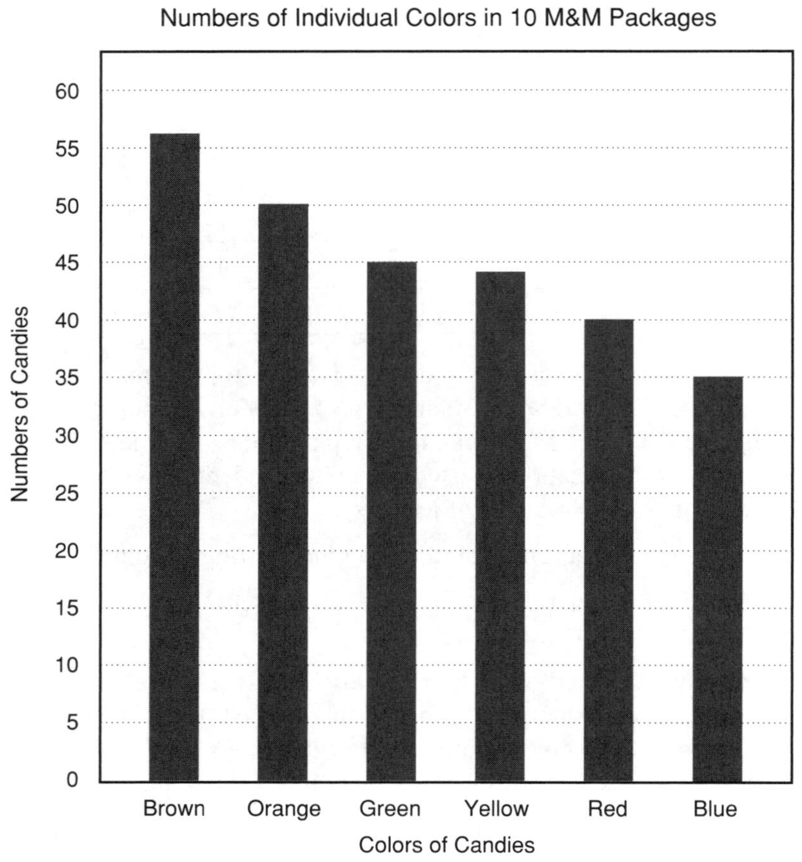

8. Provide students with graph paper and ask them to create a bar graph for their individual data. They may want to color the bars in the graphs with colored pencils or markers for effect.

9. Ask students to share their graphs with each other. Discuss the similarities and differences among the graphs.

10. Groups of students could combine their data into group bar graphs. The final activity could be a single bar graph for the total group data.

11. Refer to a bar graph in your text and help students transfer their skills. Guide students through an interpretation of the graph by asking questions and thinking aloud. Model how you go about understanding a portion of the graph and invite students to share their thinking.

CHARTS AND GRAPHS

1. Explain to students that charts and graphs are visual methods of presenting information, making comparisons, and showing relationships, rather than using lots of words.
2. Brainstorm the similarities and differences between charts and graphs. Answers might include that charts show the relationships among several parts. They may show the order in which things happen or the cause and effect, but they always show how one part relates to the others. Graphs are similar to charts in that they show relationships, but they use points and lines rather than pictures or symbols.
3. Create a chart and a graph illustrating the months when students have birthdays.
4. Demonstrate how to read the chart and graph.
5. Ask questions for which the students will have to use the graphic aids to answer (for example, Which month has the most birthdays?).

INTERPRETING LINE GRAPHS

1. Explain that a line graph is another way of arranging information that can be read at a glance. Ask students whether they have seen graphs other than bar graphs in their readings. Discuss the kinds of graphs students have seen.
2. Show students an example of a line graph on an overhead projector. Tell students about the features of the line graph including the title, the numbers, the lines, and the labels. An example of a line graph follows.

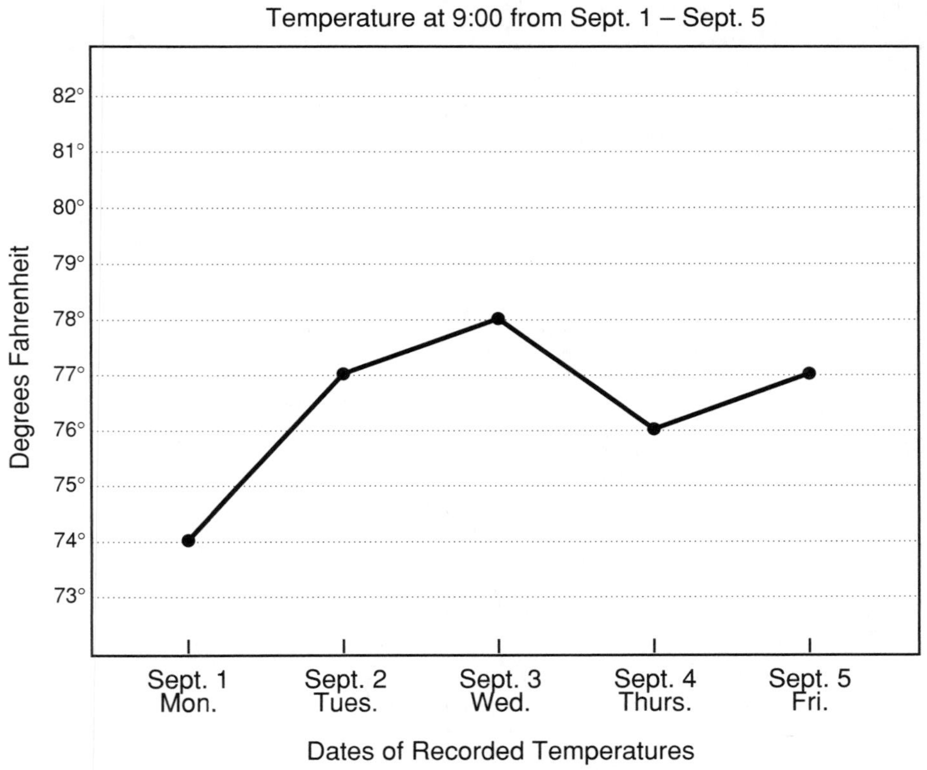

3. Ask the students to discuss the information they found on the graph. Some guiding questions and answers follow.

   Teacher: What does this graph tell us?
   Student: The temperature.
   Teacher: Where did you find that information?
   Student: From the title.
   Teacher: What else do we know from this graph?
   Student: How hot it was during the last week.
   Teacher: Can you tell me how hot it was last Wednesday?
   Student: Yes, it was 78 degrees.

4. Provide students with graph paper and help them construct a sample line graph using information from the birthday charts. See Strategy 2.
5. Ask students to compare line graphs with each other noting similarities and differences. Give them an opportunity to discuss how effective they think line graphs are at representing information.

Strategy 4 SECTION 7.3

INTERPRETING PIE CHARTS

1. Remind students that graphs and charts are visual ways of presenting information, comparisons, and relationships using few numbers and words. Explain that one of the uses of charts and graphs is to give information in a brief form and help students visualize the data without a great deal of reading.
2. Tell students that they will be learning a new kind of chart, a pie chart. Put an example of a pie chart on an overhead projector. Tell students that the information from the chart was gathered from the class family heritage unit. An example of a pie chart follow.

Mr. Thompson's Class
Percentage of members from different cultural groups

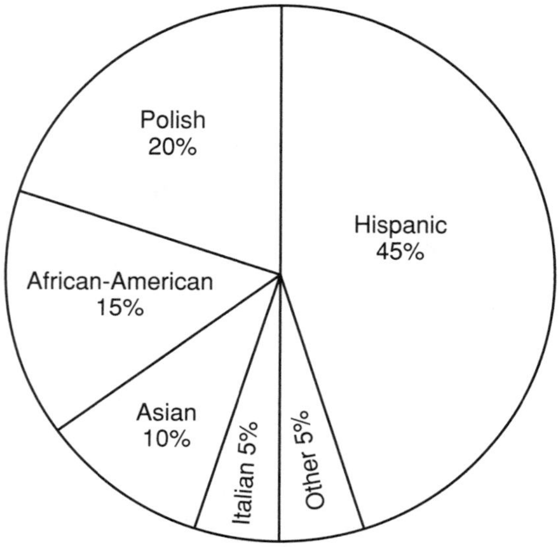

3. Ask students whether they have seen a pie chart in their reading or on television. Give students a chance to discuss the pie charts they have seen. If possible, refer to a pie chart in one of their texts.
4. Ask students what information they found on the pie chart. Remind them of the features of any graph or chart: the title, the labels, and the numbers.
5. Model for the students how you would read a pie chart for information. You might say something like what follows.

> *The first thing I look for when I see a chart is the title. This title says that the chart is the percentages of classroom members from different cultural groups. From looking at the chart, I see the largest area on the graph is made up of Hispanics. We see that 45% of the class has Hispanic origins. The second largest ethnic group in the class is made up of students of Polish ancestry. There are 20% of students who make up this group. We also see 15% of students who have African-American backgrounds; 10% of students with Asian backgrounds; 5% of students with Italian backgrounds; and 5% in a category that says Other.*

6. Ask students whether they were able to understand the information from the pie chart. Provide students with an opportunity to discuss difficulties they had with interpreting the chart. Students may ask about the category *Other* on the chart. Explain that when there are too few members in a group to be represented on the chart, they may be placed together in one category.

Practice and Reinforcement Activities

1. Ask students to think of some information they would like to know. It might be how many students wear a certain brand of clothes, the ways students get to school, or the number of rabbits in their backyards. Have students record their data for a period of time, several days at least. Ask students to make a graph for their data. All the points on the graph should be neatly plotted and connected. Share the data with the class by writing a story about it or explaining it to other students.
2. Divide the class into groups of two. Distribute two graphs to each pair of students. Ask each student to read one graph with the purpose of explaining that graph to his or her partner. Give the students time to read and think about the graphs. Then ask them to share what they have learned. After the discussions are finished, ask students whether they have questions about the information on the graphs that they were unable to understand. Answer any questions students might have.

3. Ask students to look for bar graphs, line graphs, and pie charts in newspapers, magazines or on the Internet. Invite them to bring samples of these graphs to class. Give students an opportunity to explain the graphs either to the entire class or to a small group. Post the graphs on a poster or bulletin board.
4. Locate information from the texts used in class that would be appropriate to chart or graph. Ask students to develop a graph for the information.
5. Convert some of the information you record on a daily or weekly basis into a graph. For example, you might graph the number of books the students have read, the number of books they have written, or the number of sunny days in the month. Ask a group of students to chart the information and another group to graph it on poster board for the class.
6. Integrate graph learning activities with the ongoing curriculum. Pay particular attention to graphic aids in textbooks.

Section 7.4

Inflexible Rate of Reading

Behavior Observed → **Anticipated Outcome**

The student does not vary rate of reading. The student will vary reading rate to match his or her purposes.

Background

Proficient readers have a flexible silent reading rate that is determined by their purposes. Rate of reading is better thought of as rate of comprehension to achieve the reader's purposes. It does little good to consider rate apart from comprehension; moreover, comprehension may suffer when rate is too fast or too slow. For many students experiencing difficulty in reading, lack of automaticity in identifying words may require so much of students' attention that meaning suffers. One teacher observed that it takes Jada so long to decode that she forgets what the beginning of the sentence is about by the time she gets to the end. Jada may be preoccupied with decoding. Another student is excellent at decoding but does not have the slightest idea what the passage is about. This student is a word caller. Between these two extremes are students who seldom practice flexibility in reading—quite possibly because it was never an instructional focus.

Strategic readers know that there are several factors that help determine the rate at which they read, and they know how to take these factors into account while they are reading. The chart on the following page lists some of the factors that can influence students' reading rates.

These factors influence each of the major kinds of reading such as study-type reading, rapid reading (like skimming and scanning), and technical reading. Within each of these major types of reading, rate may sometimes be faster or slower. The important point to keep in mind is whether the readers' purposes are being achieved.

Major Factors That Can Influence Reading Rates

- purpose
- type of material
- familiarity with content and/or background knowledge
- motivation and/or mood (for example, preparing for a test, relaxing with a novel)
- reading environment (for example, light quality, presence or absence of distractions)
- size of type, amount of figures, illustrations, and so on

Strategy 1 SECTION 7.4

DIFFERENT RATES

1. Be sure students understand that meaning is what reading is all about.
2. Ask students to name some of the reasons they read and to offer examples of that kind of reading. A chart similar to the following might be developed on the chalkboard.

What We Read	Why We Read
Clifford books	For fun
Our own stories	To read better
	To learn words
Lunch menu	To see what we will eat
Science book	To learn things

3. Use the chart to help students realize that they read for different purposes, especially for fun and to learn things.
4. Tell students that good readers know why they are reading something and that they should always know why they are reading a book or story. Refer to the chart as necessary and use other examples as appropriate.
5. Then tell students that sometimes they will read faster and sometimes they will read slower. Help students develop a list of times when they might speed up or slow down. See the following example.

   I speed up my reading when I—
   - already know the story.
   - am reading a story I've already practiced.
   - understand the meaning of the story.

   I slow down my reading when I—
   - don't understand.
   - am mixed up.
   - encounter unfamiliar words.

6. Spend time helping students realize that good readers will reread if they are not understanding. They also stop reading and try to get help if they are not understanding.
7. Use subsequent lessons or instructional opportunities to foster a greater awareness and understanding that everything is not read at the same speed.

Strategy 2 SECTION 7.4

READING RATE CHART

1. Begin by inviting each student to compile a list of the various kinds of reading accomplished within the last day or two and the purposes for reading. A chart like the following one might be helpful.

Day	Time	What Was Read	Why It Was Read (Purpose)

2. After students have had sufficient time for individual reflection, have them form small groups to compare their answers. Ask them to identify both common and unique items. Each group can list common and unique items on an overhead transparency or on the chalkboard.

3. Engage students in a group activity in which volunteers can share overhead transparencies or write responses on the chalkboard.

4. After responses are shared, lead students in a discussion about the rate at which the reading occurred to fulfill the intended purpose(s). Help students realize that there is a connection between purpose and rate. For example, Roger may have used a television program guide to find out whether any TV movies were showing Tuesday evening at eight o'clock. He said it took him longer to find the guide than to find out the titles of the movies by scanning the guide. Ami not only located the movies in her guide but she also read the brief blurbs about each of them. Actually, she didn't read the entire blurb for a movie once she decided that she wasn't interested. After her initial reading, she went back and reread one of the movie blurbs because she thought it might be worth watching.

5. Use the previous example or a similar one to help develop the notion of a flexible rate of reading that is governed by purpose. For example, both Roger and Ami scanned the guide to find specific information to fulfill their purposes for reading. Once the information was found, Roger and Ami read. Roger read the movie titles; Ami read the titles and blurbs and even reread one of the blurbs. Both students' reading was successful because their purposes were achieved.

Strategy 3 SECTION 7.4

INTERNET READING

1. Tell students that those students who have surfed the Internet are reading flexibly and that they can transfer those flexible reading skills to books.

2. Write the term Internet on the chalkboard. Ask students how familiar they are with the term. Most students will likely know about the Internet even if they do not have Internet connections at home.

3. Have students think about how often they use the Internet. If you are teaching younger students, you might ask how many times they look at the Internet during a week's time. For older students you might ask how often they look at the Internet each day.

4. Identify a website that is appropriate to show to students and display it on a screen. (For example, the website www.zooschool.ecsd.net at the time of this printing had no objectionable content for students.)
5. Tell students that they first come to a Home Page that lists the different types of links someone can follow. Explain to students that they would be scanning the Home Page quickly to find the information they wanted. You might say the following.

   When you open a website, you often come to the site's Home Page. If you are following a link that doesn't take you to the Home Page, you can find it on the site's menu. Let's take a look at this Home Page. We can see that there are many kinds of links to follow. Read the links quickly and decide which one you want to see first. [Give students the opportunity to tell a classmate their selection.]

6. Remind students that surveying a Home Page is similar to surveying a book by saying the following.

   This is how we survey books. We can look over a book quickly to get a sense of the entire book. Remember when you are trying to become a more flexible reader that you already know how to read quickly to get a sense of the book.

7. Click on a link on the Home Page that you have previously checked. For example, you could click on elephants. Show students the next page which is also a menu. Have students practice scanning the four menu selections (Elephants-General Information, African Elephants, Asian Elephants, and Links) and make a decision about which one to choose. For example, you might select African elephants.
8. Click on the African elephant link and ask students to suggest what you should do next. Students should respond that you should scroll down the page to see what is there. Draw a comparison to flexible reading by saying the following.

   When we open a link from a Home Page, we first scroll down to see what is on the page. We make a very quick decision about whether we want to read the page. Let's look at this page. It has pictures of elephants and then at the bottom of the page it has some information about African elephants. Once again we're scanning the page. We do this with books too when we look through a chapter of a science book before reading to see what information it will contain. We're not reading carefully yet; we're just scanning like we did on the Internet.

9. Show the print on the African elephant page. Tell students to read the information carefully paying close attention to how slowly they read. Explain to students that they are reading more slowly because they are reading for information by saying the following.

   When we read the print on an Internet page, we often slow down. We need to pay close attention to the words and try to remember what we are reading. We're not just looking for information, but we're reading to learn. We do this with books as well. When we start reading the words, we need to slow our pace so that we can comprehend what we are reading.

10. Select several informational books that are similar to the Internet page. Give students the books and ask them to practice surveying the outside and the inside of the book and reading the first few pages slowly. Remind students that they are improving their reading flexibility by doing this by saying the following.

> *You are now reading more flexibly by reading quickly and reading slowly. You can try this on your own on the Internet or with books. Remember that good readers know when to read fast and when to read slowly. You will learn this as you continue to practice reading.*

Practice and Reinforcement Activities

1. Give students a newspaper article and develop a purpose for reading the article (to find who, what, when, where, or why). Have students read at a rate that is comfortable to fulfill purposes. After students read, determine whether those purposes were achieved. Invite individual students to share insights about their reading. Several examples follow.
   - I just skimmed to find each of the answers.
   - I reread the questions so I'd know what to read for.
   - I only had trouble remembering the answer to one of the questions so I scanned the article for that specific information. Then I reread that sentence.
2. Use a selection from one of your classroom texts and model how you set purposes for reading and read flexibly to achieve those purposes.
3. Secure classroom quantities of various reading materials (telephone books, driver's license study manuals, product information sheets, maps, and so on). Identify some of the major purposes for reading each type of material and how the material might be read to fulfill particular purposes. Then have students use the material to fulfill one or more of the purposes. Share how the material was read.
4. Have students share their anticipated rate of reading prior to reading one of the materials mentioned in activity 3. Then have the students think aloud to share what they will do. Model the process by saying the following.

   > *I want to know the phone number for Sports of All Sorts. I'll look toward the back of the phone book and find the* s. *Then I'll use my knowledge of guide words to find the right page. I'm not really very good at using guide words, so I'd better take my time. I'll look on that page until I find the entry and phone number. If I can't find it, I might try the Yellow Pages under sports or sporting.*

   Then have a student actually perform the task and think aloud. Use this general procedure with other types of reading materials.
5. Give students opportunities to write down some of their insights about reading rate. For example, a chart might be developed using ideas like those listed below.

   I can usually speed up my reading when—
   - it is easy and I'm understanding.
   - I already know a lot about the topic.
   - the book is repeating what was said before.
   - the information is not related to my purposes.

I should usually slow down my reading when—

- the information is related to my purposes.
- the book has ideas that I'm interested in.
- I'm confused.
- the writing is complicated.

6. Timed silent reading exercises with comprehension questions may give students opportunities to see whether they are able to comprehend information at a faster rate. After scoring the comprehension questions, have students reinspect the text to find the correct answer or the information that formed the basis for the inferences or conclusions that they drew.
7. Remember to keep your instruction on various rates of reading linked to purpose. Helping students practice flexibility in their reading is the key.

Section 7.5

Monitoring Reading

Behavior Observed → **Anticipated Outcome**

The student does not monitor comprehension. → The student will monitor comprehension while reading.

Background

Monitoring reading involves the concepts of strategic reading and metacomprehension. Both concepts are complex; therefore, the ideas we present are concrete and visual in an effort to help students begin to grasp the concept of monitoring. You should feel free to adapt the ideas and substitute actual examples from students or from your experiences to make the concept clear and relevant. Remember to keep your students' maturity in mind.

Strategy 1 SECTION 7.5

MONITORING

1. Tell students that you are a good reader and that good readers still experience difficulty in reading. If possible, select an actual example from your own reading that represents a genuine instance of monitoring. You may also want to begin developing a file of such ideas to help with appropriate strategy lessons.
2. Share areas in which you have had difficulty, such as failing to understand a text or mispronouncing a word. Invite students to share difficulties they have experienced during reading, and write their ideas on the chalkboard.
3. Encourage discussion of the ideas presented and help students realize that:
   - All readers (not just poor readers) experience difficulty in reading.
   - Better readers keep watch over their reading to make sure they are understanding.
   - Readers fix up their reading to ensure understanding.

4. Ask students to share some of the things they do to keep watch over their reading. Encourage specific examples and discussion. Then share an example from your own reading. You could also use the following example. The actual words in the newspaper article are in italics.

   Print *Lewis slows up; so do admirers* on the chalkboard and say something like the following: "I read the title to the newspaper article you see and then began reading the article. *Carl Lewis appeared Friday at the Olympic Village, nearly starting a riot in the food court. He was reading his messages on a computer when a mob of 100 athletes and passersby surrounded him for autographs and photos.* As I finished that part of the article, I thought there were quite a few people around Carl Lewis. The headline had said that admirers had slowed up because Carl Lewis had slowed up. Although I was a bit confused because of all the people around Lewis, I continued reading. *"Carl, Carl," the controlled mob screamed, following Lewis out the double doors of the Olympic Village.* At this point I was quite certain that the title and the article were not telling me the same thing. I decided to check over my reading by going back to the title. As I reread the title, I saw my mistake; I had initially read *slows* instead of *shows.* When I read the headline correctly, the content of the article made sense. I was watching over my reading and realized that the title and the article did not seem to agree. I then decided to go back and read the title again. That's when I found my mistake. Now the article makes sense."

5. Take time to discuss this example with students and be sure they understand that rereading is one strategy that good readers sometimes use to overcome a difficulty in understanding. Use the items from number 2 and invite students to share what they have done to overcome or resolve their problems.

6. Remember that numerous lessons and modeling are needed to develop the concept of monitoring. One follow-up activity invites students to record their actual encounters with difficulties in reading. Such examples could be shared and discussed by volunteers in large or small groups to further develop the concept of monitoring.

Book or story ____________		Name ____________	
Page/Paragraph	Problem I Had	What I Did	How It Worked

Strategy 2 SECTION 7.5

WHAT'S A MONITOR?

1. Write the word *monitor* on the chalkboard and ask students to share meanings and examples of the word.

2. Explore various definitions of *monitor* by using class dictionaries or an overhead transparency with the definitions, or by distributing the definitions. A thesaurus may also be useful. Have students verify their definitions with those you provide and add new definitions. Some definitions, like a computer monitor or hall monitor, may be common. Other definitions for monitor, like a lizard or a heavily ironclad warship, may broaden students' understanding of the word.

3. Ask students to focus on what it might mean to monitor one's reading and help them identify appropriate words or phrases from the various definitions. Some examples follow.

keep track of	control
check	oversee
keep watch over	supervise

4. Invite students to share what actions they take to monitor their reading to ensure that they are understanding the text. Add appropriate examples from your own reading or the example used in Strategy 1.
5. Help students realize that a characteristic of good readers is that they monitor their reading. Many poor readers are under the mistaken notion that good readers always know the words, read fast, and never encounter difficulty in comprehension. Take time to list some of the more important actions students can take to monitor their reading. Specific items from the list could become the focus of future lessons.
6. Consider using a sheet similar to that in Strategy 1 (number 6) so students can begin to see concrete examples of how they monitor reading. These examples could also be used in future lessons and discussions.

Strategy 3 SECTION 7.5

THE CRITTER

1. Use the notion of a "critter" to help get students thinking visually about the concepts of strategic reading and metacomprehension. Enlarge and present the critter on an overhead transparency (or draw one of your own).

2. Tell students that similar critters were drawn by students who used the picture to help them remember that there is something in their heads to help them understand what they are reading. The term *inner voice* may be helpful to students.

3. Invite students to visualize a critter that they have in their heads to help them read. You may wish to give students time to draw and color their critters. You could also draw your own critter on an overhead transparency or use the sample provided.

4. Use your critter to help develop important questions with the class. Some possible questions your critter asks to help your reading make sense are listed below.

   - Do I understand what I'm reading? If yes, great! If no, what should I do about it?
   - What do I already know about this topic?
   - How is this chapter organized?
   - How can I figure out this unknown word?
   - What is my purpose for reading?
   - Have I achieved my purpose for reading?

5. A single question could be the focus of one or more lessons to develop important ideas related to strategic reading. Have students add the questions and strategies to the sheet containing their critters. For example, if the answer to "Do I understand what I'm reading?" is "no," some possible actions could include:

   - I need to concentrate on what the author is trying to tell me and visualize the message.
   - I'll reread the last paragraph.
   - I'm tired so I'll take a short break.
   - I need to ask someone for help.
   - I think I need to look up the meaning of a word.

6. Remind students to use the important ideas their critters are telling them so they understand what they are reading. The important point is for students to take control of their reading and to monitor their comprehension. A critter may help provide a concrete, visual image toward that end.

Strategy 4 SECTION 7.5

COMPREHENSION CHECKLIST

1. Tell students that there are many ways they can improve their understanding of text by applying comprehension strategies. Explain to students that comprehension is another word for knowing what you read.

2. Duplicate and distribute the Comprehension Checklist (Massey, 2003) on pages 539–540. Read each of the strategies on the checklist and provide examples for students. For example, when you read *Set a purpose for reading*, you might comment by saying something like what follows.

   > *Setting a purpose for reading means that you decide the reasons* why *you are reading the book. You might have begun reading for a class assignment, but you need to think of other reasons why you're reading as well. If you're reading a story, you might think of purposes for reading that particular book. You might read to find out more information, for enjoyment, or for many other reasons.*

3. Have students volunteer other examples for the first item on the Comprehension Checklist. If your students have a good understanding of all of the checklist items, review them in one class period. If the items are new for students, describe a few items each day for several days.
4. After students are familiar with the checklist items, tell students that they need to monitor these strategies as they read. Explain to students that you will be giving them the opportunity to monitor their reading using the Comprehension Checklist. Remind students that not every strategy that they could use will apply to this reading situation, as in the following example.

> *When you read, you need to select strategies that fit the type of text you are reading the same way you use different skills and strategies when you play basketball. When you have the ball, you need to work on your dribbling, passing, and shooting skills, but when you are playing defense you won't use these skills. It's the same when you read. Some books, for example, have a table of contents. If you are reading a book that has one, you should scan it before reading. If you are reading a book without a table of contents, you won't need that strategy at that time.*

5. Instruct students to read a story or a chapter. After they have completed reading, have them place a check by each of the strategies on the checklist that they used.
6. Meet with students individually to discuss their Comprehension Checklists. Begin the conversation with the question, "What strategies did you use while reading this text?" Encourage students to discuss the strategies they used. You may need to prompt them by asking questions on the Comprehension Checklist.
7. After you have discussed the strategies used by students, determine which strategies need to be reinforced, which ones need to be taught, and which ones you don't need to teach. Use the inside cover of this book and the table of contents to find instructional lessons for the different strategies.
8. Have students use the Comprehension Checklist frequently. Remind students that the purpose of the checklist is to help them monitor the strategies they use while reading. Tell students that you want them to eventually monitor their reading without the checklist. Additional checklists can be found in Chapter 7 Resources (pages 597–599).

COMPREHENSION CHECKLIST

Name ____ Date ____________________

Directions: When you read, ask yourself: Does it make sense? If it doesn't make sense, place a check beside each of the following comprehension strategies you used before, during, or after reading.

Before you started reading, did you

☐ Set a purpose for reading—what do you need to find or figure out?

☐ Think about what you already know about the topic—a lot or a little?

☐ Look at the pictures and predict what the story was going to be about?

☐ Read the captions?

☐ Read the bold words?

☐ Read the table of contents?

☐ Read any summaries?

☐ Read the questions at the end of the chapter?

☐ Page through the chapter?

While you were reading, did you

☐ Skip the word—is it one word that doesn't make sense? Did you try skipping that word and reading to the end of the sentence or paragraph? Did you go back to see if you knew what the word was or if you knew what it meant?

☐ Reread a paragraph and look for new information?

☐ Keep a mental picture of what's happening in your head?

☐ Summarize—stop every page or two and summarize the main points?

☐ Find that you could go on, or did you need more information from another student or teacher?

(continued)

Comprehension Checklist *(continued)*

After you finished reading, did you

- ☐ Do a text check—was this text too hard, too easy, or just right?
- ☐ Reread the section, looking for new details?
- ☐ Develop questions—what might the teacher ask? What might be on a test?
- ☐ Check your predictions—were you right? If you weren't, did you decide why?

Adapted from Massey, D.D. (2003). A comprehension checklist: What if it doesn't make sense? *The Reading Teacher*, *57*, 81–83.

THINKING ABOUT EFFECTIVE READERS

1. One of the ways readers monitor their comprehension is by thinking about how effective readers think. According to Johnson (2005), having students define good reading can help them become good readers themselves.
2. Show students pictures of students reading. You might do this by taking digital photographs of your students in various reading situations. Show the pictures on a screen to prepare students to visualize their classmates reading.
3. Tell students that they are good readers and that you are showing them pictures of good readers. Ask students to think about what that means. You might ask the following questions.
   - Do you know any readers who are good at comprehension?
   - What makes a reader good at comprehending?
   - Name some things that good readers probably do when they read.
   - Name some things that poor readers do when they read.
   - How can you become a better reader?
4. Have students write reflections to these questions. After students are finished, have them share some of their ideas with a partner.
5. Ask the class to share some of the ways good readers comprehend when they are reading. List these ideas on the chalkboard. Help students prioritize the ideas and list them on a chart or bulletin board.
6. Reinforce the strategies good readers use when they read to comprehend by reminding students occasionally to use the ideas that were placed on a chart or bulletin board.

Practice and Reinforcement Activities

1. Ask students to take out a book that they have just read and to think about the strategies they used as they read. To find out how aware students are of their reading strategies, you may want to interview them individually or reproduce the Reading Strategies Questions below and have students answer on separate sheets.

Reading Strategies Questions

Before I began reading, I ____.

When I got stuck on a word, I ____.

When I didn't understand what was happening, I ____

____.

After I finished reading, I ____

____.

2. After students have answered the above questions about their reading, ask them to read their answers and write goals for improving their monitoring. If they are not sure of the goals they could choose, use some of the suggestions from the following example and write them on the chalkboard. Then ask students to discuss their reading goals in small groups and with you. An example appears below.

   Emily was a voracious reader of easy books but was not able to verbalize any strategies for understanding reading. Before she read a book, she looked at the title and began reading. You might suggest that Emily also do any of the following activities.

   - look to see how hard or easy the book is
   - read the book jacket
   - preview the pictures or chapter titles
   - make a prediction about the book
   - look to see what genre the book is

   Because Emily usually chooses easy books, she rarely comes to a word she doesn't know. When she does come to a word she doesn't know, Emily just skips it and reads ahead. You might suggest that Emily do any of the following activities.

   - skip the word, read to the end of the sentence, then go back to the beginning and try again
   - read ahead to connect the word with other ideas
   - try to use word parts she knows
   - substitute a word that makes sense
   - use a picture clue
   - reread and connect the word to the sense of the sentence
   - ask someone what the word is
   - look up the pronunciation of the word in a dictionary
   - cross check by asking if it sounds right, if it makes sense, and if it looks right

Sometimes Emily does not have a high degree of comprehension when she reads. However, she normally continues reading without using any fix-up strategies. You might suggest that Emily do the following.

- reread the confusing part
- use pictures or subheadings to make sense of the text
- read ahead and try to connect the information
- use signal words in the text to understand

After reading, Emily usually writes the name of the book in her book log, but does little else to process the text. You might suggest that she do the following.

- tell a friend about the book
- videotape a book talk
- read the book again
- look for a similar book
- write about the book in her journal
- write a letter to the author

3. Help students monitor their reading by providing them with self-check lists. A variety of self-report lists can be found in Chapter 7 Resources (pages 597–599). Use the information to inform your instruction.

4. Some students need to monitor each sentence as they read (Buettner, 2002). For these students, stop after each sentence and ask students to tell you what the sentence was about.

Section 7.6

Summarizing Ideas

© 2010 JupiterImages Corporation.

Behavior Observed → **Anticipated Outcome**

Behavior Observed	Anticipated Outcome
The student has difficulty summarizing ideas during and after reading.	The student will learn how to summarize ideas during and after reading.

Effective readers summarize as they read.

Background

Effective readers summarize as they read. Think what you do when you read. As you read, you stop occasionally and briefly rehearse what you have read. In essence, you are summarizing. As a reader, you also summarize when you come to the end of a text. You think back to the text in its entirety and review what it said. Again, you were summarizing. You can teach students the same type of summarization strategies you use. When students use summarization strategies, they become better comprehenders of text. The teaching strategies and activities in this section emphasize summarizing both during reading and after reading.

Strategy 1 SECTION 7.6

WRITING SUMMARIES

1. Provide students with short passages at their instructional level of reading. An example follows.

> *Zebras are one of the most attractive animals in nature. Zebras come from the horse family so they look much like horses you would see at a farm or zoo. Just like horses, baby zebras are called foals, and mothers are called mares. The difference between horses and zebras, of course, is their appearance. Zebras have black and white stripes, unlike domesticated horses. Their stripes cover their entire body including their mane. Each zebra has its own unique pattern of stripes.*

2. Guide students to underline the main idea of the passage and to cross out unimportant or redundant information. An example follows.

> *Zebras are one of the most attractive animals in nature. Zebras come from the horse family ~~so they look much like horses you would see at a farm or zoo. Just like horses,~~ baby zebras are called foals and mothers are called mares. ~~The difference between horses and zebras, of course, is their appearance.~~ Zebras have black and white stripes, ~~unlike domesticated horses. Their stripes cover their entire body including their mane.~~ Each zebra has its own unique pattern of stripes.*

3. Help students make a Graphic Organizer with the remaining information. See the following example.

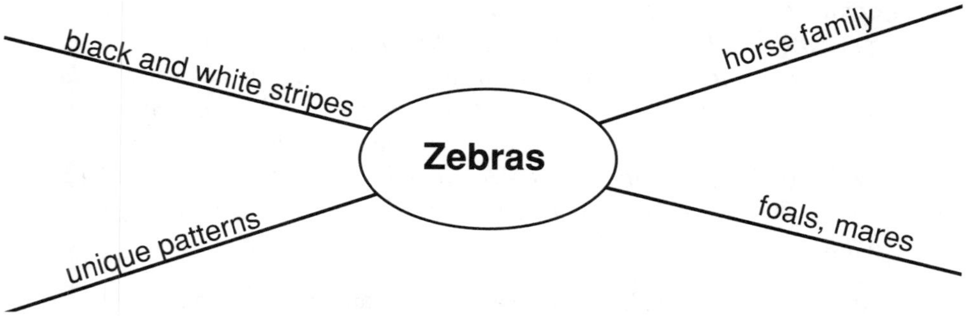

4. Together, write a short paragraph from the information on the Graphic Organizer, as in the following example.

> *Zebras come from the horse family. Babies are called foals, and mothers are called mares. Each zebra has its own pattern of black and white stripes.*

5. Review the procedure and provide students with an appropriate passage so they can begin to gain competence with the strategy. After they have completed their summaries, go through each of the above steps and discuss students' strategies. Provide guidance as needed.

Strategy 2 SECTION 7.6

GRASP: GUIDED READING AND SUMMARIZING PROCEDURE

1. Provide students with a short passage at their instructional level of reading. Explain that the students will be writing a summary of the passage. If your students do not understand the term *summary,* explain that a summary is a brief description of a longer text.
2. Ask students to read the passage independently with the purpose of remembering all that they can. After they are finished reading, they should put the passage on their desk and wait for others in the group.
3. After all students have finished reading, ask them to tell you what they remembered. List on the chalkboard all of the items they suggest.

4. Ask students to reread the passage with the purpose of making additions to and deletions from the list on the board.
5. After rereading, have the class suggest changes to the list on the chalkboard. Revise the list as needed.
6. Then ask students to suggest categories for the information. List the categories and ask students to divide the items on the list into the categories.
7. Using the outline generated by categorizing the information, write the summary. You might suggest that students begin with a main idea statement for the first main heading with details as the subheadings. An example of the Guided Reading and Summarizing Procedure (GRASP) (Hayes, 1989) strategy based on an adapted encyclopedia entry follows.

> *Otters are aquatic or semiaquatic carnivores of the weasel family. The body of the otter is lithe and muscular and covered with thick fur. Their paws are generally webbed. Otters often shut their nostrils and eyes to swim underwater. Their prey consists of small fish, eels, crayfish, and frogs. The sea otter's diet is more specialized. They have powerful teeth that are perfect for crushing sea urchins, abalones, and mussels. The sea otter floats on its back, breaking open the urchin—or mussel—shell on a stone anvil balanced on its chest. Unlike most other wild animals, otters remain playful as adults.*

Teacher: Today we are going to read a paragraph about otters. I'd like you to read it carefully trying to remember as much of the passage as you can. After you're done reading, put your paper on your desk and wait for the other students.

Teacher: Now that you have finished reading, what can you remember from the passage?

Students:

Otters like to play.	Otters eat snakes.	Otters are weasels.
They have fur.	They swim underwater.	They eat fish and frogs.
Sea otters eat seaweed.	Sea otters eat sea animals.	Their paws are webbed.

Teacher: Now reread the paragraph and think if you would like to add any more ideas, erase some of them, or change some of them.

Student: Otters shut their eyes underwater just like we do!

Teacher: Let's add that one to the list.

Student: We have some wrong things on the chalkboard. Otters don't eat snakes or seaweed.

Teacher: What do you think, class? Raise your hands if you agree that otters don't eat snakes or seaweed. I see everyone's hand is up, so I'll erase those two ideas. Now let's try to put some of the information into categories. What categories can you think of?

Student: How they look.

Teacher: What would fit under How Otters Look?

Student: They have fur and webbed feet.

Teacher: Let's make an outline with categories and information under them.

Otters in General	**How Otters Look**	**What Otters Eat**
weasels	fur	fish
swim under water with eyes shut	webbed feet	frogs
like to play		sea animals

Teacher: Let's try to write a summary using this information.

Otters are playful weasels who like to swim under water with their eyes shut. They have fur and webbed feet. Otters like to eat fish, frogs, and sea animals.

Strategy 3 SECTION 7.6

PARAPHRASING FOR COMPREHENSION

1. Select a text for students to paraphrase. The text can be a portion of a picture book, a paragraph from a content area book, or any other small amount of text.
2. Tell students that they will be Paraphrasing for Comprehension (Fisk & Hurst, 2003). Explain to students that paraphrasing is a restatement of a text. Tell students that when they read they can paraphrase the text in their minds to help them construct meaning. Tell students that they also use paraphrasing when they talk with their friends. Provide an example of paraphrasing as follows:

   Stacy: When I asked Julie if she could come to my party, she said "she had another obligation." I wonder if she really has something else to do or if she doesn't want to come to the party.

   Wylee: From the way you told me what Stacy said, I don't think she wants to come.

   Stacy: Yes, I paraphrased Julie's comments, so I think I agree with you.
3. Duplicate and distribute the reproducible on page 549. Tell students that they will be using the reproducible to learn how to paraphrase a text.
4. If you are demonstrating the strategy using a picture book, read the book to students. Otherwise, have students read the text themselves. For instance, you could use the book *Henry Climbs a Mountain* (Johnson, 2003), a picture book from the life of Henry David Thoreau.
5. Discuss the book with students. In your discussion, point out ways to restate the author's story with the author's voice. Explain to students that a paraphrase should use the author's voice.
6. Tell students that they should record any ideas from class discussion on the reproducible. An example of a class discussion of *Henry Climbs a Mountain* follows.

   Student: I noticed that the sentences were very short in this book.

   Teacher: Yes, how did the author's use of short sentences influence our reading of the story?

   Student: Well, the fast pace of the short sentences helped a rather long plot move more swiftly.

   Teacher: Good. What else did you notice from this story?

   Student: The book was written in the third person.

   Teacher: Yes, what else?

   Student: The book included lots of dialog.

7. After students have discussed the book in class, have them reread the story and write down other ideas they have. Students can use the reproducible to write down notes in the second section.
8. After students have taken notes, instruct them to write a paraphrased version of the story. Remind students that a paraphrase is a restatement that uses the same tone and voice of the original author and that a paraphrase states what happened in fewer words. An example of a paraphrase from *Henry Climbs a Mountain* (Johnson, 2003) follows.

   > *Henry didn't want to pay his taxes. The tax collector sent him to jail. Henry imagined a hiking trip in his jail cell. He sang* the bear went over the mountain. *Someone else paid Henry's taxes. He got out of jail but remembered his time there.*

9. Use Paraphrasing for Comprehension on a regular basis so that students have the opportunity to become proficient with the strategy. Continue to demonstrate paraphrasing for students and encourage students to use this strategy to expand their comprehension.

PARAPHRASING FOR COMPREHENSION

Name ________________________________ Date ____________

Title of Original Work ________________________________

1. Initial reading and discussion

2. Second reading with note-taking

3. Written paraphrase

Based on Fisk, C. & Hurst, B. (2003). Paraphrasing for comprehension. *The Reading Teacher*, *36,* 182–195.

WRITING DIFFERENT TYPES OF SUMMARIES

1. According to Gunning (2008), there are four ways that students can organize summaries: *gist*, *start-to-finish*, *point-by-point*, and *point of view*. Tell students that you are going to show them different ways to summarize fiction and informational texts.

2. Write *gist* on the chalkboard. You might start with *gist* because students are most familiar with this type of summary, even if the meaning of *gist* is unknown. If students have more experience with another type of summary, begin with that one. Explain that a *gist* summary typically lists the main ideas and supporting details or states the most important events or details. Provide students with a *gist* summary such as the following for *The Paper Bag Princess* (Munsch, 2000).

    A princess was going to marry a prince until he showed his true nature. The prince was captured by a dragon. The princess used her wits to get him free, but he didn't appreciate her efforts. At the end of the story, she walked away from him.

3. Once students are familiar with *gist*, list the other three types of summaries on the chalkboard. Explain each one to students. For example, you might say something like what follows.

    There are other ways to summarize things you have read. You can also organize by the start-to-finish *method. To do this, list the events or the details in chronological order. You could use the transition words* first, then, next, last, *and* finally. *An example from* The Paper Bag Princess *follows.*

    A dragon destroyed the castle of Princess Elizabeth and carried off Prince Ronald. Then Elizabeth came to Ronald's rescue. She tricked the dragon by making him burn 100 forests and fly around the world two times. After that she was able to free Ronald. At the end, Ronald didn't appreciate her efforts, and she left him.

4. Tell students that a third way to summarize text is to present a point-by-point description. In this case, you will list the details or events in the order of importance such as the following.

    Elizabeth and Ronald were in love and planned to marry. They encountered a traumatic experience which left Elizabeth without her castle or clothes. Ronald wasn't able to cope with Elizabeth's changed circumstances so they broke up.

5. Explain that the fourth way to summarize is by retelling with a point of view. To do this, provide a viewpoint and provide support for that viewpoint as in the following example.

    Men rely too much on outward appearance. When Elizabeth lost her looks due to her heroic attempt to rescue Ronald from the dragon, Ronald criticized her. Elizabeth did not respond to Ronald's bullying and left him to regain her shattered self-esteem.

6. Have students write each type of summary using the same text. Draw students' attention to how the summaries are the same and how they are different.

7. Remind students that they should use the *gist* summary in most school situations unless directed otherwise.

WRITING BOOK BLURBS

1. You can have students summarize fictional texts by writing Book Blurbs. Book Blurbs are the short summaries of fictional texts that include the key ideas of setting, characters, plot, and problem.
2. One way to have students think about Book Blurbs is to have them respond to the book while reading with a read-along guide (Athans & Devine, 2008). A read-along has students respond to their reading by writing to a sentence starter.
3. Select a book to read to demonstrate the strategy. For example, the book *Click, Clack, Moo, Cows That Type* (Cronin, 2000) is a picture book that you could use.
4. Remind students about the elements of fiction: setting, plot, characters, and problem. Tell students that they will be looking for the elements of fiction to develop a Book Blurb.
5. Read the first few pages of the book to students. Have them participate by thinking about the setting and characters and completing the following prompt.

   In these pages, we learn (about the setting and characters) that . . .

6. Continue reading the book, possibly finishing it. Ask students to think about the plot by considering events in a series. Have them complete the read-along prompt once again.

   In these pages, we learn (about the plot) that . . .

7. Discuss the students' responses to the book and list the settings, characters, and plot on the chalkboard. Then tell students that they can write a Book Blurb using that information.
8. Model how you would use the information to construct a Book Blurb by saying the following.

   I can use some of the information we wrote from the prompts to write a Book Blurb. In the first prompt we learned that the story took place on a farm with cows that have a typewriter. The next prompt shows how the farmer responds to the cows and how the duck begins her negotiations. We also learned from the ending prompt that the farmer did give in to the cows and the duck then made his own request. When I write the Book Blurb, I put all of this together to write something like this:

   This book is about some cows at a farm that got a typewriter. The cows began negotiating with the farmer by using notes. The farmer held his ground until the duck entered as a mediator. The farmer conceded to the cows' request. The duck then took over the typewriter and made a request of her own.

9. Have students develop Book Blurbs independently along with designs of the book covers. Post the Book Blurbs on a bulletin board to help motivate students to read a variety of books.

Practice and Reinforcement Activities

1. After teaching all three summary writing strategies (see page 550), give students a passage and ask them to use all three strategies. After they have finished, ask them which strategy they preferred, which was most useful, and when they could use each one.
2. When students are studying for tests, ask each student to summarize two important sections from the chapter. Combine the chapters into a booklet that students could use for study purposes.
3. Give students five minutes to discuss their hobbies with a partner. Then ask them to write down a summary of what their partner said. Share the summaries with the class.
4. Ask students to summarize their favorite television program. Give them an opportunity to read their summaries to a partner.
5. Have students listen to a story on tape read by a storyteller. Then have them summarize the story. They can share their summaries with the class by illustrating them and placing them on a bulletin board.
6. Have students do a one-sentence summary after you have read a book or after students have read a portion of text. Tell students to try to capture in one sentence the main point of the story or portion of text. Remind students that they should summarize in their minds when they read and that writing summaries lets them practice an important thinking skill.
7. Students can summarize their reading by creating a literacy mystery box (Pearman, Camp, & Hurst, 2004). After reading, students can select four or five items that represent the meaning of the text and place them in a box. Students then retell the story they have read using the items in the literacy mystery box as visual aids.
8. Students can have fun practicing the skill of summarizing by creating four-word movie or book reviews. To get ideas about how to teach this skill and for examples of four-word reviews for popular films, you can look at the website Four-Word Film Review (www.fwfr.com). [Note: You will not want to show this website to your class without first reading all reviews.] For example, a four-word summary for "The Wizard of Oz" could be *Lion, witch, wide road*. You might consider giving students the name of a book or movie that you know they have read or seen. List the title on the chalkboard and draw four spaces below it. Have students work in teams to come up with a four-word description that fits the book or movie. Write down the four-word summaries that students have generated. Invite students to share reasons for their selected words. Remind students that they can summarize in many different ways and that developing four-word summaries is just one way. Encourage students to try this activity during their free time.
9. Tell students that they can find summaries in many places in their every day life. Give examples of summaries students might hear. If students listen to the news, for example, they could hear a brief summary at the beginning of the broadcast. If you can, play a podcast of a news report so that students understand what you mean. Tell students that they could also hear summaries when talking with family or friends. When a friend recounts weekend events, it is an example of a summary. Provide an example such as the following: *Last weekend I went to a baseball game. Our high school was playing the team from the next town. Our team got a slow start but ended up winning the game five to two. We enjoyed seeing the team play*. Encourage students to be on the lookout for these types of summaries. Provide time occasionally for students to give their own examples of summaries they have heard or shared.

Section 7.7

Making Connections

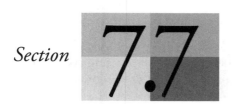

Behavior Observed → **Anticipated Outcome**

The student does not make connections while reading. → The student will make connections while reading.

Background

Students who make a wide variety of connections during reading have more possibilities for meaning making. Therefore, students who make connections to their personal experiences and to other texts as well as making connections within the text will have a richer range of ideas as they construct meaning from text. Although making connections is natural, students need to be encouraged to integrate knowledge they have from outside school with school learning. When students are guided to make connections, they generally do so. The teaching strategies and activities in this section can help students as they learn to make an expanding range of connections when reading.

Strategy 1 THINKING HATS

1. Make Thinking Hats (Moore, 1998) for each of the students in your class using six different colors of construction paper. Use the pattern for Thinking Hats on the following page to make the hats. Duplicate one sheet of hats per color. Cut out the Thinking Hats.
2. Attach each Thinking Hat to a craft stick. On the back of each hat, write one of the following types of connections: personal experiences, school subjects, other books, community, general knowledge, and people.
3. Select a story or a passage at the student's independent reading level. Provide students with ample time to read the selection.
4. Divide the class into groups with six students in each group. (One group may have fewer than six students.)
5. Give a different colored Thinking Hat to each student in a group. Be sure students understand what is meant by the word on their hats. Then tell students that the Thinking Hat that they have been given will be their focus for discussion about the story. You might say what follows.

   > *Each of you has a different color Thinking Hat. On the back of each hat is your discussion topic today. You might have a hat that has the words* personal experiences *on the back. You should tell the group what personal experiences you remembered as you read the story.*

6. Give students time to discuss the story using their Thinking Hats. After they have discussed the story in small groups, have them share their ideas by topic. For example, ask all of the students who had a hat with *other books* written on it to tell the class what other books they thought of as they read the story. Emphasize the different types of discussions that the Thinking Hats generate.
7. For variety, give each group the same kind of Thinking Hat so that one group has a *school subjects* hat, one group has a *personal experiences* hat, and so on.

THINKING HATS

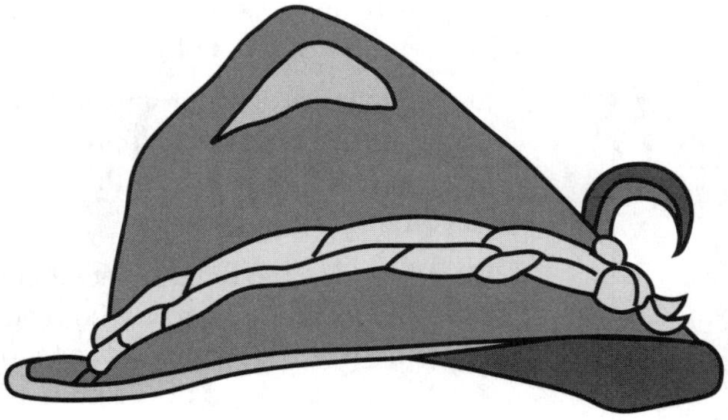

THINK SHEET

1. Select a story or a passage that students will be reading. Formulate an issue about the topic to be studied, such as the Industrial Revolution.
2. Duplicate and distribute the Think Sheet on page 557. Make a transparency of the Think Sheet to use to model the strategy.
3. Divide the class into groups of three or four students. Invite students to generate questions about the Industrial Revolution. Have groups share their ideas and write them on the section labeled *My Questions* on the Think Sheet. Some sample questions about the Industrial Revolution follow.
   - What was the biggest social change during that time period?
   - Who were the people who made up the middle class?
   - Who were the people of the working class?
   - What were some of the good points and bad points of the Industrial Revolution?
4. Tell students that the second column of the Think Sheet focuses on what students know about the issue before reading the text. Ask students to list their ideas about the changes of the Industrial Revolution before they read the text.
5. Explain to students that they should read the text to find answers to their questions and also to determine whether their ideas are supported by the text. Ask students to record facts as they read to answer their questions.
6. After students have completed the reading, have them share what they learned from the text. Guide students to make connections among their questions, their ideas, and ideas in the text. A partial example of a Think Sheet about the Industrial Revolution follows.

Think Sheet

Central Issue: What were the changes that occurred during the Industrial Revolution?		
My questions	My ideas	Text ideas
What was the biggest social change?	More money More freedom	The growing importance of the middle class
Who were the people in the middle class?	The middle class was composed of people who had some money but weren't rich.	The middle class was made up of business people who owned factories, mines, and banks.

THINK SHEET

Name ______________________________ Date ______________

Central Issue:		
My questions	*My ideas*	*Text ideas*

DIRECTED READING-CONNECTING ACTIVITY

1. Select a story or a passage that students have not read. Show students the title of the story and ask, "What do you think this story will be about?" Encourage students to draw upon their background knowledge to make predictions about the story. Write the students' predictions on the chalkboard, on chart paper, or on an overhead transparency.
2. Select a portion of text for students to read. Choose a stopping point after students have read enough of the story to have a sense of the problem but before the climax. Have students silently read the first portion of text. Tell students to stop at the predetermined point. Encourage students who finish early to think about the story thus far.
3. Write the following questions on the chalkboard or on an overhead transparency.
   - What other books does this story remind you of?
   - How does this story relate to what you've learned in school?
   - How does this story remind you of yourself?
4. Duplicate and distribute the Directed Reading-Connecting Activity (DR-CA) Chart that follows (Lenski, 1999). Have students discuss what has happened in the story up to the point they have read and write their ideas on the chart.
5. Then have students generate ideas about what they think will happen next in the story. Encourage students to think of as many possibilities as they can. Have students share their ideas.
6. Tell students that their predictions should be based on evidence from the story thus far. Have students justify their predictions with evidence from the story. Then have small groups of students share their predictions with justifications.
7. Repeat the DR-CA procedures one or two more times during the story. Have students use the DR-CA Chart for their ideas.
8. Encourage students to use the DR-CA thinking process as they read independently.

DR-CA CHART

Name ______________________________ Date ______________

Story Title ______________________________

Connections to other books		
Connections to school learning		
Connections to self		

Practice and Reinforcement Activities

1. Books on CDs are ideal for having students make connections (Labbo, 2000). Have students read and listen to a talking book on CD; then ask students to recall how events in the story are similar to other stories or to their personal experiences.
2. Create a Character Home Page (Stephens & Brown, 2000) from a book students have read. Have students identify an individual character from the story. Then have the students assume the character's identity. Help students design the Character's Home Page with the following information: personal information, characteristics, interests, hobbies, and so on. Encourage students to think of a wide variety of connections.
3. Gather students together in a literature circle. Give students the same book to read. Tell students that as they read you want them to make connections to other books, to personal experiences, and to school subjects. Encourage students to discuss the book and think of ways they can connect their story to other topics or events.
4. Have students bring family photographs to class. Tell students to place their photographs on their desks or tables and think of the many stories the photographs represent. Model using a photograph of your own. For example, say something like what follows.

   This is a picture of my family camping in Alaska. We set up our tent right next to that stream. We thought it was a wonderful camping site, but what we didn't know was that the Grizzlies in the area liked to come to that stream to catch fish. We were walking back to the tent when we saw four Grizzlies circling our tent. It didn't take us long after that to move our campsite.

   After telling one story, remind students that any memory can trigger many more memories. Continue making connections such as what follows.

   When I see that picture I think of the videos we have at home of Alaska. I also think about a book I read about the gold rush in Alaska.

   Provide students with ample time to make connections using their photographs.
5. Students can make connections by imagining themselves as someone who knows the characters in a story (Long & Gove, 2003). For example, if students are reading the story *Snow White*, they can imagine that they know Snow White or the Wicked Queen. Students should then imagine what life was like for these characters before the story took place. You might even assign students with character roles, such as best friend, neighbor, cousin, and so on. Have students create an imaginative dialog between the character and themselves. After this activity, have students make connections to their own lives.

Teachers need to be familiar with websites suggested for students.

Section **7.8**

Processing Text

Behavior Observed → **Anticipated Outcome**

The student does not process text after reading. → The student will use text-processing strategies to enhance comprehension.

Background

In order for students to have a rich comprehension of text, they need to process the information in the text in an elaborate fashion. After students have finished reading, they need to think about the text, talk about the text, manipulate the ideas, make connections to their existing knowledge, and regulate their learning (Massey, 2009). As they work with the text, students can continue learning more about the story or passage to improve their comprehension.

Strategy 1 SECTION 7.8

CHARACTER TRAITS MAP

1. Have students select a character from a story they have read.
2. Tell students that they can infer character traits from events in the story.
3. Duplicate and distribute copies of the Character Traits Map that follows.
4. Have students place the name of a character in the box.
5. Divide the class into groups of three or four students. Have students think of a character trait of the character they have chosen. For example, a character might be courageous.
6. Then have students list events from the story that provide evidence for that specific character trait.
7. Repeat the directions with a second character trait.
8. Have students share their thoughts with others in the class. Point out the similar and different perspectives students have about the same character.

CHARACTER TRAITS MAP

Name ______________________________ Date ______________

Directions: Choose a character from the story. Examine his/her actions to decide how to describe the character. Fill in two of the character's traits and the events from the story that led to your conclusions.

Name of Character

______________________ ______________________

Trait 1 Trait 2

Events Supporting Trait	Events Supporting Trait

Strategy 2

RETELLING

Retelling is a strategy to help students summarize, organize, and recognize elements in all types of printed materials. However, retellings are generally applied to literature selections and are often used in the lower grades. Students having difficulty in reading can be helped to remember story sequence and character elements in the story by using words such as *first, next, last, then,* and *finally.* Although retellings can be written, they are most often thought of as an oral activity.

Refer to the following procedures and guidelines for helpful suggestions for retelling narrative and expository text. Additional retelling suggestions can be found in Johns (2008).

Retelling Procedure for Narrative Passages

1. Ask the student to retell the passage by saying, "Tell me about (name or title of passage) as if you were telling it to someone who has never heard it before."
2. Use the following prompts only when necessary.
   - What comes next?
   - Then what happened?

   If the student stops retelling and does not continue with the prompts, ask a question about the passage that is based on that point in the passage at which the student has paused. For example, "What did the boys do after raking the leaves?"
3. When a student is unable to retell the story, or if the retelling lacks sequence and detail, prompt the retelling step by step. The following questions may help you.
   - Who was the passage about?
   - When did the story happen?
   - Where did the story happen?
   - What was the main character's problem?
   - How did he (or she) try to solve the problem? What was done first/next?
   - How was the problem solved?
   - How did the story end?

Retelling Expectations for Informational Passages

Independent level retelling will generally reflect:
- the text structure
- organization of how the material was presented
- main ideas and details contained in the text

Instructional level retelling will generally reflect:
- less content than at the independent level
- some minor misrepresentations and inaccuracies
- organization that differs from the actual text

Frustration level retelling will generally be:
- haphazard
- incomplete
- characterized by bits of information not related logically or sequentially

Strategy 3 HERRINGBONE

1. Tell students that the Herringbone pattern helps them organize information.
2. Duplicate and distribute the Herringbone pattern on page 565 or draw a Herringbone pattern on the chalkboard or on an overhead transparency.
3. Point out the features of the Herringbone pattern. Point to the horizontal line and say something like the following:

    This line is for the main idea of the story. Think about the story we have just read. What do you think was the main idea? Write it on the horizontal line.

4. Have students share their main ideas with others. Give students a chance to modify their original thoughts.
5. Show students the angled lines off the main idea.
6. Write the following words on a copy of the Herringbone pattern as in the example that follows: who, what, where, when, why, and how.

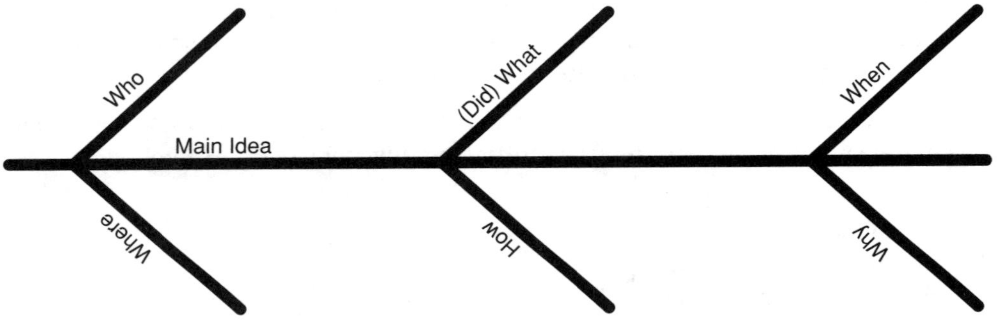

7. Have students answer the following questions on the angled lines in the Herringbone pattern.
    - Who is the passage about?
    - What is the passage about?
    - Where did the passage take place?
    - When did the action happen?
    - Why did the action happen?
    - How did the action happen?
8. Provide students with ample time to answer the questions and share their ideas with others.

HERRINGBONE

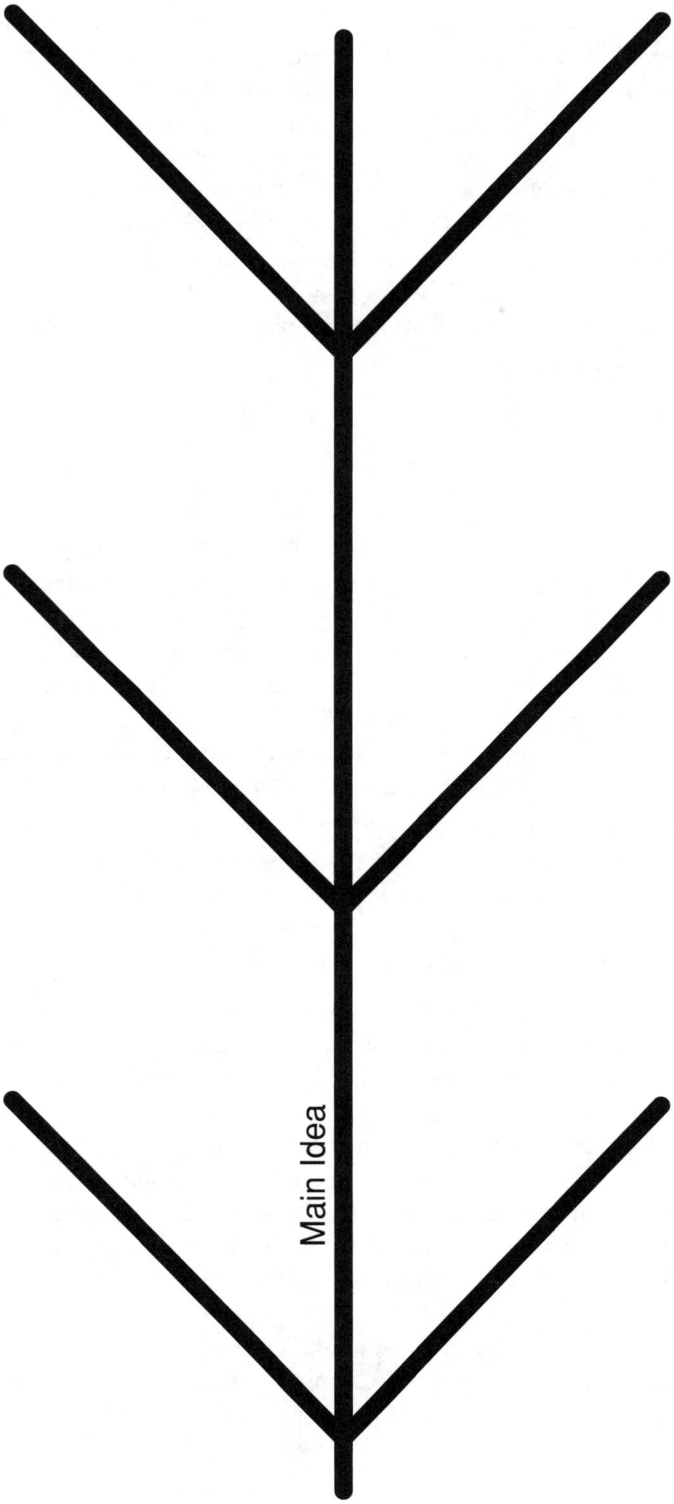

Practice and Reinforcement Activities

1. Locate a roll of adding machine paper and cut strips about three feet long. Have students divide the paper into as many sections as there are chapters in a book. Include an additional section for their names, the title of the book, and the name of the author. Have students draw a picture on each section illustrating the events of the chapters. Encourage students to include a caption under the picture. Make a slit in a small box and run the strip through the slit so that the pictures show through the opening of the box.
2. Have students bring to school large paper sacks. Slit the sack down the front and add arm holes and a scooped neck. Have students design and color the vest to represent a story that they have read.
3. Implement learning logs so students can reflect on their reading. Learning logs can be used in conjunction with any area of the curriculum. Teachers may provide daily or weekly opportunities for students to write in their learning logs. A list of learning log prompts is provided below.
   - Something important I learned is . . .
   - I don't understand . . .
   - I want to learn more about . . .
   - I wonder why . . .
   - I get confused by . . .
4. Have students participate in a paraphrase passport (Faltis, 2001). After students have read a story or a passage from a text, divide the class into groups of three or four students. Ask one student to begin to retell the story or passage. After the first student has begun the retelling, ask a second student to paraphrase the words of the first student. Then the second student should continue retelling the story, and a third student should paraphrase the second student's words and continue retelling the story and so on until the story has been completely retold.
5. After students have read a passage of text, lead a discussion to promote deep thinking. Consider the following as you prepare questions for discussions after reading (Roe, Stoodt, & Burns, 2001).
   - What are the important ideas in this selection?
   - What ideas and concepts do I want the students to remember from this selection?
   - What questions will lead students to understand these ideas and concepts?
   - What thinking abilities have students already developed?
   - What thinking abilities do students need to develop?
6. Students can become editors and experts on a specific topic by creating skinny books. Individually or in small groups, students select a specific topic related to the unit of study in the classroom. Students gather articles, pamphlets, pictures, interviews, letters, and other resources related to their topic. They identify key ideas related to their topic and develop an outline or semantic map to organize their material. They become the editor of their book as they cut, paste, write headlines, create headings and subheadings, write introductions, and create connecting information for their skinny book. Students can also highlight key vocabulary words and create a glossary, develop a table of contents, and make an index for their skinny book. Students can add illustrations, charts, graphs, tables, and other graphics to clarify their topics. Students can do presentations on their topics, and their skinny books can be added to the classroom library.
7. Encourage students to write "wish you were here" letters to clarify their learning about new places, important events, and important people. For example, students could write "wish you were here" letters about meeting with Abraham Lincoln after hearing the Gettysburg Address, traveling to Jupiter, visiting the rain forest, or participating in the Battle of the Alamo.

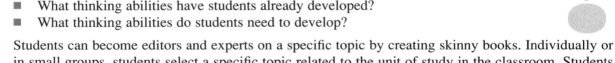

Section **7.9**

Evaluating Written Materials

Behavior Observed → **Anticipated Outcome**

The student has difficulty evaluating written materials.

The student will use information from text to evaluate written materials.

Background

The ability to read between and beyond the lines is regarded as higher-level comprehension and is often referred to as critical reading or problem solving (Wink, 2001). It involves the ability to judge, analyze, or evaluate what is read. Implicit task demands of the reader at this level include distinguishing fact from opinion; recognizing propaganda techniques; evaluating the author's bias, competence, accuracy, and viewpoint; and reacting to what has been written on the basis of one's background and experience.

Reading instruction and classroom questions often focus on the lower levels of comprehension. This emphasis is shortsighted and prevents readers from reaching their full potential. However, there are actions teachers can take to help students evaluate and react to what is read. Several strategies are presented in this section.

Strategy 1

DISTINGUISHING FACT FROM OPINION

1. Ask students whether they believe everything they read and encourage students to share their reasons. Look for the opportunity during this discussion to use the words *facts* and *opinions*.
2. Discuss the differences between facts and opinions. You may look up the words in the dictionary and discuss their meanings. List attributes of facts and opinions that are derived from each word's meaning.

Facts	**Opinions**
things known to exist	beliefs
real or true	judgments
actual events	personal attitudes
you can prove them	what someone thinks about something

3. Write the following sentence on the chalkboard: *Greg looks outside and sees that it is raining*. Have students decide whether *it is raining* is fact or opinion. Help them decide that it is a fact because Greg can see it raining.
4. Now have students assume that they asked three different people "What's the weather?" and the following responses are given.

   Tiffany: Rainy
   Roman: Great
   Ester: Terrible

   Ask students to identify each response as fact or opinion and to offer possible explanations for the two opinions. For example, Roman said the weather was "great" and may be a farmer who knows a recent planting needs rain. Ester said the weather was "terrible" because she may have planned a picnic and is disappointed.
5. Take time to stress that a person's background, feelings, attitudes, and beliefs can influence how events, actions, and even facts are interpreted. Relate these factors to the reading done by students.
6. Provide a brief passage, such as the following one, and have students decide which statements are facts and which are opinions.

   > Pennsylvania is the best state. Its capital is Harrisburg. Pennsylvania became a state on December 12, 1787. It is one of the oldest states. Almost everyone likes Pennsylvania.

   Be sure to allow ample time for students to share reasons why they identify a sentence as fact or opinion. Stress that some writers state their opinions as if they were facts.

DISCUSSION GRID

1. Provide students with a story to read or a passage from a content area textbook. Tell students that as they read they should think about the ideas from the text that interest them.
2. Duplicate and distribute copies of the Discussion Grid (Taylor, 1998) on page 571. If possible, make a transparency of the Discussion Grid to project on an overhead projector. Use the transparency to model how to use the Discussion Grid.
3. Point out to students the sections of the Discussion Grid. Tell students that the section *Ideas from the text* should be used as they read. Explain to students that when reading they should pay attention to facts in the text that are of interest to them.
4. Model how to take note of ideas from the text as in the following.

> *I am going to read a section from our science book titled* Creatures of the Night. *First, I'll preview the section. As I preview the text, I find that the author writes about raccoons, bats, flying squirrels, and opossums. After previewing the text, I begin to read. One thing I notice right away is that raccoons sleep during the day. I know from experience that raccoons often forage at night, but I never really thought about them sleeping during the day.*

5. Write *raccoons sleep during the day* in the first box of the Discussion Grid as in the following example.

Discussion Grid

Ideas from the text	Your response	Comments of others		
Raccoons sleep during the day.		Name ________	Name ________	Name ________

6. Continue reading the passage and write other ideas from the text in the additional boxes in that section.
7. Then tell students that while reading they should be thinking about the facts they have identified. Model how to write a response to the facts as in the following example.

> *As I was thinking about raccoons sleeping during the day, I wondered where they sleep and if the light and noise during the day bother them.*

8. Add your sample response to the box titled *Your response*. An example follows.

Discussion Grid

Ideas from the text	Your response	Comments of others		
Raccoons sleep during the day.	I didn't know this. I wonder where they sleep?	Name ________	Name ________	Name ________

9. After the students have read the passage, have them fill out the first two sections of the Discussion Grid. After students have listed ideas from the text and their responses, divide the class into groups of three or four students. Have students take turns sharing an idea and response. After one student has told the group an idea, have the group member make comments. Have the student who expressed an idea record the comments on the Discussion Grid.

DISCUSSION GRID

Ideas from the text	*Your response*	*Comments of others*
		Name______ Name______ Name______
		Name______ Name______ Name______
		Name______ Name______ Name______

Strategy 3 CHARACTER REPORT CARD

1. Tell students that when they read fictional books they can form judgments about the characters in the story. Explain that forming judgments about fictional characters helps readers expand their comprehension by relating in positive or negative ways to the character.
2. Select a story or a novel for students to read that gives details about a character. Provide ample time for students to read the selection.
3. Divide the class into groups of three or four students and ask students to discuss the character. Encourage students to provide factual details about the character's actions, statements, and thoughts. Then ask students to share their opinions about the character.
4. Read the Character Report Card that follows and modify it if needed. Duplicate and distribute the Character Report Card to students.
5. Have the groups of students discuss each of the character traits and assign the character a grade. Tell students that the group's grade should be unanimous.
6. After students have assigned a grade, have them discuss the reasons for the grade. Then have students list several of their reasons below the grade.
7. Ask students to complete the entire Character Report Card. After the groups have finished, have them share their grades with their classmates.

CHARACTER REPORT CARD

Name ______________________________ Date ______________

Name of character ______________________________

Title of book ______________________________

Friendship Grade ________

Reasons: ______________________________

____

Courage Grade ________

Reasons: ______________________________

____

Intelligence Grade ________

Reasons: ______________________________

____

Compassion Grade ________

Reasons: ______________________________

____

Responsibility Grade ________

Reasons: ______________________________

____

Group members: ______________________________

____

Strategy 4

DISCUSSION WEB

1. After students have read a passage from the text, introduce a central question on a Discussion Web (Alvermann, 1991). The question should be one that lends itself to opposing viewpoints. Write the question on the chalkboard or on an overhead transparency. For example, ask students the following question after they have read *Where the Red Fern Grows* (Rawls, 1961).

   Should Billy have cut down the big old sycamore tree in order to get to the coon?

2. Divide the class into groups of three or four students. Ask students to brainstorm at least three reasons for answering *yes* to the central question. Then have students generate at least three reasons for answering *no* to the central question. When students have written their reasons for answering the question in the affirmative and the negative, ask them to volunteer some of their ideas. Write the ideas in two separate columns as listed below.

No	**Yes**
It would take a long time to grow.	He shouldn't disappoint his dogs.
When it fell it could hurt something.	His dogs worked for it.
It's part of nature.	He said he would.
It was his favorite tree.	He felt he had to.

3. Discuss both sides of the question as objectively as possible. Then encourage students to take a position either for or against the issue. Some students will want to take both sides. Tell them that, although they understand both sides of the issue, they need to take one position.
4. Ask students to come to conclusions independently, defending the side they have chosen. Have them write their conclusions on index cards. Collect the index cards when students are finished and use them to learn which conclusions students have chosen. An example of a conclusion follows.

Conclusion

Billy should have cut down the tree because he wanted to keep his word.

5. A blank Discussion Web follows. Duplicate and distribute the Discussion Web for students to use with another reading selection.

DISCUSSION WEB*

Name ______________________________ Date ______________

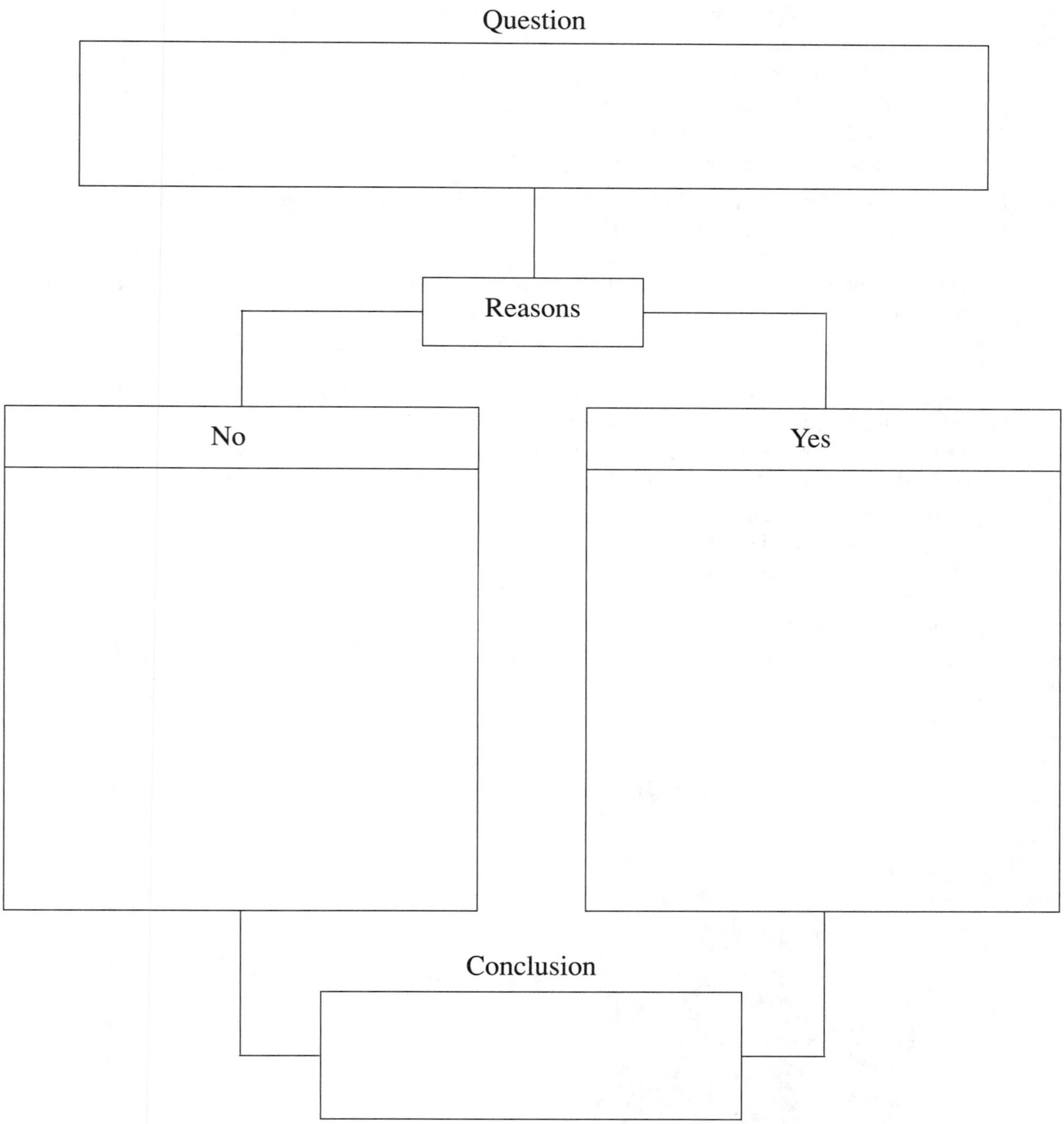

*Alvermann, 1991.

Practice and Reinforcement Activities

1. Provide sentences and have students identify them as facts (F) or opinions (O). Some sentences may require research. Take time to discuss students' responses and reasons for their decisions. An example follows.

   ___*F*___ Charles Lindbergh made the first solo flight across the Atlantic Ocean.
   ___*O*___ Lindbergh's plane is nice.
   ___*F*___ Amelia Earhart was the first woman to fly solo across the Atlantic Ocean.
   ___*F*___ Earhart wrote a book called *Soaring Wings.*
   ___*O*___ I read her book and liked it.
   ___*O*___ Generally, airplanes are the best way to travel.

2. Prepare questions for a selection and have students decide whether their answers are facts or opinions. Have students discuss their responses.
3. Present a problem and have students suggest as many solutions to the problem as possible. Then evaluate the proposed solutions and select the ones that appear to be the most workable. Use this same technique with problems in stories.
4. Additional resources for the facts-and-opinions exercises can be found in newspaper articles, advertising, editorials, columns, and cartoons.
5. Challenge students to write their own persuasive paragraph or advertisements using one of the persuasive propaganda techniques discussed. Volunteers can share them with the class.
6. Teachers can also have students evaluate written materials by engaging them in critical discussions (Bean & Moni, 2003). Students can discuss questions such as the ones that are listed below.
   - What is the background of the story?
   - What purpose does the story serve?
   - Who is the ideal reader for this story?
   - How else might the character's story be told?
   - Whose voice is left out of the story?

   Through discussions of these types of questions, students can learn to think beyond the text.

These students can be asked to evaluate the websites they are reading.

Section **7.10**

Remembering

Behavior Observed → **Anticipated Outcome**

The student has difficulty remembering what was read. → The student learns strategies to remember what was read.

Background

Part of reading is remembering. Effective readers remember much of what they read and are able to recall needed information. But remembering isn't always easy. Some students have difficulty remembering and, for those students, memory strategies are helpful. Of course, students won't remember everything they read, but a few strategies can help them remember more than they did before learning the strategies.

Part of reading is remembering.

After these students do their homework, will they remember what they read?

MEMORIZATION TECHNIQUES

1. Tell students they will need to remember parts of their reading.
2. Explain that the first thing students should do is plan to remember. Tell them that their minds will react differently to information that they have consciously intended to commit to long-term memory. To model how you would plan to remember, you might say something like what follows.

   I've got to read this section in my science book on the habitat of dolphins. I know Ms. Linder said this section was important both for our test and for a project we will be working on. I'm going to remember this information as I read it and not just gloss over it.

3. Remind students that they need to schedule time for remembering. Many students prefer to memorize information and facts last in their schedule. Ask students to write down when they will be studying and to write in times for memorizing information and facts.
4. Tell students that as they memorize they should read the entire chapter that discusses the points they want to remember. This will help them understand the relationship of the facts to other information they know.
5. Give students a chance to talk about the things they want to remember. During science class, for example, provide students with several minutes to discuss the ideas that they have been memorizing with a partner.
6. Explain the use of mnemonic devices. A mnemonic device is a memory strategy that helps you retain bits of information. Following are examples of mnemonic devices that you can teach to your class.

Mnemonic Devices

Rhyme—Create a rhyme or a song that includes the points you have to learn. *"Thirty days hath September . . ."*

Acronyms—Form words by using the first letter from each of the words to be recalled. *HOMES (Names of the Great Lakes: Huron, Ontario, Michigan, Erie, Superior)*

Pegwood—Memorize a short rhyme and then create the images that link the nouns in the rhyme with the items to be remembered.

Method of Loci—Select a spatial layout, such as your home. Mentally place the items to be recalled in each room.

Clustering—Memorize the material in categories and learn them as a pattern.

Silly Sentences—Make up a silly sentence from the first letter of each word to be remembered. *Even After Dinner, Giraffes Bend Easily (guitar strings E, A, D, G, B, E).*

Numbering—When you are memorizing a group of words, remember how many items there are to avoid missing any when you need to recall them.

Strategy 2 SECTION 7.10

DRAW

1. Choose a short article, story, or content area chapter to read to your students.
2. Prepare a series of numbered questions about the selection at the literal, inferential, and applied levels of comprehension.
3. Distribute the question sheets to students or to small groups of students. Tell students that they will DRAW (Agnew, 2000) the passage. Explain that DRAW stands for Draw, Read, Attend, and Write.
4. Cut the sheet into strips so that one question is on each sentence strip. Mix up the question strips and have each individual or group draw one question.
5. Tell students that their group will be responsible for the question that they have drawn. Then have students read the passage.
6. After students have read the passage, ask a student to read and answer his or her question to the class. Ask the other students whether they agree or disagree with the answer to the question. Encourage students to pay attention to the class discussion. Explain that they will need to remember what they read and what other students said during the class discussion.
7. When all of the questions have been answered and discussed, gather the question slips to use as a quiz. Read the questions to the students and have students write the answers. Have students correct their responses to determine how much they remembered from the text.

Strategy 3 SECTION 7.10

TRIANGLE TRIGGER WORDS

1. Select a piece of text to use that has information that you want students to remember. The selection could be from a textbook or it could be another type of informational book. For example, you might read the book *Talking Walls* by Marge Burns Knight (1992).
2. Identify several key words or phrases in advance that could help students remember portions of the text. Write the words on the chalkboard as in the following example.

Seen on Moon	Murals
Great Wall of China	Veterans
Aborigines	Iron Curtain
Cave	Pilgrimage

3. Explain to students that key words can "trigger" their memories so that they remember other information. Model how you would remember more information using trigger words.

> *When I see the word* murals, *I remember the part of the book that discussed Diego Rivera's murals all over Mexico. I remember that I was intrigued that Rivera painted big scenes on government buildings in Mexico and that he also was commissioned to paint one in New York City. The mural that was highlighted in the book looked almost like a picture from a children's book.*

4. Ask students to draw several triangles on a piece of paper. The triangles can be different types and sizes, just so they are large enough to fit a word inside.
5. Tell students that as they read they should identify key words that will help them remember. Have students write one key word in each triangle as is shown below.

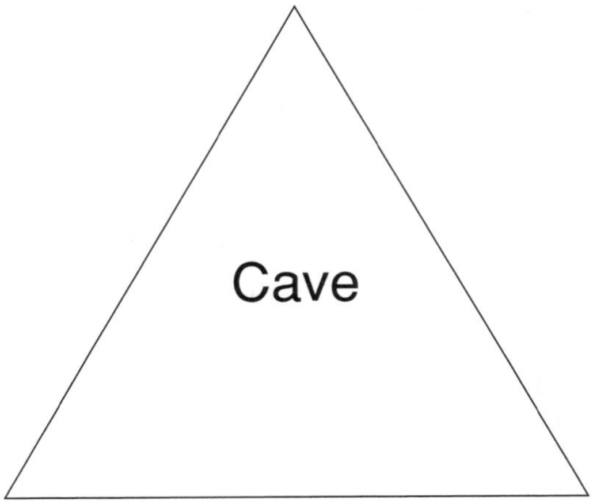

6. You might have students cut out the triangles and paste them on index cards. Tell students that these Triangle Trigger Words will help them remember what they have read.
7. Model this strategy many times, each time encouraging students to discover their own key words as they read. Remind students that they should think of key words as they read independently as well as in class.

Strategy 4 SECTION 7.10

REACTION GUIDE

1. Select a passage of text that students haven't read. Look for the most important facts that you want students to remember. An example of a passage about pyramids is on page 581. Use the passage as a guide for this strategy.
2. Develop a series of sentences based on information from the passage. Print the sentences similar to the example on page 582 called Reaction Guide for Pyramid Article. The sentences should have a before reading column and an after reading column. Each of those columns should have the words *true* and *false*.
3. Duplicate and distribute the Reaction Guide to students before they have read the passage.
4. Tell students that sometimes you will alert them to the things they should remember from the text. Tell them that you would like them to predict the answers to the statements on the Reaction Guide. Have students answer *true* or *false* for each of the statements.
5. Ask students to read the passage and look for the correct answer to the statements. As they read, remind students to remember what they have learned.
6. After students have finished reading, have them complete the second column. Determine from their answers which students are having difficulty remembering what was read.

PYRAMIDS

The Ancient Egyptians built many pyramids, but the most famous of these are the three pyramids of Giza, near Cairo, the capital of Egypt. Over the years, the city has gradually crept closer. Now there are new houses almost at the feet of the pyramids. But if you look at the pyramids across the city, they still rise up, silent and mysterious, on the edge of the great desert. For more than four thousand years, they have stood there, barely changed by the passage of time.

The largest of the three pyramids was built by King Khufu or King Cheops, to use his Greek name. This is called the Great Pyramid. It was the first to be built at Giza, in about 2500 B.C. The second largest is only a few feet lower and was built by Khafre (or Chephren in Greek), the son of Khufu. The third pyramid in this group is much smaller and was built by King Menkaure (or Mycerinus in Greek). All three pyramids were built in the space of about 80 years.

The Great Pyramid is made of limestone and is the same color as the sand and rock of the desert around it. There are no trees or other plants on this plain—just dry, open spaces. The pyramid soars to 137 meters above this—about as high as a 40-story modern skyscraper. A total of 2,300,000 blocks of stone, weighing between 2½ and 5 tons each, were used to build the Great Pyramid. It is still the biggest stone building in the world. Assuming that the pyramid was completed within Khufu's 23-year reign, this means that some 100,000 of these huge blocks of stone had to be prepared and put into position each year—or 273 every day. The Great Pyramid was the most ambitious of the pharaoh's many great building works; in view of its huge size it is not surprising that it has been called "Pharaoh's Mountain."

Enormous though this monument is, the stone blocks are so accurately cut and so carefully fitted together (without mortar) that in many cases the joints will not allow even a sheet of paper to be inserted. The actual position of the Great Pyramid is also remarkably precise: its sides face almost exactly north, east, south and west. How was all this done? How could a people who lived so long ago and who only had very simple tools plan and carry out such a great project?

REACTION GUIDE FOR PYRAMID ARTICLE

Name ______________________________ Date ______________

Directions:
- Before you read the article on pyramids, read each statement below. Depending on what you believe, circle true or false for each statement.
- After you read the article, decide if the statement is true or false based on the article. Circle the word to the right of each statement.

Before Reading			After Reading	
True	False	1. Some pyramids are located near Cairo.	True	False
True	False	2. The pyramids are over 10,000 years old.	True	False
True	False	3. The three pyramids of Giza are quite famous.	True	False
True	False	4. The Great Pyramid is called Khafre.	True	False
True	False	5. The Great Pyramid is made of granite and is the biggest stone building in the world.	True	False
True	False	6. There are over 3 million blocks of stone in the Great Pyramid.	True	False
True	False	7. The blocks of stone weigh between $2\frac{1}{2}$ and 5 tons each.	True	False
True	False	8. The Great Pyramid is taller than the Leaning Tower of Pisa.	True	False
True	False	9. Mortar was used to hold the blocks of stone together.	True	False
True	False	10. The sides of the pyramid face almost exactly north, south, east, and west.	True	False

Practice and Reinforcement Activities

1. Encourage students to use a variety of memory devices. Ask them to use several different devices on the same information. Explain that different students will find some strategies more effective than others. Ask them which ones they thought worked best for them and why.
2. Have students keep Memory Journals. Tell students to record in their Memory Journal things they especially want to remember. Provide time for students to share special memories from their journals.
3. Tell students that a location often triggers memory. Provide an example similar to what follows.

   I was trying to remember the author of a book I had just read. I just couldn't remember. Then I thought about the book and pictured where it was located on my bookshelf. As I pictured the book, I remembered how the title page looked, and I thought of the author.

   Ask students to share times they used a location for memory. Encourage students to try this strategy when they are trying to remember what they read.
4. Tell students to use Post-it® notes to write down things they want to remember as they read. Explain that thoughts can leave our memory if they are not written down. Provide students with Post-it® notes when they read independently.
5. Some students will remember what they have read if they draw pictures of the plot. After students have read the first few chapters of a fictional text, have them draw pictures of what they can remember. Then have them read the middle of the book and draw a second picture. Finally, have them read the end of the book and draw a third picture. After students have drawn three pictures illustrating the book, have them retell the story focusing on the beginning, middle, and end. Correct student misconceptions, if necessary. Once students have retold the story correctly, have them write a short summary from memory.
6. Students can remember what they have read sometimes if they listen to a book on a CD (Pearman, 2008). Students not only can hear the story, but there are often hyperlinks to words that give students definitions. These definitions are helpful for selections that have words unknown to students. When students are able to both listen and learn words, they are able to focus on comprehending, making meaning, and remembering the story.
7. Draw a stoplight with the words ready, read, and remember. Before students read, have them get ready by looking at the pictures and making predictions. While reading, students can monitor comprehension and continue making predictions. After reading, students should remember what the story was about.

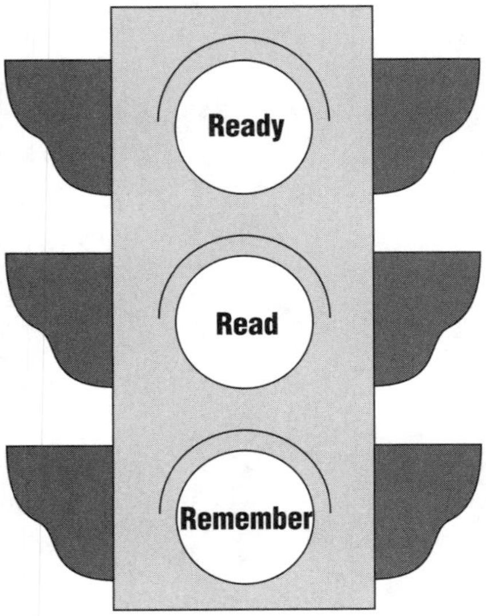

Ready

- What clues do I get from the picture?
- What do I think will happen?
- Why am I reading this book?

Read

- What will happen next?
- Does the story make sense?

Remember

- What was the story about?
- What did I learn?
- What do I want to remember about this book?

7

Resources

Note: indicates student reproducible.

STORY MAP USING STORY GRAMMAR

Name ______________________________ Date ______________

Title

Setting

Characters

Problem

Events

Solution

STORY MAP SHOWING CHARACTER CHANGE

Name ______________________________ Date ______________

Turning Point

Character at Beginning of Story	Events that Caused Change	Character at End of Story

STORY MAP USING CHRONOLOGICAL EVENTS

Name ______________________________ Date ______________

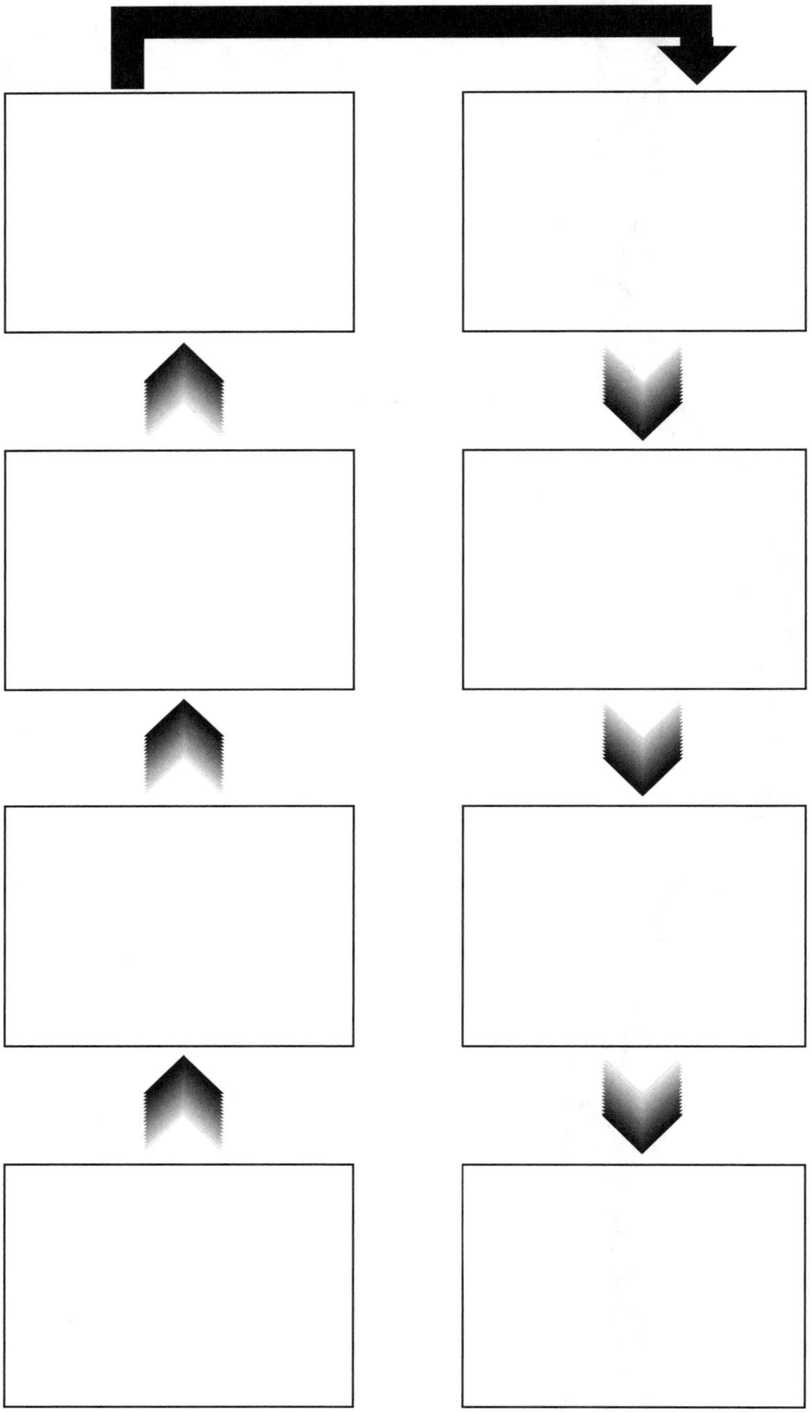

STORY MAP SHOWING EVENTS

Name ______________________________ Date ______________

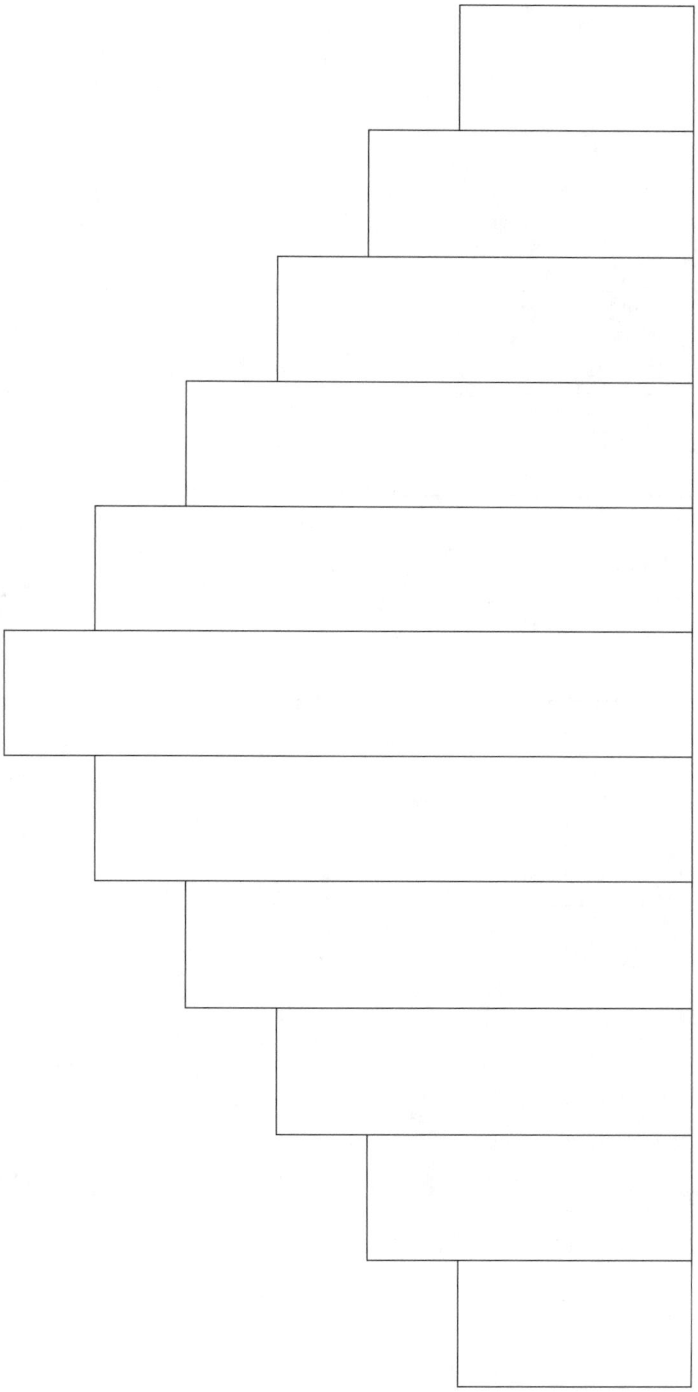

STORY SUMMARY WITH ONE CHARACTER

Name ______________________________ Date ______________

Our story is about ______________________________

______________________________.

______________________________ is an important character in the story.

______________________________ tried to ______________________________

______________________________.

The story ends when ______________________________

______________________________.

IMPORTANT IDEA OR PLOT

Name ______________________________ Date ______________

In this story the problem starts when ______________________________

____.

After that, ____.

Next, ____.

Then, ____.

The problem is finally solved when ______________________________

____.

The story ends ____

____.

SETTING

Name ______________________________ Date ______________

This story takes place ______________________________.

I know this because the author uses the words "______________________________

______________________________."

Other clues that show when and where the story takes place are ______________________________

______________________________.

MAIN IDEA-MAP

Name ______________________________ Date ______________

Topic

Details

Main Idea Sentence

COMPARE-CONTRAST IDEA-MAP

Name ____ Date ____________________

Topic:		Topic:
	=	
	=	
	=	
	≠	
	≠	
	≠	

SEQUENCE IDEA-MAP

Name ______________________________ Date ______________

Topic:

↓

↓

↓

↓

↓

CAUSE-EFFECT IDEA-MAP

Name ________________________ Date ____________

Cause:	→	Effect:

STUDENT SELF-CHECK LIST

Name ______________________________ Date ______________

	Yes	No
Before you began reading, did you		
1. ask yourself what the reading was going to be about?	☐	☐
2. think about what you already knew about the topic?	☐	☐
3. make a prediction about the contents of the passage?	☐	☐
As you were reading, did you		
4. know if you didn't understand something?	☐	☐
5. stop and read again if you didn't understand?	☐	☐
6. read ahead if you didn't know a word to see if you could figure it out from the words around it?	☐	☐
7. try to put yourself in the story?	☐	☐
8. check to see whether your prediction was correct?	☐	☐
9. make a new prediction?	☐	☐
After you finished reading, did you		
10. think about what the passage was mostly about?	☐	☐
11. think about your predictions? Were they proven correct? Why or why not?	☐	☐
12. think about how you might use the information in the future?	☐	☐

Adapted from Roberta L. Berglund and Richard J. Telfer (unpublished).

WHAT I DID WHILE READING

Name ______________________________ Date ______________

Here's my self-evaluation of what I did while I was reading ______________________________ (name of book or story).

I checked (✓) those things I did.

Strategies	*Not Much*	*A Little*	*Most of the Time*	*Almost Always*
Used text structure				
Made predictions				
Made pictures in my mind				
Found problems like hard words and not understanding				
Fixed problems by rereading, looking ahead, and checking the dictionary				
Summarized				
Asked myself questions				

Here are other strategies I used:

____

____

____

____

____

Adapted from Davey, B. (1983). Think-aloud—Modeling the cognitive processes of reading comprehension. *Journal of Reading, 27,* 44–47.

STUDENT CHECKLIST

Name ____ Date ____________________

Please draw a face in each box to show how you feel about the following sentences.

If you feel this way often, draw 

If you feel this way sometimes, draw 

If you never feel this way, draw 

I like to find things out for myself. I am curious. ☐

I like to read. ☐

I understand what I read. ☐

I try to figure out new words by myself. ☐

I use what I already know. ☐

I have lots of trouble with words. ☐

References

Adams, M.J. (1990a). *Beginning to read: Thinking and learning about print.* (A summary prepared by S.A. Stahl, J. Osborn, & F. Lear). Champaign, IL: University of Illinois.

Adams, M.J. (1990b). *Beginning to read: Thinking and learning about print.* Cambridge, MA: MIT Press.

Agnew, M.L. (2000). DRAW: A motivational reading comprehension strategy for disaffected readers. *Journal of Adolescent & Adult Literacy, 46,* 574–576.

Allington, R.L. (2009). *What really matters in fluency: Research-based practices across the curriculum.* Boston: Pearson.

Allington, R.L. (2009). *What really matters in Response to Intervention: Research-based designs.* Boston: Pearson.

Allington, R.L., & McGill-Franzen, A. (2009). Comprehension difficulties among struggling readers. In S. Israel & G. Duffy (Eds.), *Handbook of research on reading comprehension* (pp. 551–568). New York: Routledge.

Allington, R.L., & Walmsley, S.A. (Eds.) (2007). *No quick fix: Rethinking literacy programs in America's elementary schools—The RTI edition.* Newark, DE and New York: International Reading Association and Teachers College Press.

Almasi, J.F. (2003). *Teaching strategic processes in reading.* New York: Guilford.

Alvermann, D. (1991). The discussion web: A graphic aid for learning across the curriculum. *The Reading Teacher, 45,* 92–99.

Alvermann, D.E., Moon, J.S., & Hagood, M.C. (1999). *Popular culture in the classroom: Teaching and researching critical media literacy.* Newark, DE: International Reading Association and Chicago, IL: National Reading Conference.

Ames, C. (1992). Classrooms: Goal, structures, and student motivation. *Journal of Educational Psychology, 84,* 261–271.

Anderson, R.S., & Speck, B. (2001). *Using technology in K–8 classrooms.* Upper Saddle River, NJ: Prentice Hall.

Anthony, J., Lonigan, C., Driscoll, K., Phillips, B., & Burgess, S. (2003). Phonological sensiticity: A quasi-parallel progression of word structure units and cognitive operations. *Reading Research Quarterly, 38,* 470–487.

Applegate, A.J., & Applegate, M.D. (2004). The Peter Effect: Reading habits and attitudes of preservice teachers. *The Reading Teacher, 57,* 554–563.

Armbruster, B.B. (1986). Using frames to organize expository text. Paper presented at the National Reading Conference, Austin, TX.

Armbruster, B.B., Lehr, F., & Osborn, J. (2001). *Put reading first: The research building blocks for teaching children to read.* Jessup, MD: National Institute for Literacy.

Arthaud, T.J., & Goracke, T. (2006). Implementing a structured story web and outline strategy to assist struggling readers. *The Reading Teacher, 59,* 581–586.

Athans, S.K., & Devine, D.A. (2008). *Quality comprehension: A strategic model of reading instruction using Read-along Guides, Grades 3–6.* Newark, DE: International Reading Association.

Ball, E.W., & Blachman, B.A. (1991). Does phonemic awareness training in kindergarten make a difference in early word recognition and developmental spelling? *Reading Research Quarterly, 26,* 49–66.

Bannatyne-Cugnet, J. (1994). *A prairie year.* Plattsburgh, NY: Tundra.

Barr, R., Blachowicz, C., Buhle, R., Chaney, J., Ivy, C., Uchtman, A., Pigott, T., & Suarez-Silva, G. (2004). *Illinois snapshots of early literacy kindergarten/grade 1 technical manual.* Springfield, IL: Illinois State Board of Education.

Barton, J., & Sawyer, D.M. (2004). Our students *are* ready for this: Comprehension instruction in the elementary school. *The Reading Teacher, 57,* 334–347.

Base, Graeme. (1986). *Animalia.* New York: Harry N. Abrams.

Baumann, J.F. (2009). Vocabulary and reading comprehension: The nexus of meaning. In S. Israel & G. Duffy (Eds.), *Handbook of research on reading comprehension* (pp. 323–346). New York: Routledge.

Baumann, J.F., Kame'enui, E.J., & Ash, G.E. (2003). Research on vocabulary instruction: Voltaire redux. In J. Flood, D. Lapp, J.R. Squire, & J.M. Jensen (Eds.), *Handbook of research on teaching the English language arts* (pp. 752–785). Mahwah, NJ: Lawrence Erlbaum.

Bean, T.W., & Moni, K. (2003). Developing students' critical literacy: Exploring identity construction in young adult fiction. *Journal of Adolescent & Adult Literacy, 46,* 638–648.

Bear, D.R., Invernizzi, M., Templeton, S., & Johnston, F. (2000). *Words their way: Word study for phonics, vocabulary, and spelling instruction.* Upper Saddle River, NJ: Prentice Hall.

Beck, I.L., & McKeown, M.G. (2001). Text talk: Capturing the benefits of read-aloud experiences for young children. *The Reading Teacher, 55,* 10–20.

Beck, I.L., McKeown, M.G, & Kucan, L. (2002). *Bringing words to life: Robust vocabulary instruction.* New York: Guilford.

Beck, I.L., McKeown, M.G., & Kucan, L. (2003). Taking delight in words: Using oral language to build young children's vocabularies. *American Educator, 19,* 36–46.

Beck, I.L., McKeown, M.G., & Kucan, L. (2008). *Creating robust vocabulary: Frequently asked questions and extended examples*. New York: Guilford Press.

Bempechat, J. (2008). Reading success: A motivational perspective. In R. Fink & S.J. Samuels (Eds.), *Inspiring reading success: Interest and motivation in an age of high-stakes testing* (pp. 75–97). Newark, DE: International Reading Association.

Bender, W.N., & Shores, C. (2007). *Response to Intervention: A practical guide for every teacher*. Arlington, VA and Thousand Oaks, CA: Council for Exceptional Children and Corwin Press.

Bentin, S., & Leshem, H. (1993). On the interaction between phonological awareness and reading acquisition: It's a two-way street. *Annals of Dyslexia, 43,* 125–148.

Bitz, M. (2004). The Comic Book Project: Forging alternative pathways to literacy. *Journal of Adolescent & Adult Literacy, 47,* 574–586.

Blachowicz, C.L.Z. (1986). Making connections: Alternatives to the vocabulary notebook. *Journal of Reading, 29,* 643–649.

Blachowicz, C.L.Z., & Fisher, P. (2000). Vocabulary instruction. In M.L. Kamil, P.B. Mosenthal, P.D. Pearson, & R. Barr (Eds.), *Handbook of reading research* (Vol. III) (pp. 503–523). Mahwah, NJ: Erlbaum.

Blachowicz, C.L.Z., & Fisher, P. (2004). Vocabulary lessons. *Educational Leadership, 61,* 66–69.

Blachowicz, C.L.Z., & Fisher, P. (2008). Attentional vocabulary instruction: Read-alouds, word play, and other motivating strategies for fostering informal word learning. In A.E. Farstrup & S.J. Samuels (Eds.), *What research has to say about vocabulary instruction* (pp. 32–55). Newark, DE: International Reading Association.

Blachowicz, C.L.Z., & Lee, J.J. (1991). Vocabulary development in the whole literacy classroom. *The Reading Teacher, 45,* 188–195.

Blachowicz, C., & Ogle, D. (2001). *Reading comprehension: Strategies for independent learners*. New York: Guilford.

Block, C.C., & Pressley, M. (Eds.). (2002). *Comprehension instruction: Research-based best practices*. New York: Guilford.

Bluestein, A.N. (2002). Comprehension through characterization: Enabling readers to make personal connections with literature. *The Reading Teacher, 55,* 431–434.

Boehle, K., Darrow, D., Lovin, P., & White, B. (2001). Using a content area word wall. *Illinois Reading Council Journal, 28,* 62–65.

Boning, T., & Boning, R. (1957). I'd rather read than . . . *The Reading Teacher, 10,* 196–200.

Boyton, S. (1983). *A is for angry: An animal and adjective alphabet*. New York: Workman.

Bradley, L., & Bryant, P. (1983). Categorizing sounds and learning to read: A causal connection. *Nature, 301,* 419–421.

Bridges, R. (1999). *Through my eyes*. New York: Scholastic.

Bromley, K. (2007). Nine things every teacher should know about words and vocabulary instruction. *Journal of Adolescent & Adult Literacy, 50,* 528–537.

Buettner, E.G. (2002). Sentence by sentence self-monitoring. *The Reading Teacher, 56,* 34–44.

Bruel, N. (2007). *Poor puppy*. New Milford, CT: Roaring Book Press.

Burnett, F.H. (1990). *The secret garden*. New York: Dell.

Camp, D.J., & Tompkins, G.E. (1990). The abecedarius: Soldier of literacy. *Childhood Education, 66,* 298–302.

Cannon, J. (1993). *Stellaluna*. New York: Scholastic.

Carlsen, G.R., & Sherrill, A. (1988). *Voices of readers: How we come to love books*. Urbana, IL: National Council of Teachers of English.

Cecil, N.L. (2007). *Focus on fluency: A meaning-based approach*. Scottsdale: Holcomb Hathaway.

Chall, J.S. (1987). Two vocabularies for reading: Recognition and meaning. In M.G. McKeown & M.E. Curtis (Eds.), *The nature of vocabulary acquisition* (pp. 1–17). Hillsdale, NJ: Erlbaum.

Clay, M.M. (1967). The reading behavior of five-year-old children: A research report. *New Zealand Journal of Educational Studies, 2,* 11–31.

Cleland, J.V. (1999). We-can charts: Building blocks for student-led conferences. *The Reading Teacher, 52,* 588–595.

Cole, J. (1990). *The magic school bus lost in the solar system*. New York: Scholastic.

Cole, J.E. (2000). *Intrinsic motivation to read: A case study of the literacy personalities of four second-grade readers*. Unpublished doctoral dissertation. DeKalb, IL: Northern Illinois University.

Cramer, E.H. (1992). *Mental imagery and reading* (Literacy Series No. 1). Bloomington, IL: Illinois Reading Council.

Cronin, D. (2000). *Click, clack, moo, cows that type*. New York: Simon and Schuster.

Crovitz, D., & Miller, J.A. (2008). Register and charge: Using synonym maps to explore connotation. *English Journal, 97*(4), 49–55.

Csikszentmihalyi, M. (1991). Literacy and intrinsic motivation. In S.R. Graubard (Ed.), *Literacy* (pp. 115–140). New York: Noonday.

Cummings, P. (1991). *Clean your room, Harvey Moon*. New York: Bradbury.

Cunningham, P.M. (1993). Action phonics. In M.W. Olson & S.P. Homan (Eds.), *Teacher to teacher: Strategies for the elementary classroom* (pp. 9–12). Newark, DE: International Reading Association.

Cunningham, P.M. (1995). *Phonics they use: Words for reading and writing* (2nd ed.). New York: HarperCollins.

Cunningham, P.M. (2000). *Phonics they use: Words for reading and writing* (3rd ed.). New York: Longman.

Cunningham, P.M. (2003). What research says about teaching phonics. In L.M. Morrow, L.B. Gambrell, & M. Pressley (Eds.), *Best practices in literacy instruction* (2nd ed.) (pp. 65–85). New York: Guilford.

Cunningham, P.M., & Allington, R.L. (1999). *Classrooms that work: They can all read and write* (2nd ed.). New York: Addison Wesley.

Cunningham, P.M., & Cunningham, J.W. (1992). Making words: Enhancing the invented spelling-decoding connection. *The Reading Teacher, 46,* 106–107.

Cunningham, P.M., & Cunningham, J.W. (2002). What we know about how to teach phonics. In A.E. Farstrup & S.J. Samuels (Eds.), *What research has to say about reading instruction* (3rd ed.) (pp. 87–109). Newark, DE: International Reading Association.

Cunningham, P.M., & Hall, D.P. (1994a). *Making big words: Multilevel, hands-on spelling and phonics activities.* Parsippany, NJ: Good Apple.

Cunningham, P.M., & Hall, D.P. (1994b). *Making words: Multilevel, hands-on, developmentally appropriate spelling and phonics activities.* Parsippany, NJ: Good Apple.

Cunningham, P.M., & Hall, D.P. (1997a). *Making more words: Multilevel, hands-on phonics and spelling activities.* Torrence, CA: Good Apple.

Cunningham, P.M., & Hall, D.P. (1997b). *Month-by-month phonics for first grade.* Greensboro, NC: Carson-Dellosa.

Cunningham, P.M., & Hall, D.P. (1998). *Month-by-month phonics for upper grades: A second chance for struggling readers and students learning English.* Greensboro, NC: Carson-Dellosa.

Dale, E., & O'Rourke, J. (1971). *Techniques of teaching vocabulary.* Palo Alto, CA: Field Enterprises.

Davey, B. (1983). Think-aloud—Modeling the cognitive processes of reading comprehension. *Journal of Reading, 27,* 44–47.

Davey, B. (1986). Using textbook activity guides to help students learn from textbooks. *Journal of Reading, 29,* 489–494.

DeGenaro, J.J. (1993). Where there's a word, there's a vowel. In M.W. Olson & S.P. Homan (Eds.), *Teacher to teacher: Strategies for the elementary classroom* (p. 9). Newark, DE: International Reading Association.

Dole, J.A., Nokes, J.D., & Drits, D. (2009). Cognitive strategy instruction. In S. Israel & G. Duffy (Eds.), *Handbook of research on reading comprehension* (pp. 347–372). New York: Routledge.

Duffy, G.G. (2002). The case for direct explanation of strategies. In C.C. Block & M. Pressley (Eds.), *Comprehension instruction: Research-based best practices* (pp. 28–41). New York: Guilford.

Duke, K. (1992). *Aunt Isabel tells a good one.* New York: Puffin.

Duke, N.K. (2000). 3–6 minutes per day: The scarcity of informational texts in first grade. *Reading Research Quarterly, 35,* 202–224.

Duke, N.K., Bennett-Armistead, V.S., & Roberts, E.M. (2002). Incorporating informational text in the primary grades. In C. Roller (Ed.), *Comprehensive reading instruction across the grade levels* (pp. 40–54). Newark, DE: International Reading Association.

Duke, N.K., & Stewart, B.B. (1997). Standards in action in a first-grade classroom: The purpose dimension. *The Reading Teacher, 51,* 228–237.

Dunn-Rankin, P. (1968). The similarity of lower-case letters in the English alphabet. *Journal of Verbal Learning and Verbal Behavior, 7,* 990–995.

Eanes, R. (1997). *Content area literacy.* New York: Delmar.

Ehri, L., & Wilce, L. (1985). Movement into reading: Is the first stage of printed word learning visual or phonetic? *Reading Research Quarterly, 20,* 163–178.

Elkonin, D.B. (1973). USSR. In J. Downing (Ed.), *Comparative reading: Cross-national studies of behavior and processes in reading and writing* (pp. 551–579). New York: Macmillan.

Elley, W.B. (1988). Vocabulary acquisition from listening to stories. *Reading Research Quarterly, 24,* 174–187.

Elting, M., & Folsom, M. (1980). *Q is for duck: An alphabet guessing game.* New York: Clarion.

Estes, T.H. (1971). A scale to measure attitudes toward reading. *Journal of Reading, 15,* 135–138.

Eva-Wood, A.L. (2008). Does feeling come first? How poetry can help readers broaden their understanding of metacognition. *Journal of Adolescent & Adult Literacy, 51,* 564–576.

Faltis, C.J. (2001). *Joinfostering: Teaching and learning in multilingual classrooms* (3rd ed.). Upper Saddle River, NJ: Prentice Hall.

Falwell, C. (1998). *Word Wizard.* NY: Clarion.

Farstrup, A.E., & Samuels, S.J. (2008). Vocabulary instruction: A critical component for skillful reading. In A.E. Farstrup & S.J. Samuels (Eds.), *What research has to say about vocabulary instruction* (pp. 1–5). Newark, DE: International Reading Association.

Fields, M.V., Groth, L.A., & Spangler, K.L. (2004). *Let's begin reading right: A developmental approach to emergent literacy* (5th ed.). Upper Saddle River, NJ: Prentice Hall.

Fischer, K.W., & Fusaro, M. (2008). Using student interest to motivate learning. In R. Fink & S.J. Samuels (Eds.), *Inspiring reading success: Interest and motivation in an age of high-stakes testing* (pp. 62–74). Newark, DE: International Reading Association.

Fisher, D., & Frey, N. (2007). *Checking for understanding: Formative assessment techniques for your classroom.* Alexandria, VA: Association for Supervision and Curriculum Development.

Fisher, D., Frey, N., & Lapp, D. (2009). *In a reading state of mind: Brain research, teacher modeling, and comprehension instruction.* Newark, DE: International Reading Association.

Fisk, C., & Hurst, B. (2003). Paraphrasing for comprehension. *The Reading Teacher, 57,* 182–195.

Fox, B.J. (1996). *Strategies for word identification.* Columbus, OH: Merrill.

Fox, B.J. (2000). *Word identification strategies* (2nd ed.). Upper Saddle River, NJ: Prentice Hall.

Fox, E., & Alexander, P.A. (2009). Text comprehension: A retrospective, perspective, and prospective. In S. Israel & G. Duffy (Eds.), *Handbook of research on reading comprehension* (pp. 227–239). New York: Routledge.

Francis, M.A., & Simpson, M.L. (2003). Using theory, our intuitions, and a research study to enhance students' vocabulary knowledge. *Journal of Adolescent & Adult Literacy, 47*, 66–78.

Fredericks, A.D., & Rasinski, T.V. (1990). Involving parents in the assessment process. *The Reading Teacher, 44*, 346–349.

Freed, S.A., & Moon, L. (1999). *The multiple intelligences pathways to literacy*. Arlington Heights, IL: Skylight Training and Publishing.

Freeman, G., & Reynolds, E.G. (1980). Enriching basal reader lessons and semantic webbing. *The Reading Teacher, 33*, 677–684.

French, J. (2003). *Diary of a wombat*. New York: Clarion Books.

Fromherz, R.W. (2003). Create a traveling literacy trunk. *The Reading Teacher, 57*, 192–195.

Fry, E.B., Kress, J.E., & Fountoukidis, D.L. (1993). *The reading teacher's book of lists* (3rd ed.). Englewood Cliffs, NJ: Prentice Hall.

Fuchs, D., Fuchs, L.S., & Vaughn, S. (Eds.) (2008). *Response to Intervention: A framework for reading educators*. Newark, DE: International Reading Association.

Gambrell, L.B. (1996). Creating classroom cultures that foster reading motivation. *The Reading Teacher, 50*, 14–25.

Gambrell, L.B. (2007). Reading: Does practice make perfect? *Reading Today, 24*(6), 16.

Gambrell, L.B. (2008). Patterson, Proust, and the power of pleasure reading. *Reading Today, 25*(5), 18.

Gambrell, L.B., Palmer, B.M., Codling, R.M., & Mazzoni, S.A. (1996). Assessing reading motivation. *The Reading Teacher, 49*, 518–533.

Gandy, S. (2003). Increasing students' vocabulary through synonyms. *Illinois Reading Council Journal, 31*, 18–30.

Gardner, H. (1993). *Multiple intelligences*. New York: BasicBooks.

Gates, A.I. (1931). *Interest and ability in reading*. New York: Macmillan.

Gill, S.R. (2007). Learning about word parts with Kidspiration. *The Reading Teacher, 61*, 79–84.

Gillet, J.W., & Temple, C. (1990). *Understanding reading problems: Assessment and instruction* (3rd ed.). Glenview, IL: Scott Foresman.

Gillet, J.W., & Temple, C. (2000). *Understanding reading problems: Assessment and instruction* (4th ed.). New York: Longman.

Goodman, Y.M., & Marek, A.M. (1996). *Retrospective miscue analysis: Revaluing readers and reading*. Katonah, NY: Richard C. Owen.

Grant, R. (1993). Strategic training for using text headings to improve students' processing of content. *Journal of Reading, 36*, 482–487.

Graves, M.F. (2008). Instruction on individual words: One size does not fit all. In A.E. Farstrup & S.J. Samuels (Eds.), *What research has to say about vocabulary instruction* (pp. 56–79). Newark, DE: International Reading Association.

Greenlaw, J. (2001). *English language arts and reading on the internet. A resource for K–12 teachers*. Upper Saddle River, NJ: Prentice Hall.

Griffith, P.L., & Olson, M.W. (1992). Phonemic awareness helps beginning readers break the code. *The Reading Teacher, 45*, 516–523.

Gunning, T.G. (1998). *Great books for beginning readers*. Boston: Allyn and Bacon.

Gunning, T.G. (2000). *Best books for building literacy for elementary school children*. Boston: Allyn and Bacon.

Gunning, T.G. (2001). *Building words: A resource manual for teaching word analysis and spelling strategies*. Boston: Allyn and Bacon.

Gunning, T.G. (2003). *Creating literacy instruction for all children* (4th ed.). Boston: Allyn and Bacon.

Gunning, T.G. (2008). *Creating literacy instruction for all students* (6th ed.). Upper Saddle River, NJ: Pearson.

Gunning, T.G. (2008). *Developing higher-level literacy in all students: Building reading, reasoning, and responding*. Boston: Allyn and Bacon.

Guthrie, J.T., & Wigfield, A. (2000). Engagement and motivation in reading. In M.L. Kamil, P.B. Mosenthal, P.D. Pearson, & R. Barr (Eds.), *Handbook of reading research* (Vol. III) (pp. 403–422). Mahwah, NJ: Erlbaum.

Guthrie, J.T., Wigfield, A., Metsala, J.L., & Cox, K.E. (1999). Motivational and cognitive predictors of text comprehension and reading amount. *Scientific Studies of Reading, 3*, 231–256.

Haggard, M.R. (1982). The vocabulary self-collection strategy: An active approach to word learning. *Journal of Reading, 27*, 203–207.

Hall, K.P. (Ed.). (1997). *Parent letters for the intermediate grades*. Cypress, CA: Creative Teaching Press.

Hall, M. (1981). *Teaching reading as a language experience* (3rd ed.). Columbus, OH: Merrill.

Hampton, S., & Resnick, L.B. (2009). *Reading and writing grade by grade* (rev. ed.). Newark, DE: International Reading Association.

Harmin, M. (1995). *Inspiring active learning*. Edwardsville, IL: Inspiring Strategy Institute.

Harris, T.L., & Hodges, R.E. (Eds.). (1995). *The literacy dictionary: The vocabulary of reading and writing*. Newark, DE: International Reading Association.

Hayes, D.A. (1989). Helping students GRASP the knack of writing summaries. *Journal of Reading, 33*, 96–101.

Heckelman, R.G. (1969). A neurological-impress method of remedial-reading instruction. *Academic Therapy Quarterly, 4*, 277–282.

Heimlich, J.E., & Pittleman, S.D. (1986). *Semantic mapping: Classroom applications.* Newark, DE: International Reading Association.

Henk, W.A., & Melnick, S.A. (1995). The reader self-perception scale (RSPS): A new tool for measuring how children feel about themselves as readers. *The Reading Teacher, 48,* 470–482.

Herber, H.L. (1978). *Teaching reading in content areas* (2nd ed.). Englewood Cliffs, NJ: Prentice-Hall.

Herron, J. (2008). Why phonics instruction must change (the positive classroom). *Educational Leadership, 66*(1), 77–81.

Hibbing, A., & Rankin-Erickson, J. (2003). A picture is worth a thousand words: Using visual images to improve comprehension for middle school struggling readers. *The Reading Teacher, 56,* 758–770.

Hillerich, R.L. (1978). *A writing vocabulary of elementary children.* Springfield, IL: Charles C. Thomas.

Hoban, T. (1989). *Of colors and things.* New York: Greenwillow.

Hoffman, M., & Binch, C. (1991). *Amazing Grace.* New York: Dial Books for Young Readers.

Hohn, W., & Ehri, L. (1983). Do alphabet letters help prereaders acquire phonemic segmentation skills? *Journal of Educational Psychology, 75,* 752–762.

Hoose, P., & Hoose, H. (1998). *Hey, little ant.* New York: Scholastic.

Hughey, J.B., & Slack, C. (2001). *Teaching children to write.* Upper Saddle River, NJ: Prentice Hall.

International Reading Association. (1999). *Multiple methods of beginning reading instruction: A position statement of the International Reading Association.* Newark, DE: Author.

International Reading Association. (2000). *Making a difference means making it different: Honoring children's rights to excellent reading instruction.* Newark, DE: Author.

Jason, M.H., & Dubnow, B. (1973). The relationship between self-perceptions of reading abilities and reading achievement. In W.H. MacGinitie (Ed.), *Assessment problems in reading* (pp. 96–101). Newark, DE: International Reading Association.

Jenkins, E. (1997). *Ella Jenkins' song book for children.* New York: Oak Publications.

Johns, J.L. (1975). Dolch list of common nouns—A comparison. *The Reading Teacher, 28,* 338–340.

Johns, J.L. (1977). Children's conceptions of a spoken word: A developmental study. *Reading World, 16,* 248–257.

Johns, J.L. (1980). First graders' concepts about print. *Reading Research Quarterly, 15,* 529–549.

Johns, J.L. (1981). The development of the revised Dolch list. *Illinois School Research and Development, 17,* 15–24.

Johns, J.L. (1991). Literacy portfolios: A primer. *Illinois Reading Council Journal, 19,* 4–10.

Johns, J.L. (2008). *Basic reading inventory* (10th ed.). Dubuque, IA: Kendall Hunt.

Johns, J.L., & Berglund, R.L. (2006). *Fluency: Strategies and assessments* (3rd ed.). Dubuque, IA: Kendall Hunt.

Johnson, B., & Kaufman, B. (1999). *Project prevent workshop.* Des Plaines, IL: School District 62.

Johnson, D.B. (2003). *Henry climbs a mountain.* Boston: Houghton Mifflin.

Johnson, D.D. (2001). *Vocabulary in the elementary and middle school.* Boston: Allyn and Bacon.

Johnson, J.C. (2005). What makes a "good" reader? Asking students to define "good" readers. *The Reading Teacher, 58,* 776–770.

Juel, C., & Minden-Cupp, C. (2004). Learning to read words: Linguistic units and instructional strategies. In R.B. Ruddell & Norman J. Unrau (Eds.), *Theoretical models and processes of reading* (5th ed.) (pp. 313–364). Newark, DE: International Reading Association.

Kay, V. (2003). *Orphan train.* New York: Putnam's.

Keating, F. (2006). *Theodore.* New York: Simon & Schuster Books.

Kelly, M.J., & Clausen-Grace, N. (2007). *Comprehension shouldn't be silent: From strategy instruction to student independence.* Newark, DE: International Reading Association.

Klesius, J., Laframboise, K.L., & Gaier, M. (1998). Humorous literature: Motivation for reluctant readers. *Reading Research and Instruction, 37,* 253–261.

Kletzien, S.B., & Dreher, M.J. (2004). *Informational text in K–3 classrooms: Helping children read and write.* Newark, DE: International Reading Association.

Knight, M.B. (1992). *Talking walls.* Gardiner, ME: Tilbury House.

Kress, J. (1993). *The ESL teacher's book of lists.* Upper Saddle River, NJ: Prentice Hall.

Krows, J. (1993). My house. In *At my window.* Orlando, FL: Harcourt Brace Jovanovich.

Labbo, L. (2000). 12 things young children can do with a talking book in a classroom computer center. *The Reading Teacher, 53,* 542–546.

Labbo, L.D., Love, M.S., & Ryan, T. (2007). A vocabulary flood: Making words "sticky" with computer-response activities. *The Reading Teacher, 60,* 582–588.

Lamberg, W.J., & Lamb, C.E. (1980). *Reading instruction in the content areas.* Geneva, IL: Houghton Mifflin.

Lanier, E., & Lenski, S.D. (2008). *Developing an independent reading program: Grades 4–12.* Norwood, MA: Christopher-Gordon Publishers.

Layne, S.L. (1996). *Vocabulary acquisition by fourth-grade students from listening to teachers' oral reading of novels.* Unpublished doctoral dissertation, Northern Illinois University, DeKalb.

L'Engle, M. (1962). *A wrinkle in time.* New York: Dell.

Lenski, S.D. (1999). The Directed Reading-Connected Activity (DR-CA): A strategy to promote connections across texts. *Journal of Reading Education, 24,* 9–12.

Lenski, S.D., & Ehlers-Zavala, F. (2004). *Reading strategies for Spanish speakers*. Dubuque, IA: Kendall Hunt.

Lenski, S.D., & Johns, J.L. (2004). *Improving writing: Strategies, resources, and assessments* (2nd ed.). Dubuque, IA: Kendall Hunt.

Lenski, S.D., & Nierstheimer, S.L. (2002). Strategy instruction from a sociocultural perspective. *Reading Psychology, 23,* 127–143.

Long, T.W., & Gove, M.K. (2003). How engagement strategies and literature circles promote critical response in a fourth-grade, urban classroom. *The Reading Teacher*, *57,* 350–361.

Lowell, S. (1992). *The three little javelinas*. Flagstaff, AZ: Rising Moon.

Lowry, L. (1993). *The giver.* New York: Bantam Doubleday Dell.

Lundberg, I., Frost, J., & Petersen, O.P. (1988). Effects of an extensive program for stimulating phonological awareness in preschool children. *Reading Research Quarterly, 23,* 264–284.

Lyman, F. T. (1981). The responsive classroom discussion: The inclusion of all students. In A. Anderson (Ed.), *Mainstreaming digest* (pp. 109–113). College Park, MD: University of Maryland Press.

MacLachlan, P. (1987). *Sarah, plain, and tall*. New York: HarperCollins.

Manyak, P.C. (2008). What's your news? Portraits of a rich language and literacy activity for English-language learners. *The Reading Teacher*, *61*, 450–458.

Manzo, A.V., & Manzo, U.C. (1993). *Literacy disorders: Holistic diagnosis and remediation.* New York: Harcourt Brace Jovanovich.

Marcell, B. (June/July, 2007). Fluency to a fault: Put fluency in the passenger seat and let comprehension take the wheel. *Reading Today, 24*(6), 18.

Marshall, J. (1988). *George and Martha 'round and 'round.* Boston: Houghton Mifflin.

Martin, B. (2006). *"Fire! Fire!" said Mrs. McGuire*. Orlando: Harcourt.

Martin, B., Jr. (1970). *Brown bear, brown bear.* New York: Holt.

Martin, B., Jr., & Archambault, J. (1989). *Chicka chicka boom boom.* New York: Simon & Schuster.

Massey, D.D. (2003). A comprehension checklist: What if it doesn't make sense? *The Reading Teacher*, *57*, 81–83.

Massey, D.D. (2009). Self-regulated comprehension. In S. Israel & G. Duffy (Eds.), *Handbook of research on reading comprehension* (pp. 389–399). New York: Routledge.

May, F.B. (1990). *Reading as communication* (3rd ed.). Columbus, OH: Merrill.

McCormick, S. (1995). *Instructing students who have literacy problems* (2nd ed.). Columbus, OH: Merrill.

McCormick, S. (1999). *Instructing students who have literacy problems* (3rd ed.). Upper Saddle River, NJ: Prentice Hall.

McCormick, S. (2003). *Instructing students who have literacy problems* (4th ed.). Columbus, OH: Merrill Prentice Hall.

McGee, L.M., & Richgels, D.J. (1996). *Literacy's beginnings: Supporting young readers and writers* (2nd ed.). Boston: Allyn and Bacon.

McGinley, W.J., & Denner, P.R. (1987). Story impressions: A prereading/writing activity. *Journal of Reading, 31,* 248–253.

McKenna, M.C., & Kear, D.J. (1990). Measuring attitude toward reading: A new tool for teachers. *The Reading Teacher, 43,* 626–639.

McKenna, M.C., Kear, D.J., & Ellsworth, R.A. (1995). Children's attitudes toward reading: A national survey. *Reading Research Quarterly, 30,* 934–956.

McKenzie, G., & Danielson, E. (2003). Improving comprehension through mural lessons. *The Reading Teacher*, *56,* 738–742.

McLoyd, V. (1979). The effects of extrinsic rewards of differential value on high and low intrinsic interest. *Child Development, 50,* 1010–1019.

McPhail, J.C., Pierson, J.M., Freeman, J.G., Goodman, J., & Ayappa, A. (2000). The role of interest in fostering sixth grade students' identities as competent learners. *Curriculum Inquiry, 30,* 43–69.

Mesmer, E.M., & Mesmer, H.A. (2008/2009). Response to Intervention (RTI): What teachers of reading need to know. *The Reading Teacher, 62*, 280–290.

Miles, B. (1995). *Hey! I'm reading*. New York: Scholastic.

Miller, S.D., & Faircloth, B.S. (2009). Motivation and reading comprehension. In S. Israel & G. Duffy (Eds.), *Handbook of research on reading comprehension* (pp. 307–322). New York: Routledge.

Moore, D.W., & Moore, S.A. (1992). Possible sentences: An update. In E.K. Dishner, T.W. Bean, J.E. Readance, & D.W. Moore (Eds.), *Reading in the content areas: Improving classroom instruction* (3rd ed.) (pp. 196–202). Dubuque, IA: Kendall Hunt.

Moore, M. (1998). Using De Bono's thinking hats with BTN. *Practically Primary, 3,* 9–10.

Morris, D., Bloodgood, J., Lomax, R., & Perney, J. (2003). Developmental steps in learning to read: A longitudinal study in kindergarten and first grade. *Reading Research Quarterly, 38,* 302–328.

Morris, D., & Perney, J. (1984). Developmental spelling as a predictor of first-grade reading achievement. *The Elementary School Journal, 84,* 441–457.

Morrow, L.M. (1983). Home and school correlates of early interest in literature. *Journal of Educational Research, 76,* 221–230.

Moss, B. (2003). *An exploration of eight sixth graders' engagement with nonfiction trade books.* In C.M. Fairbanks, J. Worthy, B. Maloch, J.V. Hoffman, & D.L. Schallert (Eds.), 52nd Yearbook of the National Reading Conference (pp. 321–331). Oak Creek, WI: National Reading Conference.

Moss, B. (2004). Teaching expository text structures through information trade book retellings. *The Reading Teacher*, *57*, 710–718.

Mountain, L. (2002). Flip-a-Chip to build vocabulary. *Journal of Adolescent & Adult Literacy*, *46*, 62–68.

Mountain, L. (2005). ROOTing out meaning: More morphemic analysis for primary pupils. *The Reading Teacher*, *58*, 742–749.

Mountain, L. (2007/2008). Synonym success: Thanks to the thesaurus. *Journal of Adolescent & Adult Literacy*, *51*, 318–324.

Munsch, R. (2000). *The paper bag princess*. Toronto: Annick Press.

Musgrove, M. (1976). *Ashanti to Zulu: African traditions*. New York: Dial.

Nagy, W., & Anderson, R.C. (1984). How many words are there in printed school English? *Reading Research Quarterly, 19,* 304–330.

Nagy, W.E., & Scott, J.A. (2000). Vocabulary processes. In M.L. Kamil, P.B. Mosenthal, P.D. Pearson, & R. Barr (Eds.), *Handbook of reading research* (Vol. III) (pp. 269–284). Mahwah, NJ: Erlbaum.

National Association for the Education of Young Children. (2009). *Developmentally appropriate practice in early childhood programs serving children from birth through age 8*. Position Statement. Available from National Association for the Education of Young Children Web site, http://www.naeyc.org

National Reading Panel. (2000). *Teaching children to read: An evidence-based assessment of the scientific research literature on reading and its implications for reading instruction*. Washington, DC: National Institute of Child Health & Human Development.

Nelson, S., & Nelson, T. (2003). *The Nez Perce*. New York: Scholastic.

Newton, E., Padak, N., & Rasinski, T. (2008). *Evidence-based instruction in reading: A professional development guide to vocabulary*. Boston: Allyn and Bacon.

Nokes, J.D. (2008). The Observation/Inference Chart: Improving students' abilities to make inferences while reading nontraditional texts. *Journal of Adolescent & Adult Literacy*, *51*, 538–546.

Numeroff, L.J. (1991). *If you give a moose a muffin*. New York: HarperCollins.

Numeroff, L.J. (1996). *If you give a mouse a cookie*. New York: HarperCollins.

Nurss, J., Hough, R.A., & Goodson, M.S. (1981). Prereading/language development in two day care centers. *Journal of Reading Behavior, 13,* 23–31.

O'Shea, L.J., Sindelar, P.T., & O'Shea, D.J. (1985). The effects of repeated readings and attentional cues on reading fluency and comprehension. *Journal of Reading Behavior, 17,* 129–142.

Ogle, D.M. (1989). The know, want to know, learn strategy. In K.D. Muth (Ed.), *Children's comprehension of text* (pp. 205–223). Newark, DE: International Reading Association.

Opitz, M.F. (1995). *Getting the most from predictable books*. New York: Scholastic.

Opitz, M.F. (2000). *Rhymes & reasons: Literature and language play for phonological awareness*. Portsmouth, NH: Heinemann.

Opitz, M.F., & Rasinski, T.V. (2008). *Good-bye round robin: Twenty-five effective oral reading strategies* (Updated Edition). Portsmouth, NH: Heinemann.

Ortega, A., & Ramirez, J. (2002). Parent Literacy Workshops: One school's parent program integrated with the school day. *The Reading Teacher, 55,* 726–729.

Palmer, B.C., & Brooks, M.A. (2004). Reading until the cows come home: Figurative language and reading comprehension. *Journal of Adolescent & Adult Literacy*, *47*, 370–379.

Paratore, J.R. (2002). The importance of effective early intervention. In A.E. Farstrup & S.J. Samuels (Eds.), *What research has to say about reading instruction* (3rd ed.) (pp. 48–68). Newark, DE: International Reading Association.

Park, B. (1996). *Mick Harte was here*. New York: Scholastic.

Pearman, C.J. (2008). Independent reading of CD-ROM storybooks: Measuring comprehension with oral retellings. *The Reading Teacher*, *61*, 594–602.

Pearman, C.J., Camp, D., & Hurst, B. (2004). Literacy mystery boxes. *The Reading Teacher*, *57*, 766–768.

Peek, M. (1985). *Mary wore her red dress and Henry wore his green sneakers*. New York: Clarion.

Pelham, D. (1990). *Sam's sandwich*. New York: Dutton.

Pinnell, G.S., & Fountas, I.C. (1998). *Word matters: Teaching phonics and spelling in the reading/writing classroom*. Portsmouth, NH: Heinemann.

Pittleman, S.D., Heimlich, J.E., Berglund, R.L., & French, M.P. (1991). *Semantic feature analysis: Classroom applications*. Newark, DE: International Reading Association.

Powell, W.R. (1986). Teaching vocabulary through opposition. *Journal of Reading*, *29*, 617–621.

Pressley, M. (2000). What should comprehension instruction be the instruction of? In M.L. Kamil, P.B. Mosenthal, P.D. Pearson, & R. Barr (Eds.), *Handbook of reading research* (Vol. III) (pp. 545–561). Mahwah, NJ: Erlbaum.

Pressley, M. (2002). Comprehension strategies instruction: A turn-of-the-century status report. In C.C. Block & M. Pressley (Eds.), *Comprehension instruction: Research-based best practices* (pp. 11–27). New York: Guilford.

Rabe, B. (1981). *The balancing girl*. New York: E.P. Dutton.

Raines, S.C., & Isbell, R. (1988, April). *An array of teaching ideas using wordless picture books*. Paper presented at the Annual Study Conference of the Association for Childhood Education International, Salt Lake City, UT.

Rand Study Group. (2002). *Reading for understanding: Toward an R&D program in reading comprehension*. Santa Monica, CA: Author.

Raphael, T.E. (1984). Teaching learners about sources of information for answering comprehension questions. *Journal of Reading, 27,* 303–311.

Rasinski, T., & Padak, N. (2000). *Effective reading strategies: Teaching children who find reading difficult* (2nd ed.). Upper Saddle River, NJ: Prentice Hall.

Rasinski, T.V., Padak, N.D., Linek, W.L., & Sturtevant, E. (1994). Effects of fluency development on urban second-grade readers. *Journal of Educational Research, 87,* 158–165.

Rawls, W. (1961). *Where the red fern grows*. New York: Doubleday.

Readence, J.E., Bean, T.W., & Baldwin, R.S. (1998). *Content area literacy* (6th ed.). Dubuque, IA: Kendall Hunt.

Rhodes, L.K. (1981). I can read! Predictable books as resources for reading and writing instruction. *The Reading Teacher, 34,* 511–518.

Richards, J.C., & Gipe, J.P. (1993). Getting to know story characters: A strategy for young and at-risk readers. *The Reading Teacher, 47,* 78–79.

Richek, M.A., Caldwell, J.S., Jennings, J.H., & Lerner, J.W. (1996). *Reading problems: Assessment and teaching strategies* (3rd ed.). Boston: Allyn and Bacon.

Richgels, D. (2002). Invented spelling, phonemic awareness, and reading and writing instruction. In S.B. Neuman & D.K. Dickson (Eds.), *Handbook of Early Literacy Research* (pp. 142–155). NY: Guilford.

Rinne, C.H. (1998). Motivating students is a percentage game. *Phi Delta Kappan, 79,* 620–627.

Roberts, B. (1992). The evolution of the young child's concept of word as a unit of spoken and written language. *Reading Research Quarterly, 27,* 124–138.

Roe, B.D., Stoodt, B.D., & Burns, P.C. (2001). *The content areas: Secondary school literacy instruction* (7th ed.). Boston: Houghton Mifflin.

Roser, N., Martinez, M., Fuhrken, C., & McDonnald, K. (2007). Characters as guides to meaning. *The Reading Teacher*, *60*, 548–559.

Rubin, D. (1993). *A practical approach to teaching reading*. Needham Hts., MA: Allyn and Bacon.

Ruddell, M.R. (1993). *Teaching content reading and writing*. Needham Hts., MA: Allyn and Bacon.

Ruddell, R.B., & Unrau, N.J. (2004). The role of responsive teaching in focusing reader intention and developing reader motivation. In R.B. Ruddell & N.J. Unrau (Eds.), *Theoretical models and processes of reading* (5th ed.) (pp. 954–978). Newark, DE: International Reading Association.

Rupley, W.H., Logan, J.W., & Nichols, W.D. (1998/1999). Vocabulary instruction in a balanced reading program. *The Reading Teacher, 52,* 336–346.

Ryan, R.M., & Deci, E.L. (2000). Self-determination theory and the facilitation of intrinsic motivation, social development, and well-being. *American Psychologist, 55,* 68–78.

Samuels, J. (2006). Looking backward: Reflections on a career in reading. *Journal of Literacy Research, 38,* 327–334.

Samuels, S.J. (1979). The method of repeated reading. *The Reading Teacher, 32,* 403–408.

Samuels, S.J. (1994). Toward a theory of automatic information processing in reading revisited. In R.B. Ruddell, M.R. Ruddell, & H. Singer (Eds.), *Theoretical models and processes of reading* (4th ed.) (pp. 816–837). Newark, DE: International Reading Association.

Samuels, S.J. (2002). Reading fluency: Its development and assessment. In A.E. Farstrup & S.J. Samuels (Eds.), *What research has to say about reading instruction* (3rd ed.) (pp. 166–183). Newark, DE: International Reading Association.

Sanacore, J. (2000). Promoting the lifetime reading habit in middle school students. *The Clearing House, 73,* 157–161.

Sansom, I. (2005). *The case of the missing books*. New York: Harper.

Schmidt, B., & Buckley, M. (1991). Plot relationships chart. In J.M. Macon, D. Bewell, & M. Vogt (Eds.), *Responses to literature: Grades K–8* (pp. 7–8). Newark, DE: International Reading Association.

Scieszka, J. (1989). *The true story of the 3 pigs by A. Wolf*. New York: Scholastic.

Seuss, Dr. (1965). *Hop on pop*. New York: Beginning Books.

Sherman, R., & Wright, G. (1999). Let's create a comic strip. *Reading Improvement, 36,* 66–72.

Sinatra, R. (1987). *Visual literacy connections to thinking, reading and writing*. Springfield, IL: Charles C Thomas.

Slattery Gursky, R. (2003). *Effects of spontaneous phonemic awareness knowledge, contextualized phonemic awareness instruction, and decontextualized phonemic awareness training on phonemic awareness, reading, and spelling in kindergarten students*. Doctoral dissertation. DeKalb, IL: Northern Illinois University.

Smith, H.M., & Read, D. (1982). Teaching visual literacy through wordless picture books. *The Reading Teacher, 35,* 928–933.

Smith, R., & Smith, M. (2002). *B is for beaver: An Oregon alphabet*. Chelsea, MI: Sleeping Bear Press.

Smolkin, L.B., & Yaden, D.B. (1992). O is for mouse: First encounters with the alphabet book. *Language Arts, 69,* 432–441.

Snow, C.E. (2008). Foreword. In R. Fink & S.J. Samuels (Eds.), *Inspiring reading success: Interest and motivation in an age of high-stakes testing* (pp. xiii–xiv). Newark, DE: International Reading Association.

Snow, C.E., Burns, S.M., & Griffin, P. (Eds.). (1998). *Preventing reading difficulties in young children*. Washington, DC: National Academy of Education.

Snow, C.E., & Sweet, A.P. (2003). Reading for comprehension. In C.E. Snow & A.P. Sweet (Eds.), *Rethinking reading comprehension* (pp. 1–11). New York: Guilford.

Sobol, D.J. (1981). *Encyclopedia Brown's second record book of weird and wonderful facts*. New York: Dell.

Stahl, K.A.D. (2008). The effects of three instructional methods on the reading comprehension and content acquisition of novice readers. *Journal of Literacy Research, 40*, 359–393.

Stanovich, K.E. (1991). Word recognition: Changing perspectives. In R. Barr, M.L. Kamil, P. Mosenthal, & P.D. Pearson (Eds.), *Handbook of reading research* (Vol. II) (pp. 418–452). New York: Longman.

Stanovich, K.E. (1993/1994). Romance and reality (Distinguished Educator Series). *The Reading Teacher, 47*, 280–291.

Stauffer, R.G. (1969a). *Directing reading maturity as a cognitive process*. New York: Harper & Row.

Stauffer, R.G. (1969b). *Teaching reading as a thinking process*. New York: Harper & Row.

Stauffer, R.G. (1980). *The language-experience approach to the teaching of reading* (2nd ed.). New York: Harper & Row.

Stephens, E.C., & Brown, J.E. (2000). *A handbook of content literacy strategies: 75 practical reading and writing ideas*. Norwood, MA: Christopher-Gordon.

Sternberg, R.J., & Powell, J.S. (1983). Comprehending verbal comprehension. *American Psychologist, 38*, 878–893.

Swindall, V., & Cantrell, J.R. (1999). Character interviews help bring literature to life. *The Reading Teacher, 53*, 23–25.

Taba, H. (1967). *Teacher's handbook for elementary social studies*. Reading, MA: Addison-Wesley.

Taylor, G. (1998). A discussion, not a report, if you please. *Journal of Adolescent and Adult Literacy, 41*, 561–563.

Thorndike, E.L. (1941). *The teaching of English suffixes*. New York: Teachers College.

Tompkins, G.E. (1998). *50 literacy strategies: Step by step*. Upper Saddle River, NJ: Prentice Hall.

Tompkins, G.E. (2001). *Literacy for the 21st century: A balanced approach* (2nd ed.). Upper Saddle River, NJ: Prentice Hall.

Tompkins, G.E., & Blanchfield, C. (2004). *Teaching vocabulary: 50 creative strategies, Grades K–12*. Upper Saddle River, NJ: Prentice Hall.

Towell, J.H. (1999/2000). Motivating students through music and literature. *The Reading Teacher, 53*, 284–287.

Trabasso, T., & Bouchard, E. (2002). Teaching readers how to comprehend text strategically. In C.C. Block & M. Pressley (Eds.), *Comprehension instruction: Research-based best practices* (pp. 176–200). New York: Guilford.

Treiman, R., & Zukowski, A. (1991). Levels of phonological awareness. In S.A. Brady & D.P. Shankweiler (Eds.), *Phonological processes in literacy* (pp. 67–81). Hillsdale, NJ: Erlbaum.

Treiman, R., & Zukowski, A. (1996). Children's sensitivity to syllables, onsets, rimes, and phonemes. *Journal of Experimental Child Psychology, 61*, 193–215.

Tullock-Rhody, R., & Alexander, J.E. (1980). A scale for assessing attitudes toward reading in secondary schools. *Journal of Reading, 23*, 609–614.

Tumner, W.E., Herriman, M.L., & Nesdale, A.R. (1988). Metalinguistic abilities and beginning reading. *Reading Research Quarterly, 23*, 134–158.

Turkle, B. (1976). *Deep in the forest*. New York: Dutton.

Vaughn, S., & Denton, C.A. (2008). Tier 2: The role of intervention. In D. Fuchs, L.S. Fuchs, & S. Vaughn (Eds.), *Response to Intervention: A framework for reading educators* (pp. 51–70). Newark, DE: International Reading Association.

Vellutino, F.R., & Fletcher, J.M. (2005). Developmental dyslexia. In M.S.C. Hulme (Ed.), *The science of reading: A handbook* (pp. 362–378). Malden, MA: Blackwell.

Viorst, J. (1972). *Alexander and the terrible, horrible, no good, very bad day*. New York: Atheneum.

Waddell, M. (1975). *Owl babies*. Cambridge, MA: Candlewick Press.

Wedwick, L., & Wutz, J.A. (2008). *BOOKMATCH: How to scaffold student book selection for independent reading*. Newark, DE: International Reading Association.

Wharton-McDonald, R., & Swiger, S. (2009). Developing higher order comprehension in the middle grades. In S. Israel & G. Duffy (Eds.), *Handbook of research on reading comprehension* (pp. 510–530). New York: Routledge.

White, E.B. (1952). *Charlotte's web*. New York: Harper & Row.

White, T.G., Sowell, J., & Yanagihara, A. (1989). Teaching elementary students to use word-part clues. *The Reading Teacher, 42*, 302–308.

Wigfield, A., Eccels, J.S., Yoon, K.S., Harold, R.D., Arbreton, A.J.A., Freedman-Doan, C., & Blumenfeld, P.C. (1997). Change in children's competence beliefs and subjective task values across the elementary school years: A 3-year study. *Journal of Educational Psychology, 89*, 451–469.

Wilder, L.I. (1932). *Little house in the big woods*. New York: Harper.

Wilson, P.T. (1988). *Let's think about reading and reading instruction: A primer for tutors and teachers*. Dubuque, IA: Kendall Hunt.

Wilson, R.M., Hall, M., Leu, D.J., & Kinzer, C.K. (2001). *Phonics, phonemic awareness, and word analysis for teachers* (7th ed.). Upper Saddle River, NJ: Prentice Hall.

Wink, J. (2001). *Critical pedagogy: Notes from the real world* (2nd ed.). New York: Longman.

Wisendanger, K.D. (2001). *Strategies for literacy education*. Upper Saddle River, NJ: Prentice Hall.

Wood, K. (1984). Probable passages: A writing strategy. *The Reading Teacher, 37*, 496–499.

Worthy, J. (2001). A life of learning and enjoyment from literacy. *The Reading Teacher, 54*, 690–691.

Yin. (2001). *Coolies*. New York: Penguin Putnam.

Yopp, H. (1988). The validity and reliability of phonemic awareness tests. *Reading Research Quarterly, 23*, 159–177.

Yopp, H.K. (1995). A test for assessing phonemic awareness in young children. *The Reading Teacher, 49,* 20–29.

Yopp, H.K. (1995). Read-aloud books for developing phonemic awareness. An annotated bibliography. *The Reading Teacher, 48,* 538–542.

Zeigler, L.L., & Johns, J.L. (2005). *Visualization: Using mental images to strengthen comprehension.* Dubuque, IA: Kendall Hunt.

Zeno, S.M., Ivens, S.H., Millard, R.T., & Duvvuri, R. (1995). *The educator's word frequency guide.* Brewster, NY: Touchstone Applied Science.

Zwiers, J. (2004). *Building reading comprehension habits in grades 6–12: A toolkit of classroom activities.* Newark, DE: International Reading Association.

Index

G

H

I

K

Q

R

S

T

U

V

W

Y

Z